Volume 2

Western Civilization
Ideas, Politics & Society

Eighth Edition

Marvin Perry
Baruch College, City University of New York

Myrna Chase
Baruch College, City University of New York

James R. Jacob
John Jay College of Criminal Justice, City University of New York

Margaret C. Jacob
University of California, Los Angeles

Theodore H. Von Laue
Clark University

George W. Bock, *Editorial Associate*

Houghton Mifflin Company   Boston   New York

Publisher: *Charles Hartford*
Senior Sponsoring Editor: *Nancy Blaine*
Senior Development Editor: *Jeff Greene*
Senior Project Editor: *Jane Lee*
Editorial Assistant: *Kristen Truncellito*
Senior Art and Design Coordinator: *Jill Haber*
Senior Photo Editor: *Jennifer Meyer Dare*
Composition Buyer: *Chuck Dutton*
Senior Manufacturing Buyer: *Renee Ostrowski*
Senior Marketing Manager: *Sandra McGuire*
Market Specialist: *Molly Parke*

Cover image: *René Magritte, Girl at the Piano (or Georgette at the piano), 19 —. Credit: Private Collection/Art Resource, NY © 2007 C. Hersovici, Brussels/Artists Rights Society (ARS), New York.*

Printed in the U.S.A.

Library of Congress Control Number: 2005938941

Instructor's exam copy:
ISBN 13: 978-0-618-73024-7
ISBN 10: 0-618-73024-9

For orders, use student text ISBNs:
ISBN 13: 978-0-618-61302-1
ISBN 10: 618-61302-1

123456789-DOC-10 09 08 07 06

Text Credits

Page 513: From *Complete Works of Percy Bysshe Shelley,* edited by Thomas Hutchinson, 1945, p. 440. By permission of Oxford University Press.
Page 562: From Henrik Ibsen, *A Doll's House,* in *Eleven Plays of Henrik Ibsen* (New York: Modern Library, n.d.), p. 85–87.
Page 677: From Joseph Conrad, *Heart of Darkness,* 1923, Random House, Inc.

Brief Contents

Contents

Maps

Chronologies

Preface

Western civilization is a grand but tragic drama. The West has forged the instruments of reason that make possible a rational comprehension of physical nature and human culture, conceived the idea of political liberty, and recognized the intrinsic worth of the individual. But the modern West, though it has unraveled nature's mysteries, has been less successful at finding rational solutions to social ills and conflicts between nations. Science, the great achievement of the Western intellect, while improving conditions of life, has also produced weapons of mass destruction. Though the West has pioneered in the protection of human rights, it has also produced totalitarian regimes that have trampled on individual freedom and human dignity. And although the West has demonstrated a commitment to human equality, it has also practiced brutal racism.

Despite the value that westerners have given to reason and freedom, they have shown a frightening capacity for irrational behavior and a fascination for violence and irrational ideologies, and they have willingly sacrificed liberty for security or national grandeur. The world wars and totalitarian movements of the twentieth century have demonstrated that Western civilization, despite its extraordinary achievements, is fragile and perishable.

Western Civilization: Ideas, Politics, and Society examines the Western tradition—those unique patterns of thought and systems of values that constitute the Western heritage. While focusing on key ideas and broad themes, the text also provides a balanced treatment of economic, political, and social history for students in Western civilization courses.

The text is written with the conviction that history is not a meaningless tale. Without a knowledge of history, men and women cannot fully know themselves, for all human beings have been shaped by institutions and values inherited from the past. Without an awareness of the historical evolution of reason and freedom, the dominant ideals of Western civilization, commitment to these ideals will diminish. Without knowledge of history, the West cannot fully comprehend or adequately cope with the problems that burden its civilization and the world.

In attempting to make sense out of the past, the authors have been careful to avoid superficial generalizations that oversimplify historical events and arrange history into too neat a structure. They strive to interpret and to synthesize in order to provide students with a frame of reference with which to comprehend the principal events and eras in Western history.

CHANGES IN THE EIGHTH EDITION

For the eighth edition every chapter has been reworked to some extent. The hundreds of carefully selected modifications and additions significantly enhance the text. Some changes deepen the book's conceptual character, while others provide useful and illustrative historical details. The concluding essays in many chapters have been enlarged and improved. We have been particularly careful to strengthen chapters dealing with intellectual history, the text's distinguishing feature. Each chapter continues to contain a profile of a significant historical figure. Among the new personalities featured are Epictetus, Joan of Arc, Leni Riefenstahl, and Pope John Paul II. Following the suggestions of instructors who have been using the text through many editions, we have dispensed with the review questions at the end of each chapter. Instead, we have inserted several focus questions at the beginning of each chapter that serve to guide students' reading of the chapter. And to help students understand the new terms they will encounter, we have added a glossary.

Specific changes in Chapter 1, "The Ancient Near East," include an expanded treatment of Egyptian religion; as in previous editions, we made a deliberate effort to improve the final section, "The Religious Orientation of the Near East." In Chapter 2, "The Hebrews," we now discuss the scholarly debate initiated by biblical minimalists and have deepened the treatment of the prophets. Added to Chapter 3, "The Greek City-State," is a deeper analysis of the strengths and weaknesses of Athenian democracy. We added material on early Greek philosophy, the Sophists, Socrates, the Greek dramatists, and Thucydides in Chapter 4, "Greek Thought." Here too we have improved the final section, "The Greek Achievement." In Chapter 5, "The Hellenistic Age," more attention has been given to Hellenistic philosophy. Material has been added to the sections on the consequences of expansion and culture in Chapter 6, "The Roman Republic." In Chapter 7, "The Roman Empire," we have expanded the discussions of Neo-Platonism, the reigns of Diocletian and Constantine, the significance of the battle of Adrianople, and the final section, "The Roman Legacy." Changes in Chapter 8, "Early Christianity," include broader treatments of Paul and the appeal of Christianity in the Mediterranean world. The final section, "Christianity and Classical Humanism," has been significantly improved.

An expanded discussion of Muslim religion and culture is the most noteworthy addition to Chapter 9, "The Heirs of Rome." The treatment of medieval commerce and town life has been expanded in Chapter 10, "The High Middle Ages." Also significantly broadened is the treatment of medieval Christian perceptions of the Jew. In Chapter 11, "The Flowering of Medieval Culture," we have added some material on the poetry of university students. Chapter 12, "The Late Middle Ages," contains more material on the adversities of the fourteenth century, but most significant is the enrichment of the final section, "The Middle Ages and the Modern World."

The section on Renaissance art in Chapter 13, "The Renaissance," has been deleted since that topic is covered in the art essays and a new profile of Leonardo da Vinci has been added. The profile of Sir Isaac Newton in Chapter 17 is also new.

In Chapter 19, "The French Revolution," we have expanded the treatment of the relationship of the Enlightenment to the French Revolution and the Terror in the Vendée and enriched the final section, "The Meaning of the French Revolution." Also enriched is the final section, "The Legend and the Achievement," in Chapter 20, "Napoleon." In Chapter 22, "Thought and Culture in the Early Nineteenth Century," we have revised the chapter introduction and the sections on "Romanticism," "Conservatism," and "Liberalism."

In Chapter 24, "Thought and Culture in the Mid-Nineteenth Century," more attention has been given to "Darwinism" and "Religion in a Secular Age." The section on anti-Semitism has been expanded in Chapter 25, "The Surge of Nationalism." In Chapter 28, "Modern Consciousness," we continue to sharpen the treatment of major themes and thinkers. Here too we have enriched the final section, "The Enlightenment Tradition in Disarray."

The most significant changes in Chapter 29, "World War I," are a deeper treatment of the nature of combat and some additions to the final section, "The War and European Consciousness." In Chapter 30, "An Era of Totalitarianism," we have revised the analyses of Stalin's dictatorship, the rise of Hitler, and the Nazi regime. The treatment of the war, including the Holocaust, has been expanded in Chapter 32, "World War II." And, consistent with other chapters, we have improved the last section, "The Legacy of World War II."

In Chapter 34, "The Troubled Present," Russia under President Putin has been revised and updated. A new section, "The European Union," includes the expansion of the EU, a discussion of Euroskepticism among Europeans, and the defeat of the EU constitution. Treatment of the major European countries has been updated. The section dealing with international terrorism by radical Islamic jihadists has been expanded, and considerable space is given to the war in Iraq, including the role of Islamic jihadists in the insurgency.

DISTINCTIVE FEATURES

The text contains several pedagogical features, including two new ones mentioned above: focus questions and a glossary. Chapter outlines and introductions provide comprehensive overviews of key themes and give a sense of direction and coherence to the flow of history. Many chapters contain concluding essays that treat the larger meaning of the material. Facts have been carefully selected to illustrate key relationships and concepts and to avoid overwhelming students with unrelated and disconnected data. Appropriate quotations, many not commonly found in texts, have been integrated into the discussion. Each chapter contains notes and an annotated bibliography. And new to this edition, each chapter also begins with focus questions to aid students' reading of the chapter. There is also a comprehensive glossary to help students with unfamiliar terms.

Western Civilization: Ideas, Politics, and Society is available in both one-and two-volume editions, and in a third edition, *From the 1400s*. *From the 1400s* (twenty-two chapters) has been prepared for those instructors whose courses begin with the Renaissance or the Reformation.

Volume 1 of the two-volume edition treats the period from the first civilizations in the Near East through the Age of Enlightenment in the eighteenth century (eighteen chapters). Volume 2 covers the period from the growth of national states in the seventeenth century to the contemporary age (nineteen chapters). Because some instructors start the second half of their course with the period prior to the French Revolution, Volume 2 incorporates the last three chapters of Volume 1: "The Rise of Sovereignty," "The Scientific Revolution," and "The Age of Enlightenment." Volume 2 also contains a comprehensive introduction that surveys the ancient world, the Middle Ages, and the opening centuries of the modern era; the introduction is designed particularly for students who did not take the first half of the course. *From the 1400s* also contains an introduction that covers the ancient world and the Middle Ages.

ANCILLARIES

We are pleased to introduce an expanded ancillary package that will help students in learning and instructors in teaching:

Online Study Center student website

Online Study Center

Online Teaching Center instructor website
HM ClassPrep with HM Testing (powered by Diploma)
Online Instructor's Resource Manual
Computerized Test Items
PowerPoint maps and images
PowerPoint questions for personal response systems
Blackboard® and WebCT® course cartridges
Eduspace® for World History (powered by Blackboard®)
Map transparencies

The *Online Study Center* is a new companion website for students that features a wide array of resources to help students master the subject matter. The website, prepared by Gregory S. Brown of the University of Nevada, Las Vegas is divided into three major sections: "Prepare for Class" includes material such as learning objectives, chapter outlines, and pre-class quizzes for a student to consult before going to class; "Improve Your Grade" includes self-testing material like interactive flashcards, chronological ordering exercises, web activities, and interactive map and primary source exercises; and "ACE the Test" features our successful ACE brand of practice tests. Students can also find additional text resources such as an online glossary and material on how to study more effectively in the "General Resources" section. For the eighth edition, we have added icons to the text that direct students to relevant exercises and self-testing material located on the *Online Study Center*. Access the *Online Study*

Center for this text by visiting college.hmco.com/pic/perrywc8e.

The *Online Teaching Center* is a new companion website for instructors. It features all of the material on the student site plus additional password-protected resources for teaching the course such as an electronic version of the *Instructor's Resource Manual* and *PowerPoint* slides. Access the *Online Teaching Center* for this text by visiting college.hmco.com/pic/perrywc8e.

HM ClassPrep with HM Testing, the latest comprehensive instructor's resource in computerized testing, includes electronic versions of the *Instructor's Resource Manual* and *Test Items*, the *HM Testing* test generation tool, and *PowerPoint* maps and images and questions for use with personal response systems. *HM Testing* (powered by *Diploma*) offers instructors a flexible and powerful tool for test generation and test management. Now supported by the Brownstone Research Group's market-leading *Diploma*™ software, this new version of *HM Testing* significantly improves on functionality and ease of use by offering all the tools needed to create, deliver, and customize multiple types of tests. *Diploma*™ is currently in use at thousands of college and university campuses throughout the United States and Canada.

The *Instructor's Resource Manual*, prepared by John Reisbord, and *Test Items*, prepared by Joseph Y. Appiah of J. Sergeant Reynolds Community College, are both available in electronic format on *HM ClassPrep*™. The *Instructor's Resource Manual* contains advice on teaching the Western civilization course, instructional objectives, chapter outlines, lecture suggestions, paper and class activity topics, primary source and map activities, and suggestions for cooperative learning. The *Test Items* offer multiple-choice, short answer, and essay questions as well as unit, midterm, and final examination questions.

We are pleased to offer a collection of *PowerPoint* maps and images for use in classroom presentations. This collection includes all of the photos and maps in the text, as well as numerous other images from European history. PowerPoint questions and answers for use with personal response system software are also offered to adopters free of charge.

New to this edition, graded homework questions have been developed to work with the *Blackboard*® and *WebCT*® course management systems, as well as with *Eduspace*® *for Western Civilization*: Houghton Mifflin's Online Learning Tool (Powered by Blackboard®). *Eduspace*® *for Western Civilization* is a web-based online learning environment that provides instructors with a gradebook and communication capabilities, such as synchronous and asynchronous chats and announcement postings. By pairing these widely recognized course management tools with quality, text-specific and course-wide content, *Eduspace*® *for Western Civilization* makes it easy for instructors to create all or part of a course online. Developed to meet the unique needs of history curricula, *Eduspace*® *for Western Civilization* offers access to assignable resources such as over 650 gradable homework exercises, writing assignments, discussion questions for online discussion boards, and tests, which all come ready-to-use. Instructors can choose to use the content as is, modify it, or even add their own. Finally, a set of full-color map transparencies of all the maps in the text is available on adoption.

The text represents the efforts of several authors. Marvin Perry, general editor of the project, wrote Chapters 1–12, 19–20, 22–25, 28–32, the Epilogue, and the section on the American Revolution in Chapter 18. James R. Jacob is the author of Chapters 13 and 15. Margaret C. Jacob wrote Chapters 14 and 16–18. Myrna Chase is the author of Chapters 21, 26–27, and contributed to the section on reform in Britain in Chapter 23. Theodore H. Von Laue wrote much of Chapters 33 and 34 and contributed the sections on tsarist Russia to Chapter 26, and on Communist Russia to Chapter 30. Since his death, Marvin Perry and Angela Von Laue have revised these chapters. Over the years, Marvin Perry and George Bock have edited the manuscript for continuity and clarity.

ACKNOWLEDGMENTS

The authors would like to thank the following instructors for their critical reading of sections of the manuscript: Joseph Appiah, J. Sargeant Reynolds Community College; Gregory S. Brown, University of Nevada, Las Vegas; Frank Buscher, Christian Brothers University; Chiarella Esposito,

University of Mississippi; L. Edward Hicks, Faulkner University; Donald M. McKale, Clemson University; and Barbara Hensley Shepard, Longwood University. Several of their suggestions were incorporated into the final version.

We are also grateful to the staff of Houghton Mifflin Company who lent their considerable talents to the project. In particular we would like to thank Jeff Greene, senior development editor, for his conscientiousness and concern; Jane Lee, project editor, for her careful attention to detail; Jay Boggis, whose copyediting skills are reflected in the manuscript; and Linda Sykes, for supervising the choice of pictures in the text. This edition rests substantially on the editorial talents of Freda Alexander, who worked closely with us on earlier editions of the text. Both Jean Woy, senior consulting editor, who has been affiliated with the text since the first edition and Nancy Blaine, senior sponsoring editor, continue to recognize and support what we are trying to do—and for this we remain grateful. The death of my long time colleague and friend, Theodore Von Laue, deeply saddens me. Although his special talents are missed, his wife Angela Von Laue has added her literary and research skills to the project. I would like to express my personal gratitude to her and to my good friend George Bock, whose creative insights in previous editions continue to contribute to the text's distinguishing character—a concern for crucial concepts and essential relationships. Our often heated, but always fruitful discussions demonstrate to me the intrinsic value of the Socratic dialogue. And, as always, I am grateful to my wife, Phyllis Perry, for her encouragement and computer expertise, which have saved me much time and frustration.

M. P.

Introduction

The Foundations of Western Civilization

Western Civilization is a blending of two traditions that emerged in the ancient world: the Judeo-Christian and the Greco-Roman. Before these traditions took shape, the drama of civilization was well advanced, having begun some five thousand years ago in Mesopotamia and Egypt.

Religion was the central force in these first civilizations in the Near East. Religion explained the operations of nature, justified traditional rules of morality, and helped people to deal with their fear of death. Law was considered sacred, a commandment of the gods. Religion united people in the common enterprises needed for survival, such as the construction of irrigation works. Religion also promoted creative achievements in art, literature, and science. In addition, the power of rulers, who were regarded as gods or as agents of the gods, derived from the religious outlook. The many achievements of the Egyptians and the Mesopotamians were inherited and assimilated by both the Greeks and the Hebrews, the spiritual ancestors of Western civilization. But Greeks and Hebrews also rejected and transformed elements of the older Near Eastern traditions and conceived a new view of God, nature, and the individual.

The Hebrews

By asserting that God was one, sovereign, transcendent, and good, the Hebrews effected a religious revolution that separated them forever from the world-views of the Mesopotamians and Egyptians. This new conception of God led to a new awareness of the individual. In confronting God, the Hebrews developed an awareness of self, or I. The individual became conscious of his or her moral autonomy and personal worth. The Hebrews believed that God had bestowed on his people the capacity for moral freedom—they could choose between good and evil. Fundamental to Hebrew belief was the insistence that God had created human beings to be free moral agents. God did not want people to grovel before him, but to fulfill their moral potential by freely making the choice to follow, or not to follow, God's law. Thus, the Hebrews conceived the idea of moral freedom—that each individual is responsible for his or her own actions. Inherited by Christianity, this idea of moral autonomy is central to the Western tradition.

The Hebrew conception of ethical monotheism, with its stress on human dignity, is one source of the Western tradition. The other source derives from the ancient Greeks; they originated scientific and philosophical thought and conceived both the idea and the practice of political freedom.

The Greeks

In the Near East, religion dominated political activity, and following the mandates of the gods was a ruler's first responsibility. What made Greek political life different from that of earlier civilizations—and gives it enduring significance—was the Greeks' gradual realization that community problems were caused by human beings and required human solutions. The Greeks came to understand law as an achievement of the rational mind, rather than as an edict imposed by the gods. In the process, they also originated the idea of political freedom and created democratic institutions.

Greece comprised small, independent city-states. In the fifth century B.C., the city-state (*polis*) was in its maturity. A self-governing community, it expressed the will of free citizens, not the desires of gods, hereditary kings, or priests. The democratic orientation of the city-states was best exemplified by Athens, which was also the leading cultural center of Greece. In the Assembly, which was open to all adult male citizens, Athenians debated and voted on key issues of state.

Besides the idea of political freedom, the Greeks conceived a new way of viewing nature and human society. The first speculative philosophers emerged during the sixth century B.C. in Greek cities located in Ionia, in Asia Minor. Curious about the basic composition of nature and dissatisfied with earlier legends about creation, the Ionians sought physical, rather than mytho-religious, explanations for natural occurrences.

During this search, these philosophers arrived at a new concept of nature and a new method of inquiry. They maintained that nature was not manipulated by arbitrary and willful gods and that it was not governed by blind chance. The Ionians said that underlying the seeming chaos of nature were principles of order, that is, general rules that could be ascertained by human minds. The discovery marks the beginning of scientific thought. It made possible theoretical thinking and the systematization of knowledge. This is distinct from the mere observation and collection of data. Greek mathematicians, for example, organized the Egyptians' practical experience with land measurements into the logical and coherent science of geometry. The Greeks also used the data collected by Babylonian priests, who observed the heavens because they believed that the stars revealed their gods' wishes. However, the Greeks' purpose was not religious—they sought to discover the geometric laws underlying the motion of heavenly bodies. At the same time, Greek physicians drew a distinction between medicine and magic and began to examine human illness in an empirical and rational way. By the fifth century, the Greek mind had applied reason to the physical world and to all human activities. This emphasis on reason marks a turning point for human civilization.

In their effort to understand the external world, early Greek thinkers had created the tools of reason. Greek thinkers now began a rational investigation of the human being and the human community. The key figure in this development was Socrates.

Socrates' central concern was the perfection of individual human character and the achievement of moral excellence. Excellence of character was achieved, said Socrates, when individuals regulated their lives according to objective standards arrived at through rational reflection, that is, when reason became the formative, guiding, and ruling agency of the soul. Socrates wanted to subject all human beliefs and behavior to the clear light of reason and in this way to remove ethics from the realm of authority, tradition, dogma, superstition, and myth. He believed that reason was the only proper guide to the most crucial problem of human existence—the question of good and evil.

Plato, Socrates' most important disciple, used his master's teachings to create a comprehensive system of philosophy, which embraced the world of nature and the social world. Socrates had taught that there were universal standards of right and justice and that these were arrived at through thought. Building on the insights of his teacher, Plato insisted on the existence of a higher world of reality, independent of the world of things experienced every day. This higher reality, he said, is the realm of Ideas, or Forms—unchanging, eternal, absolute, and universal standards of beauty, goodness, justice, and so forth. Truth resides in this world of Forms and not in the world revealed through the human senses.

Aristotle, Plato's student, was the leading expert of this time in every field of knowledge, with the possible exception of mathematics. Aristotle objected to Plato's devaluing of the material world. Possessing a scientist's curiosity to understand the facts of nature, Aristotle appreciated the world of phenomena, of concrete things, and respected knowledge obtained through the senses. Like Plato, Aristotle believed that understanding universal principles is the ultimate aim of knowledge. But unlike Plato, Aristotle held that to obtain such knowledge the individual must study the world of facts and objects revealed through sight, hearing, and touch. Aristotle adapted Plato's stress on universal principles to the requirements of natural science.

By discovering theoretical reason, by defining political freedom, and by affirming the worth and potential of human personality, the Greeks broke with the past and founded the rational and humanist tradition of the West. "Had Greek civilization never existed," said poet W. H. Auden, "we would never have become fully conscious, which is to say that we would never have become, for better or worse, fully human."[1]

THE HELLENISTIC AGE

By 338 B.C., Philip of Macedonia (a kingdom to the north of Greece) had extended his dominion over the Greek city-states. After the assassination of Philip in 336 B.C., his twenty-year-old son Alexander succeeded to the throne. Fiery, proud, and ambitious, Alexander sought to conquer the vast Persian Empire. Winning every battle, Alexander's army carved out an empire that stretched from Greece to India. In 323 B.C., Alexander, not yet thirty-three years of age, died of a fever. His generals engaged in a long and bitter struggle to succeed him. As none of the generals or their heirs could predominate, Alexander's empire was fractured into separate states.

The period from the early city-states that emerged in 800 B.C. until the death of Alexander the Great in 323 B.C. is called the *Hellenic Age*. The next stage in the evolution of Greek civilization (*Hellenism*) is called the *Hellenistic Age*. It ended in 30 B.C., when Egypt, the last major Hellenistic state, fell to Rome.

Although the Hellenistic Age had absorbed the heritage of classical (Hellenic) Greece, its style of civilization changed. During the first phase of Hellenism, the polis had given the individual identity, and it was believed that only within the polis could a Greek live a good and civilized life. During the Hellenistic Age, this situation changed. Kingdoms eclipsed the city-states in power and importance. Although cities

retained a large measure of autonomy in domestic affairs, they had lost their freedom of action in foreign affairs. No longer were they the self-sufficient and independent communities of the Hellenic period.

Hellenistic society was characterized by a mingling of peoples and an interchange of cultures. As a result of Alexander's conquests, tens of thousands of Greek soldiers, merchants, and administrators settled in eastern lands. Greek traditions spread to the Near East, and Mesopotamian, Hebrew, and Persian traditions—particularly religious beliefs—moved westward. Cities were founded in the East patterned after the city-states of Greece. The ruling class in each Hellenistic city was united by a common Hellenism, which overcame national, linguistic, and racial distinctions.

During the Hellenistic Age, Greek scientific achievement reached its height. Hellenistic scientists attempted a rational analysis of nature, engaged in research, organized knowledge in a logical fashion, devised procedures for mathematical proof, separated medicine from magic, grasped the theory of experiment, and applied scientific principles to mechanical devices. Hellenistic science, says historian Benjamin Farrington, stood "on the threshold of the modern world. When modern science began in the sixteenth century, it took up where the Greeks left off."[2]

Hellenistic philosophers preserved the rational tradition of Greek philosophy. Like their Hellenic predecessors, they regarded the cosmos as governed by universal principles intelligible to the rational mind. The most important philosophy in the Hellenistic world was Stoicism. By teaching that the world constituted a single society, Stoicism gave theoretical expression to the cosmopolitanism and universalism of the age. Stoicism, with its concept of a world-state, offered an answer to the problems of the loss of community and the alienation caused by the decline of the city-state. By stressing inner strength in dealing with life's misfortunes, Stoicism offered an avenue to individual happiness in a world fraught with uncertainty.

At the core of Stoicism was the belief that the universe contained a principle of order: the *Logos* (reason). This ruling principle permeated all things; it accounted for the orderliness of nature. Because people were part of the universe, said the

Stoics, they also shared in the Logos, which operated throughout the cosmos. Since reason was common to all, human beings were essentially members of the same human family and fundamentally equal.

Stoicism had an enduring impact on the Western mind. To some Roman political theorists, their Empire fulfilled the Stoic ideal of a world community in which people of different nationalities held citizenship and were governed by a worldwide law that accorded with the law of reason, or natural law that operated throughout the universe. Stoic beliefs—that all human beings are members of one family; that each person is significant; that distinctions of rank are of no account; and that human law should not conflict with natural law—were incorporated into Roman jurisprudence, Christian thought, and modern liberalism. There is continuity between Stoic thought and the principle of inalienable rights stated in the American Declaration of Independence.

ROME

Rome, conquerer of the Mediterranean world and transmitter of Hellenism, inherited the universalist tendencies of the Hellenistic Age and embodied them in its law and institutions. Roman history falls into two periods: the Republic, which began in 509 B.C. with the overthrow of the Etruscan monarchy; and the Empire, which started in 27 B.C., when Octavian became, in effect, the first Roman emperor.

The Roman Republic

The history of the Roman Republic was marked by three principal developments: the struggle between patricians and plebeians, the conquest of Italy and the Mediterranean world, and the civil wars. At the beginning of the fifth century B.C., Rome was dominated by *patricians* (the landowning aristocrats). The *plebeians* (commoners) had many grievances; these included enslavement for debt, discrimination in the courts, prevention of intermarriage with patricians, lack of political

representation, and the absence of a written code of law.

Resentful of their inferior status, the plebeians organized and waged a struggle for political, legal, and social equality. They were resisted every step of the way by the patricians, who wanted to preserve their dominance. The plebeians had one decisive weapon: their threat to secede from Rome, that is, not to pay taxes, work, or serve in the army. Realizing that Rome, which was constantly involved in warfare on the Italian peninsula, could not endure without plebeian help, the pragmatic patricians begrudgingly made concessions. Thus, the plebeians slowly gained legal equality.

Although many plebeian grievances were resolved and the plebeians obtained the right to sit in the Senate, the principal organ of government, Rome was still ruled by an upper class. Power was concentrated in a ruling oligarchy, consisting of patricians and influential plebeians, who had joined forces with the old nobility.

By 146 B.C., Rome had become the dominant power in the Mediterranean world. Roman expansion occurred in three main stages: the uniting of the Italian peninsula, which gave Rome the manpower that transformed it from a city-state into a great power; the struggle with Carthage, from which Rome emerged as ruler of the western Mediterranean; and the subjugation of the Hellenistic states of the eastern Mediterranean, which brought Romans into close contact with Greek civilization.

A crucial consequence of expansion was Roman contact with the legal experience of other peoples. Roman jurists, demonstrating the Roman virtues of pragmatism and common sense, selectively incorporated elements of the legal codes and traditions of these nations into Roman law. Thus, Roman jurists gradually and empirically fashioned the *jus gentium*, the law of nations, or peoples.

Roman jurists came to identify the jus gentium with the natural law (*jus naturale*) of the Stoics. The jurists said that law should accord with rational principles inherent in nature—universal norms capable of being discerned by rational people. The law of nations—Roman civil law (the law of the Roman state), combined with principles drawn from Greek and other sources—eventually replaced much of the local law in the Empire. This evolution of a universal code of law that gave expression to the Stoic principles of common rationality and humanity was the great achievement of Roman rule.

Another consequence of expansion was increased contact with Greek culture. Gradually, the Romans acquired knowledge from Greece about scientific thought, philosophy, medicine and geography. Adopting the humanist outlook of the Greeks, the Romans came to value human intelligence and eloquent and graceful prose and oratory. Rome creatively assimilated the Greek achievement and transmitted it to others, thereby extending the orbit of Hellenism.

During Rome's march to empire, all its classes had demonstrated a magnificent civic spirit in fighting foreign wars. With Carthage and Macedonia no longer threatening Rome, this cooperation deteriorated. Rome became torn apart by internal dissension during the first century B.C.

Julius Caesar, a popular military commander, gained control of the government. Caesar believed that only strong and enlightened leadership could permanently end the civil warfare destroying Rome. Rome's ruling class feared that Caesar would destroy the Republic and turn Rome into a monarchy. Regarding themselves as defenders of republican liberties and senatorial leadership, aristocratic conspirators assassinated Caesar in 44 B.C. The murder of Caesar plunged Rome into renewed civil war. Finally, in 31 B.C., Octavian, Caesar's adopted son, defeated his rivals and emerged as master of Rome. Four years later, Octavian, now called Augustus, became, in effect, the first Roman emperor.

The Roman Empire

The rule of Augustus signified the end of the Roman Republic and the beginning of the Roman Empire—the termination of aristocratic politics and the emergence of one-man rule. Under Augustus, the power of the ruler was disguised; in ensuing generations, however, emperors would wield absolute power openly.

Augustus was by no means a self-seeking tyrant, but a creative statesman. His reforms rescued a dying Roman world and inaugurated Rome's greatest age. For the next two hundred years, the Mediterranean world enjoyed the blessings of the *Pax Romana,* the Roman peace.

The ancient world had never experienced such a long period of peace, order, efficient administration, and prosperity. The Romans called the Pax Romana a "Time of Happiness." It was the fulfillment of Rome's mission—the creation of a world-state that provided peace, security, ordered civilization, and the rule of law. The cities of the Roman Empire served as centers of Greco-Roman civilization, which spread to the furthest reaches of the Mediterranean. Roman citizenship, gradually granted, was finally extended to virtually all free men by an edict in A.D. 212.

In the third century, the ordered civilization of the Pax Romana ended. The Roman Empire was plunged into military anarchy as generals, supported by their soldiers, fought for the throne. Germanic tribesmen broke through the deteriorating border defenses to raid, loot, and destroy. Economic problems caused cities, the centers of civilization, to decay. Increasingly, people turned away from the humanist values of the Greco-Roman civilization and embraced Near Eastern religions, which offered a sense of belonging, a promise of immortality, and relief from earthly misery.

The emperors Diocletian (285–305) and Constantine (306–337) tried to contain the forces of disintegration by tightening the reins of government and squeezing more taxes out of the citizens. In the process, they divided the Empire into eastern and western halves, and transformed Rome into a bureaucratic, regimented, and militarized state.

Diocletian and Constantine had given Rome a reprieve, but in the last part of the fourth century the problem of guarding the frontier grew more acute. At the end of 406, the border finally collapsed; numerous German tribes overran the Empire's western provinces. In 410 and again in 455, Rome was sacked by Germanic invaders. German soldiers in the pay of Rome gained control of the government and dictated the choice of emperor. In 476, German officers overthrew the Roman emperor Romulus and placed a fellow German on the throne. The act is traditionally regarded as the end of the Roman Empire in the West.

EARLY CHRISTIANITY

When the Roman Empire was in decline, a new religion, Christianity, was sweeping across the Mediterranean world. Christianity was based on the life, death, and teachings of Jesus, a Palestinian Jew who was executed by the Roman authorities. Jesus was heir to the ethical monotheism of the Hebrew prophets. He also taught the imminent coming of the reign of God and the need for people to repent their sins—to transform themselves morally in order to enter God's kingdom. People must love God and their fellow human beings.

In the time immediately following the crucifixion of Jesus, his followers were almost exclusively Jews, who could more appropriately be called Jewish-Christians. To the first members of the Christian movement, Jesus was both a prophet, who proclaimed God's power and purpose, and the Messiah, whose coming heralded a new age. To Paul, another Jewish-Christian, Jesus was a resurrected redeemer who offered salvation to all peoples. Although Paul was not very precise about the divinity of Jesus and his prior existence, he did frequently refer to him as the Son of God and the Divine Wisdom, through whom all things were created and in whom God's purpose is revealed. He taught that the crucified Messiah had suffered and died for the sins of human beings, that through Jesus, God had shown his love of humanity and revealed himself to all people, both Jew and Gentile, and that this revelation supplanted the earlier one to the Jewish people. Increasingly Jesus' followers came to view the sacrificial Messiah as a savior-god, indeed as God incarnate.

The Christian message of a divine Savior, a concerned Father, and brotherly love inspired men and women who were dissatisfied with the world of the here-and-now, who felt no attachment to city or Empire, who derived no inspiration from philosophy, and who suffered from a profound sense of loneliness. Christianity offered the individual what the city and the Roman world-state could not: a personal relationship with God, a promise of eternal life, and membership in a community of the faithful (the church) who cared for each other.

Unable to crush Christianity by persecution, Roman emperors decided to gain the support of the growing number of Christians within the Empire. By A.D. 392, Theodosius I had made Christianity the state religion of the Empire and declared the worship of pagan gods illegal.

The Judeo-Christian and Greco-Roman traditions are the two principal components of Western civilization. Both traditions valued the individual. For classical humanism, individual worth derived from the human capacity to reason—to shape character and life according to rational standards. Christianity also places great stress on the individual. It teaches that God cares for each person and wants people to behave righteously, and that he made them morally autonomous.

Despite their common emphasis on the individual, the Judeo-Christian and Greco-Roman traditions essentially have different world-views. With the victory of Christianity, the ultimate goal of life shifted from achieving excellence in this world, through the full and creative development of human talent, toward attaining salvation in a heavenly city. For Christians, a person's worldly accomplishments counted very little if he or she did not accept God and his revelation. Greek classicism held that there was no authority higher than reason; Christianity taught that without God as the starting point, knowledge is formless, purposeless, and error-prone.

But Christian thinkers did not seek to eradicate the rational tradition of Greece. Rather, they sought to fit Greek philosophy into a Christian framework. In doing so, Christians performed a task of immense historical significance—the preservation of Greek philosophy.

THE MIDDLE AGES

The triumph of Christianity and the establishment of Germanic kingdoms on once Roman lands constituted a new phase in Western history: the end of the ancient world and the beginning of the Middle Ages. In the ancient world, the locus of Greco-Roman civilization was the Mediterranean Sea. The heartland of medieval civilization shifted to the north, to regions of Europe that Greco-Roman civilization had barely penetrated.

The Early Middle Ages

During the Early Middle Ages (500–1050), a common civilization evolved, with Christianity at the center, Rome as the spiritual capital, and Latin as the language of intellectual life. The opening centuries of the Middle Ages were marked by a decline in trade, town life, central authority, and learning. The Germans were culturally unprepared to breathe new life into classical civilization. A new civilization with its own distinctive style was taking root, however. It consisted of Greco-Roman survivals, the native traditions of the Germans, and the Christian outlook.

Christianity was the integrating principle of the Middle Ages, and the church the dominant institution. People came to see themselves as participants in a great drama of salvation. There was only one truth—God's revelation to humanity. There was only one avenue to heaven—the church. To the medieval mind, society without the church was as inconceivable as life without the Christian view of God. By teaching a higher morality, the church tamed the warrior habits of the Germanic peoples. By copying and preserving ancient texts, monks kept alive elements of the high civilization of Greece and Rome.

One German people, the Franks, built a viable kingdom, with major centers in France and the Rhine Valley of Germany. Under Charlemagne, who ruled from 768 to 814, the Frankish empire reached its height. On Christmas Day in the year 800, Pope Leo III crowned Charlemagne as "Emperor of the Romans." The title signified that the tradition of a world empire still survived, despite the demise of the Roman Empire three hundred years earlier. Because the pope crowned Charlemagne, this act meant that the emperor had a spiritual responsibility to spread and defend the faith.

The crowning of a German ruler as emperor of the Romans by the head of the church represented the merging of German, Christian, and Roman elements—the essential characteristic of medieval civilization. This blending of traditions was also evident on a cultural plane, for Charlemagne, a German warrior-king, showed respect for classical learning and Christianity, both non-Germanic traditions. During his reign, a distinct European civilization took root, but it was centuries away from fruition.

Charlemagne's successors could not hold the empire together, and it disintegrated. As central authority waned, large landowners began to exercise authority over their own regions. Furthering this movement toward localism and decentralization were simultaneous invasions by Muslims, Vikings from Scandinavia, and Magyars, originally from western Asia. The invaders devastated villages, destroyed ports, and killed many people. Trade was at a standstill, coins no longer circulated, and untended farms became wastelands. The European community collapsed, the political authority of kings disappeared, and cultural life and learning withered.

During these times, large landowners, or lords, wielded power formerly held by kings over their subjects, an arrangement called *feudalism.* Arising during a period of collapsing central authority, invasion, scanty public revenues, and declining commerce and town life, feudalism attempted to provide some order and security. A principal feature of feudalism was the practice of *vassalage,* in which a man in a solemn ceremony pledged loyalty to a lord. The lord received military service from his vassal, and the vassal obtained land, called a *fief,* from his lord.

Feudalism was built on an economic foundation known as manorialism. A village community (manor), consisting of serfs bound to the land, became the essential agricultural arrangement in medieval society. In return for protection and the right to cultivate fields, serfs owed obligations to their lords, and their personal freedom was restricted in a variety of ways.

Manorialism and feudalism presupposed an unchanging social order with a rigid system of estates, or orders—clergy who prayed, lords who fought, and peasants who toiled. The revival of an urban economy and the reemergence of the king's authority in the High Middle Ages (about 1050–1270) would undermine feudal and manorial relationships.

The High Middle Ages

By the end of the eleventh century, Europe showed many signs of recovery and vitality. The invasions of Magyars and Vikings had ended, and kings and powerful lords imposed greater order in their territories. Improvements in technology and the clearing of new lands increased agricultural production. More food, the fortunate absence of plagues, and the limited nature of feudal warfare contributed to a population increase.

Expanding agricultural production, the end of Viking attacks, greater political stability, and a larger population revived commerce. In the twelfth and thirteenth centuries, local, regional, and long-distance trade gained such a momentum that some historians describe the period as a commercial revolution that surpassed the commercial activity of the Roman Empire during the Pax Romana.

In the eleventh century, towns reemerged throughout Europe and in the next century became active centers of commerce and intellectual life. Socially, economically, and culturally, towns were a new and revolutionary force. Towns contributed to the decline of manorialism because they provided new opportunities for commoners, apart from food production.

A new class (the middle class) of merchants and artisans appeared; unlike the lords and serfs, the members of this class were not connected with the land. Townspeople possessed a value system different from that of lords, serfs, or clerics. Whereas the clergy prepared people for heaven, the feudal lords fought and hunted, and the serfs toiled in small villages, townspeople engaged in business and had money and freedom. Townspeople were freeing themselves from the prejudices of both feudal aristocrats, who considered trade and manual work degrading, and the clergy, who cursed the pursuit of riches as an obstacle to salvation. Townspeople were critical, dynamic, and progressive—a force for change.

Other signs of growing vitality in Latin Christendom (western and central Europe) were the greater order and security provided by the emergence of states. While feudalism fostered a Europe that was split into many local regions, each ruled by a lord, the church envisioned a vast Christian commonwealth, *Republica Christiana*, guided by the pope. During the High Middle Ages, the ideal of a universal Christian community seemed close to fruition. Never again would Europe possess such spiritual unity.

But forces were propelling Europe in a different direction. Aided by educated and trained officials who enforced royal law, tried people in royal courts, and collected royal taxes, kings enlarged their territories and slowly fashioned strong central governments. Gradually, subjects began to transfer their prime loyalty from the church and their lords to the person of the king. In the process, the foundations of European states were laid. Not all areas followed the same pattern. England and France achieved a large measure of unity during the Middle Ages; Germany and Italy remained divided into numerous independent territories.

Along with economic recovery and political stability, the High Middle Ages experienced a growing spiritual vitality. This vigor was marked by several developments. The common people showed greater devotion to the church. Within the church, reform movements attacked clerical abuses, and the papacy grew more powerful. Holy wars against the Muslims drew the Christian community closer together. During this period, the church, with great determination, tried to make society follow divine standards, that is, to shape all institutions according to a comprehensive Christian outlook.

European economic and religious vitality was paralleled by a flowering of philosophy, literature, and the visual arts. Creative intellects achieved on a cultural level what the papacy accomplished on an institutional level—the integration of society around a Christian viewpoint. The High Middle Ages saw the restoration of some learning of the ancient world, the rise of universities, the emergence of an original form of architecture (the Gothic), and the creation of an imposing system of thought (scholasticism).

Medieval theologian-philosophers, called *scholastics*, fashioned Christian teachings into an all-embracing philosophy, which represented the spiritual essence of medieval civilization. They achieved what Christian thinkers in the Roman Empire had initiated and what learned men of the Early Middle Ages were groping for: a synthesis of Greek philosophy and Christian revelation.

The Late Middle Ages

By the fourteenth century, Latin Christendom had experienced more than 250 years of growth, but during the Late Middle Ages, roughly the fourteenth and early fifteenth centuries, medieval civilization declined. The fourteenth century, an age of adversity, was marked by crop failures, famine, population decline, plagues, stagnating production, unemployment, inflation, devastating warfare, abandoned villages, and violent rebellions by the poor and weak of towns and countryside, who were ruthlessly suppressed by the upper classes. This century witnessed flights into mysticism, outbreaks of mass hysteria, and massacres of Jews; it was an age of pessimism and general insecurity. Papal power declined, heresy proliferated, and the synthesis of faith and reason erected by the Christian thinkers during the High Middle Ages began to disintegrate. All these developments were signs that the stable and coherent civilization of the thirteenth century was drawing to a close.

The Middle Ages and the Modern World

But the decline of medieval civilization in the fourteenth century brought no new dark age to Europe. Its economic and political institutions and technological skills had grown too strong. Instead, the waning of the Middle Ages opened up possibilities for another stage in Western civilization—the modern age.

The modern world is linked to the Middle Ages in innumerable ways. European cities, the middle class, the state system, English common law, universities—all had their origins in the Middle Ages. During the Middle Ages, important advances were made in business practices, such as double-entry bookkeeping and the growth of credit and banking facilities. By translating and commenting on the writings of Greek philosophers and scientists, medieval scholars preserved a priceless intellectual heritage without which the modern mind could never had evolved. During the Middle Ages, Europeans began to lead the rest of the world in the development of technology.

Medieval philosophers, believing that God's law was superior to the decrees of states, provided a theoretical basis for opposing tyrannical kings who violated Christian principles. The idea that both the ruler and the ruled are bound by a higher law would become a crucial element of modern liberal thought. The Christian stress on the sacred worth of the individual and on the higher law of God has never ceased to influence Western civilization. The Christian commandment to "love thy neighbor" has permeated modern reform movements.

Feudalism contributed to the history of liberty. The idea evolved that law should not be imposed by an absolute monarch but that it required the collaboration of kings and subjects; that a king, too, should be bound by the law; and that lords should have the right to resist a monarch who violated agreements. Related to this development was the emergence of representative institutions, notably the English Parliament. The king was expected to consult its members on matters concerning the realm's affairs.

Despite these elements of continuity, the characteristic outlook of the Middle Ages was very different from that of the modern world. Religion was the integrating feature of the Middle Ages, whereas science and secularism determine the modern outlook. Medieval thought began with the existence of God and the truth of his revelation as interpreted by the church, which set the standards and defined the purposes for human endeavor.

The medieval mind rejected the fundamental principle of Greek philosophy and modern thought—the autonomy of reason. Without the guidance of revealed truth, reason was seen as feeble. Unlike either ancient or modern thinkers, medieval scholars believed that ultimately reason alone could not provide a unified view of nature or society. To understand nature, law, morality, or the state, it was necessary to know its relationship to a supernatural order, a higher world.

In the modern view, both nature and the human intellect are self-sufficient. Nature is a mathematical system that operates without miracles or any other form of divine intervention. To comprehend nature and society, the mind needs no divine assistance; it accepts no authority above reason. The modern mind finds it unacceptable to reject conclusions of science on the basis of clerical authority and revelation or to base politics, law, and economics on religion; it rejects the medieval division of the universe into a heavenly realm of perfection and a lower earthly realm. Scientific and secular attitudes have driven Christianity and faith from their central position to the periphery of human concerns.

EARLY MODERN EUROPE

From the Italian Renaissance of the fifteenth century through the Age of Enlightenment of the eighteenth century, the outlook and institutions of the Middle Ages disintegrated and distinctly modern forms emerged. This radical change in European civilization could be seen on every level of society. On the economic level, commerce and industry expanded greatly, and capitalism largely replaced medieval forms of economic organization. In political life, central government grew stronger at the expense of feudalism. On the religious level, the unity of Christendom became fragmented by the rise of Protestantism. On the social level, middle-class townspeople, increasing in number and wealth, started playing a more important role in economic and cultural life. In consequence, the clergy lost its monopoly over learning, and the otherworldly orientation of the Middle Ages gave way to a secular outlook in literature and the arts. Theology, the queen of the sciences in the Middle Ages, surrendered its crown to mathematics and the study of nature.

The Renaissance

Many new tendencies manifested themselves dramatically during the Renaissance, a period beginning about 1350 and lasting two centuries. The word *renaissance* means rebirth, and it is used to refer to the attempt by artists and thinkers to recover and apply the learning and standards of ancient Greece and Rome. The Renaissance was an age of transition during which crucial elements of the medieval outlook were rejected, classical cultural forms were revived, and modern attitudes emerged. The Renaissance was not a complete and sudden break with the Middle Ages; many medieval ways and attitudes persisted. Nevertheless, the thesis that the Renaissance represents the birth of modernity has much in its favor.

New economic, political, and social conditions presented new challenges, for which the old order of priests and feudal lords provided no answers. So the men and women of the Renaissance reached back beyond the feudal order—which they said belonged to the "Dark Ages"—to classical antiquity, where all seemed light, refinement, and civilization. They consciously modeled themselves on the standards set by ancient Greece and Rome. They ransacked monastic libraries for manuscript records of ancient wisdom and studied ancient ruins as examples of architectural and artistic perfection. They identified much more with the urban and urbane culture of antiquity than they did with the more recent, and to their minds, barbarous past.

The Renaissance began in the independent city-states of northern Italy in the late fourteenth century; during the fifteenth and sixteenth centuries, its ideas spread to other lands in Europe. In the developed urban centers of Italy, commercial elites enjoyed the leisure and freedom that came with the wealth procured by trade. The wealthy Italian city-states acted as magnets. They attracted men of talent in every field—the military, government, business, the arts, and education—because of the rewards available to those who succeeded. Renaissance society was marked by a growing *secular outlook*. To be sure, the people were neither nonbelievers nor atheists. Increasingly, however, religion had to compete with worldly concerns. Members of the urban upper class did not allow religion to interfere with their quest for the full life. This worldliness found concrete expression in Renaissance art and literature.

Individualism was another hallmark of Renaissance society. The competitive marketplace in which they operated taught the urban elite to assert their own personalities, to demonstrate their unique talents, and to fulfill their ambitions. Individualism also found expression in portrait art, which aspired to capture a person's uniqueness. At the same time, explorers ventured into uncharted seas, conquerors carved out empires in the New World, and merchant-capitalists amassed fortunes.

The most characteristic intellectual movement of the Renaissance was *humanism,* an educational program based on the study of ancient Greek and Roman literature. Renaissance humanists valued ancient literature for its clear and graceful style and for its insights into human nature. In contrast to medieval scholastic philosophers, who used Greek philosophy to prove the truth of Christian doctrines, Italian humanists read classical literature to nourish their new interest in the worldly life.

A new curriculum was devised, aimed primarily at instructing not the clergy—as was the case in the Middle Ages—but the sons (rarely the daughters) of nobles and merchants. The new curriculum emphasized training in those skills of writing, speaking, politics and ethics that were most in demand at the Renaissance courts and that one had to master for a career in the expanding civil service. This educational ideal took such hold on the imagination of the European elite that it served until the twentieth century as the standard of what it meant to be educated.

The Renaissance wedded its vision of antiquity to its contemporary concerns. In the process, an entirely new culture was created, as different from the ancient world as it was from the Middle Ages. Thus, in art, the human form and rules of perspective were recovered from antiquity, but artists used them to represent a Christian idealism and a cult of the individual that were not antique. In politics, the ancient history of Greece and Rome was studied for clues on how to solve the problems of the Renaissance city-state, such as internal turmoil, mercenary armies, rivalries between city-states, and the menace of powerful foreign monarchies like France and Spain. Out of this intense political life came a rich experimentation in forms of government. Perhaps the most important efforts were those of the Florentines and Venetians, who tried for centuries to preserve the conditions of republican government and laid the theoretical foundations for modern republicanism.

The principal effect of this ferment was the gradual destruction of the medieval view that the world was static and the individual's place within

it fixed—whether as priest, warrior, or peasant. Instead, Renaissance culture emphasized the talents and creativity of an educated elite and the right of princes, as well as artists and merchants, to shape their own destiny. Embedded in this idea lay the germ of a completely new notion which was neither medieval nor ancient, but distinctly modern: the idea of secular progress.

The Reformation

Like the Renaissance, the Reformation, which began with Martin Luther's attack on the church, marked a break with the Middle Ages. Whereas the Renaissance turned away from medieval art and literary forms, the Reformation broke with the medieval religious outlook and ended the religious unity of the Middle Ages.

Continuing entrepreneurial activity and the intellectual curiosity fostered by Renaissance learning produced a more sophisticated and independent urban elite. By the early sixteenth century, that elite became increasingly alienated from the traditional moral authority exercised by the church. Of course, the church had always had its dissenters, such as the medieval opponents of papal authority who favored placing ecclesiastical power into the hands of the church councils, or the late-fourteenth-century followers of John Wycliffe, who attacked church corruption and repudiated certain church doctrines. Not until the early sixteenth century, however, did church critics gather enough strength to challenge successfully the rule of the papacy and the moral authority of Catholic doctrines.

The Reformation began in German cities and spread throughout western Europe. Only in countries like Spain and Italy, where ecclesiastical authority was firmly entrenched, did the church repel the Protestant advance. Protestant reformers used the newly invented printing press to appeal to the urban elite and also to the traditional nobility, who had long coveted church lands and tax revenues. During the brief period from Luther's initial confrontation with a papal representative and seller of indulgences in 1517 until the death of Henry VIII in England in 1547, nearly a quarter of the western European population had embraced one version or another of Protestantism.

Two doctrines formed the basis of this new version of Christianity: salvation comes to the believer as a result of divine mercy and not from the church's practices and rituals, and the essence of Christianity lies in the Bible itself, not in church dogma. Religion is, therefore, accessible to any literate person, and in matters of salvation, all believers act as priests in regard to their own spiritual fate. The motives of the many thousands of Europeans who embraced a Protestant creed were varied. Many were angry at the corrupt life style of some clergy and resented the clergy's authority. Moved by genuine religious feelings, many Christians sought to search Scripture for themselves rather than rely on the priests' official interpretation, and to communicate with God directly, without a priest serving as intermediary. German townspeople and lords resented tax revenues being routed to Rome and a church hierarchy dominated by Italians. Impoverished peasants hoped that rebellion against the church's authority would lead not only to religious reform but also to a social transformation—an end to their exploitation by feudal lords.

Personal faith, not adherence to the doctrines of the church, became central to the religious life of European Protestants. Like the Renaissance humanists, some Protestant leaders were trained in ancient learning, but they gave humanism a religious meaning. They wanted to restore the spirit of early Christianity, in which faith seemed purer, believers more sincere, and the clergy uncorrupted by luxury and power.

The Reformation shattered the religious unity of Europe, the chief characteristic of the Middle Ages, and weakened the church, the principal institution of medieval society. The church's moral authority was rejected by millions of Europeans, and its political power was curtailed.

By strengthening the power of kings at the expense of religious bodies, the Reformation furthered the growth of the modern state. Protestant rulers repudiated the pope's claim to temporal power and extended their authority over Protestant churches in their lands. In Catholic lands, the church, in reaction to Protestantism, tended to support rather than challenge monarchs. Protestantism did not create the modern secular state; it did, however, help to free the state from subordination to religious authority, an essential feature of modern political life.

The Reformation also promoted individualism. Protestants sought a direct and personal relationship with God and interpreted the Bible for themselves. They developed an inner confidence and assertiveness. This individualism may also have been expressed in a work ethic, compatible with capitalist forms of economic activity.

The Commercial Revolution

One of the most decisive changes occurring between 1450 and 1750 was the commercial revolution. This transformation saw the breakdown of the largely self-sufficient agrarian economy, based on the manor, which characterized the Middle Ages. In its place came increased production and commercial activity. Perhaps the most dramatic change was that for the first time in human history the problem of providing an adequate food supply was solved in a few places (England, Holland, and British North America) by the late seventeenth century.

The commercial revolution was the product of two processes: overseas expansion and the price revolution. Western European monarchies carved out empires in other parts of the world—the Portuguese in Africa, India, and the East Indies in the fifteenth and early sixteenth centuries; the Spanish in Latin America in the sixteenth century; and the French, the Dutch, and the English in North America, the East and West Indies, and India in the seventeenth and eighteenth centuries. Wherever they went, Europeans overcame armed opposition through their superior fire power in the form of the cannon, the musket, and especially the armed sailing ship. For four hundred years, one small part of the globe, western Europe, dominated and exploited much of the rest of the planet. Only in the twentieth century were the western European powers forced to relinquish their empires.

Overseas colonies played a vital role in the commercial revolution. They supplied raw materials, gold, and silver to stoke European economies; they also furnished protected markets for products made in Europe. Finally, colonies produced materials at low cost because of slave labor, which was widely used on plantations until the nineteenth century. Out of the colonies came immense profits to invest in further economic development.

The rapid and unprecedented rise in prices (inflation) throughout the sixteenth century was known as the *price revolution*. This inflation can be traced to two causes: an unexplained and perhaps inexplicable increase in population beginning in the second half of the fifteenth century and the influx of silver into western Europe from the mines of Mexico and Peru. There were more and more mouths to feed in the fifteenth and sixteenth centuries. Agricultural production expanded to meet this new demand but never expanded rapidly enough. So prices, especially for primary products like wool and grain, shot up. The flooding of western Europe with silver from New World mines was probably also inflationary in an economy of scarcity. The money supply in the form of silver coin increased faster than the supply of goods, so prices rose faster.

The effect of the price revolution can hardly be overestimated. For the first time since the thirteenth century, demand was steadily rising. Investment in increased production was bound to yield increased profits, an enormous incentive to invest and reinvest.

In early modern Europe, the largest commercial endeavor by far was agriculture. Thus, the greatest investment was in land, and the most important changes produced by that investment took place on the land. Driven by the desire for profit, landlords saw that it would be necessary to reorganize their farms in order to increase production for an expanding market. The old manorial agriculture, based on the three-field system, was geared to the needs of the manor, not those of the market. The characteristic manorial pattern of farming in strips and of having communal access to common land was inefficient. So enterprising landlords denied their peasants the use of the commons and drove them from the manor. Having eliminated peasant holdings, the landlords tore down the hedges and filled in the ditches dividing the strips, in this way consolidating the fields into single units, which they often let—if they themselves did not have the areas cultivated—at high rents to the most efficient producers.

This process of consolidation was known as *enclosure,* and its consequences were momentous. More and more land was turned over to commercial agriculture and returned increasing yields and profits. The peasants who had lost their customary use of the land either became agricultural laborers working for very low wages or left to find work in the towns or in the colonies overseas. Rural poverty and violence increased because of the displacement of the peasants.

This ruthless transformation of agriculture was matched by a comparable process in trade and industry. As commercial activity increased, the medieval guilds, which had restricted production and exchange, became obsolete. The initiative passed to rich merchants whose operations were not local like those of the guilds, but regional, national, and sometimes even international in scale.

The merchants exploited cottage industry by monopolizing raw materials. Raw wool, for example, was put out by merchants to be processed by peasants in country villages (outside of towns, where guild restrictions did not apply). This procedure saved money on overhead by using the peasants' own cottages and on labor by paying low piece rates to peasants, who were only too glad to find work. The merchants then sold the finished product where it would fetch the best price. In industry as in farming, the effect was the same: increasing profits, investment, economic expansion, and a widening gap between rich and poor.

The commercial revolution represented a crucial stage in the development of modern capitalism. It ushered in a world economy and led to European domination over the earth, a situation that would endure until the twentieth century. We shall now examine other movements that helped shape the modern world: the growth of national states, the Scientific Revolution, and the Enlightenment.

NOTES

1. W. H. Auden, ed., *The Portable Greek Reader* (New York: Viking, 1952), p. 38.

2. Benjamin Farrington, *Greek Science* (Baltimore: Penguin Books, 1961), p. 301.

Geography of Europe

The map on the following pages shows the continent of Europe and the countries around the Mediterranean Sea, together with the physical features of the land such as major rivers and other bodies of water, mountains and changes of elevation, and the names of countries and their capitals. A knowledge of the geography of this area will help give a sense of the relationship between geography and history, of how the characteristics of the terrain and the availability of rivers and other bodies of water affected the movement of people and the relationship between people and environment throughout history.

Europe is the smallest continent in the world with the exception of Australia. The other continents are Africa, Asia, North America, South America, and Antarctica. The continent of Europe, which can be viewed as the western extension of the Asian landmass, is distinctive in its configuration. Peninsulas make up a significant portion of the continent's land area. This feature gives Europe an unusually long coastline, equal in distance to one and a half times around the equator (37,877 miles). Europe's western boundary is the Atlantic Ocean, while the Ural Mountains, Ural River, and Caspian Sea—in Russia and Kazakhstan—form its eastern boundary. Europe extends southward to the Caucasus Mountains, the Black Sea, and the Mediterranean Sea. The continent extends to the Arctic Ocean in the north. Off the mainland but considered by geographers to be part of Europe are thousands of islands, most notably the British Isles to the northwest.

North Americans are often surprised to discover the small size of the European continent. The geographic area of France, for example, is less than that of Texas; England is similar in size to Alabama. The distance from London to Paris is about the same as from New York to Boston; the distance from Berlin to Moscow is comparable to that of Chicago to Denver. And the entire continent of Europe is about the size of Canada.

Major Peninsulas and Islands   There are five major European peninsulas: the Iberian (Portugal and Spain); the Apennine (Italy); the Balkan (Albania, Bulgaria, Greece, and parts of the former Yugoslavian republics and Turkey); the Scandinavian (Norway and Sweden); and Jutland (Denmark). Ireland and the United Kingdom of England, Wales, and Scotland make up the British Isles. Major islands of the Mediterranean Sea include the Balearic Islands, Corsica, Sardinia, Sicily, Crete, and Cyprus.

Seas, Lakes, and Rivers   Europe's irregular coastline encloses large areas of the surrounding waters into bays, gulfs, and seas. In the Mediterranean Sea are located, from west to east, the Tyrrhenian Sea (between Italy and Sicily, and Sardinia and Corsica), the Adriatic Sea (between Italy and the former Yugoslavian republics), the Ionian Sea (between Italy and Greece), and the Aegean Sea (between Greece and Turkey).

The Baltic Sea, in the north, is bordered by Finland, Estonia, Latvia, Lithuania, Poland, Germany, and Sweden, and connected by narrow channels to the North Sea, which lies between Great Britain and the countries of the northwestern mainland. The English Channel separates England and France, and the Bay of Biscay borders the west coast of France and the north coast of Spain. The Black Sea, on the southern border of Russia and the Ukraine, is connected by water passages to the Aegean Sea. The Caspian Sea, which lies partly in Russia and Kazakhstan, and

Elevation

Meters	Feet
4,000	13,120
2,000	6,560
500	1,640
200	656
Sea level	Sea level
Below sea level	Below sea level

✳ National capital
• Other city

NORWAY

Oslo ✳

SWEDEN

Stock✳

North

Sea

Bal

SCOTLAND

DENMARK

Se

Copenhagen ✳

NORTHERN
IRELAND

UNITED

IRELAND

Dublin ✳

KINGDOM

ENGLAND

Berlin ✳

WALES

Thames

NETHERLANDS

Elbe

London ✳

Amsterdam✳

GERMANY

POLA

ATLANTIC

English Channel

Brussels ✳

Seine

BELGIUM

LUXEMBOURG
✳Luxembourg

Prague ✳

CZECHOSLOVAKIA

OCEAN

✳ Paris

Loire

Bay

FRANCE

Bern ✳

Vienna ✳

Bu

of

SWITZERLAND

AUSTRIA

HUN

Biscay

Rhine

A L P S

SLOVENIA

Ljubljana ✳

Zagreb ✳

CROATIA

PYRENEES

Ebro

A P E N N I N E S

Adriatic

Belgrad

BOSNIA AND
HERZEGOVINA

PORTUGAL

SPAIN

Sea

Sarajevo ✳

Lisbon ✳

✳ Madrid

Tiber

(YUG

MONTENEGRO

Titograd

Corsica

✳Rome

ITALY

✳

Balearic Is.

Sardinia

ALBA

GIBRALTAR
(Gr Br)

Tyrrhenian

Ioni

Sea

Sea

Algiers ✳

✳Rabat

Sicily

Tunis ✳

MOROCCO

MALTA

TUNISIA

Tripoli ✳

ALGERIA

0	100	200	300	400	500 Km.
0	100	200	300	400	500 Mi.

LIBYA

partly in Asia, is the world's largest saltwater lake and is the lowest point in Europe at 92 feet below sea level.

Europe's many rivers have served as transportation routes for thousands of years. Several of the major rivers, including the longest, flow across the Russian plain. The Volga, Europe's longest river (2,194 miles), rises west of Moscow and empties into the Caspian Sea. It is also linked by canals and other river systems to the Arctic Ocean and the Baltic Sea. The Dnieper flows south through the agricultural heartland of the Ukraine into the Black Sea.

Europe's second longest river, the Danube (1,777 miles), is the principal waterway in the southeastern part of the continent. It originates in Germany and flows through Austria, Slovakia, Hungary, the former Yugoslavian republics, Bulgaria, and Romania into the Black Sea. The Rhine winds northward from the Alps through western Germany and the Netherlands into the North Sea, which is also the destination of the Elbe River in eastern Germany. In France, the Rhône flows south into the Mediterranean, and the Seine and Loire flow west to the English Channel and the Bay of Biscay. Other important waterways are the Po in northern Italy, the Vistula in Poland, and the Thames in England.

The proximity of most areas of the European landmass to the coastline or to major river systems is important to understanding the historical development of European civilization. Trading routes and major cities developed along these waterways, and rivers have served as natural boundaries.

LAND REGIONS   Europe, despite its small size, presents a wide range of landforms, from rugged mountains to sweeping plains. These landforms can be separated into four major regions: the Northwest Mountains, the Great European Plain, the Central Uplands, and the Alpine Mountain System. The mountains of the Northwest Region cover most of the region, running through northwestern France, Ireland, northern Great Britain, Norway, Sweden, northern Finland, and the northwest corner of Russia.

The Great European Plain covers almost all of the European part of the former Soviet Union, extending from the Arctic Ocean to the Caucasus Mountains. This belt stretches westward across Poland, Germany, Belgium, the western portion of France, and southeastern England.

The Central Uplands is a belt of high plateaus, hills, and low mountains. It reaches from the central plateau of Portugal, across Spain, the central highlands of France, to the hills and mountains of southern Germany, the Czech Republic, and Slovakia.

The Alpine Mountain System is made up of several mountain chains. Included in this system are the Pyrenees between Spain and France, the Alps in southeastern France, northern Italy, Switzerland, and western Austria, and the Apennine range in Italy. Also included are the mountain ranges of the Balkan Peninsula, the Carpathian Mountains in Slovakia and Romania, and the Caucasus Mountains between the Black and Caspian Seas. These mountain ranges have been formidable barriers and boundaries throughout history, affecting the movement of people and the relationship of people to each other and to the land.

When studying the map of Europe, it is important to notice the proximity of western areas of Asia, especially those at the eastern end of the Mediterranean Sea, to areas of North Africa. The cultures of these areas have not only interacted with those of Europe but have also played a significant role in shaping the history of Western civilization.

Western Civilization

Ideas, Politics & Society

Eighth Edition

Chapter 16

The Rise of Sovereignty: Transition to the Modern State

The Hall of Mirrors in the Royal Palace at Versailles. Immense and grand, Versailles was the wonder of the age. Like the person of the king, it said to his subjects: I am grandeur incarnate. Even by today's standards, it is an impressive building, both inside and out. (C. L. Chrysun/The Image Bank/Getty Images.)

Focus Questions

1. How were monarchs able to build strong states?

2. What enabled Spain to rise to greatness, and why was this greatness short-lived?

3. What were the achievements and failures of Louis XIV's reign?

4. What is the enduring historical significance of the English Revolution of the seventeenth century?

5. What were the distinguishing features of Prussia and Russia by the early eighteenth century?

6. Why were these developments important for the future?

Online Study Center

This icon will direct you to interactive map and primary source activities on the website http://college.hmco.com/pic/perrywc8e.

From the thirteenth to the seventeenth century, a new and unique form of political organization emerged in the West: the **dynastic,** or national, **state,** which, through taxes and war, harnessed the power of its nobility and the material resources of its territory. Neither capitalism nor technology could have enabled the West to dominate other lands and peoples had it not been for the power of the European states. They directed the energies of the landed elite into national service and international competition. A degree of domestic stability ensued, and the states encouraged commerce and industry, which could in turn be taxed. Although they nurtured the aristocracy, many states also required that both lord and peasant serve in national armies for the purpose of foreign conquest, as well as for defense.

In most emerging states, monarchs and their court bureaucracies were the key players in the process of state formation. Generally, they developed forms of government that historians describe by the term **absolutism.** For centuries, kings seemed invincible. Nevertheless, one other form of government emerged in early modern Europe: *republican,* or *constitutional,* states. By 1800, the future lay with this other, more participatory system, which gave greater power to landed or mercantile elites than to kings and their courts.

Although kings in some medieval lands had begun to forge national states, medieval political forms differed considerably from those that developed in the early modern period. During the Middle Ages, feudal lords gave homage to their kings but continued to rule over their local territories, resisting the centralizing efforts of monarchs. Local and even national representative assemblies, which met occasionally to give advice to kings, at times acted as a brake on the king's power. City-states enjoyed considerable autonomy. The clergy supported the monarch but governed as separate spiritual realms. The papacy challenged the authority of those monarchs who, it believed, did not fulfill their duty to rule in accordance with Christian teachings as interpreted by the church. In early modern times, powerful monarchs subdued these competing systems of political authority and established strong central governments at the expense of all who opposed them.

Chronology 16.1 ❖ The Rise of Sovereignty

1469	Ferdinand and Isabella begin their rule of Castile and Aragon
1485	Henry VII begins the reign of the Tudor dynasty in England
1517	The Protestant Reformation starts in Germany
1519	Charles V of Spain becomes Hapsburg emperor of the Holy Roman Empire
1556–1598	Philip II of Spain persecutes Jews and Muslims
1559	Treaty of peace between France and Spain
1560s–1609	Netherlands revolts against Spanish rule
1562–1589	Religious wars in France
1572	Saint Bartholomew's Day Massacre: Queen Catherine of France thought to have ordered thousands of Protestants executed
1579	*Vindiciae contra Tyrannos,* published by Huguenots, justifies regicide
1588	English fleet defeats the Spanish Armada
1590s	A reaction in Russia against Ivan IV, the Terrible
1593	Henry IV of France renounces his Protestantism to restore peace in France
1598	French Protestants granted limited religious toleration by the Edict of Nantes
1640–1660	Revolution in England
1648	Treaty of Westphalia ends Thirty Years' War
1649	Charles I, Stuart king of England, is executed by an act of Parliament
1649–1660	England is co-ruled by Parliament and the army under Oliver Cromwell
1660	Charles II returns from exile and becomes king of England
1683	Turks attack Vienna and are defeated
1685	Louis XIV of France revokes the Edict of Nantes
1688–1689	Revolution in England: end of absolutism; religious toleration for all Protestants
1699	Treaty of Karlowitz marks Austrians' victory over Turks and affirms Austria's right to rule Hungary, Transylvania, and parts of Croatia
1701	Louis XIV tries to bring Spain under French control
1702–1714	War of the Spanish Succession establishes a balance of power between England and France

Monarchs and Elites
as State Builders

At first, the pivotal figures in the development of states were the kings. European elites, whether landed or urban, grudgingly gave allegiance to these ambitious, and at times ruthless, authority figures. In general, a single monarch seemed the only alternative to the even more brutal pattern of war and disorder so basic to the governing habits of the feudal aristocracy. In the process of increasing their own power, the kings of Europe subordinated the aristocracy to their needs and interests and gained firm control over the Christian churches in their territories. Gradually, religious zeal was made compatible with and largely supportive of the state's goals rather than with papal dictates or even universal Christian aspirations. The demise of medieval representative assemblies—with the notable exception of the English Parliament—is a dramatic illustration of how monarchs subjected to their will all other political authorities, whether local, regional, or national.

Monarchs needed and employed a variety of tools for extending their power. All encouraged the use of vernacular languages—English, French, Spanish, and so on—to foster a common identity, as well as counteract the church's monopoly over the international language of the time, Latin. But more important than words were arms. The foundations of monarchical power were the standing army and a system of tax collection that permitted war to be waged. The two were inseparable. The goal of the monarch was to have independent wealth and power. In general, only war justified taxes. "Was [absolute monarchy] in reality ever anything but a constant search for new funds to pay for an over-ambitious foreign policy?" asks the British historian William Doyle.[1] The rise and fall of the great European powers of the early modern period, first Spain, then France and England, can be traced directly in the fortunes of their armies on the battlefield and the fullness of the king's treasury. Only the rise of the **Dutch Republic** broke with the pattern of king-army-taxes as the key to the creation of a centralized state. The Dutch case was the very antithesis of absolutism because the rich, urban, Protestant elite lent the state money at interest and in the process created

the first system of national bonds and a citizen-financed national debt. As a result, a nation was created, but one without a strong central (as opposed to local) government. Local elites held most of the power, just as they held the state bonds.

In most monarchical states, however, anything that stood in the way of royal power had to be subdued, remolded, or destroyed. Where early modern monarchs succeeded in subduing, reconstituting, or destroying local aristocratic and ecclesiastical power systems, strong dynastic states emerged. Where the monarchs failed, as they did in the **Holy Roman Empire** and Italy, no viable states evolved until well into the nineteenth century. Those failures derived from the independent authority of local princes or city-states, and in the case of Italy, from the decentralizing influence of papal authority. In the Holy Roman Empire, feudal princes found allies in the newly formed Protestant communities, and in such a situation, religion worked as a decentralizing force. Once given the power to protect the local religion, German princes also maintained their peasants as virtual serfs.

Successful early modern kings subordinated religion to the needs of the state. They did so not by separating church and state (as was later done in the United States), but rather by linking their subjects' religious identity with national identity. For example, in England, by the late seventeenth century, to be a true Protestant was to be a true English subject, while in Spain the same equation operated for the Catholic (as opposed to the Muslim or the Jew, who came to be regarded as non-Spanish).

In the thirteenth century, most Europeans still identified themselves with their localities: their villages, manors, or towns. They gave political allegiance to their local lord or bishop. They knew little, and probably cared less, about the activities of the king and his court, except when the monarch called on them for taxes or military service. By the late seventeenth century, in contrast, aristocrats in many European countries defined their political power in terms of their relationship to king and court. By then, the lives of very ordinary people were being affected by national systems of tax collection, by the doctrines and practices of national churches, and by conscription.

Increasingly, prosperous town dwellers, the bourgeoisie, also realized that their prosperity hinged, in part, on court-supported foreign and domestic policies. If the king assisted their commercial ventures, the town dwellers gave their support to the growth of a strong central state. In only two states, England and the Netherlands, did landed and mercantile elites manage to redistribute political power so that by the late seventeenth century it could be shared by monarchy and Parliament in England or, in the Netherlands, monopolized by a social oligarchy.

The effects of European state building were visible by the late seventeenth century. Commercial rivalry between states and colonial expansion, two major activities of the period, were directly related to the ability of elites to protect their interests under the mantle of the state, and to the state's willingness to encourage world trade in order to enrich its own treasury. Monarchs and the states they helped to create ushered in the modern world just as surely as did commercial expansion, capitalism, and science. They also enshrined political power as a masculine preserve, with consequences for women that persist to this day.

THE RISE AND FALL OF HAPSBURG SPAIN

The Spanish political experience of the sixteenth century stands as a model of the interconnectedness of king, army, and taxation. It was also one of the most spectacular examples in Western history of the rise and equally dramatic fall of a great power. In the course of their rise, the Spanish kings built a dynastic state that burst through its frontiers and encompassed Portugal, part of Italy, the Netherlands, and enormous areas of the New World. Spain became an intercontinental empire—the first in the West since Roman times. Until 1469, however, Spain did not exist as a political entity. In that year, Ferdinand, heir to the throne of Aragon, married his more powerful and prosperous cousin, Isabella, heiress of Castile. Yet even after the unification of Castile and the crown of Aragon (Catalonia, Aragon, and Valencia), relations among the fiercely independent provinces of Spain were often tense. Only through dynastic marriage of their offspring to a German-speaking family of central Europe, the Hapsburgs, did the Spanish monarchs emerge on

the international scene. Marriage became a key piece in the puzzle of state development.

Ferdinand and Isabella: Unity and Purity of "Blood" and Religion

During their rule (1479–1516), which took many years to establish firmly, Ferdinand and Isabella laid the foundation for the Spanish empire and Spanish domination of European affairs throughout the sixteenth century. Together, they sought to build the army and the state by waging a campaign to reconquer Spanish territory still held by the Muslims. At the same time, they strove to bring the church into alliance with the state and forge a Spanish identity based on "blood" ancestry as well as religion. It became necessary to prove that no Jews or non-Spaniards could be found in a family's lineage.

In order to develop a strong monarchy, the Spanish rulers had to bring the church's interests in line with their own. While other Europeans, partly under the impact of the Renaissance, questioned the church's leadership and attacked its corruption, the Catholic Kings (as Ferdinand and Isabella were called) reformed the church, making it responsive to their needs and also invulnerable to criticism. The crusade against the Muslims accorded with the aims of the militant Spanish church. Popular piety and royal policy led in 1492 to a victory over Granada, the last Muslim-ruled territory of Spain.

The five-hundred-year struggle for Christian hegemony in the Iberian Peninsula left the Spanish fiercely religious and strongly suspicious of foreigners. Despite centuries of intermarriage with non-Christians, by the early sixteenth century, purity of blood and orthodoxy of faith became necessary for, and synonymous with, Spanish identity. The Spanish state and church were actively engaged in persecuting Muslims and Jews, who for centuries had contributed substantially to Spanish cultural and economic life.

In 1492, in a move to enforce religious uniformity, the crown expelled from Spain Jews unwilling to accept baptism. Some 150,000 (some estimates are considerably higher) were driven out. The thousands of Jews who underwent conversion were watched by a church tribunal, **the Inquisition,**

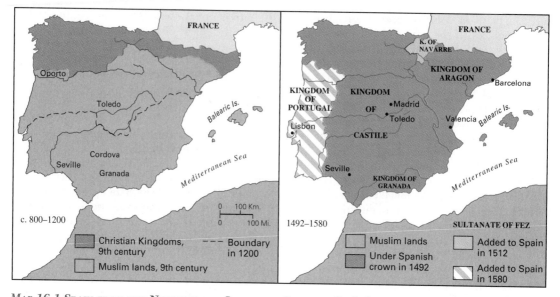

MAP 16.1 SPAIN FROM THE NINTH TO THE SIXTEENTH CENTURY Spain became a nation gradually, and eventually Portugal split away to become a separate state.

for signs of backsliding. The clerical inquisitors employed sophisticated means of interrogation and torture to ferret out newly converted Christians and their descendants suspected of practicing Judaism. Death by fire, sometimes in elaborate public ceremonies, was the ultimate penalty. Muslims also bore the pain of persecution: forced conversions; investigations, torture, and executions conducted by the Inquisition; and finally, mass expulsion in 1609–1614. The Inquisition represented the dark side of the Spanish genius for conquest and administration, and its shadow stretched down through the centuries well into the twentieth and the repressive regime of Francisco Franco.

The wars against the Muslims gave the Spanish invaluable military experience and rendered their army one of the finest in Europe. With a superior army, with the great magnates pacified, and with the church and the Inquisition under monarchical control, the Catholic Kings expanded their interests and embarked on an imperialist foreign policy in Europe and abroad, which had extraordinary consequences. Ultimately, it made Spain dominant in the New World.

Ferdinand and Isabella gambled on Columbus's voyage, and they won. Then, beginning in 1519 in Mexico, the conquistador Hernando Cortés defeated the Aztec nation with six hundred foot soldiers and sixteen horses. This feat was partly due to the superiority of Spanish technology, but it was also made possible by the condition of the Aztec nation, which was struggling to maintain a hold over its own people and over scores of other Mexican tribes that it had, in some cases, brutally subdued. The Spanish forces were led by members of the minor aristocracy, *hidalgos*. Their role was distinctive yet typical of the role played by the minor aristocracy in the building of other European nation-states. For them, as younger sons of impoverished aristocrats, war was a means to riches and land. Unlike the great and wealthy aristocrats, they would serve the crown at home and abroad as soldiers and often as bureaucrats. Their loyalty to the king was matched only by their fierce ambition. The bureaucracy and army of the early modern states were very important avenues for obtaining or retaining elite status.

The Reign of Charles V: Hapsburg, King of Spain, and Holy Roman Emperor

Through a series of shrewd marriage agreements for their children, Ferdinand and Isabella strengthened their international alliances. As a result, their grandson, Charles, who ruled from 1516 to 1556, inherited Spain, the Netherlands, Austria, Sardinia, Sicily, the kingdom of Naples, and Franche-Comté. In 1519, the same year as the conquest of Mexico, he was also elected Holy Roman Emperor (partly through bribery). Thus, he became the most powerful monarch in Europe. But in the course of his reign, he saw problems emerge that would eventually lead to Spain's decline and weaken the Hapsburg dynasty to which, through marriage, he had been heir.

Charles's inheritance was simply too vast to be governed effectively. The Lutheran Reformation proved to be the first successful challenge to Hapsburg power. It was the first phase of a religious and political struggle between Catholic Spain and Protestant Europe: a struggle that would dominate the last half of the sixteenth century and ultimately reduce Spanish influence.

The achievements of Charles V's reign rested on the twin instruments of army and bureaucracy. The Hapsburg Empire in the New World was vast, and, on the whole, effectively administered and policed. The Catholic clergy were key players in this process. Out of a sprawling empire, with its exploited native populations, came the greatest flow of gold and silver ever witnessed by Europeans. Constant warfare in Europe, in Italy and against the Turks in the Mediterranean, coupled with the immensity of the Spanish administrative network, required a steady intake of capital. But this easy access to income appears to have been detrimental in the long run to the Spanish economy. There was no incentive for the development of domestic industry, entrepreneurship, or international commerce. Moreover, constant war engendered and perpetuated a social order geared to the aggrandizement of a military class rather than to the development of a commercial class. Although war expanded Spain's power in the sixteenth century, it also sowed the seeds for the financial crises of the 1590s and beyond, and for the eventual decline of Spain as a world power.

Philip II

In the reign of Philip II (1556–1598), the strengths and weaknesses of the Spanish state became fully evident. That period is pivotal in early modern Spanish history. Philip II inherited the throne from his father, Charles V, who abdicated in 1556 and left his son with a large empire in both the Old World and the New. Philip II's zeal for Catholicism ruled his private conduct and infused his foreign policy. He waited for the moment when the crown would possess the revenue needed to launch an offensive against the Turks and international Protestantism.

To Philip II, being truly Spanish meant being Christian in faith and blood; the racist tendencies already evident in the later fifteenth century gained full expression during his reign. Increasingly, the country came to be ruled by an exclusive class of **Old Christians,** who claimed to be untainted because for centuries they had refused to marry Muslims or Jews, even if Jews were converts to Christianity—*New Christians,* as they were called. Traditional in their thinking, the Old Christians controlled the church, religious orders, and the Inquisition—all to preserve an imperial system in need of reform.

Melancholic and standoffish by temperament, Philip II worked arduously and declined most of life's enjoyments. He pored over his ministers' reports, editing and commenting, yet in the end he was strangely indecisive. Some problems remained unsolved for years, as frustrated advisers begged in vain for the king to take action.

In the 1560s, Philip sent the largest land army ever assembled in Europe into the Netherlands with the intention of crushing Protestant-inspired opposition to Spanish authority. The ensuing revolt of the Netherlands lasted until 1609, and in losing the Netherlands, Spain lost its industrial heartland. In 1576, the Spanish army, in a desperate attempt to defeat the rebels, flooded and sacked Antwerp, the leading commercial and banking city in northern Europe. Antwerp's trade and many of its educated elite gradually moved to Amsterdam, a Protestant stronghold, which

ALLEGORY OF THE ABDICATION OF CHARLES V, BY FRANS FRANCKEN II, 1556. Emperor Charles V, who ruled half of Europe and most of the Americas, abdicated in 1556, giving his German imperial crown to his brother Ferdinand, archduke of Austria, and the kingdoms of Spain and the Netherlands to his son Philip II. The Hapsburg dynasty ruled Spain until the eighteenth century and Austria and Hungary until the early twentieth century. (*Rijksmuseum, Amsterdam.*)

replaced its southern rival as an international capital and the center of the new Dutch national state.

By the 1580s, Philip's foreign policy was overextended in every direction, and his religious zeal shaped all his decisions. He intervened in the French religious wars on the Catholic side, although his intervention gave little to Spain in the way of power or influence. Philip's disastrous attempt to invade England was also born of religious zeal.

Philip regarded an assault on England, the main Protestant power, as a holy crusade against the "heretic and bastard" Queen Elizabeth; he

particularly resented English assistance to Protestant Dutch rebels. Sailing from Lisbon in May 1588, the Spanish Armada, twenty-two-thousand men strong, met with humiliating defeat. Its ships were too cumbersome to negotiate the treacherous English Channel, where the English ships easily outmaneuvered them and broke their formation by sending fire ships crashing into them. Moreover, strong winds, typical for this time of year, drove the Armada out of striking position.

The defeat had a psychological effect on the Spanish. They openly pondered what they had done to incur divine displeasure. Protestant Europe, however, hailed the victory as a sign of its election, and the "Protestant wind" stirred by divine intervention entered the mythology of English nationalism. In the rise and fall of nations, self-assurance has played a crucial, if inexplicable, role. The cultural renaissance associated with the England of Shakespeare owed its vigor and confidence in part to its pride at being Protestant and independent of Spanish influence.

The End of the Spanish Hapsburgs

After the defeat of the Armada, Spain gradually and reluctantly abandoned its imperial ambitions in northern Europe. By the first quarter of the century, enormous weaknesses had surfaced in Spanish economic and social life. In 1596, Philip II was bankrupt, his vast wealth overextended by the cost of foreign wars. Bankruptcy reappeared at various times in the seventeenth century, while the agricultural economy, at the heart of any early modern nation, stagnated. The Spanish in their golden age had never devoted enough attention to increasing domestic production.

Despite these setbacks, Spain was still capable of taking a very aggressive posture during the Thirty Years' War (1618–1648). The Austrian branch of the Hapsburg family joined forces with their Spanish cousins, and neither the Swedes and Germans nor the Dutch could stop them. Only French participation in the Thirty Years' War on the Protestant side tipped the balance decisively against the Hapsburgs. Spanish aggression brought no victories, and with the Peace of Westphalia (1648), Spain officially recognized the independence of the Netherlands and cut its ties with the Austrian branch of the family.

By 1660, the imperial age of the Spanish Hapsburgs had come to an end. The rule of the Protestant princes had been secured in the Holy Roman Empire; the largely Protestant Dutch Republic flourished; Portugal and its colony of Brazil were independent of Spain; and dominance over European affairs had passed to France. The quality of material life in Spain deteriorated rapidly, and the ever-present gap between the rich and the poor widened even more drastically. The traditional aristocracy and the church retained their land and power but failed conspicuously to produce effective leadership. With decline came rigidity of institutions and values. Spain remained authoritarian far longer than other European countries. Democratic revolutions did not occur in a country dominated exclusively by the landed elite and the church. The commercial elite that became increasingly important in England, the Netherlands, and France failed to develop in monarchical and agricultural Spain.

The Spanish experience illustrates two aspects of the history of the European state. First, the state as empire could survive and prosper only if the domestic economic base continued to expand. Living off the colonies ultimately meant economic stagnation and the absence of technological innovation at home. Second, the states where a vital and aggressive mercantile class developed generally prospered in the early modern period. In such states, the elite no longer consisted exclusively of those with landed wealth; rather, it comprised those who invested, or even participated, in the market and manufacturing. However, in Spain, the old aristocracy and the church continued to dominate and control society and its mores. They not only despised manual labor and profit taking through trade, but also showed little interest in science and technology.

Online Study Center **Improve Your Grade**
Interactive Map: Europe During the Thirty Years' War 1618–1648

THE GROWTH OF FRENCH POWER

Two states in the early modern period succeeded most effectively in consolidating the power of their central governments: France and England. Each became a model of a very different form of statehood. The English model evolved into a constitutional monarchy in which the king's power was limited by Parliament and the rights of the English people were protected by law and tradition. The French model emphasized at every turn the glory of the king and, by implication, the **sovereignty** of the state and its right to stand above the interests of its subjects. France's monarchy became absolute, although the evolution of the French state was a very gradual process, not completed until the late seventeenth century.

When Hugh Capet became king of France in 987, he was, in relation to France's other great feudal lords, merely first among equals. From this small power base, more symbolic than real, Hugh Capet's successors extended their territory and dominion at the expense of the feudal lords' power. To administer their territories, the Capetians established an efficient bureaucracy composed of townsmen and trustworthy lesser nobles who, unlike the great feudal lords, owed their wealth and status directly to the king. These royal officials, an essential element of monarchical power, collected the king's feudal dues and administered justice. At the same time, French kings emphasized that they had been selected by God to rule, a theory known as the *divine right of kings*. This theory gave monarchy a sanctity that various French kings relied on to enforce their commands to rebellious feudal lords and defend themselves against papal claims of dominance over the French church.

Yet medieval French kings never sought absolute power. Not until the seventeenth century was the power base of the French monarchy consolidated to the extent that kings and their courts could attempt to rule without formal consultations with their subjects. In the Middle Ages, the French monarchs recognized the rights of, and consulted with, local representative assemblies, which represented the three estates, or orders, in society. These assemblies (whether regional or national) consisted of deputies drawn from the various elites: the clergy, the nobility, and significantly, the leadership of cities and towns in a given region. The Estates met as circumstances—such as wars, taxes, or local disputes—warranted, and the nationally representative assembly, the Estates General, was always summoned by the king. Medieval French kings consulted these assemblies mainly to give legitimacy to their demands and credibility to their administration. They also recognized that the courts—especially the highest court, the Parlement of Paris—had the right to administer the king's justice with a minimum of royal interference. Medieval kings did not see themselves as originators of law; they were its guarantors and administrators.

War came to serve the interests of a monarchy bent on consolidating its power and authority. As a result of the Hundred Years' War (1337–1453), the English were eventually driven from France, their claims to the French throne dashed. In the process of war, the French monarchy grew richer. War enabled the French kings to levy new taxes, often enacted without the consent of the Estates General, and to maintain a large standing army under royal command. The Hundred Years' War also inspired allegiance to the king as the visible symbol of France. The war heightened the French sense of national identity; the English were a common enemy, discernibly different in manners, language, dress, and appearance.

Religion and the French State

In every emergent state, tension existed between the monarch and the papacy. At issue was control over the church within that territory—over its personnel, its wealth, and, of course, its pulpits, from which an illiterate majority learned what their leaders wanted them to know, not only in matters of religious belief but also about questions of obedience to civil authority. The monarch's power to make church appointments could ensure a complacent church, one that was willing to preach about the king's divine right to rule and that would offer no resistance to his authority. Centuries of tough bargaining with the papacy paid off when, in 1516, Francis I (1515–1547) concluded the Concordat of Bologna, by which Pope Leo X permitted the French king to nominate, and therefore effectively to appoint, men of his choice as bishops in the French church.

The Concordat of Bologna laid the foundation for what became known as the *Gallican church*—a term signifying the immense power and authority of the Catholic church in France as sanctioned and overseen by the French kings. By the early sixteenth century, religious homogeneity had strengthened the central government at the expense of papal authority and the traditional privileges enjoyed by local aristocracy. This ecclesiastical and religious settlement lay at the heart of monarchical authority. Consequently, the Protestant Reformation threatened the very survival of France as a unified state. Throughout the early modern period, the French kings had assumed that their realms must be governed by one king, one faith, and one set of laws. Any alternative to that unity offered local power elites, whether aristocratic or clerical, the opportunity to channel religious dissent into their service at the expense of royal authority. Once linked, religious and political opposition to any central government could be extremely dangerous.

During the decades that followed, partly through the efforts of the Huguenot (Protestant) underground and partly because the French king and his ministers vacillated in their attempts at persecution, the Protestant minority grew in strength and dedication. By challenging the authority of the Catholic church, Protestants were also inadvertently challenging royal authority, for the French church and the French monarchy supported each other. Protestantism became the basis for a political movement of an increasingly revolutionary nature.

From 1562 to 1598, France experienced waves of religious wars, which cost the king control over vast areas of the kingdom. In 1579, extreme Huguenot theorists published the *Vindiciae contra Tyrannos*. This anonymous attack on the rights of kings, combined with a call to action, was the first of its kind in early modern times. It justified rebellion against, and even the execution of, an unjust king. European monarchs might claim power and divinely sanctioned authority, but by the late sixteenth century, their subjects had available the moral justification to oppose their monarch's will, by force if necessary, and this justification rested on Scripture and religious conviction. Significantly, this same treatise was translated into English in 1648, a year before Parliament publicly executed Charles I, king of England.

The French monarchy struggled when faced with a combined religious and political opposition. The era of royal supremacy ushered in by Francis I came to an abrupt end during the reign of his successor, Henry II (1547–1559). Wed to Catherine de Medicis, a member of the powerful Italian banking family, Henry occupied himself not with the concerns of government but with the pleasures of the hunt. The sons who succeeded Henry—Francis II (1559–1560), Charles IX (1560–1574), and Henry III (1574–1589)—were uniformly weak. In this power vacuum, their mother, Catherine, emerged as virtual ruler—a queen despised as

an Italian and a nonaristocrat, as a woman, and as a backstairs intriguer. One of the most hated figures of her day, Catherine de Medicis defies dispassionate assessment. She probably ordered the execution of Protestants by royal troops in Paris—the beginning of the infamous Saint Bartholomew's Day Massacre (1572). The massacre, with the bloodbath that followed, became both a symbol and a legend in subsequent European history: a symbol of the excesses of religious zeal and a legend of Protestant martyrdom, which gave renewed energy to the cause of international Protestantism.

The civil wars begun in 1562 were renewed in the massacre's aftermath. They dragged on until the death of the last Valois king in 1589. The Valois failure to produce a male heir to the throne placed Henry, duke of Bourbon and a Protestant, in line to succeed to the French throne. Realizing that the overwhelmingly Catholic population would not accept a Protestant king, Henry (apparently without much regret) renounced his adopted religion and embraced the church. His private religious beliefs may never be known, but outward conformity to the religion of the Catholic majority was the only means to effect peace and reestablish political stability. Under the reign of Henry IV (1589–1610), the French throne acquired its central position in national politics. Henry granted to his Protestant subjects and former followers a degree of religious toleration through the Edict of Nantes (1598), but they were never welcomed in significant numbers into the royal bureaucracy. Throughout the seventeenth century, every French king attempted to undermine the Protestants' regional power bases and ultimately to destroy their religious liberties.

Louis XIV: The Consolidation of French Monarchical Power

The defeat of Protestantism as a national force set the stage for the final consolidation of the French state under the great Bourbon kings, Louis XIII and Louis XIV. Louis XIII (1610–1643) realized that his rule depended on an efficient and trustworthy bureaucracy, a renewable treasury, and constant vigilance against the localized claims to power by the great aristocracy and Protestant cities and towns. Cardinal Richelieu, who served as the young Louis XIII's chief minister from 1624 to 1642, became the great architect of French absolutism.

Richelieu's morality rested on one sacred principle, embodied in a phrase he invented: *raison d'état,* reason of state. Richelieu applied the principle when he brought under the king's control the disruptive and antimonarchical elements within French society. He increased the power of the central bureaucracy, attacked the power of independent, and often Protestant, towns and cities, and harassed their Huguenot inhabitants. Above all, he humbled the great nobles by limiting their effectiveness as councilors to the king and prohibiting their traditional privileges, such as using a duel rather than court action to settle grievances. Reason of state also guided Richelieu's foreign policy. It required that France turn against Catholic Spain and join the Protestant, and hence anti-Spanish, side in the war that was raging at the time in the Holy Roman Empire. France's entry into the Thirty Years' War (1618–1648) resulted in a decisive victory for French power on the Continent.

Richelieu died in 1642, and Louis XIII the following year. Mazarin, a cardinal who had never been ordained a priest and an Italian by birth, took charge during the minority of Louis XIV (he was five years old when Louis XIII died) and continued Richelieu's policies. Mazarin's heavy-handed actions produced a rebellious reaction, the *Fronde:* a series of street riots that eventually cost the government control over Paris and lasted from 1648 to 1653. Centered in Paris and supported by the great aristocracy, the courts, and the city's poorer classes, the Fronde threatened to develop into a full-scale uprising. It might have done so but for one crucial factor: its leadership was divided. Court judges (lesser nobles who had often just risen from the ranks of the bourgeoisie) deeply distrusted the great aristocrats and refused in the end to make common cause with them. And both groups feared disorders among the urban masses.

When Louis XIV finally assumed responsibility for governing in 1661, he vowed that the events he had witnessed as a child in Paris, when the Fronde had brought street rioters to the palace windows, would never be repeated. In his reign, Louis XIV crafted the absolutist state and became the source of all power, which was in turn administered by his bureaucracy. The local elites or officials were expected to look to the central government for everything, from taxes to noble titles and exclusive privileges for perfume manufacturing or coal extraction. Provincial bureaucrats reported to ministers based in Paris. Indeed, even road engineers were sent out from Paris. The army was made larger and more professional, gaining, in addition, an architecture and engineering corps. The state also established a military school and sponsored academies for science, literature, and language. Intellectuals received court patronage and pensions but were expected to say what officials liked to hear.

Under Louis XIV, the state became the major player in everything, from dredging the rivers to awarding manufacturing monopolies. No absolute monarch in western Europe had ever before held so much personal authority or commanded such a vast and effective military and administrative machine. Louis XIV's reign represents the culmination of the process of increasing monarchical authority that had been under way for centuries. Intelligent, cunning, and possessing a unique understanding of the requirements of his office, Louis XIV became the envy of his age.

Perhaps the most brilliant of Louis XIV's many policies was his treatment of the aristocracy. He simply dispensed with their services as influential advisers. He treated the aristocrats to elaborate rituals, feasts, processions, displays, and banquets, but as they played their power dwindled. The wiser members of the aristocracy stayed home on their estates. For those who ventured to Versailles in search of power and glory, the possibility of financial ruin loomed. Few could keep up with the level of the king's spending.

Louis XIV's domestic policies, not surprisingly, centered on the incessant search for new revenues. Versailles and its banquets cost a fortune. So too did his wars, which Louis XIV waged to excess. To raise capital, he used the services of Jean Baptiste Colbert, a brilliant administrator, who improved methods of tax collecting, promoted new industries, and encouraged international trade. Such ambitious national policies were possible because Louis XIV inherited the ef-

LOUIS XIV. Louis XIV sought by every gesture and pose to display grandeur and to embody monarchy. His dress and affect were meant to awe and intimidate. *(Chateaux de Versailles, France/Giraudon/Art Resource, NY.)*

ficient system of administration introduced by Richelieu. Instead of relying on the local aristocracy to collect royal taxes and to administer royal policies, Richelieu had appointed the king's own men as *intendants,* or functionaries dispatched with wide powers into the provinces. At first, their mission had been temporary and their success minimal, but gradually they became a permanent feature of royal administration. During the reign of Louis XIV, the country was divided into thirty-two districts, controlled by intendants. Operating with a total bureaucracy of about a thousand officials and no longer bothering even to consult the parlements (courts of law) or the Estates, Louis XIV ruled absolutely.

Why did such a system of absolute authority work? Did the peasants not revolt? Why did the old aristocracy not rise in rebellion? For the aristocrats, the loss of political authority was not accompanied by a comparable loss in wealth and social position; indeed, quite the contrary was true. During the seventeenth century, the French nobility—2 percent of the population—controlled approximately 20 to 30 percent of the total national income. The church, too, fared well under Louis, receiving good tax arrangements, provided it preached about the king's divinely given rights. Although there were peasant upheavals throughout the century, the sheer size of the royal army and police—more than 300,000 by the end of Louis's reign—made successful revolt nearly impossible. When in the early 1700s a popular religious rebellion led by Protestant visionaries broke out in the south, royal troops crushed it. Thus, absolutism rested on the complicity of the old aristocracy, the self-aggrandizement of government officials, the church's doctrines, the revenues squeezed out of the peasantry, and the power of a huge military machine.

Yet Louis XIV's system was fatally flawed. Without any effective check on his power and on his dreams of international conquest, no limit was imposed on the state's capacity to make war or on the ensuing national debt. By the 1680s, his domestic and foreign policies turned violently aggressive. In 1685, he revoked the Edict of Nantes, forcing many of the country's remaining Protestants to flee. In 1689, he embarked on a military campaign to gain territory from the Holy Roman Empire. And in 1701, he tried to bring Spain under the control of the Bourbon dynasty. Louis XIV, however, underestimated the strength of his northern rivals, England and the Netherlands. Their combined power, in alliance with the Holy Roman Empire and the Austrians, defeated Louis XIV's ambitions.

The War of the Spanish Succession was essentially a land war fought on the battlefields of northern Europe. Out of it, the Austrians acquired the southern Netherlands (Belgium) and thus a buffer against the possibility of a French overrun of the Low Countries. Most dramatically, however, the war created a balance of power in Europe. Britain emerged as a major force in European affairs, the counterweight against the French colossus. The relative peace of the eighteenth century has often been attributed to the creation of this real, but fragile, balance among the major European powers.

POOR WOMAN WITH CHILDREN, BY J. DUMONT (1701–1781). Louis XIV may have been grand, but he was also callous. He impoverished the poor even further, and by the end of his reign famine had returned to parts of France. (*Pushkin Museum, Moscow/Bridgeman Art Library.*)

Louis XIV's participation in these long wars emptied the royal treasury. By the late seventeenth century, taxes had risen intolerably and were levied mostly on those least able to pay: the peasants. In the 1690s, the combination of taxes, bad harvests, and plague led to widespread poverty, misery, and starvation in large areas of France. Thus, for the great majority of French people, absolutism meant a decline in living standards and a significant increase in mortality rates. Absolutism also meant increased surveillance of the population. Royal authorities censored books, spied on heretics, Protestants, and freethinkers, and even tortured and executed opponents of state policy.

By 1715, France was a tightly governed society whose treasury was bankrupt. Protestants had been driven into exile or forced to convert. Strict censorship laws closely governed publishing, causing a brisk trade in clandestine books and manuscripts. Direct taxes burdened the poor and were legally evaded by the aristocracy. Critics of state policy within the church had been effectively marginalized. And over the long run, foreign wars had brought no significant gains.

In the France of Louis XIV, the dynastic state reached maturity and began to display some of its classic characteristics: centralized bureaucracy; royal patronage to enforce allegiance; a system of taxation universally but inequitably applied; and suppression of political opposition, either through the use of patronage or, if necessary, through force. Another important feature was the state's cultivation of the arts and sciences as a means of increasing national power and prestige. Together, these policies enabled France and its monarchs to achieve political stability, enforce a uniform system of law, and channel the country's wealth and resources into the service of the state as a whole.

Yet at his death in 1715, Louis XIV left his successors a bureaucracy and onerous taxation that were vastly in need of overhaul. Because this system endorsed the traditional social privileges of the church and nobility, reforming it was virtually impossible. The pattern of war, excessive taxation of the lower classes, and spending beyond revenues had damaged French finances. Yet the bureaucracy of the absolutist state continued to grow and extend its influence into every area of trade. To this day, perfectly preserved pieces of silk and cotton cloth made in every French province sit in the Parisian archives of the government. In the eighteenth century, they had been sent there for inspection. Only when the king's ministers had approved the samples could the cloth from which they had been cut be sold in the open market, with the king's seal. By the 1780s, manufacturers clamored for freer markets, fewer, or at least faster, inspections, and more freedom to experiment. They smuggled and cheated the inspectors while looking across the Channel at England with envy at the power, wealth, and freedom of its industry and its merchants. The discontent of French manufacturers contributed to the causes of the 1789 French Revolution.

MAP 16.2 EUROPE, 1648 ▶
Europe in 1648, exhausted by war.

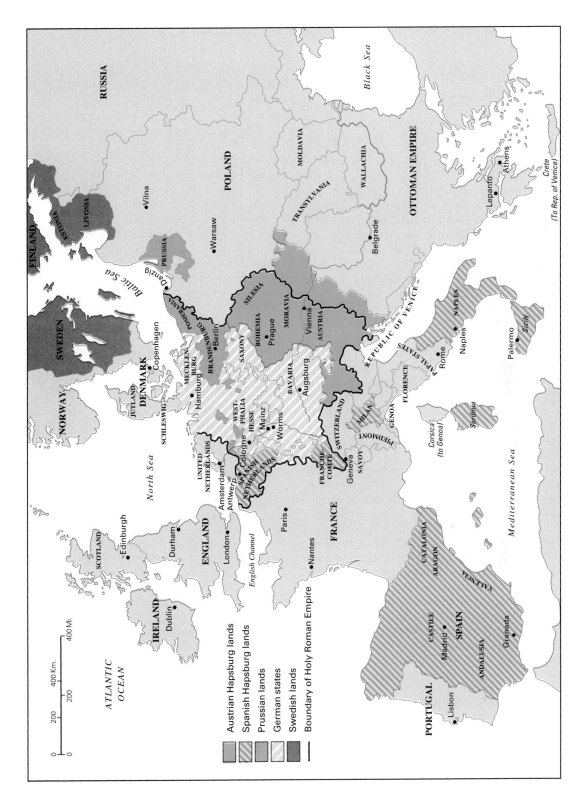

RUSSIA

Black Sea

FINLAND

SWEDEN

ESTONIA

LIVONIA

• Vilna

POLAND

MOLDAVIA

WALLACHIA

TRANSYLVANIA

Warsaw •

• Belgrade

OTTOMAN EMPIRE

PRUSSIA

Danzig

Baltic Sea

POMERANIA

SILESIA

MORAVIA

BOHEMIA

Prague •

Vienna •

AUSTRIA

REPUBLIC OF VENICE

NAPLES

Sicily

NORWAY

DENMARK

JUTLAND

SCHLESWIG

MECKLEN-BURG

BRANDENBURG

Berlin •

SAXONY

Copenhagen •

Hamburg •

WEST-PHALIA

HESSE

Mainz •

BAVARIA

Worms •

Augsburg •

SWITZERLAND

MILAN

PIEDMONT

SAVOY

GENOA

FLORENCE

PAPAL STATES

Rome •

Naples •

Palermo •

Lepanto •

Athens •

Crete
(To Rep. of Venice)

North Sea

UNITED NETHERLANDS

Amsterdam •

Antwerp •

Cologne •

SPANISH NETHERLANDS

FRANCHE-COMTÉ

Geneva •

Corsica
(to Genoa)

Sardinia

Mediterranean Sea

SCOTLAND

Edinburgh •

IRELAND

Dublin •

ENGLAND

Durham •

London •

English Channel

Paris •

FRANCE

Nantes •

CATALONIA

ARAGON

VALENCIA

CASTILE

SPAIN

Madrid •

ANDALUSIA

Granada •

PORTUGAL

Lisbon •

ATLANTIC OCEAN

400 Mi.

400 Km.

200

200

0

0

Austrian Hapsburg lands

Spanish Hapsburg lands

Prussian lands

German states

Swedish lands

Boundary of Holy Roman Empire

373

The Growth of Limited Monarchy and Constitutionalism in England

England achieved national unity earlier than any other major European state. Its island geography freed it from the border disputes that plagued emerging states in continental Europe. By an accident of fate, its administrative structure also developed in such a way as to encourage centralization. In 1066, William, duke of Normandy and vassal to the French king, had invaded and conquered England, acquiring at a stroke the entire kingdom. In contrast, the French kings took centuries to make the territory of France their domain.

As conquerors, the Norman kings pursued a policy of intermarriage and consultation. They consulted with their powerful subjects—archbishops, bishops, earls, and barons. By the middle of the thirteenth century, these consultations, or *parlays,* came to be called *parliaments.* Increasingly, the practice grew of inviting to these parliaments representatives from the counties—knights and burgesses. Gradually, these lesser-than-noble but often wealthy and prominent representatives came to regard Parliament as a means of self-expression for redressing their grievances. In turn, the later medieval kings saw Parliament as a means of exercising control and raising taxes. By 1297, the Lords (the upper house) and Commons (as the lower house was called) had obtained the king's agreement that no direct taxes could be levied without their consent. By the fourteenth century, Parliament had become a permanent institution of government. Its power was entirely subservient to the crown, but its right to question royal decisions had been established.

The English Parliament and Constitution

The medieval English Parliament possessed two characteristics that distinguished it from its many Continental counterparts, such as the various French Estates. The English Parliament was na-tional, not provincial; more important, its representatives were elected across caste lines, with voting rights dependent on property, not on noble birth or status. These representatives voted as individuals rather than collectively as clergy, nobles, or commoners, that is, as Estates. In the Middle Ages, Parliament and the monarchy were interdependent; they were seen not as rivals but as complementary forms of centralized government. That very interdependence, however, would ultimately lead to conflict.

The constitution, too, emerged during the Middle Ages in England. It comprised unwritten and written precedents, laws, and royal acts that came to embody the basic principles of government. In contrast to the French model, England developed into a *constitutional* monarchy. The most famous document, Magna Carta (1215), guaranteed certain aristocratic privileges and was read at the opening meeting of almost every Parliament the king called. This theoretical foundation—until now not written as a single document—grew out of legal practices and customs described under the generic title *common law.* Whereas feudal law applied only to a local region, common law extended throughout the realm and served as a unifying force.

The Tudor Achievement

Emphasis on the medieval evolution of Parliament and the constitution should not obscure the fact that England in the fifteenth century could be a lawless place where local nobility made war on their neighbors largely unchecked by central government. One such war, the War of the Roses (1455–1485) pitted two noble families against each other in a struggle for domination. Out of it, the Tudors emerged triumphant, in the person of Henry VII (1485–1509), who spent much of his reign consolidating and extending his authority. In the process, he revitalized and remade the institutions of central government. Henry VII's goal was to check the unruly nobility. Toward this end, he brought commoners into the government. These commoners, unlike the great magnates, could be channeled into royal service because they craved what the king offered: financial rewards and elevated social status. Although they did not fully displace the aristocracy, commoners were brought into Henry VII's inner circle, into the Privy Council, into the courts, and eventually into all the highest offices of the government. The strength and efficiency of Tudor government were shown during the Reformation, when Henry VIII (1509–1547) made himself head of the English church. He was able to take this giant step (known as the Henrican Revolution) toward increasing royal power because his father had restored order and stability.

The Protestant Reformation in England was a revolution in royal, as well as ecclesiastical, government. It attacked and defeated a main obstacle to monarchical authority: the power of the papacy. At the same time, the Reformation greatly enhanced the power of Parliament. Henry used Parliament to make the Reformation because he knew that he needed the support of the lords, the country gentry, and the merchants. No change in religious practice could be instituted by the monarchy alone. Parliament's participation in the Reformation gave it a greater role and sense of importance than it had ever possessed in the past. Nonetheless, the final outcome of this administrative revolution enhanced monarchical power. By the end of his reign, Henry VIII easily possessed as much power as his French rival, Francis I. Indeed, until the early seventeenth century, the history of monarchical power in England, with its absolutist tendencies, was remarkably similar to the Continental pattern.

At Henry's death, the Tudor bureaucracy and centralized government were strained to the utmost, yet survived. The government weathered the reign of Henry's sickly son, Edward VI (1547–1553), and the extreme Protestantism of some of his advisers, and it survived the brief and deeply troubled reign of Henry's first daughter, Mary (1553–1558), who brutally tried to return England to Catholicism. At Mary's death, England came dangerously close to the religious instability and sectarian tension that undermined the French kings during the final decades of the sixteenth century.

Henry's second daughter, Elizabeth I, became queen in 1558 and reigned until her death in 1603. The Elizabethan period was characterized by a heightened sense of national identity. The English Reformation enhanced that sense, as did the increasing fear of foreign invasion by Spain.

The fear was real enough and lessened only with the defeat of the Spanish Armada in 1588. For the English the victory was like that of David over Goliath, and its value was both symbolic and real. For the Spanish the defeat was also deeply affecting: they asked how had they gone wrong. In the seventeenth century, the English would look back on Elizabeth's reign as a golden age. It was the calm before the storm, a time when a new commercial class was formed, which, in the seventeenth century, would demand a greater say in government operations.

The social and economic changes of the Elizabethan age can be seen, in microcosm, by looking at the Durham region in northern England. From 1580 to 1640, a new coal-mining industry developed there through the efforts of entrepreneurs—gentlemen with minor lands who exploited their mineral resources. The wool trade also prospered in Durham. By 1600, social and political tensions had developed. The wool merchants and the entrepreneurial gentry were demanding a greater say in governing the region. They were opposed by the traditional leaders of Durham society: the bishops and the dozen or so aristocratic families with major landholdings and access to the court in London.

This split can be described as one between "court" and "country." In this context, *court* refers to the traditional aristocratic magnates, the church hierarchy, and royal officialdom, and *country* denotes a loose coalition of merchants and rising agricultural and industrial entrepreneurs from the prosperous gentry class, whose economic worth far exceeded their political power. The pattern found in Durham was repeated in other parts of England, generally where industry and commerce grew and prospered. The gentry gained social status and wealth. In the seventeenth century, these social and economic tensions between court and country would help foment revolution.

By the early seventeenth century in England, the descendants of the old feudal aristocracy differed markedly from their Continental counterparts. Isolation from the great wars of the Reformation had produced an aristocracy less militaristic and more ceremonial and commercial in orientation. Furthermore, the lesser ranks of the landowning aristocracy, gentlemen without

Elizabeth I, Queen of England (1558–1603)

Born in 1533, Elizabeth, the daughter of Henry VIII and his second wife, Anne Boleyn, was raised as a Protestant by her father. Fidelity to the Anglican church may have been basic to Henry's interests, but fidelity to his marriage vows was not. He put Anne Boleyn to death on charges of treason. His marriage to her had led to England's break with the Roman Catholic church, which would not grant him a divorce from his first wife, Catherine of Aragon, with whom he had failed to produce a male heir. When Henry's second mariage also did not produce the male heir he so deeply desired, he tired of Elizabeth's mother. Hence her tragic end.

The church of Rome regarded Elizabeth as a bastard and never accepted Henry's self-decreed divorce from his first wife. Not surprisingly, in her youth Elizabeth came to fear

By kind permission of the Marquess of Tavistock, and the Trustees of the Bedford Estates.

titles (the gentry), had prospered significantly in Tudor times. In commercial matters, they were often no shrewder than the great landed magnates, but they had in Parliament, as well as in their counties, an effective and institutionalized means of expressing their political interests. The great nobles, in contrast, had largely abandoned the sword as the primary expression of their political authority without putting anything comparable in its place. Gradually, political initiative was slipping away from the great lords and into the hands of a gentry that was commercially and agriculturally innovative as well as fiercely protective of its local base of political power.

Religion played a vital role in this realignment of political interests and forces. Many of the old aristocracy clung to the Anglicanism of the Henrican Reformation, with bishops and liturgy intact, and some even clung to Catholicism. The newly risen gentry found in the Protestant Reformation a form of religious worship more suited

to their independent spirit. They felt that it was their right to appoint their own preachers and that the church should reflect local tastes and beliefs rather than doctrines and ceremonies inherited from a discredited Catholicism. In late Tudor times, gentry and merchant interests fused with Puritanism—the English variety of Calvinism—to produce a political-religious vision with ominous potential.

The English Revolutions, 1640–1660 and 1688–1689

The religious and political forces threatening the monarchy were dealt with ineffectively by the first two Stuart kings: James I (1603–1625) and Charles I (1625–1649). Like their Continental counterparts, both believed in royal absolutism. Essentially, what these Stuart kings tried to do in England was what Louis XIV later tried to do in

376

marriage and to regard her claim to the English throne as precarious. She became queen in 1558—after the deaths of her half sister, Mary, and half brother, Edward, each of whom had short, tumultuous reigns. With Elizabeth's accession to the throne, England and Wales returned to the fold of the Henrican Reformation, repudiating the efforts of Queen Mary to force them to revert to Roman Catholicism. Because Mary executed Protestant leaders, she went down in history as "Bloody Mary."

At Elizabeth's accession, male contemporaries worried in print whether she would be up to the task of ruling and urged her court and Privy Council to keep her in line. They were in for a shock as Elizabeth proved to be one of the most able monarchs; she did not hesitate to set policy as she saw fit, much to the annoyance of her advisers. Even the earl of Leicester, widely regarded as one of her suitors, said in 1578 that "our conference with her Majesty about affairs is both seldom and slender."

Elizabeth faced the possibility of rebellion led by her Catholic cousin, Mary Queen of Scotland, and in the end Elizabeth saw her executed. Elizabeth's greatest test came in 1588 when the Spanish king, Philip II, sent his Armada to invade England for the purpose of restoring it to Catholicism. Consulting her astrologers but armed for battle, Elizabeth rallied the country, and the English fleet got very lucky. A gale-force wind blew the Spanish ships out of striking distance of the mouth of the Thames River, and, pursued by the faster English ships, the Armada was virtually destroyed. The wind that blew that day became known as "the Protestant wind," and Elizabeth went down in history as "good Queen Bess."

More even than her father, Elizabeth secured England, though not Ireland, for the Protestant cause. She also gave her name to the age, and Elizabethan England flourished culturally. During her reign, William Shakespeare wrote many of his greatest plays and had them performed.

France: establish crown and court administrators as the sole governing bodies within the state. The Stuarts, however, lacked an adequate social and institutional base for absolutism, not least of all a standing army. They did not possess the vast independent wealth of the French kings.

Through the established church, the Stuarts preached the doctrine of the divine right of kings. James I, an effective and shrewd administrator, conducted foreign policy without consulting Parliament. In a speech before Parliament, he stated that "it is sedition in subjects to dispute what a king may do in the height of his power . . . I will not be content that my power be disputed upon."[2]

James I made the standard moves toward creating an absolute monarchy: he centralized and consolidated the power of the government and tried to win over the aristocracy by giving them new offices and titles. He gave royal monopolies to merchants of everything from soap to coal. James I did not have a sufficient economic base to

pay for his largesse. His son and successor, Charles I, had the same problem. But he suspended Parliament in 1629 and attempted to rule through his advisers. He had two major goals: to rid the nation of Puritans and to root out the "country" opposition. Charles also tried to collect taxes without the Parliament's consent. These policies ended in disaster; by 1640, the Puritans and the gentry opposition had grown closer together.

The first English Revolution began in 1640 because Charles I needed money to defend the realm against a recent Scottish invasion. Being staunch Calvinists, the Scots had rebelled against Charles's religious policies. Moreover, their clan leaders saw rebellion as a way to get back at the Stuart kings, who long had been a thorn in their side, first when they had been in Edinburgh and now from their base in London. Charles had no alternative but to call Parliament, which could then dictate the terms: no concessions from

HENRY VIII. Although the ruler of a second-rate power, Henry VIII sought to impress upon his subjects that he was a new and powerful monarch. He sought to compete in style, if not power, with the French and the Spanish kings. (*Walker Art Gallery, Liverpool.*)

Charles, then no taxes to fight the Scots, who were also demanding money for every day they occupied the northern territory. Parliament countered the king's requests with demands for rights: consultations with Parliament in matters of taxation, trial by jury, habeas corpus, and a truly Protestant church responsive to the beliefs and interests of its laity. Charles refused these demands, viewing them as an assault on royal authority. He even tried to arrest the leaders of Parliament. In

1642, civil war began. Directed by Parliament and financed by taxes and the merchants, the war was fought by the New Model Army led by Oliver Cromwell (1599–1658), a Puritan squire with a gift for military leadership.

The two English Revolutions need to be seen as part of a constitutional crisis that lasted two generations. The crisis began in 1640, degenerated into civil war in 1642, and culminated in regicide in 1649. After the restoration of monarchy in 1660, the crisis flared up again in 1679–81 and was finally resolved by the Revolution of 1688–89—sometimes called the Glorious Revolution. The crisis affected England, Scotland, Ireland, and Wales differently, but in all cases led to the consolidation of English power over these territories. Perhaps the native Irish fared worst of all as Cromwell drove thousands to the western, barren part of the island.

The civil war of the 1640s generated a new type of military organization. The New Model Army was financed by Parliament's rich supporters and led by gentlemen farmers. Its ranks were filled by religious zealots, along with the usual cross section of poor artisans and day laborers. This citizen army defeated the king, his aristocratic followers, and the Anglican church's hierarchy.

In January 1649, Charles I was publicly executed by order of Parliament. During the interregnum (time between kings) of the next eleven years, Parliament joined with the army to govern the country as a republic. In the distribution of power between the army and the Parliament, Cromwell proved to be a key element. He had the support of the army's officers and some of its rank and file, and he had been a member of Parliament for many years. However, he gained control over the army only after it was purged of radical groups. Some of these radicals wanted to level society, that is, to redistribute property by ending monopolies and to give the vote to all male citizens. In the context of the 1650s, Cromwell was a moderate republican who also believed in limited religious toleration for Protestants, yet history has painted him, somewhat unjustly, as a military dictator.

Both English Revolutions were led by a loose coalition of urban merchants and landed gentry imbued with the strict Protestantism of the Continental Reformation. In the 1650s, their success was jeopardized by growing discontent from the poor, who made up the rank and file of the army and demanded that their economic and social grievances be rectified. The radicals of the first English Revolution—men like Gerrard Winstanley, the first theoretician of social democracy in modern times, and John Lilburne, the Leveller—demanded redistribution of property, even communal property; voting rights for the majority of the male population; and abolition of religious and intellectual elites, whose power and ideology supported the interests of the ruling classes. The radicals rejected Anglicanism, moderate Puritanism, and even, in a few cases, the lifestyle of the middle class; they opted instead for radical politics and free lifestyles. They spurned marriage, and the Quakers even allowed women to preach. The radicals terrified devoted Puritans such as Cromwell. By 1660, two years after Cromwell's death, the country was adrift, without effective leadership.

Parliament, having secured the economic interests of its constituency (gentry, merchants, and some small landowners), chose to restore court and crown and invited the exiled son of the executed king to return to the kingship. Having learned the lesson his father had spurned, Charles II (1660–1685) never instituted royal absolutism, although he did try to minimize Parliament's role in the government. His court was a far more open institution than his father's had been, for Charles II feared a similar death.

Charles's brother James II (1685–1688), however, was a foolishly fearless Catholic and admirer of French absolutism. Having gathered at his court a coterie of Catholic advisers (among them Jesuits) and supporters of royal prerogative, James attempted to bend Parliament and local government to the royal will. James's Catholicism was the crucial element in his failure. The Anglican church would not back him, and political forces similar to those that had gathered against his father, Charles I, in 1640 descended on him. The ruling elites, however, had learned their lesson back in the 1650s: civil war would produce social discontent among the masses. The upper classes wanted to avoid open warfare and preserve the monarchy as a constitutional authority but not as an absolute one. Puritanism, with its sectarian fervor and its dangerous association with republicanism, was allowed to play no part in the second English Revolution.

In early 1688, Anglicans, some aristocrats, and opponents of royal prerogative (members of the Whig party, along with a few Tories) formed a conspiracy against James II. Their purpose was to invite his son-in-law, William of Orange, stadholder (head) of the Netherlands and husband of James's Protestant daughter Mary, to invade England and rescue its government from James's control. The final outcome of this invasion was determined by William and his conspirators, in conjunction with a freely elected Parliament. This dangerous plan succeeded for three main reasons: William and the Dutch desperately needed English support against the threat of a French invasion; James had lost the loyalty of key men in the army, powerful gentlemen in the counties, and the Anglican church; and the political elite was committed and united in its intentions. William and Mary were declared king and queen by act of Parliament, and William defeated James II's army in Ireland. The last revolution in English history defeated royal absolutism forever. Ironically, while political freedom increased in England, Scotland soon lost its parliament, and Catholics in Ireland were systematically repressed.

This bloodless revolution—the Glorious Revolution—created a new political and constitutional reality. Parliament gained the rights to assemble regularly and to vote on all matters of taxation; the rights of habeas corpus and trial by jury (for men of property and social status) were also secured. These rights were in turn legitimated in a constitutionally binding document, the Bill of Rights (1689). All Protestants, regardless of their sectarian bias, were granted toleration.

Online Study Center

Improve Your Grade
Primary Source: The English Bill of Rights

The Revolution Settlement of 1688–89 resolved the profound constitutional and social tensions of the seventeenth century and laid the foundations of the English government that exists today. The year 1688 saw the creation of a new public and political order that would become the envy of enlightened reformers. The Glorious Revolution, says the historian J. H. Plumb, established "the authority of certain men of property, particularly those of high social standing, either aristocrats or linked with aristocracy, whose tap root was in land but whose side roots reached out to commerce, industry and finance."[3] Throughout the eighteenth century, England was ruled by kings and Parliaments that represented the interests of an oligarchy, whose cohesiveness and prosperity ensured social and political stability.

The English Revolutions in the end established English parliamentary government and the rule of law; they also provided a degree of freedom for the propertied. In retrospect, we can see that absolutism according to the French model probably never had a chance in England. It had too many gentlemen who possessed enough land to be independent of the crown, yet not so much that they could control whole sections of the kingdom. In addition, monarchs had no effective standing army. But to contemporaries, the issues seemed different: English opponents of absolutism spoke of their rights as granted by their ancient constitution and the feudal law, of the need to make the English church truly Protestant, and, among the radicals, of the right of lesser men to establish their property. These opponents possessed an institution—Parliament—through which they could express their grievances. Eventually, they also acquired an army, which waged war to protect property and commercial rights. In 1689, the propertied classes invented limited monarchy and a constitutional system based on laws made by Parliament and sanctioned by the king. Very gradually, the monarchical element in that system would yield to the power and authority of parliamentary ministers and state officials.

In the nineteenth and twentieth centuries, parliamentary institutions would be gradually and peacefully reformed to express a more democratic social reality. The events of 1688–89 have rightly been described as "the year one," for they fashioned a system of government that operated effectively in Britain and could also be adopted elsewhere with modification. The British system became a model for other forms of representative government, adopted in France and in the former British colonies, beginning with the United States. It was the model that offered a viable alternative to absolutism.

THE NETHERLANDS: A BOURGEOIS REPUBLIC

One other area in Europe developed a system of representative government that also survived for centuries. The Netherlands (the Low Countries, that is, the seven Dutch provinces and Belgium) had been part of Hapsburg territory since the fifteenth century. When Charles V ascended the Spanish throne in 1516, the Netherlands became an economic linchpin of the Spanish empire. Spain exported wool and bullion to the Low Countries in return for manufactured textiles, hardware, grain, and naval stores. Flanders, with Antwerp as its capital, was the manufacturing and banking center of the Spanish empire.

To the north, cities like Rotterdam and Amsterdam built and outfitted the Spanish fleet. In The Hague, printers published the Bible in Spanish and in Dutch or Flemish (actually the same language). But in the north, too, Protestantism made significant inroads.

During the reign of Charles V's successor, Philip II, a tightly organized Calvinist minority, with its popular base in the cities and its military strategy founded on sea raids, at first harassed and then aggressively challenged Spanish power. In the 1560s, the Spanish responded by trying to export the Inquisition into the Netherlands and sending an enormous standing army there under the duke of Alva. It was a classic example of overkill; thousands of once-loyal Flemish and Dutch subjects turned against the Spanish crown. The people either converted secretly to Calvinism or aided the revolutionaries. Led by William the Silent (1533–1584), head of the Orange dynasty, the seven northern provinces (Holland, Zeeland, Utrecht, Gelderland, Overijssel, Friesland, and Groningen) joined in the Union of Utrecht (1579) to protect themselves against Spanish aggression. Their determined resistance, coupled with the serious economic weaknesses of the overextended Spanish empire, eventually produced unexpected success for the northern colonies.

OLIVER CROMWELL. Cromwell wore the simple black of the Puritan gentry and sought to portray himself as a pious warrior. Yet in this portrait he does have a somewhat regal bearing, and his task demanded that he act like a king without ever becoming one. (*AKG, London.*)

By 1609, the seven northern provinces were effectively free of Spanish control and loosely tied together under a republican form of government. Seventeenth-century Netherlands (that is, the Dutch Republic) became a prosperous bourgeois state. Rich from the fruits of manufacture and trade in everything from tulip bulbs to ships—and, not least, slaves—Dutch merchants ruled their cities and provinces with a fierce pride. By the early seventeenth century, this new nation of only 1.2 million people was practicing the most innovative commercial and financial techniques in Europe.

In this fascinating instance, capitalism and Protestantism fused to do the work of princes; the Dutch state emerged without absolute monarchy, and indeed in opposition to it. From that experi-ence, the ruling Dutch oligarchy retained a deep distrust of hereditary monarchy and of central government. The exact position of the House of Orange remained a vexing constitutional question until well into the eighteenth century. The oligarchs and their party, the Patriots, favored a republic without a single head, ruled by them locally and in the Estates General meeting in The Hague. The Calvinist clergy, old aristocrats, and a vast section of the populace—all for very different reasons—wanted the head of the House of Orange to govern as stadholder of the provinces—in effect, as a limited monarch in a republican state. These unresolved political tensions between the center and the localities prevented the Netherlands from developing a form of republican government to rival the stability of the British system of limited monarchy. The Dutch achievement came in other areas.

Calvinism had provided the ideology of revolution and national identity. Capital, in turn, created a unique cultural milieu in the Dutch urban centers of Amsterdam, Rotterdam, Utrecht, and The Hague. Wide toleration without a centralized system of censorship made the Dutch book trade, which often disseminated works by refugees from the Spanish Inquisition and later by French Protestants, the most vital in Europe right up to the French Revolution. And the sights and sounds of an active and prosperous population, coupled with a politically engaged and rich bourgeoisie, fed the imagination, as well as the purses, of various artistic schools. Rembrandt van Rijn, Jan Steen, Frans Hals, Jan Vermeer, and Jan van de Velde are at the top of a long list of great Dutch artists—many of them also refugees. They left timeless images portraying the people of the only republican national state to endure throughout the seventeenth century.

THE HOLY ROMAN EMPIRE: THE FAILURE TO UNIFY GERMANY

In contrast to the English, French, Spanish, and Dutch experiences in the early modern period, the Germans failed to achieve national unity. The German failure to unify is tied to the history of the Holy Roman Empire. That union of various central European territories was created in the tenth century, when Otto I, in a deliberate attempt to revive Charlemagne's empire, was crowned "Emperor of the Romans" by the pope. Later, the title was changed to "Holy Roman Emperor." The empire consisted of mostly German-speaking principalities.

Otto and his medieval successors busied themselves not with administering their territories but with attempting to gain control over the rich Italian peninsula and dealing with the challenges presented by powerful popes. Meanwhile, the German nobility extended and consolidated their rule over their peasants and over various towns and cities within the empire. Their aristocratic power remained a constant obstacle to German unity. Only by incorporating the nobility into the fabric of the state's power, court, and army and by sanctioning their oppressive control of the peasants would Holy Roman Emperors manage to create a unified German state.

In the medieval and early modern periods, the Holy Roman Emperors depended on powerful noble lords—including archbishops and bishops—for support because the office of emperor was elective, not hereditary. German noble princes—including the archbishops of Cologne and Mainz, the Hohenzollern ruler of Brandenburg, and the duke of Saxony, who were electors responsible for choosing the Holy Roman Emperor—were fiercely independent. All belonged to the empire yet regarded themselves as autonomous powers. These decentralizing tendencies were highly developed by the thirteenth century, and the emperors gradually realized that they were losing control of the outer frontiers of the empire. The French had conducted a successful military incursion into northern Italy and on the western frontier of the empire. Hungary had fallen to the Turks, and the Swiss were hard to govern (besides, given their terrain, they were impossible to beat into submission). At the same time, Hapsburg princes maneuvered themselves into a position from which they could monopolize the imperial elections.

The Holy Roman Empire in the reigns of the Hapsburg emperors Maximilian I (1493–1519) and Charles V (1519–1556) might have achieved a degree of cohesion comparable with that in France and Spain. Certainly, the impetus of war—

against France and against the Turks—required the creation of a large standing army and the taxation to maintain it. Both could have worked to the benefit of a centralized, imperial power. But the Protestant Reformation, which began in 1517, meshed with already well-developed tendencies toward local independence and destroyed the last hope of Hapsburg domination and German unity. The German nobility were all too ready to use the Reformation as a vindication of their local power, and indeed Martin Luther made just such an appeal to their interests.

At precisely the moment in the 1520s when Charles V had to act with great determination to stop the spread of Lutheranism, he was at war with France over its claims to Italian territory. Charles had no sooner won his Italian territories, in particular the rich city-state of Milan, when he had to make war against the Turks, who in 1529 besieged Vienna. Not until the 1540s was Charles V in a position to attack the Lutheran princes. By then, they had had considerable time to solidify their position and had united for mutual protection in the Schmalkaldic League.

War raged in Germany between the Protestant princes and the imperial army led by Charles V. In 1551, Catholic France entered the war on the Protestant side, and Charles had to flee for his life. Defeated, Charles abdicated and retired to a Spanish monastery. The Treaty of Augsburg (1555) gave every German prince the right to determine the religion of his subjects. The princes had won their local territories, and a unified German state was never constructed by the Hapsburgs.

When Emperor Charles V abdicated in 1556, he divided his kingdom between his son Philip and his brother Ferdinand. Philip inherited Spain and its colonies, as well as the Netherlands. Ferdinand acquired the Austrian territories. The Spanish and Austrian branches of the Hapsburg family were thus created, and well into the late seventeenth century they defined their interests in common and often waged war accordingly. The enormous international power of the Hapsburgs was checked only by their uncertain authority over the German states within the Holy Roman Empire. Throughout the sixteenth century, the Austrian Hapsburgs barely managed to control these sprawling and deeply divided German territories. Protestantism, as protected by the Treaty of Augsburg, and the particularism and provinciality of the German nobility continued to prevent the creation of a German state.

The Austrian Hapsburg emperors, however, never missed an opportunity to further the cause of the Counter Reformation and to court the favor of local interests opposed to the nobility. No Hapsburg was ever more fervid in that regard than the Jesuit-trained Archduke Ferdinand II, who ascended the throne of the Holy Roman Empire in Vienna in 1619. He immediately embarked on a policy of Catholic revival and used Spanish officials as his administrators. His policies provoked within the empire a war that engulfed the whole of Europe.

The Thirty Years' War (1618–1648) began when the Bohemians, whose anti-Catholic tendencies can be traced back to the Hussite reformers of the early fifteenth century, attempted to put a Protestant king on their throne. The Austrian and Spanish Hapsburgs reacted by sending an army into the kingdom of Bohemia, and suddenly the whole empire was forced to take sides along religious lines. The Bohemian nobility, after centuries of enforcing serfdom, failed to rally the rural masses behind them, and victory went to the emperor. Bohemia and the German states suffered almost unimaginable devastation; ravaging Hapsburg armies sacked and burned three-fourths of each kingdom's towns and practically exterminated its aristocracy.

Until the 1630s, it looked as if the Hapsburgs would be able to use the war to enhance their power and promote centralization. But the intervention of Lutheran Sweden, led by Gustavus Adolphus and encouraged by France, wrecked Hapsburg ambitions. The ensuing military conflict devastated vast areas of northern and central Europe. The civilian population suffered untold hardships: soldiers raped women and pillaged the land, and thousands of refugees took to the roads and forests. Partly because the French finally intervened directly, the Spanish Hapsburgs emerged from the Thirty Years' War with no benefits. At the Treaty of Westphalia (1648), their Austrian cousins reaffirmed their right to govern the eastern states of the kingdom, with Vienna as their capital. Austria took shape as a dynastic state, and the German territories in the empire remained fragmented by the independent interests of their largely recalcitrant feudal nobility. In consequence, the Thirty Years' War shaped the course of German history into the nineteenth century.

THE EMERGENCE OF AUSTRIA AND PRUSSIA

Austria

As a result of the settlement at Westphalia, the Austrian Hapsburgs gained firm control over most of Hungary and Bohemia, where they installed a virtually new and foreign nobility. At the same time, they strengthened their grip on Vienna. In one of the few spectacular successes achieved by the Counter Reformation, the ruling elites in all three territories were forcibly, or in many cases willingly, converted back to Catholicism. At long last, religious predominance could be used as a force—long delayed in eastern Europe because of the Protestant Reformation—for the creation of the Austrian dynastic state.

One severe obstacle to territorial hegemony remained: the military threat posed by the Turks, who sought to control much of Hungary. In 1683 the Turks again besieged Vienna, but a Catholic and unified Austrian army, composed of a variety of peoples and assisted by the Poles, managed to defeat the Turks and recapture the whole of Hungary and Transylvania and part of Croatia. Austria's right to govern these lands was firmly accepted by the Turks at the Treaty of Karlowitz (1699).

The Austrian Hapsburgs and their victorious army had entered the larger arena of European power politics. In 1700, at the death of the last Spanish Hapsburg, Leopold I sought to place his second son, Archduke Charles, on the Spanish throne. But this attempt brought Leopold into a violent clash with Louis XIV. Once again, Bourbon and Hapsburg rivalry, a dominant theme in early modern history, provoked a major European war.

In the War of the Spanish Succession (1702–1714), the Austrians joined forces with the English and the Dutch against the French. The allies gained much: Austria acquired a colony in western Europe, what is now Belgium, and pieces of Italy including Milan. The Austrians did not capture the Spanish throne, but they did become a major force in European power politics, later to be challenged by Prussia. The English and Dutch subdued French ambitions and formed an alliance that lasted for fifty

---

years. In retrospect we can see the War as the beginning of England's rise to the status of a world power.

Prussia

The superiority of England and Austria confronted the Prussians as they sought to consolidate their authority in northern Europe. Prussia was also a state within the Holy Roman Empire, and its territorial ambitions could be checked by the other princely states or the empire. Although Prussia developed an absolute monarchy like France, its powerful aristocracy acquiesced to monarchical power only in exchange for guarantees of their feudal power over the peasantry. In 1653, the Prussian nobility granted the Hohenzollern ruler of Prussia power to collect taxes for the maintenance of a strong army, but only after he issued decrees rendering serfdom permanent.

The Hohenzollerns, the ruling dynasty of Prussia, had had a most inauspicious beginning in the later Middle Ages. These rulers were little more than dukes in the Holy Roman Empire until 1415, when Holy Roman Emperor Sigismund made one of them an imperial elector with the right to choose imperial successors. For centuries, the Hohenzollerns had made weak claims to territory in northern Germany. They finally achieved control over Prussia and certain other smaller principalities by claiming the inheritance of one wife (1608) and by single-minded, ruthless aggression.

The most aggressive of these Hohenzollerns was the elector Frederick William (1640–1688), who played a key role in forging the new Prussian state. Frederick William inherited the territories of the beleaguered Hohenzollern dynasty, whose main holding, Brandenburg in Prussia, was very poor in natural resources. Indeed, Prussia barely survived the devastation wreaked by the Thirty Years' War, especially the Swedish army's occupation of the electorate.

Distaste for foreign intervention in Prussia, and for the accompanying humiliation and excessive taxes, prompted the Junker class (the landed Prussian nobility) to support national unity and strong central government. But they would brook no threat to their economic control of their lands and peasants. Frederick William's policy of for-

MARIA THERESA AND JOSEPH. By the middle of the eighteenth century the nuclear family was being valorized even among the monarchs of Europe. Here Maria Theresa and Joseph pose with their family. (*Château de Versailles, Versailles, France/Reunion des Musees Nationaux/Art Resource, NY.*)

eign war, taxes, and military conscription led to an increase in the power of the central government. But in Prussia, in contrast to lands to the west, the bureaucracy was entirely military. No clerics or rich bourgeois shared power with the Junkers. The pattern initiated by the Great Elector (Frederick William) would be continued in the reigns of his successors: Frederick I (d. 1713), Frederick William I, and Frederick the Great.

The alliance between the aristocracy and the monarchy was especially strengthened in the reign of Frederick William I (1713–1740). In the older dynastic states, absolute monarchs tried to dispense with representative institutions once the monarchy had grown strong enough. So, too, did Frederick William finally undercut the Prussian provincial assemblies, the *Landtage*, which still had some power over taxation and army recruitment. He was able to do so only by bringing the landowning Junker class into the government—especially into the army—and by keeping the taxpaying peasants in the status of serfs. Always at

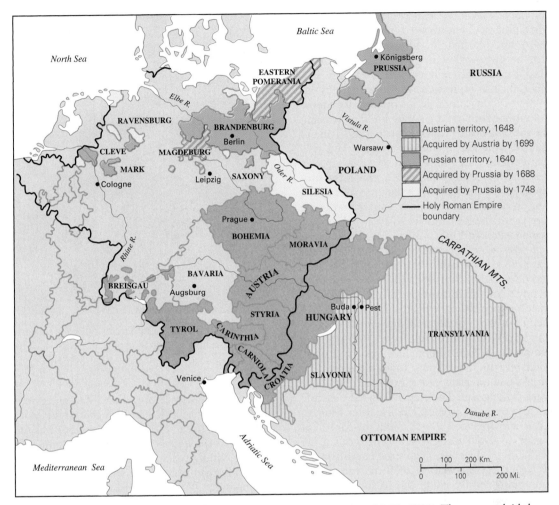

MAP 16.3 THE GROWTH OF AUSTRIA AND BRANDENBURG-PRUSSIA, C. 1650–1750 The process laid the foundation for modern Germany and also for tension between Christianity and Islam.

the heart of the Prussian state stood a military elite with little interest in reform.

RUSSIA: GREAT NOBLES AND STARVING PEASANTS

Although remote from developments in western Europe, Russia in the early modern period took on some characteristics remarkably similar to those of western European states. It relied on ab-

solute monarchy reinforced by a feudal aristocracy. As in Europe, the power of the aristocracy to wreak havoc had to be checked and its energies channeled into the state's service. But the Russian pattern of absolutism broke with the Western model and resembled that adopted in Prussia, where serfdom increased as the power of centralized monarchy grew. The award of peasants was the bribe by which the monarchy secured aristocrats' cooperation in the state's growth.

Russian absolutism experienced a false start under Ivan IV, the Terrible (1547–1584). Late in the sixteenth century, Ivan sought to impose a tsarist autocracy. He waged a futile war against Sweden and created an internal police force, which he entrusted with the administration of central Russia. His failure in war and an irrational policy of repression (fueled in part by his mental instability) doomed his attempt to impose absolutism. Much of Ivan's state building was undone with his death, which launched the Time of Troubles: a period of foreign invasion and civil warfare that endured for years.

Order was restored in 1613, when the Romanovs gained the support of the aristocracy. The accession of Michael Romanov as tsar marks the beginning of the Romanov dynasty and the emergence of a unified Russian state. Of that dynasty, by far the most important ruler was Peter the Great (1682–1725). He ruthlessly suppressed the independent aristocrats while inventing new titles and ranks for his supporters. The army was reformed in accordance with military standards in western Europe. The peasants were made the personal property of their lords. From 1700 to 1707, taxes on the peasants multiplied five times over. Predictably, the money went toward the creation of a professional army along European lines and toward making war. The preparation led this time to victory over the Swedes. Finally, Peter brought the Russian Orthodox church under the control of the state by establishing a new office, called the Holy Synod; its head was a government official.

Peter managed to wed the aristocracy to the absolutist state, and the union was so successful that strong Russian monarchs in the eighteenth century, like Catherine the Great, could embrace enlightened reforms without jeopardizing the stability of their regimes. Once again, repression and violence in the form of taxation, serfdom, and war led to the creation of a dynastic state—one that proved least susceptible to reform and was eventually dismantled in 1917 by the Russian Revolution.

THE STATE AND MODERN POLITICAL DEVELOPMENT

By the early seventeenth century, Europeans had developed the concept of the *state*: an active political entity to which its subjects owed duties and obligations. That concept became the foundation

PETER THE GREAT. Peter the Great looked westward and outward and sought to modernize Russia. (*The Art Archive.*)

of the modern science of politics. The one essential ingredient of the Western concept of the state, as it emerged in the early modern period, was the notion of *sovereignty*: the view that the state was supreme within its borders and that other institutions and organizations—by implication even the church—were allowed to exist only if they recognized the state's authority. The art of government thus entailed molding the ambitions and strength of the powerful into service to the state. The state, its power growing through war and taxation, became the basic unit of political authority in the West.

Interestingly, the concept of human liberty, now so basic to Western thought, was not articulated first in the sovereign states of Europe. Rather, the idea was largely an Italian creation, discussed with great vehemence by Italian theorists of the later Middle Ages and the Renaissance. These humanists lived and wrote in the independent city-states, and they often aimed their treatises against the encroachments of the Holy Roman Emperor—in short, against princes and their search for absolute power. In the sixteenth and seventeenth centuries, the idea of liberty was rarely discussed and was generally found only in the writings of Calvinist opponents of absolutism. Not until the mid-seventeenth century in England did a body of political thought emerge that argued that human liberty can be ensured within the confines of a powerful national state: one governed by mere mortals and not by divinely sanctioned and absolute kings. In general, despite the English and Dutch developments, absolutism in its varied forms (Spanish, French, Prussian) dominated the political development of early modern Europe.

Although first articulated in the Italian republics and then enacted briefly in England and more durably in the Netherlands, the republican ideal did not gain acceptance as a viable alternative to absolutism until the European Enlightenment of the eighteenth century. At the heart of that ideal lay the notion that the state serves the interests of those who support and create it. In the democratic and republican revolutions of the late eighteenth century, western Europeans and Americans repudiated monarchical systems of government in response to the republican ideal. By then, princes and the aristocratic and military elites had outlived their usefulness in many parts of Europe. The states they had created, mostly to further their own interests,

had become larger than their creators. Eventually, the national states of western Europe, as well as of the Americas, proved able to survive and prosper without kings or aristocrats, though they retained the administrative and military mechanisms so skillfully and relentlessly developed by early modern kings and their court officials.

By the eighteenth century, the state, not the locality, had become the focal point of Western political life. Peace depended on the art of balancing the powers of the various European states so that no single state could expect to win domination, or *hegemony,* over all the others. Whenever a European state believed that it could dominate, war resulted. In early modern times, first the Spanish under Charles V and Philip II and then the French under Louis XIV sought, and for a brief time achieved, hegemony over European politics. Ultimately, however, these great states faltered because of the internal pressures that war making created. Nonetheless, the belief persisted, until 1945, that one state could dominate Western affairs. In the twentieth century, that belief produced not simply war but world war. By then, the power of Western states had overtaken vast areas of the world, and the ability to impose a balance of power became a matter of world survival.

❖ ❖ ❖

Online Study Center ACE the Test

NOTES

1. William Doyle, *The Ancien Régime* (Atlantic Highlands, N.J.: Humanities Press, 1988), p. 19.
2. Quoted from *True Law of Free Monarchies,* excerpted in Marvin Perry et al., *Sources of the Western Tradition* (Boston: Houghton Mifflin, 1999), pp. 358–359.
3. J. H. Plumb, *The Growth of Political Stability in England: 1675–1725* (London: Macmillan, 1967), p. 69.

SUGGESTED READING

Bradshaw, B., and Peter Roberts eds., *British Consciousness and Identity: The Making of Britain, 1533–1707* (1998).

Glete, Jan, *War and the State in Early Modern Europe: Spain, the Dutch Republic and Sweden as Fiscal-military States, 1500–1660* (2001). An interesting look at states that achieved unity in this period.

Jacob, Margaret C., and W. W. Mijnhardt, eds., *The Dutch Republic in the Eighteenth Century: Decline, Enlightenment, and Revolution* (1992). Essays survey Dutch history but also look at the republic in decline.

Koenigsberger, H. G., *Monarchies, States, Generals and Parliaments* (2001). An excellent survey of the Dutch scene by a master historian.

Shorts, Russell, *The Island at the Center of the World* (2004). A delightful survey of the Dutch legacy in the new world.

Chapter 17

The Scientific Revolution: The Universe Seen as a Mechanism

When Galileo looked through his telescope, he saw shadows. But shadows meant depth and contour and that meant real, solid matter. The notion that the planets were ethereal globes of light gave way to their being just matter like the earth. (The Granger Collection.)

Focus Questions

1. What were the basic features of the medieval view of the universe?
2. Who were the leading figures of the Scientific Revolution, and what were their accomplishments?
3. What was the relationship between science and magic during this period?
4. Why was the Scientific Revolution a decisive force in the shaping of the modern outlook?

Online Study Center

This icon will direct you to interactive map and primary source activities on the website http://college.hmco.com/pic/perrywc8e.

*I*n the fifteenth century, the medieval view of the world began to disintegrate. By the late seventeenth century, educated Europeans no longer believed in it. Thus, the collapse of medieval institutions such as feudalism and serfdom had an intellectual parallel. No movement was as important in shaping the modern world-view as the Scientific Revolution of the seventeenth century. It made physical nature a valid object for experimental inquiry and mathematical calculation. For the new science to arise, a philosophical break with the medieval conception of nature had to occur. The medieval approach to nature sought to explain nature's appearances. To the naked eye, the earth seems to be in the center of our universe. Medieval philosophy explained how and why the earth was in the center; how and why heavy bodies fell toward it and light ones rose away from it. The philosophical revolution of the seventeenth century demolished such explanations. At the heart of the Scientific Revolution was the assumption that appearances could lie, that truth lay in conceptualizing the universe as an abstract entity: as matter in motion, as geometrical shapes, and as weight and number. The universe became a mechanism.

The Scientific Revolution brought a new, **mechanical conception of nature** that enabled westerners to discover and explain the laws of nature mathematically. They came to see nature as composed solely of matter, whose motion, occurring in space and measurable by time, is governed by the push and pull of bodies and by laws of force. This philosophically elegant construction rendered the physical world knowable and even possibly manageable. It also contributed decisively to the formulation of applied mechanics.

The Scientific Revolution also rested on a new, replicable methodology. Because of successful experiments performed by scientists and natural philosophers such as Galileo Galilei, William Harvey, Robert Boyle, and Isaac Newton, Western science acquired its still-characteristic methods of observation, experimentation, and replication. By the late seventeenth century, no one could entertain a serious interest in the physical order without actually doing—and recording—experiments or without observing, in a rigorous and systematic way, the behavior of physical phenomena. The mechanical concept of nature, coupled with a rigorous methodology, gave modern scientists the means to unlock and explain nature's secrets.

Mathematics increasingly became the language of the new science. For centuries, Europeans had used first geometry and then algebra to explain certain physical phenomena. With the Scientific Revolution came a new mathematics, the infinitesimal **calculus**. Even more important, philosophers became increasingly convinced that all nature—physical objects, as well as invisible forces—could be expressed mathematically. By the late seventeenth century, even geometry had become so complex that a gifted philosopher like John Locke (1632–1704), a friend and contemporary of Isaac Newton, could not understand the sophisticated mathematics used by Newton in the *Principia*. A new scientific culture had been born. During the eighteenth-century Enlightenment (Chapter 18), it provided the model for progress in the natural sciences and in the human sciences that were to imitate them.

MEDIEVAL COSMOLOGY

The unique character of the modern scientific outlook is most easily grasped through contrast with the medieval understanding of the natural world and its physical properties. That understanding rested on a blend of Christian thought with theories derived from ancient Greek writers, such as Aristotle and Ptolemy.

Aristotle (384–322 B.C.) had argued simply that it was in the nature of things to move in certain ways. A stone falls because it is absolutely heavy; fire rises because it is absolutely light. Weight is an absolute property of a physical thing; therefore, motion results from the properties of bodies, and not from the forces that impinge on them. It follows (logically but incorrectly) that if the medium through which a body falls is taken as a constant, then the speed of its fall could be doubled if its weight were doubled. Only rigorous experimentation could refute this erroneous concept of motion; it was many centuries before such experimentation was undertaken.

Aristotle's physics fitted neatly into his *cosmology*, or world picture. The earth, being the heaviest object, lay stationary and suspended at the center of the universe. The sun, planets, and moon revolved in circles around the earth. Aristotle presumed that since the planets were round themselves, always in motion, and seemingly never altered, the most "natural" movement for them should be circular, for it is perfect motion.

Aristotle's physics and cosmology were unified. He could put the earth at the center of the universe and make it stationary because he presumed its absolute heaviness; all other heavy bodies that he had observed fall toward it. Aristotle believed that everything in motion had been moved by another object that was itself in motion—a continuing chain of movers and moved. By inference, this belief led back to some object or being that began the motion. Christian philosophers of the Middle Ages argued that Aristotle's Unmoved Mover must be the God of Christianity. For Aristotle, who had no conception of a personal God or an afterlife of rewards or punishments and who believed that the universe was eternal rather than created at a specific point in time, such an identification would have been meaningless.

Although Aristotle's cosmology never gained the status of orthodoxy among the ancient Greeks, by the second century A.D. in Alexandria, Greek astronomy became codified and then rigid. Ptolemy of Alexandria produced the *Almagest* (A.D. 150), a handbook of Greek astronomy based on the theories of Aristotle. The crucial assumption in the *Almagest* was that a motionless earth stood at the center of the universe and that the planets moved about it in a series of circular orbits, interrupted by smaller circular orbits, called epicycles. The epicycles explained why at certain times a planet was visibly closer to the earth. As Ptolemy put it, if the earth moved, "living things and individual heavy objects would be left behind . . . the earth itself would very soon have fallen completely out of the heavens."[1] By the Late Middle Ages, Ptolemy's handbook had come to represent standard astronomical wisdom. As late as the 1650s, more than a hundred years after the Polish astronomer Nicolaus Copernicus had argued mathematically that the sun was the center of the universe, educated Europeans in most universities still believed that the earth held the central position.

In the thirteenth century, mainly through the philosophical efforts of Thomas Aquinas (1225–1274), Aristotle's thought was adapted to Christian beliefs, often in ingenious ways. Aquinas emphasized that order pervaded nature and that every physical effect had a physical cause. The tendency in Aquinas's thought and that of his followers, who were called **scholastics**, was to search for these causes—again, to ask *why* things move, rather than *how* they move. Aquinas insisted that nature proves God's existence; God is the First Cause of all physical phenomena. The world picture taught by the scholastics affirmed the earth and humankind as the center of the Christian drama of birth, death, and salvation.

Medieval thinkers integrated the cosmology of Aristotle and Ptolemy into a Christian framework that drew a sharp distinction between the world beyond the moon and the earthly realm. Celestial bodies were composed of the divine ether, a substance too pure and too spiritual to be found on earth; heavenly bodies, unlike earthly bodies, were immune to all change and obeyed different laws of motion. The universe was not homogeneous but divided into a higher world of the heavens and a lower world of earth. Earth could not compare with the heavens in spiritual dignity, but God had nevertheless situated it in the center of the universe. Earth deserved this position of importance, for only here did Christ live and die for humankind. This vision of the universe was to be shattered by the Scientific Revolution.

Also shattered by the **natural philosophy** articulated in the seventeenth century was the belief that all reality, natural as well as human, could be described as consisting of *matter* and *form*. Following Aristotle, the scholastics argued that matter was inchoate, lifeless, and indistinguishable, and that form gave it shape and identity. A table, for instance, possessed a recognizable shape and could be identified as a table because it possessed the form of tableness. A human being existed only because the matter of the body was given life by the soul, by its form. This doctrine was central to both medieval philosophy and theology. Important beliefs were justified by it. For example, the church taught that the priest, when performing the sacrament of the **Eucharist,** had the power to transform bread and wine into the body and blood of Christ. This was possible because, theologians argued, the matter of the bread and wine remained the same (and hence looked the same), but its form was changed by the power of the priest. Consequently, the Mass could be explained without recourse to magic, which was highly suspect. Similarly, medieval people believed that the king's power resided within him; kingness was part of his essence. So, too, nobility was a quality said to adhere to the person of the nobleman or noblewoman. The mechanical philosophy of Galileo, Boyle, and Newton, which was central to the Scientific Revolution, denied the existence of form. Matter was simply composed of **tiny corpuscles, or atoms,** which were hard and impenetrable and were governed by the laws of impact or force. Such a conception of nature threatened whole aspects of medieval and even Christian doctrine; ultimately, for society its implications proved to be democratic.

A NEW VIEW OF NATURE

Renaissance Neo-Platonism

Italian Renaissance thinkers rediscovered the importance of the ancient Greek philosopher Plato (c. 429–347 B.C.). Plato taught that the philosopher must look beyond the appearances of things to an invisible reality, which is abstract, simple, rational, and best expressed mathematically. For Plato, the greatest achievements of the human mind were mathematics and music; both revealed the inherent harmony and order within nature.

Renaissance Platonists interpreted Plato from a Christian perspective, and they believed that the Platonic search for truth about nature, about God's work, was but another aspect of the search for knowledge about God. The Italian universities and academies became centers where the revival of Plato flourished among teachers and translators, who came to be known as **Neo-Platonists.** Central to their humanist curriculum was the study of philosophy, mathematics, music, Greek and Latin, and in some cases Arabic. Those languages made available the world of pagan, pre-Christian learning and its many different philosophies of nature. The leading thinkers of the Scientific Revolution were all inspired by Renaissance Neo-Platonism. They revered Plato's search for a truth that was abstract and mathematically elegant, and they explored the ancient writers and their theories about nature. Some of the ancients had been atomists; a few had even argued that the sun might be at the center of the universe. They had also invented geometry.

With the impulse to mathematize nature came the desire to measure and experience it. The rediscovery of nature as mappable and quantifiable found expression in the study of human anatomy, as well as in the study of objects in motion. Renaissance art shows the fruits of this inquiry, for artists tried to depict the human body as exactly as possible yet to give it ideal form. The revival of artistic creativity associated with the Renaissance is linked to an interest in the natural world and to Neo-Platonism.

Magic and the Search for Nature

The thinkers of the Scientific Revolution also drew on a body of magical and mystical thought drawn from the first and second centuries A.D. Many of these anonymous students of magic believed that there had once been an ancient Egyptian priest, Hermes Trismegistus, who had possessed secret knowledge about nature's processes and the ultimate forces at work in the universe. Hermetic literature stated that true knowledge comes from a contemplation of the One, or the Whole—a spiritual reality higher than, yet embedded in, nature. Some of these ancient writings argued that the sun was the natural symbol of this Oneness, and such an argument seemed to give weight to a heliocentric picture of the universe. The Hermetic approach to nature also incorporated elements of the Pythagorean and Neo-Platonic traditions, which emphasized the inner mathematical harmony pervading nature. A follower of Hermeticism might approach nature mathematically as well as magically. For example, Johannes Kepler (see below) was both a fine mathematician and a believer in the magical power of nature. Though not directly influenced by Hermeticism as a system of belief, for much of his life Isaac Newton saw no contradiction in searching for the mathematical laws of nature while practicing alchemy—the illusive search for a way to transform ordinary metals into gold.

In early modern Europe, the practitioners of alchemy and astrology could also be mathematicians and astronomers, and the sharp distinction drawn today between magic and science—between the irrational and the rational—would not have been made by many of the leading natural philosophers who lived in the sixteenth and seventeenth centuries.

The Renaissance revival of ancient learning contributed a new approach to nature, one that was simultaneously mathematical, experimental, and magical. Although the achievements of modern science depend on experimentation and mathematics, the impulse to search for nature's secrets presumes a degree of self-confidence best exemplified and symbolized by the magician.

The Copernican Revolution

Nicolaus Copernicus was born in Poland in 1473. As a young man, he enrolled at the University of Kraków, where he may have come under the influence of Renaissance Platonism, which was spreading outward from the Italian city-states. Copernicus also journeyed to Italy, and in Bologna and Padua he may have become aware of ancient Greek texts containing arguments for the sun being the center of the universe. We know very little about his early education.

Copernicus's interest in mathematics and astronomy was stimulated by contemporary discussions of the need for calendar reform, which required a thorough understanding of Ptolemaic astronomy. The mathematical complexity of the Ptolemaic system troubled Copernicus, who believed that truth was the product of elegance and simplicity. In addition, Copernicus knew that Ptolemy had predecessors among the ancients who philosophized about a heliocentric universe or who held Aristotle's cosmology and physics in little regard. Thus, his Renaissance education gave Copernicus not a body of new scientific truth, but rather the courage to break with traditional truth taught in the universities.

Toward the end of his stay in Italy, Copernicus became convinced that the sun was at the center of the universe. So he began a lifelong task to work out mathematical explanations of how a heliocentric universe operated. Unwilling to engage in controversy with the followers of Aristotle, Coper-

COPERNICAN SYSTEM. In his *On the Revolutions of the Heavenly Spheres*, Copernicus proposed a heliocentric model in which the planets orbit around the sun. (*The Granger Collection.*)

nicus did not publish his findings until 1543, the year of his death, in a work titled *On the Revolutions of the Heavenly Spheres*. Legend says that his book, which in effect began the Scientific Revolution, was brought to him on his deathbed. Copernicus died a Catholic priest, hoping only that his book would be read sympathetically.

The treatise retained some elements of the Aristotelian-Ptolemaic system. Copernicus never doubted Aristotle's basic idea of the perfect circular motion of the planets or the existence of crystalline spheres within which the stars revolved, and he retained many of Ptolemy's epicycles—orbits within the circular orbits of the sun and planets. But Copernicus proposed a heliocentric model of the universe that was mathematically simpler than Ptolemy's earth-centered universe. Thus, he eliminated some of Ptolemy's epicycles and cleared up various problems that had trou-

bled astronomers who had based their work on an earth-centered universe.

Copernicus's genius was expressed in his ability to pursue an idea—the concept of a sun-centered universe—and to bring to that pursuit lifelong dedication and brilliance in mathematics. By removing the earth from its central position and by giving it motion—that is, by making the earth just another planet—Copernicus undermined the system of medieval cosmology and made possible the birth of modern astronomy.

But because they were committed to the Aristotelian-Ptolemaic system and to biblical statements that they thought supported it, most thinkers of the time rejected Copernicus's conclusions. They also raised specific objections. The earth, they said, is too heavy to move. How, some of Copernicus's colleagues asked, can an object falling from a high tower land directly below the point from which it was dropped if the earth is moving so rapidly?

The Laws of Planetary Motion: Tycho and Kepler

Copernicus laid the foundation for the intellectual revolution that overturned the medieval conception of the universe and ushered in modern cosmology. But it fell to other observers to fill in the important details. Tycho Brahe (1546–1601) never accepted the Copernican system, but he saw that it presented a challenge to astronomers. Aided by the king of Denmark, Tycho built the finest observatory in Europe. In 1572, he observed a new star in the heavens. Its existence offered a direct and serious challenge to the Aristotelian and scholastic assumption of unalterable, fixed, and hence perfect heavens. To this discovery of what eventually proved to be an exploding star, Tycho added his observations on the comet of 1577. He demonstrated that it moved unimpeded through the areas between the planets and passed right through the crystalline spheres. This finding raised the question of whether such spheres existed, but Tycho himself remained an Aristotelian. Although his devotion to a literal reading of the Bible led Tycho to reject the Copernican sun-centered universe, he did propose an alternative system, in which the planets revolved around the sun but the sun moved about a motionless earth.

Ultimately, Tycho's fame rests on his skill as a practicing astronomer. He bequeathed to future generations precise calculations about the movements of heavenly bodies. These calculations proved invaluable. They were put to greatest use by Johannes Kepler (1571–1630), a German who collaborated with Tycho during the latter's final years. Tycho bequeathed his astronomical papers to Kepler, who brought to these data a scientific vision that was both experimental and mystical.

Kepler searched persistently for harmonious laws of planetary motion. He did so because he believed profoundly in the Platonic ideal. According to this ideal, a spiritual force infuses the physical order, beneath appearances are harmony and unity, and the human mind can begin to comprehend that unity only through *gnosis*—a direct and mystical realization of unity—and through math-

ematics. Kepler believed that both approaches were compatible, and he managed to combine them. He believed in and practiced astrology (as did Tycho) and throughout his lifetime tried to contact an ancient but lost and secret wisdom.

In the course of his observations of the heavens, Kepler discovered the three basic laws of planetary motion. First, the orbits of the planets are elliptical, not circular as Aristotle and Ptolemy had assumed, and the sun is one focus of the **ellipse**. Unlike Tycho, Kepler accepted Copernicus's theory and provided proof for it. Kepler's second law demonstrated that the velocity of a planet is not uniform, as had been believed, but increases as its distance from the sun decreases. Kepler's third law—that the squares of the times taken by any two planets in their revolutions around the sun are in the same ratio as the cubes of their average distances from the sun—brought the planets into a unified mathematical system.

The significance of Kepler's work was immense. He gave sound mathematical proof to Copernicus's theory, eliminated forever the use of epicycles, which had saved the appearance of circular motion, and demonstrated that mathematical relationships can describe the planetary system. But Kepler left a significant question unresolved: what kept the planets in their orbits? Why did they not fly out into space or crash into the sun? The answer would be supplied by Isaac Newton, who synthesized the astronomy of Copernicus and Kepler with the new physics developed by Galileo.

Galileo: Experimental Physics

At the same time that Kepler was developing a new astronomy, his contemporary, Galileo Galilei (1564–1642), was breaking with the older physics of Aristotle. A citizen of Pisa by birth, Galileo lived for many years in Padua, where he conducted some of his first experiments on the motion of bodies. Guided by the dominant philosophy of the Italian Renaissance—the revived doctrines of Plato—Galileo believed that beyond the visible world lay certain universal truths, subject to mathematical verification. Galileo insisted that the study of motion entails not only the use of logic (as Aristotle had believed) but also the

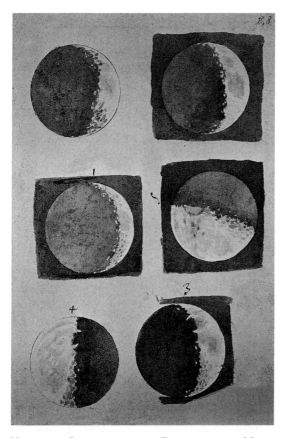

NOTEBOOK SKETCHES OF THE PHASES OF THE MOON BY GALILEO GALILEI, 1609–1610. Galileo saw only shadows when he looked into his telescope. But because he was trained as an artist in the principles of light and dark coloring to emphasize or shorten distance, he knew that what he saw represented real objects, in this case mountains and valleys. Somewhat satirically, he compared the moon to Bohemia. (*Biblioteca Nazionale Centrale, Florence.*)

application of mathematics. For this Late Renaissance natural philosopher, mathematics became the language of nature. Galileo also believed that only after experimenting with the operations of nature can the philosopher formulate harmonious laws and give them mathematical expression. Galileo was also trained in the practices of Renaissance art, in using shades to show depth and perspective. When he first looked at the moon

through his telescope, that training became very important.

In his mechanical experiments, Galileo discovered that, all other things being equal, bodies of unequal weight will experience a uniform acceleration (due to gravity). He demonstrated that bodies fall with arithmetic regularity. Motion could, therefore, be treated mathematically.

Galileo established a fundamental principle of modern science: the order and uniformity of nature. There are no distinctions in rank or quality between the heavens and earth; heavenly bodies are not perfect and changeless as Aristotle had believed. In 1609, Galileo built a telescope through which he viewed the surface of the moon. The next year, in a treatise called *The Starry Messenger*, he proclaimed to the world that the moon "is not smooth, uniform, and precisely spherical as a great number of philosophers believe it and the other heavenly bodies to be, but is uneven, rough, and full of cavities . . . being not unlike the face of the earth, relieved by chains of mountains and deep valleys."[2] In addition, Galileo noticed spots on the sun, providing further evidence that heavenly objects, like earthly objects, undergo change. There are no higher and lower worlds; nature is the same throughout. When he saw shadows through his telescope, he assumed that actual bodies were casting them, just as they do on an earthly landscape. The art and science of his age were of a piece.

Through his telescope, Galileo also observed moons around Jupiter—a discovery that helped support the Copernican hypothesis. If Jupiter had moons, then all heavenly bodies did not orbit the earth. The moons of Jupiter removed a fundamental criticism of Copernicus and opened up the possibility that the earth, with its own moon, might be just like Jupiter and that both might in turn revolve around a central point—the sun.

With Galileo, the science of Copernicus and the assault on Aristotle entered a new phase. Scholastic priests began to attack Galileo from their pulpits in Florence. They saw a threat to their own power in Galileo's public notoriety and in his following among the laity. A secret group of priests and academics, named the Liga, formed with the express purpose of silencing Galileo; they used Aristotle and the Bible to attack him. But Galileo was also a courtier with friends in high places, so he dared to challenge the clergy and to offer his science directly to the laity. He argued publicly with the theologians. In the early seventeenth century, the Catholic church saw danger on every front: Protestants in Germany, Jews and Muslims in the East, and a laity demanding new schools that would provide practical education for their children. Now Galileo offered a view of the universe that conflicted with certain scriptural texts.

Historians used to believe that the church attacked Galileo solely because he was a Copernican, that is, because he believed the sun to be at the center of the universe. New evidence from the recently opened Vatican archives suggests that the church may also have worried about his theory of matter and his abandonment of the scholastics' view of the relationship between matter and form. That view went to the heart of the doctrine of the Eucharist, and the church saw, rightly, that the new science threatened the philosophical foundations of certain key doctrines.

In 1632, Galileo's teachings were condemned, and he was placed under house arrest. These actions cut short the open pursuit of science in many Catholic countries of the seventeenth century. Where the Inquisition was strong, the new science would be viewed as subversive. Censorship worked to stifle public intellectual inquiry. By the midcentury, science had become an increasingly Protestant and northern European phenomenon.

Online Study Center

Improve Your Grade
Primary Source: Galileo Discovers the Moons of Jupiter

The Newtonian Synthesis: Experiment, Mathematics, and Theory

By 1650, the works of Copernicus and especially of Galileo had dethroned the physics and astronomy of Aristotle and Ptolemy. A new philosophy of nature tied to observation and Neo-Platonism had come into existence; its essence lay in the

mathematical expression of physical laws that describe matter in motion. Yet no single overriding law had been articulated that would bring together the experimental successes of the new science, its mathematical sophistication, and its philosophical revolution. This law was supplied by Isaac Newton.

Newton was born in 1642, in Lincolnshire, England, the son of a modest yeoman. Because of his intellectual promise, he obtained a place at Trinity College, Cambridge, and there he devoted himself to natural philosophy and mathematics. Newton's student notebooks survive and show him mastering philosophical texts while also trying to understand the fundamental truths of Protestant Christianity as taught at Cambridge. Combining Christian Neo-Platonism with a genius for mathematics, Newton produced a coherent synthesis of the science of Kepler and Galileo, which eventually captured the imagination of European intellectuals.

In 1666, Newton formulated the mathematics for the universal law of gravitation, and in the same year, after rigorous experimentation, he determined the nature of light. The sciences of physics and optics were transformed. However, for many years, Newton did not publish his discoveries, partly because even he did not grasp the immense significance of his work. Finally, another mathematician and friend, Edmund Halley, persuaded him to publish under the sponsorship of the Royal Society. The result was the *Principia Mathematica* of 1687. In 1704, Newton published his *Opticks* and revealed his theory that light was corpuscular or atomic in nature and that it emanated from luminous bodies in a way that scientists later described as waves.

Of the two books, both monumental achievements in the history of science, the *Principia* made the greater impact on contemporaries. Newton offered universal mathematical laws, as well as a philosophy of nature that sought to explain the essential structure of the universe: matter is always the same; it is atomic in structure, and in its essential nature it is dead or lifeless; and it is acted upon by immaterial forces that are placed in the universe by God. Newton said that the motion of matter could be explained by three laws: inertia, that a body remains in a state of rest or continues its motion in a straight line unless impelled to

SIR ISAAC NEWTON (1642–1727). In 1666, Newton's mathematical formulation of the law of universal gravitation and his experiments in the nature of light opened a new stage in human understanding of the physical universe. The poet Alexander Pope expressed Newton's contemporaries' view of his achievements: "Nature, and Nature's Laws lay hid in Night. God said, 'Let Newton be!' and All was Light." (*The Granger Collection.*)

change by forces impressed on it; acceleration, that the change in the motion of a body is proportional to the force acting on it; and that for every action there is an equal and opposite reaction.

Newton argued that these laws apply not only to observable matter on earth but also to the motion of planets in their orbits. He showed that planets did not remain in their orbits because circular motion was "natural" or because crystalline spheres kept them in place. Rather, said Newton, planets keep to their orbits because every body in the universe exercises a force on every other body, a force that he called *universal gravitation*. Gravity is proportional to the product of the masses of two bodies and inversely proportional to the square of the distance between them. It is operative throughout the universe, whether on

earth or in the heavens, and it is capable of mathematical expression. Newton built his theory on the work of other scientific giants, notably Kepler and Galileo. No one before him, however, had possessed the breadth of vision, mathematical skill, and dedication to rigorous observation to combine this knowledge into one grand synthesis.

The universe could now be described as matter in motion; it was governed by invisible forces that operated everywhere, both on earth and in the heavens, and these forces could be expressed mathematically. The medieval picture of the universe as closed, earthbound, and earth centered was replaced by a universe seen to be infinite and governed by universal laws. The earth was now regarded as simply another moving planet. Newtonian principles were taught by generations of

Newton's followers as, in effect, applied mechanics. A revolution in thought had changed Western ideas about nature forever.

But what was God's role in this new universe? Newton and his circle labored to create a mechanical world-view dependent on the will of God. At one time, Newton believed that gravity was simply the will of God operating on the universe. As he wrote in the *Opticks*, the physical order "can be the effect of nothing else than the wisdom and skill of a powerful ever-living agent."[3] Because of his strong religious convictions, Newton allowed his science to be used in the service of the established Anglican church, and his followers argued for social stability anchored in an ordered universe and an established church. Newton, a scientific genius, was also a deeply religious thinker committed to the maintenance of Protestantism in England. Among his contemporaries, however, were freethinkers who like John Toland (see "Skeptics, Freethinkers, and Deists" in Chapter 18) used his ideas to argue that nature can operate on its own, without the assistance of a providential God.

BIOLOGY, MEDICINE, AND CHEMISTRY

The spectacular advances in physics and astronomy in the sixteenth and seventeenth centuries were not matched in the biological sciences. Indeed, the day-to-day practice of medicine throughout western Europe changed little in the period from 1600 to 1700, for much of medical practice relied, as it had since the Middle Ages, on astrology.

Doctors clung to the teachings of the ancient practitioners Galen and Hippocrates. In general, Galenic medicine paid little attention to the discovery of specific cures for particular diseases. As a follower of Aristotle, Galen emphasized the elements that make up the body; he called their manifestations *humors*. A person with an excess of blood was sanguine; a person with too much bile was choleric. Health consisted of a restoration of balances among these various elements, so Galenic doctors often prescribed purges of one sort or another. The most famous of these was bloodletting, but sweating was also a favorite

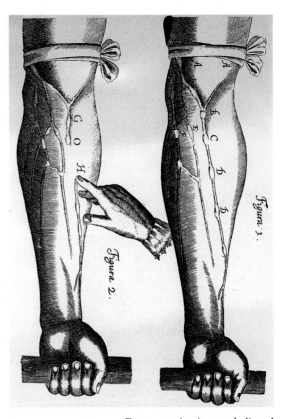

SCIENCE AND BLOOD. For centuries it was believed that blood carried character traits as well as nobility. The English experimenter William Harvey viewed blood as simply a liquid that circulated in the body in a uniform way. Illustrations such as this one made the point graphically. (*Corbis.*)

remedy. Taught devotedly in the medical schools of Europe, these methods were often as dangerous as the diseases they sought to cure.

Despite the tenacity of Galenic medicine, sixteenth- and seventeenth-century innovators and reformers did try to challenge and overturn medical orthodoxy. With an almost missionary zeal, Paracelsus (1493–1541), a Swiss-German physician and Hermeticist, introduced the concept of diagnostic medicine. He argued that particular diseases can be differentiated and are related to chemical imbalances. His treatments relied on chemicals and not on bloodletting or the positions of the stars (although he did not discount such influences), and he proclaimed an almost ecstatic vision of human vitality and longevity. In most universities, the faculties of medicine bitterly opposed his views, but by 1650 in England and later in that century in France, Paracelsian ideas had many advocates. Support for Paracelsian medicine invariably accompanied an attack on the traditional medical establishment and its professional monopoly, and it often indicated support for the new science in general. The struggle between Galenists and Paracelsians quickly took on a social dimension; the innovators saw themselves pitted against a medical elite, which, in their opinion, had lost its commitment to medical research and existed solely to perpetuate itself. In the eighteenth century, Paracelsian ideas, stripped of their magical associations, became commonplace.

The medical reforms of the eighteenth century did not rest solely on the Paracelsian approach; they also relied heavily on the experimental breakthroughs made in the science of anatomy. A pioneer in this field was the Belgian surgeon Andreas Vesalius (1515–1564), who published *The Structure of the Human Body* in 1543. Opposing Galenic practice, Vesalius argued for observation and anatomical dissection as the keys to knowing how the human body works. By the late seventeenth century, doctors had learned a great deal about the human body, its structure, and its chemistry.

The study of anatomy yielded dramatic results. In 1628, William Harvey (1578–1657) announced that he had discovered the circulation of blood. Harvey compared the functioning of the heart to that of a mechanical pump, and once again the tendency to mechanize nature, so basic to the Scientific Revolution in physics, led to a significant discovery. Yet the acceptance of Harvey's work was very slow, and the practical uses of his discovery were not readily perceived.

The experimental method in medicine produced other innovations, among them systematic examination not only of corpses but also of patients. In the late 1600s, the finest doctor of the age, Herman Boerhaave, taught his students in Leiden, in the Netherlands, by taking them on house calls, arguing that nothing in medicine can be known without a careful and rigorous examination of the body. He proclaimed that he was trying to bring the methods and philosophy of the new science to medicine, and he pioneered hands-on medical techniques.

Just as Newton applied the theory and method of science to the heavens, his contemporaries on both sides of the English Channel sought to utilize science to illuminate every object we experience. Protestantism inspired them to be aggressive in their assault on scholasticism. Indeed, the most original experimenter of the age, who codified the experimental method as we know it, was a devout English Protestant. Robert Boyle (1627–1691) believed that Aristotle's physics and the philosophy that supported it promoted Catholic teachings and thus amounted to little more than magic. At a time when English Protestants feared a revival of Catholic and absolutist monarchy, Boyle wanted to abolish the invisible forces on which Catholic theology rested. He also wished to defeat the magic of what he called "the vulgar," that is, the beliefs of the populace, whose disorder and tendencies to rebellion he feared.

To accomplish these aims, Boyle urged scientists to adopt the zeal of the magicians, but without their secretive practices and their conjuring with spirits. As an alternative to spirits, Boyle advocated the atomic explanation of matter: that matter consists of small, hard, indestructible particles that behave with regularity. According to Boyle, the existence of these particles explained the changes in gases, fluids, and solids.

Boyle pioneered the experimental method with such exciting and accurate results that by the time of his death no serious scientist could attempt chemical experiments without following his guidelines. Thus, the science of chemistry acquired its characteristic experimentalism; it was also based on an atomic theory of matter. But not until late in the eighteenth century was this new discipline applied to medical research.

BACON AND DESCARTES: PROPHETS OF THE NEW SCIENCE

The new science needed prophets and social theorists to give it direction and to assess its implications. During the early modern period, two major reformers tried, in disparate ways, to channel science into the service of specific social programs:

FONTENELLE, PORTRAIT BY BERNARD PICART.
Fontenelle understood the new science, but most important, he could make it understandable to those less learned than himself. He gave a eulogy on the death of Newton that was read throughout the century, and he also worked tirelessly for the French Academy of Sciences. *(The British Museum.)*

Francis Bacon (1561–1626) and René Descartes (1596–1650).

Bacon

The decidedly practical and empirical Francis Bacon stands as the most important English proponent of the new science, though not its most important practitioner. Bacon became profoundly suspicious of magic and the magical arts, not be-

cause they might not work but because he saw secrecy and arrogance as characteristic of their practitioners. Bacon was lord chancellor of England under James I, and he wrote about the usefulness of science partly in an effort to convince the crown of its advantages. He wanted science to serve the interests of strong monarchy.

Yet no philosopher of modern science has surpassed Bacon in elevating the study of nature to a humanistic discipline. In the *Advancement of Learning* (1605), Bacon argued that science must be open and all ideas must be allowed a hearing. Science must have human goals: the improvement of humanity's material condition and the advancement of trade and industry, but not the making of war or the taking of lives. Bacon also preached the need for science to possess an inductive methodology grounded in experience; the scientist should first of all be a collector of facts.

Although Bacon was rather vague about how the scientist as a theorist actually works, he knew that preconceived ideas imposed on nature seldom yield positive results. An opponent of Aristotle, Bacon argued that university education should move away from the ancient texts and toward the new learning. A powerful civil servant, he was not afraid to attack the guardians of tradition. The Baconian vision of progress in science leading to an improvement of the human condition and the security of the state inspired much scientific activity in the seventeenth century, particularly in England.

Descartes

René Descartes, a French philosopher of the first half of the seventeenth century, went to the best French schools and was trained by the Jesuits in mathematics and scholastic philosophy. Yet in his early twenties, he experienced a crisis of confidence. He felt that everything he had been taught was irrelevant and meaningless.

Descartes began to search within himself for what he could be sure was clear and distinct knowledge. All he could know with certainty was the fact of his existence, and even that he knew only because he experienced not his body but his mind: "I think, therefore I am." From this point of certitude, Descartes deduced God's existence.

Art of the Seventeenth and Eighteenth Centuries

1. Peter Paul Rubens. *The Betrothal of Saint Catherine*, sketch for a large altar painting, c. 1628. *(Staatliche Gemalde-Galerie, Berlin/Bridgeman Art Library.)*

The influence of political, economic, and social change permeates the visual arts of the seventeenth and eighteenth centuries. Perhaps most significant to the artists who made their living by providing paintings with religious themes for churches, as well as for private patrons, were the religious conflicts that split apart European society. Catholics and Protestants quarreled and openly fought over doctrine and dogma; as a result of the struggles, artists had to decide how best to please patrons whose religious sympathies may have changed or developed in new directions. Politically, the seventeenth and eighteenth centuries are also marked by the emergence of new

sovereign states and by a change in the nature of artistic patronage.

Although a number of terms are used to describe the seventeenth and eighteenth centuries, the one most commonly applied by art historians is *baroque*. The word literally means irregularly shaped, whimsical, grotesque, or odd. Its origin is French, but it is generally agreed that the baroque style of art originated in Rome.

Baroque art is hard to explain within the context of the social and political changes that were sweeping over Europe. Some historians see it as illustrative of the Counter Reformation; others point out that the style was equally appealing to Catholics and Protestants. Nor

2. Giovanne Benedetto Castiglione. *Melancholia*, mid-seventeenth century. *(Philadelphia Museum of Art. Pennsylvania Academy Fine Arts Collection.)*

was baroque favored only by the absolute rulers of France or other monarchs; it was also a style of the bourgeois.

One of the most famous baroque painters was Peter Paul Rubens (1577–1640) of Flanders, which, prospering from its commercial connections, was home to many successful artists and patrons in this period. To study painting, Rubens traveled to Rome in 1600 and spent many years visiting other artistic centers in Italy. There he learned to paint on large-scale canvases and play with the size and weight of his subjects. Despite the influence of his southern contemporaries, however, his style remained essentially Flemish.

In his painting *The Betrothal of Saint Catherine* (Figure 1), we immediately sense the energy and fullness of the figures typical among Italian artists. But we also notice that Rubens's palette is much lighter than theirs, and consequently, the figures of Saint Catherine and the saints who surround her seem to move lightly as well.

Noteworthy, too, in this canvas is the depiction of the figures, whose hairstyles and mode of dress is contemporary rather than suggestive of biblical times. This juxtaposition of scenes from the Bible with the flavor of everyday life in the seventeenth century reveals much about the connection between the artist and his own surroundings.

The baroque style of highly finished, realistic works is very familiar to us. But we must also recall that baroque artists were skilled draftsmen. As an example, there is Giovanne Benedetto Castiglione's *Melancholia* (mid-seventeenth century) (Figure 2), a brush drawing in oil with added red chalk. Works on paper do not always survive as well as those on board or canvas. The drawings we do have attest to the artistic skill of seventeenth-century artists, who used line and shadow as well as did their Renaissance predecessors.

Melancholia is an allegory about the human dilemma of choosing among the worlds of art, religion, science, and learning. Symbols from each of these worlds—scientific tools, musical instruments, a globe, and the like—surround the figure of Genius, who sits in a contemplative pose.

Although by and large the artists of the baroque period were not well-rounded humanists like those of the Renaissance, some of them could work in two- and three-dimensional art forms. For example, Gian Lorenzo Bernini (1598–1680) distinguished himself as a sculptor as well as an architect.

Bernini was responsible for the sculptural program of Saint Peter's Basilica in the Vatican. He also completed sculptures in other Roman churches, including the Cornaro Chapel in the Church of Santa Maria della Vittoria. His *The Ecstasy of Saint Teresa* (1644–1647) (Figure 3) is a remarkable work that tells a dramatic story. The heart of Saint Teresa of Avila was said to have been pierced by an angel's golden arrow; the pain was exquisite, for not only was it the pain of death but also the pleasure of everlasting life in the arms of God. Bernini skillfully portrays the exact moment of Saint Teresa's ecstasy, in a theatrical setting using not only sculpture but also the architectural elements of the chapel.

The saint and the angel are carved of white marble and seem to be floating on a cloud. The sculpted golden rays, which descend from a point above the figures, are bathed in light by a window hidden behind the frame that surrounds the two figures. Bernini decorated the entire chapel to follow the theme of Saint Teresa; ceiling frescoes show clouds of angels celebrating the event.

While Bernini was gaining fame in Italy, a French painter—one who spent almost his entire career in Rome—was winning an inter-

3. Gian Lorenzo Bernini. *The Ecstasy of Saint Teresa,* 1644–1647. *(Church of Santa Maria della Vittoria, Rome/Scala/Art Resource, NY.)*

national reputation. Nicolas Poussin (1593/4–1665) relied strongly on the art of the classical and especially the Hellenistic periods for his inspiration. His *The Rape of the Sabine Women* (c. 1636–37) (Figure 4), a lavish and richly painted canvas, captures action like a carefully posed photograph. Indeed, if Bernini was theatrical in his portrayal of Saint Teresa, one could say that Poussin is cinematographic.

The story depicted in *The Rape of the Sabine Women* is derived from classical mythology; the poses of the figures hark back to the Hellenistic period. Compare the positioning of the arms of the women on the left of the canvas with the tortured stance of Laocoön, in the sculpture shown in Figure 4 of the first art

4. Nicolas Poussin. *The Rape of the Sabine Women*, c. 1636–37. *(Metropolitan Museum of Art, NY.)*

essay. Other groups in the Poussin canvas are also reminiscent of that sculpture. As another bow to the ancient past, Poussin paints in the background buildings that are faithful to Roman prototypes. Such reliance on archaeology and mythology are typical of his work.

While paintings depicting mythological, historical, or religious themes dominated the major art markets during the baroque era, patrons in Holland sought paintings that related more to their own experience. For that reason, the genre of the still life—paintings of flowers, fruit, dishes, food, and other familiar objects—reached its zenith in that country.

Willem Kalf (1622–1693), among the most skilled of Dutch still-life masters, was able to take a collection of objects and turn it into an object of art. His *Still Life* (Figure 5) showcases his meticulous, almost photo-realistic style. In particular, it focuses on the way in which glass reflects light and on the juxtaposition of different textures. Although modern art historians view some still lifes as merely ornamental displays of technical skill, there was a reason for them. The popularity of still lifes, and of landscapes, probably has to do with the human desire for reassurance that "things are as they should be," that the status quo is being maintained, regardless of the religious or political turmoil affecting other aspects of life. No matter what was going on politically, no matter what religious dispute was being negotiated, people could find a degree of comfort in being surrounded by familiar objects or scenes.

While Kalf distinguished himself as a still-life painter, another Dutch master, Rembrandt van Rijn (1606–1669) gained fame for his historical and religious canvases. Rembrandt was influenced in his early years by Italian painters, especially by their use of light. But that was not his only strength. His reputation as a portrait painter brought him renown and fortune in Amsterdam.

Even more impressive were his self-portraits, which he painted not for the commissions of patrons but entirely for himself in the pursuit of truth. For an artist to paint as many self-portaits as Rembrandt did in the seventeenth century was very unusual. Self-portraits are analogous to autobiographies: in both, the artist examines himself because he believes his own self is worthy of self-examination.

Rembrandt's quest for the meaning of the inner life is compatible with the growing introspectiveness of the seventeenth century, an age that also produced Descartes's dictum that to think is to be, the soliloquies of Shakespeare's Hamlet, and the hallucinations of Cervantes' Don Quixote.

Rembrandt produced a series of sixty-two self-portraits during the course of his lifetime, an exhaustive autobiography in pictures in which he seemed to engage in a dialogue with himself in a variety of atttitudes and poses: vigorous, youthful, heroic, flamboyant, melodramatic, enigmatic, aging, distraught, struggling with despair, grimly resolved, disdainful, strong, weak. Rembrandt completed *Self-Portrait at Old Age,* 1669 (Figure 6), the fifty-fifth in a corpus of sixty-two self-portraits, in the last year of his life. It is among a cluster of self-portraits in which he appears to have "pulled himself together" and defined his identity. In it, we find Rembrandt staring back at us with the calm assurance of a man who has mastered his art and life, and surpassed his time and place.

The later part of the eighteenth century marks the beginning of the rococo and neoclassical periods in art history. Especially popular in France, the rococo and neoclassical movements owed much to political and social forces. The term *rococo* describes a style that is frothy and frivolous and compatible with the peripheral concerns of royalty. In 1698, King Louis XIV or-

5. Willem Kalf. *Still Life,* c. 1660. *(Hermitage, St. Petersburg/Scala/Art Resource, NY.)*

dered the redecoration of his palace at Versailles with works that were lighthearted and youthful instead of stodgy and serious. His dabbling with artistic matters led to quarrels and esthetic disagreements in the artistic community.

An example of the rococo is François Boucher's (1703–1770) *The Toilet of Venus* (1751) (Figure 7). Although some art historians describe his work as slick and artificial, Boucher became the darling of the French court. In his *The Toilet of Venus,* the goddess is full figured and lush, surrounded by all the sensual accouterments that the goddess of love and erotic pleasure should have. Given her appearance and her surroundings, Boucher's Venus looks as though she would have been comfortable in period dress, supervising the decor of her boudoir at the palace at Versailles. Clearly, Boucher understood his audience well.

While Boucher exemplified the light and airy sentiment of the rococo, Jacques Louis David (1748–1825) typified the neoclassical.

6. Rembrandt van Rijn. *Self Portrait at Old Age*, 1669. *(Erich Lessing/National Gallery, London/Art Resource, NY.)*

The neoclassical style represents a return to the rationality and harmony of the classical past; many of the works from this period also reflect contemporary political events.

Justice, honor for one's country, and the need to portray inspirational themes were the guideposts of the neoclassical artists. Their training ground was Italy, primarily because it was the source of the classical prototypes from which they could learn. Jacques Louis David's *The Death of Marat* (1793) (Figure 8) captures the essence of that event in a manner that combines the best of Poussin and Rubens.

The subject matter is important because it illuminates the neoclassical concept of virtue, represented by the martyrdom of Marat, a revolutionary. The style borrows from Poussin's ability to capture a scene with photographic stillness, rendering the figures in an almost sculptural way. But David has also appropriated Rembrandt's technique of skillfully juxtaposing light and shadow. While the neoclassicists sometimes paid homage to their distant past in subject matter, they also showed their reverence for the revolutionary ideals of their own time.

7. François Boucher. *The Toilet of Venus,* 1751. *(Metropolitan Museum of Art, NY.)*

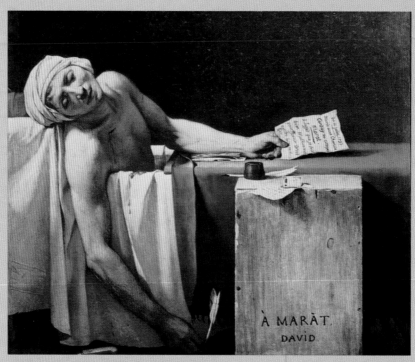

8. Jacques Louis David. *The Death of Marat*, 1793. *(Royal Museum of Fine Arts, Brussels/Giraudon/Art Resource, NY.)*

LA VÉRITÉ, BY BERNARD PICART. In the early eighteenth century, French critics of the existing order in church and state used Descartes as a symbol. Here he is pointing to the slaying of error and ignorance by truth. The engraver who created this picture was eventually forced to flee France and settle in the Dutch Republic. (*The Teylers Museum, Haarlem, The Netherlands.*)

God exists because Descartes had in his mind an idea of a supreme, perfect being, and, Descartes reasoned, this idea could have been put there only by such a being, not by any ordinary mortal. Therefore, God's existence means that the physical world must be real, for no Creator would play such a cruel trick and invent a vast hoax.

For Descartes, the new science meant confidence: in his own mind, in the knowability of the physical world, and in mathematics and reason. Scientific thought meant an alternative to everything he associated with the medieval: confusion, disorder, conflict between church and state, fear of the unknown, and magic. Turning his back on the centuries immediately preceding his own, Descartes, possibly as a result of knowing Bacon's ideas for practical science, proclaimed that "it is possible to attain knowledge which is very useful in life, and that, instead of that speculative philosophy which is taught in the schools [that is, scholasticism], we may find a practical philosophy by means of which . . . we can . . . render ourselves the masters and possessors of nature."[4] Descartes was the first person to dream about the capacity of science to control and dominate nature, though he could not imagine its potential to destroy nature.

Online Study Center

Improve Your Grade
Primary Source: Descartes' Discourse on Method Offers a New Method of Reasoning

In order to affirm the existence of anything other than the abstractions of mathematics, Descartes had to proclaim the existence of God and the Universe, largely because both were ideas in his mind. He radically separated matter from spirit, mind from nature, and in the process he widened a gap in Western thought that would haunt philosophers for centuries. What if a thinker who understood the implications of Descartes's separation of matter from spirit was to argue that only matter existed? The thinker who did so was Benedict de Spinoza (1632–1677). Born in Amsterdam of recently immigrated Jewish parents, he was trained in classical languages and Hebrew thought.

His genius drew him to the new science, and he became an early explicator of Descartes's philosophy, in which he spied a central weakness: its inability to explain the linkage between matter and spirit or to connect God to nature in any meaningful way. Spinoza's solution was radical, logical, and thoroughly heretical to Christian thinkers: he argued that God is Nature, that matter and spirit in effect are one.

To this day, philosophers dispute Spinoza's purpose. Was he an atheist who wanted to do away with the Judeo-Christian conception of God, or was he a mystic who wished to infuse God into Nature? His contemporaries of every religious persuasion (he was expelled from his Amsterdam synagogue) deemed him an atheist and thought that he had become one by reading too much science. Their condemnation made "spinozism" a byword for atheism and freethinking. In the Enlightenment, freethinkers and materialists would claim to have been inspired by Spinoza.

The thoughts and visions of Bacon and Descartes revealed the power and importance of scientific knowledge. Science could promote human well-being, as Bacon insisted; it could make human beings and nature the foundation of all meaningful knowledge, as Descartes assumed; it could express pantheism, as Spinoza showed; or it could justify a belief in Nature as God, as it did for Spinoza. Whichever position educated westerners embraced by the late 1600s, science would be used to challenge the traditional authority of the clergy, whether Catholic or fundamentalist Protestant. Why believe in dogmas and texts when nature offered another kind of truth—universal and, just as important, applicable to human problems? For good or ill, the Scientific Revolution gave its followers a sense of power and self-confidence unimagined even by Renaissance proponents of individualism or by the theorists of absolute state power.

SOCIAL IMPLICATIONS OF THE SCIENTIFIC REVOLUTION

Perhaps the critical factor in causing the historical phenomenon called the Scientific Revolution was the acceptance and use of the new science by educated elites. Without such acceptance, the science of Galileo, Kepler, Descartes, Boyle, and Newton would have remained the specialized knowledge of the few—or, worse still, a suspect, even heretical, approach to nature. Galileo could not have succeeded as much as he did in disseminating his theories (despite the hostility of the church) without his large European following and his many aristocratic patrons, particularly in Florence.

Access to the printing press in Europe was also critical to the acceptance of the new mechanical understanding of nature. Descartes understood that fact when he left France, after the condemnation of Galileo, and published and lived in the Netherlands. Persecution and censorship meant that the new science made far less of an impact in Catholic than in Protestant Europe.

Equally important, the new science offered the dream of power to both governments and early promoters of industry. In the seventeenth century, this dream enticed monarchs and statesmen to give their patronage to scientific academies and projects. The achievements of the new science were quickly institutionalized in academies dominated either by the state, as in France, or by the landed and commercial elite, as in England. Founded in the 1660s, scientific academies such as the Royal Society in England became centers for the dissemination of science at a time when many universities, still controlled by the clergy, were hostile to its attack on scholasticism.

The new mechanical learning—not widely communicated by Newton's *Principia*, which was far too technical for most people, but rather passed on as mechanical information in handbooks and lectures—began to be applied in Britain and Scotland during the second half of the eighteenth century. The applied mechanics that improved the steam engine and utilized it in coal mining and water engineering stemmed from Newtonian lectures and books, which proliferated in Britain during the 1700s. The road from the Scientific Revolution leads more directly to the Industrial Revolution than is often realized. James Watt, who perfected the steam engine, had been tutored in Newtonian mechanics. His engine revolutionized the manufacturing of cotton.

In the same period, the scientific gentleman and woman, like the French chemist Lavoisier and his wife, Marie Anne, became fashionable icons. Elite and mildly prosperous families brought microscopes and globes into their homes. Owning these objects caused the family's status to rise, even if no one in the family became an engineer or doctor. Science had captured the Western imagination.

THE MEANING OF THE SCIENTIFIC REVOLUTION

The Scientific Revolution was decisive in shaping the modern mentality; it shattered the medieval view of the universe and replaced it with a wholly different world-view. Gone was the belief that a motionless earth lay at the center of a universe that was finite and enclosed by a ring of stars. Gone, too, was the belief that the universe was divided into higher and lower worlds and that different laws of motion operated in the heavens and on earth. Nature could be mastered conceptually and mathematically.

The methodology that produced this view of nature—the new science—played a crucial historical role in reorienting Western thought from medieval theology and metaphysics to the study of physical and human problems. In the Late Middle Ages, most men of learning were Aristotelians and theologians. By the mid-eighteenth century, knowledge of Newtonian science and the dissemination of useful learning had become the goal of the educated classes. All knowledge, it was believed, could emulate scientific knowledge: it could be based on observation, experimentation, or rational deduction; and it could be systematic, verifiable, progressive, and useful. This new approach to learning used the scientists of the sixteenth and seventeenth centuries as proof that no institution or dogma had a monopoly on truth; the scientific approach would yield knowledge that might, if properly applied for the good of all people, produce a new and better age. Such an outlook gave thinkers new confidence in the power of the human mind to master nature and led them to examine European institutions and traditions with an inquiring, critical, and skeptical spirit. Scientific societies and academies sprang up all over Europe. In the Dutch Republic in 1785, a society was also founded by women interested in receiving a scientific education. Most

JAMES WATT (1736–1819). An engraved portrait of James Watt rendered in his successful years. His somewhat grim affect is consonant with the depression he often described in his letters. (*The Granger Collection.*)

scientific academies, however, excluded women into the twentieth century.

The Scientific Revolution ultimately weakened traditional Christianity. God's role in a mechanical universe was not clear. Newton had argued that God not only set the universe in motion but still intervened in its operations, thus leaving room for miracles. Others retained a place for God as Creator but regarded miracles as limitations on nature's mechanical perfection. Applied to religious doctrines, Descartes's reliance on methodical doubt and clarity of thought and Bacon's insistence on careful observation led thinkers to question the validity of Christian teachings. Theology became a separate and somewhat irrelevant area of intellectual inquiry, not fit for the interests of practical, well-informed people. Not only Christian doctrines but also various popular beliefs grew suspect. Magic, witchcraft, and astrol-

Profile

Sir Isaac Newton (1642–1727)

Today we know so much more about Sir Isaac Newton, about his beliefs and life, than did his contemporaries. Newton was very private, even secretive. He wanted to appear to the world solely as a natural philosopher interested in local motion and the motions of the heavenly bodies. He said sternly, "I do not frame hypotheses," when asked to explain what universal gravitation actually is. In his heart he believed it to be the will of God operating in the universe. This deeply religious man devoted as many hours of his workweek to theology and biblical prophecy as he did to experiments. Perhaps most surprising of all his labors are his alchemical pursuits. Like the magicians of old, he wanted to understand the secret workings of chemical action, and he believed that some day the truly pious natural philosopher would be able to transform ordinary metals into gold. Evidence of the private Newton sits amid his vast manuscript collections, which are now dispersed all over the world. At Imperial College, London, the Newton project has succeeded in putting many of these manuscripts online so that everyone can read them. Go to http://www.newtonproject.ic.ac.uk/.

(Art Resource, NY.)

ogy, still widespread among the European masses, were regarded with disdain by elite culture. The masses of people remained devoted to some form of traditional Christianity, and the uncertainty of a universe governed by devils, witches, or the stars continued to make sense to peasants and laborers.

In Catholic countries, where the Scientific Revolution began, hostility toward scientific ideas gathered strength in the early 1600s. The mentality of the Counter Reformation enabled lesser minds to exercise their fears and arrogance against any idea they regarded as suspicious. Galileo was caught in this hostile environment, and the Copernican system was condemned by the church in 1616. In Spain and Poland, it was not officially taught until the 1770s.

Gradually, the science of Newton became the science of western Europe: nature mechanized, analyzed, regulated, and mathematized. As a result of the Scientific Revolution, learned westerners came to believe more strongly than ever that nature could be mastered. Mechanical science—applied to canals, engines, pumps, and levers—became the science of industry. Thus, the Scientific Revolution, operating on both intellectual and commercial levels, laid the groundwork for two major developments of the modern West: the Age of Enlightenment and the Industrial Revolution.

❖ ❖ ❖

Online Study Center ACE the Test

NOTES

1. Quoted in Jean D. Moss, *Novelties in the Heavens* (Chicago: University of Chicago Press, 1993), p. 33.

2. Excerpted in *Discoveries and Opinions of Galileo,* ed. Stillman Drake (Garden City, N.Y.: Doubleday, 1957), p. 28.

3. Excerpted in *Newton's Philosophy of Nature,* ed. H. S. Thayer (New York: Hafner, 1953), p. 177.

4. Excerpted in *Descartes' Philosophical Writings,* ed. Norman Kemp Smith (New York: Modern Library, 1958), pp. 130–131.

SUGGESTED READING

Appleby, J., L. Hunt, and M. Jacob, *Telling the Truth About History* (1994). Discusses the issues raised by the heroic model of science that came out of the Scientific Revolution and relates the issues to today's attitudes toward science.

Burns, Williams E., *Science in the Enlightenment: An Encyclopedia* (2003). An excellent source of information.

Gleick, James, *Isaac Newton* (2004). A great read.

Hellyer, Marcus, ed., *The Scientific Revolution: The Essential Readings* (2003).

Jacob, Margaret C., and Larry Stewart, *Practical Matter. Newton's Science in the Service of Industry and Empire* (2004).

Chapter 18

The Age of Enlightenment: Reason and Reform

Madame Geoffrin's Salon. (Giraudon/Art Resource, NY.)

Focus Questions

1. What does it mean to say that someone in the eighteenth century was "enlightened"?
2. Who were the freemasons, and what role did they play in the eighteenth century?
3. What is a freethinker? A deist? An atheist? A pantheist?
4. With what economic doctrines do we associate Adam Smith?
5. To whom did Adam Smith's theories appeal? Why?
6. What is the enduring legacy of the Enlightenment? What were its political implications?

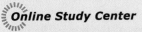

Online Study Center

This icon will direct you to interactive map and primary source activities on the website http://college.hmco.com/pic/perrywc8e.

The eighteenth century's most exciting intellectual movement is called the Enlightenment. So powerful was its dedication to toleration and rational thought that until quite recently the era was sometimes characterized as the Age of Reason. The turn toward what became known by 1750 as the Enlightenment began in the late seventeenth century. Three factors were critically important in this new intellectual ferment: revulsion against monarchical and clerical absolutism, especially as practiced by Louis XIV in France; a new freedom of publishing and, with it, the rise of a new public and a secular culture, especially in England and the Dutch Republic; and, not least, the impact of the Scientific Revolution, particularly the excitement generated by Newton's *Principia* (1687).

When Newton's great work appeared, censorship or imprisonment for ideas disliked by church or state was still commonplace. Protestants languished in French prisons. Opponents of the Calvinist clergy in the Netherlands could be detained indefinitely; one man died after three years in jail without a trial, probably a suicide. In England, Oxford University routinely expelled students whose ideas were seen to be heretical or unorthodox. In the papal territories, Jewish children were still forcibly baptized and removed from their homes. By 1750, such extreme measures were rare anywhere north of the Alps or in the American colonies.

The promoters of science and religious tolerance had secured new freedoms, many of them given by sleight of hand. Rationality and order—imitative of the order found in Newton's universe—seemed to be gaining momentum. The leaders of the Enlightenment sought to impose an ordered freedom on social and political institutions. They were prepared to attack in print, though sometimes anonymously, the attitudes and beliefs that stood in the way of tolerance, freedom, and rationality. As combative intellectuals and pundits, they earned the name *philosophes*—simply the French word for "philosophers"—now used in many languages to describe the bold and witty satirists of clergymen, courtiers, and the pious in general. Thinkers as diverse as Voltaire in France, Benjamin Franklin in America, and Immanuel Kant (1724–1804), an abstract philosopher in Germany, may be labeled *philosophes*.

Chronology 18.1 ❖ The Enlightenment

1685	Revocation of the Edict of Nantes; persecution of Protestants in France
1687	Publication of Newton's *Principia*
1688–1689	Revolution in England: the clergy's power is weakened and censorship loosened
1690	Publication of Locke's *Two Treatises of Government*
1695	Publication of Locke's *Reasonableness of Christianity*
1696	Toland's *Christianity Not Mysterious* makes the case for deism
1717	Founding of the Grand Lodge, London; the beginning of organized Freemasonry
1733	Voltaire publishes *Letters Concerning the English Nation*
1740	Frederick the Great invades Silesia; the War of the Austrian Succession ensues
1748	Hume publishes *An Enquiry Concerning Human Understanding;* Montesquieu publishes *The Spirit of the Laws*
1751	Publication of Diderot's *Encyclopedia* in Paris
1756–1763	Seven Years' War
1762	Rousseau publishes *Émile* and *The Social Contract*
1775	American Revolution begins
1776	Adam Smith publishes *The Wealth of Nations*
1785	Russian Charter of Nobility; the servitude of the peasants is guaranteed
1787	Dutch Revolution begins
1789	French Revolution begins

Late in the eighteenth century, Kant gave a succinct definition of *enlightenment:* bringing "light into the dark corners of mind," dispelling ignorance, prejudice, and superstition. Kant went to the heart of one aspect of the Enlightenment: its insistence that each individual should reason independently, without recourse to the authority of schools, churches, or clergymen.[1]

Being a political moderate and living in Prussia, Kant hoped that the call for self-education and critical thought would mean no disruption of the political order, at least at home. In his moderation he was similar to most philosophes. Distrusting the uneducated people, these intellectual leaders sought a gradual transformation of the human condition. But there were radical thinkers during the late eighteenth century, such as the American revolutionary Thomas Jefferson (1743–1826) and the feminist Mary Wollstonecraft (1759–1797), who were prepared to endorse an immediate political disruption of the traditional authority of monarchy, aristocracy, fathers, and churchmen. Whether radical or moderate, the philosophes were united by certain key ideas. They believed in **the new science,** were critical of clergy and all rigid dogma but tolerant of people's right to worship freely, and believed deeply in freedom of the press. They were also willing to entertain, though not necessarily accept, new heresies—such as **pantheism,** or the belief that the earth had gradually evolved, or the view that the Bible was a series of wise stories but not the literal word of God.

Philosophes were found most commonly in the major European cities, where they clubbed and socialized in literary and philosophical societies. By the 1770s, Paris was the center of the Enlightenment, but circles of philosophes could be found in Berlin, Moscow, Budapest, London, The Hague, and, across the Atlantic, in Philadelphia. Their writings spread far and wide because they adopted a new style for philosophical discussion: clear, direct, witty, satirical, even naughty and audacious. At times, they were more like journalists, propagandists, writers of fiction, even pornographers, who sought to live by their pens. Their success owed much to the growing literacy of urban men and women, a new prosperity that made books affordable, and the existence of an audience that liked what they had to say. The philosophes' readers, too, were fed up with all vestiges of medieval culture. They resented priestly and aristocratic privileges, monarchical decrees in place of deliberation in representative assemblies, and restrictions on who could manufacture what and where.

Appealing to the professional classes, literate merchants, and women with leisure to read, the philosophes opposed the old scholastic learning of the universities, mocked the clergy, and denied the Christian mysteries. They expressed confidence in science and reason, called for humanitarian treatment of slaves and criminals, and played a cat-and-mouse game with censors. Dedicated to freedom of thought and person, they combined these liberal values with a secular orientation and a belief in future progress. The philosophes helped shape, if not define, modern beliefs in tolerance, human rights, and free speech.

THE FORMATION OF A PUBLIC AND SECULAR CULTURE

In England and the Dutch Republic, by 1700, freedom of the press was a practical or a legal reality. During the same period, in 1685, Louis XIV outlawed Protestants from France. Faced with forced conversion or imprisonment, thousands of highly educated Protestants (as well as menial workers) fled to England or the Netherlands. They set up journals and newspapers, formed new clubs, and began a vast international discussion—conducted in French, the language of all well-educated Europeans—aiming it against the injustices of monarchical absolutism and the evils of religious persecution. In journals and newspapers, the reformers endorsed the need for political change.

At the same time, relative freedom of assembly in the cities of western Europe (even in Paris, which was too big to police) gave rise to a new public and secular sphere: a zone for social life outside the family but not attached to churches or courts. The new public sphere, found in *salons* (gatherings in private homes), coffee houses, and Masonic lodges, as well as in academies for scientific learning like the Royal Society of London, laid the ground for the emergence of the Enlightenment.

All these autonomous and voluntary groups helped create a new secular and public culture. In this new and free mental space, what we now call *civil society,* people mingled with strangers, politeness and conviviality became norms of behavior, and informal learning flourished. Lecturers gave scientific demonstrations, ordinary men learned to vote for their leaders or to debate publicly, and women met outside the home to discuss novels or politics. Indeed, in some of the Parisian salons, women were often the key organizers. By the 1780s, throughout western Europe no town of any size was without a private association, club, and newspaper. In the Dutch Republic, in 1785, the first scientific society founded by and for women met in the town of Middleburg (located in the province of Zeeland and no larger than about 17,000 souls).[2] The women chose a Freemason and follower of Voltaire to give scientific demonstrations, and they set about learning Newtonian mechanics with such dedication that their society lasted for over a hundred years.

Men and women met at these sociable gatherings not because they were relatives, belonged to the same religion, or practiced the same trade or profession, but because they had a common interest in politics, science, the new novels, or self-improvement. Members of these new clubs shared certain characteristics: they were highly literate; they possessed some surplus wealth and leisure time; and, if titled aristocrats, they were not opposed to mixing with bourgeois lawyers, doctors, civil servants, and merchants. Such cosmopolitan men and women made the theories of the philosophes come alive. The new societies thus became schools where the literate expanded their universe, learning about peoples of the Orient and the Americas and about the Newtonian heavens. In the words of Kant, they dared to think for themselves.

This training in self-governance, self-education, and social criticism helped prepare the way for the liberal revolutions that swept across Europe at the end of the eighteenth and during the first half of the nineteenth century. In the first years of the French Revolution, one of the earliest activities of the revolutionaries was to set up clubs based on equality and fraternity and modeled after the clubs and lodges of the Enlightenment. As the revolutions spread, these societies spread the principles of the French Revolution.

Salons

Perhaps the most famous of the many new forms of secular culture were the salons, often run by women and mostly found in Paris. Intellectually ambitious women, such as Madame Necker and Madame Geoffrin, organized regular evening receptions in their drawing rooms. There philosophes gathered to discuss ideas in an atmosphere that was civilized, independent of the crown and the nobility, and open. Originally, the salon was an institution found only in noble homes, where the room designated for leisure activities gave the gathering its name. The Parisian women and their philosophe friends transformed the custom into gatherings where men and women could educate themselves and where some of the most outrageous ideas of the age could be openly discussed. The habits of luxurious feasting and gaming disappeared and in their place came serious, if somewhat formal, egalitarian conversation. Salons also developed an international correspondence; letters from all over Europe were read to the assembled guests. The notion of a republic of letters and the goal of cosmopolitanism were actually experienced in the salons. Some salons, however, excluded women, who were attacked as frivolous and gossipy. The free mixing

of women and men always generated controversy in the eighteenth century.

Freemasons

As the search for a new religiosity during the Enlightenment came to mean a striving after alternatives to traditional beliefs, societies with a ritual and ethical component began to flourish. The most famous of these were the Freemasons, a fraternity that evolved in the late seventeenth century in England and Scotland. Origianlly guilds of working stonemasons, the masonic lodges evolved into fraternities of middle class and aristocratic men (and some women). By the 1720s they can be found in London and on the Continent. Keeping to the ideals of the older stonemasons they said that all men should meet "upon the level." In practice this meant holding elections for their leaders and living under rules for correct behavior, all codified in a published book of *Constitutions* (1723). In Britain after the Revolution of 1688–1689 practices that included constitutional government and frequent elections were commonplace. But on the Continent constitutional practices were new and experimental. Through them the lodges sought to make their members virtuous, disciplined, and civilized. For some men, this experience came to rival that found in the churches. Philosophes, such as Benjamin Franklin and, late in his life, Voltaire, joined lodges; in some cities, lodges became cultural centers. In Vienna, Mozart was a Freemason and wrote music for his lodge; in Berlin, Frederick the Great cultivated the lodges, which in turn became centers for the cult of enlightened monarchy.

By the middle of the eighteenth century, perhaps as many as fifty thousand men belonged to lodges in just about every major European city. British constitutionalism, as well as the old fraternal ideals of equality and liberty, took on new meaning in these private gatherings. In France, in the 1780s, the national Grand Lodge instituted a national assembly of elected representatives, as well as a monthly payment of charity for impoverished brothers. The lodges for women became places where women and men actually talked about the meaning of liberty and equality for their own lives. Many lodges were dominated by the most elite ele-

FREEMASONS' CEREMONY, VIENNA. To the right, in avid conversation, we can see one of the most famous Freemasons of the 1780s, the composer Wolfgang Amadeus Mozart. The play of light in the masonic "temple," the blindfolding, and the elegance were all intended to give importance to this new form of social life. (*Erich Lessing/Art Resource, NY.*)

ments in Old Regime society, who found themselves giving allegiance, and often considerable financial support, to a new system of belief and governance—a system that was ultimately incompatible with the principles of birth and inheritance on which their power rested. In 1738, the pope condemned membership in the lodges. At the time of the French Revolution, its opponents claimed that the lodges were responsible for the uprising. There was no truth to the claim, which opponents of all reforms and revolutions have often repeated. The subversive quality of the lodges lay not in any conspiracy but rather in the freedom they allowed for thought, self-governance, and discussion.

Scientific Academies

By midcentury, there were provincial scientific academies all over the Continent. The first scientific societies had formed in the 1660s in London and Paris. They continued to flourish and were imitated in Turin, Budapest, Berlin, and small cities of the Dutch Republic, such as Haarlem and Middelburg. Members of all these societies performed experiments of greater or lesser sophistication, listened to learned papers, and collected samples. Each society kept a cabinet of "rarities" containing everything from rocks to deformed animal bones. Any man who possessed what the age called curiosity could join one of these groups and try to become a man of science. Gradually, women were admitted—not as members but as spectators. By the 1770s, these scientific societies served as models for groups specifically interested in the application of scientific knowledge, or in useful learning. The new groups became centers for the reformers and critics of the age, who sought to turn the Enlightenment into a movement for changing society and government.

In Germany and France, where the scientific academies tended to be dominated by aristocratic leadership, new societies with a utilitarian purpose were founded and had to compete with the older societies. As a result, the turn toward the applied and the utilitarian was not as visible as in England and Scotland. In France, the academies became centers for abstract and advanced science and mathematics—for important and original contributions with little practical application. During the French Revolution, however, the academies were purged, and emphasis was then placed on applications of mechanics and chemistry.

ALTERNATIVES TO ORTHODOXY

Christianity Under Attack

No single thread had united Western culture more powerfully than Christianity. Until the eighteenth century, educated people, especially rulers and servants of the state, had to give allegiance to one or another of the Christian churches—however un-Christian their actions. The Enlightenment produced the first widely read and systematic assault on Christianity launched from within the ranks of the educated. The philosophes argued that many Christian dogmas defied logic—for example, the conversion of the substance of bread and wine into the body and the blood of Christ during the Eucharist. They also ridiculed theologians for arguing about obscure issues that seemed irrelevant to the human condi-

tion and a hindrance to clear thinking. "Theology amuses me," wrote Voltaire. "That's where we find the madness of the human spirit in all its plenitude." In the same vein, the philosophes denounced the churches for inciting the fanaticism and intolerance that led to the horrors of the Crusades, the Inquisition, and the wars of the Reformation. They viewed Christianity's preoccupation with salvation and its belief in the depravity of human nature, a consequence of Adam and Eve's defiance of God, as barriers to social improvement and earthly happiness.

Skeptics, Freethinkers, and Deists

An early attack on Christian dogma was made by the skeptic Pierre Bayle (1647–1706), who came to distrust Christian dogma and to see superstition as a social evil far more dangerous than atheism. Bayle was a French Protestant forced to flee to the Netherlands as a result of Louis XIV's campaign against Protestants. Although a Calvinist in background, Bayle also ran into opposition from the strict Calvinist clergy, who regarded him as lax on doctrinal matters. He attacked his critics and persecutors in a new and brilliant form of journalism, his *Historical and Critical Dictionary* (1697), which was more an encyclopedia than a dictionary. Under alphabetically arranged subjects and in copious footnotes, Bayle discussed the most recent learning of the day on various matters and never missed an opportunity to ridicule the dogmatic, the superstitious, or the just plain arrogant. In Bayle's hands, the ancient philosophy of skepticism—the doubting of all dogma—was revived and turned into a tool; rigorous questioning of accepted ideas became a method for arriving at new truths. As Bayle noted in his *Dictionary*, "It is therefore only religion that has anything to fear from Pyrrhonism [that is, skepticism]."[3] In this same critical spirit, Bayle, in his dictionary article entitled "David," compared Louis XIV to Goliath. The message was clear enough: great tyrants and the clergy who prop them up should beware of self-confident, independently minded citizens who are skeptical of the claims of authority made by kings and churches and are eager to use their own intellects to search for truth.

Bayle's *Dictionary,* which was in effect the first encyclopedia, had an enormous impact throughout Europe. Its very format captured the imagination of the philosophes. Here was a way of simply, even scientifically, classifying and ordering knowledge. Partly through Bayle's writings, skepticism became an integral part of the Enlightenment approach to religion. It taught its readers to question the clerical claim that God's design governs human events—that "God ordains" certain human actions. Skepticism dealt a serious blow to revealed religion and seemed to point in the direction of "natural" religion, that is, toward a system of beliefs and ethics designed by rational people on the basis of their own needs.

The religious outlook of the philosophes was also colored by late-seventeenth- and early-eighteenth-century English freethinkers. These early representatives of the Enlightenment used the term *freethinking* to signal their hostility to established church dogmas and their ability to think for themselves. They looked back to the English Revolution of 1640–1660 for their ideas about government; many English freethinkers were republicans in the tradition established by important figures of the interregnum. Indeed, the English freethinkers of the 1690s and beyond helped popularize English republican ideas at home and in the American colonies, where in 1776 these views would figure prominently in the thinking of American revolutionaries.

The freethinkers had little use for organized religion or even for Christianity itself. In 1696, the freethinker John Toland (1670–1722) published *Christianity Not Mysterious.* In it he argued that most religious doctrines seemed to contradict reason or common sense and ought to be discarded along with such beliefs as the resurrection of Jesus and the miracles of the Bible. Toland also attacked the clergy's power; in his opinion, the Revolution of 1688–89 had not gone far enough in undermining the power of the established church and the king. Toland and his freethinking associates wanted England to be a republic governed by "reasonable" people who worshiped, as Toland proposed, not a mysterious God but intelligible nature. For Toland, Newton's science made nature intelligible, and he used it as a stick with which to beat at the doctrines of revealed religion.

Combining science with skepticism, freethinking, and anticlericalism, thoughtful critics found ample reason for abandoning all traditional authority. By 1700, a general crisis of confidence in established authority had been provoked by the works of Bayle, the freethinkers, and philosophers such as Descartes. Once started in England and the Netherlands and broadcast via Dutch and French refugee printers, the Enlightenment quickly became international.

Some of the early proponents of the Enlightenment were atheists. They often published clandestinely. A particularly early and outrageous example of their thinking appeared under the title *The Treatise on the Three Imposters* (1719), which identified Jesus, Moses, and Muhammad as the impostors. However, most of the philosophes were simply **deists,** who believed only those Christian doctrines that could meet the test of reason. For example, they considered it reasonable to believe in God, for only with a creator, they said, could such a superbly organized universe have come into being. But, in their view, after God set the universe in motion, he took no further part in its operations. Thus, although deists retained a belief in God the Creator, they rejected clerical authority, revelation, original sin, and miracles. They held that biblical accounts of the resurrection and of Jesus walking on water or raising the dead could not be reconciled with natural law. Deists viewed Jesus as a great moral teacher, not as the Son of God, and they regarded ethics, not faith, as the essence of religion. Rational people, they said, served God best by treating their fellow human beings justly.

David Hume (1711–1776), a Scottish skeptic, attacked both revealed religion and the deists' natural religion. He maintained that all religious ideas, including Christian teachings and even the idea of God, stemmed ultimately from human fears and superstitions. Hume rejected the deist argument that this seemingly orderly universe required a designing mind to create it. The universe, said Hume, might very well be eternal, and the seemingly universal order simply be more in our heads than in reality. Hume laid great emphasis on social conventions, with which he associated religion. Reason should best be expressed through skepticism.

Voltaire the Philosophe

The French possessed a vital tradition of intellectual skepticism going back to the late sixteenth century, as well as a tradition of scientific rationalism exemplified by Descartes. In the early eighteenth century, however, the French found it difficult to gain access to the new literature of the Enlightenment because the French printing presses were among the most tightly controlled and censored in Europe. As a result, a brisk but risky traffic developed in clandestine books and manuscripts subversive of authority, and French-language journals poured from Dutch presses.

As a poet and writer struggling for recognition in Paris, the young François Marie Arouet, known to the world as Voltaire (1694–1778), encountered some of the new ideas that were being discussed in salons in Paris. In the French capital, those educated people who wanted to read books and discuss ideas hostile to the church or to the Sorbonne, the clerically controlled university, had to proceed with caution. Individuals had been imprisoned for writing, publishing, or owning books hostile to Catholic doctrine. Although Voltaire learned something of the new enlightened culture in Paris, it was in 1726, when he journeyed to London, that Voltaire the poet became Voltaire the philosophe. Voltaire fled Paris after he was arbitrarily arrested when defending himself in a fight with a local aristocrat.

In England, Voltaire became acquainted with the ideas of John Locke and Isaac Newton. From Newton, Voltaire learned the mathematical laws that govern the universe; he witnessed the power of human reason to establish general rules that seemed to explain the behavior of physical objects. From Locke, Voltaire learned that people should believe only the ideas received from the senses. Locke's theory of learning, his *epistemology*, impressed many of the proponents of the Enlightenment. Again, the implications for religion were most serious: if people believed only what they experienced, they would not accept mysteries and doctrines simply because they were taught by churches and clergy. Voltaire enjoyed considerable freedom of thought in England and saw a social and religious toleration that contrasted sharply with French absolutism and the power of the French clergy. He also witnessed a freer mix-

VOLTAIRE AND KING FREDERICK. The roundtable was beloved by the aristocracy because it claimed everyone as an equal. Here Voltaire visits with Frederick the Great and perhaps imagined himself as an equal. (*Bildarchiv Preussischer Kulturbesitz.*)

ing of bourgeois and aristocratic social groups than was permitted in France at this time.

Throughout his life, Voltaire fiercely supported toleration and free inquiry. He criticized churches and the Roman Catholic Inquisition. His books were banned in France, but he probably did more there than any other philosophe to popularize the Enlightenment. In *Letters Concerning the English Nation* (1733), Voltaire offered constitutional monarchy, new science, and religious toleration as models to be followed by all of Europe. In the *Letters,* he praised English society for its encouragement of these ideals. As he put it, "This is the country of sects. An Englishman, as a free man, goes to Heaven by whatever road he pleases."[4] Voltaire never ceased to ridicule the purveyors of superstition and blind obedience to religious authority, and in such works as *Candide* (1759) and *Micromegas* (1752), he castigated the clergy.

Voltaire was also a practical reformer who campaigned for the rule of law, a freer press, religious toleration, humane treatment of criminals, and a more effective system of government administration. His writings constituted a radical attack on several aspects of eighteenth-century French society. Yet, like so many philosophes, Voltaire feared the power of the people, especially if goaded by the clergy. He was happiest in the company of the rich and powerful, provided they tolerated his ideas and supported reform. Not surprisingly, Voltaire was frequently disappointed by eighteenth-century monarchs, like Frederick the Great in Prussia, who promised enlightenment but sought mainly to increase their own power and that of their armies.

Perhaps the happiest decision of Voltaire's life was to team up with the scientist and philosophe Madame du Châtelet (1706–1749). Together they read Newton, although she became the more proficient mathematician. Before her death during the birth of their child, Madame du Châtelet made the only French translation of the *Principia,* explicated it, and trained scientists who took up Newtonian ideas and spread them throughout western Europe.

Online Study Center

Improve Your Grade
Primary Source: Voltaire on Religious Toleration

POLITICAL THOUGHT

With the exception of Machiavelli in the Renaissance and Thomas Hobbes and the republicans during the English Revolution of 1640–1660, the Enlightenment produced the greatest originality in modern political thought witnessed in the West up to that time. Three major European thinkers and a host of minor ones wrote treatises on politics that remain relevant to this day: John Locke, *Two Trea-* *tises of Government* (1690); Baron de la Brède et de Montesquieu, *The Spirit of the Laws* (1748); and Jean Jacques Rousseau, *The Social Contract* (1762). All repudiated the divine right of kings and strove to check the power of monarchy; each offered different formulas for achieving that goal. These major political theorists of the Enlightenment were also aware of the writings of Machiavelli and Hobbes and, though often disagreeing with them, borrowed some of their ideas.

During the Renaissance, Machiavelli (d. 1527) analyzed politics in terms of power, fortune, and the ability of the individual ruler; he did not call in God to justify the power of princes or to explain their demise. Machiavelli also preferred a republican form of government to monarchy, and his republican vision did not lose its appeal during the Enlightenment. Very late in the eighteenth century, most liberal theorists recognized that the republican form of government, or at least the virtues practiced by citizens in a republic, offered the only alternative to the corruption and repression associated with absolute monarchy.

Political thinkers of the Enlightenment were ambivalent toward much of the writing of Thomas Hobbes (1588–1679). All, however, liked his belief that self-interest is a valid reason for engaging in political activity and his refusal to bring God into his system to justify the power of kings. Hobbes said that power did not rest on divine right but arose out of a contract made among men who agreed to elevate the state, and hence the monarch, to a position of power over them. That contract, once made, could not be broken. As a consequence, the power of the government, whether embodied in a king or a parliament, was absolute.

Hobbes published his major work, *Leviathan,* in 1651, soon after England had been torn by civil war; thus, he was obsessed with the issue of political stability. He feared that, left to their own devices, men would kill one another; the "war of all against all"[5] would prevail without the firm hand of a sovereign to stop it. Hobbes's vision of human nature was dark and forbidding. In the state of nature, the original men had lived lives that could only have been "nasty, brutish, and short." Their sole recourse was to set up a power over themselves that would restrain them. For Hobbes, the state was, as he put it, a "mortal god," the only guarantee of peace and stability. He was the first political thinker to realize the extraordinary power that had come into existence with the creation of strong centralized governments. Most Enlightenment theorists, however, beginning with John Locke, denied that governments possessed absolute power over their subjects, and to that extent they repudiated Hobbes. Many European thinkers of the eighteenth century, including Rousseau, also rejected Hobbes's gloomy view that human nature is greedy and warlike. Yet Hobbes lurks in the background of the Enlightenment. He is the first wholly secular political theorist, and he sounded the death knell for theories of the divine right of kings. The Enlightenment theorists started where he left off.

Locke

Probably the most widely read political philosopher during the first half of the eighteenth century was John Locke (1632–1704). Locke came to maturity in the late 1650s, and like so many of his contemporaries, he was drawn to science. Although he became a medical doctor, his major interest lay in politics and political theory. His *Two Treatises of Government* was seen as a justification for the English Revolution of 1688–89 and the notion of government by consent of the people. (Although the treatises were published in 1690, Locke wrote them before the Glorious Revolution; that fact, however, was not known during the Enlightenment.)

Locke's theory, in its broad outlines, stated that the right to govern derived from the consent of the governed and was a form of contract. When people gave their consent to a government, they expected it to govern justly, protect their property, and ensure certain liberties for the propertied. If a government attempted to rule absolutely and arbitrarily—if it violated the natural rights of the individual—it reneged on its contract and forfeited the loyalty of its subjects. Such a government could legitimately be overthrown. Locke believed that a constitutional government that limited the power of rulers offered the best defense of property and individual rights. He also advocated religious toleration for religious groups whose beliefs did not threaten the state. Locke denied toleration to Catholics because of their association with the Stuarts and to atheists

LOCKE ON THE CONTINENT. John Locke enjoyed an international reputation. This highly stylized portrait of him is adorned with French text. Locke had lived in the Dutch Republic, and his writings were taken and promoted by French Huguenot refugees who hated the monarchy they left behind. (*Corbis.*)

because their oaths to God could not be trusted. He also promoted the necessity for education, particularly for those who saw themselves as the natural leaders of society. And not least, he advocated commerce and trade as one of the foundations of England's national strength.

Late in the eighteenth century, Locke's ideas were used to justify liberal revolutions in both Europe and America. His *Treatises of Government* had been translated into French early in the century by Huguenot refugees. These Protestant victims of French absolutism, persecuted for their religion, saw that the importance of Locke's political philosophy was not simply in his use of contract theory to justify constitutional government; he also asserted that the community could take up arms against its sovereign in the name of the natural rights of liberty and property. Locke's ideas about the foundation of government had greater impact on the European continent and in America during the eighteenth century than in England.

Montesquieu

Baron de la Brède et de Montesquieu (1689–1755) was a French aristocrat who, like Voltaire, visited England late in the 1720s and knew the writings of Locke. Montesquieu had little sympathy for revolutions, but he did approve of constitutional monarchy. His primary concern was to check the unbridled authority of the French kings. In opposition to the Old Regime, Montesquieu proposed a balanced system of government, with an executive branch offset by a legislature whose members were drawn from the landed and educated elements in society. From his writings we derive our notion of government divided into branches. Montesquieu genuinely believed that the aristocracy possessed a natural and sacred obligation to rule and that their honor called them to serve the community. He also sought to fashion a government that channeled the interests and energies of its people, a government that was not bogged down in corruption and inefficiency.

In stressing the rule of law and the importance of nonmonarchical authority, Montesquieu became a source for legitimating the authority of representative institutions. Hardly an advocate of democracy, Montesquieu was nonetheless seen as a powerful critic of royal absolutism. His writings, particularly *The Spirit of the Laws*, established him both as a major philosophe who possessed republican tendencies and as a critic of the Old Regime in France. Once again, innovative political thinking highlighted the failures of absolutist government and pointed to the need for some kind of representative assembly in every European country. In addition, Montesquieu's ideas on a balanced system of government found favor in the new American republic.

Rousseau

Not until the 1760s did democracy find its champion: Jean Jacques Rousseau (1712–1778). Rousseau based his politics on contract theory and his reading of Hobbes. For Rousseau, the people choose their government and, in so doing, effectively give birth to civil society. But he further demanded (in contrast to Hobbes) that the contract be constantly renewed and that government be made immediately and directly responsible to the will of the people. *The Social Contract* opened with this stirring cry for reform, "Man is born free; and everywhere he is in chains," and went on to ask how that restriction could be changed. Freedom is in the very nature of man: "to renounce liberty is to renounce being a man, to surrender the rights of humanity and even its duties."[6]

Rousseau's political ideal was the city-state of ancient Greece, where men (but not women) participated actively and directly in politics and were willing to sacrifice self-interest to the community's needs. To the ancient Greek, said Rousseau, the state was a moral association that made him a better person, and good citizenship was the highest form of excellence. In contrast, modern society was prey to many conflicting interests; the rich and powerful used the state to preserve their advantages and power, and the poor and powerless viewed it as an oppressor. Consequently, the obedience to law, the devotion to the state, and the freedom that had characterized the Greek city-state had been lost.

In *The Social Contract*, Rousseau tried to resolve the conflict between individual freedom and the demands of the state. His solution was a small state, modeled after his native city of Geneva as well as after the Greek city-state. Such a state, said Rousseau, should be based on the *general will*: that which is best for the community, which expresses its common interests. Rousseau wanted laws of the state to coincide with the general will. He felt that people have the wisdom to arrive at laws that serve the common good, but to do so, they must set aside selfish interests for the good of the community. For Rousseau, freedom consisted of obeying laws prescribed by citizens inspired by the general will. The citizens themselves must constitute the lawmaking body; lawmaking cannot be entrusted to a single person or a small group.

In Rousseau's view, those who disobey laws—who act according to their private will rather than in accordance with the general will as expressed in law—degrade themselves and

JEAN JACQUES ROUSSEAU ALONE, A SELF-EXILE FROM THE CITY. Rousseau viewed nature and solitude as curative. He also advocated reading for introspection and enlightenment. (*Photographie Bulloz.*)

undermine the community. Therefore, government has the right to force citizens to be obedient, to compel them to exercise their individual wills in the proper way. He left the problem of minority rights unresolved.

No philosopher of the Enlightenment was more dangerous to the Old Regime than Rousseau. His ideas were perceived as truly revolutionary: a direct challenge to the power of kings, the power of the church, and the power of aristocrats. Although Rousseau thought that many leaders of the Enlightenment had been corrupted by easy living and the life of the salons, with their attendant aristocrats and dandies, he nevertheless earned an uneasy place in the ranks of the philosophes. In the French Revolution, his name would be invoked to justify democracy, and of all the philosophes, Rousseau would probably have been the least horrified by the early phase of that revolutionary upheaval.

SOCIAL THOUGHT

Rousseau looked on society as the corrupter of human beings, who, left to their own devices, were inherently virtuous and freedom loving. A wide spectrum of thinkers in the Enlightenment also viewed society, if not as corrupting, at least as needing constant reform. Some enlightened critics were prepared to work with those in power to bring about social reforms. Other philosophes believed that the key to reform lay not in social and political institutions but in changing the general mentality through education and knowledge. All developed new ideas about humankind as travelers told of new peoples and places where commonplace concepts, such as the Judeo-Christian God, had never existed. The societies of Native Americans fascinated Europeans, who vacillated between feeling superior and believing themselves mired in baroquely rigid customs.

Epistemology and Education

Just as Locke's *Two Treatises of Government* helped shape the political thought of the Enlightenment, his *Essay Concerning Human Understanding* (1689) provided the theoretical foundations for an unprecedented interest in education. Locke's view that at birth the mind is blank—a clean slate, or **tabula rasa**—had two important implications. First, if human beings did not come into this world with innate ideas, then they were not, as Christianity taught, inherently sinful. Second, a person's environment was the decisive force in shaping his or her character and intelligence. Nine of every ten men, wrote Locke, "are good or evil, useful or not, [because of] their education." Such a theory was eagerly received by the reform-minded philosophes, who preferred attributing wickedness to faulty institutions, improper rearing, and poor education rather than to a defective human nature.

In the Enlightenment view, the proper study of humanity addressed the process by which people can and do know. Locke had said that individuals take the information produced by their senses and reflect on it; in that way, they arrive at complex ideas. Aside from an environment promoting

Profile

Mary Wollstonecraft

One of the founders of modern feminism and a deeply committed defender of liberty, human rights, and the French Revolution, Mary Wollstonecraft (1759–1797) came to maturity in a circle of English radicals. Her friends included the Unitarian ministers Richard Price and Joseph Priestley, and she knew the British-born American radical Thomas Paine. Although she received little formal education, she taught herself languages, made a living as a translator, read Rousseau critically, and began an intellectual odyssey that took her from liberal Protestantism to freethinking and possibly atheism. She went to France during its Revolution and wanted to raise her daughter there because she believed that in France she would be freer. By far her most famous book is *The Vindication of the Rights of Women* (1792), a classic statement of women's rights and the causes of prejudice and inequality. Since the two hundredth anniversary of Wollstonecraft's famous book, her writings have been revived, and she has been placed at the center of the European Enlightenment as an embodiment of its belief in science and the possibility of human emancipation.

The Board of Trustees of the National Museums and Galleries on Merseyside, Walker Art Gallery.

learning, education obviously requires the active participation of students. Merely receiving knowledge not tested by their own sense experience is inadequate.

More treatises were written on education during the eighteenth century than in all previous centuries combined. On the Continent, where the clergy controlled many schools and all the universities, the educated laity began to demand state regulation and inspection of educational facilities. This insistence revealed a growing discontent with the clergy and their independent authority. By the second half of the century, new schools and universities in Prussia, Belgium, Austria, Hungary, and Russia attempted to teach practical subjects suited to the interests of the laity. Pre-

dictably, science was given a special place in these new institutions. In France, for all the interest in education on the part of the philosophes, by 1789 probably only 50 percent of the men and about 20 percent of the women were literate.

The standards of education for girls and women were appalling. Only a few philosophes, mostly women, and the occasional clergyman who had seen firsthand the poor quality of female education in reading and writing called for reform. But reform did not come till after 1800, when industrialization put more women in the work force and required some literacy. As for higher education, women were excluded, with a few exceptions. Madame du Châtelet in France had studied mathematics with a private tutor;

and in Italy, Laura Bassi became the first woman to teach in a European university, at Bologna. In the Netherlands, women founded a scientific academy in 1785. However, these were isolated waves in a sea of largely clerical indifference.

Generally, Protestant countries were better at ensuring basic literacy and numeracy for boys and probably also for girls. Lutheran Prussia and Presbyterian Scotland excelled in the field of education, but for very different reasons. In Prussia, Frederick the Great decreed universal public education for boys as part of his effort to surpass the level of technical expertise found in other countries. His educational policy was another example of his using the Enlightenment to increase the power of the central government. In Scotland, improvements in education were sponsored mainly by the established Presbyterian (Calvinist) church. The Protestant universities were by and large more progressive intellectually than their Catholic counterparts. The Jesuits, for instance, resisted teaching the new science. By contrast, medicine at the universities of Edinburgh—along with medicine at the University of Leiden in the Netherlands—became the most advanced of the century. But ironically, the universities were never at the forefront of the Enlightenment. For the latest ideas, one went to the salons rather than consulted the professors.

That fact fitted in very well with Locke's doctrine that knowledge comes primarily through experience. Rousseau took it up and brought it to its logical conclusion. In *Émile* (1762), he argued that individuals learn from nature, from people, or from things. Indeed, Rousseau wanted the early years of a child's education to be centered on developing the senses and not spent with the child chained to a schoolroom desk. Later, attention would be paid to intellectual pursuits, and then finally to morality. Rousseau grasped a fundamental principle of modern psychology: the child is not a small adult, and childhood is not merely preparation for adulthood but a particular stage in human development with its own distinguishing characteristics.

Rousseau appealed especially to women to be virtuous and to protect their children from social convention, that is, to teach their children about honesty and sentiment. There were problems with Rousseau's educational system. He would make the family the major educational force, and he wanted the products of such education to be cos-mopolitan and enlightened individuals, singularly free from superstition and prejudice. However, women (whom Rousseau would confine to the home) were to bear the burden of instilling enlightenment, although they had little experience of the world beyond the family, and in France their education was entirely in the hands of nuns.

Rousseau's contradictions, particularly about women, sprang in large measure from his desperate search for an alternative to aristocratic mores and clerical authority. He also shared in the gender bias of his age, although what may seem bias to us may also have reflected his belief that women sought the home as a solace and refuge. Certainly, many women read him critically, but essentially as an ally and defender.

Humanitarianism

Crime and Punishment. No society founded on the principles of the Enlightenment could condone the torture of prisoners and the inhumanity of a corrupt legal system. On those points, all the philosophes were clear, and they had plenty of evidence from their own societies on which to base their condemnation of torture and the inhumanity of the criminal justice system.

Whether an individual was imprisoned for unpaid debts or for banditry or murder, prison conditions differed little. Prisoners were often starved or exposed to disease, or both. In many continental European countries, where torture was still legal, prisoners could be subjected to brutal interrogation or to random punishment. In 1777, English reformer John Howard published a report in England and Wales that documented how prisoners went without food or medical assistance.

It was the reformers of the Enlightenment who began to agitate against the prison conditions of the day. Even if torture was illegal, as was the case only in England, prison conditions were often as harmful as torture to the physical and mental health of inmates. Conditions still present in some prisons today would have been intolerable to the philosophe-reformers.

Although there is something particularly reprehensible about the torturer, his skills were consciously applauded in many countries during the eighteenth century. Fittingly, the most powerful critique of the European system of punishment

THE INQUISITION. In one of the first histories of all the world's religions (published in 1723) the engraver, Bernard Picart, depicted the Inquisition as cold and ruthlessly interrogating (top panel), then as barbarous in its use of torture. (*Bibliothèque des Arts Decoratifs, Paris, France/Archives Charmet/ Bridgeman Art Library.*)

came from Italy, where the Inquisition and its torture chambers had reigned with little opposition for centuries. In Milan, during the early 1760s, the Enlightenment had made very gradual inroads, and in a small circle of reformers the practices of the Inquisition and the relationship between church and state in the matter of criminal justice were avidly discussed.

Out of that intellectual ferment came one of the most important books of the Enlightenment: *Of Crime and Punishment* (1764), by the Milanese reformer Cesare Beccaria (1738–1794). For centuries, sin and crime had been wedded in

the eyes of the church; the function of the state was to punish crime because it was a manifestation of sin. Beccaria cut through that thicket of moralizing. He argued that the church should concern itself with sin and should abandon its prisons and courts. Instead, the state should concern itself with crimes against society, and the purpose of punishment should be to reintegrate the individual into society. Punishment should be swift but intended to rehabilitate.

Beccaria also inquired into the causes of crime. Abandoning the concept of sin, Beccaria, rather like Rousseau, who perceived injustice and corruption in the very fabric of society, regarded private property as the root of social injustice and hence the root of crime. Pointedly, he asked, "What are these laws I must respect, that they leave such a huge gap between me and the rich? Who made these laws? Rich and powerful men. . . . Let us break these fatal connections. . . . let us attack injustice at its source."[7]

Beccaria's attackers labeled him a *socialist*— the first time (1765) that term was used—by which they meant that Beccaria paid attention only to people as social creatures and that he wanted a society of free and equal citizens. In contrast, the defenders of the use of torture and capital punishment, and of the necessity of social inequality, argued that Beccaria's teachings would lead to chaos and to the loss of all property rights and legitimate authority. These critics sensed the utopian aspect of Beccaria's thought. His humanitarianism was not directed toward the reform of the criminal justice system alone; he sought to restructure society in such a way as to render crime far less prevalent and, whenever possible, to reeducate its perpetrators.

When Beccaria's book and then the author himself turned up in Paris, the philosophes greeted them with universal acclaim. All the leaders of the period—Voltaire, Rousseau, Denis Diderot, and the atheist d'Holbach—embraced one or another of Beccaria's views. But if the criminal justice system and the schools were subject to scrutiny by enlightened critics, what did the philosophes have to say about slavery, the most pernicious of all Western institutions?

Slavery. On both sides of the Atlantic during the eighteenth century, criticism of slavery was growing. At first, it came from religious thinkers like the Quakers, whose own religious version of enlightenment predated the European-wide phenomenon by several decades. The Quakers were born out of the turmoil of the English Revolution, and their strong adherence to democratic ideas grew out of their conviction that the light of God's truth works in every man and woman. Many philosophes on both sides of the Atlantic knew Quaker thought, and Voltaire, who had mixed feelings about slavery, and Benjamin Franklin, who condemned it, admired the Quakers and their principles.

On the problem of slavery, some philosophes were strangely ambivalent. In an ideal world— just about all agreed—slavery would not exist. But the world was not ideal, and given human wickedness, greed, and lust for power, Voltaire thought that both slavery and exploitation might be inevitable. "The human race," Voltaire wrote in his *Philosophical Dictionary* (1764), "constituted as it is, cannot subsist unless there be an infinite number of useful individuals possessed of no property at all."[8] Diderot thought that slavery was probably immoral but concluded that, given the importance of slavery in the colonies and the fact that the French monarchy provided no leadership in changing the situation, there was no point in trying to abolish slavery at the time. Indeed, not until 1794, and only after agonized debate, did the French government, no longer a monarchy, finally abolish slavery in its colonies.

It must be remembered that political thinkers of the Enlightenment, among them Locke (who condoned slavery) and Montesquieu (whose ideas were used to condone it), rejected God-given political authority and argued for the rights of property holders and for social utility as the foundations of good government. Those criteria, property and utility, played right into the hands of the proslavery apologists. Montesquieu condemned slavery, but that did not stop its apologists from using his ideas about the relationship between hot climates and sloth to justify making Africans slaves. Even radicals inspired by the French Revolution, like the British manufacturer Thomas Cooper, could emigrate and become slave owners and apologists for the system.

Yet if the principle held, as so many philosophes argued, that human happiness was the greatest good, how could slavery be justified? In his short novel *Candide,* Voltaire has his title character confront the spectacle of a young African slave who has had his leg and arm cut off merely because it is the custom of a country. Candide's philosophical optimism is shattered as he reflects on the human price paid by this slave, who harvested the sugar that Europeans enjoyed so abundantly. Throughout the eighteenth century, the emphasis placed by the Enlightenment on moral sensibility produced a literature that used shock to emphasize over and over again, and with genuine revulsion, the inhumanity of slavery.

By the second half of the century, a new generation of philosophes launched strongly worded attacks on slavery. With Rousseau in the vanguard, they condemned slavery as a violation of the natural rights of man. The philosophes invented the concept of *human rights.* In a volume issued in 1755, the great *Encyclopedia* of the Enlightenment, edited by Diderot, condemned slavery in no uncertain terms: "There is not a single one of these hapless souls . . . who does not have the right to be declared free . . . since neither his ruler nor his father nor anyone else had the right to dispose of his freedom."[9] That statement appeared in thousands of copies and various editions of an encyclopedia that was probably the most influential publication resulting from the French Enlightenment. Indeed, French writers led the enlightened attacks on slavery. The Dutch novelist Betje Wolff had to translate French writers when, in 1790, she launched her attack on the Dutch slave trade.

These writers tipped the scales to put the followers of the Enlightenment in the antislavery camp. But that victory was clouded by ambiguous language coming straight from the pens of some of Europe's supposedly most enlightened thinkers and by their prejudice against blacks as non-Europeans.

Social Equality. The humanitarian impulse inevitably entailed taking a cold, hard look at social inequalities, which were very obvious in a century when dress, speech, body gestures, and even smell told all. The poor were visibly underfed; workers wore the costumes of their trade; aristocrats, both men and women, dressed in elaborate wigs, shoes, silks, jewels, and lace. Devout Calvinist women often wore black, and only their rings or headpieces betrayed their social status. How could the ideal of human equality be conceptualized in such a society?

Voltaire despised the lower classes. Kant said that women should feel and not reason: "her philosophy is not to reason, but to sense."[10] Women had few property rights, and the poor had even fewer; the Lockean contract seemed irrelevant to their circumstances. Yet in the American and French Revolutions, the leaders proclaimed human equality as an ideal. But though France freed the slaves in the colonies, the Jacobins closed down women's political clubs. In the new American republic, women began to take a more active role in civil society; slavery, however, remained (yet in every northern state, it was abolished by 1804). Modern critics condemn the Enlightenment for being inconsistent, but historical reality can be understood only in relation to the backward alternatives offered by absolute monarchs and established churches.

More than any other previous historical movement, the Enlightenment put human equality on the mental agenda of Western societies. Men and women could meet as equals at social gatherings, the new novels could depict the suffering of women at the hands of brutal men or describe the wretched life of the poor, women could travel abroad as never before, and traveling scientific lecturers frequently sought their tuition. Leisure, literacy, public and secular culture, fiery journalism, local newspapers, travelers' reports, even the new and naughty pornography, all attacked the superstitions and contradictions that centuries of custom had enshrined. The new science pointed to a universe where matter was everywhere the same—the atoms are all equal—and it universally obeyed impersonal and impartial laws. The struggle to achieve democratic equality—the dilemma of modern life—first came to the surface in countless acts of reading and conversing in the new enlightened and urban culture. It continues to this day.

ECONOMIC THOUGHT

The Enlightenment's emphasis on property as the foundation for individual rights and its search for uniform laws inspired by Newton's scientific achievement led to the development of the science of economics. Appropriately, that intellectual achievement occurred in the most advanced capitalistic nation in Europe, Great Britain. Not only were the British in the vanguard of capitalist expansion, but by the third quarter of the eighteenth century, that expansion had started the Industrial Revolution. Britain's new factories and markets for the manufacture and distribution of goods provided a natural laboratory where theorists schooled in the Enlightenment's insistence on observation and experimentation could watch the ebb and flow of capitalist production and distribution. In contrast to its harsh criticisms of existing institutions and old elites, the Enlightenment on the whole approved of the independent businessman—the entrepreneur. And there was no one more approving than Adam Smith (1732–1790), whose *Wealth of Nations* (1776) became a kind of bible for those who regarded capitalist activity as uniformly worthwhile and never to be inhibited by outside regulation.

Throughout the seventeenth century in England, there had been a long tradition of economic thought. The resulting ideology stressed independent initiative and the freedom of market forces to determine the value of money and the goods it can buy. By 1700, English economic thought was already well ahead of what could be found on the Continent, with the exception of some Dutch writings. That sophistication undoubtedly reflected the complexity of market life in cities like London and Amsterdam.

One important element in seventeenth-century economic thought, as well as in the most advanced thinking on ethics, was the role of self-interest. Far from being considered crude or socially dangerous, it was seen as a good thing, to be cautiously accepted. In the mid-seventeenth century, Hobbes took the view that self-interest lay at the root of political action. By the end of the century, Locke argued that government, rather than primarily restraining the extremes of human greed and the search for power, should promote the interests of its citizens. By the middle of the eighteenth century, enlightened theorists all over Europe—especially in England, Scotland, and France—had decided that self-interest was the foundation of all human actions and that at every turn government should aid people in

PORTRAIT OF ADAM SMITH. Portrayed here in the dress and style of a good middle-class citizen, Smith praised the freedom to trade and the wealth it brought both to nations and citizens whom he expected to act with restraint and sympathy toward others. (*The Granger Collection.*)

expressing their interests and thus in finding true happiness.

Of course, in the area of economic life, government had for centuries regulated most aspects of the market. The classic economic theory behind such regulation was mercantilism. Mercantilists believed that a constant shortage of riches—bullion, goods, whatever—existed and that governments must so direct economic activity in their states as to compete successfully with other nations for a share of the world's scarce resources.

It required faith in the inherent usefulness of self-interest to assert that government should cease regulating economic activity and that the market should be allowed to be free. The doctrine of **laissez faire**—leaving the market to its own devices—was the centerpiece of Adam Smith's

massive economic study on the origins of the wealth of nations.

As a professor in Glasgow, Scotland, Smith actually went to factories to observe the work. He was one of the first theorists to see the importance of the division of labor in making possible the manufacture of more and cheaper consumer goods. Smith viewed labor as the critical factor in a capitalist economy: the value of money, or of an individual for that matter, rested on the ability to buy labor or the byproducts of labor, namely goods and services. According to *The Wealth of Nations*, "labor is the real measure of the exchangeable value of all commodities."[11] The value of labor is in turn determined by market forces, by supply and demand. Before the invention of money or capital, labor belonged to the laborer, but in the money and market society, which had evolved since the Middle Ages, labor belonged to the highest bidder.

Smith was not bothered by the apparent randomness of market forces, although he was distressed by signs of greed and exploitation. Beneath the superficial chaos of commerce, he saw order—the same order that he saw in physical nature through his understanding of the new science. He used the metaphor of "the invisible hand" to explain the source of this order; by that he probably meant Newton's regulatory God, made very distant by Smith, who was a deist. That hand would invisibly reconcile self-interest to the common or public interest. With the image of the invisible hand, Smith expressed his faith in the rationality of commercial society and laid the first principle for the modern science of capitalist economics. He did not mean to license the oppression of the poor and the laborer. Statements in *The Wealth of Nations* such as "Landlords, like all other men, love to reap where they never sowed" or "Whenever there is great property, there is great inequality"[12] reveal Smith to be a moralist. Yet he knew of no means to stop the exploitation of labor. He believed that its purchase at market value ensured the working of commercial society, and he assumed that the supply of cheap labor was inexhaustible.

For all their differences, Smith and the French physiocrats shared certain characteristics common to enlightened economic theorists. Smith wanted to find the laws that regulated economic life; in that search they imitated the successes of the new science. In addition, they believed that progress was possible and that wealth and well-being could be increased for all. Knowledge is progressive; hence, by implication, the human condition also yields to constant improvement. This vision sometimes made the advocates of laissez faire myopic when it came to poverty and the injustice of the market. What they bequeathed to the modern age was a belief in the inevitability of progress wedded to capitalism and free trade—a belief that remains powerful to this day.

Online Study Center

Improve Your Grade
Primary Source: The Wealth of Nations: A
Natural Law of Economy (Adam Smith)

THE HIGH ENLIGHTENMENT

More than any other political system in western Europe, the Old Regime in France was directly threatened by the doctrines and reforming impulse of the Enlightenment. The Roman Catholic church was deeply entrenched in every aspect of life: landownership, control over the universities and the presses, and access to both the court and, through the pulpit, the people. For decades the church had brought its influence to bear against the philosophes, yet by 1750, the Enlightenment had penetrated learned circles and academies in Paris and the provinces. After 1750, censorship of the press was relaxed by a new censor deeply influenced by Enlightenment ideals. In fact, censorship had produced the opposite of the desired effect: the more irreligious and atheistic the book or manuscript, the more attractive and sought after it became.

By the 1740s, the fashion among proponents of the Enlightenment was to seek an encyclopedic format for presenting their ideas. After Bayle's *Dictionary,* the first successful encyclopedia was published in England by Ephraim Chambers in 1728, and before too long, a plan was under way for its translation into French. A leading Freemason in France, the chevalier Ramsay, advocated that all the Masonic lodges in Europe should make a financial contribution to this effort, but few, if any, responded to the call.

Four aggressive Parisian publishers took up the task of producing the encyclopedia. One of them had had some shady dealings in clandestine literature, which had acquainted him with the more irreligious and daring philosophes in Paris. Hence he knew the young Denis Diderot (1713–1784), who had spent six months in jail for his philosophical and pornographic writings. Out of that consortium of publishers and philosophes came the most important book of the Enlightenment, Diderot's *Encyclopedia.* Published in 1751 and in succeeding years and editions, the *Encyclopedia* initiated a new stage in the history of Enlightenment publishing. In the process, it brought to the forefront heretical ideas, which, until that time, only the most radical freethinkers in England and the Netherlands had openly written about. The new era thus ushered in, called the *High Enlightenment,* was characterized by a violent attack on the church's privileges and the very foundations of Christian belief. From the 1750s to the 1780s, Paris shone as the capital of the Enlightenment. The philosophes were no longer a persecuted minority. Instead, they became cultural heroes. The *Encyclopedia* had to be read by anyone claiming to be educated.

In his preface to the *Encyclopedia,* Diderot's collaborator, Jean D'Alembert (c. 1717–1783), summed up the principles on which it had been compiled. In effect, he wrote a powerful summation of the Enlightenment's highest ideals. He also extolled Newton's science and gave a short description of its universal laws. The progress of geometry and mechanics in combination, d'Alembert wrote in his preface, "may be considered the most incontestable monument of the success to which the human mind can rise by its efforts."[13] In turn, he urged that revealed religion be reduced to a few precepts to be practiced; religion should, he implied, be made scientific and rational. The *Encyclopedia* itself explicitly followed Francis Bacon's admonition that the scientist should first of all be a collector of facts; in addition, it gave dozens of examples of useful new mechanical devices.

D'Alembert in the preface also praised the epistemology of Locke: all that is known, is known through the senses. He declared that all learning should be catalogued and readily available, that the printing press should enlighten, and that literary societies should encourage men of

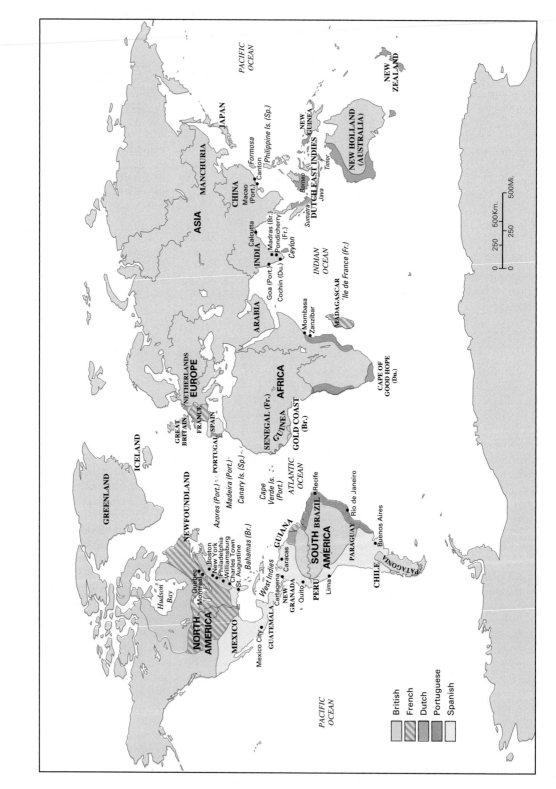

PACIFIC
OCEAN

NEW
ZEALAND

JAPAN

ASIA

MANCHURIA

NEW HOLLAND
(AUSTRALIA)

CHINA

Formosa

Macao
(Port.) •Canton

Philippine Is. (Sp.)

NEW
GUINEA

Madras (Br.)

INDIA •Calcutta
Goa (Port.)• •Pondicherry
(Fr.)
Cochin (Du.)• *Ceylon*

Borneo

DUTCH EAST INDIES

Sumatra *Java* *Timor*

*INDIAN
OCEAN*

MADAGASCAR

Ile de France (Fr.)

ARABIA

•Mombasa
Zanzibar

CAPE OF
GOOD HOPE
(Du.)

NETHERLANDS

EUROPE

AFRICA

GREAT
BRITAIN

FRANCE SPAIN

SENEGAL (Fr.)

GUINEA

GOLD COAST
(Br.)

PORTUGAL

Azores (Port.) *Madeira (Port.)*

Canary Is. (Sp.)

*ATLANTIC
OCEAN*

*Cape
Verde Is.
(Port.)*

ICELAND

GREENLAND

NEWFOUNDLAND

*Hudson
Bay*

NORTH
AMERICA

•Quebec
•Montreal

•Boston
•New York
•Philadelphia
•Williamsburg
•Charles Town
•St. Augustine

Bahamas (Br.)

West Indies

•Cartagena
NEW
GRANADA

•Caracas

GUIANA

BRAZIL •Recife

Rio de Janeiro•

SOUTH
AMERICA

PARAGUAY

Buenos Aires•

MEXICO

GUATEMALA

Mexico City•

•Quito

PERU

•Lima

CHILE

PATAGONIA

PACIFIC
OCEAN

500Km.
250 500Mi.
250
0   0

British
French
Dutch
Portuguese
Spanish

426

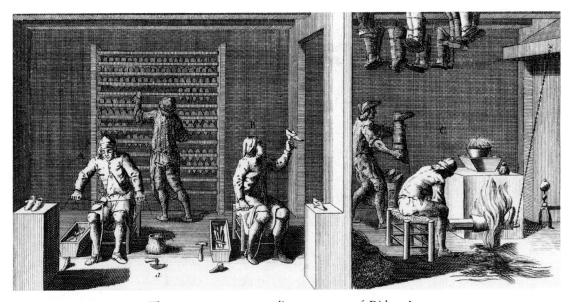

DIDEROT AND ARTISANS. There are many extraordinary aspects of Diderot's great *Encyclopedia.* Among the most noted are the quality and precision of the engravings that depict workers at their crafts. To this day the volumes remain important sources for knowledge about every craft of the age. (*Corbis.*)

talent. These societies, he added, "should banish all inequalities that might exclude or discourage men who are endowed with talents that will enlighten others."[14]

During the High Enlightenment, reformers dwelled increasingly on the Old Regime's inequalities, which seemed to stifle men of talent. The aristocracy and the clergy were not always talented, and seldom were they agitators for enlightenment and reform. Their privileges seemed increasingly less rational. By the 1780s, Paris had produced a new generation of philosophes, for whom Voltaire, Diderot, and Rousseau were aged or dead heroes. But these young authors found the life of the propagandist to be poor and solitary, and they looked at society's ills as victims rather than as reformers. They gained firsthand knowledge of the injustices catalogued so brilliantly by Rousseau in *The Social Contract.*

◀ *MAP 18.1* EUROPEAN EXPANSION, 1715 Globalization as a process began in the eighteenth century with European trade, exploration, and colonization.

The High Enlightenment's systematic, sustained, and occasionally violent attacks on the clergy and the irrationality of privilege link that movement with the French Revolution. The link did not lie in the comfortable heresies of the great philosophes, ensconced as they were in the fashionable Parisian salons. Rather, it was to be found in the way those heresies were interpreted by a new generation of reformers—Marat and Robespierre among them—who in the early days of the Revolution used the Enlightenment as a mirror on which they reflected the evils of the Old Order.

EUROPEAN POLITICAL AND DIPLOMATIC DEVELOPMENTS

Warfare

The dreams of the philosophes seemed unable to forestall imperial developments in power politics, war, and diplomacy. The century was dominated by two areas of extreme conflict: Anglo-French rivalry over control of territory in the New World and hegemony in northern Europe; and intense rivalry between Austria and Prussia over control of central Europe. These major powers, with their imperialistic ambitions, were led by cadres of aristocratic ministers or generals. The Enlightenment did little to displace the war-making role that had belonged to the aristocracy since the Middle Ages. In Berlin some philosophes enjoyed the brilliance of court life and turned a blind eye to Prussian militarism.

France and England were the great rivals in the New World, although colonization had been well under way since the early sixteenth century. Spain had been the first sovereign state to establish an empire in America; located principally in South America and Central America, this empire was based on mining gold and silver, trade, and slaves. The English and the Dutch had followed, first as settlers and then also as slave traders, but their colonies lay to the north—in Virginia, New Amsterdam (later to become New York), and New England. Farther north, the French explored and exploited Canada and the region now known as the midwestern United States. Early in the eighteenth century, the Dutch and the Spanish had largely dropped out of the race for colonies in North America, leaving the field to the French and the English.

By the middle of the eighteenth century, the rivalry of these two powers for territory in the New World increased tension in the Old World. Earlier, the British had sought to contain the French colossus and ensure their historic trading interests in the Low Countries and the Rhineland by allying themselves with the Dutch Republic and the Austrians, who controlled what is today called Belgium. The alliance of the Maritime Powers (Britain and the Netherlands) with Austria tilted the balance of power against France for the entire first half of the eighteenth century.

Meanwhile, Prussia under Frederick the Great was entering the ranks of the major powers. In 1740, Frederick launched an aggressive foreign policy against neighboring states and ruthlessly seized the Austrian province of Silesia. The forces of the new Austrian queen, Maria Theresa, were powerless to resist this kind of military onslaught. Silesia augmented the Prussian population by 50 percent. The Austrians never forgave his transgression.

In 1756, Maria Theresa formed an alliance with France against Prussia; the ensuing Seven Years' War (1756–1763) involved every major European power. Austria's alliance with France in 1756, which ended the historic rivalry between France and the House of Hapsburg, is known as the "diplomatic revolution." The Austrians had grown to fear Prussia in the north more than they feared the French. From the Austrian point of view, Prussia had stolen Silesia in 1740, and regaining it was more important than preserving historic rivalries with France. On the French side, King Louis XV longed for an alliance with a Roman Catholic power and for peace in Europe so that France would be better able to wage war against Britain in the New World.

For their part, the British sought an ally in the newer, stronger Prussia, and reneged on their traditional ally, Austria. Frederick the Great stood at the head of a new state that was highly belligerent yet insecure, for all the European powers had reasons to want to keep Prussia weak and small. The Seven Years' War—which seesawed between the opponents, with French, Austrian, and Russian forces ranged against Frederick's Prussians—changed things little in Europe but did reveal the extraordinary power of the Prussian war machine. Prussia joined the ranks of the Great Powers.

Hostilities in North America tipped the balance of power there in favor of the English. From 1754 to 1763, the French and the English fought over their claims in the New World. England's victory in this conflict—which was also part of the Seven Years' War—led ultimately to the American Revolution. England secured its claim to control the colonies of the eastern seaboard, a market that would enrich its industrialists of the next generation enormously—though, from the colonists' point of view, unjustly.

While the major western European powers were growing stronger, some eastern European countries were falling further under the domination of the Ottoman (Turkish) Empire as the result of warfare. Only Hungary decidedly benefited from the wars led by Austria against the Turks. With its new independence finally secured from the Turks in 1718, Hungary entered an era of peace and enlightenment.

Empires and nation-states were the beneficiaries of eighteenth-century war and diplomacy.

Only in the Dutch Republic did a little-noticed revolution in 1747–48 provide any indication that the Great Powers or the merchant capitalists had anything to fear from their home populations. The Dutch Revolution was led by men who identified with the Enlightenment and who wanted to reform the institutions of government. Inspired by the restoration of the House of Orange, Amsterdam rose in a democratic rebellion headed by a coalition of small merchants and minor philosophes. In 1748 they failed to effect any meaningful changes, but the calls they made for reform and renewal would be heard again in Amsterdam in 1787 and in Paris in 1789. On the latter occasion, the world would listen. For most of the eighteenth century, however, warfare seemed only to confirm the internal security and stability of the ruling monarchs and elites controlling most European states.

Enlightened Despotism

Enlightened despotism, an apparent contradiction in terms, was used as a phrase by the French philosophe Diderot as early as the 1760s. Wherever the philosophes used this phrase, it referred to an ideal shared by many of them: the strong monarch who would implement rational reforms, removing obstacles to freedom, ending book censorship, and allowing the laws of nature to work, particularly in trade and commerce. When historians use the term *enlightened despotism,* they generally are describing the reigns of specific European monarchs and their ministers: Frederick the Great in Prussia; Catherine the Great in Russia; Charles III in Spain; Maria Theresa and, to a greater extent, her son Joseph II in Austria; and Louis XV in France.

These eighteenth-century monarchs instituted specific reforms in education, trade, and commerce and against the clergy. This type of enlightened government must be understood in context: these countries developed late relative to the older states of Europe. Prussia, Austria, and Russia had to move very quickly if they were to catch up to the degree of centralization achieved in England and France. And when monarchies in France and Spain also occasionally adopted techniques associated with enlightened despotism, they generally

did so to compete against a more advanced rival—for example, France against England and Spain against France.

Austria. In the course of the eighteenth century, Austria became a major centralized state as a result of the administrative reforms of Charles VI and his successors. Though Catholic and devout at home, Charles allied himself abroad with Protestant Europe against France. In the newly acquired Austrian Netherlands, he supported the progressive and reforming elements in the nobility, which opposed the old aristocracy and clergy. His daughter Maria Theresa (1740–1780) continued this pattern, and the Austrian administration became one of the most innovative and progressive on the Continent. Many of its leading ministers, like the Comte du Cobenzl in the Netherlands or Gerard van Swieten, Joseph II's great reforming minister, were Freemasons. This movement often attracted progressive Catholics (as well as Protestants and freethinkers), who despised what they regarded as the medieval outlook of the traditional clergy.

Dynastic consolidation and warfare did contribute decisively to the creation of the Austrian state. But in the eighteenth century, the intellectual and cultural forces of the Enlightenment enabled the state to establish an efficient system of government and a European breadth of vision. With these attributes, Austria came to rival (and, in regard to Spain, surpass) older, more established states in Europe. Frustrated in their German territories, the Austrian Hapsburgs concentrated their attention increasingly on their eastern states. Vienna gave them a natural power base, and Catholic religiosity gradually united the ruling elites in Bohemia and Hungary with their Hapsburg kings. Hapsburg power created a dynastic state in Austria, yet all efforts to consolidate the German part of the empire and to establish effective imperial rule met with failure. Also problematic were Joseph II's interventions in the southern Netherlands. He offended the clergy without winning liberal support. Revolution erupted in Brussels in 1787.

Prussia. German unification proceeded very slowly, and even enlightened despotism could not achieve it. Under the most famous and enlightened

Hohenzollerns of the eighteenth century, Prussian absolutism acquired some unique and resilient features. Frederick II, the Great (1740–1786), pursued a policy of religious toleration and, in so doing, attracted French Protestant refugees, who had manufacturing and commercial skills. Intellectual dissidents, such as Voltaire, were also attracted to Prussia. Voltaire eventually went home disillusioned with this new Prussian "enlightened despotism," but not before Frederick had used him and in the process acquired a reputation for learning. By inviting various refugees from French clerical oppression, Frederick gave Berlin a minor reputation as a center for Enlightenment culture. But alongside Frederick's courtship of the French philosophes, with their enlightened ideals, there remained the reality of Prussia's militarism and the serfdom of its peasants.

Enlightened despotism was, in reality, the use of Enlightenment principles by monarchs to enhance the central government's power and thereby their own. These eighteenth-century monarchs knew, in ways their predecessors had not, that knowledge is power; they saw that application of learned theories to policy can produce useful results.

But did these enlightened despots try to create more humanitarian societies in which individual freedom would flourish on all levels? In this area, enlightened despotism must be pronounced a shallow deployment of Enlightenment ideals. For example, Frederick the Great decreed the abolition of serfdom in Prussia, but he had no means to force the aristocracy to conform because he desperately needed their support. In the 1780s, Joseph II instituted liberalized publishing laws in Austria; but when artisans began reading pamphlets about the French Revolution, the state quickly retreated and reimposed censorship. In the 1750s, Frederick the Great too had loosened the censorship laws, and writers were free to attack traditional religion; however, they were never allowed to criticize the army, the key to Frederick's aggressive foreign policy. Although Catherine the Great gave Diderot a pension, she would hear of nothing that compromised her political power, and her ministers were expected to give her unquestioning service.

Finally, if the Enlightenment means the endorsement of reason over force, and peace and cosmopolitan unity over ruthless competition, then the foreign policies of these enlightened despots were uniformly despotic. There were no major philosophes who did not grow disillusioned with enlightened monarchs on the rare occasions when their actions could be observed at close range.

THE ENLIGHTENMENT IN EASTERN EUROPE

The impact of the Enlightenment in the countries of eastern Europe varied enormously. Where it made greatest inroads, we see the subsequent emergence of discernibly modern social and political ideas and aspirations. In Hungary, for example, independence from the Ottoman Empire in 1718 left a country that was still essentially feudal yet eager for reform and renewal. In the 1720s, peace brought regeneration. The population doubled in the course of the eighteenth century; agricultural techniques markedly improved; and by midcentury, schools and universities had begun to teach the new science. Hungarian Protestants who had traveled and studied abroad came home with the ideas of the philosophes. A lay intelligentsia was created, and with it came new literature and drama, as well as Western-style civil society: lodges, salons, clubs, and societies. By 1790, the Enlightenment and the French Revolution had inspired a movement for Hungarian nationalism and against the control of the Austrians and Hapsburgs. Then in 1795, its leaders were executed. However, their nationalistic ideals survived well into the nineteenth and twentieth centuries.

In Poland and Lithuania, the influence of the Jesuits remained strong even after they were expelled from other eastern European countries, such as Hungary. In Poland, the Catholic clergy continued to control education, and the Enlightenment remained a deeply censored, almost un-

MAP 18.2 EUROPE, 1789 ▶
The Hapsburgs had vast holdings, and this situation did not make the other German states feel secure. This entire map would change after 1800 as Napoleon swept through Europe.

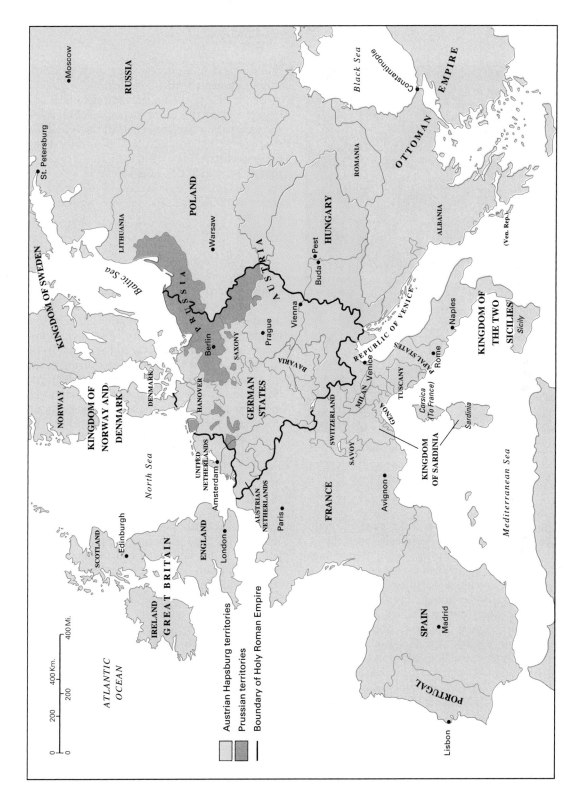

Austrian Hapsburg territories
Prussian territories
Boundary of Holy Roman Empire

CATHERINE THE GREAT. Catherine the Great adorned herself to show her aristocracy that she was its superior. (*The Luton Hoo Foundation.*)

derground movement. Yet it did exist and influence educational reform, especially after the expulsion of the Jesuits in 1773. Those who advocated the Enlightenment allied themselves with the monarchy, which they saw as the only force that might be strong enough to oppose the entrenched clergy and aristocracy. The power of the Polish nobility had dire historical consequences for the country. No central authority emerged in eighteenth-century Poland comparable in its unifying ability to the monarchs of Prussia, Austria, and Russia. Not once but three times, in 1772, 1793, and 1795, Poland was partitioned by these three potent neighbors, who took portions of it. Some Poles resisted; a Polish nobleman even appealed to Rousseau in 1771 to help draft a constitution for his beleaguered country. The document in which Rousseau expressed his thoughts on Polish government was

cautious and judicious, giving power to all the various elements within Polish elite society.

The failure of the Enlightenment to take hold in parts of eastern Europe had far-reaching consequences, with which the people of those countries continue to grapple. In the 1990s, those countries—such as Hungary and the Czech Republic—that experienced the Enlightenment seemed to show the greatest cohesiveness in the struggle to create a unified, secular, tolerant, and independent state.

THE AMERICAN REVOLUTION

England's victory over France in the Seven Years' War set in motion a train of events that culminated in the American Revolution. The war drained the British treasury, and now Britain faced the additional expense of paying for troops to guard the new North American territories that it had gained in the war. Strapped British taxpayers could not shoulder the whole burden, so the members of Parliament thought it quite appropriate that American colonists should help to pay the bill; they reasoned that Britain had protected the colonists from the French and was still protecting them in their conflicts with Indians. Thus, new colonial taxes and import duties were imposed. Particularly galling to the colonists were the Stamp Act (which placed a tax on newspapers, playing cards, liquor licenses, and legal documents) and the Quartering Act (which required colonists to provide living quarters and supplies to English troops stationed in America).

Vigorous colonial protest compelled the British Parliament to repeal the Stamp Act, but new taxes were imposed, raising the price of many everyday articles, including tea. The stationing of British troops in Boston, the center of rebelliousness, worsened tensions. In March 1770, a crisis ensued after a squad of British soldiers fired into a crowd of Bostonians who had been taunting them and pelting them with rocks and snowballs. Five Bostonians died, and six were wounded. A greater crisis occurred in 1773, when Parliament granted the East India Company exclusive rights to sell tea in America. The colonists regarded this as yet another example of British tyranny. When a crowd of Bostonians

THE BOSTON TEA PARTY. The engraver chose to depict free blacks as well as whites applauding one of the early acts that led to the American Revolution. (*AKG, London.*)

dressed as Indians climbed aboard East Indian ships and dumped about ninety thousand pounds of tea overboard, the British responded with a series of repressive measures, which included suppressing self-government in Massachusetts and closing the port of Boston.

The quarrel turned to bloodshed in April and June 1775. On July 4, 1776, delegates from the thirteen colonies adopted the Declaration of Independence, written mainly by the philosophe Thomas Jefferson. Applying Locke's theory of natural rights, this document declared that

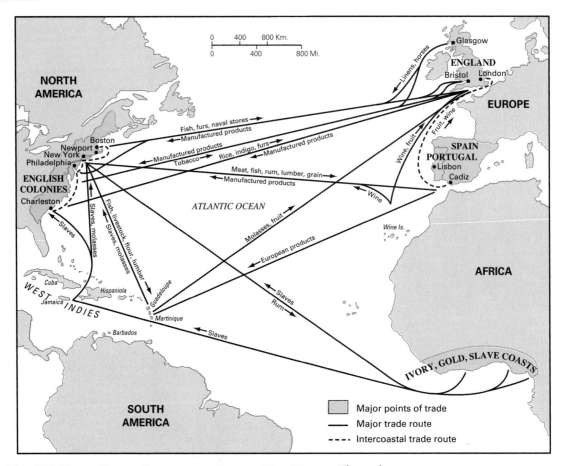

MAP 18.3 TRADE ROUTES BETWEEN THE OLD AND NEW WORLDS The trade
routes of the eighteenth century foreshadow the globalization of trade with
which we are familar.

government derives its power from the consent of
the governed, that it is the duty of a government to
protect the rights of its citizens, and that people
have the right to "alter or abolish" a government
that deprives them of their "unalienable rights."

Why were the American colonists so ready to
revolt? For one thing, they had brought to North
America a highly idealized understanding of English liberties. Long before 1776, they had extended representative institutions to include small
property owners who probably could not have
voted in England. The colonists had come to expect representative government, trial by jury, and
protection from unlawful imprisonment. Each of
the thirteen colonies had an elected assembly that
acted like a miniature parliament; in these assemblies, Americans gained political experience and
quickly learned self-government.

Familiarity with the thought of the Enlightenment and the republican writers of the English
Revolution also contributed to the Americans'
awareness of liberty. The ideas of the philosophes
traversed the Atlantic and influenced educated
Americans, particularly Jefferson and Benjamin
Franklin. Like other philosophes, American
thinkers expressed growing confidence in reason,

valued freedom of religion and of thought, and championed the principle of natural rights.

Another source of hostility toward established authority among the American colonists was their religious traditions, particularly Puritanism, which viewed the Bible as infallible and its teachings as a higher law than the law of the state. Like their counterparts in England, American Puritans challenged political and religious authorities who, in their view, contravened God's law. Thus, Puritans acquired two habits that were crucial to the development of political liberty: dissent and resistance. When transferred to the realm of politics, these Puritan tendencies led Americans to resist authority that they considered unjust.

American victory came in 1783 as a result of several factors. George Washington proved to be a superior leader, able to organize and retain the loyalty of his troops. France, seeking to avenge its defeat in the Seven Years' War, helped the Americans with money and provisions and then in 1778 entered the conflict. Britain had difficulty shipping supplies across three thousand miles of ocean, was fighting the French in the West Indies and elsewhere at the same time, and ultimately lacked commitment to the struggle.

Reformers in other lands quickly interpreted the American victory as a successful struggle of liberty against tyranny. During the Revolution, the various former colonies drew up constitutions based on the principle of popular sovereignty and included bills of rights that protected individual liberty. They also managed, somewhat reluctantly, to forge a nation. Rejecting both monarchy and hereditary aristocracy, the Constitution of the United States created a republic in which power derived from the people. A system of separation of powers and checks and balances set safeguards against the abuse of power, and the Bill of Rights provided for protection of individual rights. To be sure, the ideals of liberty and equality were not extended to all people. Slaves knew nothing of the freedom that white Americans cherished, and women were denied the vote and equal opportunity; human equality remained an issue throughout the nineteenth and twentieth centuries. To reform-minded Europeans, however, it seemed that Americans were fulfilling the promise of the Enlightenment. They were creating a freer and better society.

THE ENLIGHTENMENT AND THE MODERN WORLD

Enlightened thought culminated a trend begun by Renaissance humanists, who attacked medieval otherworldliness and gave value to individual achievement and the worldly life. It was a direct outgrowth of the Scientific Revolution, which provided a new method of inquiry and verification and demonstrated the power and self-sufficiency of the human intellect. If nature were autonomous—that is, if it operated according to natural laws that did not require divine intervention—then the human intellect could also be autonomous. Through its own powers, it could uncover the general principles that operate in the social world, as well as in nature.

The philosophes sought to analyze nature, government, religion, law, economics, and education through reason alone, with little reference to Christian teachings, and they rejected completely the claims of clerics to a special wisdom. The philosophes broke decisively with the medieval view that the individual is naturally depraved, that heaven is the true end of life, and that human values and norms derive from a higher reality and are made known through revelation. Instead, they upheld the potential goodness of the individual, regarded the good life on earth as the true purpose of existence, and insisted that individuals could improve themselves and their society by the light of reason.

In addition, the political philosophies of Locke, Montesquieu, and Rousseau were based on an entirely new (and modern) concept of the relationship between the state and the individual: states should exist not simply to accumulate power but also to enhance human happiness. From that perspective, monarchy, and even oligarchy not based on merit, began to seem increasingly less useful. And if happiness is a goal, then it must be assumed that some sort of progress is possible in history.

When we observe societies that have never experienced their own version of enlightenment, we see oftentimes the oppression of women and authoritarian governments sometimes run by clergymen. Religion can turn to intolerance or fanaticism if unchecked by questioning, or even by doubting.

The philosophes wanted a freer, more humane, and more rational society, but they feared the people and their potential for revolutionary action. As an alternative to revolution, most philosophes offered science as the universal improver of the human condition. Faith in reform without the necessity of revolution proved to be a doctrine for the elite of the salons. In that sense, the French Revolution can be said to have repudiated the essential moderation of philosophes like Voltaire, d'Alembert, and Kant.

However, the Enlightenment established a vision of humanity so independent of Christianity and so focused on the needs and abuses of the society of the time that no established institution, once grown corrupt and ineffectual, could long withstand its penetrating critique. To that extent, the writings of the philosophes point toward the democratic revolutions of the late eighteenth century. To a lesser extent, the writers of the Enlightenment also point toward ideals that remain strong in most democratic Western societies: religious toleration, freedom from torture, a disdain for prejudice and superstition, a fear of unchecked political authority, and, of course, a belief in the power of the human mind to recognize the irrational and attempt to correct it.

❖   ❖   ❖

Online Study Center ACE the Test

NOTES

1. "An Answer to the Question: 'What Is Enlightenment?'" in *Kant's Political Writings,* ed. Hans Reiss (Cambridge: Cambridge University Press, 1970), pp. 54–60.
2. *Wetten van het Natuurkundig Genootschap, door eenige Dames opgericht, binnen Middelburg den 6 August. 1785.* (Rules for the Scientific Society established by women within Middelburg on 6 August 1785), Middelburg, [1785], p. 29. The only known copy is to be found in the Provincial Library in Zeeland, the Netherlands.
3. Pierre Bayle, *Historical and Critical Dictionary,* ed. Richard H. Popkin (New York: Bobbs-Merrill, 1965), p. 195.
4. Voltaire, *Philosophical Letters* (New York: Bobbs-Merrill, 1961), p. 22.
5. Thomas Hobbes, *Leviathan,* ed. C. B. Macpherson (Harmondsworth, England: Penguin, 1977), p. 189.
6. Jean Jacques Rousseau, *The Social Contract and Discourses* (New York: Dutton, 1950), pp. 3, 9.
7. Quoted in Franco Venturi, *Utopia and Reform in the Enlightenment* (Cambridge: Cambridge University Press, 1971), p. 101.
8. Voltaire, *Philosophical Dictionary,* ed. Theodore Besterman (Harmondsworth, England: Penguin, 1974), p. 183.
9. Quoted in David B. Davis, *The Problem of Slavery in Western Culture* (Harmondsworth, England: Penguin, 1970), p. 449.
10. Immanuel Kant, *Beobachtungen,* in *Kants Werke,* ed. Dilthey, 2:230, (1900–1919).
11. Adam Smith, *The Wealth of Nations,* ed. George Stigler (New York: Appleton, 1957), p. 3.
12. Ibid., p. 98.
13. Jean Le Rond d'Alembert, *Preliminary Discourse to the Encyclopedia of Diderot,* trans. Richard N. Schwab (New York: Bobbs-Merrill, 1963), p. 22.
14. Ibid., pp. 101–102.

SUGGESTED READING

Hunt, Lynn, ed., *The Invention of Pornography: Obscenity and the Origins of Modernity* (1993). Pornography arose in the late seventeenth century and was tied to social criticism and eventually to the Enlightenment. It was very different then from what it has subsequently become.

———, ed., *Human Rights and the French Revolution* (1997). Shows how people in the eighteenth century arrived at principles that remain revolutionary in many societies today.

Jacob, Margaret, *The Enlightenment: A Brief History*

with Documents (2001). A long introduction precedes selections from Locke, Diderot, and others.

———, *Strangers Nowhere in the World. The Rise of Cosmopolitanism in Early Modern Europe* (2006).

Lukes, Steven, *The Curious Enlightenment of Professor Caritat: A Comedy of Ideas* (1995). A delightful story that makes eighteenth-century ideas accessible and relevant to today's world.

Rosenblatt, Helena, *Rousseau and Geneva* (1997).

Part Four

An Age of Revolution: Liberal, National, Industrial

1789–1848

Politics and Society	Thought and Culture
French Revolution begins (1789) Declaration of the Rights of Man and of the Citizen (1789)	Kant, *Critique of Pure Reason* (1781) Bentham, *Principles of Morals and Legislation* (1789)
France declares war on Austria (1792) Execution of Louis XVI (1793) Reign of Terror (1793–94) Napoleon seizes power (1799)	Burke, *Reflections on the Revolution in France* (1790) Wollstonecraft, *Vindication of the Rights of Woman* (1792) De Maistre, *Reflections on the State of France* (1796) Wordsworth, *Lyrical Ballads* (1798) Malthus, *Essay on the Principle of Population* (1798)
Battle of Trafalgar—French and Spanish fleets defeated by the British (1805) Napoleon defeats Prussians at Jena (1806) Napoleon defeats Russians at Friedland (1807)	Beethoven, Fifth Symphony (1807–08) Goethe, *Faust* (1808, 1832)
Napoleon invades Russia (1812) Napoleon defeated at Waterloo (1815) Congress of Vienna (1814–15)	Byron, *Childe Harold* (1812)
Revolutions in Spain, Italy, Russia, and Greece (1820–1829)	Shelley, *Prometheus Unbound* (1820) Ricardo, *Principles of Political Economy* (1817) Hegel, *The Philosophy of History* (1822–1831)
Revolutions in France, Belgium, Poland, and Italy (1830–32) Reform in Britain: Reform Act of 1832; slavery abolished within British Empire (1833); Factory Act (1833)	Fourier, *Treatise on Agrarian Domestic Fellowship* (1822) Comte, *Course in Positive Philosophy* (1830–1842)
Irish famine (1845–1849) Revolutions in France, Germany, Austria, and Italy (1848)	Proudhon, *What Is Property?* (1840) De Tocqueville, *Democracy in America* (1835–1840) Gaskell, *Mary Barton* (1848) Marx, *Communist Manifesto* (1848)

Chapter 19

The French Revolution: Affirmation of Liberty and Equality

The Storming of the Bastille, July 14, 1789. (AKG, London.)

Focus Questions

1. What were the causes of the French Revolution?
2. How did the Enlightenment and American Revolution influence the French Revolution?
3. Why are the reforms of the National Assembly described as the death warrant of the Old Regime?
4. Why and how did the French Revolution move from a moderate to a radical stage?
5. Why is the French Revolution a decisive period in the shaping of the modern West?

Online Study Center

This icon will direct you to interactive map and primary source activities on the website http://college.hmco.com/pic/perrywc8e.

The outbreak of the French Revolution in 1789 stirred the imagination of Europeans. Both participants and observers sensed that they were living in a pivotal age. On the ruins of the Old Order, founded on privilege and despotism, a new era was forming, and it promised to realize the ideals of the Enlightenment. These ideals included the emancipation of the human personality from superstition and tradition, the triumph of liberty over tyranny, the refashioning of institutions in accordance with reason and justice, and the tearing down of barriers to equality. It seemed that the natural rights of the individual, hitherto a distant ideal, would now become reality, and centuries of oppression and misery would end. Never before had people shown such confidence in the power of human intelligence to shape the conditions of existence. Never before had the future seemed so full of hope.

This lofty vision kindled emotions akin to religious enthusiasm and attracted converts throughout the Western world. "If we succeed," wrote the French poet André Chénier, "the destiny of Europe will be changed. Men will regain their rights and the people their sovereignty."[1] The editor of the Viennese publication *Wiener Zeitung* wrote to a friend: "In France a light is beginning to shine which will benefit the whole of humanity."[2] British reformer John Cartwright expressed the hopes of reformers everywhere: "Degenerate must be that heart which expands not with sentiments of delight at what is now transacting in . . . France. The French . . . are not only asserting their own rights, but they are asserting and advancing the general liberties of mankind."[3]

THE OLD REGIME

Eighteenth-century French society was divided into three orders, or **Estates,** which were legally defined groupings. The clergy constituted the First Estate, the nobility the Second Estate, and everyone else (about 96 percent of the population) the Third Estate. The clergy and nobility, totaling about 500,000 out of a population of 26 million, enjoyed special privileges, receiving pensions and profitable positions from the king. The social structure of the **Old Regime,** based on priv-

Chronology 19.1 ❖ The French Revolution

July 1788	Calling of the Estates General
May 5, 1789	Convening of the Estates General
June 17, 1789	Third Estate declares itself the National Assembly
July 14, 1789	Storming of the Bastille
Late July 1789	The Great Fear
August 4, 1789	Nobles surrender their special privileges
June 1791	Flight of Louis XVI
October 1791	Legislative Assembly succeeds the National Assembly
April 20, 1792	Legislative Assembly declares war on Austria
August 10, 1792	Parisians attack the king's palace
September 1792	September Massacres
September 20, 1792	Battle of Valmy
September 21–22, 1792	Abolition of the monarchy
January 21, 1793	Execution of Louis XVI
June 1793	Jacobins replace Girondins as the dominant group in the National Convention
July 28, 1794	Robespierre is guillotined
1795 and 1796	Failed insurrections by the poor of Paris
September 1797	Royalist coup d'état against the Directory is crushed
November 1799	Napoleon seizes power

ileges and inequalities sanctioned by law, produced tensions that contributed to the Revolution.

The First Estate

The powers and privileges of the French Catholic church made it a state within a state. As it had done for centuries, the church registered births, marriages, and deaths; collected tithes (a tax on products from the soil); censored books considered dangerous to religion and morals; operated schools; and distributed relief to the poor. Since it was illegal for Protestants to assemble publicly for prayer, the Catholic church enjoyed a monopoly on public worship. Although it owned an esti-

mated 10 percent of the land, which brought in an immense revenue, the church paid no taxes. Instead, it made a "free gift" to the state (the church determined the amount), which was always smaller than direct taxes would have been. Critics denounced the church for promoting superstition and obscurantism, impeding reforms, and being more concerned with wealth and power than with the spiritual message of Jesus.

The clergy reflected the social divisions in France. The upper clergy shared the attitudes and way of life of the nobility from which they sprang. The parish priests, commoners by birth, resented the haughtiness and luxurious living of the upper clergy. In 1789, when the Revolution began, many priests sympathized with the reform-minded people of the Third Estate.

The Second Estate

Like the clergy, the nobility was a privileged order. Nobles held the highest positions in the church, army, and government. They were exempt from most taxes (or used their influence to evade taxes), collected manorial dues from peasants, and owned between one-quarter and one-third of the land. In addition to the income they drew from their estates, nobles were becoming increasingly involved in such nonaristocratic enterprises as banking, finance, commerce, and industry. Many key philosophes—Montesquieu, Condorcet, d'Holbach—were nobles, and nobles were the leading patrons of the arts. Most nobles, however, were suspicious and intolerant of the liberal ideas advanced by the philosophes.

All nobles were not equal; there were gradations of dignity among the 350,000 members of the nobility. Enjoying the most prestige were *nobles of the sword:* families that could trace their aristocratic status back several centuries. Many of these noblemen were officers in the king's army. The highest of the ancient nobles were engaged in the social whirl at Versailles and Paris, receiving pensions and sinecures from the king but performing few useful services for the state. Most nobles of the sword, unable to afford the gilded life at court, remained on their provincial estates, the poorest of them barely distinguishable from prosperous peasants.

Alongside this ancient nobility, a new nobility had arisen, created by the monarchy. To obtain money, reward favorites, and weaken the old nobility, French kings had sold titles of nobility to members of the **bourgeoisie** and had conferred noble status on certain government offices bought by wealthy bourgeois. Particularly significant were *nobles of the robe,* who had purchased judicial offices in the parlements—the high law courts—and whose ranks included many former bourgeois.

Opinion among the aristocrats was divided. Influenced by the liberal ideals of the philosophes, some nobles sought to reform France; they wanted to end royal despotism and establish a constitutional government. To this extent, the liberal nobility had a great deal in common with the bourgeoisie. These liberal nobles saw the king's difficulties in 1788 as an opportunity to regenerate the nation under enlightened leadership. When they resisted the king, they claimed that they were attacking despotic rule. But many nobles, concerned with preserving their privileges and honorific status, were hostile to liberal ideals and opposed reform.

The Third Estate

The Third Estate comprised the bourgeoisie, peasants, and urban laborers. Although the bourgeoisie provided the leadership for the Revolution, its success depended on the support given by the rest of the Third Estate.

The Bourgeoisie. The bourgeoisie consisted of merchant-manufacturers, wholesale merchants, bankers, master craftsmen, doctors, lawyers, intellectuals, and government officials below the top ranks. Although the bourgeoisie had wealth, it lacked social prestige. A merchant, despite his worldly success, felt that his occupation denied him the esteem enjoyed by the nobility. "There are few rich people who at times do not feel humiliated at being nothing but wealthy," observed an eighteenth-century Frenchman.[4]

Influenced by the aristocratic values of the day and envious of the nobility's lifestyle, the bourgeoisie sought to erase the stigma of common birth and to rise socially by becoming landowners. By 1789, the bourgeoisie owned about 20 percent of the land. Traditionally, some members of the bourgeoisie had risen socially either by purchasing a judicial or political office that carried with it a title of nobility or by gaining admission to the upper clergy and the officer ranks of the army. Access to the nobility remained open throughout the eighteenth century. Nevertheless, since the highest and most desired positions in the land were reserved for the nobility, able bourgeois were often excluded, for a variety of reasons: the high cost of purchasing an office, the limited number of new offices created, the resistance of nobles to their advancement, or the hostility of the older nobility toward those recently ennobled. No doubt these men felt frustrated and came to resent a social system that valued birth more than talent. For most of the century, however, the bourgeoisie did not challenge the existing social structure, including the special privileges of the nobility.

By 1789, the bourgeois had many grievances. They wanted all positions in church, army, and state to be open to men of talent regardless of birth. They sought a parliament that would make laws for the nation; a constitution that would limit the king's power and guarantee freedom of thought, a fair trial, and religious toleration; and administrative reforms that would eliminate waste, inefficiency, and interference with business.

The Peasantry.   The condition of the more than twenty-one million French peasants was a paradox. On the one hand, they were better off than peasants in Austria, Prussia, Poland, and Russia, where serfdom still predominated. In France, serfdom had largely disappeared; many peasants owned land, and some were even prosperous. But most French peasants lived in poverty, which worsened in the closing years of the Old Regime.

Peasants owned between 30 and 40 percent of the land, but the typical holding was barely large enough to eke out a living. The rising birthrate (between 1715 and 1789, the population may have increased from eighteen million to twenty-six million) led to the continual subdivision of farms among heirs. Moreover, many peasants did not own land but rented it from a nobleman or a prosperous neighbor. Others worked as sharecroppers, turning over to their creditors a considerable portion of the harvest.

Owning too little land to support themselves, many peasants tried to supplement their incomes. They hired themselves out for whatever employment was available in their region: as agricultural day laborers, charcoal burners, transporters of wine, or textile workers in their own homes. Landless peasants tried to earn a living in such ways. The increasing birthrate resulted in an overabundance of rural wage earners. This worsened the plight of small landowners and reduced the landless to beggary. "The number of our children reduces us to desperation,"[5] was a common complaint of the peasants by 1789.

An unjust and corrupt system of taxation weighed heavily on the peasantry. Louis XIV had maintained his grandeur and financed his wars by milking ever more taxes from the peasants, a practice that continued throughout the eighteenth

"Let's Hope That the Game Finishes Well." This political cartoon shows a laboring-class woman carrying smug representatives of the privileged orders on her back. (*Musée de la Ville de Paris.*)

century. An army of tax collectors victimized the peasantry. In addition to royal taxes, peasants paid the tithe to the church and manorial dues to lords.

Although serfdom had ended in most parts of France, lords continued to demand obligations from peasants as they had done in the Middle Ages. Besides performing labor services on the lord's estate, peasants still had to grind their corn in the lord's mill, bake their bread in his oven, press their grapes in his winepress, and give him part of their produce in payment. (Their fees were called *banalities*.) In addition, the lord collected a land rent from peasant proprietors, levied dues on goods at markets and fairs, and exercised exclusive hunting rights on lands tilled by peasants. The last was a particularly onerous right, for the

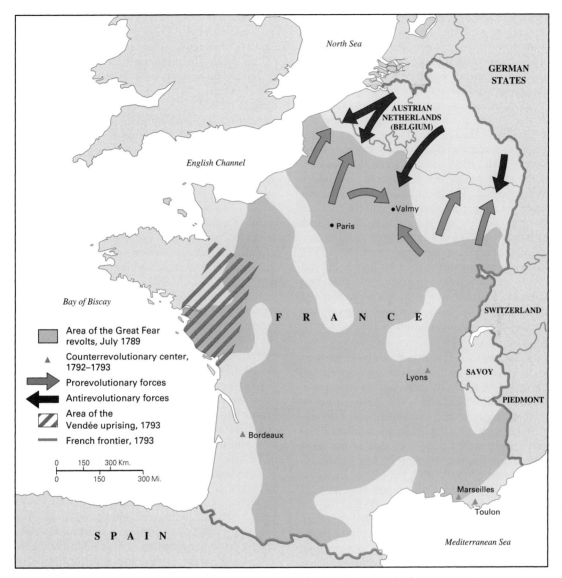

MAP 19.1 THE FRENCH REVOLUTION, 1789–1793 French revolutionaries had to deal with both internal enemies and foreign invasion.

lord's hunting parties damaged crops. Lords were determined to hold on to these privileges, not only because of the income they brought but also because they were symbols of authority and social esteem. The peasants, however, regarded these obligations as hateful legacies of the past from which they derived no benefit.

In the last part of the eighteenth century, lords sought to exact more income from their lands by reviving manorial dues that had not been collected for generations, increasing the rates on existing dues, and contracting businessmen to collect payments from the peasants. These capitalists naturally tried to squeeze as much income as possible from the peasants, making them hate the whole system of manorial obligations even more.

Inefficient farming methods also contributed to the poverty of the French peasants. In the eighteenth century, France did not experience a series of agricultural improvements comparable to those in England. Failure to invest capital in modernizing agricultural methods meant low yields per acre and a shortage of farm animals.

A rise in the price of necessities during the closing years of the Old Regime worked hardship on those peasants who depended on wages for survival. With prices rising faster than wages, only the more prosperous peasants with produce to sell benefited. The great majority of peasants were driven deeper into poverty, and the number of beggars roaming the countryside increased. A poor harvest in 1788–89 aggravated peasant misery and produced an atmosphere of crisis. The granaries were empty; the price of bread, the staple food of the French, soared; and starvation threatened. Hatred of the manorial order and worsening poverty sparked a spontaneous and autonomous peasant revolution in 1789.

Urban Laborers. The urban laboring class in this preindustrial age consisted of journeymen working for master craftsmen, factory workers in small-scale industries, and wage earners such as day laborers, gardeners, handymen, and deliverymen, who were paid by those they served. The poverty of the urban poor, like that of the peasant wage earners, worsened in the late eighteenth century. From 1785 to 1789, the cost of living increased by 62 percent, while wages rose only 22 percent. For virtually the entire decade of the Revolution, urban workers struggled to keep body and soul together in the face of food shortages and rising prices, particularly the price of their staple food, bread. Material want drove the urban poor to acts of violence that affected the course of the Revolution.

Inefficient Administration and Financial Disorder

Eighteenth-century France was in theory an absolute monarchy. The king claimed that his power derived from God, and, unlike Britain, France had no parliament that represented the people and met as a continuous body. The administration of the country was complex, confusing, and ineffective. The practice of buying state offices from the king, introduced as a means of raising money, brought in many incompetent officeholders. "When his Majesty created an office," stated one administrator, "Providence called into being an imbecile to buy it."[6] Tariffs on goods shipped from one French province to another and differing systems of weights and measures hampered trade. No single law code applied to all the provinces; instead, there were overlapping and conflicting law systems based on old Roman law or customary feudal law, which made the administration of justice slow, arbitrary, and unfair. To admirers of the philosophes, the administrative system was an insult to reason. The Revolution would sweep the system away.

Financial disorders also contributed to the weakness of the Old Regime. In the regime's last years, the government could not raise sufficient funds to cover expenses. Servicing the debt incurred during the War of the Austrian Succession (1740–1748) and the Seven Years' War (1756–1763) placed an immense burden on the treasury. This burden reached crisis proportions when France incurred additional expenses by aiding the colonists in the American Revolution. The king's gifts and pensions to court nobles and the extravagant court life further drained the treasury.

Finances were in a shambles, not because France was impoverished but because it had an inefficient and unjust tax system. Few wealthy Frenchmen, including the bourgeois, paid their fair share of taxes. Because tax revenue came chiefly from the peasants, it was bound to be inadequate. Excise duties and indirect taxes on consumer goods yielded much-needed revenue in the last decades of the Old Regime. However, instead of replenishing the royal treasury, these additional funds were pocketed by rich tax collectors, who, for a fixed payment to the state, had obtained the right to collect these indirect taxes. Although serious, the financial crisis could have been solved if the clergy, nobility, and bourgeoisie paid their fair share of taxes. Some progressive ministers recognized the need for comprehensive reforms, but nobles and clergy resisted them, clinging tenaciously to their ancient privileges. The irresolution of the king and the intrigues, rivalries, and incompetence of his ministers also impeded reform.

The nobles were able to thwart royal will mainly through the parlements, the high law courts. Many parlementaires were originally wealthy bourgeois who had purchased their offices from the state (nobles of the robe). Both the office and status of nobility remained within the family. The Paris parlement and twelve provincial parlements reviewed the judgments of lower courts and registered royal edicts. The parlements had the right to *remonstrate,* that is, to pass judgment on the legality of royal edicts before registering them. If the courts considered the king's new laws at variance with previous legislation or ancient traditions, they would refuse to register them. (Generally, it was the Paris parlement that set the example.) The king could revise the edicts in accordance with the parlements' instructions or force their registration by means of a *lit de justice:* a solemn ceremony in which the monarch appeared before the court. If the parlementaires stood firm in their resistance, the king might order the arrest of their leaders. Although the king could force his will on the parlements, their bold opposition damaged royal prestige.

With France on the brink of bankruptcy, the king's ministers proposed that the nobility and the church surrender some of their tax privileges. The parlements protested and remonstrated. Some nobles resisted because they were steadfast defenders of noble prerogatives; the more liberal nobles resisted because they saw an opportunity to check absolutism and introduce fundamental reforms that would regenerate the nation.

The resistance of the nobility forced the government, in July 1788, to call for a meeting of the Estates General—a medieval representative assembly, which had last met in 1614—to deal with the financial crisis. The body was to convene in May 1789. Certain that they would dominate the Estates General, the nobles intended to weaken the power of the throne. Once in control of the government, they would introduce financial reforms. But the revolt of the nobility against the crown had unexpected consequences. It opened the way for revolutions by the Third Estate, which destroyed the Old Regime and with it the aristocracy and its privileges.

The Roles of the Enlightenment and the American Revolution

Revolutions are born in the realm of the spirit. Revolutionary movements, says George Rudé, a historian of the French Revolution, require "some unifying body of ideas, a common vocabulary of hope and protest, something, in short, like a common 'revolutionary psychology.'"[7] For this reason, many historians see a relationship between the Enlightenment and the French Revolution. Although the philosophes themselves were not revolutionaries, their attacks on the pillars of the established order and their appeals for a freer more tolerant society helped create a revolutionary psychology. As Henri Peyre observes,

> Eighteenth-century philosophy taught the Frenchman to find his condition wretched, or in any case, unjust and illogical and made him disinclined to the patient resignation to his troubles that had long characterized his ancestors. . . . The propaganda of the "Philosophes" perhaps more than any other factor accounted for the fulfillment of the preliminary condition of the French Revolution, namely discontent with the existing state of things.[8]

As the Revolution progressed, its leaders utilized the philosophes' ideas and language to attack the foundations of the old order and to justify their own reform program.

The American Revolution, which gave practical expression to the liberal philosophy of the philosophes, also helped pave the way for the French Revolution. The Declaration of Independence, which proclaimed the natural rights of man and sanctioned resistance against a government that deprived men of these rights, influenced the framers of the Declaration of the Rights of Man and of the Citizen (see page 452). The United States showed that a nation could be established on the principle that sovereign power derived from the people. The Americans set an example of social equality unparalleled in Europe. In the United States, there was no hereditary aristocracy, no serfdom, and no state church. Liberal French aristocrats, such as the marquis de Lafayette, who had fought in the American Revolution, returned to France more optimistic about the possibilities of reforming French society.

A Bourgeois Revolution?

Because the bourgeois were the principal leaders and chief beneficiaries of the French Revolution, many historians have viewed it, along with the English Revolutions of the seventeenth century and the growth of capitalism, as "an episode in the general rise of the bourgeoisie."[9] Those who regard the Revolution as a "bourgeois revolution" argue that in the last part of the eighteenth century it became increasingly difficult for the bourgeoisie to gain the most honored offices in the land. According to this view, in the eighteenth century, a decadent and reactionary aristocracy sought to regain the powers that it had lost under Louis XIV. Through parlements, aristocrats blocked reforms proposed by the king that threatened their privileges, and they united to prevent commoners from entering their ranks. The nobility's determination to safeguard its power and social exclusiveness clashed head-on with the aspirations of a wealthy, talented, and progressive bourgeoisie. Finding the path to upward mobility and social dignity barred, the bourgeoisie, imbued with the rational outlook of the Enlightenment, came to perceive nobles as an obstacle to its advancement and the nation's progress. "The essential cause of the Revolution," concludes the French historian Albert Soboul, "was the power of a bourgeoisie arrived at its maturity and confronted by a decadent aristocracy holding tenaciously to its privileges."[10] Thus, when the bourgeois found the opportunity during the Revolution, they ended the legal division of France into separate orders.

In recent decades, some historians have challenged this interpretation. These revisionists argue that before 1789 France did not have a self-conscious bourgeois class aspiring to take control of the state in order to promote a capitalist economy, that the nobles and the bourgeoisie did not represent antagonistic classes divided by sharp differences. On the contrary, they were not clearly distinguishable from each other. The bourgeois aspired to noble status, and many nobles were involved in business enterprises—mining, metallurgy, textiles, and overseas trading companies—traditionally considered the province of the bourgeoisie. Abandoning a traditional aristocratic disdain for business, many nobles had acquired the capitalist mentality associated with the middle class. Some nobles also shared with the bourgeois the liberal values of the philosophes and a desire to do away with monarchical despotism and reform France according to rational standards. Thus, French nobles, particularly those who lived in urban centers or had traveled to Britain and the American colonies, were receptive both to new means of livelihood and to progressive ideas. Moreover, the French nobility was constantly infused with new blood from below. During the eighteenth century, thousands of bourgeois, through marriage, the purchase of an office that carried with it a title of nobility, or service as local officials—mayors, for example—had some entitlement of nobility. As the British historian William Doyle puts it, "the nobility was an open elite, not a hereditary class apart. Nor is it now possible to maintain that this elite grew less open as the eighteenth century went on thanks to some exclusive 'aristocratic reaction.'"[11]

Just prior to 1789, revisionists contend, nobles and prosperous bourgeois were no longer clearly differentiated; the traditional distinctions that had set them apart were now obsolete. France's social elite actually consisted not of a hereditary nobility but of *notables*—both nobles and bourgeois—distinguished more by wealth than by birth. Bourgeois notables were essentially moderate; they did not seek the destruction of the aristocracy that was accomplished in the opening stage of the Revolution. The elimination of aristocratic privileges was not part of a preconceived bourgeois program, revisionists maintain, but an improvised response to the violent upheavals in the countryside in July and August 1789. Moreover, not until early 1789, when a struggle erupted over the composition of the Estates General (see the next section), did the bourgeoisie start to become conscious of itself as a class with interests that clashed with those of the aristocracy. Until then, both the bourgeoisie and many aristocrats were united around a common and moderate reform program.

Finally, revisionists argue that the nobility was not as decadent or reactionary as traditional accounts would have it. The nobles resisted the king's reforming ministers because they doubted the ability of a despotic and incompetent state to solve the financial crisis. To be sure, there were aristocrats who selfishly wanted to cling to their privileges, but many also aspired to serve the public good by instituting structural changes that would liberate the nation from despotic and inefficient rule and reform its financial and administrative system. It was this desire to institute crucial changes in French political life, say revisionists, that led nobles to press for the convening of the Estates General.

THE MODERATE STAGE, 1789–91

The Clash Between the Nobility and the Third Estate

Frenchmen in great numbers met in electoral assemblies to elect deputies to the Estates General. Churchmen and nobles voted directly for their representatives. Most deputies of the clergy were parish priests, many of them sympathetic to reform. Although the majority of deputies of the Second Estate were conservative country nobles, there was a sizable liberal minority (including some who had fought in the American Revolution) that favored reform; political liberalism was not a monopoly of the bourgeoisie. The representatives from the Third Estate were elected indirectly, with virtually all taxpaying males over the age of twenty-five being eligible to vote. The delegates of the Third Estate consisted predominantly of bourgeois drawn from government service and the professions, including many articulate lawyers.

Each Estate drew up lists of grievances and suggestions *(cahiers de doléances)*. The cahiers from all three orders expressed loyalty to monarchy and church. Many cahiers of the nobility insisted on the preservation of manorial rights and honorific privileges, whereas cahiers prepared by the urban bourgeoisie often demanded the abolition of serfdom, the fees paid by peasants to lords, the lords' courts, and the lords' exclusive hunting rights. On the other hand, cahiers drawn up by liberal nobles agreed with bourgeois demands on many crucial issues. Both groups called for the establishment of a national assembly that would meet periodically and consent to taxation. Both also wanted a written constitution; financial reforms, including the surrender of tax exemptions; a guarantee of personal liberty; and freedom of the press. There was general agreement that a constitutional government that met regularly to pass laws was preferable to absolute monarchy, which ruled by decree. Both reform-minded nobles and bourgeois held great hopes for the regeneration of France and the advancement of liberty.

At this stage, then, with a significant number of nobles sympathetic to reform, there was no inseparable gulf between the Second and the Third Estates. However, it soon became clear that the hopes of reformers clashed with the intentions of many aristocrats. What had started as a struggle between the crown and the aristocracy was turning into something far more significant: a conflict between the two privileged orders on one side and the Third Estate on the other. As one keen observer noted in early 1789, "The public debate has changed. Now the King, despotism, the constitution are merely secondary: it is a war between the Third Estate and the other two orders."[12] One pamphleteer, Abbé Sieyès (1748–1836), expressed the hatred that the bourgeoisie had for the aristocracy. "The privileged order has said to the Third Estate: 'Whatever be your services, whatever be your talents, you shall go thus far and no farther. It is not fitting that you be honored.'" The higher positions in the land, said Sieyès, should be the "reward for talents," not the prerogative of birth. Without the Third Estate, "nothing can progress"; without the nobility, "everything would proceed infinitely better."[13] What triggered the conflict between them was the issue of representation in the Estates General—a medieval assembly divided into the traditional orders of clergy, aristocracy, and commoners.

Formation of the National Assembly

The Estates General convened at Versailles on May 5, 1789, but was stalemated by the question of procedure. Seeking to control the assembly, the nobility insisted that the three Estates follow the traditional practice of meeting separately and voting as individual bodies. Because the two privileged orders were likely to stand together, the Third Estate would always be outvoted, two to one. The delegates from the Third Estate, unwilling to allow the nobility and the higher clergy to dominate the Estates General, proposed instead that the three Estates meet as one body and vote by head. There were some 610 delegates from the Third Estate; the nobility and clergy together had an equivalent number. Since the Third Estate could rely on the support of sympathetic parish priests and liberal nobles, it would be assured a majority if all orders met together. As aristocrats and bourgeois became more polarized, antinoble rhetoric gained a growing audience among all segments of the Third Estate. Many commoners now saw the aristocracy as the chief obstacle to reform.

On June 10, the Third Estate broke the stalemate. It invited the clergy and nobility to join with it in a common assembly; if they refused, the Third Estate would go ahead without them. A handful of priests answered the roll call, but not one noble. On June 17, the Third Estate made a revolutionary move. It declared itself the National Assembly. On June 20, locked out of their customary meeting hall (apparently by accident), the Third Estate delegates moved to a nearby tennis court and took a solemn oath not to disband until a constitution had been drawn up for France. By these acts, the bourgeois delegates demonstrated their desire and determination to reform the state.

Louis XVI commanded the National Assembly to separate into orders, but the Third Estate held firm. The steadfastness of the delegates and the menacing actions of Parisians who supported the National Assembly forced Louis XVI to yield. On June 27, he ordered the nobility (some had already done so) and the clergy (a majority had already done so) to join with the Third Estate in the National Assembly. The Third Estate had successfully challenged the nobility and defied the king. It would use the National Assembly to institute reforms, including the drawing-up of a constitution that limited the king's power.

But the victory of the bourgeoisie was not yet secure, for most nobles had not resigned themselves to a bourgeois-dominated National Assembly.

Recognizing that France was on the threshold of a social revolution that jeopardized their power and status, many nobles now reversed their position of previous years and joined with the king in an effort to crush the National Assembly. Louis XVI, influenced by his wife, Queen Marie Antoinette, as well as his brother the comte d'Artois and court aristocrats, ordered special foreign regiments to the outskirts of Paris and Versailles. He also replaced Jacques Necker, a reform-minded minister, with a nominee of the queen. It appeared that Louis XVI, overcoming his usual hesitancy and vacillation, had resolved to use force against the National Assembly and to stop the incipient revolution. At this point, uprisings by the common people of Paris and peasants in the countryside saved the National Assembly, exacerbated hostilities between the Third Estate and the nobility, and ensured the victory of the forces of reform.

Storming of the Bastille

In July 1789, the level of tension in Paris was high for three reasons. First, the calling of the Estates General had aroused hopes for reform. Second, the price of bread was soaring: in August 1788, a Parisian laborer had spent 50 percent of his income on bread; by July 1789, he was spending 80 percent. The third element in the tension was the fear of an aristocratic plot to crush the National Assembly. Frightened that royal troops would bombard and pillage the city, Parisians searched for weapons.

On July 14, eight hundred to nine hundred Parisians gathered in front of the Bastille, a fortress used as a prison and a despised symbol of royal despotism. They gathered primarily to obtain gunpowder and to remove the cannon that threatened a heavily populated working-class district. Fearing an attack, the governor of the Bastille, Bernard Jordan de Launay, ordered his men to fire into the crowd; they killed ninety-eight and wounded seventy-three people. When the tables were turned and five cannon were aimed on the main gate of the Bastille, de Launay surrendered. Despite the promise that he would not be harmed, de Launay and five of his men were killed, and their heads were paraded on pikes through the city.

Historians hostile to the French Revolution have long depicted the besiegers of the Bastille as a destructive mob made up of the dregs of society—smugglers, beggars, bandits, degenerates. However, more recent scholarship reveals that the Bastille crowd was not drawn from the criminal elements but consisted almost entirely of small tradesmen, artisans, and wage earners—concerned citizens driven by hunger, fear of an aristocratic conspiracy, and hopes for reform.[14]

The fall of the Bastille had far-reaching consequences: a symbol of the Old Regime's darkness and despotism had fallen; some court nobles hostile to the Revolution decided to flee the country; the frightened king told the National Assembly that he would withdraw all the troops ringing Paris. The revolutionary act of the Parisians had indirectly saved the National Assembly and with it the bourgeois revolution.

Online Study Center

Improve Your Grade
Primary Source: The Taking of the Bastille and Its Aftermath: An English Perspective

The Great Fear

The uprising of the Parisians strengthened the hand of the National Assembly. Revolution in the countryside also served the interests of the reformers. The economic crisis of 1788–89 had worsened conditions for the peasantry; the price of bread soared, and the number of hungry beggars wandering the roads and spreading terror multiplied. Peasants feared that the beggars would seize their crops, which would soon be ready for harvest. Also contributing to the revolutionary mentality were the great expectations unleashed by the summoning of the Estates General, for like the urban poor, the peasants hoped that their grievances would be remedied. In the spring of 1789, peasants were attacking food convoys and refusing to pay royal taxes, tithes, and manorial dues. These revolutionary outbreaks intensified in the last weeks of July. Inflamed by economic misery and stirred by the uprisings of the Parisians, peasants began to burn manor houses and destroy the registers on which their obligations to the lords were inscribed.

The flames of the peasants' insurrection were fanned by rumors that aristocrats were organizing bands of brigands to attack the peasants. The large number of vagrants roaming the countryside helped trigger irrational fears among the peasantry. The mythical army of brigands never materialized, but the Great Fear, as this episode is called, led more peasants to take up arms against the lords. Convinced that aristocrats were plotting to block reforms, the peasants attacked the lords' chateaux with greater fury.

The peasant upheavals in late July and early August, like the insurrection in Paris, worked to the advantage of the reformers. The attacks provided the National Assembly with an opportunity to strike at noble privileges by putting into law what the peasants had accomplished with the torch—the destruction of feudal remnants. On the night of August 4, 1789, aristocrats, seeking to restore calm in the countryside, surrendered their special privileges: exclusive hunting rights, tax exemptions, monopoly on highest offices, manorial courts, and the right to demand labor services from peasants. The Assembly maintained that "the feudal regime had been utterly destroyed."*

In the decrees of August 5 and 11, the National Assembly implemented the resolutions of August 4. The Assembly also declared that the planned constitution should be prefaced by a declaration of rights. On August 26, it adopted the Declaration of the Rights of Man and of the Citizen.

October Days

Louis XVI, cool to these reforms, postponed his approval of the August Decrees and the Declaration of Rights. It would require a second uprising by the Parisians to force the king to agree to the

---

*This was not entirely true. Some peasant obligations were abolished outright. However, for being released from other specified obligations, peasants were required to compensate their former lords. The peasants simply refused to pay, and in 1793 the Jacobins, recognizing reality, declared the remaining debt null and void.

WOMEN'S MARCH TO VERSAILLES. A bread shortage and high prices sparked the protest march of thousands of women to Versailles in October 1789. The king was compelled to return to Paris, a sign of his diminishing power, and many aristocrats hostile to the Revolution fled the country. (*Bibliothèque Nationale, Paris/Giraudon/Art Resource, NY.*)

reforms and to nail down the victory of the reformers.

On October 5, 1789, Parisian housewives (and men) marched twelve miles to Versailles to protest the lack of bread to the National Assembly and the king. A few hours later, twenty thousand Paris Guards, a citizen militia sympathetic to the Revolution, also set out for Versailles in support of the protesters. The king had no choice but to promise bread and to return with the demonstrators to Paris. Two weeks later, the National Assembly abandoned Versailles for Paris.

Once again, the "little people" had aided the bourgeoisie. Louis XVI, aware that he had no control over the Parisians and fearful of further violence, approved the August Decrees and the Declaration of the Rights of Man and of the Citizen. Nobles who had urged the king to use force against the Assembly and had tried to block reforms fled the country in large numbers.

Reforms of the National Assembly

With resistance weakened, the National Assembly continued the work of reform begun in the summer of 1789. By abolishing both the special privileges of the nobility and the clergy and the absolutism based on the divine right of kings, the National Assembly completed the destruction of the Old Regime.

1. *Abolition of special privileges.* By ending the special privileges of the nobility and the clergy in the August Decrees, the National Assembly legalized the equality that the bourgeoisie had demanded. The aristocratic structure of the Old Regime, a remnant of the Middle Ages that had hindered the progressive bourgeoisie, was eliminated.

2. *Statement of human rights.* The Declaration of the Rights of Man and of the Citizen expressed liberal and universal goals of the

philosophes and the particular interests of the bourgeoisie. To contemporaries, it was a refutation of the Old Regime, a statement of ideals that, if realized, would end long-standing abuses and usher in a new society. In proclaiming the inalienable right to liberty of person and freedom of religion and thought and to equal treatment under the law, the declaration affirmed the dignity of the individual. It asserted that government belonged not to any ruler but to the people as a whole, and that its aim was the preservation of the natural rights of the individual. Because the declaration contrasted sharply with the principles espoused by an intolerant clergy, a privileged aristocracy, and a despotic monarch, it has been called the death warrant of the Old Regime.

The declaration expressed the view of the philosophes that people need not resign themselves to the abuses and misfortunes of human existence: through reason, they can improve society. But in 1789, the declaration was only a statement of intent. It remained to be seen whether its principles would be achieved. A significant example of the new leadership's commitment to equality and religious toleration was the law passed in 1791 granting civil rights to Jews. In theory, Jews were now free to leave the ghetto, to which they had been forcibly confined for centuries in order to keep them apart from gentiles, and to participate in French society as equal citizens.

3. *Subordination of church to state.* The National Assembly also struck at the privileges of the Roman Catholic church. The August Decrees declared the end of tithes. To obtain badly needed funds, the Assembly in November 1789 confiscated church lands and put them up for sale. In 1790, the Assembly passed the Civil Constitution of the Clergy, which altered the boundaries of the dioceses, reducing the number of bishops and priests, and transformed the clergy into government officials elected by the people and paid by the state.

Almost all bishops and many priests opposed the Civil Constitution. One reason was that the reorganization deprived a sizable number of clergymen of their positions. Moreover, in theory, Protestants and nonbelievers could participate in the election of Catholic clergy. In addition, the Assembly had issued the decree without consulting the pope or the French clergy as a body. When the Assembly required the clergy to take an oath that they would uphold the Civil Constitution, only about one-half would do so, and many believing Catholics supported the dissenting clergy. The Civil Constitution divided the French and gave opponents of the Revolution an emotional issue around which to rally supporters.

4. *A constitution for France.* In September 1791, the National Assembly achieved the goal at which it had been aiming since June 1789: a constitution limiting the power of the king and guaranteeing all French citizens equal treatment under the law. Citizens paying less than a specified amount in taxes could not vote. Probably about 30 percent of the males over the age of twenty-five were excluded by this stipulation, and only the more well-to-do citizens qualified to sit in the Legislative Assembly, a unicameral parliament created to succeed the National Assembly. The drafters of the constitution did not trust illiterate and propertyless men to vote and enact legislation. Nevertheless, the suffrage requirements under the constitution of 1791 were far more generous than those in Britain.

5. *Administrative and judicial reforms.* The National Assembly sought to reform the chaotic administrative system of France. It replaced the patchwork of provincial units with eighty-three new administrative units, or departments, approximately equal in size. The departments and their subdivisions were allowed a large measure of self-government.

Judicial reforms complemented the administrative changes. A standardized system of courts replaced the innumerable jurisdictions of the Old Regime, and the sale of judicial offices was ended. All judges were selected from graduate lawyers, and citizen juries were introduced in criminal cases. In the penal code completed by the National Assembly, torture and barbarous punishments were abolished.

6. *Aid for business.* The National Assembly put an end to all tolls and duties on goods transported within the country, maintained a tariff to protect French manufacturers, and insisted that French colonies trade only with the mother country. The Assembly also established a uniform system of weights and measures, eliminated the

guilds (medieval survivals that blocked business expansion), and forbade workers to form unions or to strike.

By ending absolutism, striking at the privileges of the nobility, and preventing the mass of people from gaining control over the government, the National Assembly consolidated the rule of the bourgeoisie. With one arm, it broke the power of the aristocracy and throne; with the other, it held back the common people. Although the reforms benefited the bourgeoisie, it would be a mistake to view them merely as a selfish expression of bourgeois interests. The Declaration of the Rights of Man and of the Citizen was addressed to all; it proclaimed liberty and equality as the right of all and called upon citizens to treat one another with respect. Both French and foreign intellectuals believed that the Revolution would lead ultimately to the emancipation of humanity. "The men of 1789," says the French historian Georges Lefebvre, "thought of liberty and equality as the common birthright of mankind."[15] These ideals became the core of the liberal-democratic credo that spread throughout much of the West in the nineteenth century.

THE RADICAL STAGE, 1792–94

The Sans-Culottes

Pleased with their accomplishments—equality before the law, careers open to talent, a written constitution, parliamentary government—the men of 1789 wished the Revolution to go no further. But revolutionary times are unpredictable. Soon the Revolution moved in a direction neither anticipated nor desired by the reformers. A counterrevolution, led by irreconcilable nobles and alienated churchmen, gained the support of strongly Catholic peasants. It began to threaten the changes made by the Revolution, forcing the revolutionary leadership to resort to extreme measures.

The discontent of the *sans-culottes**—small shopkeepers, artisans, and wage earners—also propelled the Revolution toward **radicalism**. Al-

though they had played a significant role in the Revolution, particularly in the storming of the Bastille and the October Days, they had gained little. The sans-culottes, says the French historian Albert Soboul, "began to realize that a privilege of wealth was taking the place of a privilege of birth. They foresaw that the bourgeoisie would succeed the fallen aristocracy as the ruling class."[16] Inflamed by poverty and their hatred of the rich, the sans-culottes insisted that it was the government's duty to guarantee them the "right of existence"—a policy that ran counter to the economic individualism of the bourgeoisie. They demanded that the government increase wages, set price controls on food supplies, end food shortages, punish food speculators and profiteers, and deal severely with counterrevolutionaries.

Although most sans-culottes upheld the principle of private property, they wanted laws to prevent extremes of wealth and poverty. Socially, their ideal was a nation of small shopkeepers and small farmers. "No one should own more than one workshop or one store," read a sans-culotte petition.[17] Whereas the men of 1789 sought equality of rights, liberties, and opportunities, the sans-culottes expanded the principle of equality to include narrowing the gap between the rich and poor. To reduce economic inequality, the sans-culottes called for higher taxes for the wealthy and the redistribution of land. Politically, they favored a democratic republic in which the common man had a voice.

In 1789, the bourgeoisie had demanded equality with the aristocrats: the right to hold the most honored positions in the nation and an end to the special privileges of the nobility. By the close of 1792, the sans-culottes were demanding equality with the bourgeois. They wanted political reforms that would give the poor a voice in the government and social reforms that would improve their lot.

Foreign Invasion

Despite the pressures exerted by reactionary nobles and clergy on the one hand and discontented sans-culottes on the other, the Revolution might not have taken a radical turn had France remained at peace. The war that broke out with Austria and Prussia in April 1792 exacerbated internal dissensions, worsened economic condi-

---

*Literally, *sans-culottes* means "without culottes" and refers to the people who wore the simple trousers of a laborer and not the knee breeches that aristocrats wore before the Revolution.

tions, and threatened to undo the reforms of the Revolution. It was in these circumstances that the Revolution moved from its moderate stage into a radical one, which historians refer to as the Second French Revolution.

In June 1791, Louis XVI and the royal family, traveling in disguise, fled Paris for the northeast of France to join with *émigrés* (nobles who had left revolutionary France and were organizing a counterrevolutionary army) and to rally foreign support against the Revolution. Discovered at Varennes by a village postmaster, they were brought back to Paris as virtual prisoners. The flight of the king turned many French people against the monarchy, strengthening the position of the radicals who wanted to do away with kingship altogether and establish a republic. But it was foreign invasion that ultimately led to the destruction of the monarchy.

In the Legislative Assembly, the lawmaking body that had succeeded the National Assembly in October 1791, one group, called the Girondins, urged an immediate war against Austria, which was harboring and supporting the émigrés. The Girondins believed that a successful war would unite France under their leadership, and they were convinced that Austria was already preparing to invade France and destroy the Revolution. Moreover, regarding themselves as crusaders in the struggle of liberty against tyranny, the Girondins hoped to spread revolutionary reforms to other lands to provoke a war of the people against kings.

On April 20, 1792, the Legislative Assembly declared war on Austria. Commanded by the duke of Brunswick, a combined Austrian and Prussian army crossed into France. French forces, short of arms and poorly led (about six thousand of some nine thousand officers had abandoned their command), could not halt the enemy's advance. Food shortages and a counterrevolution in the West increased the unrest. In an atmosphere already charged with tension, the duke of Brunswick issued a manifesto declaring that if the royal family were harmed, he would exact a terrible vengeance on the Parisians. On August 10, 1792, enraged Parisians and militia from other cities attacked the king's palace, killing several hundred Swiss guards.

In early September, as foreign troops advanced deeper into France, there occurred an event anal-

THE EXECUTION OF LOUIS XVI. The king died with dignity. His last words were, "I forgive my enemies; I trust that my death will be for the happiness of my people, but I grieve for France, and I fear that she may suffer the anger of the Lord." (*Giraudon/Art Resource, NY.*)

ogous to the Great Fear of 1789. As rumors spread that jailed priests and aristocrats were planning to break out of their cells to support the duke of Brunswick, Parisians panicked. Driven by fear, patriotism, and murderous impulses, they raided the prisons and massacred eleven to twelve hundred prisoners. Most of the victims were not political prisoners but ordinary criminals.

On September 21 and 22, 1792, the National Convention (the successor to the Legislative Assembly) abolished the monarchy and established a republic. In December 1792, Louis XVI was placed on trial, and in January 1793, he was executed for conspiring against the liberty of the

French people. The execution of Louis XVI intensified tensions between the revolutionaries and the crowned heads of Europe. The uprising of August 10, the September Massacres, the creation of a republic, and the execution of Louis XVI all confirmed that the Revolution was taking a radical turn.

Meanwhile, the war continued. Short of supplies, hampered by bad weather, and possessing insufficient manpower, the duke of Brunswick never did reach Paris. Defeated by superior artillery at Valmy on September 20, 1792, the foreign forces retreated to the frontier, and the armies of the republic took the offensive. By the beginning of 1793, French forces had overrun Belgium (then a part of the Austrian Empire), the German Rhineland, and the Sardinian provinces of Nice and Savoy. To the peoples of Europe, the National Convention solemnly announced that it was waging a popular crusade against privilege and tyranny, against aristocrats and princes.

These revolutionary political and social ideas, the execution of Louis XVI, and, most important, French expansion that threatened the balance of power frightened the rulers of Europe. Urged on by Britain, by the spring of 1793, they formed an anti-French alliance. The allies' forces pressed toward the French borders, endangering the republic.

Counterrevolutionary insurrections further undermined the fledgling republic. In the Vendée, in western France, peasants who were protesting against taxation and conscription and were still loyal to their priests and Catholic tradition, which the Revolution had attacked, took up arms against the republic. Led by local nobles, the peasants of the Vendée waged a guerrilla war for religion, royalism, and their traditional way of life. In some provinces, federalists objecting to the power wielded by the centralized government in Paris also revolted. The republic was unable to exercise control over much of the country.

The Jacobins

As the republic tottered under the weight of foreign invasion, internal insurrection, and economic crisis, the revolutionary leadership grew still more radical. In June 1793, the Jacobins replaced the Girondins as the dominant group in the National Convention. The Girondins favored a government in which the departments would exercise control over their own affairs. The Jacobins wanted a strong central government, with Paris as the center of power. The Girondins also opposed government interference in business, whereas the Jacobins supported temporary governmental controls to deal with the needs of war and economic crisis. This last point was crucial; it won the Jacobins the support of the sans-culottes.

Both the Girondins and the Jacobins came from the bourgeoisie, but some Jacobin leaders were more willing to listen to the economic and political demands of the hard-pressed sans-culottes. Besides, the Jacobins wanted an alliance with the sans-culottes in order to defend the Revolution against foreign and domestic enemies. The Jacobins had a further advantage in the power struggle: they were tightly organized, well disciplined, and convinced that only they could save the republic. On June 2, 1793, some eighty thousand armed sans-culottes surrounded the Convention and demanded the arrest of Girondin delegates—an act that enabled the Jacobins to gain control of the government.

The problems confronting the Jacobins were staggering. They had to cope with civil war, particularly in the Vendée, economic distress, blockaded ports, and foreign invasion. They lived with the terrible dread that if they failed, the Revolution for liberty and equality would perish. Only strong leadership could save the republic. It was provided by the Committee of Public Safety. Serving as a cabinet for the Convention, the Committee of Public Safety organized the nation's defenses, formulated foreign policy, supervised ministers, ordered arrests, and imposed the central government's authority throughout the nation. The twelve members of the committee, all ardent patriots and veterans of revolutionary politics, constituted "a government of perhaps the ablest and most determined men who have ever held power in France."[18]

Jacobin Achievements

The Jacobins continued the work of reform. A new constitution, in 1793, expressed Jacobin enthusiasm for political democracy. It contained a new Declaration of Rights, which affirmed and amplified the principles of 1789. By giving all adult males the right to vote, it overcame sans-culotte objections to the constitution of 1791. However, the threat of invasion and the revolts caused the implementation of the new constitution to be postponed, and it was never put into effect. Furthermore, by abolishing both slavery in the French colonies and imprisonment for debt and by making plans for free public education, the Jacobins revealed their humanitarianism and their debt to the philosophes.

Jacobin economic policies derived from the exigencies of war. To halt inflation and gain the support of the poor—both necessary for the war effort—the Jacobins decreed the *law of the maximum,* which fixed prices on bread and other essential goods. To win over the peasants, the Jacobins made it easier for them to buy the property of émigré nobles. To equip the Army of the Republic, the Committee of Public Safety requisitioned grain, wool, arms, shoes, and other items from individual citizens; required factories and mines to produce at full capacity; and established state-operated armament and munitions plants.

The Nation in Arms

For the war against foreign invaders, the Jacobins, in an act that anticipated modern conscription, drafted unmarried men between eighteen and twenty-five years of age. They mobilized all the resources of the nation, infused the army with a love for *la patrie* (the nation), and in a remarkable demonstration of administrative skill, equipped an army of more than 800,000 men. In creating the nation in arms, the Jacobins heralded the emergence of modern warfare. Inspired by the ideals of liberty, equality, and fraternity and commanded by officers who had proved their skill on the battlefield, the citizen-soldiers of the republic won decisive victories. In May and June 1794, the French routed the allied forces on the vital northern frontier, and by the end of July, France had become the triumphant master of Belgium.

By demanding complete devotion to the nation, the Jacobin phase of the Revolution also heralded the rise of modern **nationalism.** In the schools; in newspapers, speeches, and poems; on the stage; and at rallies and meetings of patriotic societies, the French people were told of the glory won by republican soldiers on the battlefield and were reminded of their duties to la patrie. "The citizen is born, lives and dies for the fatherland."[19] These words were written in public places for all citizens to read and ponder. The soldiers of the Revolution fought not for money or for a king but for the nation. "When *la patrie* calls us for her defense," wrote a young soldier to his mother, "we should rush to her. . . . Our life, our goods, and our talents do not belong to us. It is to the nation, to *la patrie,* to which everything belongs."[20] Could this heightened sense of nationality, which concentrated on the special interests of the French people, be reconciled with the Declaration of the Rights of Man, whose principles were addressed to all humanity? The revolutionaries themselves did not understand the implications of the new force that they had unleashed.

The Republic of Virtue and the Reign of Terror

Robespierre. At the same time that the Committee of Public Safety was forging a revolutionary army to deal with external enemies, it was also waging war against internal opposition. The pivotal personality in this struggle was Maximilien Robespierre (1758–1794). Robespierre, who had served in the National Assembly and was an active Jacobin, was distinguished by a fervent faith in the rightness of his beliefs, a total commitment to republican democracy, and an integrity that earned him the appellation "the Incorruptible." In the early stage of the Revolution, Robespierre had strongly supported liberal reforms. He attacked, at times with great fervor, slavery, capital punishment, and censorship; he favored civil rights for Jews; and, in what was considered a radical measure, he supported giving all men the vote regardless of how much property they owned.

Robespierre wanted to create a better society founded on reason, good citizenship, and patriotism. In his Republic of Virtue, there would be no kings or nobles; men would be free, equal, and educated; and reason would be glorified and superstition ridiculed. There would be no extremes of wealth or poverty; a person's natural goodness

M.M.J. ROBERSPIERRE
*Députés de l'Artois,
à l'Assemblée Nationale en 1789.*

A Paris, chez l'AUTEUR, quay des Augustins N° 71. au 3.º

ROBESPIERRE, AN ENGRAVING BY FIÉSINGER AFTER A DRAWING BY PIERRE-NARCISSE GUÉRIN. To create a Republic of Virtue where men would be free and equal, Maximilien Robespierre considered terror necessary. Robespierre lost favor with his own party and was himself guillotined. (*The Granger Collection.*)

would prevail over vice and greed; and laws would preserve, not violate, inalienable rights. In this utopian vision, an individual's duties would be "to detest bad faith and despotism, to punish tyrants and traitors, to assist the unfortunate, to respect the weak, to defend the oppressed, to do all the good one can to one's neighbor, and to behave with justice towards all men."[21] Motivated by a sense of integrity, people would actively put the public good ahead of private interests.

A disciple of Rousseau, Robespierre considered the national general will—a plainly visible truth that is best for the community—to be ultimate and infallible. Its realization meant the establishment of a Republic of Virtue; its denial meant the death of an ideal and a return to despotism. Robespierre believed that he and his colleagues in the

Committee of Public Safety had correctly ascertained the needs of the French people. He was certain that the committee members were the genuine interpreters of the general will, and he felt duty-bound to ensure its realization. He pursued his ideal society with religious zeal. Knowing that the Republic of Virtue could not be established while France was threatened by foreign and civil war, Robespierre urged that enemies of the republic "be prosecuted by all not as ordinary enemies, but as rebels, brigands, and assassins."[22]

To preserve republican liberty, the Jacobins made terror a deliberate government policy. Robespierre declared:

> *Does not liberty, that inestimable blessing . . . have the . . . right to sacrifice lives, fortunes, and even, for a time, individual liberties? . . . Is not the French Revolution . . . a war to the death between those who want to be free and those content to be slaves? . . . There is no middle ground; France must be entirely free or perish in the attempt, and any means are justifiable in fighting for so fine a cause.*[23]

With Robespierre playing a key role, the Jacobin leadership executed those they considered enemies of the republic: Girondins who challenged Jacobin authority, federalists who opposed a strong central government emanating from Paris, counterrevolutionary priests and nobles and their peasant supporters, and profiteers who hoarded food. The Robespierrists also executed Jacques Danton, a hero of the Revolution, who wished to end the terror and negotiate peace with the enemy. The Jacobins even sought to discipline the ardor of the sans-culottes, who had given them power. Fearful that sans-culotte spontaneity would undermine central authority and promote anarchy, Robespierrists brought about the dissolution of sans-culotte societies. In addition, they executed radical revolutionaries known as the *enragés* (literally, madmen), who had considerable influence on the Paris sans-culottes. The leaders of the enragés threatened insurrection against Jacobin rule and pushed for more social reforms than the Jacobins would allow, including setting limits on incomes and on the size of farms and businesses.

Robespierre and his fellow Jacobins did not resort to the guillotine—the instrument used to be-

THE REIGN OF TERROR. During the Terror thousands of men and women were condemned to death by the guillotine, often in front of cheering crowds. In this painting a court official reads the names of those sentenced for execution. (*Hulton/Getty Images.*)

head victims of the Terror—because they were bloodthirsty or power mad. Instead, they sought to establish a temporary dictatorship in a desperate attempt to save the republic and the Revolution. Deeply devoted to republican democracy, the Jacobins viewed themselves as bearers of a higher faith. Like all visionaries, Robespierre was convinced that he knew the right way and that the new society he envisaged would benefit all humanity. He saw those who impeded its implementation not just as opponents but as sinners who had to be liquidated for the general good.

Special courts were established in Paris and other cities to try suspects. The proceedings were carried on in haste, and most judgments called either for acquittal or execution. In the Vendée, where civil war raged, many of the arrested were executed by firing squads, without trial; some five thousand were loaded onto barges, which were then sunk in the middle of the Loire River.

Ironically, most of the executions took place after the frontiers had been secured and the civil war crushed. In many ways, the Terror was less a means

of saving the beleaguered republic and more a way of shaping the new republican society and the new individual in accordance with the radical Jacobin ideology. Of the 500,000 people imprisoned for crimes against the republic, some 16,000 were sentenced to death by guillotine and another 20,000 perished in prison before they could be tried. More than 200,000 died in the civil war in the provinces, some 40,000 summarily executed by firing squad, guillotine, and mass drownings ordered by military courts authorized by the Convention. The Terror was particularly brutal in the Vendée, where frenzied republican soldiers, under orders from their superiors, burned villages, slaughtered livestock, and indiscriminately killed tens of thousands of peasants.

The Jacobins did save the republic. Their regime expelled foreign armies, crushed the federalist uprisings, contained the counterrevolutionaries in the Vendée, and prevented anarchy. Without the discipline, order, and unity imposed on France by the Jacobins, it is likely that the republic would have collapsed under the twin blows of foreign invasion and domestic anarchy.

Profile

Gracchus Babeuf

In 1796, militant supporters of the poor conspired to overthrow the Directory, which was dominated by moderate bourgeois. Among the plotters was Gracchus Babeuf (1760–1797), whose newspaper, *Tribune of the People,* founded in 1794 shortly after the fall of Robespierre, regularly attacked the government. Made aware of the plot—known as the Conspiracy of the Equals—by informers, the Directory ordered the conspirators rounded up. Most of those indicted were freed, seven were deported, and two, including Babeuf, were executed.

The historical significance of Babeuf and his associates derives not from their inconsequential conspiracy but from their call to abolish private property and end the division of society into exploiter and exploited. Historians view the conspirators as pre-Marxist socialists who, like their Marxist successors, aspired to seize power in order to radically transform society.

Giraudon/Art Resource, NY.

Significance of the Terror. The **Reign of Terror** poses fundamental questions about the meaning of the French Revolution and the validity of the Enlightenment conception of the individual. To what extent was the Terror a reversal of the ideals of the Revolution as formulated in the Declaration of the Rights of Man? To what extent did the feverish passions and the fascination with violence demonstrated in the mass executions in the provinces and in the public spectacles in Paris— vast crowds watching and applauding the beheadings—indicate a darker side of human nature, beyond control of reason? Did Robespierre's religion of humanity revive the fanaticism and cruelty of the wars of religion, which had so disgusted the philosophes? Did the Robespierrists, who considered themselves the staunchest defenders of the Revolution's ideals, soil and subvert these ideals by their zeal? The Jacobins mobilized the might of the nation, created the mystique of *la patrie,* and imposed dictatorial rule in defense of liberty and equality; they also legalized and justified terror committed in the people's name, that is, in the cause of democracy. In so doing, were they unwittingly unleashing new forces that, in later years, would be harnessed by totalitarian ideologies consciously resolved to stamp out the liberal heritage of the Revolution? Did 1793 mark a change in the direction of Western civilization: a movement away from the ideals of the philosophes and the opening of an age of political coercion and ideological fanaticism, which would culminate in the cataclysms of the twentieth century?

Online Study Center

Improve Your Grade
Primary Source: The Reign of Terror in the Provinces: Lyon

In the spirited defense he gave at his trial, Babeuf often quoted passages from *Tribune of the People*, such as the following, which reveals the socialist character of his thought.

The masses can no longer find a way to go on living; they see that they possess nothing and that they suffer under the harsh and flinty oppression of a greedy ruling class. The hour strikes for great and memorable revolutionary events, already foreseen in the writings of the times, when a general overthrow of the system of private property is inevitable, when the revolt of the poor against the rich becomes a necessity that can no longer be postponed. . . .

Nature has placed everyone under an obligation to work. None may exempt himself from work without committing an antisocial action. Work and its fruits should be common to all. Oppression exists when one man is ground down by toil and lacks the barest necessaries of life, while another revels in luxury and idleness. It is impossible for anyone, without committing a crime, to appropriate for his own exclusive use the fruits of the earth or of manufacture.

In a truly just social order there are neither rich nor poor. The rich, who refuse to give up their superfluous wealth for the benefit of the poor, are enemies of the people.

None may be permitted to monopolize the cultural resources of society and hence to deprive others of the education essential for their wellbeing. Education is a universal human right.

The purpose of the Revolution is to abolish inequality and to restore the common welfare. The Revolution is not yet at an end, since the wealthy have diverted its fruits, including political power, to their own exclusive use, while the poor in their toil and misery lead a life of actual slavery and count for nothing in the State. *

The Defense of Gracchus Babeuf, ed. and trans. John Anthony Scott (New York: Schocken Books, 1972), pp. 45–46.

The Fall of Robespierre

The Terror had been instituted during a time of crisis and keyed-up emotions. By the summer of 1794, with the victory of the republic seemingly assured, fear of an aristocratic conspiracy had subsided, the will to punish "traitors" had slackened, and popular fervor for the Terror had diminished. As the need and enthusiasm for the Terror abated, Robespierre's political position weakened.

Opponents of Robespierre in the Convention, feeling the chill of the guillotine blade on their own necks, ordered the arrest of Robespierre and some of his supporters. On July 28, 1794, the tenth of Thermidor according to the new republican calendar, Robespierre was guillotined. Parisian sans-culottes might have saved him but made no attempt to do so. With their political clubs dissolved, they lacked the organization needed for an armed uprising. Moreover, the sans-culottes' ardor for Jacobinism had waned.

They resented Robespierre for having executed their leaders, and apparently the social legislation instituted by the Robespierrist leadership had not been sufficient to soothe sans-culotte discontent.

After the fall of Robespierre, the machinery of the Jacobin republic was dismantled. Leadership passed to the property-owning bourgeois who had endorsed the constitutional ideas of 1789–91, the moderate stage of the Revolution. The new leadership, known as Thermidoreans until the end of 1795, wanted no more of the Jacobins or of Robespierre's society. They had considered Robespierre a threat to their political power because he would have allowed the common people a considerable voice in the government. They had also viewed him as a threat to their property because he would have introduced some state regulation of the economy to aid the poor.

The Thermidorean reaction was a counterrevolution. The new government purged the army of officers who were suspected of Jacobin leanings, abolished the law of the maximum, and declared void the constitution of 1793. A new constitution, approved in 1795, reestablished property requirements for voting. The counterrevolution also produced a counterterror, as royalists and Catholics massacred Jacobins in the provinces.

At the end of 1795, the new republican government, the Directory, was burdened by war, a sagging economy, and internal unrest. The Directory crushed insurrections by Parisian sans-culottes, maddened by hunger and hatred of the rich (1795, 1796), and by royalists seeking to restore the monarchy (1797). As military and domestic pressures increased, power began to pass into the hands of generals. One of them, Napoleon Bonaparte, seized control of the government in November 1799, pushing the Revolution into yet another stage.

The Meaning
of the French Revolution

The French Revolution was a decisive period in the shaping of the modern West. It implemented the thought of the philosophes, destroyed the hierarchical and corporate society of the Old Regime, which was a legacy of the Middle Ages, promoted the interests of the bourgeoisie, and quickened the growth of the modern state.

The Revolution also weakened the aristocracy. With their ancient feudal rights and privileges eliminated, the nobles became simply ordinary citizens. Throughout the nineteenth century, France would be governed by both aristocrats and bourgeois. Property, not noble birth, determined the composition of the new ruling elite—a trend already in evidence before the Revolution.

The principle of careers open to talent gave the bourgeoisie access to the highest positions in the state. Having wealth, talent, ambition, and now opportunity, the bourgeoisie would play an ever more important role in French political life. Throughout continental Europe, the reforms of the French Revolution served as a model for progressive bourgeois who, sooner or later, would challenge the Old Regime in their own lands.

The French Revolution transformed the **dynastic state,** on which the Old Regime was based, into the **modern state:** national, liberal, secular, and rational. When the Declaration of the Rights of Man and of the Citizen asserted that "the source of all sovereignty resides essentially in the nation," the concept of the state took on a new meaning. The state was no longer merely a territory or a federation of provinces; it was not the private possession of the king claiming to be God's lieutenant on earth. In the new conception, the state belonged to the people as a whole—that for a government to be legitimate, it must derive its power from the people. And the individual, formerly a subject, was now a citizen with both rights and duties and was governed by laws that permitted no legal distinction between commoners and nobles.

The liberal thought of the Enlightenment found practical expression in the reforms of the Revolution. Absolutism and divine right of monarchy, repudiated in theory by the philosophes, were invalidated by constitutions affirming that sovereignty resides with the people, not with a monarch, and setting limits on the powers of government and by elected parliaments representing the governed. By providing for equality before the law and the protection of human rights—habeas corpus, trial by jury, full civic rights for Protestants and Jews, the abolition of slavery, freedom of speech, and the press—the Revolution struck at the abuses of the Old Regime. Because of violations and interruptions, these gains seemed at times more theoretical than actual. Nevertheless, these liberal ideals reverberated throughout the Continent. In the early nineteenth century, reformers in France and other lands, aspiring for political and social change, took the French Revolution as their inspiration, and the pace of reform quickened.

During the nineteenth century, the French Revolution served as a frame of reference for the various political constellations: **liberalism, socialism, conservatism.** Bourgeois liberals took as their model the moderate stage of the Revolution, which advanced the cause of liberty and equality and reformed a decaying Old Regime. At the same time, the Revolution presented a dilemma for bourgeois liberals, who valued reforms promoting liberty and equality but also feared the entrance into politics of the uneducated and unpropertied sans-culottes, with their demand for state intervention in the economy to improve living standards. And bourgeois moderates were haunted by memories of Jacobin radicalism. The Terror was a frightening demonstration of how liberty could degenerate into a new kind of despotism. With the demands of the sans-culottes for political democracy and for social reform, the voice of the urban poor began to be heard in politics, a phenomenon that would intensify with growing industrialization. Emerging socialists who embraced the cause of the laboring poor employed the rhetoric of the sans-culottes leaders in order to launch a social revolution that would improve the status of the downtrodden.

If European liberals embraced the philosophy of the moderate reformers of 1789–91 while rejecting the extremism of the radical Jacobins, conservatives, particularly nobles and Catholic clergy, throughout the nineteenth century regarded the Revolution in all its stages as an unmitigated disaster and wanted to undo reforms introduced by the Revolution. Hostility to the Revolution and to the Enlightenment defined extreme conservatism during the nineteenth century and found its ultimate expression in the fascist movements of the twentieth century, which explicitly attacked the universal ideals expressed in the Declaration of the Rights of Man and of the Citizen.

Prior to the Revolution, religion was still closely linked to the state. As a general rule, each state had an official religion, a state church that legitimated the ruling power. By disavowing any divine justification for the monarch's power, by depriving the church of its special position, and by no longer limiting citizenship to members of a state church, the Revolution accelerated the secularization of European political life. Sweeping aside the administrative chaos of the Old Regime, the Revolution attempted to impose rational norms on the state. The sale of public offices, which had produced ineffective and corrupt administrators, was eliminated, and the highest positions in the land were opened to men of talent regardless of birth. The Revolution abolished the peasantry's manorial obligations, which had hampered agriculture, and it swept away barriers to economic expansion. It based taxes on income and streamlined their collection. By destroying feudal remnants and eliminating internal tolls and guilds, it speeded up the expansion of a competitive market economy. In the nineteenth century, reformers in the rest of Europe would follow the lead set by France.

By showing that a decadent old order could be toppled and supplanted by a new one, the French Revolution inspired generations of revolutionaries aspiring to end long-standing abuses and re-model society. In the process, it unleashed three potentially destructive forces identified with the modern state: total war, nationalism, and a fanatic utopian mentality. All of these forces contradicted the rational and universal aims of the Declaration of the Rights of Man.

Whereas eighteenth-century wars were fought by professional soldiers for limited aims, the French Revolution, says the British historian Herbert Butterfield,

> *brings conscription, the nation in arms, the mobilization of all the resources of the state for unrelenting conflict. It heralds the age when peoples, woefully ignorant of one another, bitterly uncomprehending, lie in uneasy juxtaposition watching one another's sins with hysteria and indignation. It heralds Armageddon, the giant conflict for justice and right between angered populations each of which thinks it is the righteous one. So a new kind of warfare is born—the modern counterpart to the old conflicts of religions.*[24]

The world wars of the twentieth century were the terrible fulfillment of this new development in warfare.

The French Revolution also gave birth to modern nationalism. During the Revolution, loyalty was directed to the entire nation, not to a village or province or to the person of the king. The whole of France became the fatherland. Under the Jacobins, the French became converts to a secular faith preaching total reverence for the nation. "In 1794 we believed in no supernatural religion; our serious interior sentiments were all summed up in the one idea, how to be useful to the fatherland. Everything else . . . was, in our eyes, only trivial. . . . It was our only religion."[25] Few suspected that the new religion of nationalism was fraught with danger. Louis-Antoine de Saint-Just, a young, ardent Robespierrist, was gazing into the future when he declared: "There is something terrible in the sacred love of the fatherland. This love is so exclusive that it sacrifices everything to the public interest, without pity, without fear, with no respect for the human individual."[26] The philosophes would have deemed nationalism, which demanded total dedication of body and soul to the nation and stifled clear thinking, to be a repudiation of their universalism and hopes for rational solutions to political conflicts. It was a new dogma capable of evoking wild and dangerous passions and a setback for the progress of reason.

The French Revolution gave rise to still another potentially destructive force: a revolutionary mentality that sought to demolish an unjust traditional society and create a new social order that would restore individuals to their natural goodness. The negative side of this lofty vision was its power to whip up extremism that justified mass murder in the name of a supposedly higher good. Such was the case with Robespierre and other Jacobins. In the twentieth century, Nazis in Germany and radical socialists in Russia, China, and Cambodia, seeing themselves as idealists striving for a social regeneration of humanity, oppressed, terrorized, and murdered with intense dedication—and a clear conscience.

The Revolution attempted to reconstruct society on the basis of Enlightenment thought. The Declaration of the Rights of Man and of the Citizen, whose spirit permeated the reforms of the Revolution, upheld the dignity of the individual, demanded respect for the individual, attributed to each person natural rights, and barred the state from denying these rights. It insisted that society and the state have no higher duty than to promote the freedom and autonomy of the individual. "It is not enough to have overturned the throne," said Robespierre; "our concern is to erect upon its remains holy Equality and the sacred Rights of Man."[27] The tragedy of the Western experience is that this humanist vision, brilliantly expressed by the Enlightenment and given recognition in the reforms of the French Revolution, would be undermined in later generations. And, ironically, by its fanatical commitment to a seductive ideology that promised worldly salvation—the creation of a republic of virtue and truth—the French Revolution itself contributed to the shattering of this vision. It had spawned total war, nationalism, terror as government policy, and a revolutionary mentality that sought to change the world through coercion and violence. In the twentieth century, these dangerous forces almost succeeded in crushing the liberty and equality so valued by the French reformers.

❖ ❖ ❖

Online Study Center ACE the Test

NOTES

1. Quoted in G. P. Gooch, *Germany and the French Revolution* (New York: Russell & Russell, 1966), p. 39.

2. Quoted in Ernst Wangermann, *From Joseph II to the Jacobin Trials* (New York: Oxford University Press, 1959), p. 24.

3. Excerpted in Alfred Cobban, ed., *The Debate on the French Revolution* (London: Adam & Charles Black, 1960), p. 41.

4. Quoted in Elinor G. Barber, *The Bourgeoisie in Eighteenth-Century France* (Princeton, N.J.: Princeton University Press, 1967), p. 57.

5. Quoted in C. B. A. Behrens, *The Ancien Régime* (New York: Harcourt, Brace & World, 1967), p. 43.

6. Quoted in Leo Gershoy, *The French Revolution and Napoleon* (New York: Appleton-Century-Crofts, 1933), p. 18.

7. George Rudé, *Revolutionary Europe, 1783–1815* (New York: Harper Torchbooks, 1966), p. 74.

8. Henri Peyre, "The Influence of Eighteenth-Century Ideas on the French Revolution," *Journal of the History of Ideas*, 10 (1949):73.

9. Georges Lefebvre, *The French Revolution from 1793 to 1799*, trans. John Hall Stewart and James Friguglietti (New York: Columbia University Press, 1964), 2:360.

10. Quoted in T. C. W. Blanning, *The French Revolution: Aristocrats Versus Bourgeois?* (Atlantic Highlands, N.J.: Humanities Press, 1987), p. 9.

11. William Doyle, *Origins of the French Revolution* (New York: Oxford University Press, 1980), p. 21.

12. Quoted in Blanning, *French Revolution*, p. 38.

13. Excerpted in John Hall Stewart, ed., *A Documentary Survey of the French Revolution* (New York: Macmillan, 1951), pp. 43–44.

14. See George Rudé, *The Crowd in the French Revolution* (New York: Oxford University Press, 1959).

15. Georges Lefebvre, *The Coming of the French Revolution* (Princeton, N.J.: Princeton University Press, 1967), p. 210.

16. Albert Soboul, *The Parisian Sans-Culottes and the French Revolution, 1793–94,* trans. Gwynne Lewis (London: Oxford University Press, 1964), pp. 28–29.

17. Quoted in Soboul, *Parisian Sans-Culottes*, p. 64.

18. Alfred Cobban, *A History of Modern France* (Baltimore: Penguin, 1961), 1:213.

19. Quoted in Hans Kohn, *Nationalism: Its Meaning and History* (Princeton, N.J.: D. Van Nostrand, 1965), p. 25.

20. Quoted in Carlton J. H. Hayes, *The Historical Evolution of Modern Nationalism* (New York: Richard R. Smith, 1931), p. 55.

21. Excerpted in George Rudé, ed., *Robespierre* (Englewood Cliffs, N.J.: Prentice-Hall, 1976), p. 72.

22. Ibid., p. 57.

23. Excerpted in E. L. Higgins, ed., *The French Revolution* (Boston: Houghton Mifflin, 1938), pp. 306–307.

24. Herbert Butterfield, *Napoleon* (New York: Collier Books, 1962), p. 18.

25. Quoted in Hayes, *Evolution of Modern Nationalism,* p. 55.

26. Quoted in Hans Kohn, *Making of the Modern French Mind* (New York: D. Van Nostrand, 1955), p. 17.

27. Quoted in Christopher Dawson, *The Gods of Revolution* (New York: New York University Press, 1972), p. 83.

Suggested Reading

Blanning, T. C. W., *The French Revolution: Aristocrats Versus Bourgeois?* (1987). Summarizes recent scholarship on the question; a volume in Studies of European History series.

———, ed., *The Rise and Fall of the French Revolution* (1996). A collection of recent articles, some by prominent students of the Revolution.

Doyle, William, *The Oxford History of the French Revolution* (1990). A narrative history that incorporates new thinking on the causes and nature of the Revolution.

Forrest, Alan, *The French Revolution* (1995). Social, political, and ideological changes brought about by the Revolution.

Furet, François, and Mona Ozouf, eds., *A Critical Dictionary of the French Revolution* (1989). Articles on many topics pertaining to the Revolution.

Lefebvre, Georges, *The Coming of the French Revolution* (1967). A brilliant analysis of the social structure of the Old Regime and the opening phase of the Revolution.

Rudé, George, *The Crowd in the French Revolution* (1959). An analysis of the composition of the crowds that stormed the Bastille, marched to Versailles, and attacked the king's palace.

Chapter 20

Napoleon: Subverter and Preserver of the Revolution

Murals at Versailles, showing Napoleon reviewing his troops. (© Réunion des Musées Nationaux.)

Focus Questions

1. Why does the career of Napoleon Bonaparte continue to fascinate?

2. How did Napoleon both preserve and undermine the ideals of the French Revolution?

3. How did Napoleon speed up the modernization of Europe?

Online Study Center

This icon will direct you to interactive map and primary source activities on the website http://college.hmco.com/pic/perrywc8e.

The upheavals of the French Revolution made possible the extraordinary career of Napoleon Bonaparte. This popular general, who gained control over France in 1799, combined a passion for power with a genius for leadership. Under Napoleon's military dictatorship, the constitutional government for which the people of 1789 had fought and the republican democracy for which the Jacobins had rallied the nation seemed lost. Nevertheless, during the Napoleonic era, many achievements of the Revolution were preserved, strengthened, and carried to other lands.

RISE TO POWER

Napoleon was born on August 15, 1769, on the French-ruled island of Corsica, the son of a petty noble. After finishing military school in France, he became an artillery officer; the wars of the French Revolution gave him an opportunity to advance his career. In December 1793, Napoleon's brilliant handling of artillery forced the British to lift their siege of the city of Toulon. Two years later, he saved the Thermidorean Convention from a royalist insurrection by ordering his troops to fire into the riotous mob—the famous "whiff of grapeshot." In 1796, he was given command of the French Army of Italy. His star was rising.

In Italy, against the Austrians, Napoleon demonstrated a dazzling talent for military planning and leadership, which earned him an instant reputation. Having tasted glory, he could never do without it. Since he had experienced only success, nothing seemed impossible. He sensed that he was headed for greatness. Years later, he recalled: "[In Italy] I realized I was a superior being and conceived the ambition of performing great things, which hitherto had filled my thoughts only as a fantastic dream."[1]

In November 1797, Napoleon was ordered to plan an invasion of England. Aware that the French navy was weak, he recommended postponing the invasion. He urged instead that an expedition be sent to the Near East to strike at British power in the Mediterranean and British commerce with India, and perhaps to carve out a French empire in the Near East. With more than

Chronology 20.1 ❖ Napoleon's Career

1796	Napoleon gets command of the French Army of Italy
1798	Battle of the Nile: the British annihilate Napoleon's fleet
November 10, 1799	Napoleon helps to overthrow Directory's rule, establishing a strong executive in France
1802	He becomes first consul for life; peace is made with Austria and Britain
March 21, 1804	Civil Code (called Code Napoleon in 1807)
December 2, 1804	Napoleon crowns himself emperor of the French
October 1805	French forces occupy Vienna
October 21, 1805	Battle of Trafalgar: French and Spanish fleets are defeated by the British
December 1805	Battle of Austerlitz: Napoleon defeats Russo-Austrian forces
1806	War against Prussia and Russia
October 1806	Napoleon defeats Prussians at Jena, and French forces occupy Berlin
June 1807	French victory over Russians at Friedland
1808–1813	Peninsular War: Spaniards, aided by the British, fight against French occupation
September 14, 1812	Grand Army reaches Moscow
October–December 1812	Grand Army retreats from Russia
October 1813	Allied forces defeat Napoleon at Leipzig
1814	Paris is captured, and Napoleon is exiled to Elba
March 20, 1815	Escaping, Napoleon enters Paris and begins "hundred days" rule
June 1815	Defeated at Waterloo, Napoleon is exiled to Saint Helena

thirty-five thousand troops, Napoleon set out for Egypt, then a part of the Turkish empire. Although he captured Cairo, the Egyptian campaign was far from a success. At the battle of the Nile (1798), the British, commanded by Admiral Horatio Nelson, annihilated Napoleon's fleet. Deprived of reinforcements and supplies, with his manpower reduced by battle and plague, Napoleon was compelled to abandon whatever dreams he might have had of threatening India. Although the Egyptian expedition was a failure,

Napoleon, always seeking to improve his image, sent home glowing bulletins about French victories. To people in France, he was the conqueror of Egypt, as well as of Italy.

Meanwhile, political unrest, financial disorder, and military reversals produced an atmosphere of crisis in France. Napoleon knew that in such times people seek out a savior. A man of destiny must act. Without informing his men, he slipped out of Egypt, avoided British cruisers, and landed in France in October 1799.

Coup d'État

When Napoleon arrived in France, a conspiracy was already under way against the government of the Directory. Convinced that only firm leadership could solve France's problems, some politicians plotted to seize power and establish a strong executive. Needing the assistance of a popular general, they turned to Napoleon, whom they thought they could control. Although the hastily prepared coup d'état was almost bungled, the government of the Directory was overthrown. The French Revolution entered a new stage, that of military dictatorship.

Demoralized by a decade of political instability, economic distress, domestic violence, and war, most of the French welcomed the leadership of a strong man. The bourgeois, in particular, expected Napoleon to protect their wealth and the influence they had gained during the Revolution.

The new constitution (1799) created a strong executive. Although three consuls shared the executive office, the first consul, Napoleon, monopolized power. Whereas Napoleon's fellow conspirators, who were political moderates, sought only to strengthen the executive, Napoleon aspired to personal rule. He captured the reins of power after the coup, and his authority continued to expand. In 1802, he was made first consul for life, with the right to name his successor. And on December 2, 1804, in a magnificent ceremony at the Cathedral of Notre Dame in Paris, Napoleon crowned himself "Emperor of the French." General, first consul, and then emperor—it was a breathless climb to the heights of power. Napoleon, who once said that he loved "power as a musician loves his violin,"[2] was determined never to lose it.

Napoleon's Character

What sort of man was this on whom the fate of France and Europe depended? Napoleon's complex and mysterious personality continues to baffle biographers. However, certain distinctive characteristics are evident. Napoleon's intellectual ability was impressive. His mind swiftly absorbed and classified details, which his photographic memory stored. With surgical precision, he could probe his way to the heart of a problem while still retaining a grasp of peripheral considerations. Ideas always danced in his head, and his imagination was illuminated by sudden flashes of insight. He could work for eighteen or twenty hours at a stretch, deep in concentration, ruling out boredom or fatigue by an act of will. Napoleon, man of action, warrior par excellence, was in many ways, says Georges Lefebvre, "a typical man of the eighteenth century, a rationalist, a *philosophe* [who] placed his trust in reason, in knowledge, and in methodical effort."[3]

Rationalism was only one part of his personality. There was also that elemental, irresistible urge for action, "the romantic Napoleon, a force seeking to expand and for which the world was no more than an occasion for acting dangerously."[4] This love of action fused with his boundless ambition. Lefebvre continues:

> His greatest ambition was glory. "I live only for posterity," he exclaimed, "death is nothing, but to live defeated and without glory is to die every day." His eyes were fixed on the world's great leaders: Alexander who conquered the East and dreamed of conquering the world; Caesar, Augustus, Charlemagne. . . . They were for him examples, which stimulated his imagination and lent an unalterable charm to action. He was an artist, a poet of action, for whom France and mankind were but instruments.[5]

He also exuded an indefinable quality of personality, a charismatic force that made people feel that they were in the presence of a superior man. Contemporaries remarked that his large gray eyes, penetrating, knowing, yet strangely expressionless, seemed to possess a hypnotic power. He was capable of moving men to obedience, to loyalty, and to heroism.

The rationalist's clarity of mind and the romantic's impassioned soul, the adventurer's love of glory and the hero's personal magnetism and iron will—these were the components of Napoleon's personality. There was also an aloofness—some would say callousness—that led him to regard

CORONATION OF NAPOLEON AND JOSEPHINE, BY DAVID. Napoleon crowned himself emperor in a magnificent ceremony. To French émigrés and nobles throughout Europe, he was the "crowned Jacobin" who threatened aristocratic privileges and European stability. (*Louvre © Réunion des Musées Nationaux.*)

people as pawns to be manipulated in the pursuit of his destiny. "A man like me," he once said, "troubles himself little about the lives of a million men."[6]

Napoleon's genius might have gone unheralded and his destiny unfulfilled had it not been for the opportunities created by the French Revolution. By opening careers to talent, the Revolution enabled a young Corsican of undistinguished birth to achieve fame and popularity. By creating a national army and embroiling France in war, it provided a military commander with enormous sources of power. By plunging France into one crisis after another, it opened up extraordinary possibilities for a man with a gift of leadership and an ambition "so intimately linked with my very being that it is like the blood that circulates in my veins."[7] It was the Revolution that made Napoleon conscious of his genius and certain of his destiny.

NAPOLEON AND FRANCE

Living in a revolutionary age, Napoleon had observed firsthand the precariousness of power and the fleetingness of popularity. A superb realist, he knew that his past reputation would not sustain him. If he could not solve the problems caused by a decade of revolution and war and bind together the different classes of French people, his prestige would diminish and his power collapse. The general must become a statesman and, when necessary, a tyrant. His domestic policies, showing the influence of both eighteenth-century enlightened despotism and the Revolution, affected every aspect of society and had an enduring impact on French history. They continued the work of the Revolution in destroying the institutions of the Old Regime.

Government: Centralization and Repression

In providing France with a strong central government, Napoleon continued a policy initiated centuries earlier by Bourbon monarchs. The Bourbons, however, had not been able to overcome completely the barriers presented by provinces, local traditions, feudal remnants, and corporate institutions. Napoleon, in contrast, succeeded in giving France administrative uniformity. An army of officials, subject to the emperor's will, reached into every village, linking together the entire nation. This centralized state suited Napoleon's desire for orderly government and rational administration, enabled him to concentrate power in his own hands, and provided him with the taxes and soldiers needed to fight his wars. To suppress irreconcilable opponents, primarily die-hard royalists and republicans, Napoleon used the instruments of the police state: secret agents, arbitrary arrest, summary trials, and executions.

Napoleon also shaped public opinion to prevent hostile criticism of his rule and to promote popular support for his policies and person. In these actions, he was a precursor of twentieth-century dictators. Liberty of the press came to an end. Printers swore an oath of obedience to the emperor, and newspapers were converted into government mouthpieces. Printers were forbidden to print and booksellers to sell or circulate "anything which may involve injury to the duties of subjects toward the sovereign or the interests of the state."[8] When Napoleon's secretary read him the morning newspapers, Napoleon would interrupt, "Skip it, skip it. I know what is in them. They only say what I tell them to."[9] These efforts at indoctrination even reached schoolchildren, who were required to memorize a catechism glorifying the ruler, which ran, in part, as follows:

> *Q. What are the duties of Christians with respect to the princes who govern them, and what in particular are our duties toward Napoleon I, our Emperor?*
>
> *A. Christians owe to the princes who govern them, and we owe in particular to Napoleon I, our Emperor, love, respect, obedience, fidelity, military service; . . . we also owe him . . . prayers for his safety. . . .*
>
> *Q. Why are we bound to all these duties towards our Emperor?*
>
> *A. First of all, because God, who creates emperors and distributes them according to his will, in loading our Emperor with gifts, both in peace and war, has established him as our sovereign. . . . To honor and to serve our Emperor is then to honor and to serve God himself.*
>
> *Q. What . . . of those who may be lacking in their duty towards our Emperor?*
>
> *A. . . . they would be resisting the order established by God himself and would make themselves worthy of eternal damnation.[10]*

By repressing liberty, subverting republicanism, and restoring absolutism, Emperor Napoleon reversed some of the liberal gains of the Revolution. Although favoring equality before the law and equality of opportunity as necessary for a well-run state, Napoleon believed that political liberty impeded efficiency and threatened the state with anarchy. He would govern in the interest of the people as an enlightened but absolute ruler.

Religion: Reconciliation with the Church

For Napoleon, who was a deist, if not an atheist, the value of religion was not salvation but social and political cohesion. It promoted national unity and prevented class war. He stated:

> *Society cannot exist without inequality of fortunes, and inequality of fortunes cannot exist without religion. When a man is dying of hunger alongside another who stuffs himself, it is impossible to make him accede to the difference unless there is an authority which says to him God wishes it thus; there must be some poor and some rich in the world, but hereafter*

François Dominique Toussaint L'Ouverture

In 1791, in the midst of the French Revolution, black slaves on San Domingo, the rich French sugar colony in the West Indies, revolted, murdering their masters, burning down plantations, and crying "Vengeance! Vengeance!" Their hatred of servitude, which had ignited slave revolts in previous decades, was intensified by the ideals of liberty and equality reverberating across the Atlantic.

François Dominique Toussaint L'Ouverture (c. 1743–1803) joined the rebellion and quickly rose to a position of command. Toussaint was the son of a petty African chief from Dahomey who, like millions of other Africans, had been captured in war, sold to westerners, and brought in chains to toil on plantations in the New World. Toussaint, the eldest of eight children, was born in captivity. A remarkable old black taught him French and some Latin and geometry, and his master, recognizing Toussaint's ability, made him first a coachman and

Roger-Viollet.

and for all eternity the division will be made differently.[11]

This is what Napoleon probably had in mind when he said: "Men who do not believe in God—one does not govern them, one shoots them."[12]

Napoleon tried to close the breach between the state and the Catholic church, which had appeared during the Revolution. Such a reconciliation would gain the approval of the mass of the French people, who still remained devoted to their faith, and would reassure the peasants and bourgeoisie who had bought confiscated church lands. For these reasons, Napoleon negotiated an agreement with the pope. The Concordat of 1801 recognized Catholicism as the religion of the great majority of the French rather than as the official state religion (the proposal that the pope desired). The clergy were to be paid and nominated by the state but consecrated by the pope.

In effect, the Concordat guaranteed the reforms of the Revolution. The church did not regain its confiscated lands or its right to collect the tithe. The French clergy remained largely subject to state control. And by not establishing Catholicism as the state religion, the Concordat did not jeopardize the newly won toleration of Jews and Protestants. Napoleon had achieved his aim. The Concordat made his regime acceptable to Catholics and to owners of former church lands.

Law: The Code Napoléon

Under the Old Regime, France was plagued with numerous and conflicting law codes. Reflecting local interests and feudal traditions, these codes obstructed national unity and administrative efficiency. Efforts by the revolutionaries to draw up

then steward of the plantation's livestock, a position almost never held by a nonwhite.

At the time of the rebellion, 42,000 whites, employing brutal means of repression—whipping, chaining, roasting, and mutilation—dominated 500,000 black slaves, often working them like beasts. Complicating the social structure were mulattos, people of mixed race who were granted French citizenship in 1793 out of fear that they would side with the rebellious black slaves.

Aspiring to eliminate slavery entirely, Toussaint organized an army consisting mainly of illiterate slaves into a fighting force capable of defeating European-trained soldiers. In 1794, the Jacobins abolished slavery over the opposition of the white planters, and Toussaint, who had distinguished himself as a military commander, was appointed assistant governor. Toussaint was also a man of vision, deeply committed to the revolutionary ideals of liberty and equality and to introducing economic, administrative, and educational reforms in San

Domingo. Contrary to the wishes of the more radical black officers, he permitted whites and mulattos to hold important positions in the bureaucracy. Toussaint's reluctance to declare independence from France also angered the radicals.

In 1801, two years after seizing power in France, Napoleon sent twenty thousand troops to San Domingo to restore slavery and to subdue Toussaint, whose power had increased considerably. The old warrior, having lost none of his skills in guerrilla warfare, was at the point of defeating the French when he proposed peace. The French commander tricked Toussaint into believing that if he retired, France would negotiate a favorable settlement with San Domingo. Shortly after he retired to his farm, Toussaint was arrested and sent to prison in France, where he suffered abuse and humiliation until his death in 1803. On January 1, 1804, revolutionaries on the island established the independent state of Haiti, whose foundation Toussaint L'Ouverture had laid.

a unified code of laws bogged down. Recognizing the value of such a code in promoting effective administration throughout France, Napoleon pressed for the completion of the project. The Code Napoléon incorporated many principles of the Revolution: equality before the law, the right to choose one's profession, freedom of religion, protection of property rights, the abolition of serfdom, and the secular character of the state.

The code also had its less liberal side, denying equal treatment to workers in their dealings with employers, to women in their relations with their husbands, and to children in their relations with their fathers. By making wives inferior to their husbands in matters of property, adultery, and divorce, the code reflected both Napoleon's personal attitude and the general view of the times toward women and family stability. Of women, he once said that "the husband must possess the absolute power and right to say to his wife:

'Madam, you shall not go out, you shall not go to the theater, you shall not receive such and such a person: for the children you shall bear shall be mine!'"[13]

Adopted in lands conquered by France, the Code Napoléon helped to weaken feudal privileges and institutions and clerical interference in the secular state. With justice, Napoleon could say: "My true glory is not to have won forty battles. . . . Waterloo will erase the memory of so many victories. . . . But what nothing will destroy, what will live forever, is my Civil Code."[14]

NAPOLEON ON HIS IMPERIAL THRONE, BY JEAN-AUGUSTE-DOMINIQUE INGRES, 1806. This portrait captures the character of the self-made emperor, the daring commander, the life dedicated to glory and grandeur. (*Musée de l'Armée, Paris/Art Resource, NY.*)

Education: The Imperial University

Napoleon's educational policy was an elaboration of the school reforms initiated during the Revolution. Like the revolutionaries, Napoleon favored a system of public education, with a secular curriculum and minimum church involvement. For Napoleon, education served a dual purpose: it would provide him with capable officials to administer his laws and trained officers to lead his armies, and it would indoctrinate the young in obedience and loyalty. He established the University of France, a giant board of education that placed education under state control. To this day, the French school system, unlike that in the United States, is strictly centralized, with curriculum and standards set for the entire country.

The emperor did not consider education for girls important, holding that "marriage is their whole destination."[15] In his view, whatever education girls did receive should stress religion. "What we ask of education is not that girls should think but that they should believe. The weakness of women's brains, the instability of their ideas, the place they fill in society, their need for perpetual resignation . . . all this can only be met by religion."[16]

Economy: Strengthening the State

Napoleon's financial and economic policies were designed to strengthen France and enhance his popularity. To stimulate the economy and to retain the favor of the bourgeois, who supported his seizure of power, Napoleon aided industry through tariffs and loans. He fostered commerce (while also speeding up troop movements) by building or repairing roads, bridges, and canals. To protect the currency from inflation, he established the Bank of France, which was controlled by the nation's leading financiers. By keeping careers open to talent, he endorsed one of the key demands of the bourgeoisie during the Revolution. Fearing a revolution based on lack of bread, he provided food at low prices and stimulated employment for the laboring poor. He endeared himself to the peasants by not restoring feudal privileges and by allowing them to keep the land they had obtained during the Revolution.

Napoleon did not identify with the republicanism and democracy of the Jacobins, which he equated with mob rule. Rather, by preserving many social gains of the Revolution while suppressing political liberty, he showed himself to be an heir of enlightened despotism. Like the reforming despots, Napoleon admired administrative uniformity and efficiency; hated feudalism, religious persecution, and civil inequality; and favored government regulation of trade and industry.

NAPOLEON AND EUROPE

Although Napoleon's domestic policies gained him wide support, it was his victories on the battlefield that mesmerized the French people and gratified their national vanity. Ultimately, his popularity and his power rested on the sword. In 1802, he declared,

> My power proceeds from my reputation, and my reputation from the victories I have won. My power would fail if I were not to support it with more glory and more victories. Conquest has made me what I am; only conquest can maintain me.[17]

Napoleon, the Corsican adventurer, realized Louis XIV's dream of French mastery of Europe. Between 1805 and 1807, Napoleon decisively defeated Austria, Prussia, and Russia, becoming the virtual ruler of Europe. In these campaigns, as in his earlier successes in Italy, Napoleon demonstrated his greatness as a military commander.

Napoleon's Art of War

Although forgoing a set battle plan in favor of flexibility, Napoleon was guided by certain general principles, which constituted his art of war. He stressed the advantage of "a rapid and audacious attack" in preference to waging defensive war from a fixed position. "Make war offensively; it is the sole means to become a great captain and to fathom the secrets of the art."[18] Warfare could not be left to chance but required mastering every detail and anticipating every contingency. "I am accustomed to thinking out what I shall do three or four months in advance, and I base my calculations on the worst of conceivable circumstances."[19] Every master plan contained numerous alternatives to cover all contingencies.

Surprise and speed were essential ingredients of Napoleonic warfare. Relying heavily on surprise, Napoleon employed various stratagems to confuse and deceive his opponents: providing newspapers with misleading information and launching secondary offensives. Determined to strike unexpectedly and consequently demoralize the enemy by arriving at a battlefield ahead of schedule, he carefully selected the best routes to the chosen destination, eliminated slow-moving supply convoys by living off the countryside, and inspired his men to incredible feats of marching as they drew closer to the opposing army. In the first Italian campaign, his men covered 50 miles

in thirty-six hours; in 1805, against Austria, they marched 275 miles in twenty-three days.

His campaigns anticipated the blitzkrieg, or lightning warfare, of the twentieth century. By rapid marches, Napoleon would concentrate a superior force against a segment of the enemy's strung-out forces. Here the hammer blow would fall. Employing some troops to pin down the opposing force, he would move his main army to the enemy's rear or flank, cutting off the enemy supply line. Conducted with speed and deception, these moves broke the spirit of the opposing troops. Heavy barrages by concentrated artillery opened a hole in the enemy lines, which was penetrated first by infantry and then by shock waves of cavalry. Unlike the typical eighteenth-century commander, who maneuvered for position and was satisfied with his opponent's retreat, Napoleon sought to annihilate the enemy's army, thereby destroying its source of power.

The emperor thoroughly understood the importance of morale in warfare. "Moral force rather than numbers decides victory," he once said.[20] He deliberately sought to shatter his opponent's confidence by surprise moves and lightning thrusts. He also recognized that he must maintain a high level of morale among his own troops. By sharing danger with his men, he gained their affection and admiration. He inspired his men by appealing to their honor, vanity, credulity, and love of France. "A man does not have himself killed for a few halfpence a day or for a petty distinction," he declared. "You must speak to the soul in order to electrify the man."[21] This Napoleon could do. It was Napoleon's charisma that led the duke of Wellington to remark: "I used to say of him that his presence on the field made a difference of 40,000 men."[22]

Eighteenth-century military planners had stressed the importance of massed artillery, rapid movement, deception, living off the countryside, and the annihilation of the enemy army. Napoleon alone had the will and ingenuity to convert these theories into battlefield victories. Napoleon also harnessed the military energies generated during a decade of revolutionary war. The Revolution had created a mass army, had instilled in the republican soldier a love for *la patrie,* and had enabled promising young soldiers to gain promotions on the basis of talent rather than birth. Napoleon took this inheritance and perfected it.

The Grand Empire: Diffusion of Revolutionary Institutions

By 1810, Napoleon dominated continental Europe, except for the Balkan Peninsula. The Grand Empire comprised lands annexed to France, vassal states, and cowed allies. The French republic had already annexed Belgium and the German Left Bank of the Rhine. Napoleon incorporated several other areas into France: German coastal regions as far as the western Baltic and large areas of Italy, including Rome, Geneva and its environs, Trieste, and the Dalmatian coast. Vassal states in the Grand Empire included five kingdoms ruled by Napoleon's relatives: two kingdoms in Italy and the kingdoms of Holland, Westphalia, and Spain.

Besides the five satellite kingdoms, there were several other vassal states within the Grand Empire. Napoleon formed the Confederation of the Rhine in 1806. Its members, a loose association of sixteen (later eighteen) German states, were subservient to the emperor, as were the nineteen cantons of the Swiss confederation. The Grand Duchy of Warsaw, formed in 1807 from Prussia's Polish lands, was placed under the rule of the German king of Saxony, one of Napoleon's vassals. Finally, the Grand Empire included states compelled to be French allies—Austria, Prussia, Russia, Sweden, and Denmark.

With varying degrees of determination and success, Napoleon extended the reforms of the Revolution to other lands. His officials instituted the Code Napoléon, organized an effective civil service, opened careers to talent, and equalized the tax burden. Besides abolishing serfdom, manorial payments, and the courts of the nobility, they did away with clerical courts, promoted freedom of religion, permitted civil marriage, pressed for civil rights for Jews, and fought clerical interference in secular matters. They also abolished guilds, introduced a uniform system of weights and measures, eliminated internal tolls, and built roads, bridges, and canals. They promoted secular education and improved public health. Napoleon had launched a Europe-wide social revolution that attacked the privileges of the aristocracy and the clergy and hastened the modernization of nineteenth-century Europe.

Napoleon had a twofold purpose in implementing these reforms: promoting administrative efficiency and winning the support of conquered peoples. Pleased by the overhaul of feudal practices and the reduction of clerical power, many Europeans, particularly the progressive bourgeoisie, welcomed Napoleon as a liberator.

But there was another side to Napoleon's rule. The tyrant of Europe turned conquered lands into satellite kingdoms and exploited them for the benefit of France. In a letter to Prince Eugène, viceroy of Italy, Napoleon revealed his policy:

> All the raw silk from the Kingdom of Italy goes to England. I wish to divert it from this route to the advantage of my French manufacturers: otherwise my silk factories, one of the chief supports of French commerce, will suffer substantial losses. My principle is France first. You must never lose sight of the fact that . . . France should claim commercial supremacy on the continent.[23]

The satellite states and annexed territories were compelled to provide recruits for Napoleon's army and taxes for his war treasury. Opponents of Napoleon faced confiscation of property, the galleys, and execution.

These methods of exploitation and repression increased hatred for Napoleon and French rule. Subject peoples, including bourgeois liberals who felt that he had betrayed the ideals of the Revolution, came to view Napoleon as a tyrant ready for his downfall.

Online Study Center **Improve Your Grade**
Interactive Map: Napoleonic Europe, ca. 1812

MAP 20.1 NAPOLEON'S EUROPE, 1810 ▶
By 1810, Napoleon dominated much of the Continent. His Grand Empire comprised lands annexed to France, vassal states, and cowed allies.

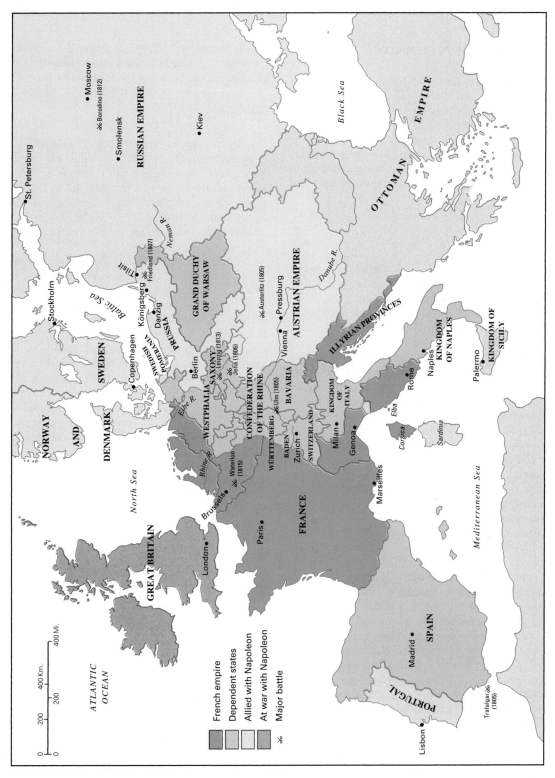

Moscow (1812)
⚔ Borodino (1812)
• Smolensk
• Kiev

RUSSIAN EMPIRE

Black Sea

OTTOMAN EMPIRE

• St. Petersburg

Neman R.

Friedland (1807)
Tilsit

Stockholm
Baltic Sea
Königsberg
Danzig

GRAND DUCHY OF WARSAW

⚔ Austerlitz (1805)
Pressburg
Danube R.
Vienna

AUSTRIAN EMPIRE

ILLYRIAN PROVINCES

PRUSSIA

SWEDISH POMERANIA

Leipzig (1813)
Berlin
SAXONY
Jena (1806)

WESTPHALIA

CONFEDERATION OF THE RHINE

BAVARIA

⚔ Ulm (1805)

KINGDOM OF ITALY

Rome

Naples
KINGDOM OF NAPLES

KINGDOM OF SICILY

Palermo

SWEDEN

Copenhagen

DENMARK

NORWAY AND

Elbe R.

Rhine R.

Waterloo (1815)
Brussels

WÜRTTEMBERG
BADEN
Zurich
SWITZERLAND

Milan
Genoa

Elba

Corsica

Sardinia

North Sea

London

GREAT BRITAIN

FRANCE

Paris

Marseilles

Mediterranean Sea

ATLANTIC OCEAN

400 Mi.
400 Km.
200
200
0
0

French empire
Dependent states
Allied with Napoleon
At war with Napoleon
⚔ Major battle

Madrid
SPAIN

PORTUGAL

Lisbon

Trafalgar (1805)

477

THE FALL OF NAPOLEON

Aside from the hostility of subject nationals, Napoleon had to cope with the determined opposition of Great Britain. Its subsidies and encouragement kept resistance to the emperor alive. But perhaps Napoleon's greatest obstacle was his own boundless ambition, which warped his judgment. From its peak, the emperor's career soon slid downhill to defeat, dethronement, and deportation.

Failure to Subdue England

Britain was Napoleon's most resolute opponent. It could not be otherwise, for any power that dominated the Continent could organize sufficient naval might to threaten British commerce, challenge its sea power, and invade the island kingdom. Britain would not make peace with any state that sought European hegemony, and Napoleon's ambition would settle for nothing less.

Since he could not make peace with Britain, Napoleon resolved to crush it. Between 1803 and 1805, he assembled an invasion flotilla in the English Channel. But there could be no invasion of Britain while British warships commanded the channel. In 1805, the battle of Trafalgar demonstrated British naval power when Admiral Nelson devastated a combined French and Spanish fleet. Napoleon was forced to postpone his invasion scheme indefinitely.

Unable to conquer Britain by arms, Napoleon decided to bring what he called "the nation of shopkeepers" to its knees by damaging the British economy. His plan, called the Continental System, was to bar all countries under France's control from buying British goods. Although hurt, Britain escaped economic ruin by smuggling goods onto the Continent and increasing trade with the New World. But the Continental System also punished European lands dependent on British imports; hundreds of ships lay idle in European ports, and industries closed down. Though generally supportive of Napoleon's social and administrative reforms, the bourgeoisie turned against him because of the economic distress caused by the Continental System. Further-

more, Napoleon's efforts to enforce the system enmeshed him in two catastrophic blunders: the occupation of Spain and the invasion of Russia.

The Spanish Ulcer

An ally of France since 1796, Spain proved a disappointment to Napoleon. It failed to prevent the Portuguese from trading with Britain and contributed little military or financial aid to France's war effort. Napoleon decided to incorporate Spain into his empire; in 1808, he deposed the Spanish ruler and designated his brother Joseph as king of Spain.

Napoleon believed that the Spanish would rally round the gentle Joseph and welcome his liberal reforms. This confidence was a fatal illusion. Spanish nobles and clergy feared French liberalism; the overwhelmingly peasant population, fanatically religious and easily stirred up by the clergy, viewed Napoleon as the Devil's agent. Loyal to the Spanish monarchy and faithful to the church, the Spanish fought a "War to the Knife" against the invaders.

Both sides in the Peninsular War displayed extreme cruelty. Guerrilla bands, aided and encouraged by priests preaching holy war, congregated in mountain hideouts. Striking from ambush, they raided French convoys and outposts. The war waged by Spanish partisans foreshadowed a twentieth-century phenomenon: the inability of a great power, using trained soldiers and modern weapons, to subdue peasant guerrillas.

The intervention of British troops, commanded by Sir Arthur Wellesley, the future duke of Wellington, led to the ultimate defeat of Joseph in 1813. The "Spanish ulcer" drained Napoleon's treasury, tied down French troops, enabled Britain to gain a foothold on the Continent from which to invade southern France, and inspired patriots in other lands to resist the French emperor.

The German War of Liberation

Anti-French feeling also broke out in the German states. Hatred of the French invaders evoked a feeling of national outrage among some Germans, who up to this time had thought only in terms of

AND THERE IS NO REMEDY, ETCHING BY FRAN-CISCO GOYA (1746–1828). Spaniards resisted the installation of Joseph, Napoleon's brother, as king of Spain. Both sides engaged in terrible atrocities in the ensuing Peninsular War. The Spanish painter Francisco Goya captured the war's brutality. (*Philadelphia Museum of Art: SmithKline Beecham Corporation Fund.*)

their own particular state and prince. Some German intellectuals, using the emotional language of nationalism, called for a war of liberation against Napoleon and, in some instances, for the creation of a unified Germany.

Besides arousing a desire for national independence and unity, the defeat of the Prussians at Jena (1806) and French domination of Germany stimulated a movement for reform among members of the Prussian high bureaucracy and officer corps. To survive in a world altered by the French Revolution, Prussia would have to learn the principal lessons of the Revolution: that aroused citizens fighting for a cause make better soldiers than mercenaries and oppressed serfs and that officers selected for daring and intelligence command better than nobles possessing only a gilded birthright. The reformers believed that the elimination of social abuses would overcome defeatism and apathy and encourage Prussians to serve the state willingly and to fight bravely for national honor. A revitalized Prussia could then deal with the French.

Among the important reforms introduced in Prussia between 1807 and 1813 were the abolition of serfdom, the granting to towns of a large measure of self-administration, the awarding of army commissions on the basis of merit instead of birth, the elimination of cruel punishment in the ranks, and the establishment of national conscription. In 1813, the reform party forced King Frederick William III to declare war on France. The military reforms did improve the quality of the Prussian army. In the War of Liberation (1813), Prussian soldiers demonstrated far more enthusiasm and patriotism than they had at Jena in 1806, and the French were driven from Germany. The German War of Liberation came on the heels of Napoleon's disastrous Russian campaign.

Disaster in Russia

The unsuccessful invasion of Russia in 1812 diminished Napoleon's glory and hastened the collapse of his empire. Deteriorating relations between Russia and France led Napoleon to his fatal decision to attack the eastern giant. Unwilling to permit Russia to become a Mediterranean power, the emperor resisted the tsar's attempts to acquire Constantinople. Napoleon's creation of the Grand Duchy of Warsaw irritated the tsar, who feared a revival of Polish power and resented French influence on Russia's border. Another source of friction between the tsar and Napoleon was Russia's illicit trade with Britain in violation of the Continental System. Napoleon reasoned that if he permitted the tsar to violate the trade regulations, other lands would soon follow and England would never be subdued. No doubt Napoleon's inexhaustible craving for power also compelled him to strike at Russia.

Napoleon assembled one of the largest armies in history: some 614,000 men, 200,000 animals, and 20,000 vehicles. Frenchmen constituted about half of the *Grande Armée de la Russie*; the other soldiers, many serving under compulsion, were drawn from a score of nationalities. The emperor intended to deal the Russians a crushing blow, forcing Tsar Alexander I to sue for peace. But the Russians had other plans: to avoid pitched battles, retreat eastward, and refuse to make peace with the invader. Napoleon would be drawn ever deeper into Russia in pursuit of the enemy.

In June 1812, the Grand Army crossed the Neman River into Russia. Fighting only rear-guard battles and retreating according to plan, the tsar's forces lured the invaders into the vastness of Russia, far from their lines of supply. In September, the Russians made a stand at Borodino, some seventy miles west of Moscow. Although the French won, opening the road to Moscow, they lost forty thousand men and failed to destroy the Russian army, which withdrew in order. Napoleon still did not have the decisive victory with which he hoped to compel the tsar to make peace. At midnight on September 14, the Grand Army, its numbers greatly reduced by disease, hunger, exhaustion, desertion, and battle, entered Moscow. Expecting to be greeted by a deputation of nobles, Napoleon found instead that the Muscovites had virtually evacuated their holy city. To show their contempt for the French conquerors and to deny the French shelter, the Russians set fire to the city, which burned for five days.

Taking up headquarters in Moscow, Napoleon waited for Alexander I to admit defeat and come to terms. But the tsar remained intransigent. Napoleon was in a dilemma: to penetrate deeper into Russia was certain death; to stay in Moscow with winter approaching meant possible starvation. Faced with these alternatives, Napoleon was forced to retreat westward to his sources of supply. On October 19, 1812, ninety-five thousand troops and thousands of wagons loaded with loot left Moscow for the long trek back.

In early November came the first snow and frost. Army stragglers were slaughtered by Russian Cossacks and peasant partisans. Hungry soldiers pounced on fallen horses, carving them up alive. The wounded were left to lie where they dropped. Some poor wretches, wrote a French officer, "dragged themselves along, shivering . . . until the snow packed under the soles of their boots, a bit of debris, a branch, or the body of a fallen comrade tripped them and threw them down. Then their moans for help went unheeded. The snow soon covered them up and only low white mounds showed where they lay. Our road was strewn with these hummocks, like a cemetery."[24]

In the middle of December, with the Russians in pursuit, the remnants of the Grand Army staggered across the Neman River into East Prussia. Napoleon had left his men earlier in the month and, traveling in disguise, reached Paris on December 18. Napoleon had lost his army; he would soon lose his throne.

Final Defeat

After the destruction of the Grand Army, the empire crumbled. Although Napoleon raised a new army, he could not replace the equipment, cavalry horses, and experienced soldiers squandered in Russia. Now he had to rely on schoolboys and overage veterans.

Most of Europe joined in a final coalition against France. In October 1813, allied forces from Austria, Prussia, Russia, and Sweden defeated Napoleon at Leipzig; in November, Anglo-Spanish forces crossed the Pyrenees into France. Finally, in the spring of 1814, the allies captured Paris. Napoleon abdicated and was exiled to the tiny island of Elba, off the coast of Italy. The Bourbon dynasty was restored to the throne of France in the person of Louis XVIII, younger brother of the executed Louis XVI and the acknowledged leader of the émigrés.

Only forty-four years of age, Napoleon did not believe that it was his destiny to die on Elba. On March 1, 1815, he landed on the French coast with a thousand soldiers. Louis XVIII ordered his troops to stop Napoleon's advance. When Napoleon's small force approached the king's troops, Napoleon walked up to the soldiers who blocked the road. "If there is one soldier among you who wishes to kill his Emperor, here I am." It was a brilliant move by a man who thoroughly understood the French soldier. The king's troops shouted, "Long live the Emperor!" and joined Napoleon. On March 20, 1815, Napoleon entered Paris to a hero's welcome. He had not lost his charisma.

Raising a new army, Napoleon moved against the allied forces in Belgium. There the British, led by the duke of Wellington, and the Prussians, led by Field Marshal Gebhard von Blücher, defeated Napoleon at Waterloo in June 1815. Napoleon's desperate gamble to regain power—the famous "hundred days"—had failed. This time the allies sent Napoleon to Saint Helena, a lonely island in

DISASTER IN RUSSIA. Lacking winter provisions, Napoleon's Grand Army abandoned Moscow in October 1812. The retreating French were decimated by hunger, winter, and Russian attacks. (*Musée de l'Armée.*)

the South Atlantic, a thousand miles off the coast of southern Africa. On this gloomy and rugged rock, Napoleon Bonaparte, emperor of France and would-be conqueror of Europe, spent the last six years of his life.

THE LEGEND
AND THE ACHIEVEMENT

"Is there anyone whose decisions have had a greater consequence for the whole of Europe?" asks the Dutch historian Pieter Geyl about Napoleon.[25] It might also be asked: Is there anyone about whom there has been such a wide range of conflicting interpretations? Both Napoleon's contemporaries and later analysts have seen Napoleon in many different lights.

Napoleon himself contributed to the historical debate. Concerned as ever with his reputation, he reconstructed his career while on Saint Helena. His recorded reminiscences are the chief source of the Napoleonic legend. According to this account, Napoleon's principal aim was to defend the Revolution and consolidate its gains. He emerges as a champion of equality and supporter of popular sovereignty who destroyed aristocratic privileges, restored order, and opposed religious intolerance. He appears as a lover of peace forced to take up the sword because of the implacable hatred of Europe's reactionary rulers. According to this reconstruction, Napoleon meant to spread the blessings of the Revolution to the Germans, Dutch, Spaniards, Poles, and Italians; he wished to create a United States of Europe, a federation of free and enlightened nations living in peace.

Undoubtedly, Napoleon did disseminate many gains of the Revolution. Nevertheless, say his critics, this account overlooks much. It ignores the repression of liberty, the subverting of republicanism, the oppression of conquered peoples, and the terrible suffering resulting from his pursuit of glory. The critics see the reminiscences as another example of Napoleonic propaganda.

Although the debate over Napoleon continues, historians agree on two points. First, his was no ordinary life. A self-made man who harnessed the revolutionary forces of the age and imposed his will on history, Napoleon was right to call his life a romance. His drive, military genius, and charisma propelled him to the peak of power; his inability to moderate his ambition bled Europe, distorted his judgment, and caused his downfall. His overweening pride, the hubris of the Greek tragedians, would have awed Sophocles; the dimensions of his mind and the intricacies of his personality would have intrigued Shakespeare; his cynicism and utter unscrupulousness would have impressed Machiavelli. His generalship led contemporaries to compare him with Alexander the Great and Hannibal, legendary commanders in the ancient world. Second, historians agree that by spreading revolutionary ideals and institutions, Napoleon made it im-

possible for the traditional rulers to restore the Old Regime intact after the emperor's downfall. He had solidified in France what the revolution had initiated—the destruction of the society based on orders and legal privileges and the opening of careers to talent regardless of birth. In conquered lands, his administrators undermined the authority of aristocrats and clergy. Napoleon's reforms furthered the rationalization and secularization of society and contributed to the transformation of the dynastic state into the modern national state and to the prominence of the bourgeoisie.

The new concept of warfare and the new spirit of nationalism also became an indelible part of the European scene. In the course of succeeding generations, the methods of total warfare in the service of a belligerent nationalism would shatter Napoleon's grandiose vision of a united Europe. They would also subvert the liberal humanism that was the essential heritage of the Enlightenment and the French Revolution.

❖   ❖   ❖

Online Study Center ACE the Test

NOTES

1. Quoted in Felix Markham, *Napoleon and the Awakening of Europe* (New York: Collier Books, 1965), p. 27.

2. Excerpted in J. Christopher Herold, ed., *The Mind of Napoleon* (New York: Columbia University Press, 1955), p. 260.

3. Georges Lefebvre, *Napoleon*, trans. J. E. Anderson (New York: Columbia University Press, 1969), 2:65.

4. Ibid., p. 67.

5. Ibid., p. 66.

6. Quoted in David Chandler, *The Campaigns of Napoleon* (New York: Macmillan, 1966), p. 157.

7. Excerpted in Maurice Hutt, ed., *Napoleon* (Englewood Cliffs, N.J.: Prentice-Hall, 1972), p. 3.

8. Excerpted in David L. Dowd, ed., *Napoleon: Was He the Heir of the Revolution?* (New York: Holt, Rinehart, & Winston, 1966), p. 42.

9. Quoted in Felix Markham, *Napoleon* (New York: Mentor Books, 1963), p. 100.

10. Excerpted in Frank Malloy Anderson, ed., *The Constitution and Other Select Documents Illustrative of the History of France* (Minneapolis: H. W. Wilson, 1908), pp. 312–313.

11. Quoted in Robert B. Holtman, *The Napoleonic Revolution* (Philadelphia: Lippincott, 1967), pp. 123–124.

12. Quoted in Holtman, *Napoleonic Revolution*, p. 121.

13. Quoted in Markham, *Napoleon*, p. 97.

14. Excerpted in Dowd, *Napoleon*, p. 27.

15. Quoted in Holtman, *Napoleonic Revolution*, p. 143.

16. Excerpted in Hutt, *Napoleon,* pp. 49–50.

17. R. M. Johnston, ed., *The Corsican: A Diary of Napoleon's Life in His Own Words* (Boston: Houghton Mifflin, 1910), p. 166.

18. Quoted in Chandler, *Campaigns of Napoleon,* p. 145.

19. Ibid.

20. Ibid., p. 155.

21. Ibid.

22. Ibid., p. 157.

23. Excerpted in Dowd, *Napoleon,* p. 57.

24. Quoted in J. Christopher Herold, *The Age of Napoleon* (New York: Dell, 1963), p. 320.

25. Pieter Geyl, *Napoleon: For and Against* (New Haven, Conn.: Yale University Press, 1964), p. 16.

SUGGESTED READING

Chandler, David, *The Campaigns of Napoleon* (1966). An analysis of Napoleon's art of war.

Herold, J. Christopher, ed., *The Mind of Napoleon* (1955). Valuable selections from the written and spoken words of Napoleon.

Hutt, Maurice, ed., *Napoleon* (1972). Excerpts from Napoleon's words and the views of contemporaries and later historians.

Markham, Felix, *Napoleon* (1963). A first-rate short biography.

———, *Napoleon and the Awakening of Europe* (1965). An exploration of Napoleon's influence on other lands.

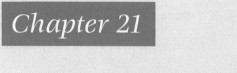

Chapter 21

The Industrial Revolution: The Transformation of Society

Railroad line from Nuremburg to Furth. The spectacle of the arrival and departure of the train attracts the townspeople of all classes. Central Europe followed England and France in railroad mania. (Art Resource, NY.)

- **Origins of the Industrial Age**
- **Society Transformed**
- **Relief and Reform**
- **Industrialism in Perspective**

Focus Questions

1. Why did England industrialize before the rest of Europe? How did political and social factors influence industrialization in England?

2. How did political and social factors promote or delay industrialization in France, in the German states, and in the Netherlands?

3. Why did cities grow so rapidly between 1800 and 1860? How did that growth influence politics?

4. Which groups were indicated by the term *middle classes,* and which were considered the *working classes* or the *lower orders* in nineteenth-century Europe? Why did contemporaries and some historians make the terms plural instead of designating all of the groups as the *middle class?*

5. How did the law discriminate against and punish the working class during the early stages of industrialization? How did it try to protect this class?

Online Study Center

This icon will direct you to interactive map and primary source activities on the website http://college.hmco.com/pic/perrywc8e.

In the second half of the eighteenth century, such significant changes took place in the ways western Europeans labored and traded that historians call the total process the Industrial Revolution. Although this revolution had no start, no single set pattern, and little planning, its effects dominated the following two centuries, changing the lives and society of Europeans and spreading throughout the world.

The term *Industrial Revolution* refers to the shift from an agrarian, handicraft, labor-intensive economy to an economy dominated by machine manufacture, specialization of tasks or division of labor, factories and cities, and a worldwide market for goods, services, and capital. These changes began in England, amazing contemporaries with inventions that, though actually simple on-the-job changes made by laborers, nonetheless "revolutionized" human tasks. Today the aspects of the Industrial Revolution that stand out for us are the increase in agricultural productivity, the population growth and the rapid development of cities, the new and more efficient ways of organizing tasks to use plentiful labor and stretch limited natural resources, and the innovative ways of expanding capital.

Industrial progress that spanned a century in Britain and as much as two centuries in the rest of the developed world hardly seems revolutionary. But the transformation of human existence between the eighteenth century and the present is so great that no terms other than *revolution* seem appropriate. In fact, historians see multiple industrial revolutions: one from 1750 to 1850 in western Europe, one from the mid-nineteenth century including the United States, another in the first half of the twentieth century, and yet another within the last fifty years.

Industrial development did not proceed at the same pace everywhere. The changes begun in England in the mid 1700s were delayed in France by political and social conflict until after the French Revolution. In the German and Italian states, the lack of political unity slowed the growth of industry. The German states began industrializing in the 1840s, nearly a century after England. Even after German unification in 1870, when industry grew phenomenally, much of the traditional economy persisted alongside the new. In Italy, too, industrialization began slowly. It was hampered by the sharp economic divisions between north and south, the comparative lack of natural resources, and the slow political unification of the peninsula. Eastern Europe did not start industrializing until the 1890s, and in some cases not until the twentieth century.

Britain, thus, had stepped out ahead. European states copied its techniques, borrowed and stole its plans, imported its engineers as advisers, borrowed its capital, and carefully studied its politics, ideas, and society to imitate whatever seemed essential to industrialization. By the second half of the nineteenth century, Germany, France, and the United States moved into genuine competition with Britain; and Italy, Russia, and Austria-Hungary raced to catch up. Almost inevitably, Europeans and Americans, and eventually other peoples around the globe, were driven to adopt the changes in agriculture and industry that had originated in England. Everywhere, as the economy changed, the conditions of labor and life were profoundly altered.

ORIGINS OF THE INDUSTRIAL AGE

Why did industrialization begin in western Europe rather than elsewhere in the world? Why had not the wealth and skills of the Chinese or the Moguls in India made these radical changes in economy and society? After all, the desire for Asia's superior products had launched Europeans on their aggressive commercial expansion in the sixteenth century. These counter-factual questions—that is, questions asking *why not* rather than *why*—furnish us with complex answers that illustrate the characteristics of the actual revolution.

From the fifteenth to the eighteenth century, western Europe accumulated substantial wealth, and this wealth was spread across more classes of people. In the late Middle Ages improved agriculture increased population. The widespread practice of diverse rural handicrafts provided the foundations for the relatively rapid expansion of trade, both overseas and on the Continent, in the next two centuries. This expansion resulted from an aggressive search for new markets rather than from new methods of production; it built on the

capitalist practices of medieval and Renaissance bankers and merchants, and it tapped the wealth of a much larger world than the Mediterranean lands accessible to earlier generations. Thus, the resources of the New World and of Africa, both human and material, fueled Europe's accumulation of wealth.

In the early modern period, the states that had centralized power in the hands of a strong monarch—England, Spain, Portugal, and France, as well as the much less centralized Netherlands—competed for markets, territory, and prestige in ways that contributed to economic expansion. Engaged in fierce military and commercial rivalries with one another, these states, with varying degrees of success, actively promoted industries to manufacture weaponry, uniforms, and ships; they also encouraged commerce for the sake of tax revenues. This growth in commerce nurtured a greatly expanded economy, in which many levels of society took part: owners of large estates, merchant princes, innovative entrepreneurs, the sugar plantation colonials, slave traders, sailors, and even peasants.

Europe's Population Explosion

Several factors, each linked to the increase in the labor supply in much of Europe, led to industrialization. In the eighteenth century, the rural population grew enormously. This increase coincided with the breakup of traditional farming. In western Europe capitalist farming for the market—an agricultural revolution—replaced traditional practices. The population explosion did not bring famine, disease, and misery to Europe as it had so many times before, and as it has in so many other regions, particularly Asia and Africa. The effects of the conjunction actually freed much of Europe's labor. Even the strong monarchs of western Europe were not powerful enough to keep labor tied to the land. In labor-scarce areas, such as Russia, the United States, and much of Latin America, however, labor remained the serfdom, slavery, and peonage deep into the nineteenth century.

The rapidly growing population provided both the laborers and the consumers of the products of economic development. Most of Europe's explosive population growth took place from the middle of the eighteenth century. In 1800, Europe

THE AGRICULTURAL REVOLUTION: THE MCCORMICK REAPER. Harvesting grain with a horse-drawn machine released great numbers of laborers from farms to work in factories and cities. The great demand for labor may explain, in part, the constant search for and investment in mechanical devices for farm and factory in the United States, a major food exporter even today. (*State Historical Society of Wisconsin.*)

had about 190 million people; by 1850, 260 million. By 1914, it had 460 million, and some 200 million other Europeans had settled throughout the world. Virtually simultaneous with this population boom, there were two major changes in agriculture: a "green revolution" of new crops, and new and different ways of utilizing land and labor. With these changes, productivity rose sufficiently to feed the increasing population and actually to improve the diet of Europeans. Better nutrition meant better health, more births, and fewer deaths of both young and old. Surviving children grew stronger and taller (the average European man was five foot six in 1900, a mere five feet in 1800). They worked harder and longer and were abler intellectually. Girls began to menstruate earlier; women married at a younger age (on average, three years earlier), which meant more births. Greater demand meant higher prices for food and profits for land entrepreneurs. At the same time, this relative agricultural prosperity contributed to the poverty of the rural poor.

Agricultural Revolution

Capitalist agriculture, born in England and the Netherlands, spread to other areas; production was for the market, not for family or village consumption. Many people, aristocrats as well as peasants, persisted in traditional patterns and mutual obligations. But powerful forces gradually drew most farmers to the marketplace, first in western, then in central, and finally in eastern and southern Europe. Land freed from traditional obligations became just another commodity to be bought, sold, traded, and managed for profit.

Peasants freed from manorial obligations joined the ranks of entrepreneurs, tenants, or wage laborers—all farming for the market. Undeveloped land was brought under cultivation; common land where villagers grazed animals was claimed as private property, generally by great landowners, whose political power gave them an advantage. This process, known as *enclosure*, took place over much of Europe. In England, most enclosure had occurred two centuries earlier, but the much smaller number of enclosures in the 1700s were, nonetheless, responsible for much rural poverty. Disposed farmers tried to eke out a living as day laborers for the commercial farming landowners, who were glad to have the cheap labor when there was work to do but resented the poor in the off-season. The pressure to make a living drove the poor to work as weavers or spinners in their own cottages. Entrepreneurs "farmed out" some manufacturing processes to displaced rural labor. In the long run, the new trends forced farmers to emigrate either to cities or to the Americas or Australia.

The agricultural revolution of the 1700s meant changes in landholding, soil usage, and animal husbandry. Land use grew more efficient. Convertible husbandry—the term given to innovation in farming—cycled land from grain production through soil-restoring crops of legumes, then pasturage, and back to grain production. Land no longer needed to lie fallow. These methods were first developed by landlords seeking to improve production but gradually extended to the peasantry. In some areas, however—within every country, and particularly in southern and eastern Europe—the old practices continued well into the 1800s.

By the middle of the nineteenth century—after two centuries of increasing agricultural productivity with little change in technology—the application of technical ingenuity to farming brought steel plows, improved reapers, horse-drawn rakes, and threshers. (The Americans were very inventive in this area; agricultural machinery formed a substantial part of their manufacturing exports.) These changes greatly increased efficiency and production; fewer men and women could produce more food and raw materials.

Britain First

Why did Britain industrialize first? At the beginning of the eighteenth century, Britain's advantages were not so apparent. The Netherlands and France were as wealthy, if not more so. They possessed an empire equal to England's in trading importance, and their populations were equally skilled and industrious. The scientific and in-tellectual life of both rivaled that of England. The French government, if anything, was more responsive than Britain's to the need for transportation and communication; it supported engineering and innovation with subsidies and prizes. It had also established schools for technicians and trained civil engineers for public works such as waterworks, canals, roads, and bridges.

The French, however, seemed less willing than the British to change the traditional ways of agriculture or craft production. The size of the landholdings, smaller than in England, may have discouraged experimentation. Well into the nineteenth century, the French produced fine goods by hand for the few, rather than cheap goods by machine for the many. A number of serious obstacles—internal tariffs, government monopolies, and strong craft guilds—hampered industrialization in France and the countries of central Europe. In England, these hindrances to the free flow of goods either were less powerful or did not exist. As a result of these commercial and cultural differences, French industrialization was slow.

The French Revolution, which gave so much political freedom and economic opportunity, perpetuated some traditional agricultural and commercial practices. Peasants who acquired land in the Revolution often gained plots so small that the new farming methods were difficult to apply. Because French peasants tried to restrict their family size in order to feed themselves, France lacked a large supply of cheap labor. Inefficient small farms did not produce a surplus for the market. Political instability made it hard for the French to develop or maintain the optimism and the willingness to take risks that contribute to economic development.

The Netherlands, too, had sufficient wealth for industrialization. During the seventeenth century, the Dutch had developed techniques of finance and commerce that every nation tried to imitate. They had a good transportation system, a fine navy, and technical know-how. They were also skilled farmers. However, they lacked natural resources.

Britain, thus, possessed several advantages enabling it to become the workshop of the world. First, it had a labor pool of hardworking, skilled farmers who could no longer earn a living on the land. Britain also possessed large and easily developed supplies of coal and iron and a long tradition of metallurgy and mining. In the early stages of industrialization, Britain's transportation system was supplemented by canals and toll roads (turnpikes), which private entrepreneurs built for profit. Private enterprise played a vital role in Britain's economic development; no other country relied as completely on private capital resources and individual entrepreneurs for its industrial development. Small wonder, then, that free trade and economic individualism had so many champions there.

The state did contribute to Britain's industrial revolution. British business thrived in a climate favorable to economic expansion—a stable environment of law, order, and protection of private property. Laws allowed the enclosure of common lands, pushing small farmers off the land and permitting the consolidation of large holdings. Parliament fostered businesses, such as toll bridge and canal builders and the East Indies Company, that expanded trade routes and enriched the British economy. By the eighteenth century, a British entrepreneur had remarkable freedom of entry into the economy, unrestricted by monopolies and guilds as were other Europeans.

Even Britain's culture spurred industrialization because it encouraged consumption and permitted social mobility. The British aspired to the lifestyles of their social superiors, creating a broad-based consuming public. Consumption was a great incentive to production and trade. Debt carried no social stigma, as it did in other cultures. Although the upper class was prejudiced against trade, there were no rigid barriers. A fortune accumulated by hard work or by marriage could overcome social handicaps within a generation or two.

Online Study Center **Improve Your Grade**
Primary Source: Life Among the Laboring Poor: A Cotton Spinner's Wife Tells Her Tale

Technological Advance

When most people think of the Industrial Revolution, they think of the inventions that changed handicrafts to machine-made goods and substituted other sources of energy for human and animal power. Innovations also led to the development of new products. In the long run, inventions would have revolutionary implications for politics and society, as well as for the economy, but the early stages of technological development grew from the simple changes workers made as they worked. Eager artisans quickly picked up on small improvements to lessen their burdens and increase their productivity and profits. Examination of some key industries indicates how the process took off.

Cotton Textiles. Cotton production was actually the first industry to grow at unprecedented rates, expanding tenfold between 1760 and 1785 and another tenfold between 1785 and 1825. In 1733, long before expansion started, a simple invention—John Kay's flying shuttle—allowed weavers to double their output. This shuttle, which could be used in the home, was a device of the wool trade for generations. It meant weavers produced faster than spinners—until James Hargreaves's spinning jenny, perfected by 1768, allowed an operator to work several spindles at once, powered only by human energy. Within five years, Richard Arkwright applied a water-frame spinning machine, which could be powered by water or animals. Samuel Crompton's spinning mule (1779) powered many spindles, first by human and later by animal and water energy. These changes improved spinning productivity so much that there were bottlenecks in weaving until Edmund Cartwright developed a power loom in 1787. To the end of the century, there was a race first speeding up the spinning and then the weaving by applying water power to looms or new, larger devices to the jenny.

These inventions drastically altered the social conditions of the workplace. At first, families worked in their cottages; women and children spun while men wove. Then, when more than human strength was needed to power the looms, and the water frame was used, it became more efficient to bring workers together than to send work out to workers' homes. Workers moved to factories located by streams for the water power. Then steam meant factories could be built anywhere. If coal was nearby, costs were cut considerably. Then, there were specialized factories for

WOMAN AT HARGREAVES'S SPINNING JENNY. The cotton textile trade was one of the first to be mechanized. In cottage industries, the whole family contributed to the making of thread and cloth. Hargreaves's spinning jenny, one of the early inventions made by the workers themselves, was an adaptation of his wife's thread-spinning tool. (*Mary Evans Picture Library.*)

weaving or spinning. Power-driven weaving was primarily men's work, spinning women's. Odd jobs were for children. Within two or three generations, the factory system revolutionized labor, changing the family. It also urbanized labor.

These were major social changes. So was the invention of Eli Whitney's cotton gin (1793). It removed seeds from raw cotton quickly and cheaply, bringing about a social revolution because farmers and plantation owners devoted more land to production. Greater demand for field labor extended and changed aspects of slavery, just as other inventions caused the shift from the domestic production system to a factory one.

Weavers and spinners—not technicians, engineers, or scientists—invented simple devices modeled after machines already in use. These inventions did not cause the cotton industry's expansion; that was the result of social and economic demand. Once begun, the expansion was so great, the demand so urgent, and the potential profits so great that more and more complicated technology developed. A role emerged for the engineer who was an expert in building or adapting machines and in utilizing different sources of power.

Steam Power. Roughly the same process took place in steam. James Watt's steam engine dates from the 1760s, but it was too expensive to be widely adapted to production. Women, children, and even men laborers were cheaper than steam-powered machinery. Within two generations, by the 1830s in England, engines and fuel became cheaper, entrepreneurs began to use them, and expansion became rapid. Steam engines ran on coal or wood, not water power, which meant flexibility in locating factories. (Any factory already located by water would continue to use that much cheaper source of power, of course.) Steam also powered transportation—trains and carts—but again cost might lead a businessman to use canal transportation. But by the midcentury, steam was widely applied, causing the incredible rate of change generally identified with the Industrial Revolution. In the two previous centuries, increasing productivity, the accumulation of capital, and the provisioning of a growing population had been powered by people, animals, and water—an extraordinary feat. With steam, work was revolutionized because weaker, younger, and less-skilled workers could perform the few simple necessary tasks. Moreover, as steam took hold, human participation in the process of manufacture diminished; engines replaced people, and workers became "hands" that drove machines.

The New Iron Age. Steam power enabled the weak to operate machinery, but it required strong machines to withstand its force. As with textiles and power, the history of the search for better iron illustrates how developments in one industry prompted change in related industries and in society.

Until the eighteenth century, making iron had not changed much since the Middle Ages. By trial-and-error methods, entrepreneurs such as the Darbys, in England, replaced the burning of scarce and valuable wood with coal or coke in the manufacture of cast iron and later wrought iron. Coal made brittle metal though, until Henry Cort copied the French practice of using a furnace with two separate compartments, one for the coke and one for the iron ore. By the 1780s, trial and error, copying, and adapting had perfected wrought iron so that it became the most widely used metal in construction and machinery. In the 1860s, steel began to be produced cheaply. Henry Bessemer converted pig iron into steel by removing impurities in the iron. William Siemens and Pierre and Émile Martin developed the open-hearth process, which could handle much greater amounts of metal than Bessemer's converter. Steel became so cheap that it quickly replaced iron. The age of steel was born.

Producing iron or steam power required coal, which was the fuel of industrial growth. Sixteen million tons were mined at the end of the Napoleonic wars; thirty million in 1836; and sixty-five million in 1856. All this coal was mined by human beings—entire families, whole villages—because steam engines were too expensive to replace human labor. Steam engines pumped water and hauled carts and miners up from the main shaft to the surface. Once steam engines

were applied to mining itself, rich veins in existing mines became accessible, stoking this early industrialization.

Transportation and Communication. Revolutionized transportation provided the network to support expansion. Major road building took place in the eighteenth century in England and in France, and later in the rest of Europe. Both Britain and the United States experienced a boom in canal construction between 1760 and 1820. But canals were quickly outmoded by railroads, which, though more expensive, were more flexible. They caught the public imagination much as automobiles and airplanes would in the twentieth century. Steam-powered engines began to replace horse-powered railroads in the 1820s. Deeming railroads essential for defense and unity, Continental governments expended major efforts to develop rail networks.

Communication changed as spectacularly as transportation. Britain inaugurated the penny post in 1840, making it possible to send a letter to any part of the kingdom for about half an American penny. But the cost of postage was so high elsewhere that letters were rare. The telegraph developed rapidly because business demanded cheap and fast communications. The first telegraphic message was sent from Baltimore to Washington, D.C., in 1844. Within seven years, the first undersea cable was laid under the English Channel, and by 1866, transatlantic cable was operating. Although certainly not cheap, the telegraph was quickly employed by ever-expanding business.

Unprecedented amounts of private British capital built Britain's system of roads, canals, railways, and steamships. Continental states were slower to adopt steam transport just because they lacked capital and skilled civil engineering. Only France invested a great percentage of private capital in building a Europe-wide transportation system. Failures of management and inadequate financing, however, led the French government to take control of its railroads. In most of Europe, state construction and control was the rule. In the United States, Congress gave enormous grants of land to railroad companies. Everywhere during the nineteenth-century railroad-building boom, financiers invested heavily. The flow of capital

The Darby Family

By trial and error, three generations of an English family of iron manufacturers developed new ways of producing the precious metal of industrialization. As in so many enterprises of the Industrial Revolution, the innovative methods and capital investments came from a single family from the seventeenth to the nineteenth century.

Abraham Darby (1677–1717), a workman in Coalbrookdale, England, built a blast furnace for casting iron. He is believed to be the first to have used coke in iron smelting while trying to replace expensive charcoal. Coke made less brittle iron than raw coal because it contained less sulphur. With larger furnaces Darby was able to make superior iron, which was used for casting quality cannon for the Royal Navy, a good contract but not a subsidy.

By the time of Abraham II (1711–1763), coke smelting was the dominant technique for making cast iron, but the Darbys had no exclusive rights to the process. The industry (still consisting of small, competing firms) was concen-

Spectrum Color Library.

from western Europe, particularly Britain and France, to other lands in Europe and America was an awe-inspiring achievement. The flow of finance across borders and oceans was matched only by the flow of labor, as Europeans and Asians built railroad networks.

The Power of Finance

The first stages of industrialization—the use of new crop mixes and tools in agriculture and the first changes in spinning and weaving—did not require much capital. Neither did the early adaptations in the iron industry. Subsequent growth, however—from the spread of factories and the extensive application of machinery in agriculture to the expansion of mining and construction in

the cities—required the investment of enormous capital. Railroads and steamship lines were often so expensive that only governments could finance them; even in Belgium, where they were privately financed at first, the king was the major investor. Large capital infusions were also needed to fund the steel industry.

In the beginning, the owning family was the source of a company's financing, its management, and even its technical innovation. Family firms dominated industry. But outside investment grew steadily from 1860 to World War I (1914). In Britain, wealthy merchants and landlords invested, and low interest rates encouraged borrowing. On the Continent, where the supply of capital was limited, the British became international investors of the first rank, furnishing much

trated in coal-rich regions such as Coalbrookdale to reduce transportation costs.

Abraham III (1750–1791) was the pride of the family and of England when in 1779 he built the first cast-iron bridge: a semicircular arch across the Severn River. The Severn bridge was a major technological feat. Darby rebuilt his grandfather's furnaces to cast large enough pieces for a bridge that is one hundred feet long with forty-five-foot-high castings. It has 378 tons of interlocking iron pieces held together by bolts or rivets. Engineers and travelers from all over Europe came to see this marvel.

The story of the Darbys and the Severn bridge symbolizes English industrialization. When John Wilkinson, another small ironmonger, failed to get together the capital for the bridge, Darby designed, cast, and built it in his small enterprise. Darby also financed the bridge. He laid out half of the total funds and got the other half from private funds—none came from government. A technological marvel, the bridge was a financial one as well, capitalized by a workman-entrepreneur who wasn't even incorporated.

of the capital for the industrialization of other nations. French investors, who were sometimes reluctant to invest at home for fear of political instability, financed railroads in central Europe. They were also the major investors in the Suez Canal and in the first canal project in Panama, which failed. Among banking families—including the Barings of London and the Rothschilds of France, England, and Germany—kinship ties joined together large amounts of investment capital. People of the same religion or region would often band together to gather capital for development, as the Protestant and Jewish bankers of France did. These investor groups fueled European industrialization.

Banking was risky business in the nineteenth century; dozens of banks failed in every financial crisis. Lacking insurance for deposits and possessing only limited resources, banks tended to be cautious about risks. They diversified their investments so as not to lose everything in the failure of a single industry. Thus, in any given country, the number of industries able to borrow substantial amounts of capital was limited. In many countries, bankers preferred safe investments in government debt, a preference that slowed the development of industry.

Financing industry was difficult until there was some organization to enable a number of people to pool their capital safely. In the existing joint-stock companies, individuals could be held responsible for all the debts of the enterprise. England was innovative in finance, permitting incorporation in 1844. Investors were liable for a corporation's debts only in proportion to the number of shares they owned. This legal change meant that investors endangered only the amount that they had paid for their stock, and not all the funds that they or their family possessed. In 1844, after nearly a century of industrial progress, England had almost 1,000 such companies, compared with only 260 in France. In the 1850s, limited liability was applied to the stock of most English businesses, and a little later it was extended to banking and insurance companies. By the 1860s, France, Germany, and the United States permitted limited liability, which released a flow of savings into industry.

Like so much of the Industrial Revolution, solving the problems of organizing, structuring, and managing firms and of acquiring funds for the development of industry was a matter of trial and error, experiment, and innovation. These inventions of the mind and culture were as important to the expanding revolution as the invention of machines.

SOCIETY TRANSFORMED

European society remained overwhelmingly rural, and much of the old life continued while the foundations of the new society were being laid. Landed property was still the principal form of wealth and the source of social and political power. Large landowners, as leaders of families and kinship groups, continued to exert political and social influence, usually on the local or regional level. From England to Russia, families of

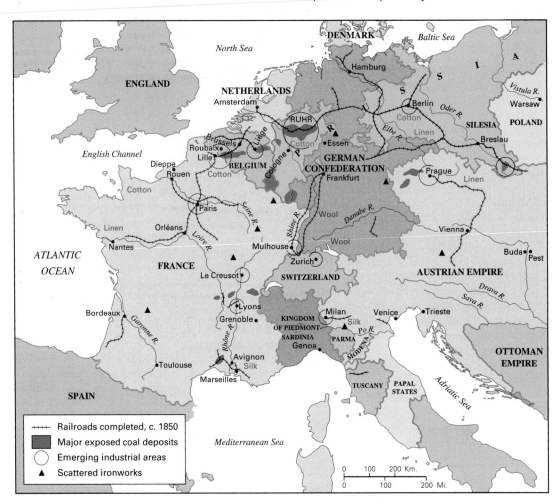

MAP 21.1 INDUSTRIAL GROWTH ON THE CONTINENT, MID 1800s   Industry created a market and production unit in northwestern Europe even before Germany and Italy were unified states.

landed wealth (often the old noble families) still constituted the social elite.

Industrialization brought a new world, with many forms of property and power. Individuals became increasingly important—before the law, in trade, in political thought, and in politics. Ultimately, the nation became more important than the province, region, or local area, but even in western Europe, this did not happen for most people until the last quarter of the nineteenth century. Contemporaries viewed the growth of cities and industrial towns as they did so many aspects of industrialization—as a sudden and complete break with the past. For them it was the shatter-ing of traditional moral and social patterns. Some people remembered the past clearly, but others idealized it as a golden age in which the relations between master and worker had been based on values other than the cash nexus—other than wages, hours, and production.

Urbanization

The urbanization of western society greatly accel-erated during the Industrial Revolution. In the nineteenth century, cities became places of manu-facture and industry, growing in number, size,

LONDON ROW HOUSES. This painting by the French artist Gustave Doré depicts overcrowded and unsanitary conditions in industrial London. Workers and their families lived side by side in row houses, each only one room wide with a tiny yard in back. (*Prints Division, New York Public Library, Astor, Lenox, and Tilden Foundations.*)

and population. Before 1800, about 10 percent of the European population lived in cities (20 percent in Great Britain and the Netherlands, the leading areas of urban living). Only forty-five cities in the *world* had more than 100,000 people. Halfway through the nineteenth century, when 52 percent of the English lived in cities, just 25 percent of the French, 36 percent of the Germans, 7 percent of the Russians, and 10 percent of U.S. inhabitants were urban dwellers.

Most of the shift from rural to urban living in the West occurred in the twentieth century, as industrialization spread. But the increase in urban population during the 1800s did occur overnight in some regions: the Midlands in England, the Lowlands in Scotland, the northern plains in France, the German Rhineland, the northeastern United States, and parts of northern Italy. Unlike capital cities, industrial ones, particularly in England, grew rapidly, without planning or much

regulation by local or national governments. Government and business were reluctant to finance remedies for poor working and living conditions, which they saw as the workers' problem or perhaps the responsibility of a particular industry or group of businessmen but not of taxpayers as a whole. Private funders were too weak and unwilling to combat the effects of unregulated private enterprise. In the rest of Europe, where industrialization came later, states were more willing to regulate industrial and urban development. They also had a bureaucracy for planning and regulation, although such efforts were still woefully inadequate.

So much growth with so little planning or control led to cities with minimal sanitation, no street lighting, wretched housing, poor transportation, and scant security. Cities had grown without planning before, but they had not been home and workplace for such large numbers of people, many of them new arrivals. Rich and poor alike suffered in this environment of disease, crime, and ugliness, although the poor obviously bore the brunt of these evils.

Major industrial cities developed similar housing patterns, mainly because of the wide disparity in economic and social power between the classes. By the middle of the nineteenth century, the wealthiest inhabitants circled the city's edge and were close to the country, living in "suburbs," which were roomier and cleaner than the city proper. As a general rule, the farther one lived from the central city, the wealthier one was. Suburban houses were not row houses; they stood alone and usually had gardens. The outermost ring of the city itself was preferred by the middle class; it had many of the characteristics of the wealthier suburbs. In an inner ring were artisans' dwellings, ranging from small detached middle-class residences to one- and two-story row houses, perhaps with small yards. In the center of industrial towns were workers' row houses, several stories high, jammed together as close to the factories as possible, separated from each other by a strip of mud or cobblestones with a pump in the middle that served all the residents in the surrounding buildings. When public transportation developed in the second half of the century, workers' districts dispersed, sometimes to encircle great governmental cities, such as London and Paris.

Almost universally, those who wrote about industrial cities—England's Manchester, Leeds, and Liverpool, and France's Lyons—described the stench, the filth, the inhumane crowding, the poverty, and the immorality. The novelists Charles Dickens, George Sand, and Émile Zola captured the horrors of urban industrial life and the plight of the poor. In *Bleak House,* Dickens, referring to one of the characters in the novel, warned about the effects of such wretchedness: "There is not an atom of Tom's slime . . . not a wickedness, not a brutality of his committing, but shall work its retribution, through every order of society, up to the proudest of the proud and the highest of the high."[1] Factual parliamentary reports read like the novels when describing a London row with its lack of toilets, its "undrained, unpaved, unventilated, uncared-for" streets.

Some reports indicated landlords' responsibility; others blamed tenants and workers, the new arrivals from rural areas in Scotland and Ireland. The parliamentary reports and the press helped mold English public opinion until it forced some regulation of urban building, transportation, sanitation, and public health. On the Continent, where the state was less committed to laissez-faire ideology, it took a much more active role in controlling urban conditions.

Changes in Social Structure

The Industrial Revolution destroyed forever the old division of society into clergy, nobility, and commoners. The development of industry and commerce created a bourgeoisie of a middle class people of common birth who engaged in trade and other capitalist ventures. Usually referred to as the middle classes (plural) because of the several economic layers, the wealthiest bourgeois were bankers, factory and mine owners, and merchants, but shopkeepers, managers, lawyers, and doctors were also included. The middle classes stressed the virtues of work, thrift, ambition, and caution. Their critics believed that the bourgeois perverted these virtues into materialism, selfishness, and callousness.

The Industrial Revolution began in an agrarian society dominated by landowning and labor-controlling aristocracy. From the eighteenth century on, as industry and commerce developed, the middle class grew in size, first in England and then throughout western Europe. Its larger size did not automatically bring greater power. The middle class struggled to end the political, economic, and social discrimination against it. Wherever industrial wealth became more important, the middle class gained political power and social respectability. The bourgeoisie was indeed able to force important changes, but its members still functioned in a political and social world that had existed long before they gained power and influence.

By the end of the century, bourgeois politicians held the highest offices in much of western Europe, sharing power with aristocrats, but in central and eastern Europe, aristocrats remained dominant into the twentieth century. Wealthy bourgeois emulated the aristocracy—buying great estates, marrying their daughters to sons of aristocrats—but they were the elite of the new industrial age, not of the Old Regime.

Although industrialization may have reduced some barriers between the landed elites and the middle class, it sharpened distinctions between the middle and laboring classes. Equally as diverse as the middle class, laborers encompassed different economic levels—rural laborers, miners, and city workers. Rural laborers included farmers and "cottage workers." In the 1700s and 1800s, an important segment of production was done in the villages, usually in the home, hence the name *domestic system*. A middleman would supply materials to a worker, who wove or spun them at piecework rates. This system, which preceded factory production, undercut workers' livelihoods and ultimately forced their children or grandchildren into urban labor.

In the first years of the Industrial Revolution, rural workers responded to the harsh conditions and low wages by destroying machinery and engaging in other acts of violence. In England, they called themselves "king Ludd's men" (*Ludd* was the name they gave to their Robin Hood, who probably did not exist). They raided farms in the night, breaking the machines or burning effigies of the farmers who they thought caused their misery. In all of Europe, peasants and artisans responded in that way to the introduction of machinery. In France, workers angrily dropped wooden shoes (*sabots*) into the works to slow the machinery, giving us the word *sabotage*.

Three broad distinctions existed among city workers; there were artisans, factory workers, and servants. Factory workers were the newest and most rapidly growing social group. At mid-century, however, they did not constitute a majority of laboring people in any large city. For example, as late as 1890, they made up only one-sixth of London's population.

The artisans were the largest group of city workers until the 1850s, and in some places for much longer. Some of them worked in construction, printing, small tailoring or dressmaking establishments, food preparation, and food processing. Others were craftspeople who produced such luxury items as furniture, jewelry, lace, and velvet. As a group, artisans were distinct from factory workers; their technical skills were difficult to learn, and traditionally their crafts were regulated by guilds, which still served both social and economic functions. Artisans were usually educated (they could read and write), lived in a city or village for generations, and maintained stable families, often securing places for their children in their crafts.

As the Industrial Revolution progressed, artisans faced competition from cheap, factory-produced goods. They began to downgrade their skills by dropping apprenticeship training, forcing journeymen to work longer hours with shoddy materials, and loosening the rules of the guilds. In 1848, artisans, rather than factory workers, were at the forefront of the revolutionary movement (see Chapter 23) as they tried to save themselves from the effects of the Industrial Revolution.

Servants, the third group of urban workers, were especially numerous in the capitals. During the first half of the nineteenth century, in cities such as Paris and London, servants outnumbered factory workers. The great increase in domestic labor—a middle-class family employed at least one servant—changed the daily life of middle-class women.

Working in a middle- or upper-class household, urban servants lived in a world apart from factory workers and artisans. They were often women from the country, where they might also have been servants. They were completely at the mercy of their employers. They might be treated decently or exploited, but they had little recourse when they were abused. Some worked their entire lives as servants; some women left service to marry working-class men. (Domestic help could not keep their jobs when they married.) Servants usually had some education. If they married and had a family, they taught their children to read and write and sometimes the manners and values of the household in which the parent had worked. Sometimes these servants taught their children their own deference to authority and their aspirations to bourgeois status.

Working-Class Life

Life was difficult for the early factory workers, who were recent arrivals from agricultural areas, where they had been driven off the land. They had no special skills or traditions of working with others in a craft. Frequently, male factory workers moved to the city without their families, leaving wives and children behind until they could support them in town. Other workers were single men or women who could find no jobs as servants or farm laborers in their villages. These people entered rapidly growing industries, where long hours—sometimes fifteen a day—were common. Farming had meant long hours, too, as had the various forms of home-based labor for piecework rates, but the pace of the machine and the routine made factory work oppressive. Machines required highly regulated human labor: generally menial, often dangerous, and usually boring.

In the mines, men, women, and small children hacked out the coal and sorted it, while horses and mules—and sometimes humans—pulled coal wagons on rails to the main shaft, where steam-powered engines lifted the coal to the surface. The miners labored to keep pace with the machines. They faced cave-ins, explosions, and deadly fumes. Deep under the earth's surface, life was dark, cold, wet, and uncertain. The work could be literally backbreaking. Their bodies stunted and twisted, their lungs wrecked, miners labored their lives away in "the pits." Technological advances, such as special lamps that would not ignite underground gases, saved their lives, but almost a century passed before working conditions improved, sometimes as a result of unions or government regulation and sometimes because labor-saving machinery became affordable.

Factory workers fared a little better than miners. Sometimes workers' standards of living rose when they moved from farms to cities, particularly if all family members found work together. The pay earned by a family might exceed what they could have earned for farm labor, but working and living conditions were terrible. Factories were dirty, hot, unventilated, and frequently dangerous. Housing was overcrowded, dirty, and badly built. Workers who were unmarried or had left their families in the country often lived in barracks. If they lost their jobs, they lost their shelter.

The lives of factory workers were depressing. They had few links to their surroundings. Like immigrants to a new country, they lived with hardship and deprivation. In the villages they had left, they had been poor but socially connected to family, to church, and even to local landlords. In

the cities, they worked with twenty to a hundred others and had little contact with their employers; instead, foremen pushed them to work hard and efficiently for long hours to keep up with the machines. They had little time to socialize; they were fined for talking to one another, as well as for lateness and for many petty infringements. To keep their jobs, they had to compete with each other. Lacking organization, comradeship, education, and experience of city life, they found little comfort when times were bad.

Yet factory workers did make lives for themselves. They married or entered into some relationship at a younger age than artisans and, on the average, had more children than other classes. A wife and children were an economic asset because they worked. When workers grew old or were disabled, their children were their only "pension." As mechanization progressed, women and children were generally driven out of the factory labor force, but in the early years they were the mainstay of the industrial process.

Many workers developed a life around the pub, the café, or some similar gathering place, where there were drinks and games and the gossip and news of the day. On Sundays, their one day off, workers drank and danced; absenteeism was so great on Monday that the day was called "holy Monday." Gin drinking was denounced on all sides; workers, their wives, and reformers alike urged temperance. Most workers did not attend church, but when they did, they frequented those churches that tried to reach them—usually not the established churches, which seemed to care only about the wealthy. In England, workers attended revivals; Methodists and other Dissenters welcomed them. The Catholic church had a particularly strong following among Irish workers. Many workers played sports, and some social organizations grew up around their sporting games. In these and other ways, workers developed a culture of their own—a culture misunderstood and often deplored by middle-class reformers.

Industrial workers rarely protested their conditions with violence. Workers lacked political and economic rights. They toiled long hours, were fined for mistakes and even for accidents, were fired at the whim of the employer or foreman, and suffered from job insecurity. Yet they rarely broke machines—unlike country laborers. Unlike

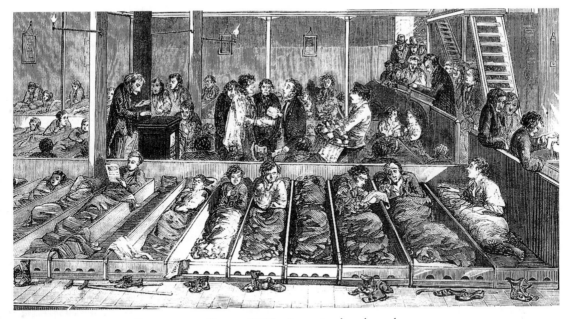

ENGRAVING FROM THE *ILLUSTRATED TIMES*, 1859. As unemployed workers flooded into the great cities of Europe, homelessness became a pressing social problem. To keep dry and warm, homeless men sometimes slept in coffins made for the living and lined up in a factory or prisonlike building. These facilities were charitable institutions—not poor-law workhouses—but they reflected the common belief that poverty was the fault of the poor, who should learn to help themselves. (*Mansell Collection.*)

craftsmen, factory workers had few organizations and no political rights; they did join with artisans in movements for political rights—the Chartists in England and the republicans in France. When workers protested, they were repressed. Even a peaceful demonstration, during which they sang hymns and prayed, might be disrupted by soldiers and gunfire. Workers who protested lost their jobs and were "blacklisted" (employers circulated their names so that other employers would not hire them). The law might say that they were equal, but workers were neither wealthy enough nor sufficiently organized to take offending employers to court for violating the law.

Workers' political agitation did not achieve much in the first half of the nineteenth century, but they made some progress toward a minimum of economic security. They formed "friendly" or "mutual aid" societies and cooperatives to help themselves when they were out of work or sick.

They paid some dues or took up special collections when one of their members died or was killed on the job. They also created clubs, where they could learn to read and write or someone could read to them or write a letter for them. Self-help organizations often developed into unions; sometimes they were unions in disguise to circumvent the law.

Many workers and radicals believed that the only hope for their class lay in unified action through trade unions, mutual aid societies, cooperatives, or political organizations. Workers developed a culture of solidarity, a sense of what was fair and unfair in relations with one another and with employers. In England and western Europe, trade unions grew, even when they were illegal. Unions made some headway in protecting their members from unemployment and dangerous working conditions, but strikes were rarely successful. The general public, which was imbued with individualist and laissez-faire principles, saw strikes as an attack on the businessman's right to carry on trade. Not until the 1870s and 1880s was widespread discontent expressed by militant trade unions.

In England, unions were legalized in 1825 but were forbidden to strike. The law made no special provision for them as it did for corporations; for example, if a union's officer ran away with its treasury, English law did not protect the workers' dues. Small unions were powerless. In 1834, there was an attempt to join all unions together in a Grand National Consolidated Trades Union. It failed because measures that would help one trade would not necessarily help another. In the 1850s, highly skilled workers joined together in a single craft union, which was more successful because employers found it difficult to replace a skilled worker. Still, the vast majority of workers were not organized during much of the nineteenth century.

RELIEF AND REFORM

If machines could produce so much wealth and so many products, why were there so many poor people living in such misery? There had always been poor people, but with industrialization, the economic and psychological hardships borne by the work force seemed worse.

Britain was the first nation to face the worsening condition of the poor. In the eighteenth century, English agricultural laborers had a higher standard of living than their counterparts on the Continent. As Britain rapidly industrialized, the changing conditions convinced observers that both rural and urban workers' lives had worsened. Parliamentary investigations by civic-minded citizens documented the suffering for all to read. Many leaders believed that only increasing economic capacity would end distress. But would the economy expand fast enough to benefit the lowliest workers through laissez faire, or did it need direction from the state? Socialists, utilitarians, and practical reformers believed that better organization of industry and government was necessary to relieve the situation.

The English Factory Acts were a series of measures, beginning in 1802, that limited the hours of those (especially women and children) who labored in mines and factories. By 1833, children under thirteen could work no more than nine hours a day, and no one aged thirteen to eighteen could work more than twelve hours or at night. The acts also required children to go to school for two hours a day, but the law did not furnish funds for schools. England was much slower than France or Germany to provide state schools; whatever initiative was taken in this regard came from private enterprise and charities rather than government. Controversy erupted among the religious sects about which of them should educate the children, who remained uneducated or self-educated amid the conflict. Sometimes there were schools for boys but not for girls. It was argued that for moral reasons the sexes should not mix in the classroom, even though they worked side by side in the factories and mines.

In 1847, women and children were no longer permitted to work more than ten hours a day. Many employers switched to a single system of ten-hour shifts, but a loophole in the Ten Hours Act allowed some to develop a "relay system," in which children worked intermittently during the day for a total of ten hours. Men could still work as much as sixteen hours but did not in actual practice because it was difficult to organize many different shifts in a large factory. At first, workers resented the regulations because family income declined if children could not work. Gradually, they realized that the humanitarian protection of women and children might make their own lives easier and safer and their wages higher. However, a ten-hour day for adult male workers was not enacted until 1874, despite two generations of agitation.

In 1834, a reform of the Poor Law, which dated from the reign of Queen Elizabeth I, tried to differentiate between the "deserving" poor and the "undeserving" poor. The New Poor Law required anyone receiving assistance to live in a prisonlike workhouse. Legislators thought only those who were truly needy would submit to such conditions just to receive a meal and shelter. They were right. The poor and the unemployed working class hated the workhouse, where families were separated by age and sex, miserably fed, and hired out to manufacturers and farmers for less than the going wage. In the "hungry forties," want was so widespread that there were not enough workhouses for the homeless and the jobless.

In contrast to Britain, people on the Continent more readily accepted the idea that the state could interfere with the market to protect labor. Most states in Europe had large bureaucracies to enforce regulations and to carry out relief measures. There was concern, however, that too much interference with employers would handicap businesses competing with the English. Governments in Germany, France, and Belgium did not always follow a laissez-faire policy, but sometimes they did. Such policies deepened class bitterness and disaffection.

Historians still debate how bad workers' conditions were in the early stages of industrialization. Workers' testimony of acute distress, particularly in the 1780–1830 period and again in the 1840s, has left a powerful impression of their misery. Their champions—humanitarians, novelists, radicals, and socialists—protested their dreadful lives. However, from the limited statistics that are available and governmental and humanitarian reports, historians generally conclude that standards of living actually improved during the eighteenth and early nineteenth centuries. They stress the higher wages, greater opportunities, and more choices for men and women. Still, few would deny that the rapidity of change caused great hardship for the workers of all countries, who endured cruel conditions in factories and slums. Machines destroyed crafts and displaced the craftsmen. A million Irish farm laborers starved during the great famine of the 1840s. Those who emigrated to England, British colonies, or the United States may have escaped starvation but still lived desperately hard lives. As for the workers who did not emigrate, statistical evidence showing an increase in their living standard does not reveal much about the radically reduced quality of life that men, women, and children experienced as they moved from rural communities to urban factories and slums—and to daily insecurity. Their grim experiences were relived by workers in the rest of Europe and the United States later in the century and in much of the world in the twentieth century.

INDUSTRIALISM IN PERSPECTIVE

Like the French Revolution, the Industrial Revolution modernized Europe. Eventually, it transformed every facet of society and even the natural world. In preindustrial society—Europe in the mid-eighteenth century—agriculture was the dominant economic activity and peasants were the most numerous class. Peasant life centered on the family and the village, which country folk rarely left. The new rational and critical spirit associated with the Enlightenment hardly penetrated rural Europe; there, religious faith, clerical authority, and ancient superstition remained firmly entrenched. The richest and most powerful class was the aristocracy, whose wealth stemmed from land and whose privileges were protected by custom and law. The French Revolution had undermined the traditional power structure of king, aristocracy, and clergy.

The Industrial Revolution accelerated the pace of modernization. In time, cities and factories eclipsed agricultural villages and handicraft manufacturing. The very geography of the world changed with the construction of dams, canals, roads, railroads, cities, and factories. In the society fashioned by industrialization and urbanization, aristocratic power and values declined. At the same time, the bourgeoisie increased in number, wealth, importance, and power. More and more, a person was judged by talent or income rather than by birth, and opportunities for upward social mobility expanded. In time, the Industrial Revolution became a great force for democratization; during the nineteenth century, first the middle class and then the working class gained the vote.

The Industrial Revolution also hastened the secularization of European life. In the cities, former villagers, separated from traditional communal ties, drifted away from their ancestral religion. Governments' power over individuals through public education and required military service contributed greatly to the molding of a secular, as well as a nationalistic, society. However, modernization did not proceed everywhere at the same pace and with the same thoroughness. Generally, premodern social and institutional forms remained deeply entrenched in eastern and southern Europe and persisted there well into the twentieth century.

As noted earlier, historians see several phases of industrial revolution: one from 1750 to 1850 in western Europe, one from the mid-nineteenth century including the United States, another in the early twentieth century, and another within the last fifty years. Despite the many problems it created, some of which still remain, the Industrial Revolution was a great triumph. Ultimately, it made possible the highest standard of living in human history and created new opportunities for social advancement, political participation, and educational and cultural development. In the second half of the nineteenth century, industrialization widened the science and technology gap between the West and the rest of the world. Western states were able to extend their power so that by the twentieth century virtually the entire globe came under Western dominance. In the twenty-first century, the world is still engaged in the process of industrialization, and the process is, indeed, worldwide, encompassing most of the peoples and places of the globe.

Online Study Center **Improve Your Grade**
Interactive Map:Continental Industrialization, ca. 1850

❖ ❖ ❖

Online Study Center **ACE the Test**

NOTE

1. Charles Dickens, *Bleak House* (Harmondsworth, England: Penguin, 1971), p. 683.

SUGGESTED READING

Crafts, N. F. R., *British Economic Growth During the Industrial Revolution* (1985). Argues that industrialization was much slower and less transforming in the nineteenth century than the phrase Industrial Revolution connotes.

Crouzet, F., *The First Industrialists: The Problem of Origins* (1985). Addresses the question of the class origins of the pioneers of industry. Were they middle class, workers, or craftsmen in social background?

Fisher, Douglas, *Industrial Revolution* (1992). Incorporates the latest scholarship on British industrialization.

Himmelfarb, Gertrude, *The Idea of Poverty: England in the Early Industrial Age* (1983). A brilliant and controversial history of English social thought focused on the condition of the poor.

Hobsbawm, Eric, *The Age of Capital* (1988). *The Age of Revolution: 1789–1848* (1964). A Marxist survey of this tumultuous period, stressing the connections among economic, social, and political revolution.

Jones, E. L., *Growth Recurring* (1988). Addresses the important question of why industrialization took place in Europe.

Landes, David, *The Unbound Prometheus: Technological Change and Industrial Development in Western Europe from 1750 to the Present* (1969). Beautifully written, this book, and Landes's subsequent studies, have influenced a generation arguing for European industrial advancement.

Langer, William L., *Political and Social Upheaval: 1832–1852* (1969). The complexities and interrelationships of economic and social change and politics are underlined in this classic. There are many monographs but this is a good overview.

Laslett, P., *The World We Have Lost* (1984). Classic discussion of the world before industrialization.

McPherson, Natalie, *Machines and Economic Growth* (1994). A return to the question of inventions and economic growth from recent scholarship.

Mokyr, Joel, *The British Industrial Revolution: An Economic Perspective* (1993). Economic emphasis rather than social or political by a scholar with wide interests.

———, *A Lever of Riches* (1990). The role of laborers and small entrepreneurs in the Industrial Revolution.

Pomerantz, Ken, *The Great Divergence: Europe, China and Making of World Economy* (2000). A "big question" study that tries to answer why northwestern Europe, which, as late as the 1700s, was comparable to China in that it was not much more advanced, industrialized first and more intensively.

Stearns, Peter, *The Industrial Revolution in World History* (1993). A readable book with a broad perspective.

Thompson, E. P., *The Making of the English Working Class* (1966). A dramatic and enormously influential classic.

Novels of Special Note

Balzac, Honoré de, *Eugénie Grandet; Père Goriot; César Birotteau.* A great novelist's studies of the decay of human character under social and economic pressures.

Dickens, Charles, *Hard Times; Our Mutual Friend; Oliver Twist; Bleak House.* The great humanitarian's social protest novels.

Eliot, George, *Adam Bede; Middlemarch.* These two great novels show a wealth of nineteenth-century life, including social attitudes and moral dilemmas.

Zola, Émile, *Germinal.* Describes the condition of miners in the 1850s and 1860s. Very interesting to compare with Richard Llewellyn's novel of Welsh miners, *How Green Was My Valley.*

Chapter 22

Thought and Culture in the Early Nineteenth Century

Traveller Looking Over a Sea of Fog, by Caspar David Friedrich. (Hamburger Kunsthalle.)

- **Romanticism: A New Cultural Orientation**
- **German Idealism**
- **Conservatism: The Value of Tradition**
- **Liberalism: The Value of the Individual**
- **Radicalism and Democracy: The Expansion of Liberalism**
- **Early Socialism: New Possibilities for Society**
- **Nationalism: The Sacredness of the Nation**

Focus Questions

1. How was the Romantic movement a reaction against the dominant ideas of the Enlightenment?

2. What was the impact of Romanticism on European life?

3. What was the attitude of conservatives and liberals toward the Enlightenment and the French Revolution?

4. How did early-nineteenth-century radicalism constitute an expansion of liberalism?

5. What did early socialists and liberals have in common? How did they differ?

6. What is the relationship between nationalism and liberalism? How do you explain nationalism's great appeal?

Online Study Center

This icon will direct you to interactive map and primary source activities on the website http://college.hmco.com/pic/perrywc8e.

*I*n 1815, the armies of France no longer marched across Europe, and Napoleon was imprisoned on an island a thousand miles off the coast of Africa. The traditional rulers of the Continent, some of them recently restored to power, were determined to protect themselves and society from future Robespierres who organized reigns of terror and Napoleons who obliterated traditional states. As defenders of the status quo, they attacked the reformist spirit of the philosophes, which had produced the French Revolution. In *conservatism,* which championed tradition over reason, hierarchy over equality, and the community over the individual, they found a philosophy to justify their assault on the Enlightenment and the Revolution.

But the forces unleashed by the French Revolution had penetrated European consciousness too deeply to be eradicated. One of them was *liberalism,* which aimed to secure the liberty and equality proclaimed by the Revolution. Another was *nationalism,* which sought to liberate subject peoples and unify broken nations. Captivated by the dream to redeem humanity, idealistic youth and intellectuals joined in the revolutionary struggle for liberty and nationhood.

The early 1800s also saw the flowering of a new cultural orientation. **Romanticism,** with its plea for the liberation of human emotions and the free expression of personality, challenged the Enlightenment stress on rationalism. Although primarily a literary and artistic movement, romanticism also permeated philosophy and political thought, particularly conservatism.

Still another force emerging in the post-Napoleonic period was socialism. Reacting to the problems spawned by the Industrial Revolution, socialists called for creating a new society, based on cooperation rather than on capitalist competition. A minor movement in the era from 1815 to 1848, socialism in its Marxist version became a major intellectual and social force in the last part of the century.

ROMANTICISM: A NEW CULTURAL ORIENTATION

The Romantic Movement, which began in the closing decades of the eighteenth century, dominated European cultural life in the first half of the

505

506 ❖ 22 Thought and Culture in the Early Nineteenth Century

nineteenth. Historians recognize the prominence of romanticism in nineteenth-century cultural life, but the movement was so complex and the differences among the various romantic writers, artists, and musicians so numerous that historians cannot agree on a definition of *romanticism*. Romantics were both liberals and conservatives, revolutionaries and reactionaries; some were preoccupied with religion and God, while others paid little attention to faith.

Most of Europe's leading cultural figures came under the influence of the Romantic Movement. Among the exponents of romanticism were the poets Shelley, Wordsworth, Keats, and Byron in England; the novelist Victor Hugo and the Catholic novelist and essayist Chateaubriand in France; and the writers A. W. and Friedrich Schlegel, the dramatist and poet Schiller, and the philosopher Schelling in Germany. Caspar David Friedrich in Germany and John Constable in England expressed the romantic mood in art, and Beethoven, Schubert, Chopin, and Wagner expressed it in music.

Exalting Imagination, Intuition, and Feelings

Perhaps the central message of the romantics was that the imagination of the individual should determine the form and content of an artistic creation. This outlook ran counter to the rationalism of the Enlightenment, which itself had been a reaction against the otherworldly Christian orientation of the Middle Ages. The philosophes had attacked faith because it thwarted and distorted reason; romantic poets, philosophers, and artists now denounced the scientific rationalism of the philosophes because it crushed the emotions and impeded creativity.

According to the romantics, the philosophes had turned flesh-and-blood human beings into soulless thinking machines. The philosophes' geometric spirit, **mechanism,** which sought to fit all life into a mechanical framework, had diminished and demeaned the individual. Such shallow thinking had stifled imagination and spontaneity, preventing people from realizing their human potential. To be restored to their true nature and made whole again, human beings must be eman-

cipated from the tyranny of excessive intellectualizing; their feelings must be nourished and expressed. Taking up one of Rousseau's ideas, romantics yearned to rediscover in the human soul the pristine freedom and creativity that had been squashed by habits, values, rules, and standards imposed by civilization.

Abstract reason and scientific knowledge, said the romantics, are insufficient guides to knowledge. They provide only general principles about nature and people; they cannot penetrate to what really matters—the uniqueness of each person, of each robin, of each tree, cloud, and lake. The philosophes had concentrated on people in general, focusing on the elements of human nature shared by all people. The romantics, in contrast, emphasized human uniqueness and diversity: the traits that set one person apart from others. Discover and express your true self, romantics commanded: cultivate your own imagination; play your own music; write your own poetry; paint your own personal vision of nature; live, love, and suffer in your own way. The philosophes had asserted the mind's autonomy—its capacity to think for itself and not depend on authority. Romantics gave primary importance to the autonomy of the personality—the individual's need and right to find and fulfill an inner self. This intense introspection, the individual's preoccupation with human feelings, is the distinguishing feature of romanticism. In the opening lines of his autobiography, *The Confessions*, Jean Jacques Rousseau, a romantic in an age of reason, expressed the passionate subjectivism that was to characterize the Romantic Movement:

> *I am commencing an undertaking, hitherto without precedent and which will never find an imitator. I desire to set before my fellows the likeness of a man in all the truth of nature, and that man myself. Myself alone! I know the feelings of my heart, and I know men. I am not made like any of those I have seen. I venture to believe that I am not made like any of those who are in existence. If I am not better, at least I am different.*[1]

Whereas the philosophes had regarded feelings as an obstacle to clear thinking, to the romantics they were the human essence. People could not live by reason alone, said the romantics. They agreed

DANTE'S INFERNO: THE WHIRLWIND OF LOVERS, BY WILLIAM BLAKE
(1757–1827). A radical romantic painter and poet, Blake totally rejected the
artistic conventions of the past. His religious and political beliefs were as unique
as his art; he spent his life trying to convey tormented inward visions. He was a
prolific illustrator, and his imaginative genius was stimulated by great literature,
such as Dante's *Divine Comedy*. (*National Gallery of Art, Washington, D.C.
Gift of W. G. Allen.*)

with Rousseau's words that "For us, to exist is to
feel and our sensibility is incontestably prior to our
reason."[2] For the romantics, reason was cold and
dreary, its understanding of people and life meager
and inadequate. Reason could not comprehend or
express the complexities of human nature or the
richness of human experience. By always dissecting
and analyzing, by imposing deadening structure
and form, and by demanding adherence to strict
rules, reason crushed inspiration and creativity and
barred true understanding. "The Reasoning Power
in Man," wrote William Blake, the British poet,

artist, and mystic, is "an Incrustation [scab] over
my Immortal Spirit."[3]

The avenue to truth for the romantics was
spontaneous human emotion rather than the intellect. By cultivating emotions, intuition, and the
imagination, individuals could experience reality
and discover their authentic selves. The romantics
wanted people to feel and to experience—"To
bathe in the Waters of Life," said Blake.[4] Or as
Johann Goethe, Germany's great poet, wrote in
Faust, "My worthy friend, gray are all theories,/
And green alone Life's golden tree."[5]

Consequently, the romantics insisted that imaginative poets had a deeper insight into life than analytical philosophers. Poetry is a true philosophy, the romantics said; it can do what rational analysis and geometric calculations cannot do—speak directly to the heart, clarify life's deepest mysteries, participate in the eternal, and penetrate to the depths of human nature. To think profoundly, one has to feel deeply, said the romantics. For reason to function best, it must be nourished by the poetic imagination; that alone extricates and ennobles feelings hidden in the soul. "I am certain of nothing but of the holiness of the Heart's affections and the truth of Imagination," wrote John Keats. "O for a Life of Sensations rather than of Thoughts."[6] In his preface to *The Lyrical Ballads* (1798), often called the manifesto of romanticism, William Wordsworth (1770–1850) held that poetry—that is, imagination and feeling—not mathematics and logic, yielded the highest truth.

The Enlightenment mind had been clear, critical, and controlled. It had adhered to standards of esthetics, thought to be universal, that had dominated European cultural life since the Renaissance. It stressed technique, form, and changeless patterns and tended to reduce the imagination to mechanical relationships. "Analysis and calculation make the poet, as they make the mathematician," wrote Étienne Condillac, a prominent French philosophe. "Once the material of a play is given, the invention of the plot, the characters, the verse, is only a series of algebraic problems to be worked out."[7] Following in this tradition, Népomucène Lemercier determined that there were twenty-six rules for tragedy, twenty-three for comedy, and twenty-four for the epic; he proceeded to manufacture plays and epics according to this formula.

Romantic poets, artists, and musicians broke with the traditional styles and uniform standards, essentially those inherited from the classical traditions, and created new cultural forms and techniques. "We do not want either Greek or Roman Models," Blake declared, "but [should be] just & true to our own Imaginations."[8] Victor Hugo (1802–1885), the dominant figure among French romantics, urged: "Freedom in art! . . . Let us take the hammer to the theories, the poetics [the analysis of poetry] and the systems."[9] Yearning for unhin-

dered self-expression, the romantics believed that one did not learn how to write poetry or paint pictures by following textbook rules, nor could one grasp the poet's or artist's intent by judging works according to fixed standards. Only by trusting their own feelings and intuition could individuals attain their creative potential and achieve self-realization. Hence, the most beautiful works of art were not photographic imitations of nature but authentic and spontaneous expressions of the artist's feelings, fantasies, intuitions, and dreams. It was the artist's inner voice that gave a work of art its supreme value. Caspar David Friedrich declared: "The artist should not only paint what he sees in front of him, but also what he sees inside himself."[10] Artists also sought to arouse the viewer's emotions by depicting nature in all its awesome glory and fury—majestic mountain peaks, raging storms and seas, thick woods, pounding waterfalls, and precipitous cliffs. Similarly, the romantics were less impressed by Beethoven's structure than by the intensity, power, and passion of his music, which expressed and touched every emotion. Thus, a contemporary of Beethoven's said that his "music moves the levers that open the floodgates of fear, terror, of horror, of pain and arouses the longing for the eternal which is the essence of Romanticism."[11]

The romantics explored the inner life of the mind, which Freud would later call **the unconscious**. "It is the beginning of poetry," wrote Friedrich Schlegel, "to abolish the law and the method of the rationally proceeding reason and to plunge us once more into the ravishing confusion of fantasy, the original chaos of human nature."[12] It was this dimension of the mind—mysterious, primitive, more elemental and more powerful than reason, the wellspring of creativity—that the romantics longed to revitalize and release. Some romantics had an intuitive awareness of the dark side of the unconscious. Buried there, they sensed, were our worst fears and most hideous desires. When we dig deeply into our "most cherished reveries," Hugo warned, we discover a spiral that

> . . . *is deep, and when one descends into it*
> *It continues ceaselessly and broadens out,*
> *And because one has touched some fatal*
>   *enigma,*
> *One often returns pale from this dark*
>   *journey.*[13]

Nature, God, History

The philosophes had viewed nature as a lifeless machine, a giant clock, all of whose parts worked together in perfect precision and harmony. Nature's laws, operating with mathematical certainty, were uncovered by the methodology of science. The romantics rejected this impersonal, mechanical model. Inspired and awed by nature's beauty and majesty, they responded emotionally to nature and sought a mystical union with it. To the romantics, nature was alive and suffused with God's presence. Nature stimulated the creative energies of the imagination; it taught human beings a higher form of knowledge. As William Wordsworth wrote,

> One impulse from a vernal [springtime]
>   wood
> May teach you more of man,
> Of moral evil and of good,
> Than all the sages can.[14]

Wordsworth felt that the poet had a unique capacity to know nature. Interaction with nature fostered self-discovery. Thus, Wordsworth saw in nature

> The anchor of my purest thoughts, the nurse,
> The guide, the guardian of my heart, and soul
> Of all my moral being.[15]

For the romantics, the poet's imagination unlocked nature's most important secrets. In perhaps the most impassioned application of this principle, English romantics decried their country's drab factories—the "dark satanic mills," which deprived life of its joy and separated people from nature.

Regarding God as a great watchmaker—a detached observer of a self-operating mechanical universe—the philosophes tried to reduce religion to a series of scientific propositions. Many romantics, on the contrary, viewed God as a spiritual force that inspired people and enriched life, and they deplored the decline of Christianity. The cathedrals and ceremonies, poetic and mysterious, satisfied the esthetic impulse; Christian moral commands, compassionate and just, elevated human behavior to a higher level. Consequently, the romantics condemned the philosophes for weakening Christianity by submitting its dogmas to the test of reason, and they recoiled with anger at the philosophes' relegation of God to the status of a watchmaker. As Samuel Taylor Coleridge (1772–1834), poet and conservative political thinker, wrote: "What indeed but the wages of death can be expected from a doctrine which degrades the Deity into a bland hypothesis, and that the hypothesis of a clockwork-maker . . . a godless nature, and a natureless, abstract God . . . the Sunday name of gravitation."[16] The romantics' call to acknowledge the individual as a spiritual being and to cultivate the religious side of human nature accorded with their aim of restoring the whole personality, which had been fragmented by the philosophes' excessive emphasis on the intellect.

The Middle Ages, too, appeared as a very different era to the philosophes and the romantics. To the former, that period was a time of darkness, when superstition and fanaticism reigned; surviving medieval institutions and traditions served only to bar progress. The romantics, in contrast, revered the Middle Ages. The wars of the French Revolution, Napoleon, and the breakdown of political equilibrium had produced a sense of foreboding about the future. Some sought spiritual security by looking back to the Middle Ages, when Europe was united by a single faith and the fabric of society seemed intact and strong. To the romantic imagination, the Middle Ages, steeped in religious faith, had nurtured social harmony and abounded with heroic and chivalrous deeds as well as colorful pageantry.

The romantics and the philosophes also diverged in their conception of history. For the philosophes, history served a didactic purpose by providing examples of human folly. Such knowledge helped people prepare for a better future, and for that reason alone history should be studied. To the romantics, a historical period, like an individual, was a unique entity with its own soul. They wanted the historian to portray and analyze the variety of nations, traditions, and institutions that constituted the historical experience, always recognizing what is particular and unique to a given time, place, and people. The romantics' feeling for the uniqueness of phenomena and their appreciation of cultural differences laid the foundation of modern historical scholarship. For

LORD BYRON (1788–1824). One of the leading romantic poets, Byron created the "Byronic hero," a lonely and mysterious figure. His own short life exalted the emotions and the senses. He went to Greece in 1824 to aid the revolutionaries and died there from poor health. (*Bettmann/CORBIS.*)

they sought to study the specific details of history and culture and to comprehend them in their own terms within the context of their own times.

Searching for universal principles, the philosophes dismissed folk traditions as peasant superstitions and impediments to progress. Rebelling against the standardization of culture, the romantics saw native languages, songs, and legends as the unique creations of a people and the deepest expression of national feeling. The romantics regarded the legends, myths, and folk traditions of a people as the wellspring of poetry and art and as the spiritual source of that people's cultural vitality, creativity, and identity. Hence they examined these earliest cultural expressions with awe and reverence. They discov-

ered the nation's past for their kinsmen. In this way, romanticism helped shape modern nationalism.

The Impact of the Romantic Movement

The romantic revolt against the Enlightenment had an important and enduring impact on European history. By focusing on the creative capacities inherent in the emotions—intuition, spontaneity, instinct, passion, will, empathy—the romantics shed light on a side of human nature that the philosophes often overlooked or undervalued. By encouraging personal freedom and diversity in art, music, and literature, they greatly enriched European cultural life. Future artists, writers, and musicians would proceed along the path cleared by the romantics. Modern art, for example, owes much to the Romantic Movement's emphasis on the legitimacy of human feeling and to its exploration of the hidden world of dreams and fantasies. The romantic emphasis on feeling sometimes found expression in humanitarian movements that fought slavery, child labor, and poverty. Romantics were among the first to attack the emerging industrial capitalism for subordinating individuals to the requirements of the industrial process and treating them as mere things. By recognizing the distinctive qualities of historical periods, peoples, and cultures, the romantics helped create the modern historical outlook. By valuing a nation's past, romanticism contributed to modern nationalism and conservatism.

However, the Romantic Movement had a potentially dangerous side: it served as background to the extreme nationalism of the twentieth century. As Ernst Cassirer points out, the romantics "never meant to politicize but to 'poeticize' the world," and their deep respect for human individuality and national diversity was not compatible with Hitler's racial nationalism. Yet by waging their attack on reason with excessive zeal, the romantics undermined respect for the rational tradition of the Enlightenment and thus set up a precondition for the rise and triumph of fascist movements. Although their intention was cultural and not political, by idealizing the past and glorifying ancient folkways, legends, native soil, and native language, the romantics introduced a highly charged nonrational component into political life. In later generations, romanticism, particularly in Germany, fused with political nationalism to produce "a general climate of inexact thinking, an intellectual . . . dreamworld and an emotional approach to problems of political action to which sober reasoning should have been applied."[17]

The philosophes would have regarded the romantics' veneration of a people's history and traditions as a barbarous regression to superstition and a triumph of myth over philosophy. Indeed, when transferred to the realm of politics, the romantics' idealization of the past and fascination with inherited national myths as the source of wisdom did reawaken a way of thinking about the world that rested more on feeling than on reason. In the process, people became committed to nationalist and political ideas that were fraught with danger. The glorification of myth and the folk community constitutes a link, however unintended, between romanticism and extreme nationalism, which culminated in the world wars of the twentieth century.

GERMAN IDEALISM

The romantics' stress on the inner person also found expression in the school of German philosophy called **idealism**. Idealists did not see the world as something objective, that is, existing independently of individual consciousness. Rather, they held that human consciousness, the knowing subject, builds the world and determines its form. German idealism arose in part as a response to the challenge posed by David Hume, the Scottish empiricist and skeptic.

The Challenge Posed by Hume's Empiricism

Enlightenment thinkers believed that physics and astronomy, epitomized by Newton, provided the kind of certainty that other forms of inquiry, notably theology, could not. But in his *Treatise of Human Nature* (1739–40) and *Enquiry Concerning Human Understanding* (1748), Hume cast doubt on the view that scientific certainty was possible. He demolished the religious argument for miracles and the deist argument for a Creator; he also called into question the very notion of scientific law.

Science rests on the conviction that regularities observed in the past and the present will be repeated in the future: that there does exist an objective reality, which rational creatures can comprehend. Hume, however, argued that science cannot demonstrate a *necessary connection* between cause and effect. Because we repeatedly experience a burning sensation when our fingers have contact with a flame, we assume a cause-and-effect relationship. This assumption is unwarranted, says Hume. All we can acknowledge is that there is a constant conjunction between the flame and the burning sensation.

According to Hume, a thoroughgoing empiricist, sense perception is the only legitimate source of knowledge, and our sense experiences can never prove a necessary connection between what we customarily perceive as cause and effect. We can see things happening, but we cannot see why they happen. Experience tells us only what happens at a particular moment; it cannot tell us with certainty that the same combination of events will be repeated in the future. Based on past experience, the mind expects the flame to burn, but we cannot prove that there is a law at work in nature guaranteeing that a specific cause will produce a specific effect. What we mean by cause and effect is simply something that the mind, through habit, imposes on our sense perceptions. For practical purposes, we can say that two events are in association with each other, but we cannot conclude with certainty that the second was caused by the first—that natural law is operating within the physical universe. Such a radical **empiricism** undermines the very foundations of science, so revered by progressive thinkers.

Immanuel Kant

In the *Critique of Pure Reason* (1781), Immanuel Kant, the German philosopher and proponent of Newtonianism and the scientific method, under-

Profile

Percy Bysshe Shelley

Percy Bysshe Shelley (1792–1822) was destined to follow his father into a parliamentary career and received a traditional classical education. Flamboyantly imaginative, he had little in common with his peers and was tormented and bullied at school. This treatment resulted in a lifelong hatred of authority, combined with recklessness, intellectual brilliance, great personal charm, and a vivid emotional temperament.

Expelled from Oxford for writing a pamphlet advocating atheism, Shelley eloped with a sixteen-year-old bride and began a life of exile, shifting from place to place in England and Europe with an ever-changing number of family members and friends. His brief, stormy life—the suicide of his first wife, his marriage to Mary Godwin (the daughter of Mary Wollstonecraft and author of *Frankenstein*), personal misfortunes, passionate friendships, financial problems, and bouts of depression—culminated in death by drowning in Italy. Throughout it all

Corbis.

took the challenge of rescuing reason and science from Hume's empiricism. Kant rejected Hume's (and Locke's) underlying premise that all knowledge derives from sense experience, which imprints impressions on the mind. The mind, said Kant, is not a tabula rasa, a blank slate, passively receiving sense impressions, but an active instrument that structures, organizes, and interprets the multiplicity of sensations coming to it. The mind can coordinate a chaotic stream of sensations because it contains its own inherent logic; it is equipped with several categories of understanding, including cause and effect. These categories are **a priori** and universal: that is, they are necessary constituents of all human minds and exist independently of and prior to experience.

For Kant, cause and effect has an objective existence; it exists as an a priori component of human consciousness. Because of the way the human mind is constituted, we presuppose a rela-

tionship of cause and effect in all our experiences with the objects of this world. The mind does not treat the physical world in an arbitrary or random way; it imposes structure and order on our sense experience. Cause and effect, space and time, and other categories of the mind permit us to attribute certainty to scientific knowledge. The physical world must possess certain definite characteristics because these characteristics conform to the categories of the mind. The object, said Kant, must "accommodate itself to the subject."

Kant rescued science from Hume's assault: the laws of science are universally valid. But in the process, Kant made scientific law dependent on the mind and its a priori categories. We see nature in a certain way because of the mental apparatus that we bring to it. The mind does not derive the laws of nature from the physical world. Indeed, the reverse is true. The mind imposes its own laws on nature—on the raw impressions re-

512

he poured out an incessant stream of poetry, prose, and translations from five languages. Like his contemporaries in the Romantic Movement, he responded emotionally to politics, the natural world, love, and poetry. "A poem," he wrote, "is the very image of life expressed in its eternal truth."

A radical in politics, Shelley was inspired by the ideals of the French Revolution, abhorred the oppressive conservatism of English politics, and was frustrated by his inability to influence events. His sonnet "England in 1819" described his disgust with a country ruled by "An old, mad, blind, despised and dying king." His lyrical poetry was composed in a spontaneous rush of feeling. He celebrated the natural world from the majesty of crashing waves and mountains to quietly radiant landscapes, and he identified himself in relation to the natural world. In "Ode to the West Wind" he compared himself to the driving wind: "A heavy weight of hours has chained and bowed/One too like thee: tameless, and swift, and proud."

Shelley was notorious for his irregular lifestyle and had little literary success in his lifetime; his life contained more pain than pleasure. In "Adonais," which he wrote on the death of fellow poet John Keats, who died in 1821 at the age of twenty-six, Shelley seemed to be prefiguring his own early death:

> He has outsoared the shadow of our night;
> Envy and calumny and hate and pain,
> And that unrest which men miscall delight,
> Can touch him not and torture not again;
> From the contagion of the world's slow stain
> He is secure, and now can never mourn
> A heart grown cold, a head grown gray in vain;
> Nor, when the spirit's self has ceased to burn,
> With sparkless ashes load an unlamented urn.*

---

*From "Adonais," in *The Complete Works of Percy Bysshe Shelley,* ed. by T. Hutchinson (London: Oxford University Press, 1945), p. 440.

---

ceived by the senses—giving the physical world form, structure, and order. By holding that objects must conform to the rules of the human mind, that it is the knowing subject that creates order within nature, Kant gave primacy to the knower rather than to the objects of knowledge. He saw the mind as an active agent, not a passive receptacle for sensations. This "turn in philosophy," which Kant considered as revolutionary as the Copernican theory had been for astronomy, gave unprecedented importance to the individual mind and its inherent capacity for knowing.

It is a fundamental principle of Kant's thought that we cannot know ultimate reality. Our knowledge is limited to the **phenomenal world,** the realm of natural occurrences. We can know only the things that we experience, that is, things we grasp through the active intervention of the mind's categories. We can have no knowledge of a thing-in-itself, that is, of an object's ultimate or real nature—its nature as it is independently of the way we experience it, apart from the way our senses receive it. The human mind can acquire knowledge only of that part of reality revealed through sense experience. We can say nothing about the sun's true nature but only describe the way the sun appears to us: that is, our impression of the sun formed by the mind's ordering of our sense experiences of it. Thus, at the same time that Kant reaffirmed the validity of scientific law, he also limited the range of science and reason.

G. W. F. Hegel

Kant had insisted that knowledge of what lies beyond the phenomena—knowledge of ultimate or absolute reality itself—is forever denied us. Georg Wilhelm Friedrich Hegel (1770–1831), another

German philosopher, could not accept this. He constructed an all-embracing metaphysical system that attempted to explain all reality and uncover the fundamental nature and meaning of the universe and human history—to grasp the wholeness of life. In the process, he synthesized the leading currents of thought of his day: the rationalism of the Enlightenment, romanticism, and Kantian philosophy.

Adopting Kant's notion that the mind imposes its categories on the world, Hegel emphasized the importance of the thinking subject in the quest for truth. However, Kant held that we can have knowledge only of how a thing appears to us, not of the thing-in-itself. Hegel, in contrast, maintained that ultimate reality, total truth, is knowable to the human mind: the mind can comprehend the principles underlying all existence and can grasp the essential meaning of human experience.

Kant had asserted the essential idealist position that it is the knowing subject that organizes our experiences of the phenomenal world. Hegel went a giant step beyond that by positing the existence of a universal Mind—Absolute Spirit— that differentiates itself in the minds of thinking individuals. He saw Mind, the thing-in-itself, as a universal agent, whose nature can be apprehended through thought.

Because Hegel viewed Absolute Spirit not as fixed and static but as evolving and developing, history plays a central role in his philosophical system. History is the development of Spirit in time. In the arena of world history, truth unfolds and makes itself known to the human mind. Like the romantics, Hegel said that each historical period has a distinctive character that separates it from every preceding age and enables us to see it as an organic whole. The art, science, philosophy, religion, politics, and leading events are sufficiently interconnected that the period may be said to possess an organic unity, a historical coherence.

Does history contain an overarching meaning? Are past, present, and future linked together by something more profound, more unifying than random chance? Hegel believed that world history reveals a rational process progressing toward a final destination. An internal principle of order underlies historical change. There is a purpose

HEGEL IN HIS STUDY. Georg Wilhelm Friedrich Hegel (1770–1831) constructed a comprehensive philosophical system that sought to explain all reality. His philosophy of history, particularly the theories of dialectical conflict and of progression toward an ultimate end, greatly influenced Karl Marx. (*Bildarchiv Preussischer Kulturbesitz, Berlin.*)

and an end to history: the unfolding of Absolute Spirit. In the course of history, an immanent Spirit manifests itself; gradually, progressively, and nonrepetitively, it actualizes itself, becoming itself fully. Nations and exceptional human beings, "World-Historical" individuals—Alexander the Great, Caesar, Napoleon—are the vehicles through which Spirit realizes its potentiality and achieves self-consciousness. Hegel's philosophy of history gives meaning, purpose, and direction to historical events. Where is history taking us? What is its ultimate meaning? For Hegel, history is humanity's progress from lesser to greater freedom: "The History of the World is none other than the progress of the consciousness of Freedom . . . [It is] the absolute goal of history."[18]

According to Hegel, Spirit manifests itself in history through a **dialectical conflict** between opposing forces; the struggle between one force (thesis) and its adversary (antithesis) is evident in all spheres of human activity. This clash of opposites gains in intensity, ending eventually in a resolution that unifies both opposing views. Thought and history then enter a new and higher stage, that of synthesis, which, by absorbing the truths within both the thesis and the antithesis, achieves a higher level of truth and a higher stage of history. Soon this synthesis itself becomes a thesis that enters into another conflict with another opposing force. This conflict too is resolved by a still higher synthesis. Thus, the dynamic struggle between thesis and antithesis—sometimes expressed in revolutions and war, and sometimes in art, religion, and philosophy—and its resolution into a synthesis accounts for movement in history. Or, in Hegelian language, Spirit is closer to realization: its rational structure is progressing from potentiality to actuality. The dialectic is the march of Spirit through human affairs. Historical change is often instituted by world-historical individuals who, unknown to themselves, are agents of Spirit in its march through history. Since Hegel held that freedom is the essence of Spirit, it is through history that human beings progress toward consciousness of their own freedom. They become self-consciously aware of their own self-determination—their ability to regulate their lives rationally according to their own consciousness. For Hegel, two developments stand out in the evolution of individual freedom: Socrates, who taught people to examine inherited values with a critical spirit, and the Protestant Reformation, which held that salvation is a matter of personal conscience.

But for individual freedom to be realized, said Hegel, social and political institutions must be rationally determined and organized; that is, the will of the individual must be harmonized with the needs of the community. For Hegel, freedom is not a matter of securing abstract natural rights for the individual, which was the goal of the French Revolution. Rather, true freedom is attained only within the social group. Thus, in Hegel's view, human beings discover their essential character—their moral and spiritual potential—only as citizens of a cohesive political community. This view goes back to the city-states of ancient Greece, which Hegel admired.

Like Rousseau, Hegel sought to bring the individual's free choice into harmony with the needs of society as a whole. Hegel linked freedom to obedience to the state's commands. In the state's laws and institutions, which are manifestations of reason, the objectivization of Spirit, individuals find a basis for rationally determining their own lives. In this way, the private interests of citizens become one with common interests of the community. For Hegel, Absolute Spirit, which is also Ultimate Reason, realizes itself in the state, the highest form of human association. The state joins fragmented individuals together into a community and substitutes a rule of justice for the rule of instincts. It permits individuals to live the ethical life and to develop their human potential. An individual cannot achieve these goals in isolation.

The rationally organized community favored by Hegel was a constitutional monarchy. Yet he also reached the perplexing conclusion that the pinnacle of the consciousness of freedom was to be found in the Germany of his day. Germans recognized the value of monarchical leadership, he said, but also assimilated the Christian principle of the individual's infinite worth.

In deeming the Prussian state, which had an autocratic king, no constitution, no popularly elected parliament, and government-imposed censorship, to be the pinnacle of freedom and the goal for which history had been striving, Hegel's thought reveals a powerful undercurrent of statism—that is, the exaltation of the state and the subordination of the individual to it. For Hegel, the national state was the embodiment of Universal Reason and the supreme achievement of Absolute Spirit:

It must . . . be understood that all the worth which the human being possesses—all spiritual reality, he possesses only through the State. . . . Thus only is he fully conscious; thus only is he a partaker of morality—of a just and moral social and political life. For Truth is the unity of the universal . . . and the Universal is to be found in the State, in its laws, its universal and rational arrangements. The state is the Divine Idea as it exists on Earth.[19]

German conservatives used Hegel's idea that existing institutions have a rational legitimacy to support their opposition to rapid change. Existing reality, even if it appears cruel and hateful, is the actualization of Absolute Spirit. Therefore, it is inherently necessary and rational and should not be altered.

Some of Hegel's followers, known as Young Hegelians, interpreted Hegel in a radical sense. They rejected his view that the Prussian state, or any German state, was the goal of world history, the realization of freedom. The Germany of their day, held the Young Hegelians, had not attained a harmony between the individual and society: it was not rationally organized and did not foster freedom. These Young Hegelians saw Hegel's philosophy as a means for radically altering the world to make existing society truly rational. The most important of the radical Young Hegelians was Karl Marx. Marx retained Hegel's overarching principles that history contains an inner logic, that it is an intelligible process, and that a dialectical struggle propels history from a lower stage to a higher stage.

CONSERVATISM: THE VALUE OF TRADITION

To the traditional rulers of Europe—kings, aristocrats, and clergy—the French Revolution was a great evil that had inflicted a near-fatal wound on civilization. As far as they were concerned, the revolutionaries heralded chaos when they executed Louis XVI, confiscated the land of the church, destroyed the special privileges of the aristocracy, and instituted the Reign of Terror. Then the Revolution gave rise to Napoleon, who deposed kings, continued the assault on the traditional aristocracy, and sought to dominate Europe. Disgusted and frightened by the revolutionary violence, terror, and warfare, the traditional rulers sought to refute the philosophes' world-view, which had spawned the Revolution. To them, natural rights, equality, the goodness of man, and perpetual progress were perverse doctrines that had produced the Jacobin "assassins." In conservatism, they found a political philosophy to counter the Enlightenment ideology.

Edmund Burke's *Reflections on the Revolution in France* (1790) was instrumental in shaping conservative thought. Burke (1729–1797), an Anglo-Irish philosopher and statesman, wanted to warn his countrymen of the dangers inherent in the ideology of the revolutionaries. Although writing in 1790, Burke astutely predicted that the Revolution would lead to terror and military dictatorship. In Burke's view, fanatics armed with abstract ideas divorced from historical experience had dragged France through the mire of revolution. Burke developed a coherent political philosophy, which served as a counterweight to the ideology of the Enlightenment and the Revolution.

The leading conservative theorists on the Continent—more aptly called *reactionaries*—were Joseph de Maistre (1753–1821) and Vicomte Louis de Bonald (1754–1840). De Maistre, who fled his native Piedmont (northern Italy) in 1792 and again in 1793, after the invasion by the armies of the new French republic, vociferously denounced the philosophes for undermining belief and authority. He called their activity an "insurrection against God." In *Reflections on the State of France* (1796) and other works, he attacked the philosophes and the French Revolution, which he blamed them for inciting. Committed to authority and order, de Maistre fought any kind of political or religious liberalism. To him, the Revolution was a satanic evil; all its pronouncements must be totally condemned and its roots expunged from the soil of Christian Europe.

Like de Maistre, de Bonald, a French émigré, detested the French Revolution, staunchly defended monarchy, and attacked the rational spirit of the Enlightenment as an enemy of faith. His Catholicism and monarchism are summarized in his famous remark: "When God wished to punish France, he took away the Bourbon from her governance."

Hostility to the French Revolution

Entranced by the great discoveries in science, the philosophes and French reformers had believed that the human mind could also transform social institutions and ancient traditions according to rational models. Progress through reason became their faith. Intent on creating a new future, the revolutionaries abruptly dispensed with old habits, traditional authority, and familiar ways of thought. For them, these traditional ways were a form of bondage that retarded progress.

To conservatives, who, like the romantics venerated the past, this was supreme arrogance and wickedness. They regarded the revolutionaries as presumptuous men who recklessly severed society's links with ancient institutions and traditions and condemned venerable religious and moral beliefs as ignorance. De Maistre called Voltaire the man "into whose hands hell has given all its power."[20] Moreover, the revolutionaries forgot—or never knew—that the traditions and institutions that they wanted to destroy did not belong solely to them. Past generations and, indeed, future generations had a claim on these creations of French genius. By attacking time-honored ways, the revolutionaries had deprived French society of moral leadership and opened the door to anarchy and terror. "You began ill," wrote Burke of the revolutionaries, "because you began by despising everything that belonged to you. . . . When ancient opinions and rules of life are taken away, the loss cannot possibly be estimated. From that moment we have no compass to govern us; nor can we know distinctly to what port we steer."[21]

The philosophes and French reformers had expressed unlimited confidence in the power of human reason to understand and to change society. Although conservatives also appreciated human rational capacities, they recognized the limitations of reason. "We are afraid to put men to live and trade each on his own private stock of reason," said Burke, "because we suspect that this stock in each man is small, and that the individuals would do better to avail themselves of the general bank and capital of nations and of ages."[22] Conservatives saw the Revolution as a natural outgrowth of an arrogant Enlightenment philosophy that overvalued reason and sought to reshape society in accordance with abstract principles.

Conservatives did not regard human beings as good by nature. Human wickedness was not due to a faulty environment, as the philosophes had proclaimed, but was at the core of human nature, as Christianity taught. Evil was held in check not by reason but by tried and tested institutions, traditions, and beliefs. Without these habits inher-

ited from ancestors, said conservatives, the social order was threatened by sinful human nature.

Because monarchy, aristocracy, and the church had endured for centuries, argued the conservatives, they had worth. The clergy taught proper moral values; monarchs preserved order and property; aristocrats guarded against despotic kings and the tyranny of the common people. All protected and spread civilized ways. By despising and uprooting these ancient institutions, the revolutionaries had hardened the people's hearts, perverted their morals, and caused them to commit terrible outrages on each other and on society.

Conservatives detested attempts to transform society according to a theoretical model. They considered human nature too intricate and social relations too complex for such social engineering. In the conservatives' view, the revolutionaries had reduced people and society to abstractions divorced from their historical settings. Consequently, they had destroyed ancient patterns that seemed inconvenient and had drawn up constitutions based on the unacceptable principle that government derives its power from the consent of the governed.

The art of politics, argued Burke, entails practical reason: pursuing limited and realizable goals for a particular community at a particular time. The wise statesman, said traditionalists, abhors abstract principles and spurns ideal models. Rather, he values the historical experiences of his nation and is concerned with real people in specific historical situations. He recognizes that institutions and beliefs do not require theoretical excellence; they do not have to meet the test of reason or of nature in order to benefit society. Statesmen who ignore these truisms and strive to reform a commonwealth according to a priori models—political formulas that do not fit the realities of history and the social order—plunge the nation into anarchy. To Burke, the revolutionaries were zealots who, like the religious radicals during the Reformation, resorted to force and terror in order to create a new man and a new society. In politics, experience is the best teacher and prudence the best method of procedure. Burke warned:

> [I]t is with infinite caution that any man ought to venture upon pulling down an edifice which

has answered in any tolerable degree for ages the common purposes of society, or on building it up again, without having models and patterns of approved utility before his eyes.[23]

For conservatives, God and history were the only legitimate sources of political authority. States were not made; rather, they were an expression of the nation's moral, religious, and historical experience. No legitimate or sound constitution could be drawn up by a group assembled for that purpose. Scraps of paper with legal terminology and philosophic visions could not produce an effective government. Instead, a sound political system evolved gradually and inexplicably in response to circumstances. For this reason, conservatives admired the English constitution. It was not a product of abstract thought; no assembly had convened to fashion it. Because it was an unwritten arrangement that grew imperceptibly out of the historical experience and needs of the English people, it was durable and effective.

Conservatives viewed society not as a machine with replaceable parts but as a complex and delicate organism. Tamper with its vital organs, as the revolutionaries had done, and it would die.

The Quest for Social Stability

The liberal philosophy of the Enlightenment and the French Revolution started with the individual. The philosophes and the revolutionaries envisioned a society in which the individual was free and autonomous. Conservatives, in contrast, began with the community; they believed that the individual could function well only as part of a social group: family, church, or state. Alone, a person would be selfish, unreliable, and frail. Through membership in a social group, however, individuals learned cooperation and manners. From the conservative perspective, by exalting the individual, the revolutionaries had threatened to dissolve society into disconnected parts. Individualism would imperil social stability, destroy obedience to law, and fragment society into self-seeking isolated atoms.

Holding that the community was more important than the individual, conservatives rejected the philosophy of natural rights. Rights were not abstractions that preceded an individual's entrance into society and pertained to all people everywhere. Rather, the state, always remembering the needs of the entire community and its links to past generations, determined what rights and privileges its citizens might have. There were no "rights of man," only rights of the French, the English, and so forth, as determined and allocated by the particular state.

Conservatives viewed equality as another pernicious abstraction that contradicted all historical experience. Since for conservatives, society was naturally hierarchical, they believed that some men, by virtue of their intelligence, education, wealth, and birth, were best qualified to rule and instruct the less able. They blamed the revolutionaries for uprooting a long-established and divinely ordained ruling elite thereby depriving society of effective leaders, causing internal disorder, and paving the way for a military dictatorship.

Whereas the philosophes had attacked Christianity for promoting superstition and fanaticism, conservatives saw religion as the basis of civil society. They were convinced that excess liberty and the weakening of religion had brutalized people and shattered the foundations of society. Conservatives denounced the Enlightenment for unshackling dangerous instincts that religion had held in check. Catholic conservatives, in particular, held that God had constituted the church and monarchy to rein in sinful human nature. "Christian monarchs are the final creation of the development of political society and of religious society," said Louis de Bonald. "The proof of this lies in the fact that when monarchy and Christianity are both abolished society returns to savagery."[24]

Conservatism exposed a limitation of the Enlightenment by pointing out that human beings and social relationships are far more complex than the philosophes had imagined. People do not always accept the rigorous logic of the philosopher and are not eager to break with ancient ways, however illogical they appear to the intellect. They often find familiar customs and ancestral religions more satisfying guides to life than the blueprints of philosophers. The granite might of tradition remains an obstacle to the visions of reformers. Conservative theorists warned that revolutionary violence in the pursuit of utopian dreams transforms politics into an ideological crusade that ends in terror and despotism. These warnings bore bitter fruit in the twentieth century.

LIBERALISM: THE VALUE
OF THE INDIVIDUAL

The decades after 1815 saw a spectacular rise of the bourgeoisie. Talented and ambitious bankers, merchants, manufacturers, professionals, and officeholders wanted to break the stranglehold of the landed nobility, the traditional elite, on political power and social prestige. They also wanted to eliminate restrictions on the free pursuit of profits.

The political philosophy of the bourgeoisie was most commonly liberalism. While conservatives sought to strengthen the foundations of traditional society, which had been severely shaken in the period of the French Revolution and Napoleon, liberals strove to alter the status quo. Believing in the goodness of human nature and the capacity of individuals to control their own lives, they hoped to realize the promise of the Enlightenment and the French Revolution.

The Sources of Liberalism

In the long view of Western civilization, liberalism is an extension and development of the democratic practices and rational outlook that originated in ancient Greece. Also flowing into the liberal tradition was the Judeo-Christian affirmation of the worth and dignity of the individual endowed by God with freedom to make moral choices. But the immediate historical roots of nineteenth-century liberalism extended back to seventeenth-century England. At that time, the struggle for religious toleration by English Protestant dissenters advanced the principle of freedom of conscience, which is easily transferred into freedom of opinion and expression in all matters. The Glorious Revolution of 1688 set limits on the power of the English monarchy. In that same century, John Locke's natural-rights philosophy proclaimed that the individual was by nature entitled to freedom, and it justified revolutions against

rulers who deprived citizens of their lives, liberty, or property. The expansion of a market economy, particularly in Britain, the American colonies, and Holland, showed the virtues of individual initiative and voluntary human actions, uncoerced by the authority of government.

The French philosophes also helped shape liberalism. From Montesquieu, liberals derived the theory of the separation of powers and of checks and balances: principles intended to guard against autocratic government. The philosophes had supported religious toleration and freedom of thought, expressed confidence in the capacity of the human mind to reform society, maintained that human beings are essentially good, and believed in the future progress of humanity—all fundamental tenets of liberalism.

The American and French Revolutions were crucial phases in the history of liberalism. The Declaration of Independence gave expression to Locke's theory of natural rights, the Constitution of the United States incorporated Montesquieu's principles and demonstrated that people could create an effective government, and the Bill of Rights protected the person and rights of the individual. In destroying the special privileges of the aristocracy and opening careers to talent, the French National Assembly of 1789 implemented the liberal ideal of equality under the law. It also drew up the Declaration of the Rights of Man and of the Citizen, which affirmed the dignity and rights of the individual, and a constitution that limited the king's power. Both Revolutions explicitly called for the protection of property rights, another basic premise of liberalism.

Individual Liberty

The liberals' primary concern was the enhancement of individual liberty. They agreed with Kant that every person exists as an end in himself or herself and not as an object to be used arbitrarily by others. If uncoerced by government and churches and properly educated, a person could develop into a good, productive, and self-directed human being.

Liberals rejected a legacy of the Middle Ages, the classification of the individual as commoner or aristocrat on the basis of birth. They held that a man was not born into a certain station in life but made his way through his own efforts. Taking their cue from the French Revolution, liberals called for an end to all privileges of the aristocracy. In the tradition of the philosophes, liberals stressed the preeminence of reason as the basis of political life. Unfettered by ignorance and tyranny, the mind could eradicate evils that had burdened people for centuries and begin an age of free institutions and responsible citizens. For this reason, liberals supported the advancement of education.

Liberals attacked the state and other authorities that prevented the individual from exercising the right of free choice, interfered with the right of free expression, and impeded the individual's self-determination and self-development. They agreed with John Stuart Mill, the British philosopher, that "over his own body and mind, the individual is sovereign . . . that the only purpose for which power can be rightly exercised over any member of a civilized community, against his will, is to prevent harm to others."[25]

To guard against the absolute and arbitrary authority of kings, liberals demanded written constitutions that granted freedom of speech, of the press, and of religion; freedom from arbitrary arrest; and the protection of property rights. To prevent the abuse of political authority, liberals called for a freely elected parliament and the distribution of power among the various branches of government. Liberals held that a government that derived its authority from the consent of the governed, as given in free elections, was least likely to violate individual freedom. A corollary of this principle was that the best government is the one that governs least—that is, one that interferes as little as possible with the economic activities of its citizens and does not involve itself in their private lives or their beliefs.

Liberal Economic Theory

Bourgeois liberals thought that the economy, like the state, should proceed according to natural laws rather than the arbitrary fiat of rulers. Adopting the laissez-faire theory of Adam Smith, they argued that a free economy, in which private enterprise was unimpeded by government regulations, was as important as political freedom to the well-being of the individual and the community. When people acted from self-interest, the liberals said, they worked harder and achieved more. Self-interest and natural competitive impulses spurred economic activity and ensured the production of more and better goods at the lowest possible price, thereby benefiting the entire nation. For this reason, the government must neither block free competition nor deprive individuals of their property, which gave them the incentive to work hard and efficiently. The state contributed to the nation's prosperity when it maintained domestic order; it endangered economic development when it tampered with the free pursuit of profits.

Believing that individuals were responsible for their own misfortunes, liberals were often unmoved by the suffering of the poor. In their eyes, the misery of the poor were due to their own moral failings, laziness, and vice. Indeed, they used the principle of laissez faire—that government should not interfere with the market—to justify their opposition to humanitarian legislation intended to alleviate the misery of the factory workers. Liberals regarded such social reforms as unwarranted and dangerous meddling with the natural law of supply and demand.

One theorist upholding this view was Thomas R. Malthus (1766–1834), an Anglican cleric and professor of history and political economy. In his *Essay on the Principle of Population* (published in 1798 and then in a second, much enlarged, edition in 1803), Malthus asserted that population grows at a much faster rate than the food supply, resulting in food shortages, irregular employment, lower wages, and high mortality. The poor's distress, said Malthus, was not due to faulty political institutions or existing social and property relations. Its true cause was the number of children they had:

> *When the wages of labour are hardly sufficient to maintain two children, a man marries and has five or six. He of course finds himself miserably distressed. . . . He accuses his parish. . . . He accuses the avarice of the rich. He accuses the partial and unjust institutions of society. . . . In searching for objects of accusation, he never alludes to the quarter from which all his misfortunes originate. The last person that he would think of accusing is himself.*[26]

The state cannot ameliorate the poor's misery, said Malthus; "the means of redress are in their own hands, and in the hands of no other persons whatever."[27] This "means of redress" would be a lowering of the birthrate through late marriages and chastity, but Malthus believed that the poor lacked the self-discipline to refrain from sexual activity. When they receive higher wages, they have more children, thereby upsetting the population-resource balance and bringing misery to themselves and others.* The view of poverty as an iron law of nature, which could not be undone by the good intentions of the state through philanthropy, buttressed supporters of strict laissez faire and eased the consciences of the propertied classes. Compassion for the poor was simply a misplaced emotion; government reforms were doomed to fail and higher wages provided no relief. Malthus's theory also flew in the face of adherents of human perfectibility and inevitable progress. Poverty, like disease, was simply a natural phenomenon—a law of nature that could not be eliminated. No wonder his contemporaries called economics "the dismal science."

In *Principles of Political Economy* (1817), David Ricardo (1772–1823) gave support to Malthus's gloomy outlook. Higher wages, said Ricardo, lead workers to have more children, causing an increase in the labor supply. Competition for jobs by an expanding labor force brings down wages. This "iron law of wages" offered bleak prospects for the working poor:

> When, however, by the encouragement which high wages give to the increase of population, the number of labourers is increased, wages again fall to their natural price [to a subsistence level] and indeed from a reaction sometimes fall below it. . . . It is a truth which admits not a doubt, that the comforts and well-being of the poor cannot be permanently secured without some regard on their part, or some effort on the part of the legislature, to regulate the increase of their numbers, and to render less frequent among them early and improvident marriages.[28]

*In later editions of his work, Malthus was more hopeful that checks on fertility through later marriage and "moral restraint" would lead to moderate improvements in the standard of living.

Liberals of the early nineteenth century saw poverty and suffering as part of the natural order and beyond the scope of government. They feared that state intervention in the economy to redress social ills would disrupt the free market, threatening personal liberty and hindering social well-being. Thus, on May 13, 1848, an editorial in the *Economist* protesting against a bill before Parliament that sought to improve housing and sanitation declared: "suffering and evil are nature's admonitions; they cannot be got rid of; and the impatient attempts of benevolence to banish them from the world by legislation . . . have always been productive of more evil than good." Government interference, liberals also argued, discouraged the poor from finding work and so promoted idleness. According to liberal political economy, unemployment and poverty stemmed from individual failings.

A particularly glaring example of the coldness and harshness of liberals toward suffering was their response to the Irish famine of 1845–1849. While the Irish were dying of starvation, the liberal leadership in Britain, fearing that government intervention would promote dependence, did little to lessen the suffering. "The more I see of government interference," wrote Sir Charles Wood, chancellor of the Exchequer, "the less I am disposed to trust it, and I have no faith in anything but private capital employed under the individual charge."[29] To some hardhearted liberals, the famine, which killed about 1.5 million people, was simply nature's way of dealing with Ireland's excess population. A dogmatic commitment to laissez faire discouraged British officials from coping humanely and creatively with this disaster.

In the last part of the century, liberals modified their adherence to strict laissez faire, accepting the principle that the state had a responsibility to protect the poor against the worst abuses of rapid industrialization.

Liberalism and Democracy

The French Revolution presented a dilemma for liberals. They supported the reforms of the moderate stage: the destruction of the special privileges of the aristocracy, the drawing up of a declaration of rights and a constitution, the establishment of a parliament, and the opening of careers to talent. But they repudiated Jacobin radicalism. Liberals were frightened by the excesses of the Jacobin regime: its tampering with the economy, which, to liberals, violated the rights of private property; its appeal to the "little people," which liberals saw as inviting mob rule; its subjection of the individual to the state, which they regarded as the denial of individual rights; and its use of terror, which awakened the basest human feelings.

To bourgeois liberals, the participation of commoners in politics meant a vulgar form of despotism and the end of individual liberty. They saw the masses—uneducated, unpropertied, inexperienced, and impatient—as lacking both the ability and the temperament to maintain liberty and protect property.

Few thinkers in the first half of the nineteenth century grasped the growing significance of the masses in politics as did Alexis de Tocqueville (1805–1859), the French political theorist and statesman. In the wake of the French Revolution, de Tocqueville, an aristocrat by birth but a liberal by temperament, recognized that the destruction of aristocracy—a system based on rank—and the march toward democracy could not be curbed. In *Democracy in America* (1835–1840), based on his travels in the United States, de Tocqueville analyzed, with cool detachment and brilliance, the nature, merits, and weaknesses of American democratic society. In contrast to the France of the Old Regime, wrote de Tocqueville, American society had no hereditary aristocracy with special privileges; the avenues to social advancement and political participation were open to all. Arguing that democracy was more just than aristocratic government, de Tocqueville saw it as the political system of the future. But he also recognized the dangers inherent in democracy.

Online Study Center

Improve Your Grade
Primary Source: A New Model: Democracy in America (Alexis de Tocqueville)

In a democratic society, he noted, people are willing to sacrifice political liberty to improve their material well-being. Consequently, democracies face an ever-present danger that people, craving equality, will surrender their liberty to a central government if it promises to provide them with property and other advantages.

According to de Tocqueville, democracy also spawns a selfish individualism, which could degenerate into vulgar hedonism. Driven by an overriding concern for possessions and profits, people can lose their taste for political participation and their concern for the public good. If narrow self-interest prevails over a sense of public duty, liberty cannot long endure.

Although recognizing the limitations of democracy, de Tocqueville did not seek to reverse its growth. In this new age that is dawning, he wrote,

> all who shall attempt . . . to base freedom upon aristocratic privilege will fail . . . all who shall attempt to draw and to retain authority within a single class, will fail. . . . All . . . who would establish or secure the independence and the dignity of their fellow-men, must show themselves the friends of equality. . . . Thus the question is not how to reconstruct aristocratic society, but how to make liberty proceed out of that democratic state of society in which God has placed us.[30]

The problems of democracy, declared de Tocqueville, must be resolved without jeopardizing freedom. The task of a democratic society is to temper extreme individualism and unrestrained acquisitiveness by fostering public spirit. Without direct participation by cooperating citizens—that is, without a concern for the common good—democracy faces a bleak future. Freedom depends less on laws than it does on cultivating the sentiments and habits of civic virtue.

Because bourgeois liberals feared that democracy could quash personal freedom as ruthlessly as any absolute monarch, they called for property requirements for voting and officeholding. They wanted political power to be concentrated in the hands of a safe and reliable—that is, a propertied and educated—middle class. Such a government would prevent revolution from below, a prospect that caused anxiety among bourgeois liberals.

When liberals of the early nineteenth century engaged in revolutions, their aims were always limited. Once they had destroyed absolute monarchy and gained a constitution and a parliament or a change of government, they quickly tried to terminate the revolution. When the fever of revolution spread to the masses, liberals either withdrew or turned counterrevolutionary, for they feared the stirrings of the multitude.

Although liberalism was the political philosophy of a middle class generally hostile to democracy, the essential ideals of democracy flowed logically from liberalism. Eventually, democracy became a later stage in the evolution of liberalism because the masses, their political power enhanced by the Industrial Revolution, would press for greater social, political, and economic equality. Thus, by the early twentieth century, many European states had introduced universal manhood suffrage, abandoned property requirements for officeholding, and improved conditions for workers.

But the fears of nineteenth-century liberals were not unfounded. In the twentieth century, the participation of common people in politics indeed threatened freedom. Impatient with parliamentary procedures, the masses, particularly when troubled by economic problems, in some instances gave their support to demagogues who promised swift and decisive action. The granting of political participation to the masses has not always made people freer. The confidence of democrats was shaken in the twentieth century by the seeming willingness of common people to trade freedom for state authority, order, economic security, and national power. Liberalism is based on the assumption that human beings can and do respond to rational argument and that reason will prevail over base human feelings. The history of the twentieth century shows that this may be an overly optimistic assessment of human nature.

RADICALISM AND DEMOCRACY: THE EXPANSION OF LIBERALISM

In the early 1800s, democratic ideals were advanced by thinkers and activists called *radicals*. Inspired by the democratic principles expressed in Rousseau's *Social Contract* and by the republican stage of the French Revolution, French radicals championed popular sovereignty—rule by the people. In contrast to liberals, who feared the masses, French radicals trusted the common person. Advocating universal manhood suffrage and a republic, radicalism gained the support of French workers in the 1830s and 1840s.

British radicals, like their liberal cousins, inherited the Enlightenment's confidence in reason and its belief in the essential goodness of the individual. In the 1790s, British radicals expressed sympathy for the French Revolution, approving its concern for natural rights and its attack on feudal privileges. In the first half of the nineteenth century, English radicals sought parliamentary reforms because some heavily populated districts were barely represented in Parliament, while lightly populated districts were overrepresented. They demanded payment for members of Parliament to permit the nonwealthy to hold office, they sought universal manhood suffrage to give the masses representation in Parliament, and they insisted on the secret ballot to prevent intimidation of and reprisals against voters. Radicals attacked the hereditary aristocracy and fought corruption. Some, like William Cobbett, a crusading journalist, supported the struggle of the working class to improve its condition. He described the workers' penury:

> *A labouring man in England with a wife and only three children, though he never lose a day's work, though he and his family be economical, frugal and industrious in the most extensive sense of these words, is not now able to procure himself by his labour a single meal of meat from one end of the year into the other. Is this a state in which the labouring man ought to be?*[31]

English radicalism embodied the desires of parliamentary reformers for broader political representation and the hopes of the laboring poor for a better life. Two important theorists of the movement were Thomas Paine and Jeremy Bentham.

Thomas Paine

Thomas Paine (1737–1809), responding to Burke's *Reflections on the Revolution in France* with *The Rights of Man* (published in two parts in 1791 and 1792), denounced reverence for tradition, defended the principle of natural rights, and praised as progress the destruction of the Old Regime. Paine shared the conviction of other Enlightenment thinkers that superstition, intolerance, and despotism had interfered with human progress in the past, and he staunchly supported the American and French Revolutions. To initiate a true age of enlightenment, he said, it is necessary to recognize that "all the great laws of society are laws of nature,"[32] and to reconstitute the social and political order in accordance with these principles inherent in nature. Paine denounced all hereditary monarchy and aristocracy as wretched systems of slavery, which deprived people of their inherent right to govern themselves and exploited them financially in order to raise money for war. The only legitimate government, he claimed, was representative democracy, in which the right of all men to participate was assured. Paine believed that republican governments would be less inclined than hereditary ones to wage war and more concerned with the welfare of the common person.

From Paine, the English radical tradition acquired a faith in reason and human goodness, a skeptical attitude toward established institutions, an admiration for the open and democratic society being shaped in the United States, and a dislike of organized religion. It also gained the belief that the goal of government was the greater happiness of ordinary people and that excluding common people from political participation was unjust.

Online Study Center

Improve Your Grade
Primary Source: A Natural Rights Defense of the French Revolution: The Rights of Man (Thomas Paine)

Jeremy Bentham

In contrast to Paine, Jeremy Bentham (1748–1832) rejected the doctrine of natural rights as an abstraction with no basis in reality, and he regarded the French Revolution as an absurd attempt to reconstruct society according to principles as misguided as those that had supported the Old Regime. Bentham's importance to the English radical tradition derives from the principle of **utility,** which he offered as a guide to reformers. The central fact of human existence, said Bentham, is that human beings seek to gratify their desires, that they prefer pleasure to pain, and that pleasure is intrinsically good and pain bad. In Bentham's view, human beings are motivated solely by self-interest, which they define in terms of pleasure and pain: "Nature has placed mankind under the governance of two sovereign masters, *pain* and *pleasure.* It is for them alone to point out what we ought to do, as well as to determine what we shall do."[33] Consequently, every political, economic, judicial, or social institution and all legislation should be judged according to a simple standard: does it bring about the greatest happiness for the greatest number? If it does not, it should be swept away.

Bentham believed that he had found an objective and scientific approach to the study and reform of society. By focusing on the necessity for change and improvement on every level of society and by encouraging a careful and objective analysis of social issues, Bentham and his followers, called *philosophical radicals,* contributed substantially to the shaping of the English reform tradition.

According to Bentham, those in power had always used what they considered the highest principles—God's teachings, universal standards, and honored traditions—to justify their political and social systems, their moral codes, and their laws. On the basis of these principles, they persecuted and abused people, instituted practices rooted in ignorance and superstition, and imposed values that made people miserable because they conflicted with human nature and the essential needs of men and women. Bentham contended that the principle of utility—that one should act always to derive the greatest happiness for the greatest number of people—permits the reforming of society in accordance with people's true nature and needs. Utilitarianism, he declared, bases institutions and laws on an objective study of human behavior rather than on unsubstantiated religious beliefs, unreliable traditions, and mistaken philosophical abstractions. Its goal is to propose measures that augment rather than diminish the community's happiness.

Bentham's utilitarianism led him to press for social and political reforms. The aristocratic ruling elite, he said, were interested not in producing the "greatest happiness of the greatest number" but in furthering their own narrow interests. Only if the rulers came from the broad masses of people would government be amenable to reforms based on the principle of greatest happiness. Thus, he supported extension of the suffrage and a secret ballot and attacked political corruption and clerical control over education. Bentham wanted to do away with the monarchy and the House of Lords and to disestablish the Anglican church. In contrast to laissez-faire liberals, Benthamites argued for legislation to protect women and children in the factories. They also sought to improve sanitation in the cities and to reform the archaic British prison system.

EARLY SOCIALISM: NEW POSSIBILITIES FOR SOCIETY

A new group, called *socialists,* went further than either the liberals or the radicals. Socialists argued that the liberals' concern for individual freedom and the radicals' demand for extension of the suffrage had little impact on the poverty, oppression, and gross inequality of wealth that plagued modern society. Asserting that the liberals' doctrine of individualism degenerated into selfish egoism, which harmed community life, socialists demanded the creation of a new society based on cooperation rather than on competition. Reflecting the spirit of the Enlightenment and the French Revolution, socialists, like liberals, denounced the status quo for perpetuating injustice and held that people could create a better world. Like liberals, too, they placed the highest value on a rational analysis of society and on transforming society in line with scientifically valid premises, whose truth rational people could grasp. Socialists believed that they had discerned a pattern in human society, which, if properly understood and acted upon, would lead men and women to an earthly salvation. Thus, early socialists were also romantics, for they dreamed of a new social order, a future utopia, where each individual could find happiness and self-fulfillment.

Although they sought to replace the existing social order with a more just arrangement, these early socialists, unlike Marx, did not advocate class warfare. They aspired to create a new harmonious social order that would reconcile different classes; for Marx, by necessity a new social order entailed the destruction of the bourgeoisie.

Saint-Simon: Technocratic Socialism

Henri Comte de Saint-Simon (1760–1825) renounced his title during the French Revolution and enthusiastically preached the opportunity to create a new society. His mission, he believed, was to set society right by instilling an understanding of the new age that science and industry were shaping. He argued that just as Christianity had provided social unity and stability during the Middle Ages, so scientific knowledge would bind the society of his time. The scientists, industrialists, bankers, artists, and writers would replace the clergy and the aristocracy as the social elite and would harness technology for the betterment of humanity. Saint-Simon's disciples championed efforts to build great railway and canal systems, including the Suez and Panama Canals. His vision of a scientifically organized society led by trained experts was a powerful force among intellectuals in the nineteenth century and is very much alive today among those who believe in a technocratic society.

Fourier: Psychological Socialism

Another early French socialist was Charles Fourier (1772–1837), who believed—like the romantics—that society conflicted with the natural needs of human beings and that this tension was responsible for human misery. Only the reorganization of society so that it would satisfy people's desire for pleasure and contentment would end that misery. Whereas Saint-Simon and his followers had elaborate plans to reorganize society on the grand scale of large industries and giant railway and canal systems, Fourier sought to create small communities that would let men and women to enjoy life's simple pleasures.

These communities of about sixteen hundred people, called *phalansteries,* would be organized

SAINT-SIMONIAN COMMUNITY AT MÉNILMONTANT. Followers of Saint-Simon established this community in a suburb of Paris. It was headed by Father Enfantin, whose iconoclastic theories of love and marriage outraged many people. (*Bibliothèque Nationale, Paris.*)

according to the unchanging needs of human nature. All the people would work at tasks that interested them and would produce things that brought them and others pleasure. Like Adam Smith, Fourier understood that specialization bred boredom and alienation from work and life. Unlike Smith, he did not believe that vastly increased productivity compensated for the evils of specialization. In the phalansteries, money and goods would not be equally distributed; those with special skills and responsibilities would be rewarded accordingly. This system of rewards conformed to nature because people have a natural desire to be rewarded.

Fourier thought that marriage distorted the natures of both men and women since monogamy restricted their sexual needs and narrowed the scope of their lives to just the family. Instead, people should think of themselves as part of the family of all humanity. Because married women had to devote all their strength and time to household and children, they had no time or energy left to enjoy life's pleasures. Fourier did not call for the abolition of the family, but he did hope that it would disappear on its own accord as society adjusted to his theories. Men and women would find new ways of fulfilling themselves sexually, and the community would be or-

ganized so that it could care for the children. Fourier's ideas found some acceptance in the United States, where in the 1840s at least twenty-nine communities were founded on Fourierist principles. None, however, lasted more than five or six years.

Owen: Industrial Socialism

In 1799, Robert Owen (1771–1858) became part owner and manager of the New Lanark cotton mills in Scotland. Distressed by widespread mistreatment of workers, Owen resolved to improve the lives of his employees and show that it was possible to do so without destroying profits. He raised wages, upgraded working conditions, refused to hire children under ten, and provided workers with neat homes, food, and clothing, all at reasonable prices. He set up schools for children and for adults. In every way, he demonstrated his belief that healthier, happier workers produced more than the less fortunate ones. Like Saint-Simon, Owen believed that industry and technology could and would enrich humankind if they were organized according to the proper principles. Visitors came from all over Europe to see Owen's factories.

Just like many philosophes, Owen was convinced that the environment was the principal shaper of character—that the ignorance, alcoholism, and crime of the poor derived from bad living conditions. Public education and factory reform, said Owen, would make better citizens of the poor. Owen came to believe that the entire social and economic order must be replaced by a new system based on harmonious group living rather than on competition. He established a model community at New Harmony, Indiana, but it was short-lived.

NATIONALISM: THE SACREDNESS OF THE NATION

Nationalism is a conscious bond shared by a group of people who feel strongly attached to a particular land and who possess a common language, culture, and history, marked by shared glories and sufferings. Nationalists contend that one's highest loyalty and devotion should be given to the nation. They exhibit great pride in their people's history and traditions and often feel that their nation has been specially chosen by God or history. They assert that the nation—its culture and history—gives meaning to an individual's life and actions. Like a religion, nationalism provides the individual with a sense of community and with a cause worthy of self-sacrifice. Identifying with the nation's collective achievements can enhance the feeling of self-worth.

In an age when Christianity was in retreat, nationalism became the dominant spiritual force in nineteenth-century European life. Nationalism provided new beliefs, martyrs, and "holy" days that stimulated feelings of reverence; it offered membership in a community, which satisfied an overwhelming psychological need of human beings for fellowship and identity. And nationalism supplied a mission—the advancement of the nation—to which people could dedicate themselves.

The Emergence of Modern Nationalism

The essential components of nationalism emerged during the French Revolution. The Revolution asserted the principle that sovereignty derived from the nation, from the people as a whole: the state was not the private possession of the ruler but the embodiment of the people's will. The nation-state was above king, church, estate, guild, or province, superseding all other loyalties. The French people must view themselves not as subjects of the king, not as Bretons or Normans, nobles or bourgeois, but as citizens of a united fatherland, *la patrie*. These two ideas—that the people possess unlimited sovereignty and that they are united in a nation—were crucial in fashioning a nationalist outlook.

As the Revolution moved from the moderate to the radical stage, French nationalism intensified. In 1793–94, when the republic was threatened by foreign invasion, the Jacobins created a national army, demanded ever greater allegiance to and sacrifice for the nation, and called for the expansion of France's borders to the Alps and the Rhine. With unprecedented success, the Jacobins used every means—press, schoolroom, and rostrum—to instill a love of country.

The Romantic Movement also awakened nationalist feelings. By examining the language, literature, and folkways of their people, romantic thinkers instilled a sense of national pride in their compatriots. Johann Gottfried Herder (1744–1803), a prominent German writer, conceived the idea of the *Volksgeist*—the spirit of the people. For Herder, each people was unique and creative; each expressed its peculiar genius in language, literature, monuments, and folk traditions. Herder did not make the theoretical jump from a spiritual or cultural nationalism to political nationalism; he did not call for the formation of states based on nationality. But his emphasis on the unique culture of a people and his assertion that an individual is defined as a member of a specific culture or nation stimulated a national consciousness among Germans and the various Slavic peoples who lived under foreign rule. Fascination with the Volksgeist prompted intellectuals to investigate the past of their own people, to rediscover their ancient traditions, and to extol their historic languages and cultures. From this cultural nationalism, it was only a short step to a political nationalism that called for national liberation, unification, and statehood.

The romantics were the earliest apostles of German nationalism. Resisting the French philosophes, who sought to impose universal norms on all peoples, German romantics stressed the uniqueness of the German nation and its history. They restored to consciousness memories of the German past, and they emphasized the distinct qualities of the German folk and the special destiny of the German nation. The romantics glorified medieval Germany and valued hereditary monarchy and aristocracy as vital links to the nation's past. They saw the existence of each individual as inextricably bound up with folk and fatherland, and they found the self-realization for which they yearned in the uniting of their own egos with the national soul. To these romantics, the national community was the source of artistic and spiritual creativity and the vital force that gave the individual both an identity and a purpose in life. The nation stood above the individual; the national spirit linked isolated souls into a community of brethren. In unmistakenly romantic tones, poet Ernst Moritz Arndt (1769–1860) demonstrated this tradition from cultural to political nationalism when he urged Germans to unite against Napoleon:

> *German man, feel again God, hear and fear the eternal, and you hear and fear also your Volk [people], you feel again in God the honor and dignity of your fathers, their glorious history rejuvenates itself in you, their firm and gallant virtue reblossoms in you, the whole German Fatherland stands again before you in the august halo of past centuries. No longer Catholics and Protestants, no longer Prussians and Austrians, Saxons and Bavarians, Silesians and Hanoverians, no longer of different faith, different mentality, and different will— be Germans, be one, will to be one by love and loyalty, and no devil will vanquish you.*[34]

Most German romantics expressed hostility to the liberal ideals of the French Revolution. They condemned the reforms of the Revolution for trying to reconstruct society by separating individuals from their national past, for treating them as isolated abstractions. They held that the German folk spirit should not be polluted by foreign French ideas.

To the philosophes, the state was a human institution, a rational arrangement between individuals that safeguarded their rights and permitted them to realize their individual goals. To German romantics such a state was an artificial and lifeless construction. The true German state was something holy, the expression of the divine spirit of the German people; it could not be manufactured to order by the intellect. The state's purpose was neither the protection of natural rights nor the promotion of economic well-being; rather, the state was a living organism that linked each person to a sacred past and reconciled and united heterogeneous wills, imbuing them with a profound sense of community, with which one entered into mystical communion. "This 'Romantic' image of a state founded not on any rational idea of the functions and purposes of a state but on love and perfect communion, is of course a formula for totalitarianism," observes R. J. Hollingdale, "and it was towards a state modeled on this formula that German nationalism continually moved."[35] Building on the romantics' views, radical German nationalists came to propound the dangerous racist idea that national identity was an inherited characteristic—that being and feeling German depended on birth rather than acculturation. Holding this belief, some German nationalists maintained that Jews, no matter how many generations they had resided in Germany, could never be truly German.

Nationalism and Liberalism

In the early 1800s, liberals were the principal leaders and supporters of nationalist movements. They viewed the struggle for national rights—the freedom of a people from foreign rule—as an extension of the struggle for the rights of the individual. There could be no liberty, said nationalists, if people were not free to rule themselves in their own land.

Liberals called for the unification of Germany and Italy, the rebirth of Poland, the liberation of Greece from Turkish rule, and the granting of autonomy to the Hungarians of the Austrian Empire. Liberal nationalists envisioned a Europe of independent states based on nationality and popular sovereignty. Free of foreign domination and tyrant princes, these newly risen states would protect the rights of the individual and strive to create a brotherhood of nationalities in Europe.

In the first half of the nineteenth century, few intellectuals recognized the dangers inherent in nationalism or understood the fundamental conflict between liberalism and nationalism. For the liberal, the idea of universal natural rights transcended all national boundaries. Inheriting the cosmopolitanism of the Enlightenment, liberalism emphasized what all people had in common, called for all individuals to be treated equally under the law, and preached toleration. Nationalists, manifesting the particularist attitude of the in-group and the tribe, regarded the nation as the essential fact of existence. Consequently, they often willingly subverted individual liberty for the sake of national grandeur. The liberal sought to protect the rights of all within the state, whereas the nationalist often ignored or trampled on the rights of individuals and national minorities. Liberalism grew out of the rational tradition of the West; nationalism derived from the emotions. Because it fulfilled an elemental yearning for community and kinship, nationalism exerted a powerful hold over human hearts, often driving people to political extremism. Liberalism demanded objectivity in analyzing tradition, society, and history, but nationalism evoked a mythic and romantic past that often distorted history.

"Nationalism requires . . . much belief in what is patently not so," wryly observes the British historian E. J. Hobsbawm.[36] Thus nationalists inflated their people's past achievements and attributed to the nation a peculiar inner spirit that set it apart from others and accounted for its superiority. While constantly declaiming the wrongs that others had inflicted on them, they turned a blind eye to their own mistreatment of other nationalities. Nationalists interpreted history to serve political ends: the unity of their people and the creation of an independent nation-state.

In the last part of the nineteenth century, the irrational and mythic quality of nationalism intensified. By stressing the unique qualities and history of a particular people, nationalism promoted hatred between nationalities. By kindling deep love for the past, for community, and for kinship, it often raised emotions to fever pitch. It shattered rational thinking, dragged the mind into a world of fantasy and myth, and introduced extremism into politics. Love of nation became an overriding passion, threatening to extinguish the liberal ideals of reason, freedom, and equality.

❖   ❖   ❖

Online Study Center ACE the Test

NOTES

1. Jean Jacques Rousseau, *The Confessions* (New York: Modern Library, 1950), p. 2.

2. Quoted in H. G. Schenk, *The Mind of the European Romantics* (Garden City, N.Y.: Doubleday, 1969), p. 4.

3. William Blake, "Milton," in *The Poetry and Prose of William Blake,* ed. David V. Erdman (Garden City, N.Y.: Doubleday, 1965), bk. 2, plate 40, lines 34–36, p. 141.

4. Ibid., plate 41, line 1.

5. Johann Goethe, *Faust,* trans. Bayard Taylor (New York: Modern Library, 1950), pt. 1, sc. 4.

6. Letter of John Keats, November 22, 1817, in *The Letters of John Keats,* ed. Hyder E. Rollins (Cambridge, Mass.: Harvard University Press, 1958), 1:184–185.

7. Quoted in John Herman Randall, Jr., *The Career of Philosophy* (New York: Columbia University Press, 1965), 2:80.

8. Blake, "Milton," Preface, bk. 1, plate 1, p. 95.

9. Quoted in Robert T. Denommé, *Nineteenth-Century French Romantic Poets* (Carbondale: Southern Illinois University Press, 1969), p. 28.

10. Quoted in T. C. W. Blanning, ed., *The Oxford Illustrated History of Modern Europe* (New York: Oxford University Press, 1996), p. 124.

11. Quoted in Frederic Ewen, *Heroic Imagination* (Secaucus, N.J.: Citadel Press, 1984), p. 276.

12. Quoted in Ernst Cassirer, *An Essay on Man* (New York: Bantam Books, 1970), p. 178.

13. Victor Hugo, "La Pente de la Rêverie," *Les Feuilles D'Automne* (Paris: J. Hetzel, 1831), p. 157.

14. From "The Tables Turned," in *The Complete Poetical Works of Wordsworth,* ed. Andrew J. George (Boston: Houghton Mifflin, 1904, rev. ed. 1982), p. 83.

15. From "Lines Composed a Few Miles Above Tintern Abbey," *The Complete Poetical Works of William Wordsworth* (Philadelphia: Porter & Coates, 1851), p. 194.

16. Quoted in R. W. Harris, *Romanticism and the Social Order, 1780–1830* (New York: Barnes & Noble, 1969), pp. 223–224.

17. Horst von Maltitz, *The Evolution of Hitler's Germany* (New York: McGraw-Hill, 1973), p. 217.

18. G. W. F. Hegel, *The Philosophy of History,* trans. J. Sibree (New York: Dover, 1956), pp. 19, 23.

19. Ibid., p. 39.

20. Quoted in George Brandes, *Revolution and Reaction in Nineteenth Century French Literature* (New York: Russell & Russell, reprint ed., n.d.), pp. 106–107.

21. Edmund Burke, *Reflections on the Revolution in France* (New York: Liberal Arts Press, 1955), pp. 40, 89.

22. Ibid., p. 99.

23. Ibid., p. 70.

24. Quoted in Frederick B. Artz, *Reaction and Revolution, 1814–1832* (New York: Harper Torchbooks, 1963), p. 73.

25. John Stuart Mill, *On Liberty,* ed. Currin V. Shields (Indianapolis: Bobbs-Merrill, 1956), chap. 1.

26. Thomas Robert Malthus, *First Essay on Population,* reprinted for the Royal Economic Society (London: Macmillan, 1926), p. 16.

27. Ibid., p. 17.

28. Excerpted in Allan Bullock and Maurice Shock, eds., *The Liberal Tradition from Fox to Keynes* (London: Adam & Charles Black, 1956), pp. 31–32.

29. Quoted in Anthony Arblaster, *The Rise and Decline of Western Liberalism* (Oxford: Basil Blackwell, 1984), p. 258.

30. Alexis de Tocqueville, *Democracy in America,* trans. Henry Reeve (New York: Oxford University Press, 1924), pp. 493–494.

31. Quoted in Raymond Williams, *Culture and Society, 1780–1945* (New York: Columbia University Press, 1983), p. 14.

32. Quoted in Francis Canavan, "Thomas Paine," in *History of Political Philosophy,* ed. Leo Strauss and Joseph Cropsey (Chicago: Rand McNally, 1963), p. 594.

33. Jeremy Bentham, *An Introduction to the Principles of Morals and Legislation,* together with *A Fragment on Government* (London: Basil Blackwell, 1948), chap. 1, sec. 1, p. 125.

34. Quoted in Hans Kohn, *Prelude to Nation-States* (Princeton, N.J.: D. Van Nostrand, 1967), p. 262.

35. R. J. Hollingdale, *Nietzsche* (London: Routledge & Kegan Paul, 1973), p. 25.

36. E. J. Hobsbawm, *Nations and Nationalism Since 1780* (Cambridge, England: Cambridge University Press, 1992), p. 12.

SUGGESTED READING

Arblaster, Anthony, *The Rise and Decline of Western Liberalism* (1984). A critical analysis of liberalism, its evolution and characteristics.

Fried, Albert, and Ronald Sanders, eds., *Socialist Thought* (1964). Selections from the writings of socialist theorists.

Harris, R. W., *Romanticism and the Social Order, 1780–1830* (1969). Involvement of English romantics in social and political questions.

Kohn, Hans, *Prelude to Nation-States* (1967). The emergence of nationalism in France and Germany.

Schenk, H. G., *The Mind of the European Romantics* (1969). A comprehensive analysis of the Romantic Movement.

Weiss, John, *Conservatism in Europe, 1770–1945* (1977). Conservatism as a reaction to social modernization.

Chapter 23

Revolution and Counterrevolution, 1815–1848

The Uprising, *by Honoré Daumier. (The Phillips Collection, Washington, D.C.)*

Focus Questions

1. Why did Metternich fear liberalism and nationalism?
2. What were the accomplishments and failures of the Congress of Vienna?
3. What were the principal reasons for the revolutions that broke out in Europe in the decades after the Congress of Vienna?
4. What reforms were introduced in Britain between 1815 and 1848?
5. Why did the Revolutions of 1848 essentially fail?
6. What were the liberal gains in 1848? Why were liberals and nationalists disappointed?

Online Study Center

This icon will direct you to interactive map and primary source activities on the website http://college.hmco.com/pic/perrywc8e.

During the years 1815 through 1848, the forces unleashed by the French Revolution clashed with the traditional outlook of the Old Regime. The period opened with the Congress of Vienna, which drew up a peace settlement after the defeat of Napoleon, and closed with the revolutions that swept across most of Europe in 1848.

Much of the Old Regime outside France survived the stormy decades of the French Revolution and Napoleon. Monarchs still held the reins of political power. Aristocrats, particularly in central and eastern Europe, retained their traditional hold on the army and administration, controlled the peasantry and local government, and enjoyed tax exemptions. Determined to enforce respect for traditional authority and to smother liberal ideals, the conservative ruling elites resorted to censorship, secret police, and armed force.

The French Revolution, however, had shown that absolutism could be successfully challenged and feudal privileges abolished. Inspired by the revolutionary principles of liberty, equality, and fraternity, liberals and nationalists continued to engage in revolutionary action.

THE CONGRESS OF VIENNA, 1814–1815

Metternich the Archconservative

After the defeat of Napoleon, representatives of European powers convened in Vienna to draw up a peace settlement. The pivotal figure at the Congress of Vienna was Prince Klemens von Metternich (1773–1859) of Austria, who had organized the coalition that triumphed over Napoleon.

A man of the Old Order, Metternich hated the new forces of nationalism and liberalism. He regarded liberalism as a dangerous disease carried by middle-class malcontents, and he believed that domestic order and international stability depended on rule by monarchy and respect for aristocracy. The misguided liberal belief that society could be reshaped according to the ideals of liberty and equality, said Metternich, had led to twenty-five years of revolution, terror, and war.

Chronology 23.1 ❖ Revolution and Reaction

1820	Revolt in Spain
1821	Austria crushes revolts in Italy
1823	French troops crush revolt in Spain
1825	Uprising in Russia crushed by Nicholas I
1829	Greece gains independence from the Ottoman Empire
1830	July Ordinances in France are followed by a revolution, which forces Charles X to abdicate
August 1830	Belgian revolution
October 1830	Belgians declare their independence from Holland, establishing a liberal government
1831	Polish revolution fails
1831–32	Austrian forces crush a revolution in Italy
1832	Reform Act extends suffrage to the middle class in Britain
1848	Year of revolution
February 1848	Revolution in Paris: Louis Philippe abdicates, and France becomes a republic
March 1848	Uprisings in capital cities of the German states lead to liberal reforms
March 18–22, 1848	"Five Glorious Days" in Milan
March 22, 1848	Citizens of Venice declare their freedom from Austria and establish a republic
June 1848	June Days of Paris: revolutionaries are beaten by professional soldiers
August 1848	Constitutional Assembly meets in Vienna and abolishes serfdom in the Austrian Empire
December 1848	Louis Napoleon is elected president of the Second Republic of France
August 1849	Hungarians' bid for independence is crushed by Hapsburg forces, aided by Russian troops

In order to restore stability and peace, the old Europe must suppress liberal ideas and quash the first signs of revolution. If the European powers did not destroy the revolutionary spirit, they would be devoured by it.

Metternich also feared the new spirit of nationalism. Because Austria was a multinational empire, it was particularly vulnerable to nationalist unrest. If its many ethnic groups—Poles, Czechs, Magyars, Italians, South Slavs, and Romanians—became infected with the nationalist virus, they would shatter the Hapsburg Empire. A highly cultured, multilingual, and cosmopolitan aristocrat, Metternich considered himself the defender of European civilization. He thought that by arousing the masses and setting people against people, nationalism could undermine the foundations of European civilization.

Metternich's critics accuse him of shortsightedness. Instead of harnessing and directing the new forces let loose by the French Revolution, he sought to stifle them. Instead of trying to rebuild

CONGRESS OF VIENNA, 1815, BY JEAN BAPTISTE ISABEY (1767–1855). The delegates to the Congress of Vienna sought to reestablish many features of Europe that existed before the French Revolution and Napoleon. They can be accused of shortsightedness; nevertheless, the balance of power that they formulated preserved international peace. Metternich is standing in front of a chair at left. (*The New York Public Library.*)

and remodel, he sought to prop up dying institutions. Regarding all reforming as an invitation to radicalism and revolution, Metternich refused to make any concessions to liberalism.

Metternich wanted to return to power the ruling families deposed by more than two decades of revolutionary warfare. He also sought to restore the balance of power so that no one country could be in a position to dominate the European continent as France under Napoleon had done. Metternich was determined to end the chaos of the Napoleonic period and restore stability to Europe. There must be no more Napoleons who obliterate states, topple kings, and dream of European hegemony. Although he served the interests of the Hapsburg monarchy, Metternich also

had a sense of responsibility to Europe as a whole. He sought a settlement that would avoid the destructiveness of a general war.

The other nations at the Congress of Vienna included Britain, Russia, France, and Prussia. Representing Britain was Robert Stewart, Viscount Castlereagh (1769–1822), the realistic British foreign secretary. Though an implacable enemy of Napoleon, Castlereagh demonstrated mature statesmanship by not seeking to punish France severely. Tsar Alexander I (1777–1825), steeped in Christian mysticism, wanted to create a European community based on Christian teachings. Alexander regarded himself as the savior of Europe, an attitude that caused other diplomats to view him with distrust. Representing France was Prince

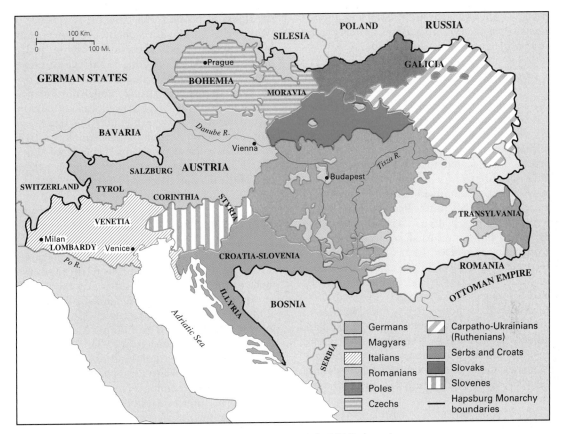

Map 23.1 PEOPLES OF THE HAPSBURG MONARCHY, 1815 In 1815, Austria was a multinational empire dominated by Germans. As nationalism among the various ethnic groups grew stronger, fear of dissolution became the principal concern of Hapsburg leaders.

Charles Maurice de Talleyrand-Périgord (1754–1838). A devoted patriot, Talleyrand sought to remove from France the stigma of the Revolution and Napoleon. The aging Prince Karl von Hardenberg (1750–1822) represented Prussia. Like Metternich, Castlereagh, and Talleyrand, the Prussian statesman believed that the various European states, besides pursuing their own national interests, should concern themselves with the well-being of the European community as a whole.

Crisis over Saxony and Poland

Two interrelated issues threatened to disrupt the conference and enmesh the Great Powers in another war. One was Prussia's intention to annex

the German kingdom of Saxony; the other was Russia's demand for Polish territories. The tsar wanted to combine the Polish holdings of Russia, Austria, and Prussia into a new Polish kingdom under Russian control. Britain and Austria saw such an extension of Russia's power into central Europe as a threat to the balance of power. Metternich declared that he had not fought Napoleon to prepare the way for the tsar. Britain agreed that Russia's westward expansion must be checked.

Prince Talleyrand of France suggested that Britain, Austria, and France form an alliance to oppose Prussia and Russia. Talleyrand's clever move restored France to the family of nations. Now France was no longer the hated enemy but a necessary counterweight to Russia and Prussia. Threatened with war, Russia and Prussia moderated their demands and the crisis ended.

The Settlement

After months of discussion, quarrels, and threats, the delegates to the Congress of Vienna finished their work. Resisting Prussia's demands for a punitive peace, the allies did not punish France severely. They feared that a humiliated France would only prepare for a war of revenge. Moreover, Metternich continued to need France to balance the power of both Prussia and Russia. France had to pay a large indemnity over a five-year period and submit to allied occupation until the obligation was met.

Despite losing most of its conquests, France emerged with somewhat more land than it possessed before the Revolution. To guard against a resurgent France, both Prussia and Holland received territories on the French border. Holland obtained the southern Netherlands (Belgium); Prussia gained the Rhineland and part of Saxony, but not as much as the Prussians had desired. Nevertheless, Prussia emerged from the settlement significantly larger and stronger. Russia obtained Finland and a considerable part of the Polish territories, but not as much as the tsar had anticipated; the Congress prevented further Russian expansion into central Europe. The northern Italian province of Lombardy was restored to Austria, which also received adjacent Venetia. England obtained strategic naval bases: Helgoland in the North Sea, Malta and the Ionian Islands in the Mediterranean, the Cape Colony in South Africa, and Ceylon in the Indian Ocean. Germany was organized into a confederation of thirty-eight (later thirty-nine) states. Norway was given to Sweden. Legitimate rulers who had been displaced by the Revolution and Napoleon were restored to their thrones in France, Spain, Portugal, the Kingdom of the Two Sicilies, the Papal States, and many German states.

The conservative delegates at the Congress of Vienna have often been criticized for ignoring the liberal and nationalist aspirations of the different peoples and turning the clock back to the Old Regime. Critics have castigated the congress for dealing only with the rights of thrones and not the rights of peoples. But after the experience of two world wars in the twentieth century, some historians today are impressed with the peacemakers' success in restoring a balance of power that effectively stabilized international relations. No one country was strong enough to dominate the Continent; no Great Power was so unhappy that it resorted to war to undo the settlement. Not until the unification of Germany in 1870–71 was the balance of power upset; not until World War I in 1914 did Europe have another general war of the magnitude of the Napoleonic wars.

REVOLUTIONS, 1820–1829

Russia, Austria, Prussia, and Great Britain agreed to act together to preserve the territorial settlement of the Congress of Vienna and the balance of power. After paying its indemnity, France was admitted into this Quadruple Alliance, also known as the Concert of Europe. Metternich intended to use the Concert of Europe to maintain harmony among nations and internal stability within nations. Toward this end, conservatives in their respective countries censored books and newspapers, imprisoned liberal activists, and suppressed nationalist uprisings.

But repression could not contain the liberal and nationalist ideals unleashed by the French Revolution. The first revolution after restoration of the legitimate rulers occurred in Spain in 1820. Fearing that the uprising, with its quasi-liberal overtones, would inspire revolutions in other lands, the Concert of Europe empowered France to intervene. In 1823, a hundred thousand French troops crushed the revolution in Spain.

Revolutionary activity in Italy also frightened the Concert of Europe. In 1821, it authorized Austria to extinguish a liberal uprising in the Kingdom of the Two Sicilies. The Austrians also

MAP 23.2 EUROPE, 1815 ▶

At the Congress of Vienna, Russia gained a considerable part of the Polish territories, Prussia acquired the Rhineland and part of Saxony, and Holland received Belgium. The northern Italian province of Lombardy was restored to the Hapsburg Empire, which also received adjacent Venetia.

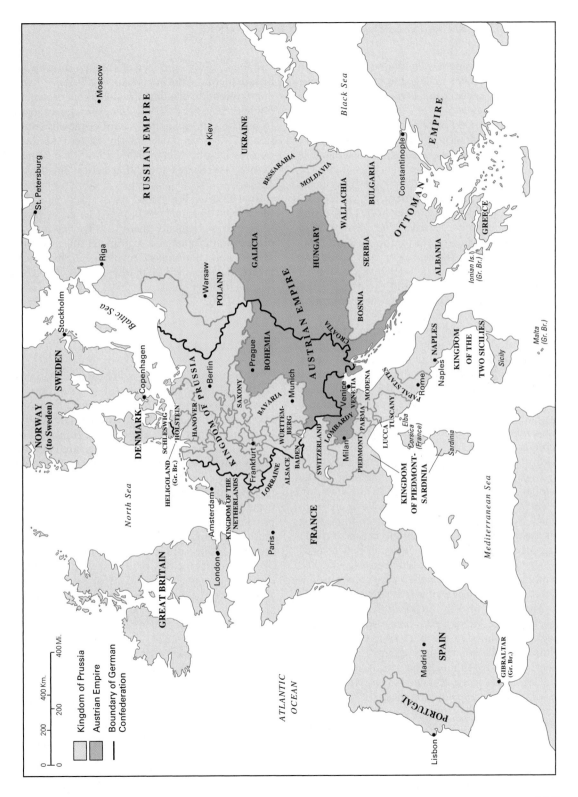

SWEDEN

NORWAY
(to Sweden)

St. Petersburg

RUSSIAN EMPIRE

Moscow

Kiev

UKRAINE

Riga

Black Sea

Baltic Sea

Warsaw

POLAND

GALICIA

BESSARABIA

MOLDAVIA

WALLACHIA

BULGARIA

OTTOMAN EMPIRE

Constantinople

Stockholm

Copenhagen

DENMARK

SCHLESWIG

HOLSTEIN

HELIGOLAND
(Gr. Br.)

KINGDOM OF PRUSSIA

HANOVER

Berlin

Prague

BOHEMIA

SAXONY

Munich

BAVARIA

AUSTRIAN EMPIRE

HUNGARY

SERBIA

BOSNIA

CROATIA

ALBANIA

GREECE

Ionian Is.
(Gr. Br.)

Venice

VENETIA

MODENA

NAPLES

KINGDOM OF THE TWO SICILIES

Sicily

Malta
(Gr. Br.)

GREAT BRITAIN

North Sea

London

Amsterdam

KINGDOM OF THE
NETHERLANDS

Frankfurt

WÜRTTEM-
BERG

BADEN

ALSACE

LORRAINE

SWITZERLAND

LOMBARDY

Milan

PIEDMONT

PARMA

LUCCA

TUSCANY

PAPAL STATES

Rome

Naples

Elba

Corsica
(France)

Sardinia

KINGDOM
OF PIEDMONT-
SARDINIA

Paris

FRANCE

ATLANTIC
OCEAN

Mediterranean Sea

Madrid

SPAIN

PORTUGAL

Lisbon

GIBRALTAR
(Gr. Br.)

400 Mi.

400 Km.

200

200

0

0

Kingdom of Prussia

Austrian Empire

Boundary of German
Confederation

537

crushed an uprising in Piedmont, in northern Italy. Rulers in other Italian states jailed and executed liberal leaders, and several thousand Italians went into exile.

In both instances, Britain strongly opposed the actions of the alliance. It interpreted the alliance differently from Austria, Prussia, and Russia. The three eastern powers wanted the alliance to smother in the cradle all subversive movements that threatened the Old Order. To Metternich, the central problem of the age was suppressing revolutions, and he regarded the alliance as a means of preserving the status quo. Britain, however, viewed the alliance solely as a means of guarding against renewed French aggression. It did not consider intervention in the domestic affairs of other nations to be in its own interest.

A revolution also failed in Russia. During the Napoleonic wars and the occupation of France, Russian officers were introduced to French ideas. Contrasting French liberal ideas and ways with Russian autocracy, some officers resolved to change conditions in Russia. Like their Western counterparts, they organized secret societies and disseminated liberal ideas within Russia. When Alexander I died, these liberal officers struck. But representing only a fraction of the aristocracy and with no mass following among the soldiers, they had no chance of success. Their uprising in December 1825 was easily smashed by the new tsar, Nicholas I, and the leaders were severely punished. To prevent Western ideas from infiltrating his realm, Nicholas imposed rigid censorship and organized the Third Section, a secret police force, which spied on suspected subversives. The Decembrists had failed, but their courage would inspire future opponents of tsarist autocracy.

The revolutions in Spain, Italy, and Russia failed, but the Metternich system also suffered setbacks. Stimulated by the ideals of the French Revolution, the Greeks revolted against their Turkish rulers in 1821. Although the Turkish sultan was the legitimate ruler, Russia, France, and Britain aided the Greek revolutionaries, for they were Christians and the Turks were Muslims. Moreover, pro-Greek sentiments were very strong among educated western Europeans, who had studied the literature and history of ancient Greece and viewed the Greeks as struggling to regain their ancestral freedom. Not only the pressure of public opinion, but also the fear of Russian motives led Britain to join in the intervention. If Russia carried out its intention of aiding the Greeks on its own, no doubt the Russian bear would never release Greece from its hug. Britain could not permit this extension of Russian power in the eastern Mediterranean. Despite Metternich's objections, Britain, France, and Russia took joint action against the Turks.

In 1829, Greece gained its independence. The Metternich system, which aimed to preserve the territorial settlements made at Vienna and to protect traditional and legitimate rulers against liberal and nationalist revolutions, had been breached. The success of the Greeks heartened liberals in other lands.

REVOLUTIONS, 1830–1832

After Napoleon's defeat, a Bourbon king, Louis XVIII (1814–1824), ascended the throne of France. Recognizing that the French people would not accept a return to the Old Order, Louis pursued a moderate course. Although his pseudoconstitution, the Charter, declared that the king's power rested on divine right, it acknowledged that citizens possessed fundamental rights: freedom of thought and religion and equal treatment under the law. It also set up a two-house parliament. But peasants, urban workers, and most bourgeois could not meet the property requirements for voting. Louis XVIII was resisted by diehard aristocrats, or *ultras,* who wanted to erase the past twenty-five years of French history and restore the power and privileges of church and aristocracy. Their leader was the king's younger brother, the comte d'Artois, who, after Louis's death in 1824, ascended the throne as Charles X (1824–1830).

The new government aroused the hostility of the bourgeoisie by indemnifying the émigrés for the property they had lost during the Revolution, censoring the press, and giving the church greater control over education. In the election of 1830, the liberal opposition to Charles X won a decisive victory. Charles responded with the July Ordinances, which dissolved the newly elected Chamber of Deputies; the ordinances also deprived rich

LIBERTY LEADING THE PEOPLE, 1830, BY EUGENE DELACROIX (1799–1863). Early-nineteenth-century reformers found their rallying cry in liberty, a legacy of the French Revolution. In this painting, Delacroix, the leader of French romantic artists, glorifies liberty. (*Louvre/Réunion des Musées Nationaux.*)

bourgeois of the vote (less wealthy bourgeois did not have the vote) and severely curbed the press.

The bourgeoisie, students, and workers rebelled. They hoped to establish a republic, but the wealthy bourgeois who took control of the revolution feared republican radicalism. They offered the throne to the duc d'Orléans; Charles X abdicated and went into exile in Britain. The new king, Louis Philippe (1830–1848), never forgot that he owed his throne to the upper bourgeois. And the Parisian workers who had fought for a republic and economic reforms to alleviate poverty felt betrayed by the outcome, as did the still-disenfranchised petty bourgeois.

The Revolution of 1830 in France set off shock waves in Belgium, Poland, and Italy. The Congress of Vienna had assigned Catholic Belgium to Protestant Holland. From the outset, the Belgians had protested. Stirred by the events in Paris, Belgian patriots proclaimed their independence from Holland and established a liberal government. Inspired by the uprisings in France and Belgium, Polish students, intellectuals, and army officers took up arms against their Russian overlords. The revolutionaries wanted to restore Polish independence, a dream that poets, musicians, and intellectuals had kept alive. Polish courage, however, was no match for Russian might, and Warsaw fell in 1831. The tsar took savage revenge on the revolutionaries. In 1831–32, Austrian forces again extinguished a revolution in Italy. As in Poland, revolutionary leaders in Italy failed to stir the great peasant masses to the cause of Italian independence and unity.

THE RISE OF REFORM IN BRITAIN

Britain was the freest state in Europe in the early decades of the nineteenth century, but it was far from democratic. A constitutional monarchy, with many limits on the powers of king and state, Britain was nonetheless dominated by aristocrats. Landed aristocrats controlled both the House of Lords and the House of Commons—the Lords because they constituted its membership and the Commons because they patronized or sponsored men favorable to their interests. The vast majority of people, from the middle class as well as from the working class, could not vote. Many towns continued to be governed by corrupt groups. New industrial towns were not allowed to elect representatives to Parliament; often lacking a town organization, they could not even govern themselves effectively.

The social separation of noble and commoner was not as rigid in Britain as on the Continent. Younger sons of aristocrats did not inherit titles and were therefore obliged to make careers in law, business, the military, and the church. The upper and middle classes mingled much more freely than on the Continent, and the wealthiest merchants tended to buy lands, titles, and husbands for their daughters. Nonetheless, Parliament, the courts, local government, the established Anglican church, the monarch—all were part of a social and political system dominated by aristocratic interests and values. This domination had changed little despite the vast changes in social and economic structure that had taken place in the process of industrialization during the second half of the eighteenth century.

Some members of Parliament urged timely reforms. In 1828, Parliament repealed a seventeenth-century act that in effect barred Catholics and Nonconformists (non-Anglican Protestants) from government positions and from universities. In 1833, slavery was abolished within the British Empire. (The slave trade had been abolished earlier.) The Municipal Corporations Act (1835) granted towns and cities greater authority over their affairs; it created local governments that could begin to solve some problems of urbanization and industrialization. These municipal corporations could institute reforms such as sanitation, which Parliament encouraged by passing the first Public Health Act in 1848.

Increasingly, reform centered on extending suffrage and on enfranchising the new industrial towns. Middle-class men, and even workers, hoped to gain the right to vote. Because of population shifts, some sparsely populated regions, called *rotten boroughs,* sent representatives to the House of Commons, while many densely populated factory towns had little or no representation. Often a single important landowner controlled many seats in the Commons. Since voting was public, it made intimidation possible, and candidates frequently tried to influence voters with drinks, food, and even money.

Bitter feelings built up during the campaign for the Reform Bill of 1832. The House of Commons passed the bill to extend suffrage by some 200,000 men, almost double the number then entitled to vote. The House of Lords, however, refused to pass the bill. There were riots and strikes in many cities, and mass meetings, both of workers and of the middle class, took place all over the country. King William IV (1830–1837) became convinced, along with many politicians, that the situation was potentially revolutionary. To defuse it, he threatened to increase the number of the bill's supporters in the House of Lords by creating new peers. This threat brought reluctant peers into line, and the bill was passed. The Reform Act of 1832 extended the suffrage to the middle class and made the House of Commons more representative. The rotten boroughs lost their seats, which were granted to towns. Suffrage did not extend to workers, however, because there were high property qualifications.

During the 1830s and 1840s, reformers called *Chartists* agitated for democratic measures, such as universal manhood suffrage, the secret ballot, salaries and the abolition of property qualifications for members of Parliament, and annual elections for Parliament. The Chartists came from the ranks of both intellectual radicals and workers. Their platform remained the democratic reform program for the rest of the century, long after the death of Chartism itself at midcentury. All of the Chartists' demands, except annual elections for members of Parliament, were eventually realized.

The last political effort by the Chartists was led by Feargus O'Connor, a charismatic Irishman, who organized a mass demonstration to present a huge petition of six demands to Parliament in 1848. The cabinet ignored the great charter, which had signatures of at least two million names. The movement died out just as most of Europe burst into revolution. The working-class

THE "PETERLOO MASSACRE". In 1819 at St. Peter's Field near Manchester, a peaceful crowd of perhaps 50,000 gathered to demand change in Britain's suffrage law—one banner calls for universal suffrage—and to listen to radical reformers. The militia charged, killing eleven and wounding hundreds. The incident provoked increased government repression. Radicals were imprisoned and large meetings were forbidden. (*Bettmann/CORBIS.*)

leadership of Chartism turned away from political programs almost exclusively to economic activity, such as trade unions, which could bring immediate benefits to workers.

Unlike the continental states, England avoided revolution. British politicians held that the reason was that they had made timely reforms in the 1830s and 1840s, and this lesson should guide the state in the future. British parliamentary govenment came to be the model of liberal, progressive, and stable politics, a symbol for all those who argued for reform rather than revolution. In the rest of Europe in 1848, however, such arguments were meeting with little success.

Online Study Center

Improve Your Grade
Primary Source: A Pro-democracy Movement in Britain: The People's Charter

REVOLUTIONS OF 1848: FRANCE

In 1848, often called *the year of revolution,* uprisings for political liberty and nationhood took place throughout Europe. The economic crisis of the previous two years had intensified unrest. Food riots broke out in many places. The decimation of the potato crop by disease and of the grain harvest by drought had caused terrible food shortages. Furthermore, a financial crisis precipitated by overspeculation had caused business failures, unemployment, and reduced wages. The common people blamed their governments for their misery and sought redress. Doubtless, economic hardship aggravated discontent with the existing regimes. But "it was the absence of liberty," concludes the historian Jacques Droz, "which . . . was most deeply resented by the peoples of Europe and led them to take up arms."[1]

The February Revolution

An uprising in Paris set in motion the revolutionary tidal wave that was to engulf much of Europe in 1848. The Revolution of 1830 had broken the back of the ultras in France. There would be no going back to the Old Regime. But King Louis Philippe and his ministers, moderates by temperament and philosophy, had no intention of going forward to democracy. A new law in 1831 broadened the franchise from fewer than 100,000 voters to 248,000 by 1846. Even so, only 3 percent of adult males qualified to vote.

The government of Louis Philippe was run by a small elite consisting of wealthy bourgeois bankers, merchants, and lawyers, as well as aristocrats who had abandoned the hope of restoring the Old Regime. This ruling elite championed the revolutionary ideas of equal treatment under the law and of careers open to talent, but fearing democracy, it blocked efforts to broaden the franchise. When the less wealthy bourgeoisie protested against the limited franchise, which still excluded professionals and small tradesmen, François Guizot, the leading minister, arrogantly proclaimed: "Get rich, then you can vote." The ruling elite had become a selfish, entrenched oligarchy, unresponsive to the aspirations of the rest of the nation. Intellectuals denounced the government for its narrow political base and voiced republican sentiments. To guard against republicanism and as a reaction to repeated attempts to assassinate the king, the government cracked down on radical societies and newspapers.

Radical republicans, or democrats, wanted to abolish monarchy and grant all men the vote. They had fought in the Revolution of 1830 but were disappointed with the results. Patriots and romantics, who looked back longingly on the glory days of Napoleon, also hated Louis Philippe's government. These French nationalists complained that the king, who dressed like a businessman and pursued a pacifist foreign policy, was not fit to lead a nation of patriots and warriors. Under Louis Philippe, they said, France could not realize its historic mission of liberating oppressed nationalities throughout Europe.

The strongest rumblings of discontent, barely heeded by the ruling elite, came from the laboring poor. Many French workers, still engaged mainly in pre–Industrial Revolution occupations, were literate and concerned with politics; they read the numerous books and newspapers that denounced social injustice and called for social change. Artisans and their families had participated in the great revolutionary outbreaks of 1789 and had defended the barricades in 1830. Favoring a democratic republic that would aid the common people, they felt betrayed by the regime of Louis Philippe, which had brought them neither political representation nor economic reform.

The few factory workers and the artisans in small workshops were becoming attracted to socialist thinkers who attacked capitalism and called for state programs to deal with poverty. Louis Blanc, a particularly popular socialist theorist, denounced capitalist competition and demanded that the government establish cooperative workshops. Owned by the workers themselves, these workshops would ensure employment for the jobless.

A poor harvest in 1846 and an international financial crisis in 1847, which drastically curtailed French factory production, aggravated the misery of the laboring poor. Prevented by law from striking, unable to meet the financial requirements for voting, and afflicted with unemployment, the urban workers wanted relief. Alexis de Tocqueville, in a speech before the Chamber of Deputies on January 29, 1848, captured the mood of the working class:

> Do you not hear them repeating unceasingly that all that is above them is incapable and unworthy of governing them; that the present distribution of goods throughout the world is unjust; that property rests on a foundation which is not an equitable foundation? And do you not realize that when such opinions take root, when they spread in an almost universal manner, when they sink deeply into the masses, they are bound to bring with them sooner or later, I know not when nor how, a most formidable revolution?
>
> This, gentlemen, is my profound conviction: I believe that we are at this moment sleeping on a volcano. I am profoundly convinced of it.[2]

The government, however, steadfastly refused to pass reforms. Its middle-class opponents sidestepped regulations against political assemblies and demonstrations by gathering at large banquets to protest. When the government foolishly tried to block future banquets, students and workers took to the streets in February 1848, denouncing Guizot and demanding reforms. Barricades went up. Attempting to defuse an explosive situation, Louis Philippe dismissed the unpopular Guizot. But the barricades, commanded by republicans, stayed, and the antigovernment demonstrations continued. When soldiers, confused by a shot that had perhaps gone off accidentally, fired directly into a crowd and killed fifty-two Parisians, the situation got out of hand. Unable to pacify the enraged Parisians, Louis Philippe abdicated. France became a republic, and the people of Paris were jubilant.

The June Days: Revolution of the Oppressed

Except for one workingman, the leadership of the provisional government established in February consisted of bourgeois. The new leaders were committed to political democracy, but only some, notably the socialist Louis Blanc, favored social reforms. Most of the ministers had little understanding of or sympathy for the plight of the laboring poor, and they viewed socialist ideas as a threat to private property. Although they considered it a sacred duty to fight for the rights of the individual, they did not include freedom from hunger and poverty among these rights. The middle class saw itself as separate from the laboring poor by reason of occupation and wealth. To the bourgeoisie, the workers were dangerous creatures, "the wild ones," "the vile mob."

Meanwhile, workers who could find jobs labored twelve and fourteen hours a day under brutalizing conditions. In some districts, one out of three children died before the age of five. Everywhere in France, beggars, paupers, prostitutes, and criminals were evidence of the struggle to survive.

The urban poor were desperate for jobs and bread. Socialist intellectuals, sympathetic to the plight of the workers, proposed that the state organize producer cooperatives run by workers.

Some wanted the state to take over insurance companies, railroads, mines, and other key industries. To the property owners of all classes, such schemes smacked of madness.

The middle-class leaders of the new republic gave all adult males the vote and abolished censorship; however, their attempts to ease the distress of the urban poor were insincere and halfhearted. The government limited the workday to ten hours and legalized labor unions, but it failed to cope effectively with unemployment. The socialist Louis Blanc called for the creation of producer cooperatives in order to guarantee employment for the city poor. The republic responded by establishing national workshops, which provided some employment on public works projects. Most workers, however, received wages for doing nothing. Drawn by the promise of work, tens of thousands of laborers left the provinces for Paris, swelling the ranks of the unemployed. The national workshops provided work, food, and medical benefits for some of the unemployed. But to the workers, this was a feeble effort to deal with their monumental distress. To the property-owning peasantry and bourgeoisie, the national workshops were a waste of government funds. They viewed the workshops as nests of working-class radicalism, where plans were being hatched to change the economic system and seize their property.

For their participation in the February uprising against Louis Philippe, the workers had obtained meager benefits. When the government closed the workshops, working-class hostility and despair turned to open rebellion. Again, barricades went up in the streets of Paris.

The June Revolution in Paris was unlike previous uprisings in France. It was a revolt against poverty and a cry for the redistribution of property; as such, it foreshadowed the great social revolutions of the twentieth century. The workers stood alone. To the rest of the nation, they were barbarians attacking civilized society. Aristocrats, bourgeois, and peasants feared that no one's property would be safe if the revolution succeeded. From hundreds of miles away, Frenchmen flocked to Paris to crush what they considered to be the madness within their midst.

Although they had no leaders, the workers showed remarkable courage. Women and children fought alongside men behind the barricades. After three days of vicious street fighting and atrocities on both sides, the army extinguished the revolt. Some 1,460 lives had been lost, including four generals. The June Days left deep scars on French society. For many years, workers would never forget that the rest of France had united against them; the rest of France would remain terrified of working-class radicalism.

In December 1848, the French people, in overwhelming numbers, elected Louis Napoleon—nephew of the great emperor—president of the Second Republic. They were attracted to the magic of Louis Napoleon's name, and they expected him to safeguard society and property from future working-class disorders. The election, in which all adult males could vote, demonstrated that most Frenchmen were socially conservative; they were unsympathetic to working-class poverty and deeply suspicious of socialist programs.

REVOLUTIONS OF 1848: GERMANY, AUSTRIA, AND ITALY

Like an epidemic, the fever of revolution that broke out in Paris in February raced across the Continent. Liberals, excluded from participation in political life, fought for parliaments and constitutions; many liberals were also nationalists who wanted unity or independence for their nations. Some liberals had a utopian vision of a new Europe of independent and democratic states. In this vision, reactionary rulers would no longer stifle individual liberty; no longer would a people be denied the right of nationhood.

Online Study Center **Improve Your Grade**
Interactive Map: Major Uprisings and Reforms, 1848–1849

The German States: Liberalism Defeated

After the Congress of Vienna, Germany consisted of a loose confederation of thirty-nine independent states, of which Austria and Prussia were the most powerful. Jealous of their independence and determined to preserve their absolute authority, the ruling princes detested liberal and nationalist ideals. In the southern German states, which had been more strongly influenced by the French Revolution, princes did grant constitutions and establish parliaments to retain the loyalty of their subjects. But even in these states, the princes continued to hold the reins of authority.

The German nationalism that had emerged during the French occupation intensified during the restoration (the post-Napoleonic period) as intellectuals, inspired in part by the ideas of the Romantic Movement, insisted that Germans, who shared a common language and culture, should also be united politically. During the restoration, the struggle for German unity and liberal reforms continued to be waged primarily by students, professors, writers, lawyers, and other educated people. The great mass of people, knowing only loyalty to their local prince, remained unmoved by appeals for national unity.

The successful revolt against Louis Philippe, hostility against absolute princes, and an economic crisis combined to produce uprisings in the capital cities of the German states in March 1848. Everywhere, liberals clamored for constitutions, parliamentary government, freedom of thought, and an end to police intimidation. Some called for the creation of a unified Germany governed by a national parliament and headed by a constitutional monarch. The poor joined the struggle. The great depression of the 1840s had aggravated the misery of the German peasant and urban masses, and as the pressures of hunger and unemployment worsened, their discontent exploded into revolutionary fervor.

In the spring of 1848, downtrodden artisans, facing severe competition from the new factories, served as the revolution's shock troops. Unable to compete with the new machines, they saw their incomes fall and their work decrease. Skilled weavers working at home earned far less than factory hands, and some unemployed craftsmen were forced to take factory jobs, which they regarded as a terrible loss of status. These craftsmen wanted to restrict the growth of factories, curtail capitalist competition, and restore the power of the guilds, which had given them security and status.

Having lost hope that the absolute princes would aid them, craftsmen gave their support to bourgeois liberals, who, without this support, could not challenge the throne or wrest power from the aristocrats. In many German states, the actions of the embittered urban craftsmen determined the successful outcome of the insurrections. (Factory workers in the emerging industries showed no enthusiasm for revolution, despite the appeals of radical socialists.) Adding to the discomfort of the ruling princes was rioting in the countryside by peasants, goaded by crop failure, debt, and oppressive demands from the aristocracy.

Terrified that these disturbances would lead to anarchy, the princes made concessions to the liberals, whom they previously had censored, jailed, and exiled. During March and April 1848, the traditional rulers in Baden, Württemberg, Bavaria, Saxony, Hanover, and other states replaced reactionary ministers with liberals, eased censorship, established jury systems, framed constitutions, formed parliaments, and ended peasant obligations to lords.

In Prussia, tensions between the army and Berliners exploded into violence. Unable to subdue the insurgents, the army urged bombarding the city with artillery. Frederick William IV opposed the idea and ordered the troops to leave Berlin. The insurgents had won the first round. The Prussian king, like the other German princes, had to agree to the formation of a parliament and the admission of prominent liberals into the government.

But the triumph of the liberals in Prussia and the other German states was not secure. Although reforms liberalized the governments of the German states, the insurrections had not toppled the ruling dynasties. Moreover, the alliance between the bourgeois and the artisans was tenuous. The artisans' violence frightened the property-owning middle class, which sought only moderate political reforms, preferably through peaceful means. In addition, the middle class saw restoration of the medieval guild system, with its restrictions on output and regulation of prices, as a reactionary economic measure.

Liberals took advantage of their successes in Prussia and other German states to form a national assembly charged with the task of creating a unified and liberal Germany. Representatives from all the German states attended the assembly, which met at Frankfurt. The delegates, including many articulate lawyers and professionals, came predominantly from the educated middle class; only a handful were drawn from the lower classes. After many long debates, the Frankfurt Assembly approved a federation of German states; it would have a parliament and would be headed by the Prussian king. Austria, with its many non-German nationalities, would be excluded from the federal union. Some radical democrats wanted to proclaim a German republic, but they were an ineffective minority. Most delegates were moderate liberals who feared that universal suffrage and the abolition of monarchy would lead to plebeian rule and the destruction of the social order. The deputies selected Frederick William as emperor of the new Germany, but the Prussian king refused; he would never wear a crown given to him by common people during a period of revolutionary agitation.

While the delegates debated, the ruling princes recovered from the first shock of revolution and ordered their armies to crush the revolutionaries. The February Revolution in Paris had shown European liberals that authority could be challenged successfully; the June Days, however, had shown the authorities that revolutionaries could be beaten by professional soldiers. Moreover, the German middle class, frightened by lower-class agitation and unsympathetic to the artisans' demands to restrict capitalism and restore guilds, was losing its enthusiasm for revolution, and so, too, were the artisans. The disintegration of the alliance between middle-class liberals and urban artisans deprived the revolutionaries of mass support. A revival of the Old Order would not face much resistance.

In Prussia, a determined Frederick William ordered his troops to reoccupy Berlin. In March, the citizens of Berlin had fought against the king's troops, but in November, no barricades went up in Berlin. Prussian forces also assisted the other German states in crushing the new parliaments. The masses of workers and peasants did

Francis Palacky

Francis Palacky (1798–1876), Czech historian and statesman, is regarded by the Czech people as the founder of their nation. Palacky was a leader in the "Czech renaissance," a cultural revival in the first half of the nineteenth century. At that time, Czech writers began to use the Czech language as a vehicle of literary expression. (Until then, German had been the dominant literary language.) This facilitated the Czechs' discovery of their historical past and helped shape a national identity.

During the revolution of 1848, Palacky became the political spokesman for his people, advocating the right of the Czech nation to exist along with the other small nations of Austria in a federation of Danubian nations under the jurisdiction of the Hapsburg Empire. He participated in the Constitutional Assembly, which met in Vienna in 1848, to draft a constitution for the Empire. After months of deliberation, the assembly was disbanded by the emperor's army.

After the revolution, Palacky concentrated on completing his monumental *History of the*

CORBIS.

not fight to save the liberal governments, which fell one by one. A small minority of democrats resisted, particularly in Baden; many of these revolutionaries died in the fighting or were executed.

German liberalism had failed to unite Germany or to create a constitutional government dominated by the middle class. Liberalism, never securely rooted in Germany, was discredited. In the following decades, many Germans, identifying liberalism with failure, turned to authoritarian Prussia for leadership in the struggle for unification. The fact that authoritarians hostile to the spirit of parliamentary government eventually united Germany had deep implications for future German and European history.

Austria: Hapsburg Dominance

The Hapsburg Empire, the product of dynastic marriage and inheritance, had no common nationality or language; it was held together only by the reigning Hapsburg dynasty, its army, and its bureaucracy. The ethnic composition of the empire was enormously complex. Germans dominated; concentrated principally in Austria, they constituted about 25 percent of the empire's population. The Magyars predominated in the Hungarian lands of the empire. The great bulk of the population consisted of Slavs: Czechs, Poles, Slovaks, Slovenes, Croats, Serbs, and Ruthenians. There were also Italians in northern Italy and Romanians in Transylvania. The Hapsburg dynasty,

Czech Nation. The entire project occupied him over forty years. In the introduction he wrote, "From my youth I have known no higher goal than to provide my beloved nation with a portrait of its past, in which, as in a mirror, it could recognize itself and remember what its needs are."

Palacky revered the ideals of the Enlightenment and supported the reforms of the French Revolution calling for constitutional government and protection of individual rights. The nationalism he advocated was liberal and cosmopolitan, not exclusive and intolerant. In contrast to many nineteenth-century nationalists who descended into a world of irrational and dangerous myths, Palacky's love of the Czech nation was circumscribed by a respect for humanity and reason. He wanted the Czechs, whom he regarded as being among the forerunners of the Enlightenment, to take their place in the modern age as an independent nation among the progressive nations of the world.

Palacky's liberal nationalism inspired twentieth-century Czech democrats, including Tomáš Masaryk, Eduard Beneš, and more recently, Václav Havel.

aided by the army and the German-dominated civil service, prevented this multinational empire from collapsing into anarchy.

Metternich, it is often said, suffered from a "dissolution complex": he understood that the new forces of nationalism and liberalism could break up the Austrian Empire. Liberal ideas could lead Hapsburg subjects to challenge the authority of the emperor, and nationalist feelings could cause the different peoples of the empire to rebel against German domination and Hapsburg rule. To keep these ideas from infecting Austrian subjects, Metternich's police imposed strict censorship, spied on professors, and expelled from the universities students caught reading forbidden books. Despite Metternich's

political police, the universities remained hotbeds of liberalism.

In 1848, revolutions spread throughout the Austrian Empire, starting in Vienna. Aroused by the abdication of Louis Philippe, Viennese liberals denounced Hapsburg absolutism and demanded a constitution, relaxation of censorship, and restrictions on the police. The government responded hesitantly and with limited force to the demonstrations of students and workers, and many parts of Vienna fell to the revolutionaries. The authorities used force that was strong enough to incense the insurrectionists and create martyrs but not strong enough to subdue them. Confused and intimidated by the revolutionaries, the government allowed freedom of the press, accepted Metternich's resignation, and promised a constitution. The Constitutional Assembly was convened and in August voted the abolition of serfdom. At the same time that the Viennese insurgents were tasting the heady wine of reform, revolts in other parts of the empire—Bohemia, Hungary, and northern Italy—added to the distress of the monarchy.

But the revolutionaries' victory was only temporary, and the defeat of the Old Order only illusory; the Hapsburg government soon began to recover its balance. The first government victory came with the crushing of the Czechs in Bohemia. In 1848, Czech nationalists wanted the Austrian Empire reconstructed along federal lines that would give Czechs equal standing with Germans. The Czechs called for a constitution for Bohemia and equal status for the Czech language in all official business. In June, students and destitute workers engaged in violent demonstrations, which frightened the middle and upper classes—both Czech and German. General Alfred zu Windischgrätz bombarded Prague, the capital of Bohemia, into submission and reestablished Hapsburg control.

In October 1848, Hapsburg authorities ordered the army to bombard Vienna. Against the regular army, the courageous but disorganized and divided students and workers had little hope. Imperial troops broke into the city, overcame resistance, and executed several of the revolutionary leaders. In March 1849, the Hapsburg leadership replaced the liberal constitution drafted by the popularly

REVOLUTION IN VIENNA. May 1848. A student leads armed railway workers. *(Historisches Museum der Stadt Wien, Vienna/Erich Lessing/Art Resource, NY.)*

elected Constitutional Assembly with a more conservative one drawn up by its own ministers.

The most serious threat to the Hapsburg realm came from the Magyars in Hungary. Some twelve million people lived in Hungary, five million of whom were Magyars. The other nationalities comprised South Slavs (Croats and Serbs) and Romanians. The upper class consisted chiefly of Magyar landowners, who enjoyed tax exemptions and other feudal privileges. Drawn to liberal and modern ideas and fearful of peasant uprisings, some Hungarian nobles pressed for an end to serfdom and the tax exemptions of the nobility. Louis Kossuth (1802–1894), a member of the lower nobility, called for both social reform and a deepening of national consciousness. The great landowners, determined to retain their ancient privileges, resisted liberalization.

Led by Kossuth, the Magyars demanded local autonomy for Hungary. Hungary would remain within the Hapsburg Empire but would have its own constitution and national army and would control its own finances. The Hungarian

leadership introduced liberal reforms: suffrage for all males who could speak Magyar and owned some property, freedom of religion, freedom of the press, the termination of serfdom, and the end of the privileges of nobles and church. Within a few weeks, the Hungarian parliament changed Hungary from a feudal to a modern liberal state.

But the Hungarian leaders' nationalist dreams towered above their liberal ideals. The Magyars intended to incorporate lands inhabited by Croats, Slovaks, and Romanians into their state (Magyars considered these lands an integral part of historic Hungary) and to transform these peoples into Hungarians. As the historian Hugh Seton-Watson has written,

Kossuth and his friends genuinely believed that they were doing the non-Hungarians a kindness by giving them a chance of becoming absorbed in the superior Hungarian culture. To refuse this kindness was nationalist fanaticism; to impose it by force was to promote

progress. The suggestion that Romanians, Slovaks, or Serbs were nations, with a national culture of their own, was simply ridiculous nonsense.[3]

In the spring of 1849, the Hungarians renounced their allegiance to the Hapsburgs and proclaimed Hungary an independent state, with Kossuth as president.

The Hapsburg rulers took advantage of the ethnic animosities inside and outside Hungary. They encouraged Romanians and Croats to resist the new Hungarian government. When Hapsburg forces moved against the Magyars, they were joined by an army of Croats, whose nationalist aspirations had been flouted by the Magyars. (The Slovaks fought alongside the Magyars.) Emperor Francis Joseph, who had recently ascended the Hapsburg throne, also appealed to Tsar Nicholas I for help. The tsar complied, fearing that a successful revolt by the Hungarians might lead the Poles to rise up against their Russian overlords. The Hungarians fought with extraordinary courage but were overcome by superior might. Kossuth and other rebel leaders went into exile; about one hundred rebel leaders were executed. Thus, through division and alliance, the Hapsburgs prevented the disintegration of the empire.

Italy: Continued Fragmentation

Italian nationalists, eager to end the humiliation of Hapsburg occupation and domination and to unite the disparate states into a unified and liberal nation, also rose in rebellion in 1848. Revolution broke out in Sicily six weeks before the February Revolution in Paris. Bowing to the revolutionaries' demands, King Ferdinand II of Naples granted a liberal constitution. The grand duke of Tuscany, King Charles Albert of Piedmont-Sardinia, and Pope Pius IX, ruler of the Papal States, also felt compelled to introduce liberal reforms.

Then the revolution spread to the Hapsburg lands in the north. The citizens of Milan, in Lombardy, built barricades and stood ready to fight the Austrian oppressor. When the Austrian sol-

diers attacked, they were fired on from nearby windows. From rooftops, Italians hurled stones and boiling water. After "Five Glorious Days" (March 18–22) of street fighting, the Austrians withdrew. The people of Milan had liberated their city. On March 22, the citizens of Venice declared their city free of Austria and set up a republic. King Charles Albert, who hoped to acquire Lombardy and Venetia, declared war on Austria. Intimidated by the insurrections, the ruling princes of the Italian states and Hapsburg Austria had lost the first round.

But soon everywhere in Italy the forces of reaction recovered and reasserted their authority. The Austrians defeated the Sardinians and reoccupied Milan, and Ferdinand II crushed the revolutionaries in the south. Revolutionary disorders in Rome had forced Pope Pius IX to flee in November 1848; in February 1849, the revolutionaries proclaimed Rome "a pure democracy with the glorious title of the Roman Republic." Heeding the pope's call for assistance, Louis Napoleon attacked Rome, destroyed the infant republic, and allowed Pope Pius to return. The last city to fall to the reactionaries was Venice, which the Austrians subjected to a merciless bombardment. After six weeks, the Venetians, weakened by starvation and cholera, surrendered. Reactionary princes still ruled in Italy; the Hapsburg occupation persisted in the north. Italy was still a fragmented nation.

REVOLUTIONS OF 1848: AN ASSESSMENT

The revolutions of 1848 in central Europe and Italy began with much promise but ended in defeat. "We stood on the threshold of paradise—but the gates slammed in our faces," wrote one dejected intellectual.[4] The revolutionaries' initial success was due less to their strength than to the governments' hesitancy to use their superior force. The reactionary rulers overcame their paralysis, however, and moved decisively to smash the revolutions. The courage of the revolutionaries was no match for regular armies. Thou-

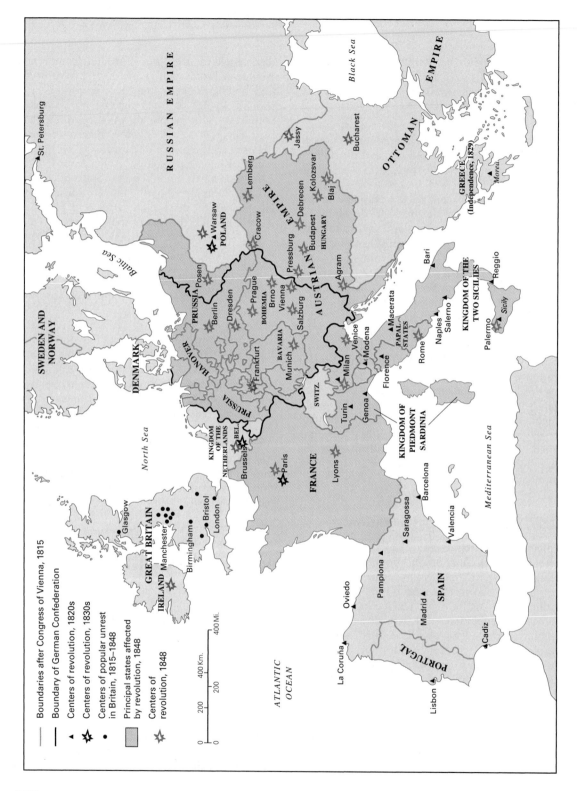

Boundaries after Congress of Vienna, 1815

Boundary of German Confederation

Centers of revolution, 1820s

Centers of revolution, 1830s

Centers of popular unrest
in Britain, 1815–1848

Principal states affected
by revolution, 1848

Centers of
revolution, 1848

RUSSIAN EMPIRE

St. Petersburg

SWEDEN AND NORWAY

Baltic Sea

DENMARK

HANOVER

North Sea

GREAT BRITAIN

IRELAND

Glasgow

Manchester

Birmingham

Bristol

London

ATLANTIC OCEAN

400 Mi.

400 Km.

200

200

0

0

KINGDOM OF THE NETHERLANDS

BEL.

Brussels

PRUSSIA

Berlin

Dresden

POLAND

Warsaw

Posen

PRUSSIA

Prague

BOHEMIA

Brno

Cracow

Lemberg

AUSTRIAN EMPIRE

Vienna

Pressburg

Budapest

HUNGARY

Debrecen

Kolozsvar

Blaj

Agram

Jassy

Bucharest

Black Sea

OTTOMAN EMPIRE

GREECE (Independence, 1829)

Morea

Frankfurt

BAVARIA

Munich

Salzburg

SWITZ.

Paris

FRANCE

Lyons

Turin

Genoa

Milan

Modena

Venice

Florence

PAPAL STATES

Macerata

Rome

Naples

Salerno

Bari

KINGDOM OF THE TWO SICILIES

Palermo

Sicily

Reggio

KINGDOM OF PIEDMONT SARDINIA

Barcelona

Saragossa

Valencia

SPAIN

Pamplona

Oviedo

Madrid

La Coruña

Cadiz

PORTUGAL

Lisbon

Mediterranean Sea

550

sands were killed and imprisoned; many fled to America.

Class divisions weakened the revolutionaries in central Europe. The union between middle-class liberals and workers, which brought success in the opening stages of the revolutions, was only temporary. Bourgeois liberals favoring political reforms—constitution, parliament, and protection of basic rights—grew fearful of the laboring poor, who demanded social reforms—jobs and bread. To the bourgeois, the workers were radical Jacobins, a mob driven by dark instincts. When the workers engaged in revolutionary violence, a terrified middle class deserted the cause of revolution or joined the old elites in subduing the workers. These class divisions showed that the liberals' concern for political reforms—the extension of suffrage and parliamentary government—did not satisfy workers who were mired in poverty. The events of 1848 also showed that social issues—the demands of the working class for an alleviation of their misery—would become a prime consideration of European political life in the generations to come.

Intractable nationalist animosities helped to destroy all the revolutionary movements against absolutism in central Europe. In many cases, the different nationalities hated each other more than they hated the reactionary rulers. Hungarian revolutionaries dismissed the nationalist yearnings of the South Slavs and Romanians living in Hungary, who in turn helped the Hapsburg dynasty to extinguish the nascent Hungarian state. The Germans of Bohemia resisted Czech demands for self-government and the equality of the Czech language with German. When German liberals at the Frankfurt Assembly debated the boundary lines of a united Germany, the problem of Prussia's Polish territories emerged. In 1848, Polish patriots wanted to recreate the Polish nation, but German delegates at the convention, by an overwhelming majority, opposed returning the Polish

lands seized by Prussia in the late eighteenth century. In addressing his fellow delegates, Wilhelm Jordan described the Poles as a people "which does not possess the same measure of human content as is given to the German kind" and denounced those Germans who would permit their kinsmen to live under Polish rule as traitors to their people. Then he justified Germany's claim to the Polish lands:

> It is high time for us to wake up . . . to a healthy national egoism . . . which places the welfare and honor of the fatherland above everything else. . . . Frankly, the rules of theoretical justice never seem more pitiful to me than when they presume to fix the fate of nations. . . . No, I admit without blinking, our right is no other than the right of the stronger, the right of conquest.[5]

Before 1848, democratic idealists envisioned the birth of a new Europe of free people and liberated nations. The revolutions in central Europe showed that nationalism and liberalism were not natural allies and that nationalists were often indifferent to the rights of other peoples. Disheartened by these nationalist antagonisms, John Stuart Mill, the English liberal statesman and philosopher, lamented that "the sentiment of nationality so far outweighs the love of liberty that the people are willing to abet their rulers in crushing the liberty and independence of any people not of their race or language."[6] In the revolutions of 1848, concludes the British historian Lewis Namier, "'nationality,' the passionate creed of the intellectuals, invades the politics of central and east-central Europe, and with 1848 starts the Great European War of every nation against its neighbors."[7]

Even though the liberal and nationalist aims of the revolutionaries were not realized, liberal gains were not insignificant. All Frenchmen obtained the right to vote; serfdom was abolished in Austria; and parliaments were established in Prussia and other German states.

Despite the establishment of parliaments, however, 1848 was a crucial defeat for German liberalism. Controlled by monarchs and aristocrats

◀ MAP 23.3 EUROPE'S AGE OF REVOLUTIONS
In the decades after the Vienna settlement, Europe experienced a wave of revolution based chiefly on liberalism and nationalism.

hostile to the democratic principles of 1848, the postrevolutionary governments, using the methods of a police state, intimidated and persecuted liberals, large numbers of whom were forced to emigrate. The failure of the revolution and the reactionary policies of the postrevolutionary governments thwarted the growth of a democratic parliamentary system in Germany. Discredited by the failure of 1848, weakened by government intimidation and the loss of many liberals to emigration, and less committed to liberal ideals—which brought no gains in 1848—the German middle class in the period immediately after 1848 became apolitical or were willing to sacrifice liberal principles in order to achieve a united and powerful Germany. Nationalism would su-persede liberalism as the principal concern of the German middle class. The failure of liberalism to take strong root in Germany would have dire consequences in the early twentieth century.

In later decades, liberal reforms, including legal guarantees of basic rights, would be introduced peacefully in several European countries—in Germany too, but there power still remained in the hands of preindustrial semifeudal elites, not with the middle class—for the failure of the revolutions of 1848 convinced many people, including liberals, that popular uprisings were ineffective ways of changing society. The Age of Revolution, initiated by the French Revolution of 1789, had ended.

❖   ❖   ❖

Online Study Center ACE the Test

NOTES

1. Jacques Droz, *Europe Between Revolutions, 1815–1848* (New York: Harper Torchbooks, 1967), p. 248.

2. *The Recollections of Alexis de Tocqueville*, trans. Alexander Teixeira de Mattos (Cleveland, Ohio: Meridian Books, 1969), pp. 11–12.

3. Hugh Seton-Watson, *Nations and States* (Boulder, Colo.: Westview Press, 1977), p. 162.

4. Quoted in Adam Zamoyski, *Holy Madness: Romantics, Patriots and Revolutionaries, 1776–1871* (London: Weidenfeld & Nicolson, 1999), p. 356.

5. Quoted in J. L. Talmon, *Political Messianism: The Romantic Phase* (New York: Praeger, 1960), p. 482.

6. Quoted in Hans Kohn, *Nationalism: Its Meaning and History* (Princeton, N.J.: Van Nostrand, 1965), pp. 51–52.

7. Lewis Namier, *1848: The Revolution of the Intellectuals* (Garden City, N.Y.: Doubleday, Anchor, 1964), p. 38.

SUGGESTED READING

Droz, Jacques, *Europe Between Revolutions* (1967). A fine survey of the period 1815–1848.

Fasel, George, *Europe in Upheaval: The Revolutions of 1848* (1970). A good introduction.

Fejtö, François, ed., *The Opening of an Era: 1848* (1973). Articles by eminent historians.

Robertson, Priscilla, *Revolutions of 1848* (1960). Vividly portrays events and personalities.

Sigmann, Jean, *1848: The Romantic and Democratic Revolutions in Europe* (1970). A useful survey.

Sperber, Jonathan, *The European Revolution, 1848–1851* (1994). A comprehensive overview.

Talmon, J. L., *Romanticism and Revolt* (1967). Forces shaping European history from 1815 to 1848.

Part Five

An Age of Contradiction: Progress and Breakdown

1848–1914

Politics and Society

Second Empire in France (1852–1870)
Commodore Perry opens Japan to trade
  (1853)
Crimean War (1853–1856)
Unification of Italy (1859–1870)

Civil War in the United States (1861–1865)
Bismarck in power in Germany (1862–1890)
Unification of Germany (1866–1871)
Settlement of 1867 splits Hapsburg territories
  into Austria and Hungary
Reform Bill of 1867 in Great Britain
Opening of Suez Canal (1869)

Franco-Prussian War (1870–71)
Third Republic in France (1870–1940)
Serbs gain independence from Ottoman
  Turks (1878)

French fight Chinese over Indochina
  (1883–85)
Berlin Conference on Africa (1884)
Reform Bill of 1884 in Great Britain

Dreyfus affair in France (1894–1906)
Sino-Japanese War (1894–95)
Spanish-American War (1898)
Battle of Omdurman in the Sudan (1898)
Boer War in South Africa (1899–1902)

Boxer Rebellion in China (1900)
Russo-Japanese War (1904–05)
Anglo-French Entente Cordiale (1904)
Anglo-Russian Entente (1907)
Congo declared a Belgian colony (1908)
Mexican Revolution (1911)

Thought and Culture

Stowe, *Uncle Tom's Cabin* (1851–52)
Dickens, *Hard Times* (1854)
Flaubert, *Madame Bovary* (1856)
Darwin, *Origin of Species* (1859)
Mill, *On Liberty* (1859)

Hugo, *Les Misérables* (1862)
Marx, *Capital* (1867)
Dostoevski, *The Idiot* (1868–69)
Tolstoy, *War and Peace* (1863–1869)
Mill, *The Subjection of Women* (1869)

Impressionism in art (1860–1886): Manet,
  Monet, Pissaro, Degas, Renoir
Darwin, *The Descent of Man* (1871)
Nietzsche, *The Birth of Tragedy* (1872)
Ibsen, *A Doll's House* (1879)

Postimpressionism in art (1880s–1890s):
  Cézanne, Gauguin, van Gogh, Munch,
  Matisse
Zola, *The Experimental Novel* (1880)
Spencer, *The Man Versus the State* (1884)
Nietzsche, *The Anti-Christ* (1888)

Le Bon, *The Crowd* (1895)
Chamberlain, *The Foundations of the
  Nineteenth Century* (1899)
Bernstein, *Evolutionary Socialism* (1899)
Durkheim, *Suicide* (1897)

Freud, *The Interpretation of Dreams* (1900)
Cubism in art: Picasso, Braque
Abstract art: Mondrian, Kandinsky,
  Duchamp
Planck: quantum theory (1900)
Lenin, *What Is To Be Done?* (1902)
Einstein: theory of relativity (1905)
Weber, *The Protestant Ethic and the Spirit of
  Capitalism* (1904–05)
Sorel, *Reflections on Violence* (1908)

Chapter 24

Thought and Culture in the Mid-Nineteenth Century: Realism and Social Criticism

The Stone Breakers (1849), by Gustave Courbet, illustrates the concern of realists for an accurate depiction of the details of everyday life. (Bildarchiv Foto Marburg/Art Resource, NY.)

- **Realism and Naturalism**
- **Positivism**
- **Darwinism**
- **Religion in a Secular Age**
- **Marxism**
- **Anarchism**
- **Liberalism in Transition**
- **Feminism: Extending the Principle of Equality**

Focus Questions

1. Why is the mid-nineteenth century described as an Age of Realism? How does realism differ from romanticism?

2. How did Darwin's theory affect conceptions of time, human origins, religious doctrines, and nationalism?

3. What did Marx have in common with the philosophes of the Enlightenment? What relationship did he see between economics and politics? Between economics and thought?

4. How was the evolution of liberalism exemplified in the theories of Mill, Green, and Spencer?

5. How may the feminist movement be regarded as an outgrowth of certain ideals that had emerged during the course of Western history?

Online Study Center

This icon will direct you to interactive map and primary source activities on the website http://college.hmco.com/pic/perrywc8e.

The second half of the nineteenth century was marked by great progress in science, a surge in industrialism, and a continuing secularization of life and thought. The principal intellectual currents of the century's middle decades reflected these trends. Realism, positivism, Darwinism, Marxism, and liberalism all reacted against romantic, religious, and metaphysical interpretations of nature and society and focused on the empirical world. In one way or another, each movement derived from and expanded the Enlightenment tradition. Adherents of these movements relied on careful observation and strove for scientific accuracy. This emphasis on objective reality helped stimulate a growing criticism of social ills; for despite unprecedented material progress, reality was often sordid, somber, and depressing. In the last part of the century, reformers, motivated by an expansive liberalism, a socially committed Christianity, or both, pressed for the alleviation of social injustice.

REALISM AND NATURALISM

Realism, the dominant movement in art and literature in the mid 1800s, opposed the romantic veneration of the inner life and romantic sentimentality. The romantics exalted passion and intuition, let their imaginations transport them to a medieval past, which they deemed idyllic, and sought subjective solitude amid nature's wonders. Realists, in contrast, turned their attention to the external world and concentrated on social conditions, contemporary manners, and the familiar details of everyday life. With clinical detachment and meticulous care, they analyzed how people actually looked, worked, and behaved.

Like scientists, realist writers and artists carefully investigated the empirical world. For example, Gustave Courbet (1819–1877), who exemplified realism in painting, sought to practice what he called a "living art." He painted common people and commonplace scenes: laborers breaking stones, peasants tilling the soil or returning from a fair, a country burial, wrestlers, bathers, family groups. In a matter-of-fact style that sought to reproduce the environment just as it is, without any attempt at glorification or deviation, realist artists also depicted floor scrapers, rag pickers, prostitutes, and beggars. Gustave Flaubert (1821–1880) said of *Madame Bovary,* his masterpiece of realist literature: "Art ought . . . to rise above personal feelings and nervous susceptibilities! It is time to give it the precision of the physical sciences by means of a pitiless method."[1] Émile de Vogüé, a nineteenth-century French writer, described realism as follows:

> They [realists] have brought about an art of observation rather than of imagination, one which boasts that it observes life as it is in its wholeness and complexity with the least possible prejudice on the part of the artist. It takes men under ordinary conditions, shows characters in the course of their everyday existence, average and changing. Jealous of the rigour of scientific procedure, the writer proposes to instruct us by a perpetual analysis of feelings and of acts rather than to divert us or move us by intrigue and exhibition of the passions. . . . The new art seeks to imitate nature.[2]

Romantic writers had written lyrics, for lyric poetry is the language of feeling. The realists' literary genre was the novel because it lends itself admirably to depicting human behavior and social conditions. Realist novels were often serialized in the inexpensive newspapers and magazines, which the many newly literate common people could read. Thus, the commoners' interests helped shape the novels' content. Seeking to portray reality as it is, realist writers frequently dealt with social abuses and the sordid aspects of human behavior and social life.

In his large output of novels, Honoré de Balzac (1799–1850) described how social and economic forces affected people's behavior. Another Frenchman, Eugène Sue, gave harrowing accounts of slum life and crime in his serialized novel, *Les Mystères de Paris* (1842–43). George Sand (a woman writing under a male pen name) portrayed the married woman as a victim in *Indiana* (1832). A reviewer praised the book for presenting

> a true, living world, which is our world . . . characters and manners just as we can

> observe them around us, natural conversations, scenes in familiar settings, violent, uncommon passions, but sincerely felt or observed and such as are still aroused in many hearts, under the apparent uniformity and monotonous frivolity of our lives.[3]

Many regard Gustave Flaubert's *Madame Bovary* (1856) as the quintessential realistic novel. It tells the story of Emma Bovary, a self-centered wife living in a drab French provincial town who, interpreting the world from the prism of the romantic stories she reads, yearns for luxury, excitement, and romance. Disillusioned with her marriage to her devoted, hard-working, but dull husband, whom she detests, Emma commits adultery.

In this work, Flaubert strove to remain detached from his characters. Unlike romantics, he was concerned not with revealing his own emotions or opinions but with the accurate depiction of characters, situations, and dialogue. His goal, he said, was a book in which "the personality of the author is *completely* absent." Commenting on the realism of *Madame Bovary,* a contemporary novelist noted that it "represents an obsession with description. Details are counted one by one, all are given equal value, every street, every house, every room, every book, every blade of grass is described in full."[4] Also described fully and in great clinical detail is Emma's death from poisoning.

Russian writers were among the leading realists. In *A Sportsman's Sketches* (1852), the novelist, dramatist, and short-story writer Ivan Turgenev (1818–1883) provided a true-to-life picture of Russian rural conditions, particularly the brutal life of serfs. In an unpolemical style, Turgenev showed that serfdom debased not only the serfs but also their masters, the rural nobility, who regarded serfs as barely human. In *War and Peace* (1863–1869), Leo Tolstoy (1828–1910) vividly described the manners and outlook of the Russian nobility and the tragedies that attended Napoleon's invasion of Europe. In *Anna Karenina* (1873–1877), he probed class divisions and the complexities of marital relationships. Anton Chekhov (1860–1904) was a physician who turned to literature. His major dramas concentrate on the realities of provincial life among in-

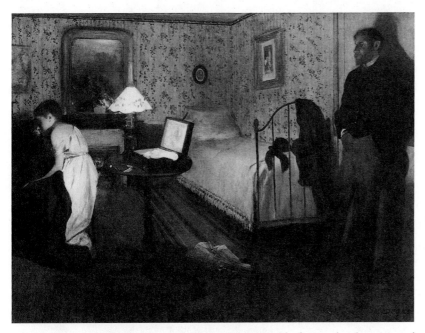

INTERIOR, 1868–69, BY EDGAR DEGAS. Set in a world of poor shopkeepers and clerks, *Thérèse Raquin* (1867) was Émile Zola's first great success as a naturalist novelist. This Degas painting depicts the sexual tension and violent emotions that Zola sought to uncover in his work. (*Philadelphia Museum of Art, The Henry P. McIlhenny Collection in Memory of Francis P. McIlhenny.*)

effectual upper-class landowners, perennially short of money, who fritter away their lives, and do nothing productive to better society. In essence, Chekhov was describing a decadent social order in its last throes. Fyodor Dostoevski (1821–1881), in his major novels *Crime and Punishment* (1866), *The Idiot* (1868), *The Possessed* (1871), and *The Brothers Karamazov* (1880), showed a superb ability to create memorable characters, to probe minds, and to describe vividly and perceptively.

Among English writers, Elizabeth Gaskell, the wife of a Unitarian minister in Manchester, dealt compassionately with the plight of industrial workers in *Mary Barton* (1848) and *North and South* (1855). The novels of Charles Dickens— *Bleak House* (1853), *Hard Times* (1854), and several others—detailed the squalor of life, the hypocrisy of society, and the drudgery of labor in British industrial cities. Dickens skillfully created

characters who, concerned only with safeguarding their privileged way of life, ignore the misery of the working class. These people run the schools, prisons, law courts, and other government agencies that oppress the poor.

Literary realism evolved into **naturalism** when writers tried to demonstrate a causal relationship between human character and the social environment: that certain conditions of life produced predictable character traits in human beings. The belief that the law of cause and effect governed human behavior reflected the immense prestige attached to science in the closing decades of the nineteenth century.

The leading naturalist novelist, Émile Zola (1840–1902), had immense confidence in the scientific method and was convinced that it applied to literature. According to Zola, the novelist should proceed like a scientist performing an experiment. The "experimental novel," he wrote, shows "the

Charles Dickens

In his novels, Charles Dickens (1812–1870) criticized oppressive institutions and practices at home and abroad. In doing so, he helped to awaken the moral conscience of his day. In his early novels, Dickens deftly blends melodrama with playful humor and comedic characters, such as the Artful Dodger and Fagin, leaders of a den of pickpockets, prostitutes, and thieves in *Oliver Twist; or The Parish Boy's Progress* (1838). Dickens also demostrates how uncaring adults mistreat children, and he evokes sympathy for society's youthful victims—the orphan Oliver Twist and his friend, Nancy, who is brutally murdered by her boyfriend, Sikes, when she tries to help Oliver escape from Sikes's gang. In *The Life and Adventures of Nicholas Nickleby* (1839), Dickens exposes the abusive treatment of children. In *Bleak House* (1853), the factory worker Gridley disparages "the system" that prevents the workers from advancing or from bettering their working conditions. Dickens

The Granger Collection.

reciprocal effect of society on the individual and the individual on society." It shows "man living in social conditions produced by himself, which he modifies daily, and in the heart of which he himself experiences a continual transformation." This type of novel, Zola claimed,

> *is a consequence of the scientific evolution of the century; it continues and completes physiology, which itself leans for support on chemistry and medicine; it substitutes for the study of the abstract and the metaphysical man the study of the natural man, governed by physical and chemical laws, and modified by the influences of his surroundings; it is in one word the literature of our scientific age, as the classical and romantic literature corresponded to a scholastic and theological age.*[5]

In his own novels, Zola probed the slums, brothels, mining villages, and cabarets of France, examining how people were conditioned by the squalor of their environment. *Germinal* (1885), his greatest novel, graphically renders the terrible toil and drudgery endured by coal miners.

Realism was not restricted to the novel alone. The leading realist playwright, Henrik Ibsen (1828–1906), a Norwegian, examined with clinical precision the commercial and professional classes, their personal ambitions, business practices, and family relationships; his dramas drew attention to bourgeois pretensions, hypocrisy, and social conventions that thwart individual growth. Although Ibsen wrote about profound social issues, he viewed himself as a dramatist relating a piece of reality and not a social reformer agitating for reform.

blamed social institutions for the misery of the downtrodden.

Hard Times takes place in an industrial town called Coketown. Dickens's description of the town is a masterful example of realist writing.

> It was a town of red brick, or of brick that would have been red if the smoke and ashes had allowed it; but, as matters stood it was a town of unnatural red and black like the painted face of a savage. It was a town of machinery and tall chimneys, out of which interminable serpents of smoke trailed themselves for ever and ever, and never got uncoiled. It had a black canal in it, and a river that ran purple with ill-smelling dye, and vast piles of buildings full of windows where there was a rattling and a trembling all day long, and where the piston of the steam-engine worked monotonously up and down, like the head of an elephant in a state of melancholy madness. It contained several large streets all very like one another, and many small streets still more like one another, inhabited by people equally like one another, who all went in and out at the same hours, with the same sound upon the same pavements, to do the same work, and to whom every day was the same as yesterday and tomorrow, and every year the counterpart of the last and the next.*

Dickens recognized that the monotony and stupefying conditions of industrial life crushed the spirit of the workers, curtailing both imagination and culture. Moreover, exploitation of the working class fostered class tensions because the workers viewed government institutions as being impervious to their needs and intent only on protecting the privileged status of the entrepreneurs and industrial elites. Dickens used *A Tale of Two Cities* (1859) to issue a warning: if the political elites of England did not effectively address the need for social reform, England, like France, would become embroiled in revolutionary violence.

---

*Charles Dickens, *Hard Times* (New York: Penguin Books, 1985), p. 65.

In *Pillars of Society* (1877), Ibsen portrayed entrepreneurs who, aspiring for wealth and status, not only betray loved ones but also engage in unscrupulous business practices at the expense of their fellow citizens. The title is ironic, for the "pillars of society" are actually corrupt hypocrites.

In *A Doll's House* (1879), Ibsen took up a theme that shocked late-nineteenth-century bourgeois audiences: a woman leaving her husband and children in search of self-realization. Nora Helmer resents being a submissive and dutiful wife to a husband who does not take her seriously, who treats her like a child, a doll. Before walking out on Torvald, Nora tells him:

> In all these eight years—longer than that— from the very beginning of our acquaintance, we have never exchanged a word on any serious subject. . . . When I was at home with papa, he told me his opinion about everything, and so I had the same opinions; and if I differed from him I concealed the fact, because he would not have liked it. He called me his doll-child, and he played with me just as I used to play with my dolls. And when I came to live with you . . . . I was simply transferred from papa's hands into yours. You arranged everything according to your own taste, and so I got the same tastes as you—or else I pretended to, I am really not sure which—I think sometimes the one and sometimes the other. . . . I have existed merely to perform tricks for you, Torvald. But you would have it so. You and papa have committed a great sin against me. It is your fault that I have made nothing of my life.

By recognizing the truth about her life up to that point in time and then by resolving "to educate myself . . . to understand myself and everything about me,"[6] Nora now has the possibility of achieving individual freedom—of becoming a person in her own right.

In striving for a true-to-life portrayal of human behavior and the social environment, realism and naturalism reflected attitudes shaped by science, industrialism, and secularism, which stressed the importance of the external world. The same outlook gave rise to positivism in philosophy.

POSITIVISM

Positivists viewed science as the higher achievement of the mind and sought to apply a strict empirical approach to the study of society. They believed that the philosopher must proceed like a scientist, carefully assembling and classifying data and formulating general rules that demonstrate regularities in the social experience. Such knowledge, based on concrete facts, would provide the social planner with useful insights. Positivists rejected metaphysics, which, in the tradition of Plato, tried to discover ultimate principles through reason alone rather than through observation of the empirical world. For positivists, any effort to go beyond the realm of experience to a deeper reality would be a mistaken and fruitless endeavor.

Auguste Comte (1798–1857), the father of positivism, called for a purely scientific approach to history and society: only through a proper understanding of the laws governing human affairs could society, which was in a state of intellectual anarchy, be rationally reorganized. Comte named his system *positivism* because he believed that it rested on sure knowledge derived from observed facts and was therefore empirically verifiable. Like others of his generation, Comte believed that scientific laws underlay human affairs and could be discovered through the methods of the empirical scientist—that is, through recording and systematizing observable data. "I shall bring factual proof," he said, "that there are just as definite laws for the development of the human race as there are for the fall of a stone."[7]

One of the laws that Comte believed he had discovered was the "law of the three stages." The human mind, he asserted, had progressed through three broad historical stages: the theological, the metaphysical, and the scientific. In the theological stage, the most primitive of the three, the mind found a supernatural explanation for the origins and purpose of things, and society was ruled by priests. In the metaphysical stage, which included the Enlightenment, the mind tried to explain things through abstractions, such as "nature," "equality," "natural rights," or "popular sovereignty," which rested on hope and belief rather than on empirical investigation. The metaphysical stage was a transitional period between the infantile theological stage and the highest stage of society, the scientific, or positive, stage. In this culminating stage, the mind breaks with all illusions inherited from the past, formulates laws based on careful observation of the empirical world, and reconstructs society in accordance with these laws. People remove all mystery from nature and base their social legislation on laws of society similar to the laws of nature discovered by Newton.

Because Comte advocated the scientific study of society, he is regarded as the principal founder of sociology; indeed, he coined the term. Comte's effort inspired many thinkers to collect and analyze critically all data pertaining to social phenomena.

DARWINISM

Many contributed to the steady advance of science in the nineteenth century. In 1808, John Dalton, an English chemist, formulated the modern atomic theory. In 1831, an English chemist and physicist, Michael Faraday, discovered the principle of electromagnetic induction, on which the electric generator and electric motor are based. In 1847, Hermann von Helmholtz, a German physicist, formulated the law of conservation of energy, which states that the total amount of energy in the universe is always the same; energy that is used up is not lost but is converted into heat. In 1887, another German physicist, Heinrich Hertz, discovered electromagnetic waves—a discovery that later made possible the invention of radio, television, and radar. Almost two decades earlier, in 1869, Dmitri Mendeleev, a Russian chemist, constructed a periodic table

A Caricature of Darwin. Darwin's theory of evolution created much controversy and aroused considerable bitterness. In this caricature, the ape-like Darwin, holding a mirror, is explaining his theory of evolution to a fellow ape. (*Hulton/Corbis-Bettmann.*)

for the elements, which helped to make chemistry more systematic and mathematical. In 1861, Louis Pasteur, a French scientist, initiated a revolution in medicine by proving that some diseases were caused by microbes, and he devised vaccines to prevent them.

Perhaps the most important scientific advance was the theory of **evolution** formulated by Charles Darwin (1809–1882). An English naturalist, Darwin did for biology what Newton had done for physics: he made it an objective science based on general principles. The Scientific Revolution of the seventeenth century had given people a new conception of space; Darwin radically altered our conception of time and biological life, including human origins.

Natural Selection

During the eighteenth century, almost all people had adhered to the biblical account of creation contained in Genesis. God had instantaneously created the universe and the various species of animal and plant life. He had given every river and mountain a finished and permanent form and made each species of animal and plant distinct from every other species. God had designed the bird's wings so that it could fly, the fish's eyes so that it could see under water, and human legs so that people could walk. All this, it was believed, had occurred some five or six thousand years ago.

Gradually, this view was questioned. In 1794, Erasmus Darwin, the grandfather of Charles Darwin, published *Zoonomia,* or *the Laws of Organic Life,* which offered evidence that the earth had existed for millions of years before the appearance of people and that animals experienced modifications, which they passed on to their offspring. Nearly forty years later, Sir Charles Lyell published his three-volume *Principles of Geology* (1830–1833), which showed that the planet had evolved slowly over many ages.

In December 1831, Charles Darwin sailed as a naturalist on the HMS *Beagle,* which surveyed the shores of South America and some Pacific islands. During the five-year expedition, Darwin collected and examined specimens of plant and animal life; he concluded that many animal species had perished, that new species had emerged, and that there were links between extinct and living species.

Influenced by Lyell's achievement, Darwin sought to interpret distant natural occurrences by means of observable processes that were still going on. He could not accept that a fixed number of distinct and separate species had been instantaneously created a mere five thousand years ago. In the *Origin of Species* (1859), and the *Descent of Man* (1871), Darwin used empirical evidence to show that the wide variety of animal species was due to a process of development over many millennia, and he supplied a convincing theory that explained how evolution operates.

Darwin adopted the Malthusian idea that the population reproduces faster than the food supply, causing a struggle for existence. Not all infant organisms grow to adulthood; not all adult organisms live to old age. The principle of **natural selection** determines which members of the species have a better chance of survival. The offspring of a lion, giraffe, or insect are not exact duplications of their parents. A baby lion might have the potential for being slightly faster or stronger than its parents; a baby giraffe might grow up to have a longer neck than its parents; an insect might have a slightly different color.

These small and random variations give the organism a crucial advantage in the struggle for food and against natural enemies. The organism favored by nature is more likely to reach maturity, to mate, and to pass on its superior qualities to its offspring, some of which will acquire the advantageous trait to an even greater degree than the parent. Over many generations, the favorable characteristic becomes more pronounced and more widespread within the species. Over millennia, natural selection causes the death of old species that cannot adjust to a changing environment. It also leads to the creation of new species, for genetic changes within a segment of a species can so differentiate its members from the rest of the species that interbreeding is no longer possible. Very few of the species that dwelt on earth ten million years ago still survive, and many new ones, including human beings, have emerged. People themselves are products of natural selection, evolving from earlier, lower, nonhuman forms of life.

Darwinism and Christianity

Like Newton's law of universal gravitation, Darwin's theory of evolution had revolutionary consequences in areas other than science. Evolution challenged traditional Christian belief. To some, it undermined the infallibility of Scripture and the conviction that the Bible was indeed the Word of God. Natural selection could explain the development of the organic world without reference to any divine design or ultimate purpose. Indeed, supernatural explanations of the origin of species now seemed superfluous and an obstacle to a scientific understanding of nature.

Darwin's theory touched off a great religious controversy between outraged fundamentalists, who defended a literal interpretation of Genesis, and advocates of the new biology. One theologian declared, "If the Darwinian theory is true, Genesis is a lie, the whole framework of the book of life falls to pieces, and the revelation of God to man, as we Christians know it, is a delusion and a snare."[8] A Methodist publication contended: "We regard this theory, which seeks to eliminate from the universe the immediate, ever-present, all pervasive action of a living and personal God, which excludes the possibility of the supernatural and the miraculous . . . as practically destructive of the authority of divine revelation, and subversive of the foundation of religion and morality."[9] In time, most religious thinkers tried to reconcile evolution with the Christian view that there was a Creation and that it had a purpose. These Christian thinkers held that God created and then directed the evolutionary process, that he steered evolution so that it would culminate in the human being.

Darwinism ultimately helped end the practice of relying on the Bible as an authority in questions of science, completing a trend initiated by Galileo. Darwinism thus contributed to the waning of religious belief and to a growing secular attitude that dismissed or paid scant attention to the Christian view of a universe designed by God and a soul that rises to heaven. For many, the conclusion was inescapable: nature contained no divine design or purpose, and the human species itself was a chance product of impersonal forces. The core idea of Christianity—that people were children of God participating in a drama of salvation—rested more than ever on faith rather than reason. Some even talked openly about the death of God. The notion that people are sheer accidents of nature was shocking. Copernicanism had deprived people of the comforting belief that the earth had been placed in the center of the universe just for them; Darwinism deprived them of the privilege of being God's special creation.

Social Darwinism

Darwin's theories were extended by others beyond the realm in which Darwin had worked. Social thinkers, who recklessly applied his conclusions to the social order, produced theories that had dangerous consequences. (Occasionally Darwin himself departed from his rigorous empiricism and drew murky conclusions about the mentally and physically handicapped and what he termed the "savage races." But he never intended his discoveries, which applied to the natural world, to serve as a guide for a ruthless social policy that glorified war and justified genocide.) **Social Darwinists**—those who transferred Darwin's scientific theories to social and economic issues—used the terms "struggle for existence" and "survival of the fittest" to buttress an often brutal economic individualism and political conservatism. Successful businessmen, they said, had demonstrated their fitness to succeed in the competitive world of business. Their success accorded with nature's laws and therefore was beneficial to society. Thus, American industrialist Andrew Carnegie (1835–1919) wrote in *The Gospel of Wealth* (1900):

> *We accept and welcome . . . the concentration of business, industrial and commercial, in the hands of a few and the law of competition . . . as being, not only beneficial, but essential to the future progress of the race. . . . We start, then, with a condition of affairs under which the best interests of the race are promoted, but which inevitably gives wealth to the few.*[10]

According to Social Darwinists, those who lost out in the socioeconomic struggle demonstrated their unfitness. Traditionally, failure had been ascribed to human wickedness or to God's plan. Now it was attributed to an inferior hereditary endowment.

Using Darwin's model of organisms evolving and changing slowly over tens of thousands of years, conservatives insisted that society, too, should experience change at an unhurried pace. Instant reforms conflicted with nature's laws and wisdom and resulted in a deterioration of the social body.

The loose application of Darwin's biological concepts to the social world, where they did not apply, also buttressed imperialism, racism, nationalism, and militarism—doctrines that preached relentless conflict. Social Darwinists insisted that nations and races were engaged in a struggle for survival in which only the fittest survive and deserve to survive. In their view, war was nature's way of eliminating the unfit. Karl Pearson, a British professor of mathematics, stated in *National Life from the Standpoint of Science* (1900):

> *History shows me only one way, and one way only in which a higher state of civilization has been produced, namely the struggle of race with race, and the survival of the physically and mentally fitter race. . . . The path of progress is strewn with the wrecks of nations; traces are everywhere to be seen of the [sacrifice] of inferior races, and of victims who found not the narrow way to perfection. Yet these dead people are, in very truth, the stepping stones on which mankind has arisen to the higher intellectual and deeper emotional life of today.*[11]

"We are a conquering race," said the U.S. senator Albert J. Beveridge. "We must obey our blood and occupy new markets, and if necessary, new lands."[12] "War is a biological necessity of the first importance," claimed the Prussian general Friedrich von Bernhardi in *Germany and the Next War* (1911).[13]

Darwinian biology was used to promote the belief in Anglo-Saxon (British and American) and Teutonic (German) racial superiority. Social Darwinists attributed to racial qualities the growth of the British Empire, the expansion of the United States to the Pacific, and the extension of German power. The domination of other peoples—American Indians, Africans, Asians, Poles—was seen as the natural right of the superior race. British naturalist Alfred Russel Wallace, who arrived at the theory of evolution independently of Darwin, wrote in 1864:

> *The intellectual and moral, as well as the physical qualities of the European are superior; the same power and capacities which have made him rise in a few centuries from the condition of the wandering savage . . . to*

his present state of culture and advancement . . . enable him when in contact with savage man, to conquer in the struggle for existence and to increase at his expense.[14]

Several writers and supporters of their countries' expansion described Native Americans, Africans, and Pacific Islanders as low forms of humanity whose subjection, even extinction, would be beneficial to the progress of civilization. For them the destruction of a "lower race" was justifiable, a biologically necessary and culturally worthy process. Thus in 1912, Paul Rohrbach, a German colonial official in Southwest Africa, wrote:

No false philanthropy or racial theory can convince sensible people that the preservation of a tribe of South Africa's kaffirs . . . is more important to the future of mankind than the spread of the great European nations and the white race in general.

Not until the native learns to produce anything of value in the service of the higher race, i.e., in the service of its and his own progress, does he gain any moral right to exist.[15]

Social Darwinism also affected racial attitudes in the United States. Too willingly, scholars, joining antiblack polemicists, attributed an inferior biological inheritance to blacks, and some predicted their extinction, seeing them as losers in the Darwinian struggle for existence. Thus in 1905, William B. Smith, a Tulane University professor, wrote: "The vision . . . of a race vanishing before its superior is not at all dispiriting, but inspiring. . . . The doom that awaits the Negro has been prepared in like measures for all inferior races."[16]

The theory of evolution was a great achievement of the rational mind, but in the hands of the Social Darwinists it served to undermine the Enlightenment tradition. Whereas the philosophes emphasized human equality, Social Darwinists divided humanity into racial superiors and inferiors. The philosophes believed that states would increasingly submit to the rule of law to reduce violent conflicts; Social Darwinists, in contrast, regarded racial and national conflict as a biological necessity, a law of history, and a means of

progress. In propagating a tooth-and-claw version of human and international relations, Social Darwinists dispensed with the humanitarian and cosmopolitan sentiments of the philosophes and distorted the image of progress. Their views promoted territorial aggrandizement and military buildup and led many to welcome World War I. The Social Darwinist notion of the struggle of races for survival became a core doctrine of the Nazi party after World War I and provided the "scientific" and "ethical" justification for genocide.

RELIGION IN A SECULAR AGE

In addition to Darwinism, other developments in the middle of the nineteenth century served to undermine traditional Christian belief. A growing secular attitude pushed religion to the periphery of human concerns for many people. Several intellectuals, in the tradition of the Enlightenment, attacked religion as an obstacle to progress. New trends in biblical scholarship questioned the established opinion about the authenticity of the text of the Bible. Fortified by the discoveries of anthropologists and psychologists, "higher critics" examined the Old and New Testaments and the rise of Christianity in a historical and critical way. Generally, Protestant scholars, particularly Germans or those trained in Germany, took the lead in the new biblical scholarship.

In his *Life of Jesus* (1835), David Friedrich Strauss (1808–1874), a German theologian, examined the Gospels in a critical spirit, attempting to discern what was historically valid. He maintained that the New Testament was replete with myths, unconscious inventions by the Gospel writers, who embellished Jesus' life and words with their own messianic longings, and with inherited legends. The Gospels contain much mythical-religious content, Strauss said, but little history. Prior to the publication of Strauss's work, most students of religion had viewed the Gospels as a reliable historical source. But Strauss argued that the Jesus of faith is not the same as the Jesus of history. The belief that history, as presented in the Gospels, provided a firm basis for belief in Christian teachings was permanently undermined.

In *Essence of Christanity* (1841), Ludwig Feuerbach (1804–1872), a German philosopher and theologian, argued that the starting point of philosophy should be the human being and the material world, not God. "Religion is the dream of the human mind," he said, and God is a human creation, a product of human feelings and wishes. Human beings believe in the divine because they seek assistance from it in life and fear death.

Feuerbach treated religion as an expression of mythical thinking and God as an unconscious projection of human hopes, fears, and self-doubts. Christianity diminishes human beings in order to affirm God, said Feuerbach; Christians deny their own worth and goodness that they might ascribe all value to God. The human being, weak and self-hating,

> sets God before him as the antithesis of himself. . . . God is the infinite, man the finite being; God is perfect, man imperfect; God eternal, man temporal; God almighty, man weak; God holy, man sinful. God and man are extremes: God is the absolutely positive, the sum of all realities; man the absolutely negative.[17]

Religion, said Feuerbach, is a form of self-alienation, for human beings diminish their humanity when they invest their finest qualities in a nonexistent God and reserve their worst qualities for themselves. God represents the externalization of an idealized human being. When individuals measure themselves against this God-ideal, they see only miserable, contemptible, and worthless creatures. "To enrich God, man must become poor; that God may be all, man must become nothing. . . . [M]an is wicked, corrupt, incapable of good; but, on the other hand, God is the only good—the Good Being."[18] Humanity liberates itself, said Feuerbach, when it rejects God's existence and religions's claim to truth. He declared that it was his aim to change the friends of God into friends of human beings and the seekers of heaven into active, productive, and life-affirming individuals.

Confronted by this assault on orthodox belief, some Christians continued to believe that the Bible was true in all its parts, that it was the divinely inspired storehouse of knowledge about God and the world. These defenders of traditional Christianity rejected evolution and any other scientific discovery that appeared to be in conflict with their reading of Scripture. Danish philosopher and Lutheran pastor Søren Kierkegaard (1813–1855) argued that true Christians commit themselves to beliefs that are seemingly unintelligible. For Kierkegaard, truth is subjective and personal, reached through passion and commitment. To find a truth that has an all-consuming meaning, to find an idea for which one can live and die—this should be the individual's highest aim. According to Kierkegaard, all philosophical systems fail because they are concerned with objective certainty and humanity in general and not with what truly matters—the individual standing alone and making choices based on passionately held beliefs. It is this experience that brings the individual face-to-face with God.

For Kierkegaard, the highest truth is that human beings are God's creatures. However, God's existence cannot be demonstrated by reason; the crucial questions of human existence can never be resolved in a logical and systematic way. In Kierkegaard's view, the individual knows God through a leap of faith, not through systematic reasoning. In contrast to the Christian apologists who sought to demonstrate that Christian teachings did not conflict with reason, Kierkegaard denied that Christian doctrines were objectively valid. For him, Christian beliefs were absurd and irrational and could not be harmonized with reason. True Christians, said Kierkegaard, confidently embrace beliefs that are incomprehensible, if not absurd.

Because Christian truths surpass reason, Kierkegaard said that true Christians, strengthened by faith, plunge, with confidence, into the absurd. But it is this leap of faith that enables Christians to conquer the agonizing feeling that life, in its deepest sense, means nothing and to give meaning to their own existence. Such a faith, based on total commitment, is thus the true avenue of self-discovery.

Modernism, a movement of Catholic intellectuals, sought to liberalize the church, to make it more accepting of modern liberal political ideals and modern science, and to reexamine the Gospels and Catholic teaching in the light of modern biblical scholarship. In many of these instances, modernists took positions that directly challenged core Catholic principles. Thus, Alfred Firmin Loiry (1857–1940), a scholarly priest, questioned the historicity of the Virgin Birth and the bodily resurrection of Jesus, rejected the infallibility of papal and council pronouncements, and contended that Jesus did not impart God's permanent truths, that both he and the Gospels have to be interpreted within the context of their historical times.

Pope Pius X (1903–1914) strongly condemned modernism for undermining revelation and fostering agnosticism. The church also suppressed modernist journals, placed a number of modernist works on the *Index of Forbidden Books,* dismissed some modernist instructors, and excommunicated a number of the movement's staunchest supporters.

MARXISM

The failure of the revolutions of 1848 and growing fear of working-class violence led liberals to abandon revolution and to press for reforms through the political process. In the last part of the nineteenth century, Marxists and anarchists became the chief proponents of revolution. Both liberalism and Marxism shared common principles derived from the Enlightenment. Their adherents believed in the essential goodness and perfectibility of human nature and claimed that their doctrines rested on rational foundations. They wanted to free individuals from accumulated superstition, ignorance, and prejudices of the past and to fashion a more harmonious and rational society. Both liberals and Marxists believed in social progress and valued the full realization of human talents.

Despite these similarities, the differences between liberalism and Marxism are profound. The goal of Marxism—the seizure of power by the working class and the destruction of capitalism—was inimical to bourgeois liberals; so, too, was the Marxist belief that violence and struggle were the essence of history, the instruments of progress, the vehicle to a higher stage of humanity. Liberals, who placed the highest value on the individual, held that through education and self-discipline people could overcome inequality and poverty.

KARL MARX. Interpreting history in economic terms, Marx predicted that socialism would replace capitalism. He called for the proletariat to overthrow capitalism and to establish a classless society. (*Corbis-Bettmann.*)

Marxists insisted that without a transformation of the economic system, individual effort by the downtrodden would amount to very little.

Karl Marx (1818–1883) was born of German-Jewish parents (both descendants of prominent rabbis). To save his job as a lawyer, Marx's father converted to Protestantism. Enrolled at a university to study law, Marx switched to philosophy. In 1842, he was editing a newspaper, which was soon suppressed by the Prussian authorities for its outspoken ideas. Leaving his native Rhineland, Marx went to Paris, where he met another German, Friedrich Engels (1820–1895), who was the son of a prosperous textile manufacturer. Marx and Engels entered into a lifelong collaboration and became members of socialist groups. In February 1848, they published the *Communist Manifesto,* which called for a working-class revolution to overthrow the capitalist system. Forced to leave France in 1849 because of his political views, Marx moved to London, where he spent the rest of his life.

Although supported by Engels, Marx was continually short of funds, and at times he and his wife and daughters lived in dreadful poverty. In London, Marx spent years writing *Capital*—a study and critique of the modern capitalistic economic system, which, he predicted, would be destroyed by a socialist revolution.

Online Study Center

Improve Your Grade
Primary Source: A Scathing Denunciation of
Socialist Reform (Marx)

A Science of History

As did other thinkers influenced by the Enlightenment, Marx believed that human history, like the operations of nature, was governed by scientific law. Marx was a strict materialist; rejecting all religious and metaphysical interpretations of both nature and history, he sought to fashion an empirical science of society. He viewed religion as a human creation—a product of people's imagination and feelings and a consolation for the oppressed. The happiness it brought he considered an illusion. Real happiness would come, said Marx, not by transcending the natural world but by improving it. Rather than deluding oneself by seeking refuge from life's misfortunes in an imaginary world, one must confront the ills of society and reform them. This last point is crucial. "The philosophers have only *interpreted* the world in different ways; the point is to *change it.*"[19]

The world could be rationally understood and changed, said Marx. People were free to make their own history, but to do so effectively, they must comprehend the inner meaning of history: the laws governing human affairs in the past and operating in the present. Marx adopted Hegel's view that history was not an assortment of unrelated and disconnected events, but a progressive development, which, like the growth of a plant, proceeded ineluctably according to its own inner laws. For both Hegel and Marx, the historical process was governed by objective and rational principles. Marx also adopted Hegel's view that history advanced dialectically: that the clash of opposing forces propelled history into higher stages.

However, Marx also broke with Hegel in crucial ways. For Hegel, it was the dialectical clash of opposing ideas that moved history into the next stage. For Marx, it was the clash of classes representing conflicting economic interests—what is called *dialectical materialism*—that accounted for historical change and progress. In Hegel's view, history was the unfolding of the Absolute Spirit, and a higher stage of development was produced by the synthesis of opposing ideas. According to Marx, Hegel's system failed because it was too metaphysical. It transcended the known world and downgraded reality to a mere attribute of Spirit. Marx saw Hegel's abstract philosophy as deflecting attention from the real world and its problems, which cried out for understanding and solution; it was a negation of life. For Marx, history was explainable solely in terms of natural processes—empirically verifiable developments.

Marx valued Hegel's insight that history is a progressive and purposeful process, but he criticized Hegel for embedding this insight in metaphysical-theological fantasy. Hegel, said Marx, had made a mystical principle the real subject of history and thought. But, in truth, it is the "real man," the person who lives in and is conditioned by the objective world, the only true reality, who is the center of history. History is not Spirit aspiring to self-actualization but people becoming fully human, fulfilling their human potential. The moving forces in history, said Marx, were economic and technological factors: the ways in which goods were produced and wealth was distributed. They accounted for historical change and were the basis of all culture—politics, law, religion, morals, and philosophy. "The history of humanity," he concluded, "must therefore always be studied and treated in relation to the history of industry and exchange."[20]

According to Marx, material technology—the methods of cultivating land and the tools for manufacturing goods—determined society's social and political arrangements and its intellectual outlooks. For example, the hand mill, the loose yoke, and the wooden plow had given rise to feudal lords, whereas power-driven machines had spawned industrial capitalists.

Class Conflict

Throughout history, said Marx, there has been a **class** struggle between those who own the means of production and those whose labor has been exploited to provide wealth for this upper class. This dialectical, or opposing, tension between classes has pushed history forward into higher stages. In the ancient world, when wealth was based on land, the struggle was between master and slave, patrician and plebeian; during the Middle Ages, when land was still the predominant mode of production, the struggle was between lord and serf. In the modern industrial world, two sharply opposed classes were confronting each other: the capitalists owning the factories, mines, banks, and transportation systems, and the exploited wage earners (the proletariat).

The class with economic power also controlled the state, said Marx and Engels. That class used political power to protect and increase its property and to hold down the laboring class. "Thus the ancient State was above all the slaveowners' state for holding down the slaves," said Engels, "as a feudal State was the organ of the nobles for holding down the . . . serfs, and the modern representative State is the instrument of the exploitation of wage-labor by capital."[21]

Furthermore, Marx and Engels asserted the class that controlled material production also controlled mental production: that is, the ideas held by the ruling class became the dominant ideas of society. These ideas, presented as laws of nature or moral and religious standards, were regarded as the truth by oppressor and oppressed alike. In reality, however, these ideas merely reflected the special economic interests of the ruling class. Thus, said Marx, bourgeois ideologists would insist that natural rights and laissez faire were laws of nature having universal validity. But these "laws" were born of the needs of the bourgeoisie in its struggle to wrest power from an obsolete feudal regime and to protect its property from the state. Similarly, nineteenth-century slaveholders convinced themselves that slavery was morally right: that it had God's approval and was good for the slave. Slave owners and capitalist employers alike may have defended their labor systems by citing universal principles that they thought were true, but in reality their systems rested on a simple economic consideration: slave labor was good for the pocketbook of the slave owner, and wage labor was good in the same way for the capitalist. They were unaware of the real forces motivating their thinking.

Destruction of Capitalism

Under capitalism, said Marx, workers knew only poverty. They worked long hours for low wages, suffered from periodic unemployment, and lived in squalid, overcrowded dwellings. Most monstrous of all, they were forced to send their young children into the factories.

Capitalism also produced another kind of poverty, according to Marx: poverty of the human spirit. Under capitalism, the factory worker was reduced to a laboring beast, performing tedious and repetitive tasks in a dark, dreary, dirty cave—an altogether inhuman environment, which deprived people of their human sensibilities. Unlike the artisans in their own shops, factory workers found no pleasure and took no pride in their work; they did not have the satisfaction of creating a finished product that expressed their skills. Work, said Marx, should be a source of fulfillment for people. It should enable people to affirm their personalities and develop their potential. By treating people not as human beings but as cogs in the production process, capitalism alienated people from their work, from themselves, and from one another.

Marx further asserted that capitalism dehumanized not only the workers but the capitalists as well. Consumed by greed and a ruthless competitiveness, they abused workers and each other and lost sight of life's true meaning: the fulfillment of the individual's creative potential. Marx's view of the individual owed much to the Western humanist tradition, which aspired to shape self-sufficient and productive human beings who strive to develop their intellectual, esthetic, and moral capacities and relate to others as subjects, not as objects. By reducing people to commodities and human relations to a cash nexus, said Marx, capitalism thwarted the realization of this humanist vision.

Marx believed that capitalist control of the economy and the government would not endure forever; capitalist society produced its own gravediggers—the working class. The capitalist system would perish just as the slave society of the ancient world and the feudal society of the Middle Ages had perished. For Marx, the destruction of capitalism was inevitable; it was necessitated by the law of historical materialism. From the ruins of a dead capitalist society, a new socioeconomic system, socialism, would emerge.

Marx predicted how capitalism would be destroyed. Periodic unemployment would increase the misery of the workers and intensify their hatred of capitalists. Small businesspeople and shopkeepers, unable to compete with the great capitalists, would sink into the ranks of the working class, greatly expanding its numbers. Society would become polarized into a small group of immensely wealthy capitalists and a vast proletariat, poor, embittered, and desperate. The monopoly of capital by the few would become a brake on the productive process. Growing increasingly conscious of their misery, the workers—aroused, educated, and organized by communist intellectuals—would revolt. "Revolution is necessary," said Marx, "not only because the *ruling* class cannot be overthrown in any other way, but also because only in a revolution *can the class which overthrows it* rid itself of the accumulated rubbish of the past and become capable of reconstructing society."[22] The working-class revolutionaries would smash the government that helped the capitalists maintain their dominance. Then they would confiscate the property of the capitalists, abolish private property, place the means of production in the workers' hands, and organize a new society. The *Communist Manifesto* ends with a ringing call for revolution:

The Communists . . . openly declare that their ends can be attained only by the forcible overthrow of all existing social conditions. Let the ruling classes tremble at a Communist revolution. The proletarians have nothing to lose but their chains. They have a world to win.
Workingmen of all countries, unite![23]

Marx did not say a great deal about the new society that would be ushered in by the socialist revolution. With the destruction of capitalism, the distinction between capitalist and worker would cease and with it the class conflict. No longer would society be divided into haves and have-nots, oppressor and oppressed. Since this classless society would contain no exploiters, there would be no need for a state, which was merely an instrument for maintaining and protecting the power of the exploiting class. Thus, the state would eventually wither away. The production and distribution of goods would be carried out through community planning and communal sharing, replacing the capitalist system of competition. People would work at varied tasks, rather than being confined to one form of employment, just as Fourier had advocated.

A revolutionary change in the conditions of life, Marx predicted, would produce a radical transformation of the human being. No longer debased by the self-destructive pursuit of profit and property and no longer victims of capitalist exploitation, people would become finer human beings—altruistic, sensitive, cooperative, and creative. United with others in a classless society free of exploitation and no longer divided by divergent interests, individuals would become truly communal and truly free beings (surpassing the merely political freedom achieved in the bourgeois state)—that is, they would become truly human.

Marxism had immense appeal for both the downtrodden and intellectuals. It promised to end the injustices of industrial society, it offered explanations that claimed the certainty of science for all the crucial events of history, and it assured adherents that history guaranteed the triumph of their cause. Far from being a scientific system, however, Marxism had the features of a religious myth., which, says Robert Tucker,

appeal[ed] to some modern men in whom the hold of traditional religion has loosened but the craving for an all-inclusive world-view remains alive and strong.[24]

Marx's influence grew during the second wave of industrialization in the closing decades of the nineteenth century, when class bitterness between the proletariat and the bourgeoisie seemed to worsen. Many workers thought that liberals and conservatives had no sympathy for their plight and that the only way to improve their lot was through socialist parties.

Critics of Marx

Critics point out serious weaknesses in Marxism. The rigid Marxist who tries to squeeze all historical events into an economic framework is at a disadvantage. Economic forces alone will not explain the triumph of Christianity in the Roman Empire, the fall of Rome, the Crusades, the French Revolution, modern imperialism, World War I, the rise of Hitler, or the mindset of contemporary Islamic terrorists. Economic explanations fall particularly flat in trying to account for the emergence of modern nationalism, whose appeal, resting on deeply ingrained emotional needs, crosses class lines. Most great struggles of the twentieth century have been not between classes but between nations.

Many of Marx's predictions or expectations have not materialized. Workers in Western lands did not become the oppressed and impoverished working class that Marx had described in the mid-nineteenth century. Because of increased productivity and the efforts of labor unions and reform-minded governments, Western workers improved their lives considerably so that they now enjoy the highest standard of living in history. The tremendous growth of a middle class of professionals, civil service employees, and small-business people belies Marx's prediction that capitalist society would be polarized into a small group of very rich capitalists and a great mass of destitute workers. Marx believed that socialist revolutions would break out in the advanced industrialized lands. But the socialist revolutions of the twentieth century occurred in underdeveloped, predominantly agricultural states. The state in communist lands, far from withering away, grew more centralized, powerful, and oppressive. In no country where communist revolutionaries seized power have people achieved the liberty that Marx desired. Nor, indeed, have orthodox communists been able to sustain a viable economic system. The phenomenal collapse of communist regimes in the former Soviet Union and Eastern Europe in recent years testifies to Marxism's failure. All these failed predictions and expectations seem to contradict Marx's claim that his theories rested on an unassailable scientific foundation.

ANARCHISM

Anarchism was another radical movement that attacked capitalism. Like Marxists, anarchists denounced the exploitation of workers and the coercive authority of government and envisioned a stateless society. Only by abolishing the state, said anarchists, could the individual live a free and full life. To achieve these ends, a small number of anarchists advocated revolutionary terrorism; others, like the great Russian novelist Leo Tolstoy, rejected all violence. These anarchists sought to destroy the state by refusing to cooperate with it.

Anarchists drew inspiration from Pierre Joseph Proudhon (1809–1865), a self-educated French printer and typesetter. Proudhon criticized social theorists who devised elaborate systems that regimented daily life, conflicted with human nature, and deprived people of their personal liberty. He desired a new society that maximized individual freedom. He looked back longingly to preindustrial society, which he saw as free of exploitation and corruption, of great manufacturers and financiers, and of powerful governments that interfered in people's lives.

Anarchism had a particular appeal in Russia, where there was no representative government and no way, other than petitions to the tsar, to legally redress injustice. A repressive regime, economic backwardness, a youth movement passionately committed to improving the lives of the masses, and a magnetic leader, Mikhail Bakunin (1814–1876), all contributed to shaping the Russian anarchist tradition. Bakunin was a man of action who organized and fought for revolution and set an example of revolutionary fervor. The son of a Russian noble, he left the tsar's army to study philosophy in the West, where he was attracted to the ideas of Marx. He was arrested for participating in the German revolution of 1848 and was turned over to tsarist officials. He served six years in prison and was then banished to Siberia, from which he escaped in 1861.

Bakunin devoted himself to organizing secret societies that would lead the oppressed in revolt. Whereas Marx held that revolution would occur in the industrial lands through the efforts of a class-conscious proletariat, Bakunin wanted all oppressed people to revolt, including the peasants (the vast majority of the population in central and eastern Europe). Toward this end, he favored secret societies and terrorism.

Marx and Bakunin disagreed on one crucial issue of strategy. Marx wanted to organize the workers into mass political parties; Bakunin held that revolutions should be fought by secret societies of fanatic insurrectionists. Bakunin feared that after the Marxists overthrew the capitalist regime and seized power, they would become the new masters and exploiters, using the state to enhance their own power. They would, said Bakunin, become a "privileged minority . . . of *ex-workers,* who, once they become rulers or representatives of the people, cease to be workers and begin to look down upon the toiling people. From that time on they represent not the people but themselves and their claims to govern the people."[25] Therefore, said Bakunin, once the workers capture the state, they should destroy it forever. Bakunin's astute prediction that a socialist revolution would lead state power to intensify rather than disappear was borne out in the twentieth century in all lands where communists had seized power.

Anarchists engaged in acts of political terrorism, including the assassination or attempted assassination of heads of state and key ministers, but they never waged a successful revolution. They failed to reverse the trend toward the concentration of power in industry and government, which would characterize the twentieth century.

LIBERALISM IN TRANSITION

In the early 1800s, European liberals were preoccupied with protecting the rights of the individual against the demands of the state. They championed laissez faire because they feared that state interference in the economy to redress social evils would threaten individual rights and the free market, which they thought were essential to personal liberty. They also favored property requirements for voting and officeholding because they were certain that the unpropertied and uneducated masses lacked the wisdom and experience to exercise political responsibility.

In the last part of the century, liberals began—not without reservation and qualification—to support extended suffrage and government action to remedy the abuses of unregulated industrialization. This growing concern for the welfare of the laboring poor coincided with and was influenced by an unprecedented proliferation of humanitarian movements on both sides of the Atlantic. Nurtured by the Enlightenment, as well as by Christian teachings, reform movements called for the prohibition of child labor, schooling for the masses, humane treatment for prisoners and the mentally ill, equality for women, the abolition of slavery, and an end to war. By the beginning of the twentieth century, liberalism had evolved into liberal democracy, and laissez faire had been superseded by a reluctant acceptance of social legislation and government regulation. But from beginning to end, the central concern of liberals remained the protection of individual rights.

John Stuart Mill

The transition from laissez-faire liberalism to a more socially conscious and democratic liberalism is seen in the thought of John Stuart Mill (1806–1873), a British philosopher and statesman. Mill's *On Liberty* (1859) is the classic statement of individual freedom and minority rights: that the government and the majority may not interfere with the liberty of another human being whose actions do no injury to others.

Mill regarded freedom of thought and expression, the toleration of opposing and unpopular viewpoints, as a necessary precondition for the shaping of a rational, moral, and civilized citizen. Political or social coercion, said Mill, is also a barrier to the full development of individuality. Liberty is a supreme good that benefits both the individual and the community. When we silence an opinion, said Mill, we hurt present and future generations. If the opinion is correct, "we are deprived of the opportunity of exchanging error for truth." If the opinion is wrong—and of this we can never be entirely certain—we "lose the clearer perception and livelier impression of truth produced by its collision with error."[26] Therefore, government has no right to force an individual to hold a view

> *because it will be better for him to do so, because it will make him happier, or because in the opinions of others, to do so would be wise, or even right. These are good reasons for remonstrating with him, or reasoning with him, or persuading him, or entreating him, but not for compelling him or visiting him with any evil in case he do otherwise.*[27]

Mill would place limits on the power of government, for in an authoritarian state citizens cannot develop their moral and intellectual potential. Although he feared the state as a threat to individual liberty, Mill also recognized the necessity for state intervention to promote individual self-development: the expansion of individual moral, intellectual, and esthetic capacities. For example, he maintained that it was permissible for the state to require children to attend school against the wishes of their parents, to regulate hours of labor, to promote public health, and to provide workers' compensation and old-age insurance.

In *Considerations on Representative Government* (1861), Mill endorsed the active participation of all citizens, including the lower classes, in the political life of the state. However, he also proposed a system of plural voting in which education and character would determine the number of votes each person was entitled to cast. In this way, Mill, a cautious democrat, sought to protect the individual from the tyranny of a politically and intellectually unprepared majority.

Online Study Center

Improve Your Grade
Primary Source: Political Reform Taken to Its Logical Conclusion: Rights for Women (Mill)

Thomas Hill Green

The leading late-nineteenth-century figures in the shaping of a new liberal position in Britain were Thomas Hill Green (1836–1882), an Oxford

University professor; D. G. Ritchie (1853–1903), who taught philosophy at Oxford and Saint Andrews; J. A. Hobson (1858–1940), a social theorist; and L. T. Hobhouse (1864–1929), an academic who also wrote for the *Manchester Guardian*. In general, these thinkers argued that laissez faire protected the interests of the economically powerful class and ignored the welfare of the nation. For example, Green valued private property but could not see how this principle helped the poor. "A man who possesses nothing but his powers of labor and who has to sell these to a capitalist for bare daily maintenance, might as well . . . be denied rights of property altogether."[28]

Green argued that the do-nothing state advocated by traditional laissez-faire liberalism condemned many citizens to destitution, ignorance, and despair. The state must preserve individual liberty and at the same time secure the common good by promoting conditions favorable for the self-development of the majority of the population. Liberalism, for Green, encompassed more than the protection of individual rights from an oppressive government. A truly liberal society, he said, gives people the opportunity to fulfill their moral potential and human capacities. And social reforms initiated by the state assisted in the realization of this broader conception of liberty. Green and other advocates of state intervention contended that the government has a moral obligation to create social conditions that permit individuals to make the best of themselves. Toward that end, the state should promote public health, ensure decent housing, and provide for education. The uneducated and destitute person cannot be morally self-sufficient or a good citizen, Green and other progressives argued.

Green and his colleagues remained advocates of capitalism but rejected strict laissez faire, which, they said, benefited only a particular class at the expense of the common good. Overcoming a traditional liberal mistrust of state power, they viewed the state as an ethical institution, assigned it a positive role in improving social conditions, and insisted that state actions need not threaten individual freedom.

In general, by the beginning of the twentieth century, liberals in Britain increasingly acknowledged the need for social legislation. The foundations for the British welfare state were being laid.

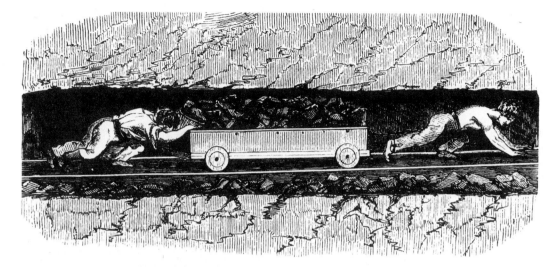

CHILD MINE LABOR, REPORT OF A PARLIAMENTARY COMMISSION OF INQUIRY, 1842. In 1842 the British Parliament passed the Mines Act, prohibiting employment of girls and boys under the age of ten in coal mines. This report, detailing children being forced to drag sledge tubs through narrow tunnels, among other abuses, convinced Parliament to act. Further legislation regulating safety and labor practices in the coal industry followed after 1850. (*The Granger Collection.*)

On the Continent, too, social welfare laws were enacted. To be sure, the motives behind such legislation were quite diverse and often had little to do with liberal sentiments. Nevertheless, in several countries liberalism was expanding into political and social democracy, a trend that would continue in the twentieth century.

Herbert Spencer: Rejection of State Intervention

Many traditional liberals regarded state intervention—"creeping socialism," they called it—as a betrayal of the liberal principle of individual freedom. They held to the traditional liberal view that the plight of the downtrodden was not a legitimate concern of the state. The new liberalism, they argued, would make people dependent on the state, thereby stifling industriousness, self-reliance, and thrift. Paternalistic government would cripple the working class morally by turning them into "grown-up babies."

In *The Man Versus the State* (1884), the British philosopher Herbert Spencer rejected the idea "that evils of all kinds should be dealt with by the State." The outcome of state intervention, he said, is that "each member of the community as an individual would be a slave to the community as a whole . . . and the slavery will not be mild."[29] Committed to a philosophy of extreme individualism, Spencer never abandoned the view that the state was an evil and oppressive institution. He favored a society in which government would play the smallest role possible and individual freedom would be maximized, for when the power of the state is extended, however well-intentioned the motive, the freedom of the individual is restricted.

Spencer's extreme laissez faire and "rugged individualism" led him to oppose various forms of government intervention, including factory inspection, sanitary laws, pure food and drug requirements, a state postal system, compulsory public education, and public relief for the poor. "The function of Liberalism in the past was that of putting a limit to the powers of kings," he declared. "The function of true Liberalism in the future will be that of putting a limit to the powers of Parliament."[30]

A thoroughgoing individualist, Spencer saw the poor as incapable, weak, imprudent, and lazy—unfit to compete in the struggle for existence. For Spencer, state action was always misguided, for it tampered with nature's laws. "Instead of diminishing suffering, it eventually increases it. It favours the multiplication of those worst fitted for existence, and, by consequence, hinders the multiplication of those best fitted for existence—leaving, as it does, less room for them."[31] Government assistance creates an attitude of dependency among the poor; because they expect things to be done for them, they do not do things for themselves.

FEMINISM: EXTENDING THE PRINCIPLE OF EQUALITY

Another example of the expansion of liberalism was the emergence of feminist movements in western Europe and the United States. **Feminism** insisted that the principles of liberty and equality expressed by the philosophes and embodied in the French Declaration of the Rights of Man and of the Citizen (1789) and the American Declaration of Independence be applied to women. Thus, Olympe de Gouges's *Declaration of the Rights of Woman* (1791), modeled after the Declaration of the Rights of Man and of the Citizen, the French Revolution's tribute to Enlightenment ideals, stated: "Woman is born free and remains equal to man in rights. . . . The aim of every political association is the preservation of the natural . . . rights of man and woman."[32] Mary Wollstonecraft's *Vindication of the Rights of Woman*, written under the influence of the French Revolution, protested against the prevailing subordination and submissiveness of women and the limited opportunities afforded them to cultivate their minds. She considered it an act of tyranny for women "to be excluded from a participation of the natural rights of mankind."[33] And in 1837, the English novelist and economist Harriet Martineau observed: "One of the funda-

Elizabeth Cady Stanton and Women's Rights

AN AMERICAN FEMINIST. Elizabeth Cady Stanton, who participated in the antislavery movement, was a principal founder of the American Woman's Suffragist Movement, which held its first convention in 1848 in Seneca Falls, New York. (*Bettmann/Corbis.*)

mental principles announced in the Declaration of Independence is that governments derive their just power from the consent of the governed. How can the political condition of women be reconciled with this?"[34]

In the United States, in the 1830s, Angelina and Sarah Grimké spoke in public—something women rarely did—against slavery and for women's rights. In 1838, Sarah Grimké published *Letters on the Equality of the Sexes and the Condition of Women*, where she stated emphatically: "Men and women were Created Equal: they are both moral and accountable beings, and whatever is *right* for man to do is *right* for women. . . . How monstrous, how anti-Christian, is the doctrine that woman is to be dependent on man!"[35] The Woman's Suffrage Movement, holding its first convention in 1848 in Seneca Falls, New York, drew up a Declaration of Statements and Principles, which broadened the Declaration of Independence: "We hold these truths to be self-evident: that all men and women are created equal." The document protested "that woman has too long rested satisfied in the circumscribed limits which corrupt customs and a perverted application of the Scriptures have marked out for her" and called for the untiring effort of both men and women to secure for women "an equal participation with men in the various trades, professions, and commerce."[36]

In their struggle for equality, feminists had to overcome deeply ingrained premises about female inferiority and deficiencies. Even the philosophes, who often enjoyed the company of intelligent and sophisticated women in the famous salons, continued to view women as intellectually and morally inferior to men. Some philosophes, notably Condorcet, who wrote *Plea for the Citizenship of Women* (1791), argued for female emancipation, but they were the exception. Most philosophes concurred with Hume, who held that "nature has subjected" women to men and that their "inferiority and infirmities are absolutely incurable."[37] Rousseau, who believed that nature had granted men power over women, regarded traditional domesticity as a woman's proper role.

> I would a thousand times rather have a homely girl, simply brought up, than a learned lady and a wit who would make a literary circle of my house and install herself as its president. A female wit is a scourge to her husband, her children, her friends, her servants, to everybody. From the lofty height of her genius, she scorns every womanly duty, and she is always trying to make a man of herself.[38]

Nevertheless, by clearly articulating the ideals of liberty and equality, the philosophes made a women's movement possible. The growing popularity of these ideals could not escape women, who measured their own position by them. More-

over, by their very nature, these ideals were expansive. Denying them to women would ultimately be seen as an indefensible contradiction.

Opponents of women's rights argued that feminist demands would threaten society by undermining marriage and the family. An article in the *Saturday Review,* an English periodical, declared that "It is not the interest of States . . . to encourage the existence of women who are other than entirely dependent on man as well for subsistence as for protection and love. . . . Married life is a woman's profession."[39] And in 1870, a member of the House of Commons wondered "what would become, not merely of woman's influence, but of her duties at home, her care of the household, her supervision of all those duties and surroundings which make a happy home . . . if we are to see women coming forward and taking part in the government of the country."[40] This concern for the family combined with a traditional biased view of woman's nature, as one writer for the *Saturday Review* revealed:

> The power of reasoning is so small in women that they need adventitious help, and if they have not the guidance and check of a religious conscience, it is useless to expect from them self-control on abstract principles. They do not calculate consequences, and they are reckless when they once give way, hence they are to be kept straight only through their affections, the religious sentiment and a well-educated moral sense.[41]

No doubt, the following comment of Jules and Edmond Goncourt, two prominent French writers, reflected the mood of many other French intellectuals:

> Men like ourselves need a woman of little breeding and education who is nothing but gaiety and natural wit, because a woman of that sort can charm and please us like an agreeable animal to which we may become quite attached. But if a mistress has acquired a veneer of breeding, art, or literature, and tries to talk to us on an equal footing about our thoughts and our feeling for beauty; if she wants to be a companion and partner in the cultivation of our tastes or the writing of our

books, then she becomes for us as unbearable as a piano out of tune—and very soon an object of dislike.[42]

In contrast to most of their contemporaries, some prominent men did support equal rights for women. "Can man be free if woman be slave?"[43] asked Shelley, who favored female suffrage. So too did Bentham and the political economist William Thompson, who wrote *Appeal of One Half of the Human Race* (1825). John Stuart Mill thought that differences between the sexes (and between the classes) were due far more to education than to inherited inequalities. Believing that all people—women as well as men—should be able to develop their talents and intellects as fully as possible, Mill was an early champion of female equality, including women's suffrage. In 1867, Mill, as a member of Parliament, proposed that the suffrage be extended to women (the proposal was rejected by a vote of 194 to 74).

In 1851, Mill had married Harriet Taylor, a long-time friend and a recent widow. An ardent feminist, Harriet Mill influenced her husband's thought. In *The Subjection of Women* (1869), Mill argued that male dominance of women constituted a flagrant abuse of power. He described female inequality as a single relic of an old outlook that had been exploded in everything else. It violated the principle of individual rights and hindered the progress of humanity:

> . . . the principle which regulates the existing social relations between the two sexes—the legal subordination of one sex to the other—is wrong in itself, and now one of the chief hindrances to human improvement . . . it ought to be replaced by a principle of perfect equality, admitting no power or privilege on the one side, nor disability on the other.[44]

Mill considered it only just that women be admitted to all the functions and occupations until then reserved for men. The struggle for female rights became a major issue in several lands at the end of the nineteenth century and the beginning of the twentieth.

❖   ❖   ❖

Online Study Center ACE the Test

NOTES

1. Quoted in George J. Becker, *Master European Realists of the Nineteenth Century* (New York: Ungar, 1982), pp. 30–31.

2. Cited in Damian Grant, *Realism* (London: Methuen, 1970), pp. 31–32.

3. Cited in F. W. J. Hemmings, ed., *The Age of Realism* (Atlantic Highlands, N.J.: Humanities Press, 1978), p. 152.

4. Quoted in Leonard J. Davis, "Gustave Flaubert," in *The Romantic Century,* ed. Jacques Barzun and George Stade, vol. 7 of *European Writers* (New York: Charles Scribner's Sons, 1985), p. 1382.

5. Émile Zola, *The Experimental Novel,* trans. Belle M. Sherman (New York: Haskell House, 1964), pp. 20–21, 23.

6. Henrik Ibsen, *A Doll's House,* in *Eleven Plays of Henrik Ibsen* (New York: Modern Library, n.d.), pp. 85–87.

7. Quoted in Ernst Cassirer, *The Problem of Knowledge,* trans. William H. Woglom and Charles W. Hendel (New Haven, Conn.: Yale University Press, 1950), p. 244.

8. Quoted in Andrew D. White, *A History of the Warfare of Science with Theology in Christendom* (New York: Appleton, 1896), 1:71.

9. Excerpted in Richard Olson, ed., *Science as Metaphor* (Belmont, Calif.: Wadsworth, 1971), p. 124.

10. Andrew Carnegie, *The Gospel of Wealth* (New York: Century, 1900), pp. 4, 11.

11. Karl Pearson, *National Life from the Standpoint of Science* (London: Adam & Charles Black, 1905), pp. 21, 64.

12. Quoted in H. W. Koch, "Social Darwinism in the 'New Imperialism,'" in *The Origins of the*

First World War, ed. H. W. Koch (New York: Taplinger, 1972), p. 341.

13. Ibid., p. 345.

14. Quoted in John C. Greene, *The Death of Adam* (New York: Mentor Books, 1961), p. 313.

15. Quoted in Sven Lindqvist, *Exterminate the Brutes,* trans. Joan Tate (New York: New Press, 1996), pp. 150–151.

16. Quoted in George M. Fredrickson, *The Black Image in the White Mind* (New York: Harper Torchbooks, 1972), pp. 26–27.

17. Ludwig Feuerbach, *The Essence of Christianity,* trans. George Eliot (New York: Harper Torchbooks, 1957), p. 33.

18. Ibid., pp. 26–28.

19. Karl Marx, *Theses on Feuerbach,* excerpted in *Karl Marx: Selected Writings in Sociology and Social Philosophy,* ed. T. B. Bottomore and Maximilien Rubel (London: Watts, 1956), p. 69.

20. Karl Marx, *The German Ideology* (New York: International Publishers, 1939), p. 18.

21. Friedrich Engels, *The Origin of the Family, Private Property & the State,* in Emile Burns, *A Handbook of Marxism* (New York: Random House, 1935), p. 330.

22. Marx, *German Ideology,* p. 69.

23. Karl Marx, *Communist Manifesto,* trans. Samuel Moore (Chicago: Henry Regnery, 1954), pp. 81–82.

24. Robert Tucker, *Philosophy and Myth in Karl Marx* (Cambridge, England: Cambridge University Press, 1972), p. 22.

25. Excerpted in G. P. Maximoff, ed., *The Political Philosophy of Bakunin* (Glencoe, Ill.: The Free Press, 1953), p. 287.

26. John Stuart Mill, *On Liberty* (Boston: Ticknor & Fields, 1863), p. 36.

27. Ibid., p. 22.

28. Thomas Hill Green, *Lectures on the Principles of Political Obligation* (Ann Arbor: University of Michigan Press, 1967), p. 219.

29. Herbert Spencer, *The Man Versus the State* (London: Watts, 1940), pp. 34, 49–50.

30. Ibid., p. 152.

31. Quoted in Anthony Arblaster, *The Rise and Decline of Liberalism* (London: Basil Blackwell, 1984), p. 290.

32. Excerpted in Eleanor S. Riemer and John C. Fout, eds., *European Women: A Documentary History, 1789–1945* (New York: Schocken Books, 1980), pp. 63–64.

33. Mary Wollstonecraft, *Vindication of the Rights of Woman* (London: Dent, 1929), pp. 11–12.

34. Excerpted in Gayle Graham Yates, ed., *Harriet Martineau on Women* (New Brunswick, N.J.: Rutgers University Press, 1985), p. 134.

35. Excerpted in Miriam Schneir, ed., *Feminism: The Essential Historical Writings* (New York: Vintage Books, 1972), pp. 40–41.

36. Ibid., pp. 76, 82.

37. Quoted in Bonnie S. Anderson and Judith P. Zinsser, *A History of Their Own* (New York: Harper & Row, 1988), 2:113.

38. Jean Jacques Rousseau, *Emile,* trans. Barbara Foxley (London: Dent, Everyman's Library, 1974), p. 370.

39. Quoted in J. A. and Olive Banks, *Feminism and Family Planning in Victorian England* (Liverpool: Liverpool University Press, 1965), p. 43.

40. Ibid., p. 46.

41. Ibid., p. 47.

42. Robert Baldick, ed. and trans., *Pages from the Goncourt Journal* (New York: Penguin Books, 1984), p. 27.

43. Percy Bysshe Shelley, "The Revolt of Islam," canto 2, stanza 43, in *The Complete Poetical Works of Percy Bysshe Shelley,* ed. Thomas Hutchinson (London: Oxford University Press, 1929), p. 63.

44. John Stuart Mill, *The Subjection of Women,* in *On Liberty and The Subjection of Women* (London: Oxford University Press, 1924), p. 427.

SUGGESTED READING

Andreski, Stanislav, ed., *The Essential Comte* (1974). An excellent collection of excerpts from Comte's works.

Becker, George J., *Master European Realists of the Nineteenth Century* (1982). Discussions of Flaubert, Zola, Chekhov, and other realists.

Bullock, Alan, and Maurice Shock, eds., *The Liberal Tradition* (1956). Well-chosen selections from the writings of British liberals; the introduction is an excellent survey of liberal thought.

de Ruggiero, G., *The History of European Liberalism* (1927). A good starting point for a study of the subject.

Farrington, Benjamin, *What Darwin Really Said* (1966). A brief study of Darwin's work.

Grant, Damian, *Realism* (1970). A very good short survey.

Greene, J. C., *The Death of Adam* (1961). The impact of evolution on Western thought.

Hemmings, F. W. J., ed., *The Age of Realism* (1978). A series of essays exploring realism in various countries.

Hofstadter, Richard, *Social Darwinism in American Thought* (1955). A classic treatment of the impact of evolution on American conservatism, imperialism, and racism.

Joll, James, *The Anarchists* (1964). A fine treatment of anarchists, their lives and thought.

Manuel, Frank E., *The Prophets of Paris* (1965). Contains a valuable chapter on Comte.

Matthews, Betty, ed., *Marx: A Hundred Years On* (1983). Eleven essays by noted authorities.

McLellan, David, *Karl Marx: His Life and Thought* (1977). A highly regarded biography.

———, ed., *Karl Marx: Selected Writings* (1977). A balanced selection of Marx's writings.

Nochlin, Linda, *Realism* (1971). The nature of realism; realism in art.

Richter, Melvin, *The Politics of Conscience* (1964). A study of Thomas Hill Green and his age.

Tucker, Robert, *The Marxian Revolutionary Idea* (1969). Marxism as a radical social philosophy.

Chapter 25

The Surge of Nationalism: From Liberal to Extreme Nationalism

Victor Emmanuel and Garibaldi at the Bridge of Teano (1860). The unification of Italy was the work of the romantic liberal Giuseppe Mazzini, the practical politician Count Cavour, and the seasoned revolutionary Giuseppe Garibaldi. Selflessly, Garibaldi turned over his conquests in the south to Victor Emmanuel in 1861. (Scala/Art Resource, NY.)

- **The Unification of Italy**
- **The Unification of Germany**
- **The Hapsburg Empire**
- **The Rise of Racial Nationalism**

Focus Questions

1. How did nationalism promote unity in some lands and division in others?

2. Why did the expressions of extreme nationalism mark a repudiation of the Enlightenment tradition and a regression to mythical modes of thought?

3. What is the relationship between medieval and modern anti-Semitism? How does anti-Semitism demonstrate the immense power of mythical thinking?

Online Study Center

This icon will direct you to interactive map and primary source activities on the website http://college.hmco.com/pic/perrywc8e.

The revolutions of 1848 ended in failure, but nationalist energies were too powerful to contain. In 1867, Hungary gained the autonomy it had sought in 1848, and by 1871, the unification of both Italy and Germany was complete.

The leading architects of Italian and German unification were not liberal idealists or romantic dreamers of the type who had fought in the revolutions of 1848; they were tough-minded practitioners of **Realpolitik**, "the politics of reality." Shrewd and calculating statesmen, they respected power and knew how to wield it; focusing on the actual world, they dismissed ideals as illusory, noble sentiments that impeded effective action. Realpolitik was the political counterpart of realism and positivism. All three outlooks shared the desire to view things coldly and objectively as they are, rather than as idealists would like them to be.

Nationalism, gaining in intensity in the last part of the nineteenth century, was to become the dominant spiritual force in European life. Once Germany was unified, Pan-Germans sought to incorporate Germans living outside the *Reich* (German empire) into the new Germany and to build a vast overseas empire. Russian Pan-Slavs dreamed of bringing the Slavs of eastern Europe under the control of "Mother Russia." Growing increasingly resentful of Magyar and German domination, the Slavic minorities of the Hapsburg Empire agitated for recognition of their national rights. In the late 1800s, nationalism became increasingly belligerent, intolerant, and irrational, threatening the peace of Europe and the liberal-humanist tradition of the Enlightenment.

THE UNIFICATION OF ITALY

In 1848, liberals failed to drive the Austrians out of Italy and to unite the Italian nation. By 1870, however, Italian unification was achieved despite many obstacles.

Forces for and Against Unity

In 1815, Italy consisted of separate states. In the south, a Bourbon king ruled the Kingdom of the Two Sicilies; the pope governed the Papal States in central Italy; Hapsburg Austria ruled Lom-

Chronology 25.1 ❖ Unification of Italy

1821	Austria suppresses Carbonari rebellion
1831–32	Austria suppresses another Carbonari insurrection
1832	Mazzini forms Young Italy
March 1848	Austrians are forced to withdraw from Milan and Venice
November 1848	Liberal revolution forces pope to flee Rome
1848–49	Austria reasserts its authority in Milan and Venice; Louis Napoleon crushes revolutionaries in Rome
1858	Napoleon III agrees to help Piedmont-Sardinia against Austria
1859	War between Piedmont-Sardinia and Austria: Piedmont obtains Lombardy from Austria; Parma, Modena, Tuscany, and Romagna vote to join with Piedmont
1860	Garibaldi invades Kingdom of the Two Sicilies
March 17, 1861	Victor Emmanuel of Piedmont is proclaimed king of Italy
1866	Italy's alliance with Prussia against Austria results in annexation of Venetia by Italy
1870	Rome is incorporated into the Italian state and unity is achieved

bardy and Venetia in the north; and Hapsburg princes subservient to Austria ruled the duchies of Tuscany, Parma, and Modena. Piedmont in the northwest and the island of Sardinia were governed by an Italian dynasty, the House of Savoy. Besides these political divisions, Italy was divided economically and culturally. Throughout the peninsula, attachment to the local region was stronger than desire for national unity. Economic ties between north and south were weak; inhabitants of the northern Italian cities felt little closeness to Sicilian peasants. Except for the middle class, most Italians clung to the values of the Old Regime. Believing that society was ordered by God, they accepted without question rule by prince and pope and rejected the values associated with the French Revolution and the Enlightenment. To these traditionalists, national unity was also hateful. It would deprive the pope of his control over central Italy, introduce liberal ideas that would undermine clerical and aristocratic authority, and depose legitimate princes.

During the wars of the French Revolution,

France had occupied Italy. The French eliminated many barriers to trade among the Italian states. They built roads, which improved links between the various regions, and they introduced a standard system of law over most of the land. The French also gave the Italian states constitutions, representative assemblies, and the concept of the state as a community of citizens.

The Italian middle class believed that expelling foreign rulers and forging national unity would continue the process of enlightened reform initiated by the French occupation and that this process would promote economic growth. Merchants and manufacturers wanted to abolish taxes on goods transported from one Italian state to another; they wanted roads and railways built to link the peninsula together; and they wanted to do away with the numerous systems of coinage and weights and measures, which complicated business transactions. Italians who had served Napoleon as local officials, clerks, and army officers resisted the restoration of clerical and feudal privileges, which denied them career opportunities.

Through works of history and literature, an intellectual elite awakened interest in Italy's glorious past. It insisted that a people who had built the Roman Empire and produced the Renaissance must not remain weak and divided, their land occupied by Austrians. These sentiments appealed particularly to university students and the middle class. But the rural masses, illiterate and preoccupied with the hardships of daily life, had little concern for this struggle for national revival.

Failed Revolutions

Secret societies kept alive the hopes for liberty and independence from foreign rule in the period after 1815. The most important of these societies was the Carbonari, which had clubs in every state in Italy. In 1820, the Carbonari, its members drawn largely from the middle class and the army, enjoyed a few months of triumph in the Kingdom of the Two Sicilies. Supported by the army and militia, they forced King Ferdinand I to grant a constitution and a parliamentary government. But Metternich feared that the germ of revolution would spread to other countries. Supported by Prussia and Russia, Austria suppressed the constitutional government in Naples and another revolution, which broke out in Piedmont. In both cases, Austria firmly fixed an absolute ruler on the throne. In 1831–32, the Austrians suppressed another insurrection by the Carbonari, in the Papal States. During these uprisings, the peasants had given little support; indeed, they seemed to side with the traditional rulers.

After the failure of the Carbonari, a new generation of leaders emerged in Italy. One of them, Giuseppe Mazzini (1805–1872), dedicated his life to the creation of a united and republican Italy—a goal he pursued with extraordinary moral intensity and determination. Mazzini was both a romantic and a liberal. As a liberal, he fought for republican and constitutional government and held that national unity would enhance individual liberty. As a romantic, he sought truth through heightened feeling and intuition and believed that an awakened Italy would lead to the regeneration of humanity. Mazzini believed that just as Rome had provided law and unity in the ancient world, and the Roman pope had led Latin Christendom during

the Middle Ages, so a third Rome, a newly united Italy, would usher in a new age of free nations, personal liberty, and equality. This era would represent great progress for humanity: peace, prosperity, and universal happiness would replace conflict, materialism, and self-interest. Given to religious mysticism, Mazzini saw a world of independent states founded on nationality, republicanism, and democracy as the fulfillment of God's plan.

After his release from prison for participating in the insurrection of 1831, Mazzini went into exile and founded a new organization, Young Italy. Consisting of dedicated revolutionaries, many of them students, Young Italy was intended to serve as the instrument for the awakening of Italy and the transformation of Europe into a brotherhood of free peoples.

Mazzini believed that a successful revolution must come from below—from the people, moved by a profound love for their nation. They must overthrow the Hapsburg princes and create a democratic republic. The Carbonari had failed, he said, because they had staged only local uprisings and had no overall plan for the liberation and unification of Italy. This could be achieved only by a revolution of the masses. Mazzini had great charisma, determination, courage, and eloquence; he was also a prolific writer. His idealism attracted the intelligentsia and youth and kept alive the spirit of national unity. He infused the *Risorgimento,* the movement for Italian unity, with spiritual intensity.

Mazzini's plans for a mass uprising against Austria and the princes failed. In 1834, a band of Mazzini's followers attempted to invade Savoy. But everything went wrong, and the invasion collapsed. Other setbacks occurred in 1837, 1841, and 1843–44. During the revolutions of 1848, however, Italian liberal-nationalists enjoyed initial successes. In Sicily, revolutionaries forced King Ferdinand to grant a liberal constitution. The rulers of Tuscany and Piedmont-Sardinia promised constitutions. After five days of fighting, revolutionaries drove the Austrians out of Milan in Lombardy. The Austrians were also forced to evacuate Venice, where a republic was proclaimed. The pope fled Rome, and Mazzini was elected to an executive office in a new Roman Republic. However, the forces of reaction, led by Hapsburg Austria, regained their courage and authority, and crushed the revolutionary movements one by one. French troops dissolved the infant Roman Republic and restored Pope Pius IX to power. Italy remained divided, and Austria still ruled the north.

Cavour and Victory over Austria

The failure of the revolutions of 1848 contained an obvious lesson: Mazzini's approach, an armed uprising by aroused masses, did not work because the masses were not committed to the nationalist cause and the revolutionaries were no match for the Austrian army. Italian nationalists now hoped that the Kingdom of Piedmont-Sardinia, ruled by an Italian dynasty, would expel the Austrians and lead the drive for unity. Count Camillo Benso di Cavour (1810–1861), the chief minister of Piedmont-Sardinia, became the architect of Italian unity.

Unlike Mazzini, Cavour was neither a dreamer nor a speechmaker but a cautious and practical statesman who realized that mass uprisings could not succeed against Austrian might. Moreover, mistrusting the common people, he did not approve of Mazzini's goal of a democratic republic. Cavour had no precise plan for unifying Italy. His immediate aim was to increase the territory of Piedmont by driving the Austrians from northern Italy and incorporating Lombardy and Venetia into Piedmont-Sardinia. But this expulsion could not be accomplished without allies, for Austria was a great power and Piedmont a small state. To improve Piedmont's image in foreign affairs, Cavour launched a reform program to strengthen the economy. He reorganized the currency, taxes, and the national debt; in addition, he had railways and steamships built, fostered improved agricultural methods, and encouraged new businesses. Within a few years, Piedmont became a progressive modern state.

In 1855, Piedmont joined England and France in the Crimean War against Russia. Cavour had no quarrel with Russia but sought the friendship of Britain and France and a chance to be heard in world affairs. At the peace conference, Cavour was granted an opportunity to denounce Austria for occupying Italian lands.

After the peace conference, Cavour continued to encourage anti-Austrian feeling among Italians and to search for foreign support. He found a supporter in Napoleon III (1852–1870), the French emperor, who hoped that a unified northern Italy would become an ally and client of France.

In 1858, Cavour and Napoleon III reached a secret agreement. If Austria attacked Piedmont, France would aid the Italian state. Piedmont would annex Lombardy and Venetia and parts of the Papal States. In return, France would obtain Nice and Savoy from Piedmont. With this agreement in his pocket, Cavour cleverly maneuvered Austria into declaring war (he did so by strengthening Piedmont's army and urging volunteers from Austrian-controlled Lombardy to join it), for it had to appear that Austria was the aggressor.

Supported by French forces and taking advantage of poor Austrian planning, Piedmont conquered Lombardy and occupied Milan. But Napoleon III quickly had second thoughts. If Piedmont took any of the pope's territory, French Catholics would blame their own leader. Even more serious was the fear that Prussia, suspicious of French aims, would aid Austria. For these reasons Napoleon III, without consulting Cavour, signed an armistice with Austria. Piedmont would acquire Lombardy, but no more. An outraged Cavour demanded that his state continue the war until all northern Italy was liberated, but King Victor Emmanuel of Piedmont accepted the Austrian peace terms.

The victory of Piedmont-Sardinia, however, proved greater than Cavour had anticipated. During the conflict, patriots in Parma, Modena, Tuscany, and Romagna (one of the Papal States) had seized power. These new revolutionary governments voted to join with Piedmont.

Garibaldi and Victory in the South

Piedmont's success spurred revolutionary activity in the Kingdom of the Two Sicilies. In the spring of 1860, some one thousand red-shirted adventurers and patriots led by Giuseppe Garibaldi (1807–1882) landed in Sicily. They were determined to liberate the land from its Bourbon ruler, and they succeeded.

An early supporter of Mazzini, Garibaldi had been forced to flee Italy to avoid arrest for his revolutionary activities. He spent thirteen years in South America, where he took part in revolutionary movements. There he learned the skills of the revolutionary's trade and toughened his body and will for the struggle that lay ahead.

Garibaldi held progressive views. He supported the liberation of all subject nationalities, female equality, the right of workers to organize, racial equality, and the abolition of capital punishment. But the cause of Italian national unity was his true religion. Whereas Cavour set his sights primarily on extending Piedmont's control over northern Italy, Garibaldi dedicated himself to the creation of a unified Italy.

Garibaldi returned to Italy just in time to fight in the revolution of 1848. He was a brilliant leader who captivated the hearts of the people and won the poor and illiterate to the cause of Italian nationality.

After the liberation of Sicily in 1860, Garibaldi invaded the mainland. He occupied Naples without a fight and prepared to advance on Rome. In this particular instance, Garibaldi's success confirmed Mazzini's belief that a popular leader could arouse the masses to heroic action.

Cavour feared that an assault on Rome by Garibaldi would lead to French intervention. Napoleon III had pledged to defend the pope's lands, and a French garrison had been stationed in Rome since 1849. Moreover, Cavour considered Garibaldi too impulsive and rash, too attracted to republican ideals, and too popular with the masses to lead the struggle for unification.

Cavour persuaded Napoleon III to approve an invasion of the Papal States by Piedmont to head off Garibaldi. A papal force offered only token opposition, and the Papal States of Umbria and the Marches soon voted for union with Piedmont, as did Naples and Sicily. Refusing to trade on his prestige with the masses to fulfill personal ambition, Garibaldi turned over his conquests to Piedmont's King Victor Emmanuel, who was declared king of Italy in 1861.

Italian Unification Completed

Two regions still remained outside the control of the new Italy: the city of Rome, ruled by the pope and protected by French troops; and Venetia, oc-

cupied by Austria. Cavour died in 1861, but the march toward unification continued. During the conflict between Prussia and Austria in 1866, Italy sided with the victorious Prussians and was rewarded with Venetia. During the Franco-Prussian War of 1870, France withdrew its garrisons from Rome; much to the anger of the pope, Italian troops marched in, and Rome was declared the capital of Italy.

Online Study Center **Improve Your Grade**
Interactive Map: The Unifications of Italy and Germany

THE UNIFICATION OF GERMANY

In 1848, German liberals and nationalists, believing in the strength of their ideals, naively underestimated the power of the conservative Old Order. After the failed revolution, some disenchanted revolutionaries retained only a halfhearted commitment to liberalism or embraced conservatism; others fled the country, weakening the liberal leadership. All liberals came to doubt the effectiveness of revolution as a way to transform Germany into a unified state; all gained new respect for the realities of power. Abandoning idealism for realism, liberals now thought that German unity would be achieved through Prussian arms, not liberal ideals.

Prussia, Agent of Unification

During the late seventeenth and eighteenth centuries, Prussian kings had fashioned a rigorously trained and disciplined army. The state bureaucracy, often staffed by ex-soldiers, perpetuated the military mentality. As the chief organizations in the state, the army and the bureaucracy drilled into the Prussian people a respect for discipline and authority.

The Prussian throne was supported by the Junkers. These powerful aristocrats, who owned vast estates farmed by serfs, were exempt from most taxes and dominated local government in their territories. The Junkers' commanding position made them officers in the royal army,

Chronology 25.2 ❖ Unification of Germany

1815	German Confederation is formed
1834	Zollverein is established under Prussian leadership
1848	Liberals fail to unify Germany
1862	Bismarck becomes chancellor of Prussia
1864	Austria and Prussia defeat Denmark in a war over Schleswig-Holstein
1866	Seven Weeks' War between Austria and Prussia: Prussia emerges as the dominant power in Germany and organizes the North German Confederation
1870–71	Franco-Prussian War
January 18, 1871	William I becomes German kaiser

diplomats, and leading officials in the state bureaucracy. The Junkers knew that a weakening of the king's power would lead to the loss of their own aristocratic prerogatives.

In France in the late 1700s, a powerful and politically conscious middle class had challenged aristocratic privileges. The Prussian monarchy and the Junkers had faced no such challenge, for the Prussian middle class at that time was small and ineffectual. The idea of individual rights did not deeply penetrate Prussian consciousness, nor did it undermine the Prussian tradition of obedience to military and state authority. Liberalism did not take firm root in Germany.

Reforms from Above. The reform movement that began after Napoleon completely routed the Prussians at Jena (in 1806) arose from distress at the military collapse and at the apathy of the Prussian population. High bureaucrats and military men demanded reforms that would draw the people closer to their country and king. These leaders had learned the great lesson of the French Revolution: a devoted citizen army fights more effectively than oppressed serfs. To imbue all classes with civic pride, the reformers abolished hereditary serfdom, gave the urban middle class a greater voice in city government, laid the foundations for universal education, and granted full citizenship to Jews. To improve the army's morale, they eliminated severe punishments and based promotions on performance rather than birth.

But the reformers failed to give Prussia a constitution and parliamentary institutions. The middle class still had no voice in the central government. Monarchical power persisted, and the economic, political, and military power of the Junkers remained unbroken. Thus, liberalism had an unpromising beginning in Prussia. In France, the bourgeoisie had instituted reforms based on the principles of liberty and equality; in Prussia, the bureaucracy introduced reforms to strengthen the state, not to promote liberty. A precedent had been established: reform in Prussia would come from conservative rulers, not from the efforts of a middle class aroused by liberal ideals.

In 1834, under Prussian leadership, the German states, with the notable exception of Austria, had established the *Zollverein*, a customs union, which abolished tariffs between the states. The customs union stimulated economic activity and promoted a desire for greater unity. Businessmen, particularly, felt that having thirty-nine states in Germany was an obstacle to economic progress. The Zollverein provided the economic foundations for the political unification of Germany, and it led many Germans to view Prussia, not Austria, as the leader of the unification movement.

Liberals' Failure. Influenced by the legacy of the French Revolution, the ideas of legal equality, political liberty, and careers open to talent found favor with the Prussian bourgeoisie. Like the French bourgeois of the Old Regime, Prussian

MAP 25.1 UNIFICATION OF GERMANY, 1866–1871 Between 1866 and 1871, Prussia fought wars against Denmark, Austria, and France, which resulted in the unification of Germany under Prussian leadership. Otto von Bismarck was the principal architect of German unification.

bankers, manufacturers, and lawyers hated a system that denied them social recognition and political influence but rewarded idle sons of the nobility with the best positions. They also denounced government regulations and taxes, which hampered business, and they loathed the rigorous censorship, which stifled free thought. Peasants and artisans, concerned with economic survival, respectful of

tradition, and suspicious of new ideas, did not identify with liberal principles.

During the revolution of 1848, liberals failed to wrest power from the monarchy and aristocracy and create a unified Germany. Frederick William IV (1840–1861) had refused the crown offered him by the Frankfurt Assembly. The Prussian monarch could not stomach German unity created by a revolution of commoners. But a German union fashioned and headed by a conservative Prussia was different and proved attractive to the Prussian monarchy.

Bismarck and the Road to Unity

Before Prussia could extend its hegemony over the other German states, Austrian influence in German affairs would have to be eliminated. This was one reason why William I (1861–1888) called for a drastic reorganization of the Prussian army. But the liberals in the lower chamber of the Prussian parliament blocked passage of the army reforms, for they feared that the reforms would greatly increase the power of the monarchy and the military establishment. Unable to secure passage, William withdrew the reform bill and asked the lower chamber for additional funds to cover government expenses. When Parliament granted these funds, he used the money to institute the army reforms. Learning from its mistake, the lower chamber would not approve the new budget in 1862 without an itemized breakdown.

A conflict had arisen between the liberal majority in the lower chamber and the crown. If the liberals won, they would, in effect, establish parliamentary control over the king and the army. At this critical hour, King William asked Otto von Bismarck (1815–1898) to lead the battle against Parliament.

Descended on his father's side from an old aristocratic family, Bismarck was a staunch supporter of the Prussian monarchy and the Junker class and a devout patriot. He yearned to increase the territory and prestige of his beloved Prussia and to protect the authority of the Prussian king, who, Bismarck believed, ruled by the grace of God. Liberals were outraged by Bismarck's domineering and authoritarian manner and his determination to preserve monarchical power and the aristocratic order. Set on continuing the reorganization of the army and determined not to bow to parliamentary pressure, Bismarck ordered the collection of taxes without Parliament's approval—an action that would have been unthinkable in Britain or the United States.

When the lower chamber continued to withhold funds, Bismarck dismissed the chamber, imposed strict censorship on the press, arrested outspoken liberals, and fired liberals from the civil service. The liberals protested against these arbitrary and unconstitutional moves, but they did not use force. Since the army fully supported the government and there was no significant popular support for challenging the government, an armed uprising would have failed. What led to a resolution of the conflict was Bismarck's extraordinary success in foreign affairs.

Online Study Center

Improve Your Grade
Primary Source: The Dual Monarchy Is Born: The Austro-Hungarian Ausgleich

Wars with Denmark and Austria. To Bismarck, a war between Austria and Prussia seemed inevitable, for only by removing Austria from German affairs could Prussia extend its dominion over the other German states. Bismarck's first move, however, was not against Austria but against Denmark. The issue that led to the war in 1864 was enormously complex. Simplified, the issue was that Bismarck (and German nationalists) wanted to free the two duchies of Schleswig and Holstein from Danish control. Both territories, which contained a large number of Germans, had been administered by Denmark, but in 1863 Schleswig was incorporated into the Danish realm. Hoping to prevent Prussia from annexing the territories, Austria joined Prussia as an ally. After Denmark's defeat, Austria and Prussia tried to decide the disposition of the territories. Bismarck used the dispute to goad Austria into war. The Austrians, on their side, were convinced that Prussia must be defeated for Austria to retain its influence over German affairs.

In the Austro-Prussian war of 1866, Prussia, with astonishing speed, assembled its forces and overran Austrian territory. At the battle of Sadowa (or Königgrätz), Prussia decisively defeated the main Austrian forces and the Seven Weeks' War ended. Prussia took no territory from Austria, but the latter agreed to Prussia's annexation of Schleswig and Holstein and a number of small German states. Prussia, moreover, organized

WILLIAM I OF PRUSSIA. German emperor, in the Hall of Mirrors at Versailles (1871). (*The Mansell Collection.*)

a confederation of North German states, from which Austria was excluded. In effect, Austria was removed from German affairs, and Prussia became the dominant power in Germany.

The Triumph of Nationalism and Conservatism over Liberalism. The Prussian victory had a profound impact on political life within Prussia. Bismarck was the man of the hour, the great hero who had extended Prussia's power. Most liberals forgave Bismarck for his authoritarian handling of Parliament. The liberal press, which had previously denounced Bismarck for running roughshod over the constitution, now li-

onized him. Prussians were urged to concentrate on the glorious tasks ahead and put aside the constitutional struggle, which, in contrast, appeared petty and insignificant.

Bismarck recognized the great appeal of nationalism and used it to expand Prussia's power over other German states and strengthen Prussia's voice in European affairs. By heralding his state as the champion of unification, Bismarck gained the support of nationalists throughout Germany. In the past, the nationalist cause had belonged to the liberals, but Bismarck appropriated it to promote Prussian expansion and conservative rule.

OTTO VON BISMARCK BY FRANZ VON LENBACH. Bismarck (1815–1899), the Iron Chancellor, was instrumental in unifying Germany. A conservative, he resisted Parliament's efforts to weaken the monarch's power. (*Bayerische Staatsgemaldesammungen, Munich.*)

Prussia's victory over Austria, therefore, was a triumph for conservatism and nationalism and a defeat for liberalism. The liberal struggle for constitutional government in Prussia collapsed. The Prussian monarch retained the right to override parliamentary opposition and act on his own initiative. In 1848, Prussian might had suppressed a liberal revolution; in 1866, liberals, beguiled by Bismarck's military triumphs, gave up the struggle for responsible parliamentary government. They had traded political freedom for Prussian military glory and power.

The capitulation of Prussian liberals demonstrated the essential weakness of the German liberal tradition. German liberals displayed diminishing commitment to the principles of parliamentary government and growing fascination with power, military triumph, and territorial expansion. Bismarck's words, written in 1858, turned out to be prophetic: "Exalt his self-esteem toward foreigners and the Prussian forgets whatever bothers him about conditions at home."[1] The liberal dream of a united Germany had been preempted by conservatives. Enthralled by Bismarck's achievement, many liberals abandoned liberalism and threw their support behind the authoritarian Prussian state. And Germans of all classes acquired an adoration for Prussian militarism and for the power state, with its machiavellian guideline that all means are justified if they result in the expansion of German power. In 1848, German liberals had called for "Unity and Freedom." What Bismarck gave them was unity and authoritarianism.

War with France. Prussia emerged from the war with Austria as the leading power in the North German Confederation; the Prussian king controlled the armies and foreign affairs of the states within the confederation. To complete the unification of Germany, Bismarck would have to draw the South German states into the new confederation. But the South German states, Catholic and hostile to Prussian authoritarianism, feared being absorbed by Prussia. Bismarck hoped that a war between Prussia and France would ignite the nationalist feelings of the South Germans, causing them to overlook the differences that separated them from Prussia.

Napoleon III, the emperor of France, was not averse to war either. The creation of a powerful North German Confederation had frightened the French, and the prospect that the South German states might one day add their strength to the new Germany was terrifying. Both France and Prussia had parties that advocated war.

A cause for war arose over the succession to the vacated Spanish throne. King William of Prussia. discussed the issue with the French ambassador and sent Bismarck a telegram informing him of what had ensued. With the support of high military leaders, Bismarck edited the telegram. The revised version gave the impression that the Prussian king and the French ambassador had insulted each other. Bismarck wanted to inflame French feeling against Prussia and arouse German opinion against France. He succeeded. In both Paris and

Berlin, crowds of people, gripped by war fever, demanded satisfaction. When France declared a general mobilization, Prussia followed suit; Bismarck had his war.

As Bismarck had anticipated, the South German states came to the aid of Prussia. Quickly and decisively routing the French forces and capturing Napoleon III, the Prussians went on to besiege Paris. Faced with starvation, Paris surrendered in January 1871. France was compelled to pay a large indemnity and to cede to Germany the border provinces of Alsace and Lorraine—a loss that French patriots could never accept.

The Franco-Prussian War completed the unification of Germany. On January 18, 1871, at Versailles, the German princes granted the title of German kaiser (emperor) to William I. A powerful nation had arisen in central Europe. Its people were educated, disciplined, and efficient; its industries and commerce were rapidly expanding; its army was the finest in Europe. Vigorous, confident, and intensely nationalistic, the new German Empire would be eager to play a greater role in world affairs. No nation in Europe was a match for the new Germany. Metternich's fears had been realized: a Germany dominated by Prussia had upset the balance of power. The unification of Germany created fears, tensions, and rivalries that would culminate in world wars.

THE HAPSBURG EMPIRE

In Italy and Germany, nationalism had led to the creation of unified states; in Austria, nationalism eventually caused the destruction of the centuries-old Hapsburg dynasty. A mosaic of different nationalities, each with its own history and traditions, the Austrian Empire could not survive in an age of intense nationalism. England and France had succeeded in unifying peoples of different ethnic backgrounds, but they did so during the Middle Ages, when ethnic consciousness was still rudimentary. The Austrian Empire, in contrast, had to weld together and reconcile antagonistic nationalities when nationalistic consciousness was high. The empire's collapse in the final stages of World War I was the culmination of years of antagonism among its different peoples.

In the first half of the nineteenth century, the Germans, constituting less than one-quarter of the population, were the dominant national group in the empire. But Magyars, Poles, Czechs, Slovaks, Croats, Romanians, Ruthenians, and Italians were experiencing national self-awareness. Poets and writers who had been educated in Latin, French, and German began to write in their mother tongues and extol their splendors. By searching their past for glorious ancestors and glorious deeds, writers kindled pride in their native histories and folklore and aroused anger against past and present injustices.

In 1848–49, the Hapsburg monarchy had extinguished the Magyar bid for independence, the Czech revolution in Prague, and the uprisings in the Italian provinces of Lombardy and Venetia. Greatly alarmed by these revolutions, the Austrian power structure resolved to resist pressures for political rights by strengthening autocracy and tightening the central bureaucracy. German and Germanized officials took over administrative and judicial duties formerly handled on a local level. An expanded secret police stifled liberal and nationalist expressions. The various nationalities, of course, resented these efforts at centralization and repression.

The defeats by France and Piedmont in 1859 and by Prussia in 1866 cost Austria its two Italian provinces. The defeat by Prussia also forced the Hapsburg monarchy to make concessions to the Magyars, the strongest of the non-German nationalities; for without a loyal Hungary, the Hapsburg monarchy could suffer other humiliations. The Settlement of 1867 split the Hapsburg territories into Austria and Hungary. The two countries retained a common ruler, Francis Joseph (1848–1916), who was emperor of Austria and king of Hungary. Hungary gained complete control over its internal affairs: the administration of justice and education. Foreign and military affairs, as well as common financial concerns, were dealt with by a ministry consisting of delegates from both lands.

With the Settlement of 1867, Magyars and Germans became the dominant nationalities in the empire. The other nationalities felt that the German-Magyar political, economic, and cultural domination blocked their own national aspirations. Nationality struggles in the half-century

THE YOUNG CZECH PARTY DEMONSTRATING IN THE AUSTRIAN PARLIAMENT
(1900). The Hapsburg Empire was burdened by conflicts between its different
nationalities. In Bohemia, Czechs and Germans often engaged in violent confrontations as Czechs pressed for recognition of their language and rights. (*Os-
terreichische Nationalbibliothek.*)

following the Settlement of 1867 consumed the
energies of the Austrians and Hungarians. In both
lands, however, the leaders failed to solve the
problem of minorities, a failure that helped pre-
cipitate World War I and led to the dissolution of
the empire during the last weeks of the war.

THE RISE OF RACIAL NATIONALISM

In the first half of the nineteenth century, nationalism and liberalism went hand in hand. Liberals
sought both the rights of the individual and national independence and unification. Liberal nationalists believed that a unified state free of foreign subjugation was in harmony with the
principle of natural rights, and they insisted that
love of country led to love of humanity. "With all
my ardent love of my nation," said Francis

Palacky, a Czech patriot, "I always esteem more
highly the good of mankind and of learning than
the good of the nation."[2] Addressing the Slavs,
Mazzini declared: "We who have ourselves arisen
in the name of our national right, believe in your
right, and offer to help you to win it. But the purpose of our mission is the permanent and peaceful
organization of Europe."[3] Liberals expected that
nationalism would unite a people in freedom and
fellowship, foster a national cultural flowering,
and promote idealism by leading people to set
aside personal concerns for the good of the nation.
They did not anticipate the emergence of an extreme nationalism that would subvert liberal values. The extreme nationalism of the late nineteenth
and early twentieth centuries contributed to World
War I and to the rise of fascism after the war. It
was the seedbed of totalitarian nationalism.

Concerned exclusively with the greatness of
the nation, extreme nationalists rejected the liberal emphasis on political liberty. Liberals re-

garded the state as a community of individuals voluntarily bonded by law and citizenship and entitled to the same rights. To extreme nationalists, however, the state was the highest development of a folkish-racial spirit inherited from their ancestors. In their eyes, profound and irreconcilable differences separated "their people" from those who did not share this ancestry. Even if they had dwelled in the land for centuries, such people were seen as dangerous aliens. Increasingly, they attacked parliamentary government as a barrier to national unity and greatness and maintained that authoritarian leadership was needed to meet national emergencies. The needs of the nation, they said, transcended the rights of the individual. Extreme nationalists also rejected the liberal ideal of equality. Placing the nation above everything, nationalists accused national minorities of corrupting the nation's spirit. In the name of national power and unity, they persecuted minorities at home and stirred up hatred against other nations. And they also glorified war as a symbol of the nation's resolve and will. At the founding of the Nationalist Association in Italy in 1910, one leader declared:

> Just as socialism teaches the proletariat the value of class struggle, so we must teach Italy the value of international struggle. But international struggle is war? Well, then, let there be war! And nationalism will arouse the will for a victorious war, . . . the only way to national redemption.[4]

Interpreting politics with the logic of emotions, extreme nationalists insisted that they had a sacred mission to regain lands once held in the Middle Ages, to unite with their kinfolk in other lands, or to rule over peoples considered inferior. They organized patriotic societies, denounced national minorities, particularly Jews, and created a cult of ancestors and a mystique of blood, soil, and a sacred national past. In these ancestral traditions and attachments, the nationalists found a higher reality akin to religious truth. Loyalty to the nation-state was elevated above all other allegiances. The ethnic state became an object of religious reverence; spiritual energies formerly

dedicated to Christianity were now channeled into the worship of the nation-state, igniting primitive, dark, cruel feelings. In 1902, Friedrich Paulsen, a German philosopher, warned of the threat that nationalism posed to reason and morality:

> A supersensitive nationalism has become a very serious danger for all the peoples of Europe; because of it, they are in danger of losing the feeling for human values. Nationalism, pushed to an extreme, just like sectarianism, destroys moral and even logical consciousness. Just and unjust, good and bad, true and false, lose their meaning; what men condemn as disgraceful and inhuman when done by others, they recommend in the same breath to their own people as something to be done to a foreign country.[5]

By the beginning of the twentieth century, conservatives had become the staunchest advocates of nationalism, and the nationalism preached by conservative extremists was stripped of Mazzinian ideals of liberty, equality, and the fellowship of nations. In Germany landholding aristocrats, generals, and clergy, often joined by big industrialists, saw nationalism as a convenient instrument for gaining a mass following in their struggle against democracy, social reform, and socialism. Championing popular nationalist myths and dreams and citing Social Darwinist doctrines, a newly radicalized right, dominated by the elite of German society, hoped to harness the instinctual energies of the masses, particularly the peasants and the lower middle class—shopkeepers, civil servants, and white-collar workers—to conservative causes. Peasants viewed liberalism and a godless Marxism as threats to traditional values, while the lower bourgeoisie feared the power of the organized proletariat. These people were receptive to the rhetoric of ultranationalists, who denounced democracy and Marxism as threats to national unity and Jews as aliens who endangered the nation. Nationalism was presented as a victory of idealism over materialism and as the subordination of class and personal interests to the general good of the nation.

Volkish Thought

Extreme nationalism was a general European phenomenon, but it was especially dangerous in Germany. Bismarck's triumphs lured Germans into a dream world. Many started to yearn for the extension of German power throughout the globe. The past, they said, belonged to France and Britain; the future, to Germany.

The most ominous expression of German nationalism (and a clear example of mythical thinking) was **Volkish thought.**[6] (*Volk* means "folk" or "people.") German Volkish thinkers sought to bind together the German people through a deep love of their language, traditions, and fatherland. These thinkers felt that Germans were animated by a higher spirit than that found in other peoples. To Volkish thinkers, the Enlightenment and parliamentary democracy were foreign ideas that corrupted the pure German spirit. With fanatical devotion, Volkish thinkers embraced all things German: the medieval past, the German landscape, the simple peasant, and the village. They denounced the liberal-humanist tradition of the West as alien to the German soul.

Among the shapers of the Volkish outlook was Wilhelm von Riehl (1823–1897), a professor at the University of Munich. He contrasted the artificiality of modern city life with the unspoiled existence in the German countryside. Berthold Auerbach (1812–1882) glorified the peasant as the ideal German. Paul de Lagarde (1827–1891), a professor of Oriental languages, called for a German faith, different from Christianity, that would unite the nation; he saw the Jews as enemies of Germany. Julius Langbehn (1851–1907) lauded a mystical and irrational life force as superior to reason and held that the Jews corrupted the German spirit.

Volkish thought attracted Germans frightened by all the complexities of the modern age: industrialization, urbanization, materialism, class conflicts, and alienation. Seeing their beloved Germany transformed by these forces of modernity, Volkish thinkers yearned to restore the sense of community, the spiritual unity, that they attributed to the preindustrial age. Only by identifying with their sacred soil and sacred traditions could modern Germans escape from the evils of industrial society. Only then could the different classes band together in an organic unity.

The Volkish movement had little support from the working class, which was concerned chiefly with improving its standard of living. It appealed mainly to farmers and villagers, who regarded the industrial city as a threat to native values and a catalyst for foreign ideas; to artisans and small shopkeepers, threatened by big business; and to scholars, writers, teachers, and students, who saw in Volkish nationalism a cause worthy of their idealism. The schools were leading agents for the dissemination of Volkish ideas.

Volkish thinkers looked back longingly to the Middle Ages, which they viewed as a period of social and spiritual harmony and reverence for national traditions. They also glorified the ancient Germanic tribes that overran the Roman Empire; they contrasted their courageous and vigorous German ancestors with the effete and degenerate Romans. A few tried to harmonize ancient Germanic religious traditions with Christianity.

Such attitudes led Germans to see themselves as a heroic people fundamentally different from and better than the English and French. It also led them to regard German culture as unique—innately superior to and, indeed, contravening the humanist outlook of the Enlightenment. Like their romantic predecessors, Volkish thinkers claimed that the German people and culture had a special destiny and a unique mission. They pitted the German soul against the Western intellect—feeling, intuition, spirit, and idealism against a drab rationalism. To be sure, the Western humanist tradition had many supporters in Germany, but the counterideology of Volkish thought was becoming increasingly widespread. This murky, irrational, radical nationalist, and antiliberal outlook shaped by these Volkish thinkers in the late nineteenth century would later undermine support for the democratic Weimar Republic established in Germany after World War I and provide Hitler with receptive listeners. Many of Hitler's supporters hoped that he would transform these Volkish longings into political realities.

Racist doctrines had a special appeal for Volkish thinkers. Racist ideologues saw race as the key to history. They maintained that not only physical features but also moral, esthetic, and intellectual qualities distinguished one race from another. In their view, a race demonstrated its vigor and achieved greatness when it preserved its purity; intermarriage between races was contamination that would result in genetic, cultural, and military decline. Unlike liberals, who held that anyone who accepted German law was a member of the German nation, racists argued that a person's nationality was a function of his or her "racial soul" or "blood."

Like their Nazi successors, Volkish thinkers claimed that the German race was purer than, and therefore superior to, all other races. Its superiority was revealed in such physical characteristics as blond hair, blue eyes, and fair skin: all signs of inner qualities lacking in other races. German racists claimed that Germans were the purest descendants of the ancient Aryans.* They held that the Aryans were a superior race and the creators of European civilization and that the Germans had inherited their superior racial qualities.

Volkish thinkers embraced the ideas of Houston Stewart Chamberlain (1855–1927), an Englishman whose fascination with Germanism led him to adopt German citizenship. In *The Foundations of the Nineteenth Century* (1899), Chamberlain asserted in pseudoscientific fashion that races differed not only physically but also morally, spiritually, and intellectually, and that the struggle between races was the driving force of history. He attributed Rome's decline to the dilution of its racial qualities through the intermixing of races. The blond, blue-eyed, long-skulled Germans, possessing the strongest strain of Aryan blood and distinguished by an inner spiritual depth, were the true ennoblers of humanity— both physically superior and bearers of a higher culture. Chamberlain denied that Christ was a Jew, saying that he was of Aryan stock. As agents of a spiritually empty capitalism and divisive liberalism, the Jews, said Chamberlain, were undermining German society. Materialistic, cowardly, and devious, they were the very opposite of the idealistic, heroic, and faithful Germans. Cham-

berlain's book was enormously popular in Germany. It was required reading in German schools and military academies, and Pan-German and other Volkish-nationalist organizations frequently cited it. Kaiser William II called *Foundations* a "Hymn to Germanism" and read it to his children.

Chamberlain's racist and anti-Semitic views make him a spiritual forerunner of Nazism, and he was praised as such by Alfred Rosenberg, the leading Nazi racial theorist in the early days of Hitler's movement. Joseph Goebbels, the Nazi propagandist, hailed Chamberlain as a "pathbreaker" and "pioneer" after meeting him in 1926. In 1923, Chamberlain, then sixty-eight years old, met Hitler, whose movement was still in its formative stage. Chamberlain subsequently praised Hitler as the savior of the Reich, and Hitler visited Chamberlain on his deathbed and attended his funeral.

German racial nationalists insisted that Germany had a unique mission; as a superior race, Germans had a right to dominate other peoples, particularly the "racially inferior" Slavs of eastern Europe. The Pan-German Association, whose membership included professors, schoolteachers, journalists, lawyers, and aristocrats, spread racial and nationalist theories and glorified war as an expression of national vitality. A statement from the association's journal sums up its philosophy:

> The racial-biological ideology tells us that there are races that lead and races that follow. Political history is nothing but the history of struggles among the leading races. Conquests, above all, are always the work of the leading races. Such men can conquer, may conquer, and shall conquer.[7]

Anti-Semitism: The Power and Danger of Mythical Thinking

German racial nationalists singled out Jews as a wicked race and a deadly enemy of the German people. **Anti-Semitism,** widespread in late-nineteenth-century Europe, affords a striking example of the perennial appeal, power, and danger of mythical thinking—of elevating to the level of ob-

---

*The Aryans emerged some four thousand years ago, probably between the Caspian Sea and India. An Aryan tongue became the basis of most European languages. Intermingling with others, the Aryans lost their identity as a people.

jective truth ideas that have no basis in fact but provide all-encompassing, emotionally satisfying explanations of life and history. By manufacturing the myth of the wicked Jew, the radical right confirmed the insight proffered by the political theorist Georges Sorel: people are moved and united by myths that offer simple, clear, and emotionally gratifying resolutions to the complexities of the modern world. Anti-Semitic organizations and political parties sought to deprive Jews of their civil rights, and anti-Semitic publications proliferated. The radical right saw Jew-hatred as a popular formula for mobilizing and uniting all social classes—a precondition for strengthening the nation and subverting liberal democracy.

In 1886, Edouard Drumont, a French journalist, published *Jewish France,* which argued that the Jews, racially inferior and believers in a primitive religion, had gained control of France. The book sold more than a million copies. Drumont blamed the Jews for introducing capitalism, materialism, and greed into France. Like medieval Christian anti-Semites, Drumont accused Jews of murdering God and of using the blood of slaughtered Christian children for ritual purposes. (In rural France, the accusation of ritual murder, a deranged survival of the Middle Ages, still persisted, at times fomented by the clergy.) French politicians played the anti-Semitic card in order to gain popularity and votes. Fully one-third of the Chamber of Deputies wanted to deprive Jews of the civil rights that they had gained during the French Revolution. During the anti-Semitic outbursts accompanying the Dreyfus affair (see Chapter 26) when the French right was shouting "Death to the Jews," Drumont's newspaper (founded with Jesuit funds) tried to inflame public opinion with sensational polemics against the Jews. It blamed all the ills of France on the Jews, called for their expulsion from the country, and predicted that they would be massacred.

Romania barred most Jews from holding office and from voting, imposed various economic restrictions on them, and limited their admission into secondary schools and universities. The Romanian government even financed an international congress of anti-Semites, which met in Bucharest in 1886.

Russia placed a quota on the number of Jewish students admitted to secondary schools and higher educational institutions, confined Jews to certain regions of the country, and, "to purify the sacred historic capital," expelled around twenty thousand Jews from Moscow. Some government officials encouraged and even organized *pogroms* (mob violence) against Jews. Between 1903 and 1906, pogroms broke out in 690 towns and villages, most of them in the Ukraine, traditionally a hotbed of anti-Semitism. (Ukrainian folk songs and legends glorified centuries-old massacres of Jews.) The attackers looted, burned, raped, and murdered, generally with impunity. In Russia, and several other lands, Jews were put on trial for the old libel of ritual murder.

In Germany and Austria, hatred of the Jews developed into a systematic body of beliefs. As the historian Hans Kohn says, "Germany became the fatherland of modern anti-Semitism; there the systems were thought out and the slogans coined. German literature was the richest in anti-Jewish writing."[8] Like conservatives in other lands, German conservatives deliberately fanned the flames of anti-Semitism to win the masses over to conservative causes. The Christian Social Workers' party, founded in 1878 by Adolf Stöcker, a prominent Protestant preacher, engaged in anti-Semitic agitation in order to recruit the lower bourgeoisie to the cause of the Protestant church and the Prussian monarchy. In German-speaking Austria, Karl Lueger, a leader of the Christian Social party, founded by conservative German nationalists, exploited anti-Semitism to win elections in overwhelmingly Catholic Vienna. Georg von Schönerer, founder of the German National party in Austria, wanted to eliminate Jews from all areas of public life.

Anti-Semitism and the success of the Italians, Germans, Serbians, and others in achieving political independence stirred nationalist feelings among Jews. Jewish nationalism took the form of **Zionism**—a movement advocating the return of Jews to Palestine, their historic homeland. A key figure in the emergence of Zionism was Theodor Herzl (1860–1904), an Austrian journalist, who was horrified by the anti-Semitism he witnessed in Paris during the Dreyfus trial. In *The Jewish State* (1896), he argued that the creation of a Jewish state was the best solution to the Jewish question.

THEODOR HERZL. Theodor Herzl is regarded as the founder of Zionism, the movement which called for Jews, the victims of persecution, to dwell once again in their ancient homeland. (*Corbis-Bettmann.*)

We are a people—one people. We have honestly endeavored to merge ourselves in the social life of surrounding communities and to preserve only the faith of our fathers. We are not permitted to do so. In vain are we loyal patriots . . . ; in vain do we strive to increase the fame of our native land in science and art, or her wealth by trade and commerce. In countries where we have lived for centuries we are still cried down as strangers . . . I think we shall not be left in peace. . . . [O]ld prejudices against us still lie deep in the hearts of people. . . . I say that we cannot hope for a change in the current . . . feeling. . . . The nations in whose midst Jews live are all either covertly or openly Anti-Semitic. . . . Palestine is our ever-memorable historic home. The very name of Palestine would attract our people with a force of marvellous potency.[9]

In 1897, in Switzerland, the first Zionist World Congress called for the establishment of a Jewish homeland in Palestine, which was then a province of the Ottoman Empire.

Anti-Semitism had a long and bloodstained history in Europe, stemming both from an irrational fear and hatred of outsiders with noticeably different ways and from the commonly accepted myth that the Jews as a people were collectively and eternally cursed for rejecting Christ. Christians saw Jews as the murderers of Christ—an image that provoked terrible anger and hatred.

During the Middle Ages, people believed and spread incredible tales about Jews. They accused Jews of torturing and crucifying Christian children in order to use their blood for religious ceremonies, poisoning wells to kill Christians, worshiping the Devil, and organizing a secret government that conspired to destroy Christianity. Jews were thought to be physically different from other people; they were said to have tails, horns, and a distinctive odor. Serving to propagate this myth was the decision of the Fourth Lateran Council (1215), which required Jews to wear a distinguishing mark on their clothing.

Although some medieval popes and bishops condemned these fables and sought to protect Jews from mob violence, the lower clergy and popular preachers spread the tales to the receptive masses. Periodically, mobs humiliated, tortured, and massacred Jews, and rulers expelled them from their kingdoms. Often barred from owning land and excluded from the craft guilds, medieval Jews concentrated in trade and moneylending—occupations that frequently earned them greater hostility. By the sixteenth century, Jews in a number of lands were forced by law to live in separate quarters of the town, called *ghettos*. Medieval Christian anti-Semitism, which depicted the Jew as vile and Judaism as repulsive, fertilized the soil for modern anti-Semitism.

In the nineteenth century, under the aegis of the liberal ideals of the Enlightenment and the French Revolution, Jews gained legal equality in most European lands. They could leave the ghetto, vote, hold offices, and participate in many activities that had been closed to them. Traditionally an urban people, the Jews, who were concentrated in the leading cities of Europe, took advantage of this new freedom and opportunity. Motivated by the fierce desire of outsiders to prove their worth and aided by deeply embedded traditions that valued education and family life, many Jews achieved striking success as entrepre-

THE PROTOCOLS OF THE ELDERS OF ZION. This infamous forgery, commissioned by the Russian secret police, became an international bestseller and contributed to outrages against Jews. Anti-Semitic organizations continue to publish and circulate it today. The picture is the actual cover of a French edition of the *Protocols,* c. 1934. (*The Wiener Library, London.*)

neurs, bankers, lawyers, journalists, doctors, scientists, scholars, and performers. For example, in 1880, Jews, who constituted about 10 percent of the Viennese population, accounted for 38.6 percent of the medical students and 23.3 percent of the law students in Vienna. Viennese cultural life before World War I was to a large extent shaped by Jewish writers, artists, musicians, critics, and patrons. All but one of the major banking houses were Jewish. By the early 1930s, German Jews, who constituted less than 1 percent of the population, accounted for 10.9 percent of the doctors, 10.7 percent of the dentists, 5.1 percent of the ed-

itors and authors, and 16.3 percent of the lawyers. Thirty percent of the Nobel Prize winners in Germany were Jews.

But most European Jews—peasants, peddlers, and laborers—were quite poor. Perhaps five thousand to six thousand Jews of Galicia in Austria-Hungary died of starvation annually, and many Russian Jews fled to the United States to escape from desperate poverty. But the anti-Semites saw only "Jewish influence," "Jewish manipulation," and "Jewish domination." Aggravating anti-Semitism among Germans was the flight of thousands of Russian Jews into Austria and Germany. Poor, speaking Yiddish, a form of medieval German that sounded peculiar to nineteenth-century Germans, and having noticeably different customs, these Jews triggered primitive fears and hates among Germans.

Like other bourgeois, the Jews who were members of the commercial and professional classes gravitated toward liberalism. Moreover, as victims of persecution, they naturally favored societies that were committed to the liberal ideals of legal equality, toleration, the rule of law, and equality of opportunity. As strong supporters of parliamentary government and the entire system of values associated with the Enlightenment, the Jews became targets for those conservatives and Volkish thinkers, who repudiated the humanist and cosmopolitan outlook of liberalism and professed a militant nationalism. To Volkish thinkers, the West represented an alien culture hostile to German racial-national identity, and the Jews, an alien race, symbolized the West. "Anti-Semitism was a manifestation of a rejection of the 'West' with which the Jews were identified," says the German historian Karl Dietrich Bracher, "because the Enlightenment and democracy were essential pre-conditions for their acceptance and progress."[10]

Anti-Semites invented a mythical evil to be blamed for all the social and economic ills caused by the rapid growth of industries and cities and for all the new ideas that were undermining the Old Order. Their anxieties and fears concentrated on the Jews, to whom they attributed everything they considered to be wrong with the modern age, all that threatened the German Volk.

The thought processes of Volkish anti-Semites demonstrate the mind's monumental capacity for self-delusion and irrational thinking. In the mythical world of Volkish thinkers, Jews were regarded

Richard Wagner

Richard Wagner (1813–1883), Germany's most important musical composer, was also instrumental in giving German nationalism an irrational component that contributed to its dangerousness. Wagner's immensely popular operas glorified ancient, pre-Christian Germanic myths and warriors and heroines. To many Germans, his operas, particularly the *Ring* cycle, represented true German idealism, a heroic spirit now corrupted by materialism and greed. This hoary Teutonic past bound Germans together and set them apart from other Europeans; the Enlightenment and parliamentary democracy, associated with France and Britain, were foreign ideas that corrupted the true German spirit. Wagner also promulgated Jew-hatred, a central doctrine of militant German nationalists, who regarded Jews as an alien and dangerous element in their midst.

In his *Judaism in Music*, first published in 1850 under a pseudonym and republished in 1869 under his own name, Wagner, who resented the fame of the Jewish composers Felix Mendelssohn (who had converted to Lutheranism) and Giacomo Meyerbeer, asserted that Jews debased German music. They could not possess nor express the feelings that animated the German soul; they had their own folk soul, which had been shaped by a degenerate cul-

Nationalarchive der Richard-Wagner-Stiftung/ Richard-Wagner-Gededkstatte, Bayreuth.

as foreign intruders who could never be loyal to the fatherland; as a lower form of humanity that could infect and weaken the German race and debase its culture; and as international conspirators who were plotting to dominate Germany and the world. That last accusation was an updated version of the medieval myth that Jews were plotting to destroy Christendom. In an extraordinary display of irrationality, Volkish thinkers held that Jews throughout the world were gaining control over political parties, the press, and the economy in order to dominate the planet.

The myth of a Jewish world conspiracy found its culminating expression in a notorious forgery, the *Protocols of the Elders of Zion*. The *Protocols*, written in France by someone in the service of the Russian secret police, sought to justify the tsarist regime's anti-Semitic policies. The forger concocted a tale of an alleged meeting of Jewish elders in the Jewish cemetery of Prague. In these eerie surroundings, the elders plot to take over the world. First published in Russia in 1903, the *Protocols* was widely distributed after World War I and widely

ture. Devoid of a creative imagination and concerned only with self-centered materialist pursuits, said Wagner, Jews were incapable of making a creative contribution to European culture. The German people, he stated, have "the most profound repugnance for the Jewish nature." And in the concluding passage of the essay, Wagner wrote: "There is only one possible way of redeeming the Jews from the terrible curse that hangs over them—annihilation."*

In later essays published in the Wagnerian journal, the *Bayreuther Blätter,* and in private correspondence and conversations, Wagner's anti-Semitism grew even more vitriolic and racist. "I hold the Jewish race to be the born enemy of pure humanity and everything noble in it. It is certain that it is running us Germans to the ground.** Wagner and his immediate circle, including his wife Cosima, reviled Judaism as a curse, considered Jews inferior, and maintained that they were taking over Germany. They frequently referred to Jews as vermin, bacilli, and lice, the very language that Nazi mass murderers would employ. Holding that aristic creativity was a function of ethnicity, Wagner saw Jews as the deadly opponent of the German spirit, the contaminators of the arts in Germany, and rejected their participation in the regeneration of the nation's culture, which he hoped to inspire. He also doubted that Jesus was Jewish and called for severing Christianity's relationship from its Jewish roots, believing that such a connection ruined it.

German anti-Semites regarded Wagner as their apostle: they sent him their anti-Semitic publications for approval and viewed the master's home as a shrine. A young Adolf Hitler was obsessed with Wagner's music, which he felt embodied the Germanic soul; it may have inspired him to believe that he was the man of destiny needed to regenerate Germany and save it from the Jews, whom Wagner accused of dominating the country. Wagner's family and disciples viewed Hitler as the savior of the German soul. Once in power, the Nazis utilized, for propaganda purposes, the music and words of Wagner, whom they unreservedly revered.

At the time that Wagner, and many other German intellectuals, were spreading their venomous anti-Semitic myths, Jews, who constituted less than one percent of Germany's population, considered themselves loyal German's, were devoted to German culture, and were making immense contributions to medicine, science, the arts, and commerce.

---

*Quoted in Jacob Katz, *The Darker Side of Genius: Richard Wagner's Anti-Semitism* (Hanover, NH: Brandeis University Press and University Press of New England, 1986), pp. 35–36.
**Ibid., p. 115.

believed. Influenced by the *Protocols,* Russian anti-Semites interpreted the Russian Revolution of 1917 as an attempt by Jews to subjugate Christian Russia. German anti-Semites regarded the *Protocols* as convincing evidence that the Jews were responsible for starting World War I, for Germany's defeat, and for the revolution that toppled the monarchy. Nazi propagandists exploited the *Protocols* to justify their quest for power. Even after the *Protocols* was exposed as a blatant forgery, it continued to be translated and distributed. For anti-Semites, the myth of a Jewish world-conspiracy had become an integrating principle; it provided satisfying answers to the crucial questions of existence.

In the Middle Ages, Jews had been persecuted and humiliated primarily for religious reasons. In the nineteenth century, national-racial considerations augmented the traditional, biased Christian perception of Jews and Judaism. Christian anti-Semites believed that, through conversion, Jews could escape the curse of their religion. Racial anti-Semites, however, used the language of Social Darwinism. They said that Jews belonged to a different species of the human race, that they were indelibly stained and eternally condemned by their biological makeup, and that their evilness and worthlessness derived from inherited racial characteristics, which could not be altered by conversion. As one anti-Semitic deputy stated in a speech before the German Reichstag (the lower chamber of the German parliament) in 1895,

> *If one designates the whole of Jewry, one does so in the knowledge that the racial qualities of this people are such that in the long run they cannot harmonize with the racial qualities of the Germanic peoples and that every Jew who at this moment has not done anything bad may nevertheless under the proper conditions do precisely that, because his racial qualities drive him to do it. . . . the Jews . . . operate like parasites . . . the Jews are cholera germs.*[11]

The Jewish population of Germany was quite small. In 1900, it was only about 497,000, or 0.95 percent of the total population of 50,626,000. Jews were proud of their many contributions to German economic and cultural life; they considered themselves patriotic Germans, relished German literature and music, and regarded Germany, a land of high civilization, as an altogether desirable place to live—a place of refuge in comparison with Russia, where Jews lived in terrible poverty and suffered violent attacks. German Jews, who felt that they already had a homeland, had little enthusiasm for Zionism.

German anti-Semitic organizations and political parties failed to get the state to pass anti-Semitic laws, and by the early 1900s, these groups had declined in political power and importance. But the mischief had been done. In the minds of many Germans, even in respectable circles, the image of the Jew as an evil and dangerous creature had been firmly planted. It was perpetuated by the schools, youth groups, the Pan-German Association, and an array of racist pamphlets and books. Late-nineteenth-century racial anti-Semites had constructed an ideological foundation on which Hitler would later build his movement. In words that foreshadowed Hitler, Paul de Lagarde said of the Jews: "One does not have dealings with pests and parasites; one does not rear them and cherish them; one destroys them as speedily and thoroughly as possible."[12]

It is, of course, absurd to believe that a nation of fifty million was threatened by a half-million citizens of Jewish birth, or that the eleven million Jews of the world (by 1900) had organized to rule the planet. The Jewish birthrate in Germany was low, the rate of intermarriage high, and the desire for complete assimilation into German life great. Within a few generations, the Jewish community in Germany might well have disappeared. Moreover, despite the paranoia of the anti-Semites, the German Jews and the Jews in the rest of Europe were quite powerless. There were scarcely any Jews in the ruling circles of governments, armies, civil services, or heavy industries. As events were to prove, the Jews, with no army or state and dwelling in lands where many despised them, were the weakest of peoples. But the race mystics, convinced that they were waging a war of self-defense against a satanic foe, were impervious to rational argument. Anti-Semites, said Theodor Mommsen, the great nineteenth-century German historian, would not listen to

> *logical and ethical arguments. . . . They listen only to their own envy and hatred, to the meanest instincts. Nothing else counts for them. They are deaf to reason, right, morals. One cannot influence them. . . . [Anti-Semitism] is a horrible epidemic, like cholera—one can neither explain nor cure it.*[13]

Racial nationalism, a major element in nineteenth-century intellectual life, attacked and undermined the Enlightenment tradition. Racial nationalists denied equality, scorned toleration, dismissed the idea of the oneness of humanity, and made myth and superstition vital forces in political life. They distorted reason and science to demonize and condemn an entire people and to justify humiliation and persecution. They presented a pathogenic racial ideology, fraught with unreason and hate, as something virtuous and idealistic. That many people, including the educated and the enlightened, accepted these racial doctrines was an ominous sign for Western civilization. It made plain the tenuousness of the rational tradition of the Enlightenment and showed how receptive the mind is to dangerous myths, and how easily human behavior can degenerate into inhumanity.

❖   ❖   ❖

Online Study Center ACE the Test

NOTES

1. Quoted in Otto Pflanze, *Bismarck and the De-velopment of Germany: The Period of Unification* (Princeton, N.J.: Princeton University Press, 1963), p. 232.

2. Quoted in Hans Kohn, *Pan-Slavism* (Notre Dame, Ind.: University of Notre Dame Press, 1953), pp. 66–67.

3. Quoted ibid., p. 44.

4. Cited in Edward R. Tannenbaum, *1900: The Generation Before the Great War* (Garden City, N.Y.: Doubleday, 1976), p. 337.

5. Quoted in Friedrich Meinecke, *The German Catastrophe* (Boston: Beacon Press, 1963), pp. 23–24.

6. This discussion is based largely on the works of George L. Mosse, particularly *The Crisis of German Ideology* (New York: Grosset & Dunlap Universal Library, 1964).

7. Cited in Horst von Maltitz, *The Evolution of Hitler's Germany* (New York: McGraw-Hill, 1973), p. 33.

8. Hans Kohn, *Nationalism: Its Meaning and History* (Princeton, N.J.: Van Nostrand, Anvil Books, 1955), p. 77.

9. Theodor Herzl, *The Jewish State* (New York: American Zionist Emergency Council, 1946), pp. 76–77, 85, 96.

10. Karl Dietrich Bracher, *The German Dictatorship*, trans. Jean Steinberg (New York: Praeger, 1970), p. 36.

11. Quoted in Raul Hilberg, *The Destruction of the European Jews* (Chicago: Quadrangle, 1967), pp. 10–11.

12. Quoted in Helmut Krausnick, Hans Buchheim, Martin Broszat, and Hans-Adolf Jacobsen, *Anatomy of the SS State,* trans. Richard Barry et al. (London: William Collins Sons, 1968), p. 9.

13. Quoted in Peter G. J. Pulzer, *The Rise of Political Anti-Semitism in Germany and Austria* (New York: Wiley, 1964), p. 299.

SUGGESTED READING

Beales, Derek, *The Risorgimento and the Unification of Italy* (1971). A comprehensive overview, followed by documents.

Fischer, Klaus P., *The History of an Obsession* (1998). A superb study of German-Jewish relations, particularly the delusional character of anti-Jewish thinking.

Holborn, Hajo, *A History of Modern Germany, 1840–1945* (1969). A standard reference work.

Kohn, Hans, *Nationalism: Its Meaning and History* (1955). A concise history of modern nationalism by a leading student of the subject.

Mosse, George L., *The Crisis of German Ideology* (1964). Explores the dark side of German nationalism.

Perry, Marvin and Frederick M. Schweitzer, *Antisemitism: Myth and Hate from Antiquity to the Present* (2002). Analyzes the lies, misperceptions, and myths that have been used to justify persecution of Jews throughout the centuries.

Rodes, John E., *The Quest for Unity: Modern Germany, 1848–1970* (1971). A good survey of German history.

Chapter 26

The Industrial West: Responses to Modernization

Krupps metalworks factory. (Bettmann/CORBIS.)

Focus Questions

1. Why was England seen by many as the model liberal nation in the middle decades of the nineteenth century?

2. In England, the middle class and the workers often strove together for reform from 1860 to 1914. In France they rarely did so. Why?

3. What was the general crisis of liberalism after 1870?

4. How did the conservatives attempt to win over the masses after 1870?

5. How did the ideology of official nationality undermine liberal reforms and inhibit industrialization in tsarist Russia?

Online Study Center

This icon will direct you to interactive map and primary source activities on the website http://college.hmco.com/pic/perrywc8e.

A "second industrial revolution" quickened the pace of industrialization, forcing even more rapid change in European society between 1870 and World War I than the "first industrial revolution." Mechanized industry, powered by new forms of energy, spread to all European states, though not to every region within them; it vastly increased the quantity of goods available to large segments of the population, not just to the wealthy. Indeed, new groups rose to authority and wealth. The generation before the First World War was truly the golden age of the middle classes, which gained wealth, power, and influence as social discrimination against them steadily diminished. Dazzled by the material benefits of a mass-producing society, many Europeans saw progress as inevitable. Those who were still left out of the consuming society struggled for their share.

The **mechanization** of basic goods industries had proceeded slowly and unevenly in the first half of the nineteenth century (see Chapter 21). Traditional economic production and social arrangements persisted alongside new technology and new methods of organizing labor. At midcentury, only Britain had become predominantly urban and an importer of food. Yet even Britain retained many aspects of an earlier rural, agrarian, privileged society as the new mercantile and manufacturing groups were gaining political and social power. In every country, traditional society ignored, resisted, and repressed the emerging forces and social groups as they reshaped basic institutions.

To deal with the major changes brought about by industrialization, governments expanded the role of the state, strengthening the central power over the diverse interests, regions, classes, and even nationalities. Civil wars, unification movements, and struggles for political representation usually ended with a stronger central government. Sometimes the new balance of classes and regions meant the repression of dissent, regionalism, and tradition—the American Civil War, the Irish struggle for home rule, and the subjugation of minorities in newly unified Germany or tsarist Russia or Austria-Hungary are just some of the examples. In the half-century before the First World War, governments developed the machin-

Chronology 26.1 ❖ Europe in the Age of Industrialization

1845–47	Great famine in Ireland
1851	Louis Napoleon Bonaparte overthrows the Second Republic, becoming Emperor Napoleon III
1860s	Irish movement for republican form of government (the Fenians); Civil War in the United States; unification movements in German and Italian states; Dual Monarchy in Austria-Hungary
1861	Kingdom of Italy is formed; Tsar Alexander II emancipates the serfs and institutes reforms in Russia
1863	Emancipation of slaves in the United States
1864	Marx founds the First International Workingmen's Association
1867	Second Reform Bill passes, doubling the English electorate
1870–71	Franco-Prussian War; Paris Commune; creation of the German Empire
1873	Great Depression; the *Kulturkampf* in Germany
1875	German Social Democratic party founded
1880s	Parnell leads the Irish home rule movement
1881	Tsar Alexander II is assassinated
1884	Reform Bill grants suffrage to most English men
1889	Second International Workingmen's Association is founded
1891	Trans-Siberian Railroad constructed
1894–1906	The Dreyfus affair in France
1903–1905	Russo-Japanese War
1905	Revolution of 1905 in Russia
1909	Lloyd George introduces "people's budget"
1911	House of Lords limited by act of Parliament

ery to control great numbers of citizens through military **conscription**, public education, broad taxation, and, in some places, social legislation. Some governments encouraged nationalism, once thought dangerously democratic, as a way of absorbing masses of previously excluded people. Industrialization influenced the outcome of each of these struggles.

Industrialization affected international affairs as well. Population, area, and the size of the army were no longer adequate measures of national power. The amount of coal and iron production, the mileage and tonnage of railways and navies, the mechanization of industry, and the skill of the populace became important components. By 1914, production, trade, foreign markets, and political empires altered the balance of power, changing the positions of France, Russia, and Austria and tipping the scale toward the superior industrial might of Germany and the United States.

THE ADVANCE OF INDUSTRY

Industry developed on the foundation of cheap labor and plentiful agricultural commodities, which were made easily and cheaply available by the development of a relatively inexpensive transportation and communication system. It took more than a century to lay that foundation, but by the 1850s, it was in place for almost all of Europe and parts of the Americas. On it was built a new economic world of growth and prosperity such as had not been seen before. *Revolution* accurately describes the radically new forms of business and labor organization, the massive accumulation of capital, the scientific and technological advance, and the new modes of marketing, distribution, and production. The apparently limitless change fostered a mentality that assumed people could be replaced, raw materials replenished, nature rearranged, and even homelands exchanged.

Comparison with the midcentury quickly indicates the scope of the second industrial revolution. In 1850, most people were still farmers and much of industry produced tools and materials for farming. Even Britain had more domestic servants than factory hands and twice as many agricultural laborers as textile and clothing workers. Large factories were few; handicrafts still flourished. Electricity was too expensive to power lighting or drive machines; steel was too expensive to build with. Sailing ships still outnumbered steamships, and horses carried more freight than trains. On-the-job training was more common than schooling. Construction and machine making were a result of trial and error, not architectural and engineering knowledge.

This situation changed radically in two spurts: the first between 1850 and 1870; the second after the Great Depression of 1873, from the 1870s until World War I. During the first spurt, most of Europe and America consolidated earlier industrialization, extending it to previously untouched areas. The shift to machine production became permanent, steam power and other forms of energy were harnessed, and more sophisticated tools were introduced. The concentration of factory workers and production in industrial cities spurred many social changes. Labor organized unions primarily in the crafts. Social legislation was passed, especially laws for the protection of women and children. Governments, usually municipal rather than national, struggled to control water pollution, improve sanitation, and regulate housing conditions. In the more advanced industrial areas, the workplace changed; women

and children were pushed out by unskilled male labor.

During the second spurt, beginning in the late 1870s but turning into a clear trend by the 1890s, in the major industrial countries of Germany and the United States, heavy industry became concentrated in large firms, capitalized by specialist banks. Cartels and monopolies—groups of companies that joined together in order to fix prices and giant firms able to dominate entire industries nationally and internationally—drastically altered the scale of development. Monopolies, run by boards of directors, some professional managers, and financiers, operated far-flung enterprises of enormous mechanized factories, staffed by unskilled, low-paid, often seasonal workers. These industrial giants controlled the output, price, and distribution of commodities; they dominated smaller firms, financed and controlled research and development, utilized scientific advances, and expanded far beyond their national frontiers. Giant firms welded alliances with specialized banks all over Europe.

The "captains of industry"—the owners or managers of these large firms—possessed such extraordinary economic power that they often commanded political power as well. In much of Europe, such men were **ennobled**. Britain's railroad barons are early examples. In the United States, bankers and entrepreneurs were called "robber barons"; industrial titans could order politicians to represent their interests as "the oil senator" or "the railroad senator." These dynamic and powerful men, who could "cause" depressions or "own" cities, fascinated the public and obsessed their critics. Their images obscured the fact that the second industrial revolution was a broad movement, including thousands of small businesses.

The rapid growth and the powerful figures in great industries hid from contemporaries the fact that economic development was extremely uneven, even in advanced industrial states. Uneven development intensified political conflicts and social animosities, which, in turn, contributed to the uneven development. Industrialized Britain, for example, included rural, backward Ireland, which furnished foodstuffs and laborers but hardly shared in the benefits of industrialization. This economic deprivation, together with cultural and religious differences, fueled the Irish desire for autonomy. Until 1914, the central, southern, and eastern parts of Europe were also backwater areas, with some large-scale industries. In these regions economic oppression and repression of minorities went hand in hand. Often the lowest workers and the poorest peasants were ethnic and national minorities, who resented the power of the dominant groups. From the backwater areas hundreds of thousands of peasants and craftsmen, searching for a livelihood, immigrated to the Americas or British colonies. The movement from rural to urban areas was matched by an exodus on a scale unknown in history.

Britain alone developed industry according to free trade principles. Other governments built or subsidized "essential" industries (broadly defined to include transportation, communication, national banks, and above all, the production of war goods). The eastern empires—Russia and Austria-Hungary—remained economically and socially backward: overwhelmingly agricultural, with craftspeople manufacturing in consumer-oriented, small-scale operations of textiles and food processing. Even in industrially advanced Germany, megacartels such as the Krupp steelworks existed alongside handicraft labor.

Industrial work and wealth were unevenly and unequally distributed. The bourgeoisie included families rich enough to be elevated to the House of Lords or move in the German emperor's circle, as well as white-collar workers—the clerks in stores and government offices—and the poor but respected schoolteachers. In the second half of the century, middle-class values and interests provided standards of education, morality, and consumption for others to imitate. Traditional groups—artisans and peasantry—suffered considerable social dislocation as factory skills replaced craft skills and the use of agricultural machinery increased. Craftsmen and peasants became part of the industrial labor supply just when the introduction of heavy equipment reduced the total numbers of workers needed. Forced to move to cities, they competed for jobs. Men replaced women and children in rural and urban work. National and religious minorities replaced workers of the dominant groups.

Wages remained relatively stable after the 1870s, while the price of food and some other goods dropped. As a result, employed workers' purchasing power rose, and they spent more of their income on cheap consumer goods. Yet even the employed struggled, for they had lost family income when the state required their children to be trained in schools, something many workers resented. Their wives' income was lost, too, unless the women could find low-paying work as domestics, pieceworkers, seamstresses, or laundresses. Economic and social changes drastically altered the family and the role of each of its members. The cultural ideal of women in the home (the "cult of domesticity"), which appealed even to working-class wives in the prewar generation, depended on the ability of labor to support a family. To the degree that it could be achieved, it left the world of work a male domain.

The socioeconomic trends strongly affected political and social movements. As the middle class strove to inhibit and control labor, labor responded by broadening its organization to buttress its political and economic position. The rise in workers' standard of living and the improved working conditions did not narrow the gap between the workers and the owners. Indeed, the gap between the poor and the well-off, the powerless and the powerful, widened.

Technological Takeoff

Technology revolutionized production in undreamed-of ways, multiplying rather than merely adding to the goods and services. At midcentury, the trial-and-error tinkering of the artisan or the inventor began to be replaced by practical applications of scientific research to engineering, production, transportation, and communication. By 1900, German electrical, chemical, and mechanical industries routinely hired engineers and applied scientists to solve technical problems and produce new commodities, including artificial ones, of dyestuffs, fertilizers, and fuels. The Americans were not far behind. The Americans were early champions of scientific management—or "Taylorism," as it was called after Frederick Taylor, one of its leading proponents. Americans taught Taylorism in their new professional schools of business. Even European socialist critics of capitalism talked of "Taylorizing" production and management, taking the inefficiency out of capitalism.

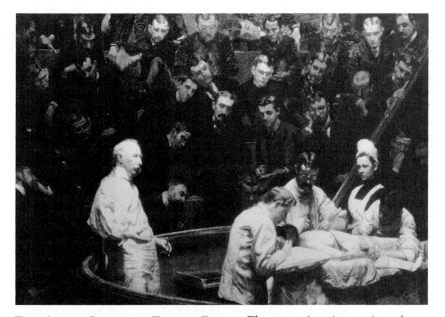

THE AGNEW CLINIC, BY THOMAS EAKINS. The great American painter has caught the atmosphere of medical school in the nineteenth century. Here, well-dressed and for the most part interested physicians observe a mastectomy operation. The combination of scientific study, expertise, and professional specialization lifted the practice of medicine from a trade to a science in the public's mind. (*University of Pennsylvania Art Collection, Philadelphia, Penn.*)

The result was a "takeoff" of technology, connecting industries to technological and scientific advances. A few key industries—railroads, communications, and energy—illustrate.

Railroads thrilled the public, along with investors and politicians, for railroads had the aura of progress that the cheaper, equally efficient, and labor-intensive (rather than capital-intensive) canals and roads did not. Railroads were the engine of industrial growth in Britain, stimulating the demand for coal and iron, steel, gravel, wood and tar, engineering training, and electronic signaling. Bessemer and Siemens processes quality steel made cheaply and abundantly, causing a boom in the railroad and construction industries. Stronger steel machinery allowed a wider application of steam power in these industries, as well as others, including mining.

In the first period of consolidation, from 1850 to the 1870s, many railroad firms competed with each other. Further expansion required an un-

precedented amount of capital accumulation, and the acquisition and use of funds was just as innovative as the invention of better engines and cars. Railroad moguls who commanded the greatest amounts of capital soon swallowed up their rivals, acquiring immense personal and corporate fortunes. In countries without moguls, government stepped in to amass the capital, build railroads, take over failing ones, and subsidize private builders by land or monopoly grants and contracts. It did so to foster commerce, maintain military power, and strengthen the central authority by bringing regions and groups into the national market. Railroads transformed North America and Eurasia, opening up vast unsettled areas. In the United States, there were more miles of railway (176,000) by 1870 than in all of Europe. It was the same in Canada. Railroads linked India's various regions. In Russia, in the 1890s, the Trans-Siberian Railroad, a fledgling line financed with reluctant French capital, carried millions of settlers eastward to central Asia.

Online Study Center Improve Your Grade
Interactive Map: European Rails

Shipping paralleled the epic expansion of railroads, bringing distant parts of the world together. The application of the steam-powered engine to ships was prohibitively expensive at first, just as it was for railroads and mining. In 1870, sailboats carried 4.5 million tons of goods, and steamships less than a million tons; by 1913, steam carried 11 million tons of goods, and sail only 800,000. The whole world was open to cheap, plentiful goods, products that often could swamp local crafts; simultaneously, Europe became the marketplace for much of the world.

Steam power fueled the massive increase in productivity from the middle of the century until its monopoly was broken at the turn of the century. Electricity became more competitive, powering whole industries and lighting great cities. Two German engineers, Gottlieb Daimler and Karl Benz, perfected the internal combustion engine fueled by petroleum products and applied it to a carriage. The automobile age was born. Ultimately, petroleum power democratized many aspects of the industrial process, fostering changes in production, organization, and consumption. Daimler developed a luxury automobile, the Mercedes; the American Henry Ford (1863–1947) produced his 1908 Model T for the "ordinary man." By 1914, his **mass-production,** conveyer-belt assembly-line techniques revolutionized industrial production. Another German's development of the diesel engine made the fuel for giant cargo ships, warships, and luxury liners much cheaper, more powerful, and more efficient. Steam, oil and gas, and electricity would power the twentieth century.

As they do today, communications pushed expansion, and industrial growth stretched communications. At the time, the rapid improvement of everyday postal services was much more important than inventions of the telegraph, the telephone, and the radio. Development costs were so prohibitive for the telephone (invented by Alexander Graham Bell in 1876) and the wireless, or radio (invented by Guglielmo Marconi in 1895) that it took almost twenty-five years after invention for either device to be widely used even in industrial countries. Once costs were cut, however, communications grew exponentially, shrinking distances between markets and time between orders and delivery.

By the end of the nineteenth century, the scientific and the industrial revolutions had joined forces. Scientific knowledge quickly became applied practice; inventions and inventors played a great role in industrial expansion. More than half a century elapsed between Michael Faraday and James Maxwell's discovery of the fundamentals of electricity and the inventions of Thomas Edison, Bell, and Marconi. In a much shorter time, electricity provided power for lights, for urban and suburban trains, and for some factory engines. This same trend was evident in industrial chemistry. In 1850, almost all industrial materials were the ones people had been using for centuries: wood, stone, cotton, wool, flax, hemp, leather, plant dyes, and the base metals such as copper, iron, lead, and tin and their various alloys. Particularly in Germany, chemists discovered new elements and perfected formulas for alloys, dyes, and coal-tar products. In medicine, too, the marriage of science and technology produced miraculous progeny—anesthetics and antiseptics, the discovery and isolation of disease-causing bacteria by Louis Pasteur, a French chemist. By the end of the century, researchers had identified the causes of several killer diseases: typhoid, tuberculosis, cholera, tetanus, diphtheria, and leprosy.

Each new scientific breakthrough was quickly published for the general public in the popular scientific, medical, and technological press. Science exposed poor sanitation and squalor as the breeders of disease, and industrialized countries worked harder to ameliorate those conditions. Life expectancy increased, the death rate decreased, and the population in the more advanced industrialized countries boomed despite the fact that couples practiced contraception as a way to maintain their standard of living.

In all, each advance—and we have discussed only a few key industries—brought changes in the political and social power of individuals, groups,

PAINTING OF THE BOWERY BY LOUIS SONTAG (1895). This New York City street scene bursts with commercial energy and activity as the night is lighted by blazing electricity. The artist puts pushcarts, trolleys, horse-drawn cabs, and trains side by side, as he does the classic architecture of the theater and the four-story buildings housing shops and families on the Bowery. The city throbs with the energy of modern technology. (*Museum of the City of New York #32.275.2. Gift of William B. Miles.*)

and nations and pushed industrial and commercial development still further.

Accelerated Urbanization

Rapid industrial development urbanized northwestern Europe and the United States. More and larger cities, more densely populated, drew people from rural life and labor to mix with those who were city born and bred. Although the majority of England's population lived in cities of ten thousand as early as 1800, most other Europeans did not until the twentieth century, and most of the world waited in the countryside until after the Second World War. Although a commercial and not an industrial city, London had become a megalopolis of five million people by 1880; it was home to seven million by 1914. Between 1866 and the First World War, Berlin grew from half a million to two million. At unification, Germany had just three cities of more than a hundred thousand inhabitants; by 1903, it had fifteen. Paris increased in population from two

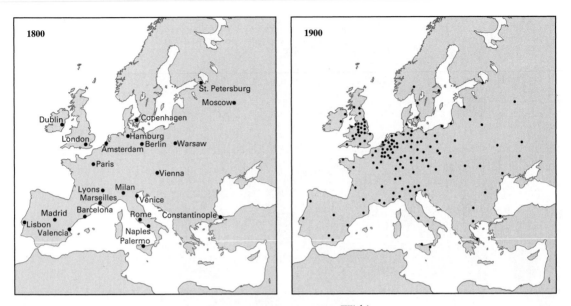

MAP 26.1 EUROPEAN CITIES OF 100,000 OR MORE, 1800–1900 Within a
century, industrialization brought about the urbanization of northwestern
Europe, particularly England, Belgium, western Germany, and northern France.

million to three million between 1850 and World
War I. By 1900, the United States was more heavily urbanized than Europe and had more cities of
a million inhabitants than any other nation.
These millions were immigrants, recently European peasants, or American farmers attracted to
industrial labor.

By the end of the century, most of western Europe had taken some steps to provide sanitation,
a public water supply, policing, and public transport. Streets were being laid and widened, housing was constructed, and some regulations were
imposed on housing and commercial property.
New professions of urban planner, transport and
sanitation engineer, and social worker joined then
replaced the well-meaning, civic-minded, urban-
dwelling men and women volunteers who worked
to alleviate the worst effects of urban industrial
living.

The draw of the factory, the drama of the
train, and the squalor and poverty of rural life
brought village and rural people to the city. Responding to the various pressures of education,
the press, and patriotic campaigns, they became
loyal to their nation. Maintaining traditional loy-

alties and minority identity became increasingly
difficult. There were exceptions: industrialization
actually heightened minority identity among such
industrially advanced peoples as the Czechs in
Austria-Hungary and the Basques in Spain. Generally, however, if a minority culture managed to
resist the pressures for integration, its success reflected the relative economic backwardness of the
area. In Russia, the Austro-Hungarian Empire,
the Iberian Peninsula, and southern Italy, discontented peasants rejected pressures for national integration. There, the peasants barely eked out a
living, often working on great estates for landlords who paid them little despite the abundance
they produced for export. As the landlord often
spoke another language, the peasant's discontent
stemmed from a mix of national or ethnic identity and economic woe.

Labor's Responses

Around the world, labor, too, was caught in the
changing conditions of the second wave of industrialization. Giant enterprises required great

"MATCH GIRLS." The "Match Girls" strike taught the public the human cost of cheap and dangerous products. Here the women pack phosphorus matches in a London factory. (*Hackney Archives Department, London.*)

armies of unskilled workers who toiled for low pay, usually by the day or by the job, if they were lucky enough (or shared enough of their wages with the foreman) to be chosen to work. When workers had low pay, irregular work, and minimal skills, the building of unions was almost impossible. Unskilled workers could not be fitted into craft unions. Technology increased the number of the unskilled, and it "deskilled" the craft workers, often pitting the two groups against each another. Skilled craftspeople watched as machines and unskilled workers—often foreigners or minorities or displaced peasants—took their places. Labor standards, the quality of goods, and wages all declined. Rising wages in any industry became an incentive to invent a machine to drive them back down.

Where workers could vote, they pressed for government action against the social evils of industrialization and urbanization. In some countries, such as the United States, workers voted for the same political parties that other classes voted for. In Britain, workers did so at first but then organized their own party. In France, Germany, and Italy, workers joined socialist parties calling for the end of capitalism; in Italy, Spain, and

parts of France, even more radical, anarchist parties gained worker support. Beginning in the 1860s and 1870s, workers demanded union recognition, minimum wages, maximum hours, and better working conditions even for nonunion workers. Laborers had to win over the general public, which was imbued with individualist, property-protecting values as well as class prejudices. Labor won public sympathy for the poorest of workers and for exploited women and children. In 1888, an English strike of women and girls who worked in match factories, where phosphorus endangered lives, drew public and press support, including sympathy strikes of other workers. The "match girls" made some gains. But the next year, when impoverished British dockworkers struck, there was little public sympathy for these rough-and-ready men. It was Australian and American dockworkers who rescued them from sure defeat. They knew the horrible conditions of the job and realized how vulnerable a union of unskilled day laborers in any country actually was.

Between the "hungry forties" and the outbreak of World War I, the standard of living of many workers, both skilled craftspeople and factory hands, did improve, thanks to trade union organization, government intervention in the economy, and the general increase in productivity. Nevertheless, most workers—and their families—lived in overcrowded, bleak, cold tenements, without ventilation or running water. They worked long hours—as many as fifty-five per week in trades where governments restricted the length of the workweek, and from seventy to seventy-five in unregulated trades. Their jobs were exhausting and monotonous. Women workers had a particularly hard life, spending the regulated number of hours in the factory and then doing piecework at home to make ends meet. In addition, they took care of the home and the children, of which there were usually five or more. Workers suffered from malnutrition, diseases (particularly tuberculosis), and lack of medical care for childbirth or accidents, even those that maimed and killed.

Governments paid attention, taking the first steps to protect women and children and then extending reforms to male workers as laborers were drawn to socialist or labor parties, which believed that exploitation was built into the capitalist profit system. In the 1880s, Bismarck instituted reforms (see below), and by 1914, Britain, France, Austria, Italy, Denmark, and Switzerland provided some benefits for sick, injured, and elderly workers. These social welfare measures, however, offered only minimum assistance—much less than organized labor provided for itself from dues and welfare funds.

Socialist parties, which by the 1890s were often Marxist, grew phenomenally in Germany and rapidly in much of the rest of Europe. Even in England, where Marxism was unimportant and democracy assumed, unionists organized the socialist Independent Labour party. Even backward Russia had a Marxist socialist party. Socialists did not always agree on tactics; their views depended on their ideology and their country's political environment. Some socialists—men such as Wilhelm Liebknecht and August Bebel of Germany or Jules Guesde of France—insisted that reform would come only through a socialist-led revolution. Others—"revisionist" Marxists—argued that an improving standard of living and universal manhood **suffrage** required socialists to build democracy.

In the decade before 1914, a wave of strikes swept through every industrial and industrializing country. Strikes were put down with violence: the dock strikes in London and Liverpool, the railroad workers' strike in France, and the miners' strikes in England and France, for example. Strikes and the growth of socialist parties accentuated the fear of class warfare among the middle and upper classes.

GREAT BRITAIN: AN INDUSTRIAL MODEL

In 1850, foreigners and Englishmen alike believed England to be the most modern and progressive of states. It had made phenomenal industrial progress, and most of its people began to share a higher standard of living in the era of free trade after 1847. England was the model parliamentary government; it balanced an incomparable degree of political liberty with economic and social reforms, avoiding the extremes of revolution and reaction. Political parties competed to govern and in the process reformed evils and extended membership in the political community to previously excluded groups, such as labor or the Irish. That was the widely held view of Victorian England. The reality differed. "Country gentlemen" dominated British politics: titled aristocrats staffed the cabinets and commanded the army and navy just as they did in central Europe. Great social mobility existed, but wealthy industrialists, merchants, and entrepreneurs who wanted a public life had to demonstrate a large measure of social conformity.

A century of industrial and commercial changes—and some good luck, like the discovery of gold in California and Alaska—brought prosperity and a sense of well-being, which shaped the politics of the time. Two men of quite different personalities and values were the central political figures whose competition stimulated reform: William E. Gladstone (1809–1898), a pious, sober man for whom politics was a struggle between the forces of liberal good and conservative evil; and the flamboyant Benjamin Disraeli (1804–1881), a novelist and a conservative, who loved the fascinating game of politics. They laid down the rules of the parliamentary game for others to admire and imitate. If the prime minister and his party failed to get a bill passed, the rules required a change in the governing party. He and his cabinet (men of his party drawn from the Parliament to run the government) had to resign or call a new election.

In 1867, when Gladstone failed to pass a bill to let some of the working class vote, Disraeli proposed suffrage for most city workers, not at all what anyone expected of the leader of the Conservatives. The measure carried, and suddenly the electorate was doubled. Both parties feared democracy, yet in the competition for power, democracy had become a reality. Overnight, compulsory elementary education became a necessity (other European states had state schools and compulsory education, but not England). In 1884, Gladstone's party extended the vote to most Englishmen. Women and many Irishmen still could not vote, but the belief grew that it was only a matter of time before liberal democracy would include even them. Would "country gentlemen" admit women, the Irish, and labor into the political community? Could Britain be truly democratic? On the eve of the First World War, the demands for justice by each of these groups created a prolonged crisis for parliamentary government.

Labor Unrest

In the stable, prosperous middle decades of the century, British workers created the strongest labor movement in Europe. After the depression of 1873, English self-confidence declined. As in all the countries of Europe, technology altered conditions in whole industries, leading, in the 1880s, to a rise in militant industrial unions, termed "new unions." Unlike workers on the Continent, British workers were relatively untouched by Marxist ideas, managing to express their interests within the Liberal party. In the 1880s, however, widespread hardship caused by foreign competition and the general industrial downturn led some labor leaders to advocate English socialism. In 1893, J. Kier Hardie, a colorful nonconformist who represented a poor Welsh mining district in the House of Commons,

formed the Independent Labour party. Sometimes in alliance with middle-class socialists, such as the Fabians, sometimes with Liberals, he and other union leaders hammered out a political and economic program.

The Labour party might never have gotten off the ground if it had not been for the Taff Vale decision (1901). The courts awarded damages to an employer picketed by a union. If workers could be fined for picketing or other actions "restraining trade," their unions would be broken and their treasuries depleted. This happened just as labor was mounting a campaign for protection against unemployment, accidents, sickness, and old age—benefits that German workers had obtained in the 1880s. Labor took to politics. By 1906, in a Liberal landslide, the new Labour party gained twenty-nine seats. The Liberals, led by David Lloyd George (1863–1945) and the then Liberal Winston Churchill (1874–1965), introduced a series of important social measures. They repealed the Taff Vale decision. Aided by the Labour party, they enacted a program of old-age pensions, labor exchanges to help the unemployed find work, minimum wages for certain industries, unemployment, and health insurance—in short, a program deeply influenced by Bismarck's social legislation. The House of Lords rejected the budget, forcing a constitutional crisis. The Lords took this extreme action because "the people's budget" financed the social legislation by raising the income tax and levying inheritance taxes ("death duties") and "unearned" income taxes on rents, investments, and increases in the value of land. All these taxes were directed at the wealthy and the privileged.

The Liberals waged an all-out fight with the Lords, who saw their struggle as the defense of Britain and its empire against the Liberals' "socialist" campaign. Lloyd George sarcastically described the dukes as "five hundred men, ordinary men, chosen accidentally from among the unemployed." Class hatreds, unacknowledged for a couple of generations as part of the political balance that Britain had achieved, intensified and were bitterly and freely expressed. Miners, railway workers, and dockhands allied, calling a general strike. The people's budget ultimately passed.

Later, the Parliament Act of 1911 stipulated that the Lords could only delay the passage of a bill passed by the Commons, not prevent it. The machinery for democratic government in Britain was in place. Excluded groups had focused on democracy as the way to gain justice—not on social revolution. But a long coal strike in 1912 involved a million and a half workers, and only government intervention could stop it. Whether British liberal democracy would survive was uppermost in the minds of many on the eve of World War I.

The Irish Question

For members of Parliament, the Irish were a "question," and a troublesome one, for much of the nineteenth century. The great famine of 1845–47 brought unparalleled suffering to the Irish: a million of them died and another million emigrated. The sufferers saw England if not as the cause, then as callously indifferent to their plight. A revolutionary republican group, the Fenians, called for Irish independence, developing a variety of protests against British policy in Ireland. Fenian protests were remarkably successful; Gladstone said the Fenians provoked him to take up Irish reform. Like many English liberals, he thought that economic and religious reforms would end Irish discontent; therefore, he ended the **tithe** the mostly Catholic Irish paid to the Anglican church and passed land legislation for Irish tenant farmers. Had these reforms been made in the 1840s and 1850s, they might have appeased the Irish. By the 1880s, however, they were too little, too late; the issue had become home rule—that is, self-government within the British Empire. In the Commons, the Irish, led by the Protestant Charles Stewart Parnell, formed a separate bloc to force the Conservatives and the Liberals to reckon with the issue of home rule. Parnell's supporters used every known parliamentary tactic, and invented some new ones, to secure their goals. They denounced violence, but others urged violence. Terrorist acts aroused public passions; Parliament enacted extreme measures, suspending trial by jury and many other liberties in Ireland, which only intensified the hostilities. At the end of his life, Gladstone had split his party and failed, as would his Liberal successors, to achieve a reconciliation with the Irish. Parnell, whose political aura faded in a scandalous love affair, had also failed.

The continuing bitter struggle for home rule made prewar British politics extremely volatile. The House of Lords, dominated by Tory imperialists (Conservatives), could not prevent the passage of home rule once the Parliament Act of 1911 became law. The Liberals pushed for the reform, but Tory imperialists thought the empire more important than elections and majority rule. Militant groups took the law into their own hands. The Irish Republican Brotherhood and the Gaelic League pressed for full independence; fearing Catholic domination, the Protestant Irish organized a private army, the Ulster Volunteers. Gangs smuggled guns (many from America), soldiers fired on demonstrators, and civil war seemed close. Some English Tory leaders threatened mutiny; one actually reviewed eighty thousand volunteer soldiers willing to fight against the English for the Protestant cause in Ireland.

In 1914, when Great Britain declared war on Germany, Ireland was uppermost in British minds. On the day the archduke of Austria was assassinated, the front pages of the British papers were filled with news of Irish protest, not with foreign affairs. With the onset of war, women and labor suspended their militant campaigns, pledging their loyalty to king and country. Many Irish fought for Britain in World War I, but the deferred promise of home rule angered many others. Some, like Sir Roger Casement, joined the Germans to fight for Ireland's independence. In 1916, on Easter Sunday, a group of Irish nationalists seized the Dublin post office in an insurrection; it was suppressed and the leaders executed.

After the war, Lloyd George negotiated a settlement. Ireland was divided, the south gaining self-government and the predominantly Protestant northern six counties of Ulster remaining part of the United Kingdom.

The Woman Question

The "woman question"—the issue of women's equality—was much older than the nineteenth-century political movement for the right to vote. This question was more than an English or American political concern. The suffrage movement was stronger there than elsewhere in Europe. On the Continent, including Scandinavia, Germany,

POSTER PUBLISHED BY THE ARTISTS' SUFFRAGE LEAGUE, DESIGNED BY EMILY HARDING ANDERES, C. 1908. This suffragette poster illustrates the fact that British women could not vote in the early twentieth century. The cap and gown of the woman college graduate does not help her find the key that will release her from the imprisoning categorization with felons and the mentally ill, who couldn't vote for Parliament either. Women were leaders in local government—where they were in charge of schools, orphanages, and hospitals—but were unable to vote for members of the House of Commons until after World War I. *(Library of Congress.)*

and even Russia, the "new woman" of the end of the century demanded sexual freedom, the right of divorce, child custody, and property ownership. Those demands would have been **utopian** dreams if the Industrial Revolution had not made it possible for women to work and to support themselves and their families. Nonetheless, husbands and fathers still had control of their children and the family property, education was

unattainable for most women, and employment was scarce and low paying. During the wave of industrial change on the eve of the First World War, the woman question came up again. Artists and intellectuals, such as Henrik Ibsen, George Bernard Shaw, and H. G. Wells, supported women's emancipation, and others, such as August Strindberg, opposed it. Socialist feminists, such as the German Clara Zetkin, argued that only socialism could liberate women from responsibility for their children and from their lives of hard work in the home and in the economy. Conservatives, in contrast, were unified in their view that women's rights would destroy the family and undermine the nation. Ironically, radicals in France, Italy, and Spain, who ordinarily would have championed equality, opposed women's suffrage because they feared that priests and husbands would dominate the women. Finally, women themselves were torn between their role as wives and mothers and their desire for equality and some measure of protection.

Women had greater freedom in England than in most countries; there they could vote for and serve on school and local government boards. Without their volunteer work in schools and charity organizations, the educational and social support system of Britain would have floundered. But they could not vote for members of Parliament, their education was stunted, and they suffered from enormous social pressure to conform to traditional women's roles. The women's movement was far from united. Middle-class women and working-class women led very different lives. Many of the latter were much more concerned with economic security than with the right to vote. Although no longer limited to the most miserable and sometimes degrading labor, working-class women remained particularly vulnerable to the ups and downs of the economy. Even middle-class women were divided. Some feminists—Millicent Fawcett and Josephine Butler, for instance—thought that women should concentrate on self-improvement and legal efforts to raise their status in society rather than focus on the vote. Others proposed radical and immediate action. Still others thought that the political road was the wrong one to take; if women wanted to be free, they needed to liberate themselves economically and socially from their dependence on men.

Despite the many aspects of women's rights, in England the "question" was posed as a suffrage issue. It was posed in particularly vivid ways—ways that threatened the accepted forms and norms of liberal politics. In the campaign for women's suffrage, suffragist tactics and government repression steadily escalated in violence. Many Liberals and some Labourites supported women's suffrage. Still, the leader of the Liberals advised women "to keep on pestering . . . but exercise the virtue of patience." A family of feminists called for an end to patience. Emmeline Pankhurst and her daughters Sylvia and Christabel urged demonstrations and disruptions of the House of Commons. When their petitions were ignored, they moved to more shocking actions: breaking windows, starting fires in mailboxes, etching with acid slogans in the golf greens, and chaining themselves to the gates of Parliament. In 1913, one militant killed herself in protest by jumping in front of the king's horse at the races. The suffragists' opponents argued that women were not rational enough to discuss politics. When law-breaking feminists were arrested, they staged hunger strikes. Ugly situations resulted. The police force-fed the demonstrators and subjected them to ridicule and rough treatment. Often the police would release half-starved suffragists to recover their health, then reimprison them ("cat and mouse" it was called). Ridiculed, humiliated, and punished—but, above all, legally ignored—feminists refused to accept the passive role that male-dominated society assigned them.

Women played a major part on the home front in World War I, and in 1918, women over thirty years of age were enfranchised in Britain. In some colonies (Australia, New Zealand), women had the right to vote. Finally, in 1928, British women gained the right to vote on the same terms as men, that is, they had to be twenty-one years old and to have six months' residency. After the war, women gained the right to vote in the United States, Germany, and the Soviet Union, but they would have to wait a long time for this right in France, Spain, Italy, and Switzerland.

Britain on the Eve of War

The bitter conflicts of prewar Britain showed the cracks in the country's self-image as a stable, liberal, constitutional regime. The elite learned that the tactics of the new politics—strikes, demonstrations, passive resistence, and terrorism—would destroy the liberal parliamentary institutions that many saw as the basis of Britain's greatness. Parliamentary government proved able to win a grueling world war, but issues of empire and economic depression would test the constitution once again as excluded groups fought for full democracy.

FRANCE: DEMOCRATIC OR AUTHORITARIAN?

The political fortunes of France in the nineteenth century differed greatly from Britain's. France's slow and uneven industrialization greatly affected its national and international affairs. Virtually each generation faced revolution and reaction, swinging from democratic revolution to authoritarian stability, from active participation of the people to rule by a single man or small group of men.

Napoleon "le Petit"

At midcentury, the personality and politics of Louis Napoleon Bonaparte (1808–1873), the nephew of the great Napoleon I, dominated France. By an overwhelming majority, in an election in which all French males could vote, "the small" or "little" Bonaparte ("le Petit") was elected president of the Second French Republic, which a democratic social revolution had established in 1848. Within three years, he was dictator-emperor, the republic destroyed by a **plebiscite.** This vote and subsequent elections were rigged. Bonaparte's imperialism, his support of Catholics in Rome and in France, and the end of the republic outraged liberals and republicans, including Alexis de Tocqueville and Victor Hugo. The working class wanted the republic, but most other French men accepted its end.

Bonapartism was a mix of democratic, socialist, nationalist, and authoritarian ideas. It promised national glory, strong leadership, and social progress. Bonaparte combined the appearance of democracy—elections by universal manhood suffrage, plebiscites, a press, and intellectual debate—with economic expansion. At the same time, he suppressed opposition, censored the press, rarely convened the parliament, and manipulated both elections and debate. His close friends and his relatives were his advisers and administrators. Property owners, who liked stability at home, expansion abroad, railroad construction, and the rebuilding of Paris, liked him. He expressed concern for workers, whose suffering became acute as industrialization took hold. After a decade of authoritorian rule, he loosened the controls on the press and the legislature, legalized strikes, and granted workers a limited right to unionize. In 1869, when members of the opposition were elected, a new constitution with liberal safeguards for individual liberties was written. It turned Louis Napoleon Bonaparte into a constitutional parliamentary monarch like Queen Victoria in England. Was he a liberal nationalist who wanted to give France reforms once he had established his power? Or did he, like the great Napoleon, accept liberal change only when he feared an overthrow? Such questions became irrelevant the very next year in the Franco-Prussian War (1870–71) when France was defeated and occupied by Prussian troops.

After the Fall

As French armies collapsed, the people of Paris rose, refusing to accept defeat or the peace terms of the provisional government. The Paris Commune (1871) simply refused to obey. The Communards included a wide range of opinion: the followers of anarchist Pierre Joseph Proudhon; groups of republican and socialist veterans of the Revolution of 1848 suddenly and unexpectedly liberated from prisons, hiding, and exile; and many ordinary republicans and patriots. For two months, the revolutionaries ruled Paris, inspired by the Jacobins of 1793 and the radicals of June 1848. Then Adolph Thiers who had accepted Bismarck's peace terms, ordered French soldiers to attack Paris. The fighting was bitter and desperate, with many acts of terrorism and violence on both sides of this civil war. The defeated Communards were treated as traitors: twenty thousand men and women were executed without trial, and those who were tried received harsh sentences of death, life imprisonment, and transportation to prison colonies.

The Commune became legendary. It alarmed governing classes across Europe, who feared revolutionary socialism or anarchism. Many thought that the people should be ruled with an iron fist. International revolutionaries, too, thought that the Communards were the radicalized masses, forgetting that they had risen to save their country. Convinced that political leaders everywhere would be just as brutal in defending private property as Thiers had been, revolutionaries like Marx urged the masses to train themselves for violent insurrection. Other radicals, appalled by the bloodbath, argued that the revolutionary days of 1789, 1830, and 1848 were over because the modern state was too powerful. Workers would have to express their protests by votes and demonstrations.

The suppression of the Paris Commune marked a turning point in French political life. To French property owners, republican government meant radicalism, despite the fact that republicans had destroyed the Commune. A much wider public supported a republican regime either by action or by apathy. Burdened by an indemnity and the loss of Alsace and part of Lorraine in the Franco-Prussian War and embittered by the experience of war and civil war, republican France slowly rebuilt national unity and regained its place in Europe.

Threats to the Republic

The government born from the next few years of political crisis would be the longest-lasting republic in the history of France (1870–1940). Its birth was accidental; with no king willing to rule, republicans did. The Third Republic had a powerful bicameral legislature—a senate and a chamber of deputies, which resembled the House of Commons—and a prime minister, who had to have its support. The president was a figurehead; republicans wanted no new Napoleon. Unlike Britain, France had many political parties, which expressed the deep differences—regional, political, religious, economic, and historical—among the French, but also exaggerated them.

Critics of the Third Republic gathered around a dashing republican general, Georges Boulanger (1837–1891), whose popularity reminded many of Napoleon III. Was France to swing back to authoritarianism again? The threat faded when Boulanger dramatically committed suicide on the grave of his former mistress. Almost immediately, another scandal was exposed. Several republican deputies were involved in a giant stock swindle

AFTER THE FALL: LAROQUETTE PRISONERS BEFORE THE FIRING SQUAD. The repression of the Paris Commune, which resisted the French provisional government when it tried to make peace with the Prussians, was a brutal bloodbath with atrocities on both sides. When it was over, almost eight thousand were sent into exile, five thousand imprisoned and fined, and many executed. Few could have predicted that the republic established then would survive to World War II. (*Corbis-Bettmann.*)

involving the financing of the Panama Canal. They tried to cover up the taking of bribes. The low level of public morality shocked the people. Many viewed all politics as immoral; others thought democracy was prone to corruption as in the United States and France. Prime ministers resigned in rapid succession; cabinets rose and fell frequently, giving the impression of a state without direction; politics seemed to consist of wheeling and dealing. The Third Republic survived, but not without more trouble; in the process, politics took to the streets and the press.

The Dreyfus affair tore France apart for more than a decade. In 1894, Captain Alfred Dreyfus, an Alsatian-Jewish artillery officer, was wrongly accused of selling military secrets to the Germans.

He was condemned to life imprisonment on Devil's Island, off the coast of French Guiana in South America. Anti-Semitic elements joined the Republic's opponents, including the army, the Catholic church, and monarchists, to block every attempt to clear Dreyfus. In the beginning, he had few friends; the vast majority felt that the honor of France and the army was at stake. Then a few radical republicans, including the writers Anatole France, Émile Zola, and the future war leader, Georges Clemenceau, came to Dreyfus's defense, mobilizing public opinion. University students demonstrated, insisting on a retrial. Dreyfus was finally cleared in 1906.

The radical republicans launched a fierce campaign to root out the antirepublicans and anti-

Semitic elements. **Anticlericalism** had been strong in France for more than a century among certain groups; the Dreyfus case exacerbated the divisions in French society. The radicals attacked the Catholic church, expelled religious orders, and confiscated their property. They tried to replace the influence of the parish priest with that of the district schoolmaster. Complete separation of church and state was ordered, making France a secular state.

France on the Eve of War

French economic development lagged. France had fewer and smaller industries than Britain or Germany, and more French people lived in rural areas or in small communities. In general, industry, trade unions, and socialist groups tended to be decentralized rather than national; artisans were much more influential than proletarians. For a generation after the suppression of the Paris Commune, militants refused to cooperate with the Republic or any bourgeois government. In the 1880s, both trade unions and socialist political parties turned to democratic politics to gain social reform, such as pensions and regulations governing working conditions, wages, and hours. The ruling elite opposed such measures, which might have improved the lives of ordinary people. Socialists were ambivalent, thinking such reforms mere tokens to buy off workers. Many workers and intellectuals supported radical **syndicalism** (which advocated bringing industries and government under the control of workers) and even anarchism.

The Third Republic was not popular. The church, the army, socialism, and even memories of the monarchy and the empire inspired deeper passions than the Republic. The Republic survived because its enemies were divided. Few would have believed that France could fight and win the first World War.

GERMANY: AN AUTHORITARIAN STATE?

The Prussian Bismarck created a German empire under his and Prussia's control. Prussia's king

was emperor. All roads led to Berlin's Brandenburg Gate, where Bismarck decided the great issues, shaping the political environment for the next generation. For conservatives and liberals alike, the "Iron Chancellor" was the man of the hour because he had united Germany.

Bismarck's constitution, like that of Napoleon III, was hardly liberal. Both men granted universal manhood suffrage and then manipulated the votes and elections. The German government was federal, the twenty-four states had some powers, but foreign affairs and defense were in the hands of the emperor and his chancellor. The German kaiser, unlike Britain's monarch, had considerable control over lawmaking, foreign affairs, and the military. Aristocrats held the important positions in the military, the diplomatic corps, and the top echelon of the bureaucracy. The German Empire did not have Britain's two-party system, cabinet responsibility, or guarantees of civil liberties. Technically, the Reichstag could refuse to pass the budget, but politicians were usually unwilling to do that. Only the king-emperor could remove the chancellor or the cabinet members from office. Bismarck saw political parties as merely interest groups incapable of making policy for the country as a whole. He treated them as lobbyists. He cared little for liberal and democratic measures, maintaining an authoritarianism that would have significant consequences for Germany's future.

Bismarck's "Struggle for Culture"

To Bismarck, Catholics and socialists were internationalists who did not put Germany's interests first. Bismarck took advantage of the prejudice and non-Catholics' misunderstanding of the declaration of papal infallibility of 1871 to pass discriminatory laws against Catholics, restricting the Jesuits and requiring government supervision of the church and the education of priests in state schools. All marriages had to be performed by state officials. Churchmen who rejected these laws were imprisoned or exiled. Almost 40 percent of Germany's people were Roman Catholic, and Bismarck's persecution actually strengthened the German Catholics' loyalty to their church and to the Catholic Center party. It weakened the lib-

Profile

Jean Jaurès

Jean Jaurès (1859–1914) was the most important socialist in the Third French Republic. A brilliant student, he advanced to the highest ranks of the university. He soon tired of teaching philosophy, however, and chose politics. He was the youngest member elected to the Chamber of Deputies. Deeply concerned about workers' problems, Jaurès believed that capitalism was creating a new feudalism in which the rich controlled the society. He led a socialist party convinced that only the working class struggled for justice and that their struggle could win over others.

Jaurès brought liberal republicans and socialists together for social reforms. He championed Alfred Dreyfus and argued that socialists had just as much at stake as liberals in questions of justice. Jaurès and French workers joined with intellectuals and students in demonstrating for and demanding a fair trial and freedom for the convicted Jewish officer. Many

Roger-Viollet.

erals, who did not defend Catholic civil liberties. Prussian conservatives, though Protestant, resented Bismarck's anticlerical policy, which could be turned against Lutherans as well as Catholics. When Leo XIII became pope in 1878, Bismarck quietly opened negotiations to end the "struggle for culture" (**Kulturkampf**).

In the late 1870s, Bismarck attacked socialists—the other internationalists. Socialists were divided. One group, the German Workers' Association, was formed by Ferdinand Lassalle (1825–1864), a charismatic lawyer-reformer who had the support of workers and trade unionists, as well as some influence with Bismarck himself. Lassalle believed that if Germany enacted social reforms, workers would be just as patriotic as any other group. Marxists scoffed, opposing cooperation with the state, but there were more Lassalleans than Marxists. When Lassalle was

killed in a duel, they joined forces in 1875 to create a German Social Democratic party, the SPD. To crush the socialists, Bismarck sought to drive a wedge between workers and their leaders. He was sure that the liberals would respond as they had when he had attacked the Catholics. When in 1878 two attempts were made on the emperor's life, Bismarck, manipulating the public, blamed the socialists and demanded that the party be outlawed and its leaders imprisoned. The few socialists were not a threat; their immediate practical program called for civil liberties and democracy in Germany. Only those with the narrowest of conservative views would have labeled the socialists as dangerous, but many in Germany, particularly the Prussian Junker class, held such a narrow view. Once again Bismarck was right about the liberals, who scarcely objected when special legislation outlawed subversive organiza-

socialists refused to take part in parliamentary politics; they thought Jaurès a bourgeois politician because he had been a university professor and never a worker. But those credentials brought a wide range of support as Jaurès campaigned vigorously for reforms that French workers still had not won. In 1905, the socialist parties of France joined together under his leadership during a time of strikes and repression. On the international scene, in the Second International, Jaurès was brilliant in his opposition to war, calling for all workers, not just French ones, to refuse to fight should their governments become belligerents.

In the last days before World War I, Jaurès was assassinated by a French nationalist fanatic who was afraid that the great speaker would convince his socialist followers to resist the war. The assassin was wrong. French workers—even socialists—defended their country in 1914 because they believed it to be the most democratic nation.

tions and authorized the police to ban meetings and newspapers.

The Social Democratic party, like the Catholic Center party before, survived and strengthened its disciplined organization. The liberals grew weaker. Meanwhile, Bismarck wooed workers with social legislation. The effects of the rapid industrialization of the 1850s and 1860s disturbed Bismarck, as they did many conservatives. Germany was the first state to enact social legislation: insurance against sickness, disability, accidents, and old age. The employer, the state, and the worker each contributed small amounts to an insurance fund. Many people considered such measures socialist because the government taxed citizens to support workers.

German socialists became the model for socialists in other nations because they had greater numbers and superior organization and leadership and because Bismarck's social legislation had given German workers some protection. The Social Democratic party was not just a party but also a way of life, offering members political activities, youth and women's divisions, athletic leagues, and cultural societies. Before World War I, union membership stood at roughly three million, and the Social Democratic party was the largest single party in Germany. The socialists talked revolution, but many members favored gradual reform, and most German workers were patriotic, even imperialistic.

Germany on the Eve of War

When Kaiser William II (1889–1918) ascended the throne, Germany possessed the most extensive sector of large-scale, concentrated industrial and corporate capitalism, as well as the largest and most powerful unions. Only the United States could rival the German giant capitalist in scale and concentration of industry.

In 1914, Germany was the most highly industrialized and powerful European nation, with the largest and most successful socialist party. Yet it was governed by a political regime that preserved aspects of an absolute monarchy. The constitution was a peculiar mixture of aristocratic Prussian power in the upper house and in the lower, democratic universal male suffrage manipulated to illiberal ends. The bureaucracy, the military, and the chancellor remained out of the reach of the voting populace. Bismarck's hostility to liberalism and his authoritarian rule had undermined the development of a viable parliamentary government. The Social Democrats, ostensibly the party of revolution, were the only party that campaigned for chancellor responsibility, that is, for power of the Reichstag to reject the chancellor. In other countries such a measure would be advocated by liberals, but in Germany democratic and liberal measures were part of the campaign of socialists.

ITALY: UNFULFILLED EXPECTATIONS

Italian nationalists expected greatness from the unification of their country, so long conquered, plundered, divided, and ruled by absolute princes. But the newly unified Italy faced serious problems. An overwhelmingly Roman Catholic country, like France, it was split by religious controversy. Liberals and republicans wanted a secular state, with civil marriage and public education, which was **anathema** to the church. Another divisive factor was Italy's long tradition of separate and rival states—an extreme version of the regional conflicts of other states. Many Italians doubted that the central government would deal justly with every region. Furthermore, few Italians could actually participate in the constitutional monarchy. Of the twenty-seven million citizens, only about two million could vote, even after the reforms of 1881, which tripled the electorate. Liberals could point out that almost every literate male could vote, but this achievement was small consolation to those who had fought for unification but were denied voting privileges when they failed a literacy test.

Among Italian workers, cynicism about the government was so deep that many turned to extreme radical movements, which advocated the rejection of authority and the tactics of terrorism, assassination, and general strikes. Disgust with parliamentary government led workers to believe that direct action would gain more than elections and parties. Advocates of direct action were much stronger in Italy than in France. Other alienated Italians included peasants from the poor rural south. Catholic, loyal to their landlord, and bitterly unhappy with their economic situation, they saw few signs of the new state aside from taxation and conscription.

The ruling elite brushed aside Italy's difficult social and economic problems. It concentrated instead on issues more easily expressed to an inexperienced political nation: nationalism, foreign policy, and military glory. The politicians trumpeted Italy's ambitions for great power status, justifying military expenditures beyond the means of such a poor state. They presented Italy's scramble for African and Mediterranean territories as the solution to its social ills. Exploiting others would pay for badly needed social reforms, and the raw materials gained would fuel industry. The failure of these promises deepened the cynicism of a disillusioned people. On the eve of World War I, Italy was deeply divided politically. A wave of strikes and rural discontent gave sufficient warning to political leaders so that they

declared neutrality, deciding, unlike Russia, not to risk the shaky regime by entering the war. But the appeals of expansionism were too great for them to maintain this policy.

RUSSIA: TSARIST EMPIRE

To the east, bordering on Germany, the vast Russian empire was considered part of Europe, although it differed fundamentally from western Europe. Stretching through the Eurasian landmass from Germany to China and Japan, covering one-sixth of the world's land surface, it suffered from incurable weaknesses. Unprotected by natural boundaries in its vast open spaces, it had been created by conquest. Its rulers lived in permanent dread of foreign invasion and internal breakup. Large distances, an adverse climate, and poor communications, as well as extensive ethnic, religious, and cultural diversity held together by force, made Russia a backward country. The great movements that had shaped the outlook of the modern West—the Renaissance, the Reformation, the Scientific Revolution, the Enlightenment, and the Industrial Revolution—had barely penetrated the lands to the east. Yet Russia's rulers, intermarrying with European royalty, always claimed, along with the western-educated elites, that their country was part of Europe. Their capital, Saint Petersburg, at the westernmost point of the Russian empire, was built to match the splendor of French royal architecture.

Russia's fortunes depended on its political order, which centered on the commands of the ruler. Peter the Great, in the early eighteenth century, had reorganized the tsarist government, centralizing the administration and forcing the nobility to serve the state; he also founded the Russian Academy of Sciences. At the end of the century, an exceptionally energetic ruler, Catherine the Great, inspired by French intellectuals such as Voltaire, strengthened the authority of the tsarist regime. Her successors, however, had reason to fear the liberal views of the Enlightenment. Russian officers, returning from western Europe after the defeat of Napoleon, asked why their country could not share in the civilized life they had just

Art of the Late Nineteenth and Twentieth Centuries

During the late nineteenth century, a number of art movements emerged that redefined both the objectives and the techniques of painters, sculptors, architects, and artisans. What set nineteenth-century art apart from works that came before was the realization among artists that they did not need to devote themselves to capturing reality as it was. They began to move away from representational art, pursuing instead a course that would bring them far along the road to abstraction—so far that by the early twentieth century, images bore almost no resemblance to the objects from which they were drawn.

As a point of departure, it is useful to consider the work of Jean François Millet (1814–1875), a French realist who brought scenes from everyday life to his canvas. Like the neoclassicists, Millet aspired to visual accuracy. Nonetheless, his work was innovative,

1. Jean François Millet. *The Gleaners*, 1857. *(Musée d'Orsay, Paris/Erich Lessing/Art Resource, NY.)*

2. Paul Cézanne. *Madame Cézanne in the Conservatory*, c. 1880. *(Metropolitan Museum of Art, NY.)*

for he did not paint heroic, highly dramatic scenes but rather portrayed peasants and other common people at their usual tasks.

In *The Gleaners* (Figure 1) from 1857, Millet depicts, in a rhythmic composition, three heavy, slow-moving women harvesting a field of wheat. He uses color and light to convey their solid simplicity. In turning to everyday matters and bringing his canvas outside, Millet broke with tradition and set a prece-

dent for the colorists of the later part of the century.

Art movements of the mid- and late nineteenth century include impressionism, a style that began in France and gained popularity both in Europe and in the newest emerging art center, the United States. A host of artists responded to the tenets of the impressionist movement, which heralded changes in color, line, and style. One hallmark of impressionists

3. Georges Seurat. *Sunday Afternoon on the Island of La Grande Jatte*, 1884–86. *(Art Institute of Chicago.)*

was their urge to paint *en plein air*, in nature—to take their easels out of the confining studio and set them down in fields, meadows, or anywhere else they could experience nature and put it on canvas, as Millet had done.

Art historians describe the impressionist movement as a revolution in color, in part because impressionist painters did not laboriously mix their paints on palettes but rather mixed colors on the canvas itself. But the impressionist movement, and the postimpressionists who followed, also heralded a revolution in line, in dimension, and in painting itself. What impressionists had in common was the desire to record realistically their immediate visual impression of a subject—for example, how a landscape appeared in a fleeting moment when light and atmosphere randomly coalesced.

The artists who followed are loosely called postimpressionists. Generally speaking, the term *postimpressionist* can be applied to almost any artist who worked after the 1880s. Usually, the artist had an impressionist phase and then experimented further not only with color but with form and space as well.

The paintings of Paul Cézanne (1839–1906) are some of the finest work of the postimpressionist era. He is best known for still lifes, but his portraits are also important reminders of the developments in the visual arts during the nineteenth century. The portrait of his wife, *Madame Cézanne in the Conservatory* (c. 1880) (Figure 2), illustrates many of the qualities of a postimpressionist work: overlapping brush strokes create depth and volume, and their rhythmic patterning adds texture to the flat canvas. Cézanne seems to be working at once in both a realistic and an impressionist genre. The face of the subject is rendered realistically, as are the tree behind her and some other elements of the composition. But her

4. Vincent Van Gogh. *Self-Portrait*, 1889. *(Musée d'Orsay, Paris/Erich Lessing/Art Resource, NY.)*

hands, her dress, and most aspects of the background are impressionistic. This blending of styles and the experimentation with different vantage points and different elements that go into the overall composition demonstrate the approach tried by many artists of this period.

In his brief career, Georges Seurat (1859–1891) was able to take the lessons of the impressionists and give them a new twist. He, too, shared the impressionists' love of color and worked at using color in a wholly new way. Called pointillism, the technique used by Seurat required meticulous brush control and a deep understanding of the mechanics of color. Seurat's first pointillist work, *Sunday Afternoon on the Island of La Grande Jatte*

(1884–86) (Figure 3) illustrates the care with which the artist rendered his images.

Typically, a painting by Seurat, which more often than not was preceded by a great many preliminary sketches and drawings, comprises literally millions of tiny individual dots and strokes of pure color applied in such a way that the viewer's eye blends them into their final form. Thus, pointillism foreshadows the digitization used in electronic images today.

Seurat's contemporary, Vincent Van Gogh (1853–1890), is one of the best-known painters. The subject of biography, music, and endless fascination, Van Gogh could be classified as either a postimpressionist or an expressionist, although probably neither term would

5. Paul Gauguin. *Ea Haereia oe (Where Are You Going?)* (Hermitage, St. Petersburg, Russia/Scala/Art Resource, NY.)

have found favor with the artist himself. Van Gogh's career spanned only ten years—even less time than that of Seurat—and some art historians call him the greatest Dutch artist since Vermeer and other painters of the seventeenth century.

Van Gogh's strengths lie in his use of color and his understanding of the medium of oil paint. His thickly applied brush strokes add light and shadow to his luminous canvases. He did not hesitate to depart from realism, to distort shape and exaggerate color to suggest energy and motion and to express feeling.

He painted a whole gamut of subjects from still lifes, to landscapes, to portraits and self-portraits. He was particularly fascinated by the human face. He said that there was something in the eyes—the soul, the inner life—whether those of a beggar or a streetwalker, that was more beautiful than a cathedral. His aim was to capture the human essence in such pictures.

In *Self-Portrait* (1889) (Figure 4), he scrutinized his own face one more time, shortly before his suicide. It is a stark testament to a life tormented by mental illness yet driven to sublime heights of creative expression.

6. Pablo Picasso. *Les Demoiselles d'Avignon*, 1907. *(Musem of Modern Art, NY/Art Resource, NY/ ©2005 Estate of Pablo Picasso/Artists Rights Society [ARS], New York.)*

Among the other *-isms* that defined art in the late nineteenth century was primitivism, a movement "discovered" by progressive artists such as Pablo Picasso. Picasso looked to various sources for his inspiration, including Africa and the Far East. He also championed other artists who worked outside the mainstream.

In line with this tendency was the work of Paul Gauguin (1848–1903), who renounced not only impressionism but also the entire Western notion that a painter should reproduce the physical world as it actually appears. In 1891, attempting to escape what he viewed as a corrupt civilization, Gauguin abandoned France for the island of Tahiti, in the South Pacific. During his first two years in Tahiti, Gauguin painted sixty-six canvases, one of which was *Ea Haereia oe* (*Where Are You Going?*)

Figure 5). In the two-dimensionality, intentional disproportion, rich coloration, and ambiguity of content of this painting, we see an attempt to revert to the pristine viewpoint of primitivism, in which the artist's work is predominated more by imagination and feeling than by the restraints of sensory perception.

In the twentieth century, no single style prevailed. It was a period of great experimentation and great changes. One of the most important movements of the early decades was abstraction, more easily defined visually than in words. Pablo Picasso (1881–1974) was one of the champions of the abstract movement. His *Les Demoiselles d'Avignon* (1907) (Figure 6) redefines the female form. This is not Boucher's *Venus*. Picasso's female forms are reductive— angular distortions of female bodies—and they hint at a number of cultural influences. While some may see suggestions of the classical in the forms of the three women to the left, there are also echoes of African sculpture; indeed, Picasso was influenced by both. But he was also inventive and sophisticated. His work reduces the visual to its most abstract elements. Changes in his style over his long and productive career indicate his receptiveness to influences from non-Western cultures as well as from his own Western heritage.

The genre of abstraction that Picasso pioneered is called *cubism*. Among the host of cubist followers, many developed their own distinct cubist subcategories. Marc Chagall (1887–1985), a Russian painter whose works often strongly reflected his Jewish roots, worked in a cubist style that combined fantasy and reality. In *The Fiddler* (1911) (Figure 7), he blends elements of Russian and Jewish folktales with cubist renderings of scenes from everyday life.

By World War I, avant-garde artists had experimented with a multitude of abstract styles. At the Armory Show in New York City in 1913, many abstract painters made their debut on the North American continent. Generally favorably received by the art community (though not as welcomed by the average viewer), abstract painting began to gain a foothold outside Europe. Given the disfavor with which the National Socialists in Germany viewed nonrepresentational art, it was a good thing that America was willing to welcome avant-garde artists and their work.

In 1939, the Nazis—either by auction or destruction—got rid of many of the most famous abstract works in German museums. Some pieces were sold to museums or collectors in other European cities, only to fall victim once again to the strict anti-abstract sentiments of the Nazis as the war progressed; other works, and artists, were saved in the United States.

During and after World War II, art continued to be a compendium of various themes and movements. Not every artist worked in the abstract; some preferred to stick to realism. Still others painted in a style that came to be known as abstract expressionism.

7. Marc Chagall. *The Fiddler*, 1911. *(Kunstsammlung Nordrhein-Westfalen, Duesseldorf, Germany/ Erich Lessing/ Art Resource/ ©2005 Artists Rights Society [ARS], New York/ADAGP, Paris.)*

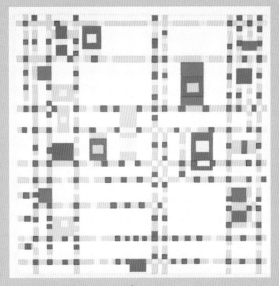

8. Piet Mondrian, *Broadway Boogie-Woogie*, 1942. *(Museum of Modern Art, NY/Art Resource, NY/HCR International.)*

9. Edward Hopper. *Nighthawks*, 1942. *(Art Institute of Chicago.)*

The art of Piet Mondrian (1872–1944) may summarize the path taken by many abstract artists whose careers spanned both world wars. A Dutch painter, Mondrian started his career by working with representational images. Soon, however, he began to strip away all the elements of the representational, replacing reality with abstraction and reducing his canvases to simple, rhythmical, almost mathematically precise shapes and primary colors. He described his own work as neoplasticism; the paintings themselves suggest strict rules for balancing the horizontal and vertical, and color and space.

One of Mondrian's last works, *Broadway Boogie-Woogie* (1942–43) (Figure 8), amply illustrates the flatness and geometric precision of his neoplastic vision. The canvas shows only three colors and is divided only into horizontal and vertical space, yet it possesses a rhythmic sense that reveals great skill and a fine grasp of how space and color can be used.

Not all art of the twentieth century was abstract. Some of the best representational art of any era belongs to this period. This is exemplified by the work of the American painter Edward Hopper (1882–1967). His haunting *Nighthawks* (1942) (Figure 9), painted the same year as Mondrian completed *Broadway Boogie-Woogie*, shows the reality of loneliness. It placed Hopper in the school of social realists, who painted true-to-life images of the world around them. Hopper depicted not cathedrals or temples but diners, barber shops, and movie theaters, using light and shadow as skillfully as Rembrandt.

observed. They turned into revolutionaries and attempted a futile uprising in December 1825 at the accession of Nicholas I. Thereafter, fear of revolution always haunted the tsarist government.

To counter the subversive influence of western ideals and institutions, Nicholas I decreed an ideology of Russian superiority; called *official nationality*, it remained in force until 1917. The government's version of Russian nationalism taught the Russian people that the Orthodox church, the autocratic rule of the tsar, and Russia's Slavic culture made the Russian empire superior to the West. With the help of the secret police, the government tried to re-create the largely spontaneous unity of the leading western states by all-inclusive political controls, drawing a virtual iron curtain around the country to keep out dangerous foreign influences. The ideal was a monolithic regime, run like an army by a vigorous administration centered on the monarch; all Russians were to obey his wise and fatherly commands. But Nicholas's ambition to make Russia victorious in all comparisons with western Europe was thwarted in the Crimean War (1854–56), fought on Russian soil. English and French expeditionary forces defeated the Russian army and frustrated Russian efforts to gain political influence in the eastern Mediterranean area. Nicholas died before the war ended. A new regime began under Alexander II (1855–1881) in a mood of profound and widespread crisis. Alexander II was determined to preserve autocratic rule in Russia. However, he wanted Russia to achieve what had made western Europe strong: the energetic support and free enterprise of all its citizens. Whether stimulating popular initiative was possible without undermining **autocracy** was the key puzzle for him and for his successors to the end of the tsarist regime.

Alexander's boldest reforms included the emancipation of the serfs in 1861. They were liberated from bondage to the nobility and given land of their own, but not individual freedom. They remained tied to their villages and to their households, which owned the land collectively. Emancipation did not transform the peasants into enterprising and loyal citizens. For the nonpeasant minority, a package of other reforms brought new opportunities: limited self-government for selected rural areas and urban settlements, an independent judiciary, and the rule of law. Trial by jury was introduced, as well as a profession novel to Russians: the practice of law.

Meanwhile, Alexander reopened the borders, allowing closer ties with Europe. The rising class of businesspeople and professional experts looked west and conformed to western European middle-class standards. There was some relaxation in the repression of non-Russian minorities. The construction of railroads facilitated agricultural exports to the west and permitted the importing of goods and capital from the west. For some years, the economy boomed.

More significant in the long run was the flowering of Russian thought and literature among the intelligentsia. These were educated Russians who were shaped by Western schooling and travel yet still were prompted by the "Russian soul" and an intensity of inward feeling unknown in Western society. They quarreled with fierce sincerity about whether Russia should pursue superiority by imitating the West or by cultivating its own Slavic genius, possibly through a Pan-Slavic movement. Pan-Slavism, which glorified the solidarity of Russians with other Slavic peoples of eastern Europe, was a popular cause. Even more than the tsars, the intelligentsia hoped for a glorious Russia that would outshine the West.

The tsar, however, would not permit open discussion likely to provoke rebellion. Liberals advocating gradual change were thwarted by censorship and the police. The 1860s saw the rise of self-righteous fanatics ready to match the chicanery of the police and foment social revolution. By the late 1870s, they organized themselves into a secret terrorist organization, and in 1881, they assassinated Alexander II. The era of reforms ended, but the revolutionary underground continued, soon led by Marxist intellectuals.

The next tsar, Alexander III (1881–1894), a firm though unimaginative ruler, returned to the principles of Nicholas I. In defense against the revolutionaries, he perfected the police state, even enlisting anti-Semitism in its cause. He updated autocracy and stifled dissent, but he also promoted economic development. Russia had relied too heavily on foreign loans and goods; it had to build up its own resources. It also needed more railroads to bind its huge empire together, so in 1891, the tsar ordered the construction of the Trans-Siberian Railroad. Soon afterward, Minister of Finance Sergei Witte used the railroad expansion to boost heavy industry and industrialization generally.

In 1900, Witte addressed a farsighted memorandum to the young Nicholas II (1894–1917), who was hopelessly unprepared and out of tune with the times when he succeeded his father:

> *Russia more than any other country needs a proper economic foundation for its national policy and culture. . . . International competition does not wait. If we do not take energetic and decisive measures so that in the course of the next decade our industry will be able to satisfy the needs of Russia and of the Asiatic countries which are—or should be—under our influence, then the rapidly growing foreign industries will . . . establish themselves in our fatherland and the Asiatic countries mentioned above. . . . Our economic backwardness may lead to political and cultural backwardness as well.*[1]

Forced industrialization, however, also brought perils. It propelled the country into alien and often hated ways of life, created a discontented new class of workers, and impoverished agriculture. In addition, it promoted mobility, literacy, and contact with western Europe. Thus, it helped to increase political agitation among the professional classes, workers, peasants, and subject nationalities. Indispensable for national self-assertion and survival, industrialization strained the country's fragile unity.

The first jolt, the revolution of 1905, resulted from the Russo-Japanese War, in which Russia was defeated. Autocracy survived, although it was now saddled with a parliament, called the Imperial Duma, a concession to the revolution. The new regime, privately resisted by Nicholas II, started auspiciously. Russian art and literature flourished and the economy progressed. Agrarian reforms introduced the incentives of private property and individual enterprise in the villages. Nevertheless, popular resentment against government-sponsored modernization festered, waiting for opportunities to explode.

The four imperial rulers of Russia between 1825 and 1914 had labored under enormous difficulties in their efforts to match the power and prestige of the great states of Europe. Two of them met a violent end: Alexander II was assassinated, and Nicholas II was murdered. The other two died in weariness and failure. Although the awe that the tsars inspired among their subjects was real, their splendor was hollow. The tsars' high hopes for Russia's prominence in the world were frustrated by their failure to cope with the massive adversities confronting the country. Its hugeness and scarce means of communication, along with its ethnic, religious, and regional diversity, prevented the emergence of a collective national identity. The country also lacked an effective middle class. The members of the Russian intelligentsia and professional class were as ignorant as the tsars about their country's realities; some even dreamed of a Russia superior to the West. And the abysmally backward peasant masses, scattered over the largest country in the world, were poor material for building a modern state. Outwardly impressive, the Russian empire faced a grim future as the international competition for power escalated in World War I.

Online Study Center

Improve Your Grade
Primary Source: What Is to Be Done with Russia? (Vladimir I. Lenin)

THE UNITED STATES: DEMOCRATIC GIANT

Within a generation of its bloody Civil War (1861–1865), the United States moved into the ranks of giant industrial powers, then to the status of a great power, and, by the end of World War I, to world leadership. In the mid-nineteenth century, however, the United States was essentially a nation of farmers, producing primary goods or raw materials. In the northeastern part of the country, craft industries supplied consumer goods for a domestic market. Advancing beyond basic craft goods was just as slow a process as it

PEASANTS IN RUSSIA. This photograph from the late nineteenth century shows Russian peasants in front of their home. (*Corbis-Bettmann.*)

was in France and most of central Europe. Before the Civil War, the economy was primarily mercantile. Merchants were the commercial cement bonding the many small artisans, farmers, and exporters. Despite immigration from Europe and the use of slaves, there was a steady demand for cheap labor. Capital was even scarcer than labor. Americans were inventive, competitive, and socially democratic.

In many ways the early industrialization of the United States resembled that of Britain. Unskilled European immigrants and rural laborers furnished the manpower for New England textile mills, just as Irish and rural laborers had in England. Both shared the blessings of a single government, able to provide a stable framework for commerce, and in the case of the United States, maintain tariffs against British competition. In both, government was noninterventionist—unwilling and unable to regulate private enterprise. In both the exploitation of resources as private property rather than public property

was characteristic. Once a large internal market for cheap, standardized goods developed, entrepreneurs took the risks of investment and production on a large scale. Even more than the British, perhaps because of the much larger market for cheap goods, Americans took to machines that had standardized and interchangeable parts to produce such goods. (Eli Whitney, inventor of the cotton gin, began by producing interchangeable parts for handguns, for example.) Unlike Britain, however, the United States depended on an influx of capital (most of it English)—a dependence that continued even after the Civil War, when great sectors of the American economy moved from the work of artisans to modern concentrated industry. American industrialization gained momentum with the westward expansion. Unlike Britain, American industrialization required substantial foreign investment in large-scale corporations in heavy industries such as coal mining and iron and steel manufacture.

The role of government has often been underestimated in the United States. On both the regional and the national level, government encouraged free enterprise by allowing individuals and corporations to claim the nation's resources. It also fostered railroad building, tariff regulation, and free immigration—all of which contributed to the construction of an industrial giant. In terms of social problems, however, government took a laissez-faire stance. American politicians did much less than Europeans to support social legislation, including pensions and minimum wages; there was no Bismarck, Lloyd George, or Churchill to write social legislation. Yet until the end of the century, the United States had less labor strife than Europe and a relative absence of class conflict. Why? Did American workers share the dream of entrepreneurial success? Was the difficulty of forging class solidarity among varied ethnic groups of different cultures and languages decisive? Each new immigrant group (and later the rural blacks) did enter at the bottom, supplying cheap and competitive labor and experiencing violent reactions from their fellow workers from other ethnic and racial groups. At the end of the century, assimilated and politically active workers were able to prohibit Asian immigration. Congress closed the doors to Chinese workers after they had built the transcontinental railroad. A **gentleman's agreement** excluded the Japanese.

Labor conflict between workers and employers did flare up, however, in the decade before World War I. Generally, workers voted for one of the two major parties, but in the election of 1912, more than a million voted for the socialist candidate. In that election about 70 percent of the votes cast were either socialist or progressive. Not all of these voters were "foreigners" or recent immigrants, as contemporaries pretended. Many Americans were critical of the money power of giant cartels and monopolies, and both Theodore Roosevelt of the Republicans and Woodrow Wilson of the Democrats called for restrictions on monopolies, or trusts. Unrestricted competition, which gave cartels and trusts an unfair advantage, upset many Americans. Corporate ethics shocked them; business leaders as "robber barons" was not the American dream.

By 1914, the American market was the largest, most homogeneous, and most rapidly growing in the world. The United States was the largest industrial nation, producing more steel and coal than any other country. It was also the world's leader in automobiles, farming technology, electricity, and petroleum sectors. Its labor was the most productive and had the highest standard of living. The United States had achieved this commanding position in a little more than a generation.

A GOLDEN AGE?

To thoughtful Europeans living in 1915, after a year of World War I, the nineteenth century must have seemed a golden era. They might have viewed it as a period of unparalleled peace and progress, full of the promise of all that well-meaning people considered modern: liberal institutions and democratic movements, autonomous nations, scientific and industrial progress, and individual human development. The century that had just ended seemed one of progress in the production of goods, the alleviation of want, the development of technology, and the application of science to industry and medicine. Part of that progress, in most minds, was the extension of constitutional and liberal government and the expression of humanitarian concern for others. Serfdom had been abolished in Europe; so had slavery in the United States and Brazil. Europeans spoke of self-government as a right. The importance of democracy had been acknowledged, and in most of Europe, universal manhood suffrage, if not universal suffrage, was in effect before the outbreak of the war.

The world had become smaller, more interdependent, and more cosmopolitan. Many westerners were more educated and probably better fed, housed, and clothed than their counterparts in preceding eras. Europe was at the height of its power in the nineteenth century. European productive capacities had reached out to most areas of the world, and European culture was brilliant—whether considered in the aggregate, or individually as German, French, English, or Italian culture.

A New York Sweatshop, Photo by Jacob Riis (1849–1914). The latter half of the nineteenth century saw a proliferation of sweatshops. Adults and children alike, usually immigrants, labored long hours in appalling conditions for little pay. (*Corbis-Bettmann.*)

Yet people looking back from the vantage point of 1915 must have realized, too, that something had gone wrong in the nineteenth century. Authoritarian governments persisted in central, eastern, and southern Europe. Traditional institutions and groups still exercised their privileges at the expense of others, often by brutally repressing opposition, especially regional and minority loyalties. Some had begun to have doubts when the revolutions of 1848 failed to reconcile national and class conflicts. Perhaps the bitter reaction to 1848, the harsh reality of the midcentury wars of unification, and the building of the centralized state had perverted the ideals of liberal government and individual freedom. Many doubted the wisdom of democratic government as they saw cynical leaders manipulate the passions of the masses. Perhaps the ideals of liberal government, individual freedom, national autonomy, and economic progress were not equally suited to every situation. In the last part of the nineteenth century and the first part of the twentieth, liberal-democratic ideals fell prey to authoritarianism, extreme nationalism, imperialism, class conflict, and racism. But despite a world war and mass destruction, liberal ideals would survive and spread.

❖   ❖   ❖

Online Study Center ACE the Test

NOTE

1. Theodore Von Laue, *Sergei Witte and the Industrialization of Russia* (New York: Columbia University Press, 1963), p. 3.

SUGGESTED READING

Anderson, Bonnie, and Judith Zinsser, *A History of Their Own: Women in Europe from Prehistory to the Present,* vol. 2 (1988). A comprehensive survey of the movement for women's independence.

Blackbourn, David, and Geoff Eley, *The Peculiarities of German History* (1984). Critically examines traditional assumptions about Bismarck's Germany.

Foster, R. F., *Modern Ireland (1600–1972)* (1988). The best single-volume history.

Hobsbawm, Eric, *Nations and Nationalism Since 1780* (1992). A good introduction to a complex subject.

——, *Nations and Nationalism Since 1780: Program, Myth, Reality* (1993). A sophisticated survey of developments in Europe.

Johnson, D., *France and the Dreyfus Affair* (1967). The best of many books on this topic.

Joll, James, *Europe Since 1870* (1973). A valuable general survey, particularly good on socialism in the individual nations.

Kemp, Tom, *Industrialization in Nineteenth-Century Europe* (1985). A readable general survey incorporating recent scholarship.

Kropotkin, Peter, *Memoirs of a Revolutionist* (1967). A classic autobiography (written in 1889) of an aristocratic anarchist in tsarist Russia.

Mack Smith, Denis, *Italy: A Modern History,* rev. ed. (1969). An excellent survey, with emphasis on the failure of Italy to develop viable liberal institutions or economic solutions.

Montgomery, David, *The Fall of the House of Labor: The Workplace, the State, and American Labor Activism, 1865–1925.* An important book for the changes of work life in the Industrial Revolution.

Nelson, Daniel, *Managers and Workers: Origins of the New Factory System in the United States, 1880–1920* (1975). An intelligent examination of the industrial growth that made the United States a Great Power.

Perkin, Harold, *The Third Revolution: Professional Elites in the Modern World* (1998). A comparative study of the rise of professional elites in the major powers.

Ragsdale, Hugh, *The Russian Tragedy: The Burden of History* (1996). A short history of Russia that sets the tsarist empire in historical perspective.

Seton-Watson, Christopher, *Italy from Liberalism to Fascism* (1981). An excellent survey of Italian history.

Sheehan, J. J., *German History (1770–1866)* (1989). The best on the subject.

Weber, E., *Peasants into Frenchmen: Modernization of Rural France, 1870–1914* (1976). Describes the most important aspects of nation building.

Wehler, Hans, *The German Empire 1871–1918* (1986). A revisionist analysis in keeping with Blackbourn and Eley.

Wright, Gordon, *France in Modern Times,* 2nd ed. (1974). A good survey of the entire period.

Imperialism: Western Global Dominance

Lithograph by Joseph Keppler, showing the Great Power of the West fighting over China.
(Library of Congress.)

- **Emergence of the New Imperialism**
- **European Domination of Asia**
- **The Scramble for Africa**
- **Latin America**
- **The Legacy of Imperialism**

Focus Questions

1. How did industrialization change Europeans' relations with China, India, and Japan?

2. What explanations for imperialism or European expansion were offered at the end of the nineteenth century?

3. What were the obstacles to Indian unity and independence?

4. Why was Africa divided up in such a short time?

Online Study Center

This icon will direct you to interactive map and primary source activities on the website http://college.hmco.com/pic/perrywc8e.

I n the last two decades of the nineteenth century, European nations very rapidly laid claim to great portions of the world's surface. Russia and the United States pushed to the territorial limits of their continents and beyond. Westerners exploited the weakness of Japanese and Chinese dynasties to gain economic and political advantage in the Far East. They separated one by one the territories of the Ottoman Turkish ruler. The British deprived India of all semblance of independence, ruling it directly or through puppet princes. Europeans grabbed most of Africa, seizing goods, annexing territories, and carving out empires if local rulers were too weak or too self-interested to prevent it. Latin American development and prosperity became absolutely dependent on Europe and the United States.

From about 1880 to 1914, Europeans confronted each other, willing to fight over stretches of desert or rain forest that they could scarcely locate on the map. Asians and Africans who could not resolve conflicts among themselves found their lives controlled and their lands occupied by Europeans. Even those who united could not counter Western military and technological superiority.

European domination of most of the world continued until after World War II. The impact of **imperialism**—the domination by a country of the political, economic, or cultural life of another country, region, or people—contributed to both world wars and to the conflicting ideologies and crises of the cold war. Today's interdependent global economy and culture is, in part, the result of more than a century of imperialism.

EMERGENCE OF THE NEW IMPERIALISM

From the long perspective, European history has been one of expansion. It has also been a history of a struggle for domination of others—from the sixteenth-century explorations, conquests, and settlements of the Americas and the aggressive inroads in Southeast Asia and Africa for lucrative trade in spices, silks, luxury goods, and slaves to the eighteenth-century wars over trade and claims

Chronology 27.1 ❖ Expansion of Western Dominance

1830	The French move into Algeria
1839–1842	Opium War: the British defeat the Chinese, annexing treaty ports in China and opening them to Western trade
1853	U.S. naval forces open Japan to Western trade
1857–58	Sepoy Mutiny; Britain replaces the East India Company and governs India directly
1867	Mexicans led by Juárez execute Maximilian; Meiji Restoration in Japan
1869	Opening of Suez Canal
1876	Stanley sets up posts in the Congo for Leopold II of Belgium
1878	Congress of Berlin: Great Powers prevent Russia from upsetting the balance of power in the Near East
1878–1881	British and Russian troops occupy Afghanistan
1881	The French take control of Tunisia
1882	Britain occupies Egypt
1883–85	The French force the Chinese out of Indochina
1884	Berlin Conference on Africa
1894–95	Sino-Japanese War: the British, Russians, and French intervene to take away Japan's gains
1896	Ethiopians defeat Italian invaders at Adowa
1898	Spanish-American War: the United States annexes the Philippines and Puerto Rico and occupies Cuba; the battle of Omdurman in the Sudan
1899–1902	Boer War between the British and the Afrikaners
1900	Boxers rebel against foreign presence in China
1904–05	Russo-Japanese War: the Japanese defeat the Russians
1911	Mexican Revolution; Manchu dynasty is overthrown in China, a republic formed, and Sun Zhongshan (Sun Yat-sen) becomes its president; civil war breaks out in China
1919	Britain grants a legislative assembly in India; Gandhi's passive resistance movement broadens in response to the Amritsar Massacre; Kemal Atatürk emerges as the Turkish national leader; League of Nations mandate system established

to colonies. By the early 1800s, however, the old slaving stations in Africa had declined, as had the Caribbean sugar trade and the mines of Central and South America. Revolutionary wars had liberated the United States and Latin America and seemed to usher in a new era of trade and investment without political control. For most of the nineteenth century Europeans—at least those engaged in the growth of industry and the development of the nation—showed little interest in adding to the remnants of colonial empires. Advocates of free trade argued that commerce would go to whichever country could produce the best goods most cheaply. Efforts to add colonies would be better expended in improving industry, they said.

Meanwhile, European influence over the rest of the world grew as European nations industrialized, expanding world trade and drawing previously untouched peoples into the network of supply and demand of raw materials, finished goods, and capital. The expansion of world trade and the spread of Western ideas and technology continued even without any extensions of political empires. Masses of European immigrants made new homes in North and South America, Australia, and New Zealand.

Suddenly, however, in the last decades of the century, Europeans switched abruptly from commercial penetration to active conquest, political control, and exploitation of previously unclaimed and, in many ways, untouched territories. Why did Europeans strive to claim and control the entire world?

Conflicting Interpretations

Some historians suggest that the new imperialism (to differentiate it from the **colonialism** of settlement and trade of the 1500s and 1600s) was a direct result of industrialization. With intensified economic activity and competition, Europeans struggled for raw materials, markets for their manufactured goods, and places to invest their capital for higher rates of return. In the late 1800s, many politicians and industrialists believed that annexing overseas territories was the only way for their nations to ensure the economic necessities for their people. Trusting the free market might mean triumph for competitor states. Captains of industry defended the search for new empires to their sometimes reluctant governments and compatriots, predicting dire economic consequences if their countries failed to get their share of the world markets.

Historians today, however, point out that most of the areas claimed by Europeans and Americans were not profitable sources of raw materials or wealthy enough to be good markets. For Europeans and Americans, the primary trading and investment venues were Europe and America rather than Asia or Africa. Some individual businesses made colonial profits, but most colonies proved unprofitable for the Western taxpayer. Between 1865 and 1914, for example, only 39 percent of British investment went to lands of the empire outside the British Isles, 28 percent of that amount going to the self-governing dominions. The average rate of return did not surpass that from home investments. In general, the colonies did not attract surplus European population that could contribute to the mother country's economy. The Americas and the British settlements drew most of the European emigrants, who also streamed to Australia, Canada, New Zealand, and South America—lands already dominated by westerners. Two-thirds of British emigrants went outside the empire, mostly to the United States. Italians certainly did not migrate to Italy's African territories, and the French scarcely migrated at all.

The economic justifications of imperialism are inseparable from the intensely nationalistic ones. Policymakers hoped that possession of empires would solve economic problems, which were particularly pressing after the crash of 1873, and join together disparate social groups with pride in national power. The newly unified states, Germany and Italy, demanded colonies as recognition of their Great Power status; leaders in those two nations were convinced that Britain's standing depended on colonies and naval power. They were aware of the heavy tax burden on British subjects, the expenses of empire, and the greatly increased possibility of war with rival nations or resistant subjects. Nevertheless, these leaders chose an imperial course. Having lost ingloriously to Prussia in 1870, France also turned its attention overseas, hoping to recoup prestige and to add to its work force and wealth for future European struggles. Many leaders hoped that imperialism would win them the loyalty of their own people. Some argued that the well-being of the workers depended on colonies. Others argued from strength: Americans, who built one of the world's great industrial powers after the Civil War, trumpeted their achievements by defeating the once-imperial Spain in Cuba and the Philippines. In the 1890s, Japan announced that it had joined the world's Great Powers by attacking China for control of Korea's raw materials and markets. Still others urged imperialism from weakness. Economically backward Russia pushed east to the Pacific and south toward India for ports and resources to develop its commerce and industry. Thus, both economically powerful states and struggling ones turned to imperialism.

On the eve of World War I, many socialists, including Vladimir Lenin, a revolutionary Marxist who would become one of the leaders of the Russian Revolution in 1917, argued that imperialism was inevitable in a highly advanced **capitalist** country. These socialists asserted that capitalist nations maintained their monopolistic economy and their political system by exploiting the less-developed world. Monopoly capitalism was condemned to periodic depressions due to lack of materials, markets, and capital, Lenin said. Unless the governments of capitalist countries could ensure high wages and profits for their own people by exploiting colonial peoples, working-class revolutions would break out. Powerful business interests also pushed their governments to the verge of war to safeguard their profits. At the same time, Lenin said, imperialism greatly accelerated both the development of capitalism and opposition to it among the victims of imperialism in Asia, Africa, and Latin America. He predicted that the struggle for empire would end in war between the Great Powers, which would draw the colonies into European affairs even faster than the operations of the market.

Nationalistic competition among the Europeans led them as much as economic motives to extend their power struggles to Africa and Asia. Far away from their European boundaries, leaders acquired territories for strategic reasons or to keep rivals out. For example, Britons worked to keep the Germans out of the Middle East because it might open the Indian Ocean—and the British-dominated Indian sub-

continent—to them. They had to keep the Russians out of Afghanistan too. Bismarck actually encouraged French expansion in Africa, hoping the inevitable conflict with the Italians and the British would distract them from Alsace and Lorraine, which Germany had taken in 1870. Overseas expansion could create yet another political rift to weaken the French government; at the least it would be expensive for France to maintain. But when Germany expanded its navy for glory and power, Britain moved quickly to ally with its rival France.

The British liked to think that they were merely defending their empire, particularly India. They defined enormous amounts of territory and water as essential. Other nations saw Britain as their primary rival for the spoils of imperialism—for "a place in the sun," as the Germans liked to phrase it. In Russia, a small clique of nobles and officers urged expansion, knowing that a move into Asia would bring conflict with Britain. Later, such a move meant conflict with Japan, driving the British and Japanese together. Because the conflicts between Europeans were played out in Asia and Africa, perhaps for a while they helped keep Europe itself relatively peaceful. In the long run, however, the tense atmosphere of imperialism—the **militarism** and the racism—contributed to an even more devastating conflict in Europe, World War I, which engaged the empires as well.

The most extreme ideological expression of nationalism and imperialism was Social Darwinism. In the popular mind, the concepts of evolution justified the exploitation of "lesser breeds without the law" by superior races. This language of race and conflict, of superior and inferior people, had wide currency in the Western states. Social Darwinists vigorously advocated the acquisition of empires, saying that strong nations—by definition, those that were successful at expanding industry and empire—would survive and that others would not. To these elitists, all white men were more fit than nonwhites to prevail in the struggle for dominance; even among Europeans, some nations were deemed more fit than others for the competition. Usually, Social Darwinists thought their own nation the best, which sparked their competitive enthusiasm. But some feared that their people were incapable of endurance and sacrifice. They hoped the struggle for colonies would strengthen the nation's biological inheritance, its racial stock.

A GERMAN MISSIONARY WITH STUDENTS. Throughout the nineteenth century, Christian missionaries had gone to Asia, Africa, and Latin America to preach and carry on the crusade against slavery. Many of these Christians devoted their lives to accomplishing their goals; at the same time, many carried with them the ethnocentric values and judgments of their compatriots who thought that non-Europeans were backward and uncivilized. (*Ullstein/The Granger Collection.*)

Not all advocates of empire were Social Darwinists. Some did not think of themselves as racists; but when they believed extending empire, law, order, and industry would raise "backward peoples" up the ladder of evolution to equality, they shared the assumptions of the Social Darwinists. In the nineteenth century, in contrast to the seventeenth and eighteenth centuries, Europeans, except for missionaries, rarely adopted the customs or learned the languages of local people. They had little sense that other cultures and other peoples had merit and deserved respect.

Many westerners believed that it was their duty as Christians to set an example and to educate others. Missionaries were the first to meet and learn

about many peoples and the first to develop writing for those without a written language. Christian missionaries were ardently opposed to slavery, and throughout the century they went to unexplored African regions to preach against slavery, which was still carried on by Arab and African traders. But even missionaries thought preaching would not end the enslavement of those Africans who were vanquished in tribal wars. Some, like David Livingstone, hoped an expanding European economy would bring Africa to the world market and ultimately to freedom and progress.

Some of the passion for imperialism was sparked by interest in exotic places. At the end of the eighteenth century, the expeditions of Mungo

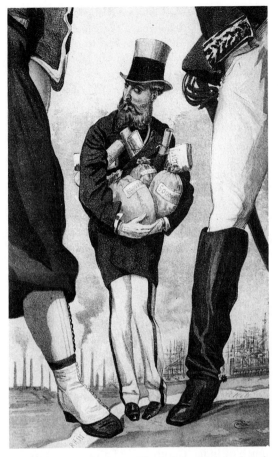

LEOPOLD II OF BELGIUM. The Belgian king had such extravagant tastes and habits that he operated as a private entrepreneur in the Congo, amassing a great fortune. His moneymaking created conditions that were so bad, akin to slavery, that Belgium's parliament took the territory away from him. His claim to the Congo, however, sparked the great powers into laying claim to much of Africa. (*Corbis-Bettmann.*)

Park, a Scottish explorer, on the Niger River in West Africa stimulated the romantic imagination. The explorations of Livingstone in the Congo Basin and of Richard Burton and John Speke (who raced with each other and with Livingstone to find the source of the Nile River) fascinated many Europeans during the second half of the nineteenth century. In the early 1800s, expeditions were a matter of adventure and scientific curiosity; they often included explorers from several countries. After the midcentury, national prestige became a goal in these forays. Sponsored by national geographic and exploratory societies and encouraged by their nation's military, explorers captured the public imagination in much the same way that astronauts do today. Explorers became public personalities; both the public and these celebrities saw exploration as an escape from a humdrum or stultifying existence at home.

Individuals and nations competed to find the highest mountain, the longest river, the highest waterfall, and the land never before seen by white men. Such challenges called men and women away from their ordinary lives to dream of adventure. The mass press—the media of the day—spread stories of exotic peoples and customs, European bravery, and self-sacrificing heroes. The fiction of English authors Rudyard Kipling (1865–1936) and H. Rider Haggard (1856–1925) and their many inferior imitators stimulated the passion for faraway places and unknown peoples and helped shape the attitudes of the next generation. Kipling wrote: "Take up the White Man's Burden—/Send forth the best ye breed—/Go bind your sons to exile/To serve your captives' need." He also wrote of the Indian Gunga Din, whose brave death while serving his white masters won him their respect. Authors usually depicted heroism and glory and rarely described the exploitation, cruelty, and abuses of empire—until twentieth-century writers like Joseph Conrad, George Orwell, Olive Schreiner, and E. M. Forster began to probe imperialism's darker side.

A Global Economy

The Western economy became truly global by the end of the nineteenth century, thanks to new markets, new technology, and overseas trade and investment. As the Western powers industrialized, even small, backward European countries exploited raw materials and markets in the rest of the world. In many parts of Europe, even the working classes and the peasantry could buy goods from faraway places that had previously been available only to the very wealthy.

The underdeveloped areas of the world, in turn, found markets for their crops and were able to buy

European goods—at least the wealthy could. But being part of the world economy also made these areas subject to the smallest tremors on the European and American stock exchanges and to changing fashions of consumption. Participation in the world market brought wealth to a few people but meant hardship for many. It also meant the loss of traditional customs and social relationships.

Increasing crop production to satisfy European and American markets often created problems. Producing for the Western market meant turning land that had grown food for families over to export crops like coffee or **indigo,** thus reducing the local food supply. It often meant consolidation of small peasant holdings in the hands of richer peasants or landlords. Thus, market forces drove the poorer peasants off the land, into debt to the landlord or to the usurer, and into cities. For most of the nineteenth century, the peasants felt bonded to their traditional masters, but in the twentieth century, they came to see themselves as enslaved by foreigners who either controlled the government or the world market. The passionate desire to escape this bondage has fueled revolutionary and nationalist movements throughout the world.

Economic interdependence operated to the great advantage of Europeans and Americans, enriching the lives of consumers. Many Europeans and Americans dressed in Egyptian cotton, Australian wool, Chinese silk, and Argentinian leather and consumed Chinese tea or Colombian coffee; some had homes or offices furnished in hardwoods from Burma, Malaya, or Africa. Westerners could purchase all these goods, and many more, at prices so favorable that many luxury items became available to those who were not rich. Europeans and Americans could travel anywhere, using gold or easily available foreign currency, exchanged at a rate almost always favorable to them. They could invest their money in the raw materials or the government bonds of virtually any area of the world and expect a good return. They also expected their investments to be secure and their property and themselves to be protected. Non-Western political authorities unable to guarantee that security, for whatever reason, risked intervention, perhaps occupation, by European or American forces. In some non-Western areas, the governors had to grant **extraterritoriality,** or the right of Europeans

to trial by their own laws in foreign countries. Europeans also often lived a segregated and privileged life in quarters, clubs, and whole sections of foreign lands or cities that were closed to native inhabitants.

Control and Resistance

Changing technology widened the gap between industrialized states and Asia and Africa. Europeans possessed the enormous power of industry and of military technology. European nation-states could mobilize the support of all their citizens. These facts made it unlikely that a non-European country or people could successfully resist an industrialized European state intent on conquest. Yet Ethiopia was able to resist Italy's incursions, North Africans kept the French on the defensive in Algeria and Morocco, and the Japanese held off potential invaders.

Europeans established varying degrees of political control over much of the rest of the world. Control meant Europeans had to have the help of native elites, which perpetuated traditional powers or created a new class of leaders. Control could mean outright annexation and the governing of a territory as a colony. In this way, Germany controlled Tanganyika (East Africa) after 1886, France governed Algeria, and Britain ruled much of India. Control could also mean status as a **protectorate,** in which the local ruler continued to rule but was directed, or "protected," by a great power. In this way, the British controlled Egypt after 1882 and maintained authority over their dependent Indian princes, and France guarded Tunisia. There were also spheres of influence, where, without military or political control, a European nation had special trading and legal privileges that other Europeans did not have. At the turn of the century, the Russians and the British, each recognizing the other's **sphere of influence,** divided Persia (Iran). Some peoples were so completely dependent for trade and finance that they seemed politically independent only in the most technical sense. Cuba and the Philippines, for example, dared take no action that might upset their economic connections to the United States in the 1930s, not even action that might ease their debt crisis.

Nevertheless, many non-Europeans resisted American and European economic and political control. Resistance shaped their history and their self-awareness. In many areas, such as the Ottoman Empire, China, and Japan, ruling governments found ways of limiting the political influence of Western trading interests. Some countries tried, as Egypt and Turkey did, to seek economic independence through modernization.

These forms of resistance were carried out by rulers who could command loyal subjects. Other resisters—individuals, groups, and regional communities—retained traditional ways, rejecting Western education and **secularization,** even renewing institutions, particularly religious ones, that were falling into disuse when the Europeans arrived. Such resistance became a statement of both national and individual identity. A few of the many instances of such resistance include the Sudanese Muslims' holy war led by the Mahdi Mohammed Ahmed. His followers attacked Egyptian fellow Muslims as agents of the European nonbelievers. The Boxer Rebellion in China and the Sepoy Mutiny in India are other examples of traditionalist resistance to outsiders. Still other resisters reacted with strongly nationalistic feelings and fought to strengthen the nationalism of their people, sometimes even going to Western universities, military schools, and factories to master the West's advanced technology. Mohandas Gandhi, Jawaharlal Nehru, Sun Yat-sen (Sun Zhongshan), Chiang Kai-shek (Jiang Jieshi), and Kemal Atatürk are national heros for resistance to the West.

In most cases, however, resistance brought non-European peoples more firmly under Western control. When their interests were threatened, Europeans generally responded by annexing the rebellious region or establishing a protectorate. Resistance continued, nonetheless. Whole peoples in Africa moved from place to place to escape European religion, taxes, and laws; and insurgent mountain people in Indochina and Algeria evaded French cultural influence or restricted it to the coastline for generations.

Europeans might dominate the ruler and perhaps the ruling elite, and they might make entire sectors of the economy dependent on their trade. They could also see the influence of their ideas and language on the youth and observe the decline of local traditions. But the level of European power differed in each area, and in many places Europeans were never fully in control. Each region has had a different history of European intervention. Nevertheless until the Second World War, Western domination seemed, to westerners and nonwesterners alike, a relentless force.

EUROPEAN DOMINATION OF ASIA

India, China, and Japan were powerful kingdoms when the first European traders arrived in the fifteenth- and sixteenth-century explorations. For several hundred years, there were trading connections in which the European was the weaker party, dependent on the goodwill and interest of the Asians. In China and India, native craftspeople produced goods superior to European products, so Asians had little reason to trade with the West; however, Europeans had many incentives for commerce with the East. In the nineteenth century, when many more and much more powerful Europeans came to Asia, they encountered Chinese and Mogul empires that were weakened by internal problems. The situation gave Europeans an edge. The Asian kingdoms possessed a sense of cultural unity based on traditions and on the great religious and ethical systems of Hinduism, Buddhism, Islam, and Confucianism. Their loyalties were cultural and religious, not nationalist as Europeans knew it. Within a short time, the resentment of European domination developed into a national feeling, unifying diverse social and religious communities.

Online Study Center **Improve Your Grade**
Interactive Map: European Colonization, Nineteenth and Twentieth Centuries

India

When Italian, Portuguese, and Spanish merchants came as traders, admirers, and imitators of the Mogul Empire, they found it ruled by a dynasty of highly advanced, wealthy, and religiously tolerant Muslim princes. When British traders arrived in the eighteenth century, the empire was

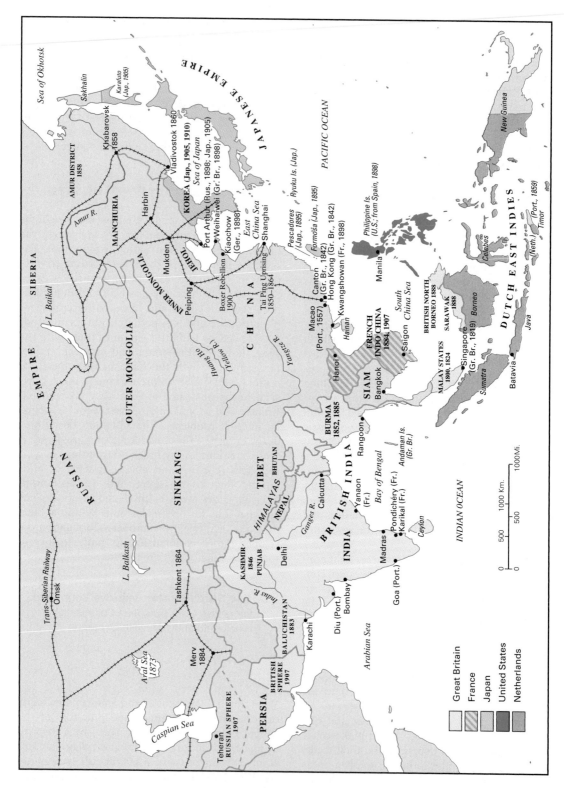

Sea of Okhotsk

JAPANESE EMPIRE

Sakhalin

Karafuto (Jap., 1905)

AMUR DISTRICT 1858

Khabarovsk 1858

Vladivostok 1860

Sea of Japan

MANCHURIA

Harbin

KOREA (Jap., 1905, 1910)

Port Arthur (Rus., 1898; Jap., 1905)

Weihaiwei (Gr. Br., 1898)

Kiaochow (Ger., 1898)

East China Sea

Shanghai

Ryuku Is. (Jap.)

PACIFIC OCEAN

Philippine Is. (U.S. from Spain, 1898)

New Guinea

RUSSIAN EMPIRE

SIBERIA

L. Baikal

Trans-Siberian Railway

Omsk

OUTER MONGOLIA

INNER MONGOLIA

JEHOL

Mukden

Peiping

Boxer Rebellion 1900

Hwang Ho (Yellow R.)

CHINA

Tai Ping Uprising 1850–1864

Yangtze R.

Pescadores (Jap., 1895)

Formosa (Jap., 1895)

South China Sea

Manila

Canton (Gr. Br., 1842)

Macao (Port., 1557)

Hong Kong (Gr. Br., 1842)

Kwangshowan (Fr., 1898)

Hainan

FRENCH INDO CHINA 1884, 1907

Saigon

BRITISH NORTH BORNEO 1888

SARAWAK 1888

Borneo (Gr. Br., 1819)

Celebes

DUTCH EAST INDIES

(Neth.) 1859

Timor (Port., 1859)

SINKIANG

L. Balkash

TIBET

NEPAL BHUTAN

HIMALAYAS

Hanoi

SIAM Bangkok

MALAY STATES 1800, 1824

Singapore (Gr. Br., 1819)

Sumatra

Java

Batavia

Tashkent 1864

KASHMIR 1846

PUNJAB

Delhi

Indus R.

Ganges R.

BRITISH INDIA

INDIA

BURMA 1852, 1885

Rangoon

Yanaon (Fr.)

Bay of Bengal

Calcutta

Madras

Pondichéry (Fr.)

Karikal (Fr.)

Ceylon

Andaman Is. (Gr. Br.)

INDIAN OCEAN

Merv 1884

Aral Sea 1873

BALUCHISTAN 1883

Karachi

Diu (Port.)

Bombay

Goa (Port.)

Arabian Sea

BRITISH SPHERE 1907

PERSIA

RUSSIAN SPHERE 1907

Teheran

Caspian Sea

1000 Mi.

1000 Km.

500

500

0

0

Great Britain

France

Japan

United States

Netherlands

disintegrating. The Muslim zealot Emperor Aurangzeb Alamgir (1658–1707) had launched a holy war that would tear apart Hindus and Muslims, as well as Sikhs, for half a century. The rivalries of powerful native princes, each of whom wished to succeed the emperor, worked to foreign advantage. India fell prey to the Europeans, and by the end of the century the British cleared out their rivals one by one. India became the jewel of the British Empire, the most completely governed Asian state.

British Rule. At first, British **rule** was **indirect.** Britain's East India Company was a regulated chartered monopoly enterprise under the control of Parliament, which exercised little control until the Sepoy Mutiny of 1857–58. (The Indians call this massive act of resistance the *Great Rebellion.*) This major popular uprising joined Muslim and Hindu soldiers with some native princes, who finally perceived that the British, rather than neighboring princes, posed the true threat to their authority. Peasants, who were victims of both their local landlords and the market, also participated. In a fierce war, the British, with the aid of faithful troops from the Punjab, repressed the uprising. The British ruled some states through dependent Indian princes, but after the Rebellion about two-thirds of the subcontinent was ruled directly by about a thousand British officials. Unlike the Chinese and the Japanese, the peoples of India lost all semblance of independence.

The men of the East India Company had mixed with the Indians, often marrying local women and adopting their customs and languages. But the British community felt so threatened by the uprising that it not only took all the authority it could into its hands but also maintained a social and legal separation from Indians. The civil service was British, trained in England and sent out to govern according to English law and customs. Later, an elite of Indians, educated in English and trained in law and administration, became part of the civil service. Along with soldiers drawn from the peoples with a military tradition, the Indian civil service (about four thousand Europeans and half a million Indians in 1900) ruled some three hundred million Indians of almost two hundred language groups, and several religions, races, and cultures. Today the territories that were British India are India, Pakistan, Bangladesh, and Myanmar (Burma). The British allowed friendly native princes to rule. Thus, the British created a powerful state with a single system of law, administration, and language. The subcontinent had some political unity, an English-educated elite, and a common resentment of British control. The British created the state; the many Indian communities created a nation.

India also acquired a modern railroad and communications system and an economy in which a segment was geared to meet the needs of the world market. The rest of the economy tried to supply local and regional demands. The railroad linked areas of food surplus with areas of need, reducing the incidence and impact of local famines, which had plagued India's history. Population increased as fewer people died of starvation and lives were saved with public projects of sanitation, hygiene, water and flood control, and Western medicine.

British rule also ended the century of war and disorder that accompanied the disintegration of the Mogul Empire, but it did not end the control that local landlords and usurers had over the lives of peasants. Many observers believe that the Indian masses benefited little from economic progress because landlords demanded payments that the poor could not afford. Moneylenders cheated the poor. In addition, the increase in population more than matched the increase in food. Even if they did not starve, most people suffered from malnutrition. What further aggravated the situation, these critics claim, was that the British flooded the Indian market with cheap, machine-produced English goods, thus driving native artisans out of business or even deeper into debt. Such detrimental consequences were not unique to India. They could be noted in many areas where the market economy and European rule disrupted traditional arrangements; their effect was most severe on the poorest and the weakest.

◄ *Map 27.1* Asia, 1914 This map of Asia is deceptive. There are no markings or colors that can indicate the level of influence and control European and U.S. powers exercised over the technically sovereign states of China, Siam (Thailand), and Persia (Iran).

THE SEPOY REBELLION: REPELLING A SORTIE BEFORE DELHI. When Indian troops (Muslims and Hindus) rebelled against foreigners in 1857–58, the British presence was seriously threatened. Here British rifles defending Delhi sounded the retreat. Thinking the rifles had withdrawn, the Sepoys were badly defeated when they advanced. "The Mutiny," as the British saw it, or "the Great Rebellion," as Indians saw it, was short-lived, but relations between Indians and Britons changed forever as the British segregated themselves socially from the people they governed. (*Bettmann/CORBIS.*)

British racism excluded the Indian elite from clubs, hotels, and social gatherings and declared top government positions off-limits for Indians. Many of the traditional elite who profited from British connections resented the lack of respect for India's culture. In the 1880s, educated Indians demanded equality and self-government. They created the Indian National Congress, which, however, was neither national, because its members were upper-class Hindus, nor a congress, because it had no power to represent. At first, the Congress party sought home rule, or self-government within the empire. Eventually, it organized masses of Indians to gain independence.

The Anticolonial Campaign. Resistance to colonialism grew in militance throughout Asia when the Japanese defeated the Russians in 1904–1905 in the Russo-Japanese War. That victory inspired Indian nationalists. World War I brought greater solidarity among Indians, who, though opposed to British rule, had been far from united. Muslims had founded the Muslim League to speak for their minority community. (Many Hindus believed that the British favored the Muslims as part of a divide-and-conquer strategy.) The Indian elite found grounds for cooperation among the disparate communities, but the masses continued to be divided by differences of religion, class, and culture. These differences made Indian self-government seem distant even to Britons who wanted it.

In 1919, partly in response to agitation and partly as a reward for Indian loyalty during the war, the British granted India a legislative assembly, which would represent almost a million of the three hundred million people in the subcontinent. Representation was by groups (Hindus, Muslims, Europeans, Anglo-Indians, and Sikhs) and by economic and social functions (that is, to rural, urban, university, landholding, and commercial classes).

In the same year, agitation and unrest became most bitter. At Amritsar in the Punjab, a British officer commanded his Gurkha troops to fire into a peaceful demonstration until their ammunition was exhausted; 379 Indians died and 1,200 were wounded. Women and children were among the victims. The government punished the officer, but the British community in India gave him a fortune, honoring him for what he had done. The massacre and British behavior stung Indians to action—even those Indians who had advocated self-government within the British Empire.

Out of this feverish period emerged a gentle but determined revolutionary leader, Mohandas K. Gandhi (1869–1948). He had led resistance to racial discrimination in South Africa and, in the process, developed a doctrine of **civil disobedience** and nonviolent resistance. He believed that Indians' love of one another would overthrow British rule. His was a spiritually uplifting message, and a shrewd political tactic as well. Gandhi called on the Indian elite to give up their privileges, resign their positions in British firms and government, boycott British schools, and boycott all foreign goods. Freeing India required mass support as well as sacrifice. Gandhi rallied this support dramatically with "the march to the sea": a mass refusal to pay taxes on salt. Thrown in prison, Gandhi and his followers fasted for spiritual discipline, threatening the British with the possibility that they would starve to death, setting off more civil disturbances. Gandhi boycotted foreign goods by spinning cotton and wearing simple native dress. To gain independence, he was even willing to sacrifice the higher standard of living that an industrial economy could bring to India. Most important, he was able to join traditional religious and cultural beliefs into political tactics that inspired Indian nationalism.

Independence finally came after World War II exhausted Britain's resources, reduced its power, and stirred much of the world to struggle against racism and for liberty and democracy. There was no war between Britain and India—an accomplishment that many credit to the strength of Gandhi's moral leadership. But even his leadership could not prevent the partition of the country into Muslim Pakistan and predominantly Hindu India. Nor could it prevent bloody communal massacres and his own death at the hands of a Hindu nationalist assassin.

China

European intervention in China was very different. For centuries, Europeans had admired China for its wealth, art, and culture, and even for its imperial government, which ruled through mandarins (men who passed tests of Chinese learning). Unlike India, China excluded foreigners, whether they were missionaries, traders, or soldiers and sailors, in an effort to preserve traditional beliefs and shield them from Christianity, Western science, and secular ideologies.

When the British defeated the Chinese in the Opium War of 1839–1842, the Manchu dynasty was forced to open trade. Previously the emperor had granted trading privileges to native monopolists. When the Chinese destroyed Indian opium traded by the East India Company, the British aggressively asserted their right to trade. In the subsequent war, Britain seized several trading cities along the coast, including Hong Kong. In the Treaty of Nanking (1842), the British insisted on determining Chinese tariffs. Furthermore, British subjects in China would be tried according to their own law (the right of extraterritoriality). These provisions undermined the emperor's ability to control the foreigners in his country.

Defeat forced the emperor to change. He revitalized the Manchu bureaucracy and cleaned up the official corruption, which weighed heavily on the poorest taxpayers. Nevertheless, widespread economic discontent led to the Taiping Rebellion of 1850–1864. This uprising seriously threatened the dynasty, which called on westerners to suppress the rebels. Britain and France extorted additional concessions. They forced the emperor to allow Chinese people to emigrate to become cheap, exploited laborers in South Africa and the United States.

For a time, the Europeans seemed content with trading rights in coastal towns and preferential treatment for their subjects. But Japan's easy victory in the Sino-Japanese War of 1894–95 encouraged Europeans to mutilate China. Britain,

Gandhi

Even before the First World War, there was growing opposition to colonialism in Asia and Africa, but who would become the leaders of the national movements and what would be their demands? A most unlikely leader emerged in India. In a series of struggles a diminutive, gentle, pacifist, Mohandas Karamchand Gandhi (1869–1948), came to represent the most populous, most diverse, and largest colony in its stuggle for independence.

Gandhi began modestly within the framework of British government and law, asking that poor Indian immigrants in South Africa not be discriminated against. Returning to India, he joined the Congress party, but he was not one of the elite who dominated that group. Eventually Gandhi transformed the Congress into a mass party that became a model and inspiration for other national movements. Victims of oppression throughout the world found his method of nonviolent resistance (*satyagraha*) the least bloody way to counter those who held all the weapons. Satyagraha called for a high degree of self-control and self-awareness, which Gandhi expressed in the language of the Indian religious and cultural tradition: Indians could free themselves once they thought of themselves

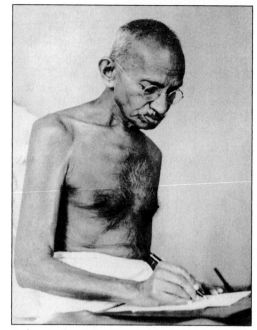

Hulton Archive/Getty Images.

France, Russia, and Germany all scrambled for concessions, protectorates, and spheres of influence. China might have been carved up like Africa; however, each Western nation resisted any partition that might give an advantage to a rival. To ensure American interests in China, the United States proclaimed the **"Open Door"** policy: that trade should be open to all and that the great powers should respect the territorial integrity of China. Whether the American action restrained the Western powers from further partitioning China is unclear. The important treaty ports had already been apportioned. Market capitalism, which Americans championed, was the most powerful threat to China's independence.

Chinese traditionalists organized secret societies to expel foreigners and punish those Chinese

who accepted westernization. In 1900, encouraged by Empress Tzu-hsi, the Society of Righteous and Harmonious Fists (called the Boxers by Europeans) attacked foreigners throughout the north of China. An international army of Europeans, Japanese, and Americans suppressed the rebellion, seized Chinese treasures, and forced China to pay an indemnity. They also made China station foreign troops on its soil.

Chinese discontent with the dynasty deepened, and nationalistic opposition to the foreigners increased. When Japan defeated Russia in 1905, many Chinese urged their country to imitate Western ways as the Japanese had done. Growing nationalism led to a boycott of American goods in 1905 to protest U.S. restrictions on Chinese immigrants. In 1911, nationalist revolutionaries, particularly strong

as a nation and refused to carry out the commands of their rulers, but they must not lose control and respond to the savage acts of their rulers with savage acts of revenge. It was a difficult political message to accept for people who were not yet one nation and who had suffered repeated injustice and discrimination.

In 1919 at Amritsar in Punjab region, British governors brutally repressed a peaceful demonstration in which 1,500 Indians were killed or injured. Thereafter, Gandhi led thousands in a march to protest the British monopoly of salt; journalists and photographers from all over the world covered the protest. This simple man was turning the world of power and wealth upside down. Indians seemed willing to do without the benefits of industrialization and modern society to be free. Sophisticated Congress party leaders, such as Jawaharlal Nehru (1889–1964), supported Gandhi's strategy. In the 1930s the British jailed demonstrators repeatedly; Gandhi protested with hunger strikes. Rather than face his angry followers, British governors released him. Finally, in 1935 and 1937, Britain granted India provincial assemblies, but by then India's religious groups (Hindu and Muslim) were fragmented on every issue but independence, and radicals, including a communist party, regarded the aims of Gandhi and the Congress party as reactionary and bound to fail.

When World War II broke out, the British declared war on behalf of India, arousing the nation. Although hundreds of thousands of Indian soldiers fought for the colonial rulers in the war, India refused to put its demands on hold. Gandhi spent months on a hunger strike for independence, and independence now became the country's slogan. At war's end, the British no longer had the power, the wealth, or the will to hold on to India. In 1947, the promise to partition India in two states, one Muslim and one Hindu, broke the subcontinent into violence, which all the efforts of the nonviolent movement could not prevent. Gandhi fasted once again—this time to calm his people and prevent civil war. Six months later an angry Hindu nationalist shot and killed Gandhi as he walked to morning prayers. The world mourned and India took another path.

among soldiers, workers, and students, overthrew the Manchu and declared a republic. Sun Zhongshan (Sun Yat-sen, 1866–1925) became president of the republic and head of the Nationalist party.

Espousing the Western ideas of democracy, nationalism, and social welfare (the three principles of the people, as Sun called them), the republic struggled to establish its authority over a China torn by civil war and ravaged by foreigners. Russia was claiming Mongolia; Britain, Tibet. Japan posed a danger as well. The northern warlords resisted any attempt to strengthen the republic's army because it might diminish their power. However, in the south, the republic more or less maintained control.

After Sun's death, the Guomindong (Kuomintang), under the **authoritarian** leadership of Jiang Jieshi (Chiang Kai-shek, 1887–1975), tried to modernize, using the military power of the state and introducing segments of a modern economic system. But faced with civil war, and attacked from both the right and the communist left under Mao Zedong (Mao Tse-tung, 1893–1976), and by the Japanese after 1931, the Guomindong made slow progress. A divided China continued to be at the mercy of outside interests until after World War II.

Japan

Like China, Japan was forced open by the West. By the 1850s, as in India and China, social dissension within Japan and foreign pressure combined to force the country to admit outside trade. In 1853,

Commodore Matthew C. Perry sailed into Tokyo Bay, making a show of American strength. The Japanese signed treaties that granted westerners extraterritoriality and control over tariffs.

A flood of violence ensued. The warrior nobility, the samurai, attacked foreigners and murdered members of their own government. They thought that trade would enhance the status of merchants, a social class they despised. In response to the samurai actions, U.S. and European ships destroyed important Japanese fortresses. Samurai seized the government, determined to preserve Japan's independence. This takeover—the Meiji Restoration of 1867—returned power to the emperor, or Meiji, from the feudal aristocracy, which had ruled in his name for almost seven hundred years.

The new government enacted a series of reforms, turning Japan into a powerful centralized state. Large landowners gave their estates to the emperor in exchange for compensation and high-level positions in the government. All classes were made equal before the law. As in France and Germany, universal military service was required, which diminished social privilege and helped to imbue Japanese of all classes with nationalism. The Japanese modeled their constitution on Bismarck's: there was a **bicameral diet,** or parliament, but the emperor kept authority.

The Meiji regime introduced modern industry and economic competition. The Japanese visited factories all over the West and hired westerners to teach industrial skills. The government, like central and eastern European governments, built defense industries, backed heavy industry and mining, and developed a modern communication system of railroads, roads, and telegraph. The government encouraged competitive consumer industries as well; it sold factories to wealthy family monopolies, the *zaibatsu,* which came to dominate the Japanese economy. Industry in Japan adopted traditional Japanese values and emphasized cooperation more than competition, paternalism rather than individualism, and deference rather than conflict. Westerners regarded the close cooperation of government and powerful families as something peculiar to the Japanese (neither capitalist nor socialist). Within little more than a generation of the Meiji Restoration, Japan moved from economic backwardness to a

place among the top ten industrial nations. To underdeveloped countries, Japan became a model of a nation that borrowed from the West yet preserved its traditional values and social structure.

By 1900, Japan ended the humiliating treaties with the West and became an imperialist power. Japan won Taiwan and Korea in its war with China in 1894–95 despite great power intervention. The great powers grabbed greater spheres of influence from the helpless Chinese, infuriating the Japanese. In 1904, conflict over influence in Manchuria brought Japan and Russia to war, which Japan won. The victory of an Asian power over a Western power had a tremendous impact inspiring anti-Western nationalist movements throughout Asia.

In World War I, Japan fought on the side of the Allies, emerging as the most powerful Asian state. It took over the former German holdings north of the equator, except for Germany's sphere of influence in China. (U.S. president Woodrow Wilson blocked that move at the Paris peace conference.) In the 1920s, the prosperous economy strengthened the middle class and increased the importance of the working class, reinforcing democratic institutions. But Japan's dependence on foreign trade meant that the nation was hard hit by the Great Depression of 1929, when the major states subjected its trade to tariffs. The depression weakened elements that contributed to peace, stability, and democracy in Japan and strengthened militarist and imperialist groups, which were set on control of Manchuria and China.

In the 1930s, nationalists in Burma, India, Indochina, and Indonesia looked to Japan for support against Western imperialism. World War II, however, brought Japanese **occupation** and exploitation, not the independence and equality that these leaders hoped for.

The Ottoman Empire

Throughout the nineteenth century the great powers competed to inherit the estate of the "Sick Man of Europe" as Turkey was called then. Their competition ensured the sick man's demise. They claimed parts of the Balkans, central Asia, North Africa, and the Middle East. By the early twentieth century the traditional rivalry between Russia and

COMMODORE PERRY AND THE U.S. SQUADRON MEETING JAPANESE IMPERIAL COMMISSIONERS AT YOKOHAMA (1854). Commodore Matthew Perry had opened Japan, against its will, to the West the preceding year. With the Meiji Restoration of 1867, a strong central government pushed Japan until it became one of the top ten industrial nations by 1900. Japan's imperialistic expansion brought it into conflict with China, Russia, and the Western imperialist powers. (*Culver Pictures.*)

Britain over central Asia was overshadowed by the German and British conflict in the Middle East.

A group of German financiers proposed a railroad from central Turkey to Baghdad, on the Tigris River, with a connection down the Euphrates River to Basra and the Persian Gulf. Because the proposed new railroad would further open Turkey and its empire to the world market, the sultan was enthusiastic and offered to subsidize the project by guaranteeing the bonds and profits for the syndicate. The German backers of the railroad offered British and French investment groups a 25 percent share each, with 25 percent control to the Turks; the Germans kept the final quarter for themselves. The deal seemed fair, but the British government refused to allow British businessmen to invest because they feared Ger-

man ascendancy in an area so close to India and the Suez Canal. The Germans came to see the British as their number one rival. In World War I, the Ottomans sided with the Germans, partly because of German influence over a generation of the Turkish elite and partly for fear of a Russian presence in the Caucasus, the Balkans, and the Black Sea areas. In all these moves politics dominated economics.

Throughout World War I, the Allies secretly negotiated the division of the Ottoman Empire. Hoping to weaken the Ottoman contribution to the German war effort, Britain sponsored Arab independence movements in the Arabian peninsula and in the territories that are today Iraq, Syria, Lebanon, Jordan, and Israel. In the 1917 Balfour Declaration, Britain promised the Zionists a Jewish homeland in Palestine. The Allies also promised Greece and Italy Turkish lands.

When the war was over, the Turks, led by Mustafa Kemal Atatürk, refused to accept the dismemberment of Turkish-speaking territory. They did accept the loss of Arab lands. The Turks drove the Allies out of Anatolia, declared a republic in 1923 under Atatürk's presidency, and moved the capital to Ankara, far away from the cosmopolitan city of Constantinople (Istanbul). Turkey, which became a secular state, was no longer the spiritual leader of millions of Muslims throughout the world. During Atatürk's presidency (1923–1938), the Turkish government banned traditional practices, such as veils for women, harems, and polygamy. European education and ideas flourished in the new republic. In Turkey the conflict between the modern and the traditional was resolved in favor of modern nationalism.

Among the Arabs, several forces fostered the desire for national **self-determination,** which grew during and after World War I. The Arab chiefs welcomed British aid against the Turks but deeply resented intervention in their spiritual and local political affairs. They suspected that the Europeans were primarily interested in the area's oil. Arab nationalism, once encouraged against the Ottomans, could not be controlled by Europeans when the Turks ceased to be a power. As nationalism developed, it sometimes joined with Islam to foment opposition to the imperialists between the world wars and after. At other times, the nationalists rejected Islam or controlled it because they hoped to secularize and modernize as in Turkey.

Southeast and Central Asia

The great power rush to claim territory was evident everywhere in Asia. When China, India, and the Ottoman Empire lost the ability to control border territories, European states tried to grab them. Indochina, Tibet, Korea, Burma, Afghanistan, and Persia were each the object of some power's design.

In southeast Asia, the French claimed Indochina (Vietnam, Laos, and Cambodia today) and waged war with China (1883–85) to gain it.

The French parliament threw out the government that gained the faraway and not obviously valuable territory, but France annexed the land nonetheless. Indochina was a prosperous agricultural region trading with other Asians and hardly at all with France. Some French may have profited from the colony—merchants, civil servants, soldiers, priests, and scholars—but France as a whole was indifferent to its new acquisition.

From Indochina the French might have expanded into Siam (Thailand) as might the British from their base in Burma (Myanmar). Neither power was willing to let the other take Siam. Like Turkey in the Middle East, Siamese rulers were able to play the powers against each other to preserve some territorial integrity. Only fear of Germany led Britain and France to put colonial differences aside.

Elsewhere throughout southeast Asia, Germany, the United States, Britain, and France competed for island naval stations and trading places. The Netherlands held on to a remnant of their seventeenth-century empire in the East Indies (Indonesia). Even colonies began to acquire colonies, as New Zealand and Australia pushed claims to Borneo and Tasmania. After World War I, they claimed German colonies south of the equator. Some may have had economic motives, but national identity was equally important.

Just as the French and British competed in southeast Asia, and the Japanese and all the great powers competed in northern China and Korea, the Russians and the British confronted one another in central Asia. Russia's moves, south into Afghanistan and Persia (Iran), both of which bordered India, alarmed the British. They were sure that hostile forces on the borders would inspire rebellious Indian movements. In Persia the British and Russians vied with one another to lend money to the shah to build a railroad to Teheran. At that moment Russians were borrowing money from the French for their own industrialization, but to create a claim they were willing to borrow more. At stake was control of the "top of the world," the passages to India. British and Russian troops fought each other in Afghanistan. When Britain was fighting the Boer War (see below) in South Africa, the Russians moved toward Persia, Tibet, and Afghanistan. These moves had little to do with economics and much to do with strategic control. The entire situation indicated the volatility of relations between the great powers outside of Europe itself.

The rise of Germany made both Britain and Russia, longtime foes, willing to compromise. The Russians agreed to a British puppet ruler in Afghanistan. They divided Persia into three zones: one in the north for the Russians, one in the south for the British, and one in the middle for the Persians, to keep the two European powers separate.

This resolution of difficulties made possible British and Russian cooperation in Europe. An important piece in the system of alliances that led to World War I was in place. It had tremendous impact on Persia as well. Torn between Britain and Russia, Persia was neither independent nor stable. Its situation was further complicated after World War I, when its vast reserves of oil became valuable to the great powers. Reza Shah of the Pahlavi family gained control in 1925, abolishing foreigners' special privileges. In 1934, the shah granted the concession over the Bahrain Islands to an American firm, Standard Oil, thinking that foreigners whose interests seemed to be merely economic might be more easily controlled than foreigners with geopolitical designs. Yet as British power receded in the region during and after World War II, U.S. power took its place.

The response to European expansion and control throughout Asia before and after the First World War was nationalism. In a short time, in areas divided for centuries by ethnic and religious differences, states began organizing patriots into powerful movements to resist foreign domination. Those resistance movements would become nations in the aftermath of World War II.

THE SCRAMBLE FOR AFRICA

The most rapid European expansion took place in Africa. As late as 1880, European nations ruled only a tenth of the continent. By 1914, Europeans claimed everything except Liberia (a small territory of freed slaves from the United States) and Abyssinia (Ethiopia).

In the early nineteenth century, European powers laid some claims to Africa. The French moved into Algeria in 1830 only to spend a gen-

eration trying to pacify the populace. During the Napoleonic wars, Britain gained Capetown in South Africa, a useful provisioning place for ships bound for India and the East. The Boer cattlemen and farmers, who had migrated there from the Netherlands in the seventeenth century, were unwilling to accept British rule. To get away from the British, the Boers moved northward in a migration known as the Great Trek (1835–37), warring with native tribes along the way. By 1880, the Boers were firmly established in the interior of South Africa, in the Transvaal and the Orange Free State. In general, though, until the 1870s, interest in Africa seemed marginal and likely to decline.

Then the astounding activities of Leopold II, the king of Belgium, changed the picture. In 1876, as a private entrepreneur, he formed the International Association for the Exploration and Civilization of Central Africa. Leopold sent Henry Stanley (1841–1904) to the Congo River Basin to establish trading posts, sign treaties with the chiefs, and claim the territory for the association. Stanley, an adventurer and a newspaper reporter who had fought on both sides during the American Civil War, had earlier led an expedition to central Africa in search of David Livingstone, the popular missionary-explorer whom the public believed to be in danger. The human-interest adventure story delighted thousands of readers. Imperialism became the fashion. For men like Stanley, Leopold's enterprise promised profit and adventure. For the Africans, it promised brutal exploitation. The French immediately established a protectorate on the north bank of the Congo.

Online Study Center

Improve Your Grade
Primary Source: European Imperialism in Africa: A Veteran Explains the Rules of the Game

The Berlin Conference

The scramble for African territory threatened European stability. Bismarck and Jules Ferry, the premier of France, called an international conference in Berlin in 1884 to lay some ground rules for the

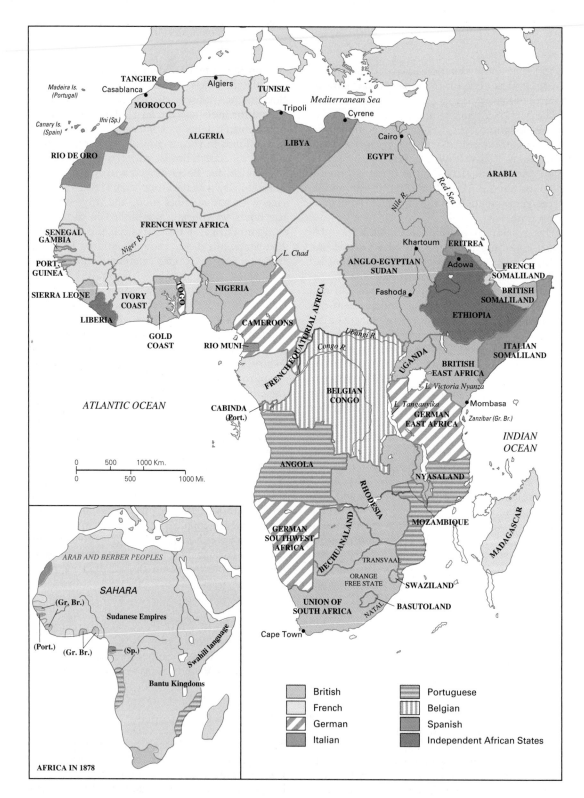

TANGIER
Casablanca
Madeira Is.
(Portugal)
MOROCCO
Canary Is.
(Spain)
Ifni (Sp.)
RIO DE ORO

Algiers
TUNISIA
Tripoli
LIBYA
Cyrene
Mediterranean Sea
Cairo
EGYPT

ALGERIA

ARABIA

Red Sea
Nile R.

FRENCH WEST AFRICA

Niger R.

SENEGAL
GAMBIA
PORT.
GUINEA
SIERRA LEONE
LIBERIA
IVORY
COAST
GOLD
COAST
RIO MUNI
TOGO
NIGERIA
L. Chad

Khartoum
ANGLO-EGYPTIAN
SUDAN
Fashoda
ERITREA
Adowa
FRENCH
SOMALILAND
BRITISH
SOMALILAND
ETHIOPIA

CAMEROONS
FRENCH EQUATORIAL AFRICA
Ubangi R.
Congo R.

ITALIAN
SOMALILAND

ATLANTIC OCEAN

CABINDA
(Port.)

BELGIAN
CONGO

UGANDA
BRITISH
EAST AFRICA
L. Victoria Nyanza
L. Tanganyika
Mombasa
GERMAN
EAST AFRICA
Zanzibar (Gr. Br.)

INDIAN
OCEAN

0   500   1000 Km.
0   500   1000 Mi.

ANGOLA

RHODESIA
NYASALAND
MOZAMBIQUE

GERMAN
SOUTHWEST
AFRICA
BECHUANALAND
TRANSVAAL
ORANGE
FREE STATE
NATAL
UNION OF
SOUTH AFRICA
SWAZILAND
BASUTOLAND
Cape Town

MADAGASCAR

ARAB AND BERBER PEOPLES
SAHARA
(Gr. Br.)
Sudanese Empires
(Port.)
(Gr. Br.)
(Sp.)
Swahili language
Bantu Kingdoms
AFRICA IN 1878

British
French
German
Italian
Portuguese
Belgian
Spanish
Independent African States

650

development of Africa south of the Sahara. Leopold (as businessman rather than as the king of Belgium) was declared the personal ruler of the Congo Free State. The Congo Basin was made a free trade zone for merchants of every nation.

The nations at the conference agreed to stop slavery and the slave trade in Africa, which still engaged Arabs and Africans. Before long, however, the Congo Association was trying to turn a profit with practices as vicious as those of the African slave traders. Edward D. Morel, an English humanitarian, and Roger Casement, a British civil servant who later became an Irish national hero, waged a vigorous campaign against Leopold for the Aborigines' Protection Society. They produced evidence that slavery, mutilation, brutality, and murder were commonly practiced to force blacks to work for rubber plantations in the Congo. The outcry of world public opinion led the Belgian parliament to declare the territory a Belgian colony in 1908, putting an end to Leopold's private enterprise.

Britain in Africa

Great Britain's activities in Africa exemplify the complicated motives, operations, and results of European imperialism. In the second half of the nineteenth century, Britain maintained only a few outposts along the coast of West Africa; even its hold on South Africa appeared to be loosening. From time to time, the British navy interfered with slave traders in Africa, but overall British interest there was minimal. In principle, Britain rejected empire. Its practice was another thing entirely.

Egypt. Local conditions in Egypt, complicated by the construction of the Suez Canal (1859–1869), led to British occupation. For a generation (1805–1847), Mohammed Ali, governor of Egypt, had struggled for independence from the sultan of

◀ MAP 27.2 AFRICA, 1914 Africa's rapid dismemberment is pictured in these two maps. In 1878, there were few enclaves of Europeans along the coasts. By 1914, Africa had been carved up, and all but Ethiopia and Liberia had been claimed.

the Ottoman Empire. Thereafter, strong *khedives* (Turkish governors), with British and French support, maintained Egypt's autonomy. Foreign investment and influence grew; successive khedives spent lavishly to modernize. Egypt fell deeply into debt to Europeans. The building of the Suez Canal, in which the khedive and British and French capitalists were the principal stockholders, brought the country to the verge of bankruptcy. In the long run, the existence of the canal promised Egypt trade and contact with the world economy, but its cost brought immediate disaster. When European creditors demanded cuts in the army as a way for Egypt to pay its debts, Egyptian soldiers rebelled. The combination of national bankruptcy and the khedive's inability to keep law and order was sufficient pretext for the British to become "protectors" in 1882.

The canal was the important waterway to India for the British. It was merely an investment to the French. The British invited France to join the occupation. Domestic politics prevented French invasion, but they deeply resented the "insult" to French national honor. Meanwhile, British citizens hired ships to watch the naval bombardment of Egyptian ports as if war were a fireworks display.

Prime Minister William Gladstone, a "little Englander" (one who opposed empire), promised to withdraw British troops once the situation stabilized. Every day that the British remained, Egyptian discontent grew, further threatening the markets, investments, and even government. Egyptian opposition took two irreconcilable forms. Some Egyptians wanted a strong government and army so that they could throw the British out. Others hated all modernization, regarding it as a threat to Islam. As the British became entrenched, resistance grew more violent.

The British did not withdraw from Egypt; in fact, they moved farther south into the Sudan, where devout Muslims led by Mohammed Ahmed, the Mahdi or "divinely guided one," were waging holy war against Egyptian authority. They resented foreign, non-Muslim influence over the khedive. The British, trying to strengthen the khedive's authority so that taxes would be collected, Egypt's budget balanced, and debts paid, were making the situation worse. An English general led ten thousand of the khedive's

THE SECRET OF ENGLAND'S GREATNESS, BY THOMAS JONES BARKER. In this painting, Queen Victoria presents a Bible in the audience chamber at Windsor. (*National Portrait Gallery, London.*)

troops against the Sudanese Muslim followers of the Mahdi. The Egyptians were annihilated.

Costly occupation angered British financiers. Gladstone's Liberal party rejected further action in the Sudan, but public opinion demanded action. In 1885, Gladstone sent General Charles "Chinese" Gordon, famous for suppressing the Taiping Rebellion, as an observer to the Sudan. At Khartoum, the garrison was killed, and Gordon's head severed and placed on a pike. An enraged public accused Gladstone of having martyred the famous hero. Gladstone refused to annex the Sudan. In 1898, a Conservative government sent General Herbert Kitchener to Africa. His men, armed with machine guns, mowed down charging Muslims at Omdurman. The casualties were reported to be eleven thousand Sudanese, twenty-eight Britons, and hundreds of Egyptians.

The battle of Omdurman was an ugly victory; 1898 became a year of ugly confrontations and dubious victories for the British Empire. Immedi-

ately after the battle, British forces confronted a French exploratory mission under the command of Major Jean Baptiste Marchand at Fashoda in the Sudan. The French had marched from West Africa to the Sudan en route to Somaliland on the Red Sea to lay claim to territory from one side of Africa to the other. The British were moving south from Egypt and north from Kenya into the same territory. In the **diplomatic crisis** that followed, Britain and France were brought to the brink of war. Public passions were inflamed. Too divided by the Dreyfus affair at home (see Chapter 26) to risk a showdown with Britain, the French cabinet ordered Marchand to retreat. French public opinion was incensed. Behind the scenes, however, French diplomats began to negotiate with Britain to reconcile their two nations' ambitions. France could not challenge both Germany across the Rhine and Britain in Africa and Asia. The British, facing problems in Egypt and the Sudan, as well as mounting troubles in South Africa, also realized their limits. "Splendid isolation" was risky business if the whole world could be your battlefield and each of the great powers your enemy.

South Africa. Nothing underlined Britain's isolation more than the Boer War, which began in 1899. British relations with the Boers had been difficult since the Great Trek. They were aggravated when rich deposits of gold and diamonds were discovered in Boer territory.

The opposing leaders in these territories were strong and unyielding. Paul Kruger (1825–1904), the Boer president of the Transvaal, wanted independence, power, and access to the sea. He aimed to restrict the foreign prospectors, who were flooding into Boer territory by the thousands. The prime minister of Cape Colony, Cecil Rhodes (1853–1902), who had made a fortune in diamonds and gold in South Africa, acquired Rhodesia (Zimbabwe), a sizable and wealthy territory, for Britain. He dreamed of British red coloring the map of Africa from Cape Town to Cairo.

In 1895, Rhodes's close friend Leander Jameson led about six hundred armed men into the Transvaal to spark an uprising against Kruger, expecting British support. The raid failed, both men were disgraced, and suspicions of conspiracy reached as high as the cabinet. Kaiser William II of Germany impetuously sent President Kruger a congratulatory telegram; the British took the diplomatic insult to heart. Accustomed to French opposition in every area of the globe, they now had to face the Germans.

Everything about the Boer War was unfortunate for the British. The Boers were formidable opponents—farmers by day and commandos by night, armed with the latest French and German rifles. Hatred for the British in the press of Europe was almost universal. The war was exceptionally costly both in money and lives; it roused many Britons to a hysterical patriotism. Anti-imperialism gained strength, too. Humanitarians in London found some British tactics shameful. To deal with their stubborn foe, for example, the British herded, or "concentrated," whole settlements of Boers into compounds surrounded by barbed wire. The British won the major battles but had to contend with bitter **guerrilla** resistance.

The nasty war ended in 1902. Hoping to live together in peace with the Boers, the British made many concessions to them, including the right to use their own language, Afrikaans (English remained the official language). They also offered amnesty to any Boer who would swear allegiance to the British king. The settlement, which appeared generous to the belligerents, boded ill for the majority black population of South Africa. Boer autonomy meant that London would be able to do little to protect the rights of black Africans in the Boer territories. Few safeguards for blacks were written into the treaty or the constitution of the new Union of South Africa.

Costs of Colonialism

The cost of imperialism in Africa seemed high not only to the British and French but also to other imperialists. Defeat at Adowa (1896) by Ethiopians belied Italian dreams of empire and national glory. Victory would not have alleviated Italy's economic problems, although it might have reduced political discontent. Germans could take little heart from their African acquisitions— Southwest Africa (Namibia), Southeast Africa (Tanzania, but not Zanzibar, which was British), the Cameroons, and Togo. The German colonies were the most efficiently governed (critics said ruthlessly controlled) but yielded few benefits, other than pride of ownership. The Belgians obviously gained no prestige from the horrors perpetrated in the Congo. Serious thinkers contemplating the depths to which Europeans would sink in search of fortune and fame suggested the Europeans were more barbarous than the Africans.

For the most part, honor was fleeting and profits illusory in African empires. Yet it appeared that Europeans might go to war with each other for African lands with few people and fewer resources. Such a war promised to be more deadly than the colonial conflicts between the technologically superior Europeans and the Africans and Asians. Only patient diplomacy and the growing threat of Germany kept England and France from coming to blows. Germany expressed its aggressive imperialism in a naval arms race with the British, which threatened the latter's power and national self-image. The "**Teutonic cousins**" eyed each other with deepening suspicion. This tension contributed to the alliances that the Great Powers made in the decade before World War I.

LATIN AMERICA

The growing European influence in Latin America in the nineteenth century was yet another variety of imperialism. Although it involved neither direct rule, as in Africa and parts of Asia, nor a foreign threat, as in China and southeast Asia, it nonetheless gave Europeans and Americans control over much of Latin American life.

In the era of the American Revolution of 1776 and the French Revolution of 1789, Latin American colonists had rebelled against Spain. Britain and the United States encouraged them, in part to gain a free hand for trade that Spain had not allowed. They successfully forestalled attempts of the other Great Powers to restore Spain or to extend colonies after Napolean's fall. (The American president Monroe had warned against intervention and colonization there.)

For the entire nineteenth century, European trade and immigration penetrated South America. Argentina, Brazil, Chile, and other countries took in the Irish, Germans, Italians, eastern Europeans and Spaniards; like the United States, they became primarily immigrant nations. (A few countries—notably Mexico and Peru—attracted fewer Europeans, preserving an Amerindian or mestizo society.) Europeans also invested heavily. Britain and to a lesser degree France dominated the economy; they cooperated commercially with local merchants, loaned money, and negotiated favorable trade treaties for their citizens. By the end of the century, the United States was their competitor.

Both the Europeans and the local merchants and landowner elite exploited the lower classes. Brazil relied on African slave labor to produce for European markets; it was the last American nation to abolish slavery. Native Indians were pushed off their lands just as ruthlessly as they had been in North America.

Europe also dominated the Western Hemisphere culturally. In Latin America, a small, wealthy upper class imitated continental European culture. At Manaus in the Amazon region, using profits of rubber farms worked by enslaved Indians, rich South Americans built an ornate opera house resembling Milan's La Scala. Using the profits of cotton or coffee labor, wealthy North Americans lived like the British gentry. In Buenos Aires, Rio de Janeiro, and Santiago, merchants discussed the latest European intellectual fads. Both upper-class South and North Americans sent their children to Europe to attend school and to acquire "culture" before they entered business, agriculture, and government in their native lands. In these matters, the Latin American elite behaved much the same as westernizers among the elites of India, the Middle East, and southeast Asia. Some people in both Latin and North America, however, felt that New World countries must develop their own cultures, not imitate Britain or France. Significant local cultures did evolve.

The wealthy classes in Latin America depended on Europe for trade as well as culture. They became indebted to Europeans for funds to support their governments and build their railroads. For their part, the Europeans were content to gain the profits from commerce without direct colonization. If political dissension threatened to interfere with peaceful trade, Europeans had ways of letting the merchant class know the costs of that dissension.

An exception to this general policy of nonintervention was Napoleon III's attempt in 1867 to conquer Mexico and to install an Austrian archduke (Maximilian) on a bogus throne. The Mexicans, led by Benito Juárez (1806–1872), resisted the French invasion; the United States threatened. Napoleon thought better of his dreams of easy glory and abandoned the campaign, undertaken more to please members of his military than the French business community. The Mexicans executed Maximilian; the experience intensified Mexican nationalism.

The business interests of Britain and the United States prevented other European interventions, but by the end of the century, the United States was able to energetically pursue its own interests, first in the Caribbean and Central America and then throughout Latin America. After the Spanish-American War (1898), the U.S. occupied Cuba and annexed Puerto Rico and the Philippines. It also restated the **Monroe Doctrine** when it announced in 1904 that Europeans could not

SLAVES DRYING COFFEE ON A PLANTATION IN TERREIROS, RIO DE JANEIRO (c. 1882). Brazilian slaves toiled to produce one of Brazil's main exports to the world market. The world economy, which developed during the commercial revolution, emerged full force with the age of imperialism as more and more resources of the non-European world were produced, bought, and sold for overseas consumption. (*Photograph by Marc Ferrez; courtesy of Gilberto Ferrez.*)

intervene in the western hemisphere even to protect their citizens or their business interests.

U.S. citizens engineered the secession of Panama from Colombia in 1903 to obtain the rights to build the Panama Canal on favorable terms. The United States intervened repeatedly in the Caribbean, sending U.S. marines to occupy the Dominican Republic, Haiti, Nicaragua, and the port of Veracruz in Mexico. Seizing customs revenues for payment of debts and threatening Latin American governments, American "**gunboat diplomacy**" replaced English and French commercial power. Like Britain, the United States used force to maintain its interests while at the same time articulating a policy of free competition for trade and commerce—of open doors around the world, including Latin America.

In many ways, U.S. behavior resembled European imperialism. Like the European nations that acquired bases in China, the United States took Guantanamo Bay in Cuba, Fonseca in Nicaragua,

and the Canal Zone in Panama. Like European businesses, U.S. entrepreneurs invested so heavily in underdeveloped areas that they frequently controlled governments and ruling elites. In 1923, 43 percent of all U.S. foreign investment went to Latin America, 27 percent to Canada, only 22 percent to Europe (at a time when the United States was underwriting German recovery from World War I), and 8 percent to Asia and Africa. Foreign investment may have been a mere fraction of total American wealth, but it was significant to important segments of the national economy.

The United States practiced "**dollar diplomacy**" in Latin America. It used its economic power to influence politics just as Europeans had in Morocco, Tunisia, Egypt, Persia, Turkey, and China. When corrupt members of dictatorial regimes borrowed money for national development or for their personal use and were unable to repay, the U.S. treated governments like private companies or private individuals in default. The U.S. marines took customs, taxes, and treasuries until the debts were repaid. The customs revenues of Haiti (1915) and Santo Domingo (1904, 1916–1924) were collected for American bankers just as Britain and France had taken Egyptian revenues. Governments in Central America were U.S. puppets or clients just as European countries had controlled the Middle East or central Asia. The influence of the U.S. on Mexico under Porfirio Díaz (1876–1880, 1884–1911) resembled that of Germany and Britain on the Ottoman Empire.

The Latin American response to U.S. imperialism was opposition and resistance. The strongest challenge to U.S. interests came with the Mexican Revolution of 1911. Mexican leaders—Emiliano Zapata, Victoriano Huerta, and Francisco "Pancho" Villa—had different motives for the overthrow of Díaz, but each saw the United States as part of the problem. Zapata wanted land reform, to break up the great estates and give land to the peasants; Huerta wanted to increase foreign investment in industry but keep Mexico, not the foreigners, in control. In 1916, Villa led a raid across the U.S. border. Woodrow Wilson ordered U.S. troops to chase him into Mexico. At that very moment, Wilson was preaching self-determination for European nations and expressing concern about the wrongs done to the weak by the strong in Europe.

After World War I, relations between the United States and Latin America remained troubled, particularly during the Great Depression, which had devastating effects on the countries that had begun to industrialize and build an export market. Only recently have U.S.–Latin American relations substantially improved.

THE LEGACY OF IMPERIALISM

World War I was a turning point in the history of imperialism, although neither mother countries nor colonies seemed aware of it at the time. Britain and France divided the German colonial spoils and replaced Turkish power in the Middle East. Both empires were at their territorial peak in 1919. But the origins of **decolonization** also date from the postwar era. Wilson and Lloyd George, championed national self-determination at the Paris Peace

Conference. They meant their slogans to apply to Europeans, not to the colonial world, but many intellectuals, both in the colonies and in Europe, argued that the principle of self-determination should also apply to Asians and Africans. Liberal democrats in the West began to talk of training the colonies for eventual self-government or independence. In the colonies, forces for independence grew. Colonial intellectuals thought the democrats' timetable for equality or for self-government was too slow. Some found leadership in the anti-imperialist campaign of Lenin and the Bolsheviks.

Less than three decades later, World War II exhausted the European colonial powers. It depleted their soldiery, financial resources, and willingness to wage war against their rebellious colonies. During this war, the Allies relied on colonies for labor, soldiers, bases, and supplies. Colonies and British Commonwealth states like Australia made giant strides toward industrialization. At the very moment that colonies were most important to their mother countries, they were taking steps toward greater economic independence. Furthermore, after fighting against Nazi racism, it was difficult for Europeans to justify European rule over nations yearning for self-determination.

Today, almost a century after the rapid division of the world among the European and U.S. powers and decades after the decolonization of most of the world, the results of imperialism persist. Imperialism left a legacy of deep animosity in the countries of Asia, Africa, and Latin America. Although most nations have political independence, Western economic and cultural domination still exists and often influences the policies of autonomous governments. Much of the world is still poor and suffers from insufficient capital, unskilled leaders, and unstable governments. Many people in these poor areas believe that their countries' condition is the result of a century of Western exploitation.

Imperialism has been a source of great bitterness to former colonial peoples, not just because of economic exploitation but also because it was accompanied by racism and callous disregard for other cultures. Thus, many non-Westerners see little to admire in the values of the West. Their non-Western nationalism usually includes a strong anti-Western strain, some of which is expressed in religious and cultural conservatism or "fundamentalism." Politically, this anti-Western bent led some groups in some countries to procommunist or pro-Russian positions during the cold war or to the creation of their own versions of socialism, such as African socialism or Latin American revolutionary movements. In the aftermath of the cold war and decolonization, fundamentalism or traditionalism became a new political force opposing Western technological and economic competition. This political opposition is directed at the local elites as well. Local elites, even nationalist leader-heroes, are thought corrupted by the profits and values of globalism, which threatens to destroy traditional values, particularly religious ones, and livelihoods.

In today's economically interdependent world, the influence of Western ideas, institutions, technologies, and economic practices is apparent everywhere. English is an international language. The languages of computer technology are universal. African and Asian lands have adopted and adapted democracy, parliamentary and party government, military strategy and technology, socialism, and national boundaries left by Western powers. Intellectuals speak of a global village, so closely connected is the community of ideas shared by leading Africans, Asians, and Latin Americans with Europeans and North Americans. At the same time, many countries are acutely conscious of their hard-won nationhood and of their dependence on shifts in the world markets, which they cannot control.

❖   ❖   ❖

Online Study Center ACE the Test

SUGGESTED READING

Ascherson, Neil, *The King Incorporated: Leopold the Second and the Congo* (2001).

Brown, Judith, *Gandhi: Prisoner of Hope* (1990). An excellent biography illustrating the political wisdom of Gandhi.

Bulmer-Thomas, V., *The Economic History of Latin America Since Independence* (1994). An important contribution to our understanding of the development of Latin America.

Bushnell, D., and N. Macaulay, *The Emergence of Latin America in the 19th Century* (1994).

Cain, P. A., and A. G. Hopkins, *British Imperialism: Innovation and Expansion, 1688–1914* (1993). This study emphasizes the importance of empire to Britain when banking, insurance, and service economics surpassed manufacturing.

Darby, Phillip, *Three Faces of Imperialism* (1987). British and American approaches to Asia and Africa.

Gordon, Andrew, *The Modern History of Japan: From Tokugawa to the Present* (2003). Excellent survey by a leading scholar.

Headrick, Daniel, *The Tools of Empire: Technology and European Imperialism in the Nineteenth Century* (1981) and *Tentacles of Progress: Technological Transfer in the Age of Imperialism, 1850–1940* (1988). Interesting argument for the role of technology in imperialism.

Hobsbawm, Eric, *The Age of Empire* (1988). The third volume of a Marxist interpretation of the history of modern Europe.

Hochschild, Adam, *King Leopold's Ghost: A Story of Greed, Terror, and Heroism in Colonial Africa* (1998).

Jeal, Tim, *Livingstone* (1974). A very readable biography of a fascinating life, with good background on Africa.

Keddi, N., *Religion and Politics in Iran* (1983). Essays on the crucial area of modern Iran.

Langer, William, *Diplomacy of Imperialism, 1890–1902,* (1950). Old but valuable for the important impact of diplomacy on the fate of disparate peoples.

Lieven, Dominic, *Empire: The Russian Empire and Its Rivals* (2000). A comparison of the great empires.

Mortimer, E., *Faith and Power: The Politics of Islam* (1982).

Packenham, Thomas, *The Scramble for Africa* (1991). Colorful narrative history.

Phillips, Richard, *Mapping Men and Empire: A Geography of Adventure* (1997). Explores the role of science and adventure in imperialism.

Porter, Bernard, *The Lion's Share: A Short History of British Imperialism, 1850–1970* (1975). A good survey history.

Spence, J. D., *The Search for Modern China* (1990). Thorough study and a good read.

Wolpert, S., *A New History of India* (1982). Good reference work.

CLASSIC TEXTS ON IMPERIALISM

These works shaped the debate on imperialism for politics, history, and ideology.

Hobson, J. A., *Imperialism: A Study* (1902). The original analysis of imperialism as the inevitable result of capitalism.

Lenin, V. I., *Imperialism: The Highest Stage of Capitalism* (1917).

Luxemburg, Rosa, *The Accumulation of Capital* (trans. 1963).

Chapter 28

Modern Consciousness: New Views of Nature, Human Nature, and the Arts

Evening on Karl Johan Street, by Edvard Munch. Munch's works often depicted anguish and horror. (Corbis-Bettmann.)

- **Irrationalism**
- **Freud: A New View of Human Nature**
- **Social Thought: Confronting the Irrational and the Complexities of Modern Society**
- **The Modernist Movement**
- **Modern Physics**
- **The Enlightenment Tradition in Disarray**

Focus Questions

1. In what ways did late modern thought and the arts break with the Enlightenment tradition?

2. How did the thought of Nietzsche, Dostoevski, Bergson, and Sorel exemplify the growing power and appeal of irrationalism?

3. What did Freud contribute to an understanding of irrationalism? What is his relationship to the Enlightenment tradition?

4. How did the modernist movement in the arts break with the standards of esthetics that had governed European culture since the Renaissance?

5. How did modern physics alter the Newtonian conception of the universe?

6. In what ways was the Enlightenment tradition in disarray by the early twentieth century?

Online Study Center

This icon will direct you to interactive map and primary source activities on the website http://college.hmco.com/pic/perrywc8e.

The modern mentality may be said to have passed through two broad phases: early modernity and late modernity. Formulated during the era of the Scientific Revolution and the Enlightenment, early modernity stressed confidence in reason, science, human goodness, and humanity's capacity to improve society for human betterment. Then in the late nineteenth and early twentieth centuries, a new outlook took shape. Late modern thinkers and scientists achieved revolutionary insights into human nature, the social world, and the physical universe; and writers and artists opened up hitherto unimagined possibilities for artistic expression.

These developments produced a shift in European consciousness. The mechanical model of the universe, which had dominated the Western outlook since Newton, was fundamentally altered. The Enlightenment view of human rationality and goodness was questioned, and the belief in natural rights and objective standards governing morality came under attack. Rules of esthetics that had governed the arts since the Renaissance were discarded. Shattering old beliefs, late modernity left Europeans without landmarks—without generally accepted cultural standards or agreed-on conceptions about human nature and life's meaning.

The late modern period was marked by extraordinary creativity in thought and the arts. Yet imaginative and fruitful as these changes were for Western intellectual and cultural life, they also helped create the disoriented, fragmented, and troubled era that characterized the twentieth century.

IRRATIONALISM

While many intellectuals continued to adhere to the outlook identified with the Enlightenment, some thinkers in the late nineteenth century challenged the basic premises of the philosophes and their nineteenth-century heirs. In particular, they repudiated the Enlightenment conception of human rationality, stressing instead the irrational side of human nature. Regarding reason as sovereign, the philosophes had defined human beings by their capacity to think critically; now thinkers saw blind strivings and animal instincts as the primary fact of human existence. It seemed that reason exercised a very limited influence over human conduct, that impulses, drives, and instincts—all forces below the surface—determined behavior much more than did logical consciousness.

The problem of **irrationalism** is manifold. Some thinkers, while recognizing the weakness of reason, continued to value it and sought to preserve it as an essential ingredient of civilized life. Some studied manifestations of the irrational in myth, religion, the arts, and politics in a logical and systematic way in order to gain understanding of human nature and human behavior. Others, concentrating on the creative potential of the irrational, urged nourishing the feelings, which they considered vital to artistic creativity and a richer existence. Still others celebrated violence as a healthy expression of the irrational.

The new insights into the irrational side of human nature and the growing assault on reason had immense implications for political life. In succeeding decades, these currents of irrationalism would become ideologized and politicized by unscrupulous demagogues who sought to mobilize and manipulate the masses. The popularity of fascist movements, which openly denigrated reason and exalted race, blood, action, and will, demonstrated the naiveté of nineteenth-century liberals, who believed that reason had triumphed in human affairs.

Nietzsche

The principal figure in the dethronement of reason and the glorification of the irrational was the German philosopher Friedrich Nietzsche (1844–1900). Nietzsche's writings are not systematic treatises but rather collections of aphorisms, often containing internal contradictions. Consequently, his philosophy lends itself to misinterpretation and misapplication. Nazi theorists, for example, distorted Nietzsche to justify their notions of the German master race.

Nietzsche attacked the accepted views and convictions of his day as a hindrance to a fuller and richer existence. He denounced social reform, parliamentary government, and universal suffrage; ridiculed the vision of progress through sci-

FRIEDRICH NIETZSCHE (1844–1900). Possessing the intuitive genius of a great poet, Nietzsche grasped the crucial problem afflicting the modern European soul: What path should the individual take in a world where God is dead? Nietzsche's answer to this question—the superman who creates his own values—lent itself to considerable misinterpretation and distortion and had little constructive social value. (*Bettmann/CORBIS.*)

ence; condemned Christian morality; and mocked the liberal belief in man's essential goodness and rationality. According to Nietzsche, man must understand that life, which is replete with cruelty, injustice, uncertainty, and absurdity, is not governed by rational principles. There exist no absolute standards of good and evil whose truth can be demonstrated by reflective reason. Nothing is true; there is no higher purpose or sense to the universe or human existence. There is only the naked individual living in a godless and absurd world.

Modern bourgeois society, said Nietzsche, is decadent and enfeebled—a victim of the excessive development of the rational faculties at the expense of will and instinct. Against the liberal-rationalist stress on the intellect, he urged recognition of the dark, mysterious world of instinctual desires, the true forces of life. If the human will is smothered with excessive intellectualizing, the spontaneity that sparks cultural creativity and ignites a zest for living is destroyed. The critical and theoretical outlook destroys the creative instincts. For man's manifold potential to be realized, he must stop relying on the intellect and nurture again the instinctual roots of human existence.

Christianity, with all its prohibitions, restrictions, and demands to conform, also crushes the human impulse for life, said Nietzsche, the son of a Lutheran pastor. Christian morality must be obliterated, for it is fit only for the weak, the slave. The triumph of Christianity in the ancient world, said Nietzsche, was a revolution of the lowest elements of society, the meek, the weak, and the ignoble, who sought to inherit the earth from their aristocratic superiors. It was nothing less than an attempt of resentful slaves and slavelike plebeians to prevent their aristocratic superiors from expressing their heroic natures and to strike back at the noble spirits whom they envied. They did so by condemning as evil the very traits that they themselves lacked—strength, power, assertiveness, and a zest for life—and by making their own base, wretched, and life-negating values the standard of all things. Then they saddled with guilt all those who deviated from the standard. This transvaluation of values engineered by Christianity, said Nietzsche, led to a deterioration of life and culture. In *The Anti-Christ* (1888), Nietzsche wrote:

> *Christianity has waged a war to the death against this* higher *type of man. . . . Christianity has taken the side of everything weak, base, ill-constituted, it has made an ideal out of opposition to the . . . instincts of strong life. . . . Christianity is a revolt of everything that crawls along the ground directed against that which is elevated.*[1]

The Christian virtues of love, compassion, and pity, Nietzsche added, are really only a facade hiding Christians' true feelings of envy, resentment, hatred, and revenge against their superiors, betters, and tormentors and desire for their own power.

Although the philosophes rejected Christian doctrines, they largely retained Christian ethics. Unlike the philosophes, Nietzsche did not attack Christianity because it was contrary to reason. He attacked it because, he said, it gave man a sick soul. It was life-denying. Blocking the free and spontaneous exercise of human instincts, it made humility, weakness, and self-abnegation virtues and pride a vice. In short, Christianity extinguished the spark of life. This spark of life, this inner yearning that fosters self-creation, must again burn.

"God is dead," Nietzsche proclaimed. God is man's own creation. Christian morality is also dead. Dead also are all the inherited truths based on nature and reason. There are no higher worlds, no transcendental or metaphysical truths, no morality derived from God or nature, and no natural rights, scientific socialism, or inevitable progress. We are wandering through an eternal nothing in which all the old values and truths have lost their intelligibility. This **nihilism**—the belief that moral and social values have no validity—has caused a crisis in European life. But the death of God and of all transcendental truths can mean the liberation of man, insisted Nietzsche. Man can surmount nihilism by adopting a new orientation that gives primacy to the superior man—the **overman** or **superman** who asserts his will, gives order to chaotic passions, makes great demands on himself, and lives life with a fierce joy. The overman aspires to self-perfection; without fear or guilt, he creates his own values and defines his own self, his own life. Such a man can overcome the deadening uniformity and mediocrity of modern civilization. He can undo democracy and socialism, which have made masters out of cattlelike masses, and surmount the shopkeeper's spirit, which has made man soft and degenerate. European society lacks heroic figures; everyone belongs to a vast herd, but there are no leaders.

According to Nietzsche, Europe could be saved only by the emergence of such a higher type of man, who would not be held back by the egalitarian rubbish preached by democrats and socialists. "A declaration of war on the masses by *higher* man is needed," said Nietzsche, to end "the dominion of *inferior* men." Europe requires "the annihilation of *suffrage universal,* i.e., the system through which the lowest natures prescribe themselves as laws for the higher."[2] Europe needs a new breed of rulers, a true aristocracy of masterful men. The overman is a new kind of man who breaks with accepted morality and sets his own standards. He does not repress his instincts but asserts them. He destroys old values and asserts his prerogative as master. Free of Christian guilt, he proudly affirms his own being; dispensing with Christian "thou shalt not," he instinctively says, "I will." He dares to be himself. Because he is not like other people, traditional definitions of *good* and *evil* have no meaning for him. He does not allow his individuality to be stifled. He makes his own values, those that flow from his very being.

The overman understands and exemplifies the ultimate fact of life: that "the most fearful and fundamental desire in man [is] his drive for power,"[3] that human beings crave and strive for power ceaselessly and uncompromisingly. It is perfectly natural for human beings to want to dominate nature and other human beings; inherent in human nature is the desire "to overpower, overthrow, . . . to become master, a thirst for enemies and antagonisms and triumphs."[4] This will to power is not a product of rational reflection but flows from the very essence of human existence. As the motivating force in human behavior, it governs everyday life and is the determining factor in political life. The enhancement of power brings supreme enjoyment: "The love of power is the demon of men. Let them have everything—health, food, a place to live, entertainment—they are and remain unhappy and low-spirited; for the demon waits and waits and will be satisfied. Take everything from them and satisfy this and they are almost happy—as happy as men and demons can be."[5] The masses, cowardly and envious, will condemn the overman as evil; this has always been their way. Thus, Nietzsche castigates democracy because it "represents the disbelief in great human beings and an elite society,"[6] and Christianity because it imposes an unnatural morality, one that affirms meekness, humility, and compassion.

The German philosopher Arthur Schopenhauer (1788–1860) had declared that beneath the conscious intellect is the will, a striving, demanding, and imperious force, which is the real determinant of human behavior. Schopenhauer held that the intellect is merely a tool of an alogical and irrational will. Life is an endless striving to fulfill ceaseless desires. Blind animal impulses, not the capacity for rational choice, are a human being's true essence. Schopenhauer sought to repress the will. He urged people to stifle desires and retreat into quietude to escape from life's agonies.

Nietzsche learned from Schopenhauer to appreciate the power of unconscious strivings that dominate human behavior, but he rejected Schopenhauer's condemnation and negation of the will, his flight from life. Instead, Nietzsche called for the heroic and joyful assertion of the will and the affirmation of life in order to redeem life from nothingness.

Overmen cast off all established values. Free of all restrictions, rules, and codes of behavior imposed by society, they create their own values. They burst on the world propelled by that something that urges people to want, take, strike, create, struggle, seek, dominate. They know that life is purposeless but live it laughingly, instinctively, fully. Overmen are people of restless energy who enjoy living dangerously, have contempt for meekness and humility, and dismiss humanitarian sentiments; they are noble warriors, hard and ruthless. Only a new elite, which distances itself from the masses and holds in contempt the Christian belief that all people are equal before God, can save European society from decadence.

The influence of Nietzsche's philosophy is still a matter of controversy and conjecture. Perhaps better than anyone else, Nietzsche grasped the crucial problem of modern society and culture: that with the "death of God," traditional moral values had lost their authority and binding power. In a world where nothing is true, all is permitted. Nietzsche foresaw that the future, an age without values, would be violent and sordid, and he urged individuals to face themselves and life free of illusion, pretense, and hypocrisy. Nietzsche is also part of a general nineteenth-century trend that sought to affirm the human being and earthly aspirations rather than God or salvation.

But no helpful social policy could be derived from Nietzsche's heroic individualism, which taught that "there are higher and lower men and that a single individual can . . . justify the existence of whole millennia."[7] Nietzsche thought only of great individuals, humanity's noblest specimens, who overcome mediocrity and the artificiality of all inherited values. The social community and social injustice did not concern him. "The weak and ill-constituted shall perish: first principle of our philanthropy. And one shall help them to do so."[8] Surely, these words offer no constructive guidelines for dealing with the problems of modern industrial civilization.

Likewise, Nietzsche had no constructive proposals for dealing with the disintegration of rational and Christian certainties. Instead, his vitriolic attack on European institutions and values helped to erode the rational foundations of Western civilization. This assault appealed immensely to intellectuals in central Europe, who saw Nietzsche's philosophy as liberating an inner energy. Thus, many young people, attracted to Nietzsche, welcomed World War I; they viewed it as an esthetic experience and thought that it would clear a path to a new heroic age. They took Nietzsche's words literally: "A society that definitely and *instinctively* gives up war and conquest is in decline."[9]

Nazi theorists tried to make Nietzsche a forerunner of their movement. They sought philosophical sanction for their own thirst for power, contempt for the weak, ruthlessness, and glorification of action, as well as for their cult of the heroic and their Social Darwinistic revulsion for human equality. Recasting Nietzsche in their own image, the Nazis saw themselves as Nietzsche's overmen: members of a master race, who, by force of will, would conquer all obstacles and reshape the world according to their own values. Some German intellectuals were drawn to Nazism because it seemed a healthy affirmation of life, the life with a new purpose, for which Nietzsche called.

Nietzsche himself, detesting German nationalism and militarism, scoffed at the notion of German racial superiority, disdained (despite some unfortunate remarks) anti-Semitism, and denounced state worship. He would have abhorred Hitler and been dismayed at the twisting of his idea of the will to power into a prototype fascist principle. The men whom he admired were passionate but self-possessed individuals who, by mastering their own chaotic passions, would face life and death courageously, affirmatively, and creatively. Such men make great demands on themselves. Nevertheless, as Janko Lavrin points out, "Practically all the Fascist and Nazi theories can find some support in Nietzsche's texts, provided one gives them the required twist."[10] Nietzsche's extreme and violent denunciation of Western democratic principles, including equality; his praise of power; and his call for the liberation of the instincts; as well as his elitism, which denigrates and devalues all human life that is not strong and noble; and his spurning of humane values provided a breeding ground for violent, antirational, antiliberal, and inhumane movements. His philosophy, which included loose talk about the virtues of pitiless warriors, the breeding of a master race, and the annihilation of the weak and the ill, is conducive to a politics of extremes that knows no moral limits.

Dostoevski

Like Nietzsche, the Russian novelist and essayist Fyodor Dostoevski (1821–1881) attacked the fundamental outlook of the Enlightenment, particularly as expressed by liberals and socialists. In contrast to their view that human beings are innately good, responsive to reason's promptings, and capable of constructing the good society through reason, Dostoevski perceived human beings as inherently depraved, irrational, and rebellious.

In *Notes from Underground* (1864), the narrator (the Underground Man) rebels against the efforts of rationalists, humanists, positivists, liberals, and socialists to define human nature according to universal principles and to reform society so as to promote greater happiness. He rebels against science and reason, against the entire liberal and socialist vision. He does so in the name of human subjectivity: the uncontainable, irrepressible, whimsical, and foolish human will. Human nature, says the Underground Man, is too volatile, too diversified to be schematized by the theoretical mind; it will struggle against reason's yoke.

For the Underground Man, there are no absolute and timeless truths that precede the individual and to which the individual should conform. There is only a terrifying world of naked wills vying with one another. In such a world, people do not necessarily seek happiness, prosperity, and peace—all that is good for them, according to "enlightened" thinkers. To the rationalist who aims to eliminate suffering and deprivation, Dostoevski replies that some people freely choose suffering and depravity because it gratifies them—for some, "even in a toothache there is enjoyment"—and they are repelled by wealth, peace, security, and happiness. They do not want to be robots in a rigorously planned and regulated social order, which creates a slot for everything, and they consider excessive intellectualizing—"over-acute consciousness"—a disease that keeps them from asserting their autonomy, their "independent choice."

> [I]t seems that something that is dearer to almost every man than his greatest advantages must really exist . . . for which, if necessary, a man is ready to act in opposition to all laws, that is, in opposition to reason, honor, peace, prosperity. . . . One's own free unfettered choice, one's own fancy, however wild it may be, one's own fancy worked up at times to frenzy—why that is that very "most advantageous advantage" which we have overlooked, which comes under no classification and through which all systems and theories are continually being sent to the devil. . . . What man needs is simple independent choice, whatever that independence may cost and wherever it may lead.[11]

It is this irrational will, Dostoevski tells us, that defines the individual's uniqueness and leads him to resist the blueprints drawn up by social theorists. For such crystal palaces—secular utopias designed to satisfy all human needs—do not satisfy what the individual needs most: the expression of one's own desires, no matter how foolish or capricious they might appear to the rational mind. So much for any theory that tries to reduce human nature, which is essentially peculiar, irrational, and incomprehensible, to a formula. If Dostoevski is right, if individuals do not act out of enlightened self-interest, if they are driven by instinctual cravings that resist reason's appeals, then what hope is there for social planners wishing to create the "good" society?

The Underground Man maintains that by following irrational impulses and engaging in irrational acts, human beings assert their individuality; they prove that they are free. The Underground Man is totally free. He struggles to define his existence according to his own needs rather than the standards and values created by others. For him, freedom of choice is a human being's most priceless possession, and it derives not from the intellect but from impulses and feelings that account for our essential individuality. He considers the "rational faculty" as "simply one-twentieth of all my faculties of life"; life is more than reasoning, more than "simply extracting square roots."[12]

In rejecting external security and liberal and socialist concepts of progress—in aspiring to assert his own individuality even if this means acting against his own best interests—the Underground Man demonstrates that a powerful element of irrationality underlies human nature, an element that reason can neither understand, control, nor satisfy.

Bergson

Another thinker who reflected the growing irrationalism of the age was Henri Bergson (1859–1941), a French philosopher of Jewish background. Originally attracted to positivism, Bergson turned away from the positivistic claim that science could explain everything and fulfill all human needs. Such an emphasis on the intellect, said Bergson, sacrifices spiritual impulses, imagination, and intuition and reduces reality and the soul to mere mechanisms. The methods of science cannot reveal ultimate reality, Bergson insisted. European civilization must recognize the limitations of scientific rationalism. Our capacity for intuition, whereby the mind grasps the inner life of the object—becomes one with it—tells us more about reality than the method of analysis employed by science. The intuitive experience—something like the artist's instant comprehension of a natural scene—is a direct avenue to truth, which is closed to the calculations and measurements of science. Bergson's philosophy pointed away from science toward religious mysticism.

To his admirers, Bergson's philosophy liberated the person from the constraints of positivism, mechanism, and materialism. It also extolled the creative potential of intuition, the mystical experience, and the poetic imagination: those forces of life that resist categorization by the scientific mind. A protest against modern technology and bureaucracy—against all the features of mass society that seemed to stifle individual uniqueness and spontaneity—it sought to reaffirm the primacy of the individual in an increasingly mechanized and bureaucratic world. The popularity of Bergson's philosophy with its depreciation of reason, symptomized the unsuspected strength and appeal of the nonrational—another sign that people were searching for new alternatives to the Enlightenment world-view.

Sorel

Nietzsche and Dostoevski proclaimed that irrational forces constitute the essence of human nature; Bergson held that a nonrational intuition provides insights unattainable by the scientific mentality. The French social theorist Georges Sorel (1847–1922), who had given up engineering to follow intellectual pursuits, recognized the political potential of the nonrational. Like Nietzsche, Sorel was disillusioned with contemporary bourgeois society, which he considered decadent, unheroic, and life-denying. Like Nietzsche, he also denounced the liberal-democratic foundations of middle-class society. Whereas Nietzsche called for the overman to rescue society from decadence and mediocrity, Sorel placed his hopes in the workers, whose position made them courageous and virile. He saw them as bearers of higher values: as noble and determined producers struggling against exploiters and parasites.

Sorel wanted the proletariat to destroy the existing bourgeois-liberal-capitalist order and rejuvenate society by infusing it with dynamic and creative energy and a sense of moral purpose. The overthrow of decadent bourgeois society would be accomplished through a general strike: a universal work stoppage, which would bring down governments and give power to the workers. Sorel applauded violence, for it intensified the revolutionaries' dedication to the cause and spurred them to acts of heroism. It also accorded with his general conception that life is an unremitting battle and that history is a perpetual conflict between decay and vitality, between passivity and action. In his view, struggle purified, invigorated, and promoted creative change.

Sorel saw the general strike as having the appeal of a great mobilizing myth. What was important was not that the general strike actually take place, but that its image stir all the anticapitalist resentments of the workers and inspire them to carry out their revolutionary responsibilities. Sorel understood the extraordinary potency of myth: it structures and intensifies feelings, unifies people, and mobilizes and channels their energy into heroic action. Because they appeal to the imagination and the emotions, myths are an effective way of organizing the masses, buoying up their spirits, and moving them to revolt. By believing in the myth of the general strike, workers would soar above the moral decadence of bourgeois society and bear the immense sacrifices that their struggle called for.

Like Marx, Sorel believed that the goals of the worker could not be achieved through peaceful parliamentary means. He, too, wanted no reconciliation between bourgeois exploiters and oppressed workers. The only recourse for workers was direct action and violence. However, Marx considered violence simply as a means to a revolutionary end and would dispense with it once the end was achieved. Regarding violence as sublime—a means of restoring grandeur to a flabby world—Sorel valued it as an end in itself.

Sorel's condemnation of liberal democracy and his conviction that fabricated myths could serve as a powerful political weapon found concrete expression in the fascist movements after World War I. Sorel heralded the age of mass political movements committed to revolutionary violence and of myths manufactured by **propaganda** experts determined to destroy the liberal-rational tradition of the Enlightenment.

Freud and His Daughter, Anna (1912). Sigmund Freud (1856–1939), the father of psychoanalysis, penetrated the world of the unconscious in a scientific way. He concluded that powerful drives govern human behavior more than reason does. His explorations of the unconscious produced an image of the human being that broke with the Enlightenment's view of the individual's essential goodness and rationality. (*Mary Evans Picture Library.*)

FREUD: A NEW VIEW OF HUMAN NATURE

In many ways, Sigmund Freud (1856–1939), an Austrian-Jewish physician who spent most of his adult life in Vienna, was a child of the Enlightenment. Like the philosophes, he identified civilization with reason and regarded science as the avenue to knowledge. But in contrast to the philosophes, Freud focused on the massive power and influence of nonrational drives. Marx had argued that, although people believe that they think freely, in truth their beliefs and thoughts reflect the interests and ideology of the ruling class. Freud, too, believed that our conscious thoughts are determined by hidden forces—namely, unconscious impulses.

Whereas Nietzsche glorified the irrational and approached it with a poet's temperament, Freud recognized its potential danger. He sought to comprehend it scientifically and wanted to regulate it in the interests of civilization. Unlike Nietzsche, Freud did not belittle the rational but always sought to salvage respect for reason. In a letter to the Austrian novelist Stefan Zweig, Freud wrote that the essential task of **psychoanalysis** was "to struggle with the demon" of irrationality in a "sober way," to make it "a comprehensible object of science."[13] By "a sober way," he meant the scientific method, not Bergson's intuition or Nietzsche's inspired insights. Better than anyone, Freud recognized reason's limitations and the power of the nonrational, but he never wavered in his support of reason:

> We may insist as often as we like, that man's intellect is powerless in comparison with his instinctual life, and we may be right in this. Nevertheless, there is something peculiar about his weakness. The voice of the intellect is a soft one, but it does not rest until it has gained a hearing. Finally, after a countless succession of rebuffs, it succeeds. This is one of the few points on which one may be optimistic about the future of mankind.[14]

Freud's explorations of the world of the unconscious had a profoundly upsetting impact on our conception of the self. Freud himself viewed his theories as a great blow to human pride, to "man's craving for grandiosity":

> Humanity has, in the course of time, had to endure from the hands of science two great outrages upon its naive self-love. The first was when it realized that our earth was not the center of the universe, but only a tiny speck in a world-system of a magnitude hardly conceivable; this is associated in our minds with

the name of Copernicus. . . . The second was when biological research robbed man of his peculiar privilege of having been specially created, and relegated him to a descent from the animal world, implying an ineradicable animal nature in him: this transvaluation has been accomplished in our own time upon the investigations of Charles Darwin. . . . But man's craving for grandiosity is now suffering the third and most bitter blow from present-day psychological research which is endeavoring to show the "ego" of each of us that he is not even master in his own house, but that he must remain content with the veriest scrap of information about what is going on unconsciously in his own mind.[15]

Freud held that people are not fundamentally rational and that human behavior is governed primarily by powerful inner forces, which are hidden from consciousness. Within the human mind, intense mental activity takes place that is independent of and unknown to consciousness. Primitive drives, strivings, and thoughts influence our behavior, often without our awareness, so that we may not know the real reasons for our actions. Freud considered not just the external acts of a person but also the inner psychic reality underlying human behavior.

Freud, of course, did not discover the unconscious. Romantic poets had sought the wellspring of creativity in a layer of mind below consciousness. The Greek tragedians, Shakespeare, Schopenhauer, Nietzsche, and Dostoevski, among others, had all penetrated the tangled world of the passions and marveled at its elemental power. Freud, who believed that artistic and literary creativity ultimately derives from primal instincts rooted in the unconscious, paid tribute to creative writers' intuition: "they are apt to know of a whole host of things between heaven and earth of which our philosophy has not yet let us dream. In their knowledge of the mind they are far in advance of us everyday people, for they draw upon sources which we have not yet opened up for science."[16] He described Nietzsche as a philosopher "whose guesses and intuitions often agree in the most astonishing way with the laborious findings of psychoanalysis."[17] Freud's great achievement was to explore the unconscious methodically and

systematically with the tools and temperament of a scientist. He showed that the irrational contained a structure that could be empirically explained and rationally explored.

After graduating from medical school, Freud specialized in the treatment of nervous disorders. His investigations led him to conclude that childhood fears and experiences, often sexual in nature, accounted for neuroses: disorders in thinking, feeling, and behavior that interfere with everyday acts of personal and social life. Neuroses can take several forms, including hysteria, anxiety, depression, and obsessions. So painful and threatening were these childhood emotions and experiences that his patients banished them from conscious memory to the realm of the unconscious. To understand and treat neurotic behavior, Freud said, it is necessary to look behind overt symptoms and bring to the surface emotionally charged experiences and fears—childhood traumas—that lie buried in the unconscious, along with primitive impulses.

Freud probed the unconscious by urging his patients to say whatever came to their minds. This procedure, called *free association,* rests on the premise that spontaneous and uninhibited talk reveals a person's underlying preoccupations, his or her inner world, and the "demons" that are at the root of the person's emotional distress. A second avenue to the unconscious is the analysis of dreams. An individual's dreams, said Freud, reveal his or her secret wishes, often socially unacceptable desires, and frightening memories. Finding them too painful to bear, we lock up these wishes and memories in the deepest dungeons of the unconscious. But repressed emotions do not disappear; even in their cages, the demons remain active, continuing to haunt us and to generate conflicts. Our distress is real and even excruciating, but we do not know its source.

The **id,** the subconscious seat of the instincts, said Freud, is "a cauldron full of seething excitations" that constantly demand gratification. The id is primitive and irrational. It knows no values; it has no awareness of good and evil. Unable to endure tension, it demands sexual release, the termination of pain, or the cessation of hunger. When the id is denied an outlet for its instinctual energy, people become frustrated, angry, and unhappy. Gratifying the id is our highest pleasure.

But the full gratification of instinctual demands is detrimental to civilized life. That is why the **ego**, which stands for reason, seeks to hold the id in check, to bring it in line with reality.

Freud postulated a harrowing conflict between the relentless strivings of our instinctual nature and the requirements of civilization. In Freud's view, civilization requires the renunciation of instinctual gratification and the mastery of animal instincts, a thesis he developed in *Civilization and Its Discontents* (1930). Although Freud's thoughts in this work were, no doubt, influenced by the great tragedy of World War I, the main theme could be traced back to his earlier writings. Human beings derive their highest pleasure from sexual fulfillment, said Freud, but unrestrained sexuality drains off psychic energy needed for creative artistic and intellectual life and directs human energies away from work needed to preserve communal life. Hence society, through the family, the priest, the teacher, and the police, imposes rules and restrictions on our animal nature. But this is immensely painful. The human being is caught in a tragic bind. Society's demand to repress the instincts in the interest of civilization causes terrible frustration; equally distressing, the violation of society's rules under the pressure of instinctual needs evokes feelings of guilt. Either way, people suffer; civilized life simply entails too much pain for people. It seems that the price we pay for civilization is neurosis, mental distress. Most people cannot endure the amount of instinctual renunciation that civilization requires. There are times when our elemental human nature rebels against all the restrictions and "thou shalt nots" demanded by society, against all the misery and torment imposed by civilization.

"Civilization imposes great sacrifices not only on man's sexuality, but also on his aggressivity,"[18] said Freud. People are not good by nature, as the philosophes had taught; on the contrary, they are "creatures among whose instinctual endowments is to be reckoned a powerful share of aggressiveness." Their first inclination is not to love their neighbor but to "satisfy their aggressiveness on him, to exploit his capacity for work without compensation, to use him sexually without his consent, to seize his possessions, to humiliate him, to cause him pain, to torture and to kill him."[19] Man is wolf to man, concluded Freud.

"Who has the courage to dispute it in the face of all the evidence in his own life and in history?"[20] Civilization "has to use its utmost efforts in order to set limits to man's aggressive instincts," but "in spite of every effort these endeavors of civilization have not so far achieved very much."[21] People find it difficult to do without "the satisfaction of this inclination to aggression."[22] When circumstances are favorable, this primitive aggressiveness breaks loose and "reveals man as a savage beast to whom consideration towards his own kind is something alien."[23] For Freud, "the inclination to aggression is an original self-subsisting disposition in man," and it "constitutes the greatest impediment to civilization." Civilization attempts "to combine single human individuals and after that families, then races, peoples and nations into one great unity. . . . But man's natural aggressive instinct, the hostility of each against all and of all against each, opposes this program of civilization."[24] Aggressive impulses drive people apart, threatening society with disintegration. For Freud, an unalterable core of human nature is ineluctably in opposition to civilized life. To this extent, everyone is potentially an enemy of civilization.

Freud's awareness of the irrational and his general pessimism regarding people's ability to regulate it in the interests of civilization did not lead him to break faith with the Enlightenment tradition, for Freud did not celebrate the irrational. He was too aware of its self-destructive nature for that. Civilization is indeed a burden, but people must bear it, for the alternative is far worse. In the tradition of the philosophes, Freud sought truth based on a scientific analysis of human nature and believed that reason was the best road to social improvement. Like the philosophes, he was critical of religion, regarding it as a pious illusion—a fairy tale in conflict with reason. Freud wanted people to throw away what he believed was the crutch of religion: to break away from childlike dependency and stand alone.

Also like the philosophes, Freud was a humanitarian who sought to relieve human misery by making people aware of their true nature, particularly their sexuality. He wanted society to soften its overly restrictive sexual standards because they were injurious to mental health. As a practicing psychiatrist, he tried to assist his patients in dealing with emotional problems. Freud wanted to raise to the level of consciousness hitherto un-recognized inner conflicts that caused emotional distress. One enduring consequence of the Freud-ian revolution is the recognition of the enormous importance played by childhood in the shaping of the adult's personality. The neurotic disorders that burden adults begin in early childhood. Freud urged that we show greater concern for the emotional needs of children.

Yet Freud also differed from the philosophes in crucial ways. Dismissing the Christian doctrine of original sin as myth, the philosophes had believed human nature to be essentially good. If people took reason for their guide, evil could be elimi-nated. Freud, however, asserted, in secular and sci-entific terms, a pessimistic view of human nature. He saw evil as rooted in human nature rather than as a product of a faulty environment. Education and better living conditions would not eliminate evil, as the philosophes had expected, nor would abolition of private property, as Marx had de-clared. In a socialist state where economic dispari-ties have been eliminated, said Freud, people will lust after power and privilege. The philosophes venerated reason; it had enabled Newton to un-ravel nature's mysteries and would permit people to achieve virtue and reform society. Freud, who wanted reason to prevail, understood that its soft voice had to compete with the thunderous roars of the id. Freud broke with the optimism of the philosophes. His awareness of the immense pres-sures that civilization places on our fragile egos led him to be generally pessimistic about the future.

Unlike Marx, Freud had no vision of utopia. He saw the crude, untameable, and destructive character of human nature as an ever-present ob-stacle to harmonious social relations. That Freud was hounded out of Vienna by the Nazis just be-fore WW II and his four sisters were later mur-dered by them simply for being Jewish is a telling footnote to his view of human nature, the power of the irrational, and the fragility of civilization.

Online Study Center

Improve Your Grade
Primary Source: The Interpretation of Dreams: Psychoanalysis Is Born (Freud)

SOCIAL THOUGHT: CONFRONTING THE IRRATIONAL AND THE COMPLEXITIES OF MODERN SOCIETY

The end of the nineteenth century and the begin-ning of the twentieth mark the great age of socio-logical thought. The leading sociological thinkers of the period all regarded science as the only valid model for correct thinking, and all claimed that their thought rested on a scientific foundation. They struggled with some of the crucial problems of modern society: How can society achieve co-herence and stability when the customary associa-tions and attachments that characterized village life are ruthlessly dissolved by the rapidly devel-oping industrial-urban-capitalist order, which ele-vates often selfish individualism over integrative communal ties that had characterized pre-indus-trial society, and when religion no longer unites people? What are the implications of the nonra-tional for political life? How can people preserve their individuality in a society that is becoming increasingly regimented? In many ways, twenti-eth-century dictatorships were responses to the dilemmas of modern society analyzed by these social theorists. And twentieth-century dictators would employ these social theorists' insights into group and mass psychology for the purpose of gaining and maintaining power.

Durkheim

Émile Durkheim (1858–1917), a French scholar of Jewish background and heir to Comte's positivism, was an important founder of modern sociology. Like Comte, he considered scientific thought to be the only valid model for modern society. A crucial el-ement of Durkheim's thought was the effort to show that the essential ingredients of modern times—sec-ularism, rationalism, and individualism—threaten society with disintegration. In traditional society, the social order was derived from God, and a per-son's place and function were assigned by God and determined by birth and custom. However, modern people, skeptical and individualistic, do not accept such restraints. Instead, they seek to uplift themselves and demand that society allow them the opportunity. In the process, they reject or ignore the restraints that society must impose if it is to function. Their attitude leads to anarchy. Durkheim wanted to prevent modern society from disintegrating into a disconnected mass of self-seeking, antagonistic individuals.

The weakening of those traditional ties that bind the individual to society constituted, for Durkheim, the crisis of modern industrial society. Without collective values and common beliefs, he felt, society was threatened with disintegration and the individual with disorientation. To a Western world intrigued by scientific progress, Durkheim emphasized the spiritual malaise of modern society. Modern people, said Durkheim, suffer from **anomie**—a collapse of values. They do not feel integrated into a collective community and find no purpose in life. In *Suicide* (1897), Durkheim maintained that "the exceptionally high number of voluntary deaths manifests the state of deep disturbances from which civilized societies are suffering and bears witness to its gravity."[25] The high level of boredom, anxiety, and pessimism also evidence the pathology of modern society. Modern people are driven to suicide by intense competition and the disappointment and frustration resulting from unfulfilled expectations and a lack of commitment to moral principles. People must limit their aspirations and exercise discipline over their desires and passions. They must stop wanting more. Religion once spurred people to view restraint and the renunciation of desires as virtues, but it can no longer do so.

Although Durkheim approved of modernity, he noted that modern ways have not brought happiness or satisfaction to the individual. Modern scientific and industrial society requires a new moral system, which would bind the various classes into a cohesive social order and help overcome the feelings of restlessness and dissatisfaction tormenting people. Like Saint-Simon, Durkheim called for a rational and secular system of morals to replace Christian dogma, which had lost its power to attract and to bind.

Durkheim focused on a crucial dilemma of modernity. On the one hand, modern urban civilization has provided the individual with unparalleled opportunities for self-development and material improvement. On the other, the break-

down of traditional communal bonds caused by the spread of rationalism and individualism has produced a sense of isolation and alienation. In modern mass society, the individual feels like an outsider, a condition that has been exacerbated by the decline of Christianity. Twentieth-century totalitarian movements sought to integrate these uprooted and alienated souls into new collectivities: a proletarian state based on workers' solidarity or a racial state based on ethnic purity and nationalism (see Chapter 30).

Pareto

Like Comte, Vilfredo Pareto (1848–1923), an Italian economist and sociologist, aimed to construct a system of sociology on the model of the physical sciences. His studies led him to conclude that social behavior rests primarily not on reason but rather on nonrational instincts and sentiments. These deeply rooted and essentially changeless feelings are the fundamental elements in human behavior. Although society may change, human nature remains essentially the same. Whoever aims to lead and to influence people must appeal not to logic but to elemental feelings. Most human behavior is nonrational; nonlogical considerations also determine the beliefs that people hold. Like Marx and Freud, Pareto believed that we cannot accept a person's word at face value; we find the real cause of human behavior in human instincts and sentiments. People do not act according to carefully thought-out theories. They act first from nonlogical motivations and then construct a rationalization to justify their behavior. Much of Pareto's work was devoted to studying the nonrational elements of human conduct and the various beliefs invented to give the appearance of rationality to behavior that derives from feeling and instinct.

Pareto divided society into two strata: the elite and the masses. Elites have always existed, said Pareto, because human beings are unequal by nature and because the goods that all people seek cannot be shared equally. Because struggle is a general law of life, elites and masses will exist in all societies. The belief that a democracy constitutes rule by a people is a myth, said Pareto. In actuality, a small group of party leaders controls the political system. Pareto also rejected as naive Marx's vision of the end of the class struggle.

In the tradition of Machiavelli, Pareto held that a successful ruling elite must, with cunning, and if necessary with violence, exploit the feelings and impulses of the masses to its own advantage. Democratic states, he said, delude themselves in thinking that the masses are really influenced by rational argument. A staunch opponent of parliamentary democracy, Pareto predicted that new political leaders would emerge who would master the people through propaganda and force, appealing always to sentiment rather than to reason. To this extent, Pareto was an intellectual forerunner of fascism, which preached an authoritarian elitism (see Chapter 30). Mussolini praised Pareto and proudly claimed him as a source of inspiration. The extent to which Pareto, who died one year after Mussolini came to power, welcomed the fascist regime is a matter of conjecture. But the triumph of fascism did seem to confirm his convictions that democracy was ready to collapse and that a small minority of determined men, willing to use violence, could gain control of the state if the holders of power were reluctant to counter with force.

Le Bon

Gustave Le Bon (1841–1931), a French social psychologist, concentrated on mass psychology as demonstrated in crowd behavior, a phenomenon of considerable importance in an age of accelerating industrialization and democratization. "The substitution of the unconscious action of crowds for the conscious activity of individuals is one of the principal characteristics of the present age,"[26] Le Bon declared in the preface to *The Crowd* (1895). In the past, said Le Bon, rivalries between monarchs dominated Europe's political stage; "the opinion of the masses scarcely counted, and most frequently did not count at all."[27] But Europe has experienced a great transformation. In this new age, he said, the masses organized in socialist parties, and unions are starting to determine the destinies of nations. Le Bon, who had contempt for democracy, intended his work to be a justification for rule by an authoritiarian elite.

Le Bon applied the term *crowd* to a large group of people in which individuality is submerged in the mass, and the individual loses control over his or her ideas and emotions. A psychological crowd could be a street mob, a political party, or a labor union. An agglomeration of individuals "presents new characteristics very different from those of the individuals composing it. The sentiments and ideas of all the persons in the gathering take one and the same direction, and their conscious personality vanishes."[28] The crowd acquires a collective mind, in which critical thinking is swamped and "unconscious qualities obtain the upper hand."[29] Becoming increasingly intolerant and fanatical, the crowd member "descends several rungs in the ladder of civilization. Isolated, he may be a cultivated individual; in a crowd, he is a barbarian—that is, a creature acting by instinct."[30] Crowd behavior demonstrates convincingly that "the part played by the unconscious in all our acts is immense and that played by reason very small."[31] In a contest with aroused emotions, human reason is utterly powerless.

Le Bon also discussed the leaders of crowds and their means of persuasion. "A crowd is a servile flock that is incapable of ever doing without a master," he stressed. Leaders "are more frequently men of action than thinkers"; they are "morbidly nervous, excitable, . . . bordering on madness." Fanatically committed to their beliefs, they do not respond to logical argument. The masses, "always ready to listen to the strong-willed man,"[32] respond to the intensity of the leader's faith.

Both Mussolini and Hitler, who deliberately sought to seduce, manipulate, and dominate the masses, absorbed Le Bon's ideas, which had become commonplace in the early twentieth century. "I don't know how many times I have re-read *Psychologie des Foules* [*The Crowd*]," declared Mussolini. "It is an excellent work to which I frequently refer."[33] Hitler's analysis of the crowd—"sober reasoning determines their thoughts far less than emotion and feeling"—restates many of Le Bon's observations.

Weber

Probably the most prominent social thinker of the age, the German academic Max Weber (1864–1920) was a leading shaper of modern sociology. In Weber's view, Western civilization, unlike the other civilizations of the globe, had virtually eliminated myth, mystery, and magic from its conception of nature and society—the "disenchantment of the world," Weber called it. Most conspicuous in Western science, this process of rationalization, or "calculated action," was also evident in politics, law, and economics. Weber considered Western science to be an attempt to understand and master nature through reason, and Western capitalism an attempt to organize work and production in a rational manner. The Western state has a rational written constitution, rationally formulated law, and a bureaucracy of trained government officials who administer the affairs of state according to rational rules and regulations. Justice is not dispensed by wise elders but proceeds from codified law and established procedures. The question of why the West, and not China or India, engaged in this process of rationalization intrigued Weber, and much of his scholarly effort went into answering it.

Weber understood the terrible paradox of reason. Reason accounts for brilliant achievements in science and economic life, but it also despiritualizes life by ruthlessly eliminating centuries-old traditions, denouncing deeply felt religious beliefs as superstition, and regarding human feelings and passions as impediments to clear thinking. While giving people knowledge, the process of disenchantment has shattered the basis for belief in transcendental values; in a thoroughly disenchanted world, life is without ultimate purpose and the individual is soulless. This is the dilemma of modern individuals, said Weber. Secular rationality is shaping a world in which standards cannot claim ultimate sanction. A disenchanted world contains no inherited truths, no God-given answers to the human being's desperate need for meaning. We are now confronted with an immense and unprecedented burden: how to create for ourselves values that give meaning to life in a world deprived of certainty.

Secular rationality has produced still another awesome problem, said Weber. It has fostered self-liberation, for it enables human beings to overcome illusions and take control of the environment and of themselves, but it is also a means of self-enslavement, for it produces institutions, giant public and corporate bureaucracies, that in their relentless pursuit of efficiency encourage uniformity and depersonalization. Modern officials, said Weber, are emotionally detached. Concerned only with the efficient execution of tasks, they employ reason in a cold and calculating way; human feelings such as compassion and affection are ruled out as hindrances to effectiveness. In the name of efficiency, people are placed in "steel cages,"—that is, treating them impersonally as mere objects—depriving them of their individuality, personal liberty, and humanity. In the form of private and public bureaucratic hierarchies, reason has created the means for self-enslavement:

> It is horrible to think that the world could one day be filled with nothing but those little cogs, little men clinging to little jobs and striving towards bigger ones. . . . This passion for bureaucracy . . . is enough to drive one to despair. . . . That the world should know no men but these: it is in such [a process] that we are already caught up, and the great question is, therefore, not how we can promote and hasten it, but what can we oppose to this machinery in order to keep a portion of mankind free from this parceling-out of the soul, from this supreme mastery of the bureaucratic way of life.[34]

Like Freud, Weber was aware of the power of the nonrational in social life. One expression of the irrational that he analyzed in considerable depth was the charismatic leader who attracts people by force of personality. Charismatic leaders may be religious prophets, war heroes, or others who possess this extraordinary ability to attract and dominate others. People yearn for charismatic leadership, particularly during times of crisis. The leader claims a mission—a sacred duty—to lead the people during the crisis. The leader's authority rests on the people's belief in the mission and their faith in the leader's extraordinary abilities; a common allegiance to the charismatic leader unites the community. In an era that has seen its share of dictators and demogogues, the question of why people are drawn to the charismatic savior—why they succumb to his authority, and why they alter their lives in order to implement his vision—is of crucial concern to historians and social theorists.

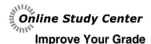

Online Study Center

Improve Your Grade
Primary Source: Science and Art Compared
(Weber)

THE MODERNIST MOVEMENT

Breaking with Conventional Modes of Esthetics

At the same time as Freud and social thinkers were breaking with the Enlightenment view of human nature and society, artists and writers were rebelling against the traditional forms of artistic and literary expression that had shaped European cultural life since the Renaissance. Rejecting both classical and realist models, they subordinated form and objective reality to the inner life—to feelings, imagination, and the creative process. These avant-garde writers and artists found new and creative ways to express the explosive primitive forces within the human psyche that increasingly had become the subject of contemporary thinkers. Their experimentations produced a great cultural revolution, called **modernism,** which still profoundly influences the arts. In some ways, modernism was a continuation of the Romantic Movement, which had dominated European culture in the early nineteenth century. Both movements subjected to searching criticism cultural styles that had been formulated during the Renaissance and had roots in ancient Greece.

Even more than romanticism, modernism aspired to an intense introspection—a heightened awareness of self—and saw the intellect as a barrier to the free expression of elemental human emotions, the wellspring of creativity. Modernist artists and writers abandoned conventional literary and artistic models and experimented with new modes of expression. They liberated the imagination from the restrictions of conventional forms and enabled their audience, readers and viewers alike, to share in the process of creation, often unconcious, and to discover fresh insights into objects, people, and social conditions. They believed that there were further discoveries to be made in the arts, further possibilities of expression, that past masters had not realized. The consequence of

their bold venture, wrote the literary critic and historian Irving Howe, was nothing less than the "breakup of the traditional unity and continuity of Western culture."[35]

Like Freud, modernist artists and writers probed beyond surface appearances for a more profound reality hidden in the human psyche. Writers such as Thomas Mann, Marcel Proust, James Joyce, August Strindberg, D. H. Lawrence, and Franz Kafka explored the inner life of the individual and the psychopathology of human relations in order to lay bare the self. They dealt with the predicament of alienated and estranged men and women who rejected the values and customs of their day, and they depicted the anguish of people burdened by guilt, torn by internal conflicts, and driven by inner self-destructiveness. Besides showing the overwhelming might of the irrational and the seductive power of the primitive and the instinctual, they also broke the silence about sex that had prevailed in Victorian literature.

From the Renaissance through the Enlightenment and into the nineteenth century, Western esthetic standards had been shaped by the conviction that the universe embodied an inherent mathematical order. A corollary of this conception of the outer world as orderly and intelligible was the view that art should imitate reality. According to the sociologist Daniel Bell, from the Renaissance on, art was seen as "a mirror of nature, a representation of life. Knowledge was a reflection of what was 'out there' . . . a copy of what was seen."[36] Since the Renaissance, artists had deliberately made use of laws of perspective and proportion; musicians had used harmonic chords, which brought rhythm and melody into a unified whole; and writers had produced works according to a definite pattern, which included a beginning, middle, and end.

Modernist culture, however, acknowledged no objective reality of space, motion, and time that has the same meaning for all observers. Rather, reality can be grasped in a variety of ways; a multiplicity of frames of reference apply to nature and human experience. Consequently, reality is the way the viewer apprehends it to be through the prism of the imagination. "There is no outer reality," said the modernist German poet Gottfried Benn, but "only human consciousness, constantly building, modifying, rebuilding new worlds out of its own creativity."[37] Modernism is concerned less with the object itself than with how the artist transforms it, with the sensations that an object evokes in the artist's inner being, and with the meaning that the artist's imagination imposes on reality. "Conscientious and exact imitation of nature does not create a work of art," wrote Emil Nolde, a German expressionist painter. "A work becomes a work of art when one re-evaluates the values of nature and adds one's own spirituality."[38] Bell makes this point in reference to painting:

> *Modernism . . . denies the primacy of an outside reality, as given. It seeks either to rearrange that reality, or to retreat to the self's interior, to private experience as the source of its concerns and aesthetic preoccupations. . . . There is an emphasis on the self as the touchstone of understanding and on the activity of the knower rather than the character of the object as the source of knowledge. . . . Thus one discerns the intentions of modern painting . . . to break up ordered space . . . to bridge the distance between object and spectator, to "thrust" itself on the viewer and establish itself immediately by impact.*[39]

Dispensing with conventional forms of esthetics, which stressed structure and coherence, modernism propelled the arts onto uncharted seas. Modernists abandoned the efforts of realists and naturalists to produce a clinical and objective description of the external world; instead they probed subjective views and visions and the inner world of the unconscious. Recoiling from the middle-class, industrial civilization, which prized rationalism, organization, clarity, stability, and definite norms and values, modernist writers and artists were fascinated by the bizarre, the mysterious, the unpredictable, the primitive, the irrational, and the formless.

Writers experimented with new techniques to convey the intense struggle between the conscious and the unconscious and to connote the aberrations and complexities of human personality and the irrationality and absurdity of human behavior. In particular, they devised a new way, the **stream of consciousness**, to reveal the mind's

every level—both conscious reflection and unconscious strivings—and to capture how thought is punctuated by spontaneous outbursts, disconnected assertions, random memories, undifferentiated and freely associated words and sounds, hidden desires, and persistent fantasies. The stream of consciousness is not narrated memory but a flow of feelings and thoughts in which the boundary between consciousness and unconsciousness is blurred. It attempts to reveal the mystery and complexity of the inner person, the hidden drives, desires, torments, and obsessions that intrigued Freud.

Modern artists deliberately plunged into the world of the unconscious in search of the instinctual, the fantastic, the primitive, and the mysterious, which they believed yielded a truth higher than that given by analytical thought. They embarked on a voyage into the mind's interior in the hopes of finding stimulants that would spark the creative imagination. Composers engaged in open revolt against the conventional rules and standards of musical composition. For example, the Austrian composer Arnold Schönberg (1874–1951) purposefully abandoned traditional scale and harmonic chords to produce atonal music that "seeks to express all that swells in us subconsciously like a dream."[40] The Russian composer Igor Stravinsky (1882–1971) experimented with both atonality and primitive rhythms. When Stravinsky's ballet *The Rite of Spring* was performed in Paris in 1913, the theater audience rioted to protest the composition's break with tonality, its use of primitive, jazzlike rhythms, and its theme of ritual sacrifice.

The modernist movement, which began near the end of the nineteenth century, was in full bloom before World War I and would continue to flower in the postwar world. Probably the clearest expression of the modernist viewpoint is found in art.

Modern Art

In the late nineteenth century, artists began to turn away from the standards that had characterized art since the Renaissance. Increasingly, artists sought to penetrate the deepest recesses of the unconscious, which they saw as the source of

Joseph Conrad

Behavior driven by the unconscious and the human being's capacity to act irrationally and cruelly—the dark side of human nature, which was the subject of Freud's investigations—intrigued many modernist writers, including the British novelist Joseph Conrad (1857–1924), born Josef Teodor Konrad Korzenlowski. In 1862, when Conrad was not yet five years old, his father, who had participated in an insurrection to liberate Poland from Russian rule, was exiled to nothern Russia. In this harsh environment, his mother died of tuberculosis in 1865. His father, who translated the works of French and English authors in Polish, which the precocious young Conrad read voraciously, made the difficult decision to place his only child in the care of Joseph's maternal uncle in Poland, where he attended school. Joseph lost his father when he was twelve, and five years later, he left school to become an apprentice seaman on a French merchant ship. In 1878, speaking only a few words of English, he joined the British merchant navy.

During his twenty years at sea, Conrad visited exotic lands and experienced danger. These adventures found literary expression in Conrad's novels and short stories, including *An Outcast of the Islands* (1896), *Lord Jim* (1900), *Heart of Darkness* (1902), *Nostromo* (1904), and *The Secret Agent* (1907). But Conrad was far more than a masterful renderer of adventure

The Granger Collection.

creativity and the abode of a higher truth. Drawing inspiration from dreams, nightmares, and powerful emotions, they often represented the world in a startling manner which deviated from the Renaissance's search for precise form or the ideal. Paul Klee (1879–1940), a prominent twentieth-century artist, described modern art as follows: "Each [artist] should follow where the pulse of his own heart leads. . . . Our pounding heart drives us down, deep down to the source of all. What springs from this source, whether it may be called dream, idea or phantasy—must be taken seriously."[41]

Between 1909 and 1914, a new style, called *cubism*, was developed by Pablo Picasso (1881–1973) and Georges Braque (1882–1963). They explored the interplay between the flat world of the canvas and the three-dimensional world of visual perception, to paint a reality deeper than what the eye sees at first glance. Cu-

stories. His reputation as one of England's finest novelists derives from both his compelling prose and his creative exploration of human depravity, a phenomenon to which he seemed irresistibly drawn. In 1891, after a four-month stay in the Congo Free State, a land notoriously exploited and brutalized by agents of the Belgian king Leopold II, Conrad suffered psychological trauma. His experiences in the heart of Africa led him to write his most compelling work, *Heart of Darkness*.

Kurtz, the principal character in *Heart of Darkness,* runs a very successful ivory trading post deep in the Congo. A poet, musician, and painter, Kurtz came to Africa imbued with humanitarian sentiments, intending to bring enlightenment to "savage" Africans. But in the primeval African jungle, his other self, long repressed by European values, comes to the fore. Kurtz becomes a depraved tyrant who decorates the fence poles around his house with human heads. The charismatic Kurtz has made disciples of the villagers, who view him as a godlike figure; they heed his every word and, at his command, launch murderous raids against nearby villages for more ivory. Kurtz engages in mysterious ceremonies—Conrad leaves the nature of these ceremonies to the reader's imagination, but it is likely that they are human sacrifices—that contribute to his uncanny power over the Africans.

Heart of Darkness expressed Conrad's revulsion for avaricious European imperialists, who, in their quest for riches, plundered and destroyed African villages and impressed the natives into forced labor. Their greed, callousness, and brutality belied the altruism that they claimed was their motivation for coming to Africa. *Heart of Darkness* is also a tale of moral deterioration. The forbidding jungle environment, far from the restraints of European civilization, and the repulsive scramble for riches disfigure Kurtz, who is transformed into a sadist driven by dark urges no longer buried within his unconscious. The wilderness "whispered to him things about himself which he did not know, things of which he had no conception till he took counsel with this great solitude—and the whisper had proved irresistibly fascinating."[*]

When the dying Kurtz cries out, "The horror! The horror!" in what Conrad says is "that supreme moment of complete knowledge,"[†] was he referring to his own moral collapse? Civilization, as Freud maintained, is very fragile; only a thin barrier separates it from barbarism. Given the right circumstances, all human beings are capable of the moral disfigurement experienced by Kurtz. Thus "darkness" refers not only to the jungle interior but also to the destructive tendencies that are at the core of human nature.

---

[*]Joseph Conrad, *Heart of Darkness* (New York: Barnes and Noble, 1994), p. 102.
[†]Ibid, p. 123.

bist art presents objects from multiple viewpoints simultaneously. The numerous fragmentary images of cubist art make one aware of the complex experience of seeing. One art historian describes cubism as follows: "The cubist is not interested in usual representational standards. It is as if he were walking around the object he is analyzing, as one is free to walk around a piece of sculpture for successive views. But he must represent all these views at once."[42] The cubists' effort to depict something from multiple perspectives rather than from a single point in space and their need to deliberately deform objects in order to achieve this effect mark a radical break with artistic conventions.

Throughout the period 1890 to 1914, avant-garde artists were de-emphasizing subject matter. It is not surprising that some artists such as Piet Mondrian (1872–1944) and Wassily Kandinsky (1866–1944) finally created abstract art, a non-

THE STARRY NIGHT (1889), BY VINCENT VAN GOGH. Van Gogh experienced wide mood swings—from extreme agitation to melancholy. His tumultuous temperament found expression in his paintings. *The Starry Night* conveys van Gogh's impression of a night sky. (*The Museum of Modern Art, New York. Acquired through the Lillie P. Bliss Bequest.*)

objective art totally devoid of reference to the visible world that bears no resemblance to the natural world. In declaring that he "painted . . . subconsciously in a state of strong inner tension,"[43] Kandinsky explicitly expressed a distinguishing quality of modern Western art: the artist's private inner experience of the world.

The revolution in art that took place near the turn of the twentieth century is reverberating still. These masters of modern art continue to inspire with their passion and vision. By breaking with the Renaissance view of the world as inherently orderly and rational and by stressing the power of the imagination, modern artists opened up new possibilities for artistic expression. They also exemplified the growing power and appeal of the nonrational in European life.

MODERN PHYSICS

Until the closing years of the nineteenth century, the view of the universe held by the Western mind was based mainly on the classical physics of Isaac Newton (1642–1727). This view included the following principles: (1) Time, space, and matter are objective realities, existing independently of the observer. (2) The universe is a giant machine whose parts obey strict laws of cause and effect. (3) The atom, indivisible and solid, is the basic unit of matter. (4) Heated bodies emit radiation in continuous waves. (5) Through further investigation, it will be possible to gain complete knowledge of the physical universe. Between the 1890s and the 1920s, this view of the universe was shattered by a second Scientific Revolution.

HARMONY IN RED (1908), BY HENRI MATISSE. In this early example of French fauvism, Matisse broke away from the representational renderings of his predecessors and set the tone for much of twentieth-century expressive painting. His use of line, color, and rhythmic motifs transforms the visual surface into brilliant designs and establishes a new pictorial language. (*The State Hermitage Museum, St. Petersburg.*)

The discovery of x-rays by Wilhelm Konrad Roentgen in 1895, of radioactivity by Henri Bequerel in 1896, and of the electron by J. J. Thomson in 1897 led scientists to abandon the conception of the atom as a solid and indivisible particle. Rather than resembling a billiard ball, they said, the atom consists of a nucleus of tightly packed protons, separated from orbiting electrons by empty space.

In 1900, Max Planck, a German physicist, proposed the quantum theory, which holds that a heated body radiates energy not in a continuous unbroken stream, as had been believed, but in intermittent spurts, or jumps, called quanta. Planck's theory of discontinuity in energy radiation challenged a cardinal principle of classical physics: that action in nature was strictly continuous.

In 1905, Albert Einstein, a German-Swiss physicist of Jewish lineage, substantiated and elaborated Planck's theory by suggesting that all forms of radiant energy—light, heat, x-rays—move through space in discontinuous packets of energy. Then, in 1913, Niels Bohr, a Danish scientist, applied Planck's theory of energy quanta to the interior of the atom and discovered that the Newtonian laws of motion could not fully explain what happens to electrons orbiting an atomic nucleus.

As physicists explored the behavior of the atom further, it became apparent that its nature was fundamentally elusive and unpredictable.

LES DEMOISELLES D'AVIGNON (1907), BY PABLO PICASSO. Picasso's painting exemplified new trends in art. Rather than conforming with classical and Renaissance conventions of representation, Picasso aimed to interpret visual reality in accord with his own sensibilities. (*Collection, The Museum of Modern Art, New York. Acquired through the Lillie P. Bliss Bequest/Art Resource, NY © 2005 Estate of Pablo Picasso/Artistic Rights Society [ARS], New York.*)

They soon observed that radioactive atoms throw off particles and transform themselves from atoms of one element into atoms of an entirely different element. But the transformation of a single atom in a mass of radioactive material could not be predicted according to inexorable laws of cause and effect. For example, it is known that over a period of 1,620 years half the atoms of the element radium decay and transform themselves into atoms of another element. It is impossible, however, to know when a particular atom in a lump of radium will undergo this transformation. Scientists can make accurate predictions only about the behavior of an aggregate of radium atoms. The transformation of any given radium atom is the result of random chance rather than of any known physical law. The fact that we cannot predict when a particular radioactive atom will decay calls into question the notion of classical physics that physical nature proceeds in an orderly fashion in accordance with strict laws of cause and effect.

Newtonian physics says that, given certain conditions, we can predict what will follow. For example, if an airplane is flying north at four hundred miles per hour, we can predict its exact

BLACK WEFT, BY WASSILY KANDINSKY. Kandinsky was a leader of a group of avant-garde painters in Munich, called *Der Blaue Reiter* (The Blue Rider), whose goal was to challenge the limits of artistic expression. In this painting, he has removed virtually all traces of the physical world, thereby creating a nonobjective artwork that bears little, or no, resemblance to the natural world. (*Musée des Beaux-Arts, Nantes, France/RMN/Art Resource, NY.*)

position two hours from now, assuming that the plane does not alter its course or speed. Quantum mechanics teaches that in the subatomic realm we cannot predict with certainty what will take place; we can only say that, given certain conditions, it is probable that a certain event will follow. This principle of uncertainty was developed in 1927 by the German scientist Werner Heisenberg, who showed that it is impossible to determine at one and the same time both an electron's precise speed and its position. This means that the law of cause and effect does not apply to elementary particles such as electrons. We cannot describe an electron in terms of absolute certainties. In the small-scale world of the electron, we enter a universe of uncertainty, probability, and statistical relationships. No improvement in measurement techniques will dispel this element of chance and provide us with complete knowledge of the universe.

Einstein himself could not accept a core principle of modern physics—that complete comprehension of reality was unattainable. Nevertheless, his theory of relativity was instrumental in shaping modern physics, for it altered classical conceptions of space and time. Newtonian physics had viewed space as a distinct physical reality, a stationary and motionless medium through which light traveled and matter moved. Time was deemed to be a fixed and rigid framework, the

ALBERT EINSTEIN (1879–1955), A PRINCIPAL ARCHITECT OF MODERN PHYSICS. Forced to flee Nazi Germany, Einstein became a U.S. citizen. He was appointed to the Institute for Advanced Study at Princeton, New Jersey. (AP/Wide World.)

same for all observers and existing independently of human experience. For Einstein, however, neither space nor time had an independent existence, and neither could be divorced from human experience. When asked to explain briefly the essentials of relativity, Einstein replied: "It was formerly believed that if all material things disappeared out of the universe, time and space would be left. According to the relativity theory, however, time and space disappear together with the things."[44]

Contrary to all previous thinking, relativity theory holds that time differs for two observers traveling at different speeds. Imagine twin brothers involved in space exploration, one as an astronaut, the other as a rocket designer who never leaves earth. The astronaut takes off in the most advanced spaceship yet constructed, one that achieves a speed close to the maximum attainable in our universe—the speed of light. After traveling several trillion miles, the spaceship turns around and returns to earth. According to the experience of the ship's occupant, the whole trip

took about two years. But when the astronaut lands on earth, he finds totally changed conditions. For one thing, his brother has long since died, for according to earth's calendars some two hundred years have elapsed since the rocket ship set out on its journey. Such an occurrence seemed to defy all commonsense experience, yet experiments supported Einstein's claims.

Motion, too, is relative. The only way we can describe the motion of one body is to compare it with another moving body. This means that there is no motionless, absolute, fixed frame of reference anywhere in the universe.

In his famous equation, $E = mc^2$, Einstein showed that matter and energy are not separate categories but two different expressions of the same physical entity. The source of energy is matter, and the source of matter is energy. Tiny quantities of matter could be transformed into staggering amounts of energy. The atomic age was dawning.

The discoveries of modern physics transformed the world of classical physics. Whereas nature had been regarded as something outside the individual—an objective reality existing independently of ourselves—modern physics teaches that our position in space and time determines what we mean by reality and that our very presence affects reality itself. When we observe a particle with our measuring instruments, we are interfering with it, knocking it off its course; we are participating in reality. Nor is nature fully knowable, as the classical physics of Newton had presumed. Uncertainty, probability, and even mystery are inherent in the universe.

We have not yet felt the full impact of modern physics, but there is no doubt that it has been part of a revolution in human perceptions. As Jacob Bronowski, a student of science and culture, concludes,

> One aim of the physical sciences has been to give an exact picture of the material world. One achievement of physics in the twentieth century has been to prove that that aim is unattainable. . . . There is no absolute knowledge. . . . All information is imperfect. We have to treat it with humility. That is the human condition; and that is what quantum

physics says. . . . The Principle of Uncertainty . . . fixed once and for all the realization that all knowledge is limited.[45]

That we cannot fully comprehend nature must inevitably make us less certain about our theories of human nature, government, history, and morality. That scientists must qualify and avoid absolutes has no doubt made us more cautious and tentative in framing conclusions about the individual and society. Like Darwin's theory of human origins, Freud's theory of human nature, and the transformation of classical space by modern artists, the modifications of the Newtonian picture by modern physicists contributed to the sense of uncertainty and disorientation that characterized the twentieth century.

THE ENLIGHTENMENT TRADITION IN DISARRAY

Most nineteenth-century thinkers carried forward the spirit of the Enlightenment, particularly in its emphasis on science and its concern for individual liberty and social reform. In the tradition of the philosophes, nineteenth-century thinkers regarded science as humanity's greatest achievement and believed that through reason society could be reformed. The spread of parliamentary government and the extension of education, along with the many advances in science and technology, seemed to confirm the belief of the philosophes in humanity's future progress.

But at the same time, the Enlightenment tradition was being undermined. In the early nineteenth century, the romantics revolted against the Enlightenment's rational-scientific spirit in favor of human will and feelings. Romantic nationalists valued the collective soul of the nation—ancient traditions rooted in a hoary and dateless past—over reason and individual freedom. Conservatives emphasized the limitations of reason and attacked the political agenda of the Enlightenment and the French Revolution.

In the closing decades of the nineteenth century, the Enlightenment tradition was challenged by Social Darwinists, who glorified violence and saw conflict between individuals and between nations as a law of nature and the avenue to progress. They considered the right of the powerful to predominate to be a right of nature beyond good and evil, and they castigated humanitarianism as weakness. Orthodox Marxists continued to teach that conflict between the proletariat and the industrial bourgeoisie was necessary for humanity's progress. Echoing Sorel, several thinkers trumpeted the use of force in social and political controversies. A number of thinkers, rejecting the Enlightenment view of people as fundamentally rational, held that subconscious drives and impulses govern human behavior more than reason does. If this is so, then the individual is not essentially autonomous, master of his or her own self. Several of these thinkers urged celebrating and extolling the irrational, which they regarded as the true essence of human beings and life. They glorified an irrational vitality, or Nietzsche's will to power, which transcended considerations of good and evil. "I have always considered myself a voice of what I believe to be a greater renaissance—the revolt of the soul against the intellect—now beginning in the world," wrote the Irish poet William Butler Yeats.[46] German advocates of "life philosophy" explicitly called the mind "the enemy of the soul."

Even theorists who studied the individual and society in a scientific way pointed out that below a surface of rationality lies a substratum of irrationality, which constitutes a deeper reality. The conviction was growing that reason was a puny instrument in comparison with the volcanic strength of nonrational impulses, that these impulses pushed people toward destructive behavior and made political life precarious, and that the nonrational did not bend very much to education. The Enlightenment's image of the autonomous individual who makes rational decisions after weighing the choices (a fundamental premise of liberalism and democracy) no longer seemed tenable. Often the individual was not the master of his or her own person; human freedom was limited by human nature.

Liberalism was also undermined by theorists who rejected the idea of natural rights. The view that all individuals are born with inalienable rights had provided the philosophical basis of classical liberalism. It was now argued, however, that natural rights were not a law of nature or a higher truth; rather, they were simply a human creation, a product of a specific set of circumstances at a particular stage in history, notably the emergence of the bourgeoisie. Could commitment to parliamentary government, the rule of law, and other liberal-democratic institutions and practices survive this assault on the core principle of liberalism?

Other theorists argued that ideas of right, truth, and justice do not have an independent value but are merely tools used by elites in their struggle to gain and maintain power. Opponents of liberalism and democracy utilized the theory of elites advanced by Pareto, as well as the new stress on human irrationality, as proof that the masses were incapable of self-government and that they had to be led by their betters. Many intellectuals of the right employed the new social theories to devalue the individualist and rational bases of liberal democracy bequeathed by the Enlightenment.

A fundamental feature of European civilization was the conviction that the universe contained self-evident moral norms and that obedience to these laws promoted the good life. For Christians these norms were ordained by God and revealed to human beings. The philosophes, like the ancient Greeks, maintained that universal moral standards did indeed exist but that they were ascertained by reason, not by revelation. In the late nineteenth century, several thinkers, particularly Nietzsche, proclaimed that no such universal standards existed. Could the Enlightenment's vision of a more humane and peaceful future be realized in a world where moral values had lost their authority, when neither religion nor reason could demonstrate their certainty?

At the beginning of the twentieth century, the dominant mood remained that of confidence in Europe's future progress and in the values of European civilization. However, certain disquieting trends were already evident; they would grow to crisis proportions in succeeding decades. Although few people may have realized it, the Enlightenment tradition was in disarray.

The thinkers of the Enlightenment believed in an orderly, machinelike universe; the operation of natural law and natural rights in the social world;

objective rules that gave form and structure to artistic productions; the essential rationality and goodness of the individual; and science and technology as instruments of progress. This coherent world-view, which had produced an attitude of certainty, security, and optimism, was in the process of dissolution by the early twentieth century. The commonsense Newtonian picture of the physical universe, with its inexorable laws of cause and effect, was fundamentally altered; the belief in natural rights and objective standards governing morality was undermined; and rules and modes of expression that were at the very heart of Western esthetics were abandoned. Confidence in human rationality and goodness weakened. Furthermore, science and technology were accused of forging a mechanical, bureaucratic, and materialistic world that stifled intuition and feelings, thereby diminishing the self. To redeem the self, some thinkers urged a heroic struggle, which was easily channeled into primitive nationalism and martial crusades. They romanticized violence as a release of elemental and instinctual forces that liberated the human personality from unhealthy constraints imposed by traditional morality. Thus, the radical attack on the moral and intellectual values of the Enlightenment, as well as on liberalism and democracy, included the denunciation of reason, the exaltation of force, a quest for the heroic, and a yearning for a new authority. This critique constitutes the intellectual background of the fascist movements that emerged after World War I. Holding the Enlightenment tradition in contempt and fascinated by power and violence, many people, including intellectuals, would exalt fascist ideas and lionize fascist leaders.

In the early twentieth century, then, the universe no longer seemed an orderly system, an intelligible whole; it seemed something fundamentally inexplicable. Human nature, too, seemed intrinsically unfathomable and problematic. To the question "Who is man?" Greek philosophers, medieval scholastics, Renaissance humanists, and eighteenth-century philosophes had provided a coherent and intelligible answer. By the early twentieth century, the old spiritual and intellectual certainties were rapidly eroding, Western intellectuals no longer possessed a clear idea of who the human being was. Individuals had become strangers to themselves, and life seemed devoid of an overriding purpose. Nietzsche sensed this:

> *Disintegration characterizes this time, and thus uncertainty: nothing stands firmly on its feet or on a hard faith in itself; one lives for tomorrow as the day after tomorrow is dubious. Everything on our way is slippery and dangerous, and the ice that still supports us has become thin: all of us feel the warm, uncanny breath of the thawing wind; where we still walk, soon no one will be able to walk.*[47]

This radical new disorientation led some intellectuals to feel alienated from Western civilization and even hostile toward it. At the beginning of the twentieth century, says the Dutch historian Jan Romein, "European man, who only half a century earlier had believed he was about to embrace an almost totally safe existence, and paradoxically enough did so in many ways, found himself before the dark gate of uncertainty."[48]

When the new century began, most Europeans were optimistic about the future, some even holding that European civilization was on the threshold of a golden age. Few suspected that European civilization would soon be gripped by a crisis that threatened its very survival. The powerful forces of irrationalism, which had been celebrated by Nietzsche, analyzed by Freud, and creatively ex-

pressed in modernist culture, would erupt with devastating fury in twentieth-century political life, particularly in the form of extreme nationalism and racism, which extolled violence. Disoriented and disillusioned people searching for new certainties and values would turn to political ideologies that openly rejected reason, lauded war, and scorned the inviolability of the human person. Dictators, utilizing the insights into the unconscious and the nonrational offered by Freud and social theorists, succeeded in manipulating the minds of people to an unprecedented degree.

These currents began to form at the end of the nineteenth century, but World War I brought them together in a tidal wave. World War I accentuated the questioning of established norms and the dissolution of Enlightenment certainties and caused many people to regard Western civilization as dying and beyond recovery. The war not only exacerbated the spiritual crisis of the preceding generation, but also shattered Europe's political and social order. It gave birth to totalitarian ideologies that nearly obliterated the legacy of the Enlightenment. The world wars of the twentieth century, with their millions of dead and mutilated, and the totalitarian experiments, which trampled on human dignity, bore out Nietzsche's warning that in a nihilistic world all is permitted.

❖   ❖   ❖

NOTES

1. Friedrich Nietzsche, *Twilight of the Idols* and *The Anti-Christ,* trans. R. J. Hollingdale (New York: Penguin, 1972), pp. 117–118.

2. Friedrich Nietzsche, *The Will to Power,* trans. Walter Kaufmann and R. J. Hollingdale, ed. Walter Kaufmann (New York: Vintage Books, 1968), pp. 458–459.

3. Ibid., pp. 383–384.

4. Friedrich Nietzsche, *The Genealogy of Morals,* Essay I, sec. 13 (New York: Modern Library, 1954), p. 656.

5. Quoted in R. J. Hollingdale, *Nietzsche* (London: Routledge & Kegan Paul, 1973), p. 82.

6. Nietzsche, *Will to Power,* p. 397.

7. Ibid., p. 518.

8. Nietzsche, *Anti-Christ,* p. 116.

9. Nietzsche, *Will to Power,* p. 386.

10. Janko Lavrin, *Nietzsche* (New York: Charles Scribner's Sons, 1971), p. 113.

11. Fyodor Dostoevski, *Notes from Underground and The Grand Inquisitor,* trans. Ralph E. Matlaw (New York: Dutton, 1960), pp. 20, 23.

12. Ibid., p. 25.

13. Quoted in Peter Gay, *Freud: A Life for Our Time* (New York: Norton, 1988), p. xvii.

14. Sigmund Freud, *The Future of an Illusion,* trans. W. D. Robeson-Scott, rev. James Strachey (Garden City, N.Y.: Doubleday, 1964), p. 87.

15. Sigmund Freud, *A General Introduction to Psychoanalysis,* trans. Joan Riviere (Garden City, N.Y.: Garden City Publishing Co., 1943), p. 252.

16. Sigmund Freud, "Delusions and Dreams in Jensen's 'Gradiva,'" trans. James Strachey, in *The Standard Edition of the Complete Psychological Work of Sigmund Freud,* 2nd ed. (London: Hogarth Press, 1959), 9:8.

17. Sigmund Freud, "An Autobiographical Study," ibid., 20:60.

18. Sigmund Freud, *Civilization and Its Discontents* (New York: Norton, 1961), p. 62.

19. Ibid., p. 58.

20. Ibid.

21. Ibid., p. 59.

22. Ibid., p. 61.

23. Ibid., p. 59.

24. Ibid., p. 69.

25. Émile Durkheim, *Suicide: A Study in Sociology,* trans. John Spaulding and George Simpson (New York: Free Press, 1951), p. 391.

26. Gustave Le Bon, *The Crowd: A Study of the Popular Mind* (New York: Viking, 1960), p. 3.

27. Ibid., pp. 14–15.

28. Ibid., p. 23.

29. Ibid., p. 30.

30. Ibid., p. 32.

31. Ibid., p. 7.

32. Ibid., p. 118.

33. Quoted in Robert A. Nye, *The Origin of Crowd Psychology* (Beverly Hills, Calif.: Sage, 1975), p. 178.

34. Quoted in Robert Nisbet, *The Social Philosophers* (New York: Crowell, 1973), p. 441.

35. Irving Howe, ed., *The Idea of the Modern in Literature and the Arts* (New York: Horizon Press, 1967), p. 16.

36. Daniel Bell, *The Cultural Contradictions of Capitalism* (New York: Basic Books, 1976), p. 110.

37. Quoted in Howe, *Idea of the Modern,* p. 15.

38. Excerpted in Herschel B. Chipp, ed., *Theories of Modern Art* (Berkeley: University of California Press, 1968), p. 146.

39. Bell, *Cultural Contradictions,* pp. 110, 112.

40. Excerpted in Piero Weiss and Richard Taruskin, eds., *Music in the Western World: A History in Documents* (New York: Schirmer Books, 1984), p. 428.

41. Paul Klee, *On Modern Art,* trans. Paul Findlay (London: Faber & Faber, 1948), p. 51.

42. John Canaday, *Mainstreams of Modern Art* (New York: Holt, 1961), p. 458.

43. Quoted in G. H. Hamilton, *Painting and Sculpture in Europe, 1880–1940* (Baltimore: Penguin Books, 1967), p. 133.

44. Quoted in A. E. E. McKenzie, *The Major Achievements of Science* (New York: Cambridge University Press, 1960), 1:310.

45. Jacob Bronowski, *The Ascent of Man* (Boston: Little, Brown, 1973), p. 353.

46. Quoted in Roland N. Stromberg, *Redemption by War* (Lawrence: Regents Press of Kansas, 1982), p. 65.

47. Nietzsche, *Will to Power,* p. 40.

48. Jan Romein, *The Watershed of Two Eras,* trans. Arnold J. Pomerans (Middletown, Conn.: Wesleyan University Press, 1978), p. 658.

SUGGESTED READING

Aschheim, Steven E., *The Nietzsche Legacy in Germany, 1890–1990* (1992). How Germans, including Nazis, interpreted Nietzsche.

Baumer, Franklin, *Modern European Thought* (1977). A well-informed study of modern thought.

Bradbury, Malcolm, and James McFarlane, eds., *Modernism, 1890–1930* (1974). Essays on various phases of modernism; valuable bibliography.

Gay, Peter, *Freud: A Life for Our Times* (1988). A highly recommended study.

Hamilton, G. H., *Painting and Sculpture in Europe, 1880–1940* (1967). An authoritative work.

Hollingdale, R. J., *Nietzsche* (1973). A lucid study.

Masur, Gerhard, *Prophets of Yesterday* (1961). Studies in European culture, 1890–1914.

Monaco, Paul, *Modern European Culture and Consciousness, 1870–1980* (1983). A useful survey.

Roazen, Paul, *Freud's Political and Social Thought* (1968). The implications of Freudian psychology.

Part Six

World Wars and Totalitarianism: The West in Crisis

1914–1945

Politics and Society

World War I (1914–1918)
United States declares war on Germany (1917)
Bolshevik Revolution in Russia (1917)
Wilson announces his Fourteen Points (1918)
Treaty of Versailles (1919)

Mussolini seizes power in Italy (1922)
First Five-Year Plan starts rapid
    industrialization in the Soviet Union (1928)
Forced collectivization of agriculture in the
    Soviet Union (1929)
Start of the Great Depression (1929)

Hitler becomes chancellor of Germany (1933)
Hitler sends troops into the Rhineland (1936)
Rome-Berlin Axis (1936)
Stalin orders mass purges in the Soviet
    Union (1936–38)
Spanish Civil War (1936–1939)
Franco establishes a dictatorship in Spain
    (1939)
Nazi-Soviet Non-Aggression Pact (1939)
German troops invade Poland: World War II
    begins (1939)

Germany invades Belgium, Holland,
    Luxembourg, and France (1940)
Japan attacks Pearl Harbor: United States
    enters war against Japan and Germany
    (1941)
War in Europe ends (1945)
United States drops atomic bombs on Japan;
    Japan surrenders (1945)

Thought and Culture

Bohr: Quantum theory of atomic stucture
    (1913)
Stravinsky, *The Rite of Spring* (1913)
Pareto, *Treatise on General Sociology* (1916)
Spengler, *The Decline of the West* (1918,
    1922)
Dadaism in art (1915–1924)
Barth, *The Epistle to the Romans* (1919)

Wittgenstein, *Tractatus Logico-Philosophicus*
    (1921–22)
Eliot, *The Waste Land* (1922)
Cassirer, *The Philosophy of Symbolic Forms*
    (1923–1929)
Mann, *The Magic Mountain* (1924)
Surrealism in art (c. 1925)
Hitler, *Mein Kampf* (1925–26)
Hemingway, *The Sun Also Rises* (1926)
Benda, *The Treason of the Intellectuals* (1927)
Heidegger, *Being and Time* (1927)
Lawrence, *Lady Chatterley's Lover* (1928)
Remarque, *All Quiet on the Western Front*
    (1929)

Freud, *Civilization and Its Discontents* (1930)
Ortega y Gasset, *The Revolt of the Masses*
    (1930)
Jaspers, *Man in the Modern Age* (1930)
Jung, *Modern Man in Search of a Soul* (1933)
Toynbee, *A Study of History* (1934–1961)
Keynes, *The General Theory of Employment,
    Interest, and Money* (1936)
Steinbeck, *The Grapes of Wrath* (1939)

Hemingway, *For Whom the Bell Tolls* (1940)
Koestler, *Darkness at Noon* (1941)
Fromm, *Escape from Freedom* (1941)
Camus, *The Stranger* (1942)
Sartre, *Being and Nothingness* (1943)
Orwell, *Animal Farm* (1945)

Chapter 29

World War I:
The West in Despair

For many people, the declaration of war was a cause for celebration. Few Europeans realized what a horror the war would turn out to be. (Archives Larousse-Giraudon.)

Focus Questions

1. How did the nationality problem in Austria-Hungary contribute to the outbreak of World War I?

2. In assessing responsibility for the war, what arguments have been advanced by historians for each of the major countries involved?

3. Why did many Europeans celebrate the coming of war?

4. What was Wilson's peace program? What obstacles did he face?

5. Why did the Provisional Government and liberal democracy fail in Russia in 1917?

6. How did World War I transform the consciousness of Europeans?

Online Study Center

This icon will direct you to interactive map and primary source activities on the website http://college.hmco.com/pic/perrywc8e.

rior to 1914, the dominant mood in Europe was one of pride in the accomplishments of Western civilization and confidence in its future progress. Advances in science and technology, the rising standard of living, the spread of democratic institutions, and Europe's position of power in the world all contributed to a sense of optimism, as did the expansion of social reform and the increase in literacy for the masses. Furthermore, since the defeat of Napoleon (1815), Europe had avoided a general war, and since the Franco-Prussian War (1870–71), the Great Powers had not fought one another. Reflecting on the world he knew before World War I, the historian Arnold Toynbee recalled that his generation had

expected that life throughout the World would become more rational, more humane, and more democratic and that, slowly, but surely, political democracy would produce greater social justice. We had also expected that the progress of science and technology would make mankind richer, and that this increasing wealth would gradually spread from a minority to a majority. We had expected that all this would happen peacefully. In fact we thought that mankind's course was set for an earthly paradise, and that our approach towards this goal was predestined for us by historical necessity.[1]

Few people recognized that the West's outward achievements masked inner turbulence that was propelling Western civilization toward a cataclysm. The European state system was failing. By 1914, national states, fueled by explosive nationalism, were grouped into alliances that faced each other with ever-mounting hostility. Nationalist passions, overheated by the popular press and expansionist societies, poisoned international relations. Nationalist thinkers propagated pseudoscientific racial and Social Darwinist doctrines, which glorified conflict and justified the subjugation of other peoples. Committed to enhancing national power, statesmen lost sight of Europe as a community of nations sharing a common civilization. Caution and restraint gave way to belligerency in foreign relations.

Chronology 29.1 ❖ World War I

June 28, 1914	Archduke Francis Ferdinand of Austria assassinated at Sarajevo
August 4, 1914	Germans invade Belgium
August 1914	Russians invade East Prussia and are defeated by Germans at the battle of Tannenberg
September 1914	The first battle of the Marne saves Paris
April 1915–January 1916	Gallipoli campaign: Allies withdraw after suffering 252,000 casualties
May 1915	Italy enters war on Allies' side
Spring 1915	Germany launches offensive that forces Russia to abandon Galicia and most of Poland
February 1916	General Pétain leads French forces at Verdun; Germans fail to capture the fortress town
June 1916	Russians suffer more than a million casualties in an offensive against Austrian lines
July–November 1916	Battle of the Somme: Allies suffer 600,000 casualties
January 1917	Germany launches unrestricted submarine warfare
March 1917	Tsarist regime is overthrown
April 6, 1917	United States declares war on Germany
May 1917	General Pétain restores French army's morale and discipline
July–November 1917	British defeat at Passchendaele
Fall 1917	Italian defeat at Caporetto
November 1917	Bolsheviks, led by Lenin, take command in Russia
January 1918	U.S. president Woodrow Wilson announces his Fourteen Points
1918–1920	Civil war and foreign intervention in Russia
March 1918	Russia signs Treaty of Brest-Litovsk, losing territory to Germany and withdrawing from the war
March 21, 1918	Germans launch a great offensive to end the war
June 3, 1918	Germans advance to within fifty-six miles of Paris
August 8, 1918	British victory at Amiens
October 1918	Turks are forced to withdraw from the war after several British successes
November 3, 1918	Austria-Hungary signs armistice with the Allies
November 11, 1918	Germany signs armistice with the Allies, ending World War I
January 1919	Paris Peace Conference
June 28, 1919	Germany signs Treaty of Versailles

The failure of the European state system was paralleled by a cultural crisis. Some European intellectuals attacked the rational tradition of the Enlightenment and celebrated the primitive, the instinctual, and the irrational. Increasingly, young people felt drawn to philosophies of action that ridiculed liberal bourgeois values and viewed war as a purifying and ennobling experience. Colonial wars, colorfully portrayed in the popular press, ignited the imagination of bored factory workers and daydreaming students and reinforced a sense of duty and an urge for gallantry among young men. These "splendid" little colonial wars helped fashion an attitude that made war acceptable, if not laudable. Yearning to break loose from their ordinary lives and to embrace heroic values, many Europeans regarded violent conflict as the highest expression of individual and national life.

"This peace is so rotten," complained a young German writer, George Heym, in 1912, longing for "a war, even an unjust one."[2] That same year, a survey of French students between the ages of eighteen and twenty-five showed that

> the most cultivated elite among [them] find in warfare an aesthetic ideal. . . . These young men impute to it all the beauty with which they are in love and of which they have been deprived in ordinary life. Above all, [W]ar, in their eyes is the occasion for the most noble of virtues . . . energy, mastery, and sacrifice for a cause which transcends ourselves."[3]

The popular historian Heinrich von Treitschke (1834–1896), whose lectures influenced many students who were to rise to positions of importance in the German army and administration, expressed the prevailing mood: "Those who preach the nonsense about everlasting peace do not understand the life of the [German] race. . . . [T]o banish war from history would be to banish all progress."[4] Friedrich von Bernhardi (1849–1930), a German general and influential military writer, considered war "a biological necessity of the first importance." In *Germany and the Next War* (1911), he wrote:

> War is a biological necessity of the first importance, a regulative element in the life of mankind which cannot be dispensed with,

> since without it an unhealthy development will follow, which excludes every advancement of the race, and therefore all real civilization. . . .
> The struggle for existence is, in the life of Nature, the basis of all healthy development. . . . The law of the stronger holds good everywhere. . . .The weaker succumb. . . .
> The knowledge, therefore, that war depends on biological laws leads to the conclusion that every attempt to exclude it from international relations must be demonstrably untenable.[5]

Although technology was making warfare more brutal and dangerous, Europe retained a romantic illusion about combat. "Even if we end in ruin it was beautiful," exclaimed General Erich von Falkenhayn, the future chief of the German general staff, at the outbreak of World War I.[6]

Although Europe was seemingly progressing in the art of civilization, the mythic power of nationalism and the primitive appeal of conflict were driving European civilization to the abyss. Few people recognized the potential crisis—certainly not the statesmen whose reckless blundering allowed the Continent to stumble into war.

Online Study Center **Improve Your Grade**
Interactive Map: World War I: Territorial Boundaries Before and After

AGGRAVATED NATIONALIST TENSIONS IN AUSTRIA-HUNGARY

On June 28, 1914, a young terrorist, with the support of the secret Serbian nationalist society called Union or Death (more popularly known as the Black Hand), murdered Archduke Francis Ferdinand, heir to the throne of Austria-Hungary. Six weeks later, the armies of Europe were on the march; an incident in the Balkans had sparked a world war. An analysis of why Austria-Hungary felt compelled to attack Serbia and why the other powers became enmeshed in the conflict shows how explosive Europe was in 1914. And nowhere were conditions more volatile than in Austria-Hungary, the scene of the assassination.

With its numerous nationalities, each with its own history and traditions and often conflicting aspirations, Austria-Hungary stood in opposition to nationalism, the most powerful spiritual force of the age. Perhaps the supranational Austro-Hungarian Empire was obsolete in a world of states based on the principle of nationality. Dominated by Germans and Hungarians, the empire remained unable either to satisfy the grievances or to contain the nationalist aims of its numerous minorities, particularly the Czechs and South Slavs (Croats, Slovenes, and Serbs).

The more moderate leaders of the ethnic minorities did not call for secession from the empire. Nevertheless, heightened agitation among several nationalities, which increased in the decade before 1914, greatly perturbed Austrian leaders. The fear that the empire would be torn apart by rebellion caused Austria to react strongly to any country that fanned the nationalist feelings of its Slavic minorities. This policy increased the tensions between Austria and small Serbia, which had gained its independence from the Ottoman Empire in 1878.

Captivated by Western ideas of nationalism, the Serbs sought to create a Greater Serbia by uniting with their racial kin, the seven million or so South Slavs living in the Hapsburg Empire. The shrill appeals by Serbian nationalists made Austrian leaders fear that the South Slavs might press for secession. Some of these leaders, notably Foreign Minister Count Leopold von Berchtold and Field Marshal Franz Conrad von Hötzendorf, urged the destruction of Serbia to eliminate the threat to Austria's existence.

Another irritant to Austria-Hungary was Russian Pan-Slavism, which called for the solidarity of Russians with their Slavic cousins in eastern Europe—Poles, Czechs, Slovaks, South Slavs, and Bulgarians. Pan-Slavism was based on a mystic conception of the superiority of Slavic civilization to Western civilization and of Russia's special historic mission to liberate its kin from Austrian and Turkish rule. Although Russian Pan-Slavs were few and did not dictate foreign policy, they constituted a significant pressure group. Moreover, their provocative and semireligious proclamations frightened Austria-Hungary, which did not draw a sharp line between Pan-Slavic aspirations and official Russian policy.

The tensions stemming from the multinational character of the Austro-Hungarian Empire in an age of heightened nationalist feeling set off the explosion in 1914. Unable to solve its minority problems and fearful of Pan-Slavism and Pan-Serbism, Austria-Hungary felt itself in a life-or-death situation. This sense of desperation led it to lash out at Serbia after the assassination of Archduke Francis Ferdinand.

THE GERMAN SYSTEM OF ALLIANCES

Perhaps the war might have been avoided, or at least limited to Austria and Serbia, if Europe in 1914 had not been split into two hostile **alliance systems.** Such a situation contains inherent dangers. Counting on the support of its allies, a country might pursue a more provocative and reckless course and be less conciliatory during a crisis. Furthermore, a conflict between two states might spark a chain reaction that draws in the other powers, transforming a limited war into a general war. That is what happened after the assassination. This dangerous alliance system originated with Bismarck.

The New German Empire

With its unification in 1870–71, Germany became an international power of the first rank, upsetting the balance of power in Europe. For the first time since the wars of the French Revolution, one nation was in a position to dominate the European continent. How a united and powerful Germany would fit into European life was the crucial problem in the decades following the Franco-Prussian War.

To German nationalists, unification both fulfilled a national dream and pointed to an even more ambitious goal: extending German power in Europe and the world. As the nineteenth century drew to a close, German nationalism became more extreme. Believing that Germany must either grow or die, nationalists pressed the government to build a powerful navy, acquire colonies, gain a much

EMPEROR WILLIAM II OF GERMANY AND EMPEROR
FRANZ JOSEPH OF AUSTRIA ATTENDING A PARADE IN
BERLIN 1889. (*Bettmann/CORBIS.*)

greater share of the world's markets, and expand
German interests and influence in Europe. Sometimes these goals were expressed in the language of
Social Darwinism: nations are engaged in an eternal struggle for survival and domination.

Militant nationalists preached the special destiny of the German race and advocated German
expansion in Europe and overseas. Decisive victories against Austria (1866) and France (1871), the
formation of the German Reich, rapid industrialization, and the impressive achievements of German science and scholarship had molded a
powerful and dynamic nation. Imbued with great
expectations for the future, Germans became increasingly impatient to see the fatherland gain its
"rightful" place in world affairs—an attitude that
alarmed non-Germans.

Bismarck's Goals

Under Bismarck, who did not seek additional territory but wanted only to preserve the recently
achieved unification, Germany pursued a moderate and cautious foreign policy. One of Bismarck's
goals was to keep France isolated and friendless.
Deeply humiliated by its defeat in the Franco-
Prussian War and the loss of Alsace and Lorraine,
France found its nationalists yearning for a war of
revenge against Germany. Victor Hugo expressed
the "sacred anger" of the French: "France will
have but one thought: to reconstitute her forces,
gather her energy, . . . raise her young generation to
form an army of the whole people. . . . Then one
day she will be irresistible. Then she will take back
Alsace-Lorraine."[7] Even though the French government, aware of Germany's strength, was unlikely to initiate a conflict, the issue of Alsace-
Lorraine increased tensions between the two
countries. Annexing the French provinces proved
to be a serious blunder by Germany, for it made
reconciliation impossible.

Bismarck also hoped to prevent a war between
Russia and Austria-Hungary since it could lead to
German involvement, the breakup of Austria-
Hungary, and Russian expansion in eastern Europe. To maintain peace and Germany's existing
borders, Bismarck forged complex alliances. In
the 1880s, he created the Triple Alliance, consisting of Germany, Austria-Hungary, and Italy, as
well as an alliance with Russia.

A major weakness marred Germany's alliance
system, however, for Austria and Russia were potential enemies. Austria feared Russian ambitions
in the Balkans and felt threatened by Russian
Pan-Slavs. Bismarck knew that an alliance with
Austria was essentially incompatible with Germany's treaty obligations to Russia. But he hoped
that the arrangement would enable him to exercise a moderating influence over both eastern
powers and prevent a war from erupting and upsetting the status quo. Besides, the treaty with
Russia deprived France of a valuable ally.

Bismarck conducted foreign policy with restraint. He formed alliances not to conquer new
lands but to protect Germany from aggression by
either France or Russia. His aim was to preserve
order and stability in Europe, not to launch war.

However, when the young Kaiser William II (1888–1918) ascended the throne, he clashed with the aging prime minister, and in 1890, Bismarck was forced to resign. Lacking Bismarck's diplomatic skills, his cool restraint, and his determination to keep peace in Europe, the new German leaders pursued a belligerent and imperialistic foreign policy in the ensuing years.

The first act of the new leadership was to let the treaty with Russia lapse, allowing Germany to give full support to Austria, which was deemed a more reliable ally. Whereas Bismarck had warned Austria to act with moderation and caution in the Balkans, his successors not only failed to hold Austria in check but actually encouraged Austrian aggression. This proved fatal to the peace of Europe.

The Triple Entente

Fear of Germany

When Germany broke with Russia in 1890, France was quick to take advantage of the situation. Worried by Germany's increasing military strength, expanding industries, growing population, and alliance with Austria and Italy, France eagerly courted Russia as an ally. It urged its bankers to invest in Russia, supplied weapons to the tsar, and arranged for the French and Russian fleets to exchange visits. In 1894, France and Russia entered into an alliance; the isolation forced on France by Bismarck ended.

Germany's growing military might also alarmed Great Britain. In addition, Germany had become a potent trade rival and strove to become a great colonial power as well—a goal demanded by German nationalists. But what troubled Britain most was Germany's decision to build a great navy. Germany was already the strongest land power on the Continent. Achieving naval parity with England would give Germany the potential to threaten Britain's overseas empire and to blockade the British Isles, depriving Britain of food and supplies. Germany's naval program was the overriding reason why Britain moved closer first to France and then to Russia. Germany's naval construction, designed to increase its stature as a Great Power but not really necessary for its security, was one indication that German leaders had abandoned Bismarck's policy of good sense. Eager to add the British as an ally and demonstrating superb diplomatic skill, France moved to end long-standing colonial disputes with Britain. The Entente Cordiale of 1904 accomplished this conciliation; England emerged from its self-imposed isolation.

Although the Franco-British understanding intensified German anxiety, Germany doubted that France and England, which had almost gone to war in 1898 in the Sudan, had overcome their deep animosities. Consequently, Chancellor Bernhard von Bülow (1849–1929) decided to test the Entente Cordiale by provoking a crisis; he chose Morocco because earlier the British had resisted French imperialist designs there. He prodded a reluctant Kaiser William II to visit the Moroccan port of Tangier, a sign that Germany would support the Moroccan sultan against France. In January 1906, however, at the conference held in Algeciras, Spain, to resolve the crisis, Britain sided with France, which was given special rights in Morocco. Germany's efforts to disrupt the Anglo-French Entente Cordiale had failed.

Eager to counter Germany's Triple Alliance with a strong alliance of their own, French diplomats sought to ease tensions between their Russian ally and their new British friend. Two events convinced Russia to adopt a more conciliatory attitude toward Britain: an unexpected and humiliating defeat in the Russo-Japanese War of 1904–1905 and a working-class revolution in 1905. Shocked by defeat, its army bordering on disintegration, its workers restive, Russia was receptive to settling its imperial disputes with Britain over Persia, Tibet, and Afghanistan—a decision encouraged by France. In the Anglo-Russian Entente of 1907, as in the Anglo-French Entente Cordiale of 1904, the former rivals conducted themselves in a conciliatory, if not friendly, manner. In both instances, what engendered this spirit of cooperation was fear of Germany; both agreements represented a triumph for French diplomacy. The Triple Entente, however, was not a firm alliance, for there was no certainty that Britain, traditionally reluctant to send its troops to the Continent, would give more than diplomatic support to France and Russia in case of a showdown with Germany.

Europe was now broken into two hostile camps: the Triple Entente of France, Russia, and Britain and the Triple Alliance of Germany, Austria-Hungary, and Italy. The costly arms race and the maintenance of large standing armies by all the states except Britain served to increase fear and suspicion between the alliances.

German Reactions

Germany denounced the Triple Entente as a hostile anti-German coalition designed to encircle and crush Germany. To survive, Germany must break this ring. In the past, German arms had achieved unification; German military might would also end this threat to the fatherland. Considering Austria-Hungary its only reliable ally, Germany resolved to preserve the power and dignity of the Hapsburg Empire. If Austria-Hungary fell from the ranks of the Great Powers, Germany would have to stand alone against its enemies. At all costs, Austria-Hungary must not be weakened.

This assessment, however, suffered from dangerous miscalculations. First, Germany overstressed the hostile nature of the Triple Entente. In reality, France, Russia, and Britain drew closer together not to wage aggressive war against Germany but to protect themselves against burgeoning German military, industrial, and diplomatic power. Second, by linking German security to Austria, Germany greatly increased the chance of war. Growing more and more fearful of Pan-Serbism and Pan-Slavism, Austria might well decide that only a war could prevent its empire from disintegrating. Confident of German support, Austria would be more likely to resort to force; afraid of any diminution of Austrian power, Germany would be more likely to support Austria. In contrast to Bismarck, the new leadership thought not of restraining Austria but of strengthening it, by war if necessary.

DRIFTING TOWARD WAR

The Bosnian Crisis

After 1908, several crises tested the competing alliances. Particularly significant was the Bosnian affair, for it contained many of the ingredients that eventually ignited the war in 1914. The defeat by Japan in 1905 had diminished Russia's stature as a Great Power. The new Russian foreign minister, Alexander Izvolsky, hoped to gain a diplomatic triumph by compelling the Ottoman Turks to allow Russian warships to pass through the Dardanelles, fulfilling a centuries-old dream of extending Russian power into the Mediterranean. Izvolsky hoped that England and France, traditional opponents of Russia's Mediterranean ambitions but now Russia's allies, would not block the move. But certainly Austria would regard it as a hostile act.

Russia made a deal with Austria: if Austria would support Russia's move to open the Dardanelles, Russia would permit Austrian annexation of the provinces of Bosnia and Herzegovina. Officially part of the Ottoman Empire, these provinces had been administered by Austria-Hungary since 1878. The population consisted mainly of ethnic cousins of the Serbs. A formal annexation would certainly infuriate the Serbs, who hoped one day to make the region part of Greater Serbia. In 1908, Austria proceeded to annex the provinces, but Russia met stiff resistance from England and France when it presented its case for opening the strait to Russian warships. Austria had gained a diplomatic victory, while Russia suffered another humiliation. Even more enraged than Russia, Serbia threatened to invade Bosnia to liberate its cousins from Austrian oppression. The Serbian press proclaimed that Austria-Hungary must perish if the South Slavs were to achieve liberty and unity. A fiery attitude also prevailed in Vienna: Austria-Hungary could not survive unless Serbia was destroyed.

During this period of intense hostility between Austria-Hungary and Serbia, Germany supported its Austrian ally. To keep Austria strong, Germany would even agree to the dismemberment of Serbia and to its incorporation into the Hapsburg Empire. The crisis led Austria and Germany to coordinate battle plans in case a conflict between Austria and Serbia involved Russia and France. Unlike Bismarck, who tried to hold Austria in check, German leadership now coolly envisioned an Austrian attack on Serbia, and just as coolly offered German support if Russia intervened.

Balkan Wars

The Bosnian crisis pushed Germany and Austria closer together, brought relations between Austria and Serbia to the breaking point, and in-

Map 29.1 THE BALKANS, 1914 Prior to 1914, the Balkans, with its different ethnic groups, was considered a powder keg. The most serious problem, which triggered World War I, was Austria-Hungary's fear of Serbian nationalists eager to create a Greater Serbia.

flicted another humiliation on Russia. The first Balkan War (1912) continued these trends. The Balkan states of Montenegro, Serbia, Bulgaria, and Greece attacked a dying Ottoman Empire. In a brief campaign, the Balkan armies captured the Turkish Empire's European territory, with the exception of Constantinople. Because it was on the victorious side, landlocked Serbia gained the Albanian coast and thus a long-desired outlet to the sea. Austria, however, was determined to keep its enemy from reaping this reward, and Germany, as in the Bosnian crisis, supported its ally. Unable to secure Russian support, Serbia was forced to surrender the territory, which in 1913 became the state of Albania.

During a five-year period, Austria-Hungary had twice humiliated Serbia. Russia shared these humiliations, for it had twice failed to help its small Slavic friend and had been denied access

to the Dardanelles at the time of the Bosnian crisis. Incensed Serbian nationalists accelerated their campaign of propaganda and terrorism against Austria. Believing that another humiliation would irreparably damage its prestige, Russia vowed to back Serbia in its next confrontation with Austria. And Austria, its patience exhausted and emboldened by German encouragement, wanted to end the Serbian threat once and for all. Thus, the ingredients for war between Austria and Serbia, a war that might easily draw in Russia and Germany, were present. Another incident might well start a war. It came on June 28, 1914.

Assassination of Francis Ferdinand

Archduke Francis Ferdinand (1863–1914), heir to the throne of Austria, was sympathetic to the grievances of the South Slavs and favored a policy that would place the Slavs on an equal footing with Hungarians and Germans within the Hapsburg Empire. If such a policy succeeded, it could soothe the feelings of the Austrian Slavs and reduce the appeal of a Greater Serbia, the aim of the Black Hand.

On June 28, 1914, Francis Ferdinand was assassinated while making a state visit to Sarajevo, the capital of Bosnia. Young Gavrilo Princip, part of a team of Bosnian terrorists, fired two shots at close range into the archduke's car. Francis Ferdinand and his wife died within fifteen minutes. The conspiracy was organized by Dragutin Dimitrijevic, chief of intelligence of the Serbian army, who was linked to the Black Hand.* By killing the archduke, the terrorists hoped to bring to a boiling point tensions within the Hapsburg Empire and prepare the way for revolution.

Feeling that Austria's prestige as a Great Power and indeed its very survival as a supranational empire were at stake, key officials, led by the foreign minister, Count Leopold von Berchtold, decided to use the assassination as a pretext to crush Serbia. For years, Austrian leaders had

*Serbia's prime minister, Nikola Pasic, learned of the plot and, through the Serbian envoy in Vienna, tried to get Austria to cancel Francis Ferdinand's visit. The Austrians, however, were not told of a specific assassination attempt, for Pasic did not want to admit that such an act of terrorism was being plotted on Serbian soil.

THE ASSASSINATION OF ARCHDUKE FRANCIS FERDINAND. Immediately after the
assassination, Austrian authorities arrest one of the assassins. (*Bettmann/Corbis.*)

yearned for war with Serbia in order to end agitation for the union of the South Slavs. Now, they
reasoned, the hour had struck. But war with Serbia would require Germany's approval. Believing
that Austria was Germany's only reliable ally and
that a diminution of Austrian power and prestige
threatened German security, German statesmen
backed Austria, encouraging it to take up arms
against Serbia. Both Germany and Austria
wanted a quick strike to overwhelm Serbia before
other countries were drawn in.

Germany Abets Austria

Confident of German backing, on July 23 Austria
presented Serbia with an ultimatum and demanded a response within forty-eight hours. The
terms of the ultimatum were so harsh that it was

next to impossible for Serbia to accept them. This
reaction was the one that Austria intended, as it
sought a military solution to the crisis rather than
a diplomatic one. But Russia feared that an Austrian conquest of Serbia was just the first step in
an Austro-German plan to dominate the Balkans.
Such an extension of German and Austrian
power in a region close to Russia was unthinkable to the tsar's government. Moreover, after
suffering repeated reverses in foreign affairs, Russia would not tolerate another humiliation. As
Germany had resolved to back its Austrian ally,
Russia determined not to abandon Serbia.

Serbia responded to Austria's ultimatum in a
conciliatory manner, agreeing to virtually all Austrian demands. But it refused Austrian officials
entry to investigate the assassination. Having already decided against a peaceful settlement, Aus-

tria insisted that rejecting one provision meant rejecting the entire ultimatum, and it ordered the mobilization of its army.

This was a crucial moment for Germany. Would it continue to support Austria, knowing that an Austrian attack on Serbia would most likely bring Russia into the conflict? Determined not to desert Austria and believing that a showdown with Russia was inevitable anyway, the German war party, with the military cajoling and persuading civilian authorities, continued to urge Austrian action against Serbia. They argued that it was better to fight Russia in 1914 than a few years later, when the tsar's empire, which already had a huge reserve of manpower and was rapidly building strategic railroads and expanding its Baltic fleet, would be stronger. The war party claimed that Germany's superior army could defeat both Russia and France, that Britain's army was too weak to make a difference, and that, in any case, Britain might remain neutral. Although Germany would have preferred a limited war, involving only Austria and Serbia, the idea of a general war did not dismay it. Indeed, the prospect of a war with Russia and France exhilarated some military leaders and statesmen. The permanent weakening of Russia and France would break the ring of encirclement, increase German territory, and establish Germany as the foremost power in the world.

On July 28, 1914, Austria declared war on Serbia. Russia, with the assurance of French support, proclaimed partial mobilization aimed at Austria alone. But the military warned that partial mobilization would throw the slow-moving Russian war machine into total confusion if the order had to be changed suddenly to full mobilization. Moreover, the only plans, particularly railway schedules, the Russian general staff had drawn up called for full mobilization, that is, for war against both Austria and Germany. Pressured by his generals, the tsar gave the order for full mobilization on July 30. Russian forces would be arrayed against Germany as well as Austria.

Because the country that struck first gained the advantage of fighting according to its own plans rather than having to improvise in response to the enemy's attack, generals tended to regard mobilization by the enemy as an act of war. Therefore, when Russia refused a German warning to halt mobilization, Germany, on August 1, ordered a general mobilization and declared war on Russia. Two days later, Germany also declared war on France, believing that France would most likely support its Russian ally. Besides, German battle plans were based on a war with both Russia and France; therefore, a war between Germany and Russia automatically meant a German attack on France.

When Belgium refused to allow German troops to march through Belgian territory into France, Germany invaded the small nation, which brought Britain, pledged since 1839 to guarantee Belgian neutrality, into the war. Britain could never tolerate German troops directly across the English Channel in any case, nor could it brook German mastery of western Europe. A century before, Britain had fought Napoleon to prevent France from becoming master of Europe; now it would fight Germany for the same reason. It was this fear that led Britain's naval and military commands to enter into joint planning with their French counterparts, which linked the two powers more closely. Should France be attacked, Britain would be unlikely to stay neutral.

The Question of Responsibility

The question of whether any one power was mainly responsible for the war has intrigued historians. In assessing blame, historians have focused on Germany's role. The German historian Fritz Fischer argues that Germany's ambition to dominate Europe was the underlying cause of the war. Germany encouraged Austria to strike at Serbia, knowing that an attack on Serbia could mean war with Russia and its French ally. Believing that it had the military advantage, Germany was willing to risk such a war. Hence, "her leaders must bear a substantial share of the historical responsibility for the outbreak of general war in 1914."[8]

Attracted by Social Darwinist ideas that foresaw an inevitable racial struggle between Germans and Slavs, by militarist doctrines that glorified war, and by a nationalist drive for **Lebensraum**—more living space—continues Fischer, Germany sought to become the foremost economic and political power in Europe and to play a far greater role in world politics; to achieve this goal, it was willing to go to war. Fischer supports his position by pointing to Germany's war aims, drawn up immediately after the outbreak of war, which called for the annexation of neighboring territories and the creation of satellite states.

Fischer's critics, however, stress that Social Darwinism and militarism enthralled other European nations besides Germany. They argue furrther that Germany would have preferred a limited war between Austria and Serbia and before the war had no plans to dominate Europe. The plans for territorial acquisition, drawn up during the war, not before it, were not the reason why Germany went to war.

Historians also attribute blame to the other powers. Austria bears responsibility for its determination to crush Serbia and for its insistent avoidance of a negotiated settlement. Serbia's responsibility stems from pursuing an aggressive Pan-Serbian policy, which set Serbia on a collision course with Austria-Hungary. In 1913, the British ambassador to Vienna warned: "Serbia will some day set Europe by the ears, and bring about a universal war on the Continent. I cannot tell you how exasperated people are getting here at the continual worry which that little country causes to Austria."[9] Russia bears responsibility for instituting general mobilization, thereby turning a limited war between Austria-Hungary and Serbia into a European war; France, for failing to restrain Russia and indeed for encouraging its ally to mobilize; and England, for failing to make clear that it would support its allies. Had Germany seen plainly that Britain would intervene, it might have been more cautious. Finally, blame falls on diplomats and statesmen for their ineptness and lack of imagination in dealing with a crisis that could have been resolved without war.

Some historians, dismissing the question of responsibility, regard the war as an obvious sign that European civilization was in deep trouble. Viewed in the broad perspective of European history, the war marked a culmination of dangerous forces in European life: the glorification of power; fascination with violence and the nonrational; general dissatisfaction and disillusionment with bourgeois society; and, above all, explosive nationalism. It also underscored the diminishing confidence in the capacity of reason to solve the problems created by the Industrial Revolution and pointed to the flaws and perils of the alliance system.

WAR AS CELEBRATION

When war was certain, an extraordinary phenomenon occurred. Crowds gathered in capital cities, demonstrating allegiance to the various fatherlands and readiness to fight. Even socialists, who had pledged their loyalty to an international workers' movement, devoted themselves to their respective nations. War and its violence seemed to offer an escape from the dull routine of classroom, job, and home and from the emptiness, drabness, mediocrity, and pettiness of bourgeois society—from "a world grown old and cold and weary," as Rupert Brooke, a young British poet, put it.[10] To some, war was a "beautiful . . . sacred moment" that satisfied an "ethical yearning."[11] To many people, especially youth and intellectuals, war seemed a healthy and heroic antidote to what they regarded as an unbearably decadent and soul-destroying machine age and to bourgeois preoccupation with work, profits, and possessions. More significantly, the outpouring of patriotic sentiments demonstrated the power that nationalism exerted over the European mind. Overcoming bitter class animosities, nationalism welded millions of people into a collectivity ready to commit body and soul to the nation, especially in its hour of need. For decades, state-directed education had indoctrinated youth with nationalist attitudes, beliefs, and myths designed to promote social cohesion. This training proved extraordinarily successful.

In Paris, men marched down the boulevards singing the stirring words of the French national anthem, the "Marseillaise," while women showered young soldiers with flowers. A participant recollected: "Young and old, civilians and military men burned with the same excitement. . . . thousands of men eager to fight would jostle one another outside recruiting offices, waiting to join up. . . . The word 'duty' had a meaning for them, and the word 'country' had regained its splendor."[12] These sentiments were echoed by another French soldier, Andre Fribourg, traveling to the front:

Our hearts beat with enthusiasm. A kind of intoxication takes possession of us. My muscles and arteries tingle with happy strength. The spirit is contagious. Along the track walkers wave to us. Women hold up their children. We are carried away by the greeting of the

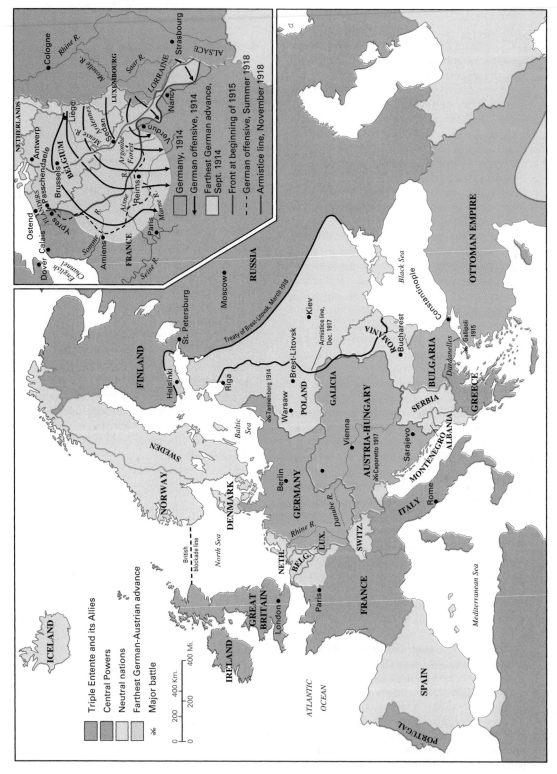

Germany, 1914
German offensive, 1914
Farthest German advance,
Sept. 1914
Front at beginning of 1915
German offensive, Summer 1918
Armistice line, November 1918

Cologne
Rhine R.
NETHERLANDS
Antwerp
Ostend
Passchendaele
BELGIUM
Brussels
Liège
FLANDERS
Ypres
Dover
Calais
English Channel
Amiens
Somme R.
FRANCE
Seine R.
Paris
Marne R.
Reims
Aisne R.
Argonne Forest
Verdun
Meuse R.
Sedan
Ardennes
LUXEMBOURG
Saar R.
Moselle R.
LORRAINE
Nancy
Strasbourg
ALSACE

Triple Entente and its Allies
Central Powers
Neutral nations
Farthest German-Austrian advance
Major battle

ICELAND

NORWAY

SWEDEN

FINLAND
Helsinki

St. Petersburg

Moscow

RUSSIA

Treaty of Brest-Litovsk, March 1918

Riga
Baltic Sea
Tannenberg 1914
Warsaw
Brest-Litovsk
POLAND
Armistice line, Dec. 1917
Kiev
GALICIA
ROMANIA
Bucharest
Black Sea
Constantinople
OTTOMAN EMPIRE
Dardanelles
Gallipoli 1915
GREECE
ALBANIA
MONTENEGRO
Sarajevo
SERBIA
BULGARIA
Vienna
AUSTRIA-HUNGARY
Caporetto 1917
ITALY
Rome

Berlin
GERMANY
Danube R.
SWITZ.
LUX.
BELG.
NETH.
Rhine R.

DENMARK

North Sea
British blockade line

GREAT BRITAIN
London

IRELAND

Paris
FRANCE

SPAIN

PORTUGAL

ATLANTIC OCEAN

Mediterranean Sea

400 Mi.
400 Km.
200
200
0
0

702

land, the mystery that the future holds, the thought of glorious adventure, and the pride of being chosen to share it.[13]

Similarly, a German newspaper editorialized, "It is a joy to be alive. We wished so much for this hour. . . . The sword which has been forced into our hand will not be sheathed until our aims are won and our territory extended as far as necessity demands."[14] Writing about those momentous days, the British mathematician-philosopher Bertrand Russell (1872–1970) recalled his horror and "amazement that average men and women were delighted at the prospect of war. . . . [T]he anticipation of carnage was delightful to something like ninety per cent of the population. I had to revise my views on human nature."[15]

Soldiers bound for battle and wives and sweethearts seeing them off at train stations were in a holiday mood. "My dear ones, be proud that you live in such a time and in such a nation and that you . . . have the privilege of sending those you love into so glorious a battle," wrote a young German law student to his family.[16] The young warriors yearned to do something noble and altruistic, to win glory, and to experience life at its most intense.

The martial mood also captivated many of Europe's most distinguished intellectuals. They shared Rupert Brooke's sentiments: "Now God be thanked Who has matched us with His hour,/And caught our youth, and wakened us from sleeping."[17] In November 1914, Thomas Mann, the distinguished German writer, saw the war as "purification" and "liberation." "How could . . . the soldier in the artist," he asked, "not praise God for the collapse of a peaceful world with which he was fed up, so exceedingly fed up."[18] To the prominent German historian Friedrich Meinecke, August 1914 was "one of the great moments of my life which suddenly filled my soul with . . . the profoundest joy."[19]

Some intellectuals also welcomed the war because it unified the nation in a spirit of fraternity, which eliminated party squabbles and class differences and overcame individual isolation. Stefan Zweig (1881–1942), an Austrian writer, recalled how news of the war was greeted in Vienna:

As never before, thousands and hundreds of thousands felt what they should have felt in peace time, that they belonged together. . . . All differences of class, rank, and language were flooded over at that moment by the rushing feeling of fraternity. Strangers spoke to one another in the streets, people who had avoided each other for years shook hands, everywhere one saw excited faces. Each individual experienced an exaltation of his ego . . . he had been incorporated into the mass . . . and his person, his hitherto unnoticed person, had been given meaning.[20]

War, in the view of some intellectuals, would spiritually regenerate the nation. It would resurrect glory, honor, and heroism; it would awaken a spirit of self-sacrifice and dedication and give life an overriding purpose in a world suffocating from bourgeois materialism and drabness.

Thus, a generation of European youth marched off to war joyously, urged on by their teachers and cheered by their delirious compatriots. It must be emphasized, however, that both the soldiers who went off to war singing and the statesmen and generals who welcomed war or did not try hard enough to prevent it expected a short, decisive, and gallant conflict. Few envisioned what World War I turned out to be: four years of barbaric, senseless slaughter. The cheers of chauvinists, naive and deluded idealists, and fools drowned out the words of those, principally socialists, labor leaders, pacifists, and left-leaning liberals, who realized that Europe was stumbling into darkness. "The lamps are going out all over Europe," said British Foreign Secretary Edward Grey. "We shall not see them lit again in our lifetime."

STALEMATE IN THE WEST

On August 4, 1914, the German army invaded Belgium. German war plans, drawn up years earlier, chiefly by General Alfred von Schlieffen, called for the army to swing through Belgium to outflank French border defenses, envelop the French forces,

◀ MAP 29.2 WORLD WAR I, 1914–1918
This map shows Europe divided into competing alliances and German advances into France and eastern Europe once war broke out.

TROOPS LEAVING BERLIN, 1914. "The sword has been forced into our hand," said Germans at the outbreak of war. German troops mobilized eagerly and efficiently; here a trainload is leaving for the western front. (*Historical Pictures Service/Stock Montage.*)

and destroy the enemy by attacking its rear. With the French army smashed and Paris isolated, German railroads—an extensive system of tracks, carefully planned by the general staff, had been constructed in the previous decade—would rush the victorious troops to the eastern front to bolster the small force that had been assigned to hold off the Russians. The German military felt certain that the spirit and skill of the German army would ensure victory over the much larger Russian forces. But everything depended on speed. France must be taken before the Russians could mobilize sufficient numbers to invade Germany. The Germans were confident that they would defeat France in two months or less.

French strategy called for a headlong attack into Alsace and Lorraine. Inspired by Napoleon's stress on offensive warfare and convinced of French soldiers' unconquerable will and irresistible nerve, the French army prepared its soldiers only for offensive warfare. The field regulations proclaimed: "Battles are . . . struggles of morale. Defeat is inevitable as soon as the hope of conquering ceases to exist. Success comes . . . to him whose will is firmest and morale strongest."[21]

The French doctrine proved an instant failure. Although bayonet charges against machine-gun emplacements demonstrated the valor of French soldiers, they also revealed the incompetence of French generals. Making no effort at concealment or surprise and wearing striking red and blue uniforms, French soldiers were perfect targets. Marching into concentrated fire, they fell like pins. Everywhere the audacious attack was failing, but French generals, beguiled by the mystique of the offensive, would not change their tactics. In the first six weeks of the war, the French suffered an astounding 385,000 casualties, including 100,000 dead.

German success was not complete, however. Moving faster than anticipated, the Russians invaded East Prussia. In response, General Helmuth von Moltke transferred troops from the French front, hampering the German advance. By early September, the Germans had reached the Marne River, forty miles from Paris. With their capital at their backs, the regrouped French forces, aided by the British, fought with astounding courage. Meanwhile, the Germans were exhausted by long marches and had outrun their supplies. Moreover, in their rush toward Paris, they had unknowingly exposed their flank, which the French attacked. The British then penetrated a gap that opened up between the German armies, forcing the Germans to retreat. The first battle of the Marne had saved Paris. Now the war entered a new and unexpected phase: the deadlock of trench warfare.

For over four hundred miles across northern France, from the Alps to the North Sea, the opposing sides constructed a vast network of trenches. These trenches had underground dugouts, and barbed wire stretched for yards before the front trenches as a barrier to attack. Behind the front trenches were other lines, to which soldiers could retreat and from which support could be sent. Between the opposing armies lay "no man's land," a wasteland of mud, shattered trees, torn earth, and broken bodies. In the trenches soldiers were reduced to a primitive existence. Sometimes they stood knee-deep in freezing water or slimy mud; the stench from human waste, rotting corpses, and unwashed bodies overwhelmed the senses; rats, made more fecund by easy access to food, including decaying flesh, swarmed over the dead and scampered across the wounded and the sleeping; and ubiquitous lice caused intense discomfort and disease, which frequently required hospitalization for several weeks. After days of fearsome, earsplitting bombardments, even the most stouthearted were reduced to shivering, whimpering creatures. The agonizing cries and pleas of the wounded, left

to die on the battlefield because it was too dangerous to attempt a rescue, shattered the nerves of the men in the trenches. Trench warfare was a futile battle of nerves, endurance, and courage, waged to the constant thunder of heavy artillery, which from many miles away pulverized both ramparts and men. And in April 1915, the Germans introduced poison gas that added to the war's horror.

But the most distinctive feature of trench warfare was butchery. As attacking troops climbed over their trenches and advanced bravely across no man's land, they were decimated by heavy artillery and chewed up by rapid machine-gun fire, which could fire 500 or more rounds a minute. If they did penetrate the frontline trenches of the enemy, they were soon thrown back by a counterattack.

Despite a frightful loss of life, little land changed hands in this war of attrition. So much heroism, sacrifice, and death achieved nothing. The Allied generals in particular, unfeeling and totally lacking in imagination, ordered still greater attacks, hoping to wear down German manpower, which was inferior to their own. Once German reserves could not replenish losses, they reasoned, a breakthrough would be possible. But this strategy only increased the death toll, for the advantage was always with the defense, which possessed machine guns, magazine rifles, and barbed wire. Aided by radio and aerial reconnaissance, the defense could rush reinforcements to thwart an enemy attack. Tanks could redress the balance, but the generals, committed to old concepts, did not make effective use of them. And whereas the technology of the machine gun had been perfected, the motorized tanks often broke down. Gains and losses of land were measured in yards, but the lives of Europe's youth were squandered by the hundreds of thousands. In 1915, for example, France launched numerous attacks against German lines but never gained more than three miles in any one place. Yet these small gains cost France 1,430,000 casualties.

In 1915, neither side could break the deadlock. Hoping to bleed the French army dry and force its surrender, the Germans in February 1916 attacked the town of Verdun, which was protected by a ring of forts. They chose Verdun because they knew the French could never permit a retreat from this ancient fortress. The Germans hoped that France, compelled to pour more and more troops into bat-

BRITISH MUNITIONS WORKERS. With millions of men in the military, women took jobs formerly held only by men. Women drove trucks and buses, operated cranes, and worked in armament factories. Resistance to granting them equal rights diminished, as politicians recognized the essential contribution of women to the war effort. (*Brown Brothers.*)

tle, would suffer such a loss of men that it would be unable to continue the war. However, the leadership of General Henri Philippe Pétain, the tenacity of the French infantry, and the well-constructed concrete and steel forts enabled the French to hold on. When the British opened a major offensive on July 1, the Germans had to channel their reserves to the new front, relieving the pressure on Verdun. Verdun was World War I's bloodiest battle. France and Germany together suffered perhaps a million casualties, including some 300,000 dead.

At the end of June 1916, the British, assisted by the French, attempted a breakthrough at the Somme River. On July 1, after seven days of intense bombardment intended to destroy German defenses, the British climbed out of their trenches and ventured into no man's land. But German positions had not been destroyed. Emerging from their deep dugouts, German machine gunners fired repeatedly at the British, who had been ordered to advance in rows. Marching into concentrated machine-gun fire and continuous artillery barrages while desperately searching for a way through the still intact German wire, few British troops ever made it across no man's land. Out of 110,000 who attacked, 60,000 fell dead or wounded—most in the first hour of the assault—"the heaviest loss ever suffered in a single day by a British army or by any army in the First World War," observes the British historian A. J. P. Taylor.[22] Some reached the German wire, only to become entangled in it. The Germans killed them with rifle fire and bayonets. For days the wounded lay in no man's land, their shrieks unheeded. The Germans suffered only 8,000 casualties, another powerful sign that in trench warfare advantage lay with the defense.

After this initial disaster, common sense and a concern for human life demanded that the attack be called off, but the generals, who rarely made an appearance at the front to observe the actual conditions of battle, continued to feed soldiers to the German guns. When the battle of the Somme ended in mid-November, Britain and France had lost more than 600,000 men; yet the military situation remained essentially unchanged. In December 1916, the new commander in chief of the French forces, General Robert Nivelle, ordered another mass attack for April 1917. The Germans discovered the battle plans on the body of a French officer and withdrew to a shorter line on high ground, constructing the strongest defense network of the war. Although Nivelle knew that the French had lost the element of surprise, he went ahead with the offensive, which proved to be another bloodbath. Sometimes the fire was so intense that the French could not make it out of their own trenches. Although French soldiers fought with courage, the situation was hopeless. Still Nivelle persisted with the attack. After ten days, French casualties numbered 187,000.

The soldiers could endure no more. Spontaneous revolts, born of despair and military failure, broke out in rest areas as soldiers refused to return to the slaughter ground. In some instances, they shouted "Peace" and "To hell with the war." Mobs of soldiers seized trains to reach Paris and stir up the population against the war. Mutineers took control of barracks and threatened to fire on officers who interfered. The mutiny spread to the frontlines as soldiers told their officers that they would defend the trenches but not attack. The French army was disintegrating. "The slightest

German attack would have sufficed to tumble down our house of cards and bring the enemy to Paris," recalled a French officer.[23]

General Pétain, the hero of Verdun, replaced the disgraced Nivelle. To restore morale, Pétain granted more leave, improved the quality of food, made the rest areas more comfortable, and ordered officers to show concern for their men. He visited the troops, listened to their complaints, and told them that France would engage in only limited offensives until the United States, which had just entered the war, reinforced the Allies in large numbers. These measures, combined with imprisonments and executions, restored discipline. The Germans, unaware of the full magnitude of the mutiny, had not put pressure on the front. By the time the Germans attacked, General Pétain had revitalized the army.

OTHER FRONTS

While the western front hardened into a stalemate, events moved more decisively on the eastern front. In August 1914, according to plan, the bulk of the German army invaded France, hoping for a speedy victory, while a small force defended the eastern frontier against Russia. Responding to French requests to put pressure on Germany, the Russians, with insufficient preparation, invaded East Prussia. Defeated at the battle of Tannenberg (August 26–30, 1914), the Russians withdrew from German territory, which remained inviolate for the rest of the war.

Meanwhile, Germany's ally Austria was having no success against Serbia and Russia. Germany had to come to Austria's rescue. In the spring of 1915, the Germans made a breakthrough that forced the Russians to abandon Galicia and most of Poland. But Germany did not gain the decisive victory it had sought. Although badly battered, Russia remained in the war, forcing Germany to fight on two fronts.

In June 1916, the Russians launched an offensive, opening a wide breach in the Austrian lines. However, a German counteroffensive forced a retreat and cost the Russians more than a million casualties. Russia's military position deteriorated and its domestic unrest worsened.

In March 1917, food shortages and disgust with the great loss of life exploded into a spontaneous

Manfred Freiherr von Richthofen (the "Red Baron")

During World War I, airplanes were first used to gather intelligence about enemy positions. To thwart these reconnaissance planes, the other side sent up its own planes, arming pilots first with revolvers and grenades and later with machine guns. Thus, aerial combat was born. The daredevil pilots who dueled in the air captured the imagination of the people back home, and their exploits were widely publicized in the press.

The most famous ace of the war was Manfred Freiherr von Richthofen (1892–1918). Known as the "Red Baron" because he painted his plane scarlet so that both friend and foe could identify it, Richthofen is credited with shooting down eighty Allied aircraft. Richthofen's parents were typical Junker landowners. As a young man, Manfred acquired a passion for hunting and later transferred his marksmanship skills to aerial combat. A fellow pilot said that Richthofen "has to thank his hunter's eye for his incredible success. Watching like an eagle, he spots the weakness of his opponent and like a bird of prey he dives on the victim, which is inescapably in his

Bettmann/CORBIS.

revolution. The tsar abdicated. Dominated by liberals, the new government opted to continue the war, despite the weariness of the Russian masses. In November 1917, a second revolution brought to power the Bolsheviks, or communists. In March 1918, the Bolsheviks ended Russia's role in the war by signing the punitive Treaty of Brest-Litovsk, in which Russia surrendered Poland, the Ukraine, Finland, and the Baltic provinces.

Some major battles involved belligerents who joined the conflict after August 1914—notably, the Ottoman Turks, who sided with the Germans, and the Italians, who joined the Allies. Intent on seizing the Dardanelles, the Allies met fierce Turkish resistance on the Gallipoli Peninsula. The Gallipoli campaign (1915–16) cost the Allies 252,000 casualties,

and they gained nothing. In 1917, the Italians were badly defeated by a combined German and Austrian force at Caporetto. Germany and Austria took some 275,000 prisoners.

COLLAPSE

OF THE CENTRAL POWERS

American Entry

The year 1917 seemed disastrous for the Allies. The Nivelle offensive had failed, the French army had mutinied, a British attack at Passchendaele did not bring the expected breakthrough and added some three hundred thousand casualties to the list

clutches."* Following in his father's footsteps, Manfred pursued a military career. Learning to fly in 1915, he soon was given command of a squadron of fighter pilots. An enthusiastic huntsman, Richthofen confessed that shooting down Allied planes satisfied his passion for the hunt and a compulsive need for glory.

In drawing comparisons between German and Allied pilots, he stressed the superiority of the Germans' "aggressive spirit," which he believed he exemplified. He noted some of that spirit in the English pilots as well, ascribing it to their "German blood."

> The Frenchman lies in wait for his prey to surprise him in a trap. That is hard to do in the air. Only a beginner will let himself be taken unawares. Ambush does not work, for one cannot hide and the invisible airplane has not yet been invented. Now and then, however, the Gallic blood rages in him and he launches an attack, but it is comparable to carbonated soda. For a moment there is an awful lot of spirit that suddenly goes flat. He is lacking in tenacious endurance.
>
> The Englishman, on the other hand, shows some of his Germanic blood. These sportsmen take readily to flying, but they lose themselves in sport. They have enough amusement looping, diving, flying upside-down and demonstrating similar stunts for our men in the trenches. This would make a good impression during the Johannistal Sportsweek, but the men in the trenches are not as appreciative.[†]

April 1917 was a particularly successful month for Richthofen. He shot down twenty-one British planes, including four in one day, and was promoted to captain. One year later, in a furious dogfight above the Somme involving more than twenty German and British planes, the Red Baron's plane was hit by a Canadian pilot. When Australian soldiers reached the crashed plane, they found the Red Baron dead, his nose and jaw crushed from having smashed into the machine-gun butts in front of him. (Since the Australians on the ground were also firing at his plane, it is not certain who inflicted the fatal bullet.)

---

*Quoted in Peter Kilduff, *The Red Baron: Beyond the Legend* (London: Cassell, 1999), p. 7.
[†]Manfred Freiherr von Richthofen, *The Red Baron*, trans. Peter Kilduff (Garden City, N.Y.: Doubleday, 1969), p. 67.

of butchery, and the Russians, torn by revolution and gripped by war weariness, were close to making a separate peace. But there was one encouraging development for the Allies. In April 1917, the United States declared war on Germany.

From the outset, America's sympathies lay with the Allies. To most Americans, Britain and France were democracies threatened by an autocratic and militaristic Germany. These sentiments were reinforced by British propaganda, which depicted the Germans as cruel "Huns." Since most war news came to the United States from Britain, anti-German feeling gained momentum. What precipitated America's entry was the German decision of January 1917 to launch a campaign of unrestricted submarine warfare. To deprive Britain of war supplies and to starve it into submission, the Germans resolved to torpedo both enemy and neutral ships in the war zone around the British Isles. Since the United States was Britain's principal supplier, American ships became a target of German submarines.

Angered by American loss of life and materiel, as well as by the violation of the doctrine of freedom of the seas, and fearful of a diminution of prestige if the United States took no action, President Woodrow Wilson (1856–1924) pressed for American entry. Also at stake was American security, which would be jeopardized by German domination of western Europe. As Secretary of State Robert Lansing wrote in a private memorandum just before the United States entered the war, "The

Allies must not be beaten. It would mean the triumph of Autocracy over Democracy; the shattering of all our moral standards; and a real, though it may seem remote, peril to our independence and institutions."[24]

In initiating unrestricted submarine warfare, Germany gambled that the United States, even if it became a belligerent, could not intervene in sufficient numbers quickly enough to make a difference. The Germans lost their gamble. The United States broke diplomatic relations with Germany immediately on learning of the submarine campaign. Three weeks later, the British gave the Americans a message sent by German Foreign Secretary Arthur Zimmerman to the German ambassador in Mexico City and deciphered by British code experts. In the Zimmerman telegram, Germany proposed that in case of war between Germany and the United States, Mexico should join Germany as an ally; in return, Mexico would receive Texas, New Mexico, and Arizona. This fantastic proposal further exacerbated anti-German feeling in the United States. As German submarines continued to attack neutral shipping, President Wilson, on April 2, 1917, urged Congress to declare war on Germany, which it did on April 6.

Although the United States may have entered the war to protect its own security, President Wilson told the American people and the world that the United States was fighting "to make the world safe for democracy." With America's entry, the war was transformed into a moral crusade: an ideological conflict between democracy and autocracy. In January 1918, Wilson enunciated American war aims in "Fourteen Points," which called for territorial changes based on nationality and the application of democratic principles to international relations. An association of nations would be established to preserve peace; it would conduct international relations with the same respect for law as was evidenced in democratic states. Thus, Wilson placed his hope for the future peace of the world in liberal nationalism and democracy, the two great legacies of the nineteenth century.

Germany's Last Offensive

With Russia out of the war, General Erich Ludendorff prepared for a decisive offensive before the Americans could land sufficient troops in France to help the Allies. A war of attrition now favored the Allies, who could count on American supplies and manpower. Without an immediate and decisive victory, Germany could not win the war. Ludendorff hoped to drive the British forces back to the sea, forcing them to withdraw from the Continent. Then he would turn his full might against the French. The great offensive began on March 21, 1918. The Germans breached the enemy lines, and the British retreated. Expanding their offensive, the Germans sought to split the British and French forces by capturing Amiens, the Allies' major communications center, and to drive the British back to the channel ports.

Suddenly, the deadlock had been broken; it was now a war of movement. Within two weeks, the Germans had taken some 1,250 square miles. But British resistance was astonishing, and the Germans, exhausted and short of ammunition and food, called off the drive. A second offensive against the British in April also had to be called off as the British contested every foot of ground. Both campaigns depleted German manpower while the Americans were arriving in great numbers to strengthen Allied lines and uplift morale.

At the end of May, Ludendorff resumed his offensive against the French. Attacking unexpectedly, the Germans broke through and by June 3 advanced to within fifty-six miles of Paris. General John Pershing, head of the American forces, cabled Washington that "the possibility of losing Paris has become apparent."[25] But the offensive was already winding down as reserves braced the French lines. In the battle of Belleau Wood (June 6–25, 1918), the Americans checked the Germans. There would be no open road to Paris.

In mid July, the Germans tried again, crossing the Marne River in small boats. By August 3, the second battle of the Marne ended with the Germans being forced back over the river. Although they had thrown everything they had into their spring and summer offensives, it was not enough. The Allies had bent, but reinforced and encouraged by American arms, they did not break. Now they began to counterattack. On August 8, the British, assisted by the French and using tanks to great advantage, broke through east of Amiens. Ludendorff called August 8 "the black day of the German Army." The kaiser himself declared to his generals: "We have nearly reached the limit of our powers of resistance. The war must be ended."[26] The Allies, their confidence surging, continued to attack with great success in August and September.

Meanwhile, German allies, deprived of support from a hard-pressed Germany, were unable to cope. An Allied army of French, Britons, Serbs, and Italians compelled Bulgaria to sign an armistice on September 29. Shortly afterward, British successes in the Middle East forced the Turks to withdraw from the war. In the streets of Vienna, people were shouting, "Long live peace! Down with the monarchy!" The Austro-Hungarian Empire was rapidly disintegrating into separate states based on nationality.

By early October, the last defensive position of the Germans crumbled. The army's spirit collapsed as well; war-weary soldiers, sensing that the war was lost, surrendered in large numbers and refused orders to return to the front. Fearing an Allied invasion of Germany, Ludendorff wanted an immediate armistice. But he needed to find a way to obtain favorable armistice terms from President Wilson and to shift the blame for the lost war from the military and the kaiser to the civilian leadership. Cynically, he urged the creation of a popular parliamentary government in Germany. But events in Germany went further than the general had anticipated. Whereas Ludendorff sought a limited monarchy, the shock of defeat and hunger sparked a revolution that forced the kaiser to abdicate.

On November 11, the new German Republic signed an armistice ending the hostilities. At 11 A.M., soldiers from both sides walked into no man's land and into a new day. A newspaper correspondent with the British army in France wrote: "Last night for the first time since August in the first year of the war, there was no light of gunfire in the sky, no sudden stabs of flame through darkness, no spreading glow above black trees where for four years of nights human beings were smashed to death. The Fires of Hell had been put out."[27]

THE PEACE CONFERENCE

Wilson's Hope for a New World

In January 1919, representatives of the Allied powers assembled in Paris to draw up peace terms; President Wilson was also there. The war-weary masses turned to Wilson as the prophet who would have the nations beat their swords into plowshares. In Paris, two million people lined the streets to cheer Wilson and throw bouquets; his carriage passed under a huge banner proclaiming "Honor to Wilson the Just." In Rome, hysterical crowds called him the god of peace; in Milan, wounded soldiers sought to kiss his clothes; in Poland, university students spoke his name when they shook hands with each other.

For Wilson, the war had been fought against autocracy. He hoped that a peace settlement based on liberal-democratic ideals would sweep away the foundations of war. Wilson proclaimed his message with a spiritual zeal that expressed his Presbyterian background and his faith in American democracy.

None of Wilson's principles seemed more just than the idea of self-determination: the right of a people to have its own state, free of foreign domination. In particular, this goal meant (or was interpreted to mean) the return of Alsace and Lorraine to France, the creation of an independent Poland, readjustment of the frontiers of Italy to incorporate Austrian lands inhabited by Italians, and an opportunity for Slavs of the Austro-Hungarian Empire to form their own states. Although Wilson did not demand the liberation of all colonies, the Fourteen Points did call for "a free, open-minded and absolutely impartial adjustment of all colonial claims" and a territorial settlement "made in the interest and for the benefit of the population concerned."

Aware that a harshly treated Germany might well seek revenge, engulfing the world in another cataclysm, Wilson insisted that there should be a "peace without victory." A just settlement would encourage a defeated Germany to work with the victorious Allies in building a new Europe. But on one point he was adamant: Prussian militarism, which he viewed as a principal cause of the war, must be eliminated. To create a better world, Wilson urged the formation of a League of Nations, an international parliament to settle disputes and discourage aggression. Wilson wanted a peace of justice to preserve Western civilization in its democratic and Christian form.

Online Study Center

Improve Your Grade
Primary Source: A New Diplomacy: The Fourteen Points

Problems of Peacemaking

How could such moralistic pronouncements translate into concrete peace provisions? "[N]o mortal man . . . could have hoped to bring about all the things that the world came to expect of Wilson," concludes the American historian Thomas A. Bailey. "Wilson's own people were bound to feel disillusioned; the peoples of the neutral and Allied countries were bound to feel deceived; and the peoples of the enemy countries were bound to feel betrayed."[28]

Wilson's negotiating position had also been undermined by the Republican party's victory in the congressional elections of November 1918. Wilson had appealed to the American people to elect Democrats as a vote of confidence in his diplomacy. But instead Americans sent twenty-five Republicans and fifteen Democrats to the Senate. Although the Republicans' success apparently stemmed from local and national, rather than international, issues, the outcome diminished Wilson's prestige at the conference table. In the view of his fellow negotiators, Wilson was trying to preach to Europe even though he lacked the support of his own country. Since the Senate had to ratify any American treaty, European diplomats worried that what Wilson agreed to the Senate might reject, which is precisely what happened.

Attending the conference in person also weakened Wilson's negotiating position. As leader of the nation that had rescued the Allies and as initiator of a peace program that held the promise of a new world, Wilson occupied a position of honor, from which he could exert considerable influence and authority. But by haggling with the other representatives, he was knocked from his lofty pedestal and became all too human. "Messiahs tend to arouse less enthusiasm the more they show themselves," notes Bailey; "the role requires aloofness and the spell of mystery."[29]

A major obstacle to Wilson's peace program was France's demand for security and revenge. Nearly the entire war on the western front had been fought on French territory. France mourned the loss of half its young men. Many French industries and farms had been ruined. Particularly galling to the French was the flooding of mines and the general destruction of property carried out by the Germans in their retreat at the war's

WILSON AND CLEMENCEAU ARRIVE AT VERSAILLES, JUNE 28, 1919. The idealism of President Wilson (center) clashed with Premier Clemenceau's (left) determination to enhance France's security. (*Hulton Deutsch Collection/Getty Images.*)

end. Viewing the Germans as savages and vandals, many in France were skeptical of Wilson's idealism. France's representative at the conference table, Georges Clemenceau (1841–1929), did not share Wilson's hope for a new world or his confidence in the future League of Nations. Instead, he demanded that Germany be severely punished and its capacity to wage war destroyed. He wanted guarantees that the wars of 1870–71 and 1914–18 would not be repeated. The latter war had shown that without the help of Britain and the United States, France would have been at the mercy of Germany. Because there was no certainty that these states would again aid France, Clemenceau wanted to use his country's present advantage to cripple Germany.

The intermingling of nationalities was another barrier to Wilson's program, for no one could create a Europe completely free of minority problems. Some nationalities would always feel that they had been treated shabbily, and the various nationalities were not willing to moderate their demands or lower their aspirations. "To most Europeans," states the German-American historian Hajo Holborn, "the satisfaction of their national dreams was an absolute end even when their realization violated the national determination of others."[30] For example, the Fourteen Points called for an independent Poland with secure access to the sea. But between Poland and the sea lay land populated by Germans. Giving this land to Poland would violate German self-determination; denying it to Poland would mean that the new country had little chance of developing a sound economy. No matter what the decision, one people would regard it as unjust. Similarly, to provide the new Czechoslovakia with defensible borders, it would be necessary to give it land inhabited principally by Germans. This, too, could be viewed as a denial of German self-determination, but not granting the area to Czechoslovakia would mean that the new state would not be able to defend itself against Germany.

Secret treaties drawn up by the Allies during the war also interfered with Wilson's program. These agreements, dividing up German, Austrian, and Ottoman territory, did not square with the principle of self-determination. For example, to entice Italy into entering the war, the Allies had promised it Austrian lands that were inhabited predominantly by Germans and Slavs. Italy was not about to repudiate its prize because of Wilson's principles.

Finally, the war had aroused great bitterness, which persisted after the guns had been silenced. Both the masses and their leaders demanded retribution and held exaggerated hopes for territory and reparations. In such an atmosphere of postwar enmity, the spirit of compromise and moderation could not overcome the desire for spoils and punishment. A century earlier, when the monarchs had defeated Napoleon, they sought a peace of reconciliation with France. But setting aside their hatreds proved harder for democratic statesmen and nations than it had been for despotic monarchs and aristocratic diplomats.

The Settlement

After months of negotiations, often punctuated by acrimony, the peacemakers hammered out a settlement. Five treaties made up the Peace of Paris: one each with Germany, Austria, Hungary, Bulgaria, and Turkey. Of the five, the Treaty of Versailles, which Germany signed on June 28, 1919, was the most significant.

France regained Alsace and Lorraine, the territory lost to Germany in the Franco-Prussian War of 1870–71. The Treaty of Versailles also barred Germany from placing fortifications in the Rhineland. The French military had wanted to take the Rhineland from Germany and break it up into one or more republics under French suzerainty. Under this arrangement French control would extend to the Rhine River, which was a natural defensive border; French forces had only to destroy the bridges to prevent a German invasion of France. With Germany deprived of this springboard for invasion, French security would be immensely improved. Recognizing that the German people would never permanently submit to the amputation of the Rhineland, which was inhabited by more than five million Germans and contained key industries, Wilson and British Prime Minister David Lloyd George (1863–1945) resisted these French demands. They did not want to create an Alsace-Lorraine in reverse by awarding France a region that was overwhelmingly German. Nor could Wilson ever agree to such a glaring violation of the principle of self-determination.

Faced with the opposition of Wilson and Lloyd George, Clemenceau backed down and agreed instead to Allied occupation of the Rhineland for fifteen years, its demilitarization, and an Anglo-American promise of assistance if Germany attacked France in the future. This last point, considered vital by France, proved useless. The alliance went into effect only if both the United States and Britain ratified it. Since this so-called Security Treaty did not get past the U.S. Senate, Britain also refused to sign it. France had made a great concession on the Rhineland issue but received nothing in exchange. The French people felt that they had been duped and wronged.

A related issue concerned French demands for annexation of the coal-rich Saar Basin, which adjoined Lorraine. By obtaining this region, France would weaken Germany's military potential. France argued that this would be just compensation for the deliberate destruction of the French coal mines by the retreating German army at the end of the war. But here, too, France was disappointed. The final compromise called for a League of Nations commission to govern the Saar Basin for fifteen years, after which the inhabitants would decide whether their territory would be ceded to France or returned to Germany.

In eastern Germany, in certain districts of Silesia that had a large Polish population, a plebiscite determined the future of the region. As a result, part of Upper Silesia was ceded to Poland. The settlement also gave Poland a corridor cut through West Prussia and terminating in the Baltic port of Danzig, and Danzig itself was declared an international city to be administered by the League of Nations. The Germans would never resign themselves to this loss of territory that separated East Prussia from the rest of Germany.

The victorious nations were awarded control of German and Ottoman colonies. However, these nations held the colonies not outright but as mandates under the supervision of the League, which would protect the interests of the native peoples. Thus, the division of Ottoman and German colonies represented a compromise between traditional imperialism and Wilsonian idealism. The mandate system implied the ultimate end of colonialism, for it clearly opposed the exploitation of colonial peoples and asserted independence as the rightful goal for subject nations.

To strip Germany of any offensive capacity, the settlement abolished the German general staff and forbade military conscription in Germany. The German army was limited to a hundred thousand volunteers and deprived of heavy artillery, tanks, and warplanes. The German navy was limited to a token force, which did not include submarines.

The issue of war reparations caused great bitterness between Wilson and his French and British adversaries. The American delegation wanted the treaty to fix a reasonable sum that Germany would have to pay and specify the period of years allotted for payment. But, instead, the Treaty of Versailles left Germany with an open-ended bill, which would probably take generations to pay. Wilson had lost on the issue of reasonable reparations. Moreover, Article 231, which preceded the reparation clauses, placed sole responsibility for the war on Germany and its allies. The Germans responded to this accusation with contempt.

In separate treaties, the conference dealt with the dissolution of the Hapsburg Empire. In the closing weeks of the war, the Austro-Hungarian Empire had crumbled as the various nationalities proclaimed their independence from Hapsburg rule. In most cases, the peacemakers ratified with treaties what the nationalities had already accomplished in fact. Serbia joined with Austro-Hungarian lands inhabited by South Slavs to become Yugoslavia. Czechoslovakia arose from the predominantly Czech and Slovak regions of Austria. Hungary, which broke away from Austria to become a separate country, had to cede a considerable amount of land to Romania and Yugoslavia. Austria had to turn over to Italy the South Tyrol, which was inhabited by two hundred thousand Austrian Germans. This clear violation of the principle of self-determination greatly offended liberal opinion. Deprived of its vast territories and prohibited from union with Germany, the new Austria was a third-rate power.

Assessment and Problems

The Germans unanimously denounced the Treaty of Versailles, for in their minds the war had ended not in German defeat but in a stalemate. They regarded the armistice as the prelude to a negotiated settlement among equals, based on Wilson's call for a peace of justice. Instead, the Germans were barred from participating in the negotiations. And they viewed the terms of the treaty as humiliating and vindictive—designed to keep Germany militarily and economically weak. What standard of justice, they asked, allowed the Allies to take the German colonies, reduce the German military to a pitiful size without disarming themselves, ban Germany from the League of Nations, and saddle the country with impossible reparations? Why should Germany lose approximately one-eighth of its territory and one-tenth of its population? Why should the Allies blame the war on Germany, provide for the self-determination of Poles while precluding the union of German-speaking Austria with Germany, hand over to Italy some two hundred thousand Austrian Germans, place Germans under Polish rule, and declare the German port of Danzig a free city?

MAP 29.3 POST–WORLD WAR I: BROKEN EMPIRES AND CHANGED BOUNDARIES ▶
World War I led to the breakup of the Russian, Austro-Hungarian, and Ottoman Empires and the creation of several new countries, including Poland, Czechoslovakia, Yugoslavia, Lithuania, Latvia, and Estonia.

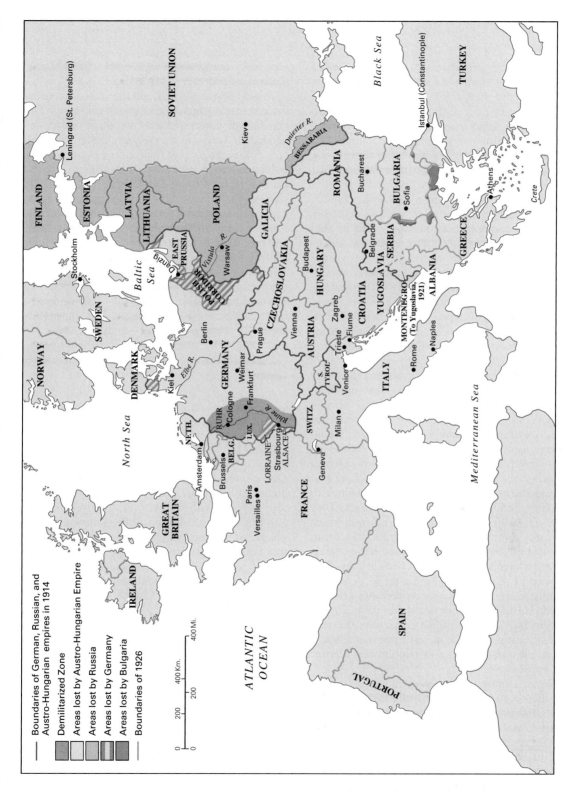

Boundaries of German, Russian, and Austro-Hungarian empires in 1914

Demilitarized Zone
Areas lost by Austro-Hungarian Empire
Areas lost by Russia
Areas lost by Germany
Areas lost by Bulgaria

Boundaries of 1926

0   200   400 Km.

0   200   400 Mi.

SOVIET UNION

FINLAND

ESTONIA

LATVIA

LITHUANIA

POLAND

EAST PRUSSIA

POLISH CORRIDOR

Danzig

Warsaw

Vistula R.

Kiev

Dniester R.

BESSARABIA

ROMANIA

Bucharest

BULGARIA

Sofia

Black Sea

Istanbul (Constantinople)

TURKEY

GREECE

Athens

Crete

SERBIA

YUGOSLAVIA

CROATIA

MONTENEGRO
(To Yugoslavia, 1921)

ALBANIA

Belgrade

Zagreb

Fiume

Trieste

Venice

ITALY

Rome

Naples

Milan

S. TYROL

AUSTRIA

HUNGARY

Budapest

Vienna

CZECHOSLOVAKIA

GALICIA

Prague

GERMANY

Berlin

Weimar

Frankfurt

Cologne

RUHR

Rhine R.

Elbe R.

LUX.

LORRAINE

ALSACE

Strasbourg

SWITZ.

Geneva

FRANCE

Paris

Versailles

BELG.

Brussels

NETH.

Amsterdam

Leningrad (St. Petersburg)

NORWAY

SWEDEN

Stockholm

DENMARK

Kiel

Baltic Sea

North Sea

GREAT BRITAIN

IRELAND

ATLANTIC OCEAN

Mediterranean Sea

SPAIN

PORTUGAL

The Germans protested that, when the United States entered the war, Wilson had stated that the enemy was not the German people but their government. Surely, the Germans now argued, the new German democracy should not be punished for the sins of the monarchy and the military. To the Germans, the Treaty of Versailles was not the dawning of the new world that Wilson had promised but a vile crime.

Worn out by war, torn by revolutionary unrest, and desperately short of food, with its economy in disarray and with the Allies poised to invade, the new German republic had no choice but to sign the treaty. However, the sentiments of the German people were clearly and prophetically expressed by the Berlin *Vorwärts,* the influential Social Democratic newspaper: "We must never forget it is only a scrap of paper. Treaties based on violence can keep their validity only so long as force exists. Do not lose hope. The resurrection day comes."[31]

Critics in other lands also condemned the treaty as a punitive settlement, warning that it would only exacerbate old hatreds and enflame German nationalism. The treaty's defenders, however, insisted that had Germany won the war, it would have imposed a far harsher settlement on the Allies. They pointed to German war aims, which called for the annexation of parts of France and Poland, the reduction of Belgium and Romania to satellites, and German expansion in Africa. They pointed also to the Treaty of Brest-Litovsk, which Germany compelled Russia to sign in 1918, as an example of Germany's ruthlessness. An insatiable Germany deprived Russia of 34 percent of its population, 32 percent of its farmland, 54 percent of its industrial enterprises, and 89 percent of its coal mines. Furthermore, they noted that the peace settlement did reflect Wilson's principles: the new map of Europe was the closest approximation of the ethnic distribution of its peoples that Europe had ever known.

What is most significant about the Treaty of Versailles is that it did not solve the German problem. Germany was left weak but unbroken—its industrial and military power only temporarily contained, and its nationalist fervor not only undiminished but stoked by a peace treaty that all political parties viewed as unjust, dictated, and offensive to national pride. The real danger in Europe was German unwillingness to accept defeat or surrender the dream of expansion.

Would France, Britain, and the United States enforce the treaty against a resurgent Germany? The war had demonstrated that an Allied victory depended on American intervention. But in 1920, the U.S. Senate, angry that Wilson had not taken Republicans with him to Paris and fearing that membership in the League of Nations would involve America in future wars, refused to ratify the Treaty of Versailles. Britain, feeling guilty over the treatment of Germany, lacked the will for enforcement and even came to favor treaty revision. The responsibility for preserving the settlement therefore rested primarily with France, which was not encouraging. The Paris peace settlement left Germany resentful but potentially powerful—German industrial capacity was considerable, and only Russia had a larger population—and to the east lay small and weak states, some of them with sizable German minorities, that could not check a rearmed Germany.

THE RUSSIAN REVOLUTION OF 1917

One consequence of the war that influenced the course of European and world history in momentous ways was the Russian Revolution of 1917 and the resultant triumph of the Bolsheviks. The people of Russia had initially responded to the war with a show of patriotic fervor. But the realities of war quickly dimmed this ardor. The ill-equipped and poorly led Russian armies suffered huge losses. In July 1915, the minister of war wrote this dismal report:

> *The soldiers are without doubt exhausted by the continued defeats and retreats. Their confidence in final victory and in their leaders is undermined. Ever more threatening signs of impending demoralization are evident. Cases of desertion and voluntary surrender to the enemy are becoming more frequent. It is difficult to expect enthusiasm and selflessness from men sent into battle unarmed and ordered to pick up the rifles of their dead comrades.*[32]

By 1916, the home front began to fall apart. Shops were empty, money had no value, and hunger and cold stalked the working quarters of cities and towns. Factory workers, many of them women replacements for husbands, brothers, and sons who were at the front, toiled long hours for wages that could not keep up with the accelerating inflation. When they protested, the goverment resorted to heavy-handed repression. By January 1917, nearly all Russians, soldiers and civilians alike, had lost trust in their autocratic government. But Tsar Nicholas II, determined to preserve autocracy, resisted any suggestion that he liberalize the regime for the sake of the war effort.

Autocracy was ready to collapse at the slightest blow. In early March (February 23 by the calendar* then in use), a strike, riots in the food lines, and street demonstrations in Petrograd (formerly Saint Petersburg) flared into sudden, unpremeditated revolution. The soldiers, who in 1905 had stood by the tsar, rushed to support the striking workers. The Romanov dynasty, after three hundred years of rule (1613–1917), came to an end. A Provisional Government was set up—provisional until a representative Constituent Assembly, to be elected as soon as possible, could establish a permanent regime.

Problems of the Provisional Government

The collapse of autocracy was followed by what supporters in Russia and the West hoped would be a liberal democratic regime pledged to give Russia a constitution. In reality, however, the course of events from March to November 1917 resembled a free-for-all—a no-holds-barred fight for the succession to autocracy, with only the fittest surviving. Events demonstrated the desperate state of the Russian Empire. Its vast size promoted internal disunity; increasing hardships raised the fury of the accumulated resentments to raw brutality among the masses. National minorities took advantage of the anarchy to dismember the country.

*Until March 1918, events in Russia were dated by the Julian calendar, thirteen days behind the Gregorian calendar used in the West. By the Julian calendar the first revolution occurred in February, the second in October.

Among the potential successors to the tsars, liberals of various shades seemed at first to enjoy the best chances. They represented the educated and forward-looking elements in Russian society that had arisen after the reforms of the 1860s: lawyers, doctors, professional people of all kinds, intellectuals, businesspeople and industrialists, many landowners, and even some bureaucrats. Liberals had opposed autocracy and earned a reputation for leadership.

Liberals had joined the March revolution reluctantly, for they were afraid of the masses and the violence of the streets. They dreaded social revolution that could result in the seizure of factories, dispossession of landowners, and tampering with property rights. Although most leaders of the Provisional Government had only modest means, they were "capitalists," believing in private enterprise as the best way of promoting economic progress. Their ideal was a constitutional monarchy, its leadership entrusted to the educated and propertied elite familiar with the essentials of statecraft.

Unfortunately, the liberals misunderstood the mood of the people. Looking to the Western democracies—including, after April 1917, the United States—for political and financial support, the liberals decided to continue the war on the side of the Allies. Moreover, the new leadership considered it a matter of national honor to stand with their allies and to regain Russian land occupied by Germany. The decision antagonized the war-weary masses, along with the Russian soldiers, almost two million of whom had deserted. The liberals also antagonized the Russian peasants by not confiscating and redistributing the landlords' lands free of charge. As Russian nationalists who wanted their country to remain undivided, the liberals opposed national minorities—Finns, Ukrainians, Georgians, and others—who sought self-determination; hence, they lost the minorities' support.

The peasants began to divide the landlords' land among themselves, and more soldiers deserted in order to claim a share. The breakdown of the railways stopped factory production; enraged workers ousted factory managers and owners. Consumer goods grew scarce and prices soared, and the peasants could see no reason to sell their crops if they could buy nothing in return. Thus, the specter of

THE TSAR IN EXILE. Nicholas II and his children, living in reduced circumstances, take the sun on a roof in Tobolsk, Siberia. The imperial family was later transferred to Ekaterinburg and then murdered in 1918. (*Hulton Deutsch Collection/Getty Images.*)

famine in the cities arose. Hardships and anger mounted. Adding to the disorder were the demands of the non-Russian nationalities for self-determination and even secession.

Freedom in Russia was leading to dissolution and chaos. The largely illiterate peasant masses had no experience with or understanding of the institutions, habits, and attitudes of a free society. Without their cooperation, Russian liberalism collapsed. This outcome demonstrated the difficulty of establishing Western liberal democratic forms of government in countries lacking a sense of unity, a strong middle class, and a tradition of responsible participation in public affairs.

By July 1917, when Aleksandr Kerensky (1881–1970), a radical lawyer of great eloquence, took over the leadership of the Provisional Government, it had become clear that law and order could be upheld only by brute force. In late August and early September, a conspiracy led by an energetic young general, Lavr Kornilov, sought to establish a military dictatorship. Kornilov had the support not only of the officer corps and the tsarist officials but also of many liberals fed up with anarchy. What stopped the general was not Kerensky's government (which had no troops) but the workers of Petrograd. Their agitators demoralized Kornilov's soldiers, proving that a dictatorship of the right had no mass support. The workers also repudiated Kerensky and the Provisional Government, as well as their own moderate leaders; henceforth, they supported the Bolsheviks.

Lenin and the Rise of Bolshevism

Revolutionary movements had a long history in Russia, going back to the early nineteenth century, when educated Russians began to compare their country unfavorably with western Europe. They, too, wanted constitutional liberty and free speech in order to make their country modern. Prohibited from speaking out in public, they went underground, giving up their liberalism as ineffective. They saw revolutionary socialism, with its idealis-

WOMEN DEMONSTRATE IN PETROGRAD in 1917. The collapse of the tsarist regime was followed by a period of political fermentation, meetings, and concern about food shortages. Women demonstrated for increased bread supplies. The poster reads, "Comrades, workers, and soldiers, support our demands!" (*Sovfoto.*)

tic vision and compassion for the multitude, as a better ideology in the harsh struggle with the tsar's police. By the 1870s, many socialists had evolved into austere and self-denying professional revolutionaries who, in the service of the cause, had no moral scruples, just as the police had no scruples in the defense of the tsars. Bank robbery, murder, assassination, treachery, and terror were not seen as immoral if they served the revolutionary cause.

In the 1880s and 1890s, revolutionaries learned industrial economics and sociology from Marx; from Marxism they also acquired a vision of a universal and inevitable progression toward socialism and communism, which satisfied their semireligious craving for salvation in this world, not the next. Marxism also allied them with socialist movements in other lands, giving them an internationalist outlook. History, they believed, was on their side, as it was for all the proletarians and oppressed peoples in the world.

By 1900, a number of able young Russians had rallied to revolutionary Marxism; almost all of them were educated or came from privileged families. The most promising was Vladimir Ilyich Ulyanov, known as Lenin (1870–1924), the son of a teacher and school administrator who had attained the rank of a nobleman. Lenin had studied law but practiced revolution instead. His first contribution lay in adapting Marxism to Russian conditions; to do so, he took considerable liberties with Marx's teaching. His second contribution followed from the first: outlining the organization of an underground party capable of surviving against the tsarist police. It was to be a tightly knit conspiratorial elite of professional revolutionaries. Its headquarters would be safely located abroad, and it would have close ties to the masses, that is, to the workers and other potentially revolutionary elements.

Two other prominent Marxists were Leon Trotsky (1879–1940) and Joseph Stalin (1879–1953). Trotsky, whose original name was Lev

Bronstein, was the son of a prosperous Jewish farmer from southern Russia and was soon known for his brilliant pen. Less prominent until after the Revolution, Stalin (the man of steel) was originally named Iosif Dzhugashvili; he was from Georgia, beyond the Caucasus Mountains. Bright enough to be sent to the best school in the area, he dropped out for a revolutionary career. While they were still young, Lenin, Trotsky, and Stalin were all hardened by arrest, imprisonments, and exile to Siberia. Lenin and Trotsky later lived abroad, while Stalin, following a harsher course, stayed in Russia; for four years before 1917, he was banished to bleakest northern Siberia and conditioned to ruthlessness for life.

In 1903, the Russian Marxists split into two factions, the moderate Mensheviks, so named after finding themselves in a minority (*menshinstvo*) at a rather unrepresentative vote at the Second Party Congress, and the extremist **Bolsheviks,** who at that moment were in the majority (*bolshinstvo*). They might more accurately have been called the "softs" and the "hards." The "softs" (Mensheviks) preserved basic moral scruples; they would not stoop to crime or undemocratic methods for the sake of political success. For that the "hards" (Bolsheviks) ridiculed them, noting that a dead, imprisoned, or unsuccessful revolutionary was of little use.

Meanwhile, Lenin perfected Bolshevik revolutionary theory. He violated Marxist tradition by paying close attention to the revolutionary potential of peasants (thereby anticipating Mao Zedong). Lenin also looked closely at the numerous peoples in Asia who had recently fallen under Western imperialist domination. These people, he sensed, constituted a potential revolutionary force. In alliance with the Western—and Russian—proletariat, they might overthrow the worldwide capitalist order. The Bolsheviks, the most militant of all revolutionary socialists, were ready to assist in that gigantic struggle.

Lenin was a Russian nationalist as well as a socialist internationalist; he had a vision of a modern and powerful Russian state destined to be a model in world affairs. Russian communism was thus nationalist communism. The Bolsheviks saw the abolition of income-producing property by the dictatorship of the proletariat as the most effective way of mobilizing the country's resources. Yet the Bol-

V. I. LENIN. Red Army soldiers leaving for battle in the civil war are addressed by Lenin in Moscow in May 1920. (*Sovfoto.*)

shevik mission was also internationalist. The Russian Revolution was intended to set off a world revolution, liberating all oppressed classes and peoples around the world and achieving a higher stage of civilization.

Lenin's Opportunity

On April 16, 1917, Lenin, with German help, arrived in Petrograd from exile in Switzerland. (The Germans provided Lenin with a secret train to take him to Petrograd; they hoped that the Bolshevik leader, who wanted Russia to withdraw from the "capitalist" war, would initiate a revolution and gain power.) The Provisional Government, he said, could not possibly preserve Russia from disintegration. Most of the soldiers, workers, and peasants would repudiate the Provisional Government's cautious liberalism in favor of a regime expressing their demand for peace and land. Nothing would stop them from avenging themselves for centuries of oppression. Lenin also felt that only complete state control of the economy could rescue the country from disaster. The sole way out, he insisted, was the dictatorship of the proletariat backed by *soviets* (councils) of soldiers, workers, and peasants, particularly the poorer peasants.

Lenin prepared his party for the second stage of the Revolution of 1917: the seizure of power by the Bolsheviks. His slogan, "Peace, Land, and Bread," held a magnetic attraction for the desperate Russian masses. The Bolsheviks' determined effort to win over the disheartened soldiers proved particularly effective. Many of the people who supported the Bolsheviks interpreted Lenin's other powerful slogan—"All Power to the Soviets"—to mean that the Bolsheviks aimed to create a democratic socialist state that would institute needed social reforms. They did not anticipate the creation of Bolshevik dictatorship.

Conditions favored the Bolsheviks, as Lenin had predicted. The Bolsheviks obtained majorities in the soviets. The peasants were in active revolt, seizing the land themselves. The Provisional Government lost all control over the course of events; three years of warfare had caused the disintegration of Russian society. On November 6 (October 24 by the old calendar), Lenin urged immediate action: "The government is tottering. It must be *given the death blow* at all costs." On the following day, the Bolsheviks, meeting little resistance, seized power. Lenin permitted elections for the Constituent Assembly that had been scheduled by the Provisional Government. In a free election, the Bolsheviks received only 24 percent of the vote. After meeting once in January 1918, however, the Constituent Assembly was disbanded by the Bolsheviks.

The Bolsheviks Survive

Lenin contended that he was guiding the Russian proletariat and all humanity toward a higher social order, symbolizing—in Russia and much of the world—the rebellion of the disadvantaged against Western (or "capitalist") dominance. That is why, in 1918, he changed the name of his party from Bolshevik to Communist, which implied a concern for the human community. For Lenin, as for Marx, a world without exploitation was humanity's noblest ideal.

But staggering adversity confronted Lenin after his seizure of power. In the prevailing anarchy, Russia lay open to the German armies. Under the Treaty of Brest-Litovsk, signed in March 1918—the lowest point in Russian history for over two hundred years—Russia lost Finland, Poland, and the Baltic provinces, all regions inhabited largely by non-Russians. It also lost the rebellious Ukraine, its chief industrial base and breadbasket. Yet Lenin, with the country in shambles, had no choice but to accept the humiliating terms.

THE WAR AND EUROPEAN CONSCIOUSNESS

"There will be wars as never before on earth," predicted Nietzsche. World War I bore him out. Modern technology enabled the combatants to kill with unprecedented efficiency; modern nationalism infused both civilians and soldiers with the determination to fight until the enemy was totally beaten. Exercising wide control over its citizens, the modern state mobilized its human, material, and spiritual resources to wage total war. As the war hardened into a savage stalemate, statesmen did not press for a compromise peace but rather demanded ever more mobilization, ever more escalation, and ever more sacrifices.

The Great War profoundly altered the course of Western civilization, deepening the spiritual crisis that had produced it. How could one speak of the inviolability of the individual when Europe had become a slaughterhouse, or of the primacy of reason when nations permitted the slaughter to go unabated for four years? How could the mind cope with this spectacle of a civilization turning against itself, destroying itself in an orgy of organized violence? How could it explain students leaving their schoolbooks to become, as one participant said, "nocturnal beasts of prey hunting each other in packs"?[33] A young French soldier, shortly before he was killed at Verdun, expressed the disillusionment that gripped the soldiers in the trenches: "Humanity is mad! It must be mad to do what it is doing. What a massacre! What scenes of horror and carnage, I cannot find words to translate my impressions. Hell cannot be so terrible. Men are mad!"[34] The war, said British poet Robert Graves, provoked an "inward scream" that still reverberates. The agony caused by the astronomical casualty figures—some 9.4 million dead and twenty-one million wounded, many of them pathetically mutilated and disfigured—touched millions of homes. Now only the naive could believe in continuous progress, a principal dogma of nineteenth-century liberal culture. Western civilization had entered an age of violence, anxiety, and doubt.

World War I was a great turning point in the history of the West. The war left many with the gnawing feeling that Western civilization had lost its vitality and was caught in a rhythm of breakdown. It seemed that Western civilization was fragile and perishable, that Western people, despite their extraordinary accomplishments, were never more than a step or two away from barbarism. Surely, any civilization that could allow such senseless slaughter to last four years had entered its decline and could look forward to only the darkest of futures.

European intellectuals were demoralized and disillusioned. The orderly, peaceful, rational world of their youth had been destroyed. The Enlightenment world-view, weakened in the nineteenth century by the assault of romantics, Social Darwinists, extreme nationalists, race mystics, and glorifiers of the irrational, was now disintegrating. The enormity of the war had shattered faith in the capacity of reason to deal with crucial social and political questions. It appeared that civilization was fighting an unending and seemingly hopeless battle against the irrational elements in human nature and that war would be a continuous phenomenon in the twentieth century.

Scientific research had produced more efficient weapons to kill and maim Europe's youth. The achievements of Western science and technology, which had been viewed as a boon for humanity and the clearest testament to the superiority of European civilization, were called into question. Confidence in the future gave way to doubt. The old beliefs in the perfectibility of humanity, the blessings of science, and ongoing progress now seemed an expression of naive optimism, if not post-Christian myths that the war had exposed as fraudulent. As A. J. P. Taylor concludes,

> *The First World War was difficult to fit into the picture of a rational civilization advancing by ordered stages. The civilized men of the twentieth century had outdone in savagery the barbarians of all preceding ages, and their civilized virtues—organization, mechanical skill, self-sacrifice—had made war's savagery all the more terrible. Modern man had developed powers which he was not fit to use. European civilization had been weighed in the balance and found wanting.*[35]

Western civilization had lost its spiritual center. The French writer Paul Valéry summed up the mood of a troubled generation, for whom the sun seemed to be setting on the Enlightenment:

> *The storm has died away, and still we are restless, uneasy as if the storm were about to break. Almost all the affairs of men remain in a terrible uncertainty. We think of what has disappeared, and we are almost destroyed by what has been destroyed; we do not know what will be born, and we fear the future, not without reason. We hope vaguely, we dread precisely; our fears are infinitely more precise than our hopes; we confess that the charm of life is behind us. There is no thinking man . . . who can hope to dominate this anxiety, to escape from this impression of darkness. . . . But among all these injured things is the Mind. The Mind has indeed been cruelly wounded; its complaint is heard in the hearts of intellectual men; it passes a mournful judgment on itself. It doubts itself profoundly.*[36]

Having lost confidence in the power of reason to solve the problems of the human community, in liberal doctrines of individual freedom, and in the institutions of parliamentary democracy, many people turned to fascism as a simple saving faith. Far from making the world safe for democracy, as Wilson and other liberals had hoped, World War I gave rise to totalitarian movements, which would nearly destroy democracy.

KÄTHE KOLLWITZ: THE SURVIVORS (1922). With an estimated ten million dead and twenty-one million wounded, World War I shattered the hope that western Europe had been making continuous progress toward a rational and enlightened civilization. (*National Gallery of Art, Washington, D.C., Rosenwald Collection © Estates of Käthe Kollwitz, Artistic Rights Society [ARS], New York 1991.*)

The war produced a generation of young people who had reached their maturity in combat. Violence had become a way of life for millions of soldiers hardened by battle and for millions of civilians aroused by four years of propaganda. The relentless massacre of Europe's young men had a brutalizing effect. Violence, cruelty, suffering, and even wholesale death seemed to be natural and acceptable components of human existence. The sanctity of the individual seemed to be liberal and Christian claptrap.

The fascination with violence and contempt for life persisted in the postwar world. Many returned veterans yearned for the excitement of battle and the fellowship of the trenches—what one French soldier called "the most tender human experience." After the war, a young English officer reminisced: "There was an exaltation, in those days of comradeship and dedication, that would have come in few other ways."[37] A fraternal bond united the men of the trenches. Many veterans also shared a primitive attraction to war's fury. A Belgian veteran expressed it this way:

> *The plain truth is that if I were to obey my native animal instincts—and there was little hope for anything else while I was in the trenches—I should enlist again in any future*

war, or take part in any sort of fighting, merely to experience again that voluptuous thrill of the human brute who realizes his power to take away life from other human beings who try to do the same to him. What was first accepted as a moral duty became a habit and the habit . . . had become a need.[38]

And no doubt Julian Grenfell spoke for many other combat soldiers when he declared in November 1914: "I *adore* war. I have never been so well or so happy. . . . The fighting excitement vitalizes everything, every sight and word and action."[39] The brutalizing effect of the war is evident in this statement by a German soldier, for whom the war never ended:

People told us that the War was over. That made us laugh. We ourselves are the War. Its flame burns strongly in us. It envelops our whole being and fascinates us with the enticing urge to destroy. We . . . marched onto the battlefields of the postwar world just as we had gone into battle on the Western Front: singing, reckless, and filled with the joy of adventure as we marched to the attack; silent, deadly, remorseless in battle.[40]

The British novelist D. H. Lawrence (1885–1930) understood that the brutality and hate unleashed by the war had ruined old Europe and would give rise to even greater evils. On the day the armistice was signed, he warned prophetically:

I suppose you think the war is over and that we shall go back to the kind of world you lived in before it. But the war isn't over. The hate and evil is greater now than ever. Very soon war will break out again and overwhelm you. . . .The crowd outside thinks that Germany is crushed forever. But the Germans will soon rise again. Europe is done for. . . . The war isn't over. Even if the fighting should stop, the evil will be worse because the hate will be dammed up in men's hearts and will show itself in all sorts of ways.[41]

The veterans who aspired to recapture the exhilaration experienced in combat made ideal recruits for extremist political movements that glorified action and promised to rescue society from a decadent liberalism. Hitler and Mussolini, both ex-soldiers imbued with the ferocity of the front, knew how to appeal to them. The lovers of violence and the harbingers of hate who took control of fascist parties would come within a hairsbreadth of destroying Western civilization. The intensified nationalist hatreds following World War I also helped fuel the fires of World War II. The Germans vowed to regain lands lost to the Poles. Some Germans, like the embittered Hitler, were consumed by anguish over a defeat that they believed never should have happened and over the humiliating Treaty of Versailles; a desire for revenge festered in their souls. Italy, too, felt aggrieved because it had not received more territory from the dismembered Austro-Hungarian Empire. Mussolini would cleverly exploit these feelings in his bid for power.

Yet, while some veterans clung to an aggressive militarism, others aspired to build a more humane world. Such veterans embraced democratic and socialist ideals and resolved that the bloodbath would never be repeated. Tortured by memories of war, European intellectuals wrote pacifist plays and novels and signed pacifist declarations. Indeed, in the 1930s, an attitude of "peace at any price" discouraged resistance to Nazi Germany in its bid to dominate Europe.

During World War I, new weapons were introduced, particularly the tank and the fighter plane, which revolutionized the future of warfare. Just prior to World War II, imaginative military planners recognized that planes and tanks, properly deployed, could penetrate and smash the enemy's defenses, circumventing the stalemate of trench warfare. Planes also meant terror from the skies, for bombs could pulverize a city, killing and maiming tens of thousands of civilians.

World War I was total war; it encompassed the entire nation and had no limits. States demanded total victory and total commitment from their citizens. They regulated industrial production, developed sophisticated propaganda techniques to strengthen morale, and exercised ever greater control over the lives of their people, organizing and disciplining them like soldiers. This total mobilization of nations' human and material resources provided a model for future dictators. With ever-greater effectiveness and ruthlessness, dictators would centralize power and manipulate thinking.

The ruthless dictatorships that emerged in Russia, Germany, and Italy were products of the war. The war gave Communists the opportunity to seize power in Russia, and the mentality of the front helped to mold the fascist movements that emerged in Italy and Germany. And both Hitler and Stalin

drew a moral lesson from the immense loss of life in the trenches: a desired political end justifies vast human sacrifices. The barbarism of the trenches would be eclipsed in the postwar era by the horrors inflicted on people by totalitarian regimes.

❖   ❖   ❖

Online Study Center ACE the Test

NOTES

1. Arnold Toynbee, *Surviving the Future* (New York: Oxford University Press, 1971), pp. 106–107.

2. Quoted in Roland N. Stromberg, *Redemption by War* (Lawrence: Regents Press of Kansas, 1982), p. 24.

3. Excerpted in John W. Boyer and Jan Goldstein, eds., *Twentieth Century Europe*, vol. 9 of *University of Chicago Readings in Western Civilization*, ed. John W. Boyer and Julius Kirshner (Chicago: University of Chicago Press, 1987), p. 26.

4. Heinrich von Treitschke, *Politics*, excerpted in *Germany's War Mania* (New York: Dodd, Mead, 1915), pp. 222–223.

5. Friedrich von Bernhardi, *Germany and the Next War,* trans. Allan H. Fowles (New York: Longmans, Green, and Company, 1914), pp. 18, 24.

6. Quoted in James Joll, "The Unspoken Assumptions," in *The Origins of the First World War*, ed. H. W. Koch (New York: Taplinger, 1972), p. 325.

7. Quoted in Barbara Tuchman, *The Guns of August* (New York: Macmillan, 1962), pp. 46–47.

8. Fritz Fischer, *Germany's Aims in the First World War* (New York: Norton, 1967), p. 88.

9. Quoted in Joachim Remak, *The Origins of World War I* (New York: Holt, 1967), p. 135.

10. Rupert Brooke, "Peace," in *Collected Poems of Rupert Brooke* (New York: Dodd, Mead, 1941), p. 111.

11. Quoted in Joachim C. Fest, *Hitler* (New York: Harcourt Brace Jovanovich, 1973), p. 66.

12. Roland Dorgelàs, "After Fifty Years," in *Promise of Greatness*, ed. George A. Panichas (New York: John Day, 1968), pp. 14–15.

13. Excerpted in Joe H. Kirchberger, ed., *The First World War: An Eyewitness to History* (New York: Facts on File, 1992), p. 45.

14. Quoted in Tuchman, *The Guns of August*, p. 145.

15. Bertrand Russell, *The Autobiography of Bertrand Russell, 1914–1944* (Boston: Little, Brown, 1968), pp. 4, 6.

16. Quoted in Robert G. L. Waite, *Vanguard of Nazism* (New York: Norton, 1969), p. 22.

17. Brooke, "Peace," p. 111.

18. Quoted in Peter Gay, *Freud: A Life for Our Time* (New York: Norton), p. 348.

19. Quoted in Koch, *Origins of the First World War*, p. 318.

20. Stefan Zweig, *The World of Yesterday* (New York: Viking, 1970), p. 223.

21. Quoted in Tuchman, *Guns of August*, p. 51.

22. A. J. P. Taylor, *A History of the First World War* (New York: Berkeley, 1966), p. 84.

23. Quoted in Richard M. Watt, *Dare Call It Treason* (New York: Simon & Schuster, 1963), p. 215.

24. Quoted in Daniel M. Smith, *The Great Departure* (New York: Wiley, 1965), p. 20.

25. Quoted in S. L. A. Marshall, *The American Heritage History of World War I* (New York: Dell, 1966), p. 334.

26. Quoted in John Terraine, *To Win a War: 1918, the Year of Victory* (Garden City, N.Y.: Doubleday, 1981), p. 102.

27. Excerpted in Louis L. Snyder, ed., *Historic Documents of World War I* (Princeton, N.J.: Van Nostrand, 1958), p. 183.

28. Thomas A. Bailey, *Woodrow Wilson and the Lost Peace* (Chicago: Quadrangle Books, 1963), p. 29.

29. Ibid., p. 209.

30. Hajo Holborn, *The Political Collapse of Europe* (New York: Knopf, 1966), p. 102.

31. Quoted in Bailey, *Woodrow Wilson,* p. 303.

32. Excerpted in Ronald Kowalski, *The Russian Revolution, 1917–1921* (New York: Routledge, 1997), p. 20.

33. Quoted in Michael Adas, *Machines as the Measure of Man* (Ithaca, N.Y.: Cornell University Press, 1989), p. 376.

34. Quoted in Alistair Horne, *The Price of Glory* (New York: Harper, 1967), p. 240.

35. A. J. P. Taylor, *From Sarajevo to Potsdam* (New York: Harcourt, Brace & World, 1966), pp. 55–56.

36. Paul Valéry, *Variety* (New York: Harcourt, Brace, 1927), pp. 27–28.

37. Quoted in Modris Eksteins, *Rites of Spring: The Great War and the Birth of the Modern Age* (New York: Doubleday Anchor Books, 1989), p. 232.

38. Quoted in Eric J. Leed, *No Man's Land: Combat and Identity in World War I* (New York: Cambridge University Press, 1979), p. 201.

39. Quoted in Reginald Pound, *The Lost Generation of 1914* (New York: Coward-McCann, 1964), p. 80.

40. Quoted in Robert G. L. Waite, *Vanguard of Nazism* (New York: Norton, 1969), p. 42.

41. Quoted in Samuel Hynes, *A War Imagined* (New York: Atheneum, 1991), p. 266.

Suggested Reading

Joll, James, *The Origins of the First World War* (1984). Excellent work of synthesis.

Koch, H. W., ed., *The Origins of the First World War* (1972). Useful essays, particularly those dealing with the glorification of war before 1914.

Lafore, Laurence, *The Long Fuse* (1971). A beautifully written study of the causes of the conflict.

Leed, Eric J., *No Man's Land: Combat and Identity in World War I* (1979). The impact of the war on the men who participated in it.

Service, Robert, *The Russian Revolution, 1900–1927* (1990). A brief overview.

Strachan, Hew, ed., *The Oxford Illustrated History of the First World War* (1998). Essays by an international team of specialists on many phases of the war.

Stromberg, Roland N., *Redemption by War: The Intellectuals and 1914* (1982). Analysis of the reasons why so many intellectuals welcomed the war.

Tuchman, Barbara, *The Guns of August* (1962). A beautifully written account of the opening weeks of World War I.

Winter, J. M., *The Experience of World War I* (1995). Excellent illustrations and eyewitness accounts are integrated into a gripping narrative.

Chapter 30

An Era of Totalitarianism

Carefully orchestrated to show the irresistible might of the Nazi movement, the Nuremberg rallies were among the greatest theatrical performances of the twentieth century. (Bettmann/CORBIS.)

Focus Questions

1. What are the distinctive features of a totalitarian state?

2. What motivated Stalin to make terror a government policy? What motivated Communist bureaucrats to participate in Stalin's inhumanities?

3. What were the essential features of the fascist movements that arose in Europe after World War I?

4. What were Hitler's attitudes toward liberalism, war, race, the Jews, and propaganda?

5. In what ways did Nazism conflict with the core values of both the Enlightenment and Christianity? Why did the Nazi regime attract so many supporters?

6. What lessons might democratic societies draw from the Nazi experience?

Online Study Center

This icon will direct you to interactive map and primary source activities on the website http://college.hmco.com/pic/perrywc8e.

*I*n the 1930s, the term **totalitarianism** was used to describe the Fascist regime in Italy, the National Socialist regime in Germany, and the Communist regime in the Soviet Union. To a degree that far exceeds the ancient tyrannies and early modern autocratic states, these dictatorships aspired to and, with varying degrees of success, attained control over the individual's consciousness and behavior and all phases of political, social, and cultural life. To many people it seemed that a crises-riddled democracy was dying and that the future belonged to these dynamic totalitarian movements.

Totalitarianism is a twentieth-century phenomenon, for such all-embracing control over the individual and society could be achieved only in an age of modern ideology, technology, and bureaucracy. The totalitarian state was more completely established in Germany and the Soviet Union than in Italy, where cultural and historic conditions impeded the realization of the totalitarian goal of monolithic unity and total control.

In *Totalitarian Dictatorship and Autocracy* (1956), Carl J. Friedrich and Zbigniew K. Brzezinski viewed fascist and communist dictatorships as "historically unique and **sui generis**"[1]—different in nature from ancient oriental despotisms, the Roman Empire, the tyrannies of the Renaissance city-states, or the absolute monarchies of modern Europe. "Broadly speaking, totalitarian dictatorship is a new development; there has never been anything quite like it before." They contended further that "fascist and communist totalitarian dictatorships are basically alike."[2] True the ideological aims and social and economic policies of Hitler and Stalin differed fundamentally. However, both Soviet Russia and Nazi Germany shared the totalitarian goal of total domination of the individual and institutions and employed similar methods to achieve it. Mussolini's Italy is more accurately called *authoritarian,* for the party-state either did not intend to control all phases of life or lacked the means to do so. Moreover, Mussolini hesitated to use the ruthless methods that Hitler and Stalin employed so readily.

THE NATURE OF TOTALITARIANISM

Striving for total unity, control, and obedience, the totalitarian dictatorship is the antithesis of liberal democracy. It abolishes all competing political parties, suppresses individual liberty, eliminates or regulates private institutions, and utilizes the modern state's bureaucracy and technology to impose its ideology and enforce its commands. The one party-state determines what people should believe—what values they should hold. There is no room for individual thinking, private moral judgment, or individual conscience. The individual possesses no natural rights that the state must respect. The state regards individuals merely as building blocks, human material to be hammered and hewed into a new social order. It seeks to create an efficiently organized and stable society—one whose members do not raise troublesome questions or hold unorthodox opinions.

Nevertheless, the totalitarian dictatorship is also an unintended consequence of liberal democracy. It emerged in an age in which, because of the French and Industrial Revolutions, the masses had become a force in political life. The totalitarian leader seeks to gain and preserve power by harnessing mass support. Hitler, in particular, built a party within the existing constitutional system and exploited the electoral process in order to overthrow the democratic government.

Unlike previous dictatorial regimes, the dictatorships of both the left and the right sought to legitimatize their rule by gaining the masses' approval. They claimed that their governments were higher and truer expressions of the people's will. The Soviet and Nazi dictatorships established their rule in the name of the people—the German Volk or the Soviet proletariat.

A distinctive feature of totalitarianism is the overriding importance of the leader, who is seen as infallible and invincible. The masses' slavish adulation of the leader and their uncritical acceptance of the dogma that the leader or the party is always right promote loyalty, dedication, and obedience and distort rational thinking.

Totalitarian leaders want more than power for its own sake; in the last analysis, they seek to transform the world according to an all-embracing ideology, a set of convictions and beliefs that, says Hannah Arendt, "pretend[s] to know the mysteries of the whole historical process—the secrets of the past, the intricacies of the present, the uncertainties of the future."[3] The ideology constitutes a higher and infallible truth based on a law of history or social development that, says Karl Dietrich Bracher, "reduce[s] the past and the future to a single historical principle of struggle, no matter whether by state, nation, people, race, or class."[4] The ideology contains a dazzling vision of the future—a secular New Jerusalem—that strengthens the will of the faithful and attracts converts. "This utopian and **chiliastic** outlook of totalitarian ideologies," declare Friedrich and Brzezinski, "gives them a pseudoreligious quality. In fact, they often elicit in the less critical followers a depth of conviction and a fervor of devotion usually found only among persons inspired by a transcendent faith."[5] Like a religion, the totalitarian ideology provides its adherents with beliefs that make society and history intelligible, that explain all of existence in an emotionally gratifying way. A distinguishing feature of both communist and Nazi ideologies was the dogmatic belief that conflict—between classes for Marxists and between nations and races for Nazis—was the driving force in history.

The ideology—a "grand transcendent fiction [or] *metamyth*" in Brzezinski's apt phrase—promises to transform the social order in accordance with an ultimate and exclusive truth propagated by the party, thereby satisfying a human yearning for complete certitude.[6] Like a religion, it creates true believers, who feel that they are participating in a great cause—a heroic fight against evil—that gives meaning to their lives. During World War II, a German soldier fighting on the eastern front wrote to his brother that the battle "is for a new ideology, a new belief, a new life! I am glad that I can participate. . . . in this war of light and darkness."[7]

Also like a religion, the totalitarian party gives isolated and alienated individuals a sense of belonging, a feeling of camaraderie; it enables a person to lose himself or herself in the comforting and exhilarating embrace of a mass movement. The radical Russian anarchist Bakunin had sensed the seductive power of the community when he stated: "I do not want to be I, I want to be We."[8]

Not only did the totalitarian religion-ideology supply followers with a cause that claimed absolute goodness; it also provided a Devil. For the Soviets, the source of evil and the cause of all the

Chronology 30.1 ❖ Totalitarianism

November 1917	Bolsheviks, led by Lenin, take command in Russia
1918–20	Civil war and foreign intervention in Russia
March 1918	Treaty of Brest-Litovsk
July 1918	Nicholas II of Russia and his family are murdered
March 1919	Communist International is formed
1921–28	New Economic Policy
1922	Stalin becomes general secretary of the Communist party
1922	Mussolini rises to power
1923	Hitler's failed Beer Hall Putsch and subsequent imprisonment
January 1924	Lenin dies
1924	Constitution of the Union of Soviet Socialist Republics takes effect
1928	First Five-Year Plan starts rapid industrialization in Russia
October 1929	The Great Depression begins
1929	Stalin in sole command in Russia; collectivization of agriculture begins
1933	Hitler elected chancellor of Germany
1936	Stalin constitution: socialism achieved
1936–38	Stalin's terror purges
1936–39	Spanish Civil War
November 1938	Nazi pogrom—*Kristallnacht*
1939	Hitler invades Poland; World War II breaks out
June 1941	Hitler invades the Soviet Union

people's hardships were the degenerate capitalists, reactionary peasants who resisted collectivization, the traitorous Trotskyites, or the saboteurs and foreign agents, who impeded the realization of the socialist society. For the Nazis, the Devil was the conspirator Jew. These "evil" ones must be eliminated in order to realize the totalitarian movement's vision of the future.

Thus, totalitarian regimes liquidate large segments of the population designated as "enemies of the people." Historical necessity or a higher purpose demands and justifies their liquidation. The appeal to historical necessity has all the power of a great myth. Presented as a world-historical struggle between the forces of good and the forces of evil, the myth incites fanaticism and numbs the conscience. Traditional rules of moral-

ity have no meaning; seemingly decent people engage in terrible acts of brutality with no remorse, convinced that they are waging a righteous war.

Totalitarians are utopians inspired by idealism; they seek the salvation of their nation, their race, or humanity. They believe that the victory of their cause will usher in the millennium, a state of harmony and bliss. Such a vision is attractive to people burdened by economic insecurity or spiritual disorientation. The history of the twentieth century demonstrates how easily utopian beliefs can be twisted into paranoid fantasies, idealistic sentiments transformed into murderous fanaticism, and destructive components of human nature mobilized and directed by demagogues.

Unlike earlier autocratic regimes, the totalitarian dictatorship is not satisfied with its subjects' outward obedience; it demands the masses' unconditional loyalty and enthusiastic support. It strives to control the inner person: to shape thoughts, feelings, and attitudes in accordance with the party ideology, which becomes an official creed. It does not rule by brute force alone but seeks to create a "new man," one who dedicates himself body and soul to the party and its ideology. Such unquestioning, faithful subjects can be manipulated by the party. The disinterested search for truth, justice, and goodness—the exploration of those fundamental moral, political, and religious questions that have characterized the Western intellectual tradition for centuries—is abandoned. Truth, justice, and goodness are what the party deems them to be, and ideological deviation is forbidden.

The totalitarian dictatorship deliberately politicizes all areas of human activity. Ideology pervades works of literature, history, philosophy, art, and even science. It dominates the school curriculum and influences everyday speech and social relations. The state is concerned with everything its citizens do: there is no distinction between public and private life, and every institution comes under the party-state's authority. If voluntary support for the regime cannot be generated by indoctrination, then the state unhesitatingly resorts to terror and violence to compel obedience. People live under a constant strain. Fear of the secret police is ever present; it produces a permanent state of insecurity, which induces people to do everything that the regime asks of them and to watch what they say and do.

COMMUNIST RUSSIA

In 1918, Lenin's infant Communist government was threatened with civil war. Tsarist officers had gathered troops in the south; other anticommunist centers rose in Siberia, and still others in the extreme north and along the Baltic coast. The political orientation of these anticommunist groups, generally called *Whites* in contrast to the communist *Reds,* combined all shades of opinion, from moderate socialist to reactionary, the latter usually predominating. The Whites received support from foreign governments, which freely intervened. Until their own revolution in November 1918, the Germans occupied much of southern Russia. England, France, and the United States sent troops to points in northern and southern European Russia; England, Japan, and the United States also sent troops to Siberia. At first they wanted to offset German expansion, but later they hoped to overthrow the Communist regime. In May and June 1918, Czech prisoners of war, about to be evacuated, precipitated anticommunist uprisings along the Trans-Siberian Railroad, bringing the civil war to fever pitch.

In July 1918, Communists murdered Nicholas II and his entire family. In August, a noncommunist socialist nearly assassinated Lenin, while White forces in the south moved to cut off central Russia from its food supply. In response, the Communists speeded the buildup of their own Red Army. Recruited from the remnants of the tsarist army and its officer corps, the Red Army was reinforced by compulsory military service and strict discipline; Trotsky reintroduced the death penalty, which had been outlawed by the Provisional Government. Threatened with death if they refused, many tsarist officers served in the Red Army. They were closely watched by Trotsky's ruthless political commissars, who were also responsible for the political reliability and morale of the troops. Trotsky ordered the formation of "blocking units" to machine-gun retreating soldiers. The civil war was brutal; both sides butchered civilians and their own comrades.

In November 1918, thanks to the Allied victory and the American contribution to it, the German menace ended. Yet foreign intervention stepped up in response to the formation of the Communist International (Comintern), an organization founded by Lenin to guide the international revolutionary movement that he expected to issue from the world war. Lenin sought revolutionary support from abroad for strengthening his hand at home; his enemies reached into Russia to defeat at its source the revolution that they feared in their own countries. At the same time, the civil war rose to its climax.

Hard-pressed as Lenin's party was, by the autumn of 1920 it had prevailed over its enemies. The Whites were divided among themselves and discredited by their association with the tsarist regime; the Communists had greater popular support, the advantage of interior communications, and superior political skills. The war-weary foreign interventionists called off their efforts to overthrow the Communist regime by force.

The communist victory in the civil war exacted a staggering price. Reds and Whites alike carried the tsarist tradition of political violence to a new pitch of horror (some of it later described in novels by Boris Pasternak and Mikhail Sholokhov). The entire population, including the Communist party and its leaders, suffered in the war. Some 1.2 million combatants on both sides perished. In addition, the Communists killed some 250,000 peasants who resisted grain requisitions and executed tens of thousands of political opponents. Adding to the death toll were some 100,000 Jews, victims of pogroms perpetrated largely by the Whites. Compounding the nation's anguish was the famine of 1921–22, which claimed some five million victims.

War Communism and the New Economic Policy

Besides the extreme misery brought on by the world war and civil war, the Russian people had to endure the rigors of the policy known as "war communism." It was introduced in 1918 to deal with the plummeting agricultural and economic production, rampant inflation, and desperate hunger in the cities. Under war **communism,** the state took over the means of production and greatly limited private ownership; it conscripted labor and, in effect, confiscated grain from the peasants. War communism devastated the economy even further and alienated workers and peasants. The state-run factories were mismanaged, workers stayed away from their jobs or performed poorly, and peasants resisted the food requisition detachments that the government sent to seize their grain.

There was even open rebellion. In March 1921, sailors at the Kronstadt naval base and workers in nearby Petrograd—people who in 1917 had been ready to give their lives for the Revolution—rose against the repression that had been introduced during the civil war; they called for the establishment of socialist democracy. Trotsky ruthlessly suppressed that uprising, but the lesson was clear: the Communist regime had to retreat from war communism and to restore a measure of stability to the country.

In 1921, the Communist party adopted the New Economic Policy (NEP), which lasted until 1928. Under a system that Lenin characterized as "state socialism," the government retained control of finance, industry, and transportation—"the commanding heights" of the economy—but allowed the rest of the economy to return to private enterprise. Peasants, after giving part of their crops to the government, were free to sell the rest in the open market; traders could buy and sell as they pleased. With the resumption of small-scale capitalism, an air of normal life returned.

One-Party Dictatorship

While the Communists were waging a fierce struggle against the Whites, they instituted a militant dictatorship run by their party. Numbering about five hundred thousand members in 1921, the Communist party was controlled by a small, intimate group, the politburo (political bureau), which assumed a dictatorial role. The key leaders—Lenin, Trotsky, Stalin, and a few others—determined policy, assigned tasks, and appointed important officials. The party dominated all public agencies; its leaders held the chief positions in government. No other political parties were tolerated, and trade unions became agents of the regime. Never before had the people of Russia been forced into such compulsory unity and abject dependence on their government.

Impatient with the endless disputes among righteous and strong-willed old revolutionaries, Lenin, in agreement with other top leaders, demanded unconditional submission to his decisions. He even ordered that dissidents be disciplined and political enemies be terrorized. No price was too high to achieve monolithic party unity. Believing that they were creating a new and better society that would serve as a model for the rest of humanity, the Communists felt no moral objection to the use of force or even terror, including executions and forced-labor camps. The dreaded Cheka, a ruthless secret police organization, executed some two hundred thousand people from 1919 to 1925. The means Lenin employed for ruling his backward country denied the human values that Marx had taken from the Enlightenment and put into his vision of a socialist society. Lenin was perfectly willing to use state terror to promote the class struggle.

The Communists abolished the power of the Orthodox church, which was the traditional ally of tsarism and the enemy of innovation. They were militant atheists, believing with Marx that religion was the "opium of the people"; God had no place in their vision of a better society. Above all, they wiped out—by expropriation, discrimination, expulsion, and execution—the educated upper class of bureaucrats, landowners, professional people, and industrialists.

The Communist party promised "to liberate woman from all the burdens of antiquated methods of housekeeping, by replacing them by house-communes, public kitchens, central laundries, nurseries, etc."[9] But traditional values, particularly in the Asian parts of the Soviet Union, hardly favored equality between the sexes, especially in political work. The practical necessity of combining work with family responsibility, moreover, tended to keep women out of managerial positions in the party and the organizations of the state, but the ideal remained alive.

The Communists never ceased to stress that they worked strenuously for the welfare of the vast majority of the population. They received much acclaim for their emphasis on providing housing, food, and clothing and making education, theater, and other cultural activities, previously reserved for the elite, available to the masses. Although the Communists were not opposed to some private ownership of property, they outlawed income-producing property that enabled capitalists to employ (or exploit, as the Communists said) others for their own profit.

For Lenin, socialism meant reeducating the unruly masses to higher standards of individual conduct and economic productivity that would be superior to capitalism. In the spring of 1918, he complained that Russian workers had not yet matched capitalist performance: "The Russian worker is a bad worker compared with the workers of the advanced, i.e., western countries." To overcome this deficiency, Lenin urged competition—socialist competition—and hammered home the need for "iron discipline at work" and "unquestioning obedience" to a single will, that of the Communist party. There was no alternative: "Large-scale machinery calls for absolute and strict unity of will, which directs the joint labors of hundreds and thousands and tens of thousands of people. A thousand wills are subordinated to one will."[10]

In those words lay the essence of subsequent Soviet industrialization. The economy was to be monolithic, rationally planned, and focused on pursuing a single goal: overcoming the weaknesses of Russia so disastrously demonstrated in the war. Allowing workers to make their own decisions, Lenin held, would perpetuate Russian backwardness. Instead, he called for a new "consciousness," a hard-driving work ethic expressed in the Russian Marxist revolutionary vocabulary.

In attempting to transform their Soviet Russia into a modern industrialized state that would serve as a model for the world, the Communists imposed a new autocracy even more authoritarian than the old. In order to survive, Russia would be rebuilt against the people's will, if necessary. In the view of the party leaders, the masses always needed firm guidance. The minds of the people, therefore, came under unprecedented government control. In education, from kindergarten through university, in the press, on radio, and in literature and the arts, the Communist party tried to fashion people's thoughts to create the proper "consciousness."

The party made Marxism-Leninism the sole source of truth, eliminating as best it could all rival creeds, whether religious, political, or philosophical. Thinking was to be as reliably uniform as a machine process and totally committed to the party. Moreover, thoughts were to be protected against subversive capitalist influences. Soviet Russia, the party boasted, had risen to a superior plane of social existence and would attract other revolutionary states to its federal union until eventually it covered the entire world. Lest Soviet citizens doubt their new superiority, the party prohibited all uncontrolled comparison with other countries.

Lenin molded Soviet Russia into an international revolutionary force, the champion of anticapitalism and of the liberation of colonial peoples. The Russian Revolution inspired nationalistic ambitions for political self-determination and cultural self-assertion among a growing number of peoples around the world, especially in Asia. It appealed particularly to intellectuals educated in the West (or in westernized schools) yet identifying themselves with their downtrodden compatriots.

To have a political tool for world revolution, Lenin created the Communist—or Third—International (Comintern). The most radical successor to earlier socialist international associations, it helped organize small Communist parties in western Europe, which in time became dependable, though rather powerless, agents of Soviet Russia. In Asia, where no proletariat existed, Lenin tried to work closely with incipient nationalist movements. Lenin and the Bolshevik Revolution gained the admiration and instinctive loyalty of colonial and semicolonial people in what would come to be called the Third World.

In 1923, a new constitution laid down federal guidelines for Soviet Russia, henceforth officially known as the Union of Soviet Socialist Republics (U.S.S.R.) or the Soviet Union. Having captured the attention of the world, the Soviet Union now stood out as the communist alternative to the capitalist West.

The Stalin Revolution

Lenin died in 1924, and the task of achieving the goal that he had set was taken up by Stalin. The "man of steel" was crude and vulgar, toughened by the revolutionary underground and tsarist prisons and by the roughest aspects of Russian life. Relentlessly energetic but relatively inconspicuous among key Bolsheviks, Stalin had been given, in 1922, the unwanted and seemingly routine task of general secretary of the party. He used this position to his own advantage, building up a reliable party cadre—apparatus men, or *apparatchiki*, as they came to be called—and dominating the party as not even Lenin had done. When he was challenged, particularly by Trotsky and his associates, in the protracted struggles for the succession to Lenin, it was too late to unseat him. None of Stalin's rivals could rally the necessary majorities at the party congresses; none could match Stalin's skill in party infighting or in making rough and anarchic people into docile members of the Communist party apparatus.

Online Study Center

Improve Your Grade
Primary Source: Stalin's Rise to Power: A Biased but Accurate Analysis

Industrialization. To Stalin, Russia's most pressing need was not world revolution but the fastest possible buildup of Soviet power through industrialization. The country could not afford to risk near-annihilation again, as it had done in the world war and then in the civil war. Communist pride dictated that the country be made as strong as possible. Stalin set forth the stark reckoning of Russian history in a speech delivered in 1931, three years after launching a program of massive industrialization:

> *Those who fall behind get beaten, But we do not want to be beaten. No, we refuse to be beaten. One feature of the history of old Russia was the continual beatings she suffered for falling behind, for her backwardness. All beat her—for her backwardness, for military backwardness, cultural backwardness, political backwardness, for industrial backwardness, for agricultural backwardness. She was beaten because to do so was profitable and could be done with impunity. . . . You are backward, you are weak—therefore you are wrong, hence you can be beaten and enslaved. You are mighty, therefore you are right, hence we must be wary of you. Such is the law of the exploiters. . . . That is why we must no longer lag behind.*[11]

Stalin decided on all-out industrialization at the expense of the toiling masses. Peasants and workers, already poor, would be required to make tremendous sacrifices of body and spirit to overcome the nation's weaknesses.

Abandoning the NEP, Stalin decreed a series of Five-Year Plans, the first and most experimental one commencing in 1928. The industrialization drive was heralded as a vast economic and social revolution, undertaken by the state according to a rational plan. The emphasis lay on heavy industry: the construction of railroads, power plants, steel mills, and military hardware, such as

FORCED LABOR IN THE GULAG. All those accused of disloyalty to the party and not killed outright ended up in one of the gulags, or forced-labor camps. Forced labor was designed as a punishment and also as a means of obtaining raw materials from inhospitable regions in the far north. In this photo, deported peasants and political prisoners using primitive technology are engaged in constructing the canal linking Leningrad with the White Sea. Millions perished in the gulags. (*David King Collection, London, England.*)

tanks and warplanes. Production of consumer goods was cut to the minimum, and all small-scale private trading, revived under the NEP, came to an end—with disastrous results for the standard of living. Having just come within sight of their pre-1914 standard of living, Russians now found their expectations dashed.

A new grim age of drastic material hardships and profound anguish began. Harsh punishments, including denial of food cards and imprisonment, were meted out for lateness, slowness, or incompetence. Many people, however, particularly the young, were fired to heroic exertions. They were proud to sacrifice themselves for the building of a superior society. And many common factory workers had the opportunity to attend school and become engineers and administrators, tying them to the regime. When the Great Depression in the capitalist countries put millions out of work, no Soviet citizen suffered from unemployment; in the 1930s, gloom pervaded the West, but confidence and hope, artificially fostered by the party, buoyed up many people in Soviet Russia. The first two Five-Year Plans dramatically and rapidly increased Russia's industrial infrastructure as factories, mines, dams, and railroads were feverishly constructed. At no time, though, did the planning produce Western-style efficiency, and workers, who labored in a herculean way, actually suffered a decline in real wages. The regime concentrated on heavy industry, not consumer goods or improving the standard of living.

Collectivization. Meanwhile, a different and far more brutal revolution overtook Soviet agriculture: peasants were forcibly integrated into the planned economy through collectivization. Agriculture—peasants, their animals, and their fields—was subjected to the same rational control as industry. Collectivization meant the pooling of farmland, animals, and equipment to achieve efficient, large-scale production. The Communist solution for the backwardness of Russian agriculture was for peasants to become organized like factory workers. But knowing the peasants' distaste for the factory, their attachment to their own land, and their stubbornness, the party had hesitated to carry out its ambitious scheme. In 1929, however, Stalin believed that, for the sake of industrialization, he had no choice. If the Five-Year Plan was to succeed, the government had to receive planned crops of planned size and quality at planned times. This could be accomplished, Stalin thought, only by destroying the independent peasantry and creating huge agricultural factories. With collectivization, the ascendancy of the party over the people of Russia became almost complete.

The peasants paid a ghastly price. Stalin declared war on the Russian countryside. He ordered that the *kulaks*, the most enterprising and well-to-do peasants, be "liquidated as a class." Many were killed outright, and millions were deported to forced-labor camps in the far north, where most ultimately perished from hunger, cold, or abuse. Their poorer and less efficient neighbors were herded onto collective farms at the point of a bayonet.

The peasants struck back, sometimes in pitched battles. The horror of forced collectivization broke the spirit even of hardened officials. "I am an old Bolshevik," sobbed a secret police colonel to a fellow passenger on a train; "I worked in the underground against the Tsar and then I fought in the civil war. Did I do all that in order that I should now surround villages with machine guns and order my men to fire indiscriminately into crowds of peasants? Oh, no, no!"[12] Typically, however, the local officials and activists who stripped the peasants of their possessions and searched for hidden grain viewed themselves as idealists building a new society that was in the best interests of a suffering humanity; they infused their own ruthlessness into the official orders. Their dedication to the triumph of communism overcame all doubts caused by the sight of starving people and the sounds of wailing women and children.

Defeated but unwilling to surrender their livestock, the peasants slaughtered their animals, gorging themselves in drunken orgies against the days of inevitable famine. The country's cattle herds declined by one-half, inflicting irreparable secondary losses as well. The number of horses, crucial for rural transport and farm work, fell by one-third. Crops were not planted or not harvested, the Five-Year Plan was disrupted, and from 1931 to 1933 millions starved to death.

The suffering was most cruel in the Ukraine, where famine killed approximately six million people, many after extreme abuse and persecution. In order to buy industrial equipment abroad so that industrialization could proceed on target, the Soviet Union had to export food, as much of it as possible and for prices disastrously lowered by the Great Depression. Let the peasants in the Ukrainian breadbasket starve so that the country could grow strong! Moreover, Stalin relished the opportunity to punish the Ukrainians for their disloyalty during the civil war and their resistance to collectivization.

By 1935, practically all farming in Russia was collectivized. The kulaks had been wiped out as a class, and the peasants, ever rebellious under the tsars, had been cowed into permanent submission. In theory, the collective farms were run democratically, under an elected chairman; in practice, they followed as best they could the directives handed down from the nearest party office. People grumbled about the rise of a new serfdom. Agricultural development had been stifled.

Stalin had hoped to create technically efficient "factory farms" that would provide inexpensive food for the massive industrial labor force. But in reality, collectivization stifled agricultural production. Resentful peasants had slaughtered half the country's livestock rather than turn it over to the state; mismanagement and unenthusiastic collective farmers resulted in a precipitous decline in agricultural production. For decades collective farming failed to achieve the levels of production previously reached in the 1920s.

Total Control. To quash resistance and mold a new type of suitably motivated and disciplined citizen, Stalin unleashed a third revolution, the revolution of totalitarianism. Only communist regimentation, he believed, could liberate Russia from its historic inferiority. Moreover, the totalitarian state accorded with his desire to exercise total control over the party and the nation. Stalin's totalitarianism aimed at a complete reconstruction of state and society, down to the in-

A COLLECTIVE FARM FESTIVAL, BY SERGEI GERASIMOV, 1936–37. This propaganda painting of a festival on a collective farm glorifies the new agricultural system that Stalin imposed on the Russian peasantry by force. *(Galleria Statale Tret'jakov, Moscow/Art Resource, NY.)*

nermost recesses of human consciousness. It called for "a new man," suited to the needs of Soviet industrialism.

The revolution of totalitarianism encompassed all cultural activity. All media of communication—literature, the arts, music, the stage—were forced into subservience to the Five-Year Plan and Soviet ideology. In literature, as in all art, an official style was promulgated. Called *socialist realism*, it was expected to describe the world as the party saw it or hoped to shape it. Novels in the social realist manner told how the romances of tractor drivers and milkmaids or of lathe operators and office secretaries led to new victories of production under the Five-Year Plan. Composers found their music examined for remnants of bourgeois spirit; they were to write simple tunes suitable for heroic times. Everywhere huge, high-color posters showed men and women hard at work with radiant faces, calling others to join them; often Stalin, the wise father and leader, was shown among them. In this way, artistic creativity was locked into a dull, utilitarian straitjacket of official cheerfulness; creativity was allowed only to boost industrial productivity. Behind the

scenes, all artists were disciplined to conform to the will of the party or be crushed.

Education, from nursery school to university, was likewise harnessed to train dutiful and loyal citizens, and Soviet propaganda made a cult of Stalin that bordered on deification. Thus, a writer declared in 1935:

> *Centuries will pass and the generations still to come will regard us as the happiest of mortals, as the most fortunate of men, because we . . . were privileged to see Stalin, our inspired leader. Yes, and we regard ourselves as the happiest of mortals because we are the contemporaries of a man who never had an equal in world history. The men of all ages will call on thy name, which is strong, beautiful, wise, and marvellous. Thy name is engraved on every factory, every machine, every place on the earth, and in the hearts of all men.*[13]

To break stubborn wills and compel conformity, Stalin unleashed raw terror. Terror had been used as a tool of government ever since the Bolsheviks seized power. Lenin, who had provided theo-

MAP 30.1 THE UNION REPUBLICS OF THE UNION OF SOVIET SOCIALIST
REPUBLICS (U.S.S.R.) The Soviet Union consisted of many different
nationalities whose nationalist aspirations were held in check by the repressive
regime.

retical justification for terror in the struggle against
tsarism, employed it after the Revolution (and the
tsars had also used it, moderately and intermittently). After the start of the first Five-Year Plan,
show trials were staged in which engineers who
disagreed with Stalin's production timetable were
denounced as saboteurs. The terror used to herd
the peasants onto collective farms was even
greater. Stalin also used terror to crush opposition
and to instill abject fear in the ranks of the party
and in Russian society at large.

Purges had long been used to rid the party of
weaklings. After 1934, however, they became an
instrument of Stalin's drive for unchallenged personal power. In 1936, his vindictive terror broke
into the open. The first batch of victims, including
many founders of the Communist party, were ac-

cused of conspiring with the exiled Trotsky to set
up a "terrorist center" and of scheming to terrorize
the party. After being sentenced to death, they
were immediately executed. In 1937, the next
group, including prominent Communists of
Lenin's day, were charged with cooperating with
foreign intelligence agencies and wrecking "socialist reconstruction," the term for Stalin's revolution; they too were executed. Shortly afterward, a
secret purge decimated the military high command—almost half the country's seventy thousand
officers were either shot or sent to the camps—for
which the country paid a heavy price when Germany attacked in 1941.

In 1938, the last and biggest show trial advanced the most bizarre accusation of all: sabotage, espionage, and attempting to dismember the

Soviet Union and kill all its leaders (including Lenin in 1918). In the public hearings, some defendants refuted the public prosecutor, but in the end all confessed, usually after torture and threats to their family, before being executed. Western observers were aghast at the cynical charges and at the physical and mental tortures used to obtain the confessions.

The great trials, however, involved only a small minority of Stalin's victims; many more perished in silence without benefit of legal proceedings. The terror first hit members of the party, especially the Old Bolsheviks, who had joined before the Revolution; they were the most independent-minded members and therefore the most dangerous to Stalin. But Stalin also decimated the cultural elite that had survived the Lenin revolution. Thousands of engineers, scientists, industrial managers, scholars, and artists disappeared; they were shot or sent to forced-labor camps, where most of them perished. Their relatives also suffered, often fired from their jobs, evicted from their apartments, exiled to remote regions, and even sentenced to labor camps. No one was safe. To frighten the common people in all walks of life, men, women, and even children were dragged into the net of Stalin's secret police, leaving the survivors with a soul-killing reminder: submit or else. "In the years of the terror," recalled one victim, "there was not a house in the country where people did not sit trembling at night."[14]

The forced labor camps to which Stalin's victims were deported played an important role in the Soviet economy. Slave labor constructed the White Sea–Baltic Canal, which the regime held up as a monument of Communist achievement. Mining, logging, and construction enterprises in remote parts of the country also depended on forced labor. It is estimated that from 1929 until the death of Stalin in 1953, some 18 million people were confined to the Gulag, as Stalin's system of concentration camps came to be known. Many perished from abuse, starvation, and bone-crushing labor in freezing weather. As in Nazi concentration camps, administrators and guards deliberately dehumanized and brutalized the prisoners, whom the regime designated as "filth" and "enemies of the people."

Stalin may have orchestrated the terror, but large numbers of party members believed that terror, which was decimating their own ranks, was necessary. The memory of the vicious civil war, when domestic and foreign enemies sought to overthrow the new Bolshevik regime, and the resistance of the kulaks to collectivization created a siege mentality among the Communist leadership. Everywhere they saw anti-Soviets plotting against the party; they defined these enemies as Trotskyites, former kulaks, Whites who had fought in the civil war, members of outlawed anti-Soviet political parties, foreign agents, and criminals—cattle and horse thieves, contraband smugglers, bandits, and so on. Party officials saw terror as a legitimate way both of protecting the party to which they were ideologically committed and from which they derived prestige, power, and material benefits, and of protecting the Soviet experiment, which they viewed as humanity's best hope.

The toll of the purges is reckoned in many millions; it included Trotsky, who in 1940 was murdered in Mexico. The bloodletting was ghastly, as Stalin's purge officials themselves followed each other into death and ignominy. Stalin, however, was untroubled by the waste of life. By showing party officials and the Russian masses how vulnerable they were, how dependent they were on his will, he frightened them into servility. No doubt, the terror was also an expression of his craving for personal power and his vengeful and suspicious, some say clinically paranoid, nature. He saw enemies everywhere, took pleasure in selecting victims, and reveled in his omnipotence. For good reason, Stalin has been called a twentieth-century Ivan the Terrible. Like the sixteenth-century tsar, for whom he expressed admiration, Stalin stopped at no brutality in order to establish personal autocracy.

But more than a craving for personal power motivated Stalin. He regarded himself as Lenin's heir, responsible for securing and expanding the Revolution and defending it against foreign and domestic enemies. The only way to do this was to create a powerful Soviet Union through rapid modernization. Stalin, who had passed through the hands of the tsarist police and participated in the carnage of the civil war, believed that without the total obedience of the Russian people the Soviet state and society could not be effectively modernized and that terror was necessary to compel compliance. Stalin, as much a Russian patriot as a Marxist, did not forget the threat to Russia's survival after World War I. He was keenly aware of the political ambitions of Mussolini, of Japanese expansionism in the Far East, and eventually of German rearmament under Hitler. As he had said in 1931, if the Soviet Union did not make the utmost effort to strengthen itself within ten years, it could not withstand another attack; its peoples would perish under foreign domination. In Stalin's mind, totalitarianism was necessary to save Russia from foreign enemies that would devour it. Ten years after Stalin's warning of 1931, Hitler's armies invaded the Soviet Union, ready to exploit, enslave, and annihilate its citizens and seize its territory. The expansion of industrial capacity under Stalin was a key reason why Russia ultimately defeated the Nazi invaders.

THE NATURE OF FASCISM

Liberals viewed the Great War as a conflict between freedom and autocracy and expected an Allied victory to accelerate the spread of democracy throughout Europe. Right after the war, it seemed that liberalism would continue to advance as it had in the nineteenth century. The collapse of the autocratic German and Austrian Empires had led to the formation of parliamentary governments throughout eastern and central Europe. Yet within two decades, in an extraordinary turn of events, democracy seemed in its death throes. In Spain, Portugal, Italy, and Germany, and in all the newly created states of central and eastern Europe except Czechoslovakia, democracy collapsed, and various forms of authoritarian government emerged. The defeat of democracy and the surge of authoritarianism was best exemplified by the triumph of totalitarian fascist movements in Italy and Germany; with brutal frankness, their leaders proclaimed that individual freedom, a relic of a dying liberal age and a barrier to national greatness, would be dispensed with.

The emergence of fascist movements in more than twenty European lands after World War I was a sign that liberal society was in a state of disorientation and dissolution. The cultural pessimism, disdain for reason, elitism, romantic glorification of action and heroism, and contempt for liberal values voiced by many intellectuals and nationalists

before the war found expression after the war in the antidemocratic and irrational fascist ideologies, which altered European political life. Fascism marked the culmination of the counter-Enlightenment mentality inherent in the extreme nationalism and radical conservatism of the late nineteenth century and in the repudiation of modern Western civilization by disenchanted intellectuals.

As a Europe-wide phenomenon, fascism was a response to a postwar society afflicted with spiritual disintegration, economic dislocation, political instability, and thwarted nationalist hopes. A general breakdown of meaning and values led people to search for new beliefs and new political arrangements. Fascism was an expression of fear that the Bolshevik Revolution would spread westward. It was also an expression of hostility to democratic values and a reaction to the failure of liberal institutions to solve the problems of modern industrial society. Disillusioned with liberal government that failed to cope with massive social and economic problems, particularly during the Depression, many Europeans were tempted by authoritarian alternatives that would dispense with parliamentary government and the protection of individual rights. Anything seemed better than the ineffectual parliaments that appeared helpless in the face of mounting misery. Moreover, in many European lands, democracy had shallow roots. Having little familiarity with or appreciation of the procedures and values of constitutional government, people were susceptible to antidemocratic ideologies.

Fascist movements were marked by a determination to eradicate liberalism and Marxism—to undo the legacy of the French Revolution of 1789 and the Bolshevik Revolution of 1917. Fascists believed that theirs was a spiritual revolution, that they were initiating a new era in history and building a new civilization on the ruins of liberal democracy. "We stand for a new principle in the world," said Mussolini. "We stand for the sheer, categorical, definitive antithesis to the world of democracy . . . to the world which still abides by the fundamental principles laid down in 1789."[15] The chief principle of Nazism, said Hitler, "is to abolish the liberal concept of the individual and the Marxist concept of humanity, and to substitute for them the Volk community, rooted in the soil and united by the bond of its common blood."[16] The fascists' uniforms, songs, flags, parades, mass rallies, and cult of physical strength and violence all symbolized this call for a reawakened and reunited people.

Fascists accused liberal society of despiritualizing human beings and transforming them into materialistic creatures whose highest ideal was moneymaking. Regarding liberalism as bankrupt and parliamentary government as futile, many people yearned for a military dictatorship. To fascists and their sympathizers, democracy seemed an ineffective and enfeebled Old Order ready to be overthrown. Idealistic youth and intellectuals rejoiced in fascist activism. They saw fascism as a revolt against the mediocrity of the liberal state and modern mass society and a reaffirmation of the noblest human qualities: heroism and dedication to one's people. Fascists saw themselves as participants in a dynamic mass movement that would rectify the weaknesses and irresolution of parliamentary government and rid the nation of corrosive foreign influences. For them, the triumph of fascism would mark a new beginning for their nation and a new era in world history.

The fascist vision of a regenerated nation—a New Order led by a determined and heroic elite—arising from the ruins of a decadent Old Order had the appeal of great myth; it evoked belief, commitment, and loyalty. The myth of rebirth—a nation cured of evil and building a new and vigorous society—had a profound impact on people dissatisfied with liberal society and searching for new beliefs. The myth of the nation reborn answered a metaphysical yearning to give meaning to life and history. It provided an emotionally gratifying world-view at a time when many people had lost confidence in liberal-democratic ideals and institutions.

Fascists regarded Marxism as another enemy, for class conflict divided and weakened the state. To fascists, the Marxist call for workers of the world to unite meant the death of the national community. Fascism, in contrast, would reintegrate the proletariat into the nation and end class hostilities by making people at all levels feel that they were a needed part of the nation. Fascism thus offered a solution to the problem of insecurity and isolation in modern industrial society.

Attacking the rational tradition of the Enlightenment, fascism exalted will, blood, feeling, and instinct. Intellectual discussion and critical analysis, said fascists, cause national divisiveness; reason promotes doubt, enfeebles the will, and hinders in-

stinctive, aggressive action. Fascism made a continual appeal to the emotions as a means of integrating the national community. This flow of emotion fueled irrational and dangerous desires, beliefs, and expectations, which blocked critical judgment and responsible action. Glorifying action for its own sake, fascists aroused and manipulated brutal and primitive impulses and carried into politics the combative spirit of the trenches. They formed private armies, which attracted veterans—many of them rootless, brutal, and maladjusted men who sought to preserve the loyalty, camaraderie, and violence of the front.

Fascist ideology exalted the leader, who, it was believed, intuitively grasped what was best for the nation. It also called for rule by an elite of dedicated party members. The leader and the party would relieve the individual of the need to make decisions. Convinced that the liberal stress on individual freedom promoted national divisiveness, fascists pressed for monolithic unity: one leader, one party, one ideology, and one national will.

Fascism drew its mass support from the lower middle class: small merchants, artisans, white-collar workers, civil servants, and peasants of moderate means, all of whom were frightened both by big capitalism and by Marxism. They hoped that fascism would protect them from the competition of big business and prevent the hated working class from establishing a Marxist state, which would threaten their property. The lower middle class saw in fascism a noncommunist way of overcoming economic crises and restoring traditional respect for family, native soil, and nation. Furthermore, many of these people saw fascism as a way of attacking the existing social order, which denied them opportunities for economic advancement and social prestige.

Although a radicalized middle class gave fascist movements their mass support, the fascists could not have captured the state without the aid of existing ruling elites: landed aristocrats, industrialists, and army leaders. In Russia, the Bolsheviks had to fight their way to power; in Italy and Germany, the old ruling order virtually handed power to the fascists. In both countries, fascist leaders succeeded in reassuring the conservative elite that they would not institute widespread social reforms or interfere with private property and would protect the nation from communism. Even though the old elite often abhorred fascist violence and demagoguery, it entered into an alliance with the fascists to protect its interests. In Germany, the elite could not have installed Hitler in power had he not had the electoral backing of a significant number of Germans.

In their struggle to bring down the liberal state, fascist leaders aroused primitive impulses and tribal loyalties; they made use of myths and rituals to mobilize and manipulate the masses. Organizing their propaganda campaigns with the rigor of a military operation, fascists stirred and dominated the masses and confused and undermined their democratic opposition, breaking its will to resist. Fascists were most successful in countries with weak democratic traditions. When parliamentary government faltered, it had few staunch defenders, and many people were drawn to charismatic demagogues who promised direct action.

The proliferation of fascist movements demonstrated that the habits of democracy are not quickly learned, easily retained, or even desired. Particularly during times of crisis, people lose patience with parliamentary discussion and constitutional procedures, sink into nonrational modes of thought and behavior, and are easily manipulated by unscrupulous politicians. For the sake of economic or emotional security and national grandeur, they will often willingly sacrifice political freedom. Fascism starkly manifested the immense power of the irrational; it humbled liberals, making them permanently aware of the limitations of reason and the fragility of freedom.

The fascist goal of maximum centralization of power was furthered by developments during World War I: the expansion of bureaucracy, the concentration of industry into giant monopolies, and the close cooperation between industry and the state. The instruments of modern technology—radio, motion pictures, public address systems, telephone, and teletype—made it possible for the state to indoctrinate, manipulate, and dominate its subjects.

The Rise of Fascism in Italy

Postwar Unrest

Although Italy was on the winning side in World War I, it resembled a defeated nation. Food shortages, rising prices, massive unemployment, violent strikes, workers occupying factories, and peasants squatting on the uncultivated periphery of large estates created a climate of crisis. These dismal conditions contrasted sharply with the vision of a postwar world painted by politicians during the war. Italy required effective leadership and a reform program, but party disputes paralyzed the liberal government. With several competing parties, the liberals could not organize a solid majority that could cope with the domestic crisis.

The middle class was severely stressed. To meet accelerating expenses, the government increased taxes, but the burden fell unevenly on small landowners, small business owners, civil service workers, and professionals. Moreover, the value of war bonds, purchased primarily by the middle class, declined considerably because of inflation. Instead of being able to retrieve the good old days and their former status once the war ended, these solid citizens found that their economic position continued to deteriorate.

Large landowners and industrialists feared that their nation was on the verge of a Bolshevik-style revolution. They took seriously the proclamations of the socialists: "The proletariat must be incited to the violent seizure of political and economic power and this must be handed over entirely and exclusively to the Workers' and Peasants' Councils."[17] In truth, Italian socialists had no master plan to seize power. Peasant squatters and urban strikers were responding to the distress in their own regions and did not significantly coordinate their efforts with those in other localities. Besides, when workers realized that they could not keep factories operating, their revolutionary zeal waned and they started to abandon the plants. The workers' and peasants' poorly led and futile struggles did not portend a Red revolution. Nevertheless, the industrialists and landlords, with the Bolshevik Revolution still vivid in their minds, were taking no chances.

Adding to the unrest was the national outrage at the terms of the peace settlement. Italians felt that despite their sacrifices—five hundred thousand dead and one million wounded—they had been robbed of the fruits of their victory. Although Italy had received the Brenner Pass and Trieste, it had been denied the Dalmatian coast, the Adriatic port of Fiume, and territory in Africa and the Middle East. Nationalists blamed the liberal government for what they called a "mutilated victory." In

MUSSOLINI WITH HIS TROOPS. The Italian dictator deliberately tried to sustain an image of a virile warrior. Although Mussolini established a one-party state, he was less successful than Hitler or Stalin in creating a totalitarian regime. (*AP/Wide World.*)

1919, a force of war veterans, led by the poet and adventurer Gabriele D'Annunzio (1863–1938), seized Fiume, to the delirious joy of Italian nationalists and the embarrassment of the government. D'Annunzio's occupation of the port lasted more than a year, adding fuel to the flames of Italian nationalism and demonstrating the weakness of the liberal regime in imposing its authority on rightist opponents.

Mussolini's Seizure of Power

Benito Mussolini (1883–1945) was born in a small village in east-central Italy. Proud, quarrelsome, violent, and resentful of the humiliation he suffered for being poor, the young Mussolini was a trouble-

maker and was often brought before school authorities. But he was also intelligent, ranking first on final examinations in four subjects. After graduation, Mussolini taught in an elementary school, but this work did not suit his passionate temperament. From 1902 to 1904, he lived in Switzerland, where he broadened his reading, lectured, and wrote. He also came under the influence of anarchists and socialist revolutionaries.

Returning to Italy, Mussolini was labeled a dangerous revolutionary by the police. As a reward for his zeal and political agitation, which led to five months in prison for inciting riots, in 1912 he was made editor of *Avanti*, the principal socialist newspaper. During the early days of World War I, he was expelled from the Socialist party for advocating Italian intervention in the war. After Italy entered the war, Mussolini served at the front and, during firing practice, suffered a serious wound, for which he was hospitalized.

In 1919, Mussolini organized the Fascist party to realize his immense will to power. The quest for power, the yearning for action and a release of dynamic energy, more than a set of coherent doctrines, characterized the young movement. A supreme opportunist rather than an ideologist, Mussolini exploited the unrest in postwar Italy in order to capture control of the state. He attracted converts from among the discontented, the disillusioned, and the uprooted. Many Italians, particularly the educated bourgeois who had been inspired by the unification movement of the nineteenth century, viewed Mussolini as the leader who would gain Fiume, Dalmatia, and colonies and win Italy's rightful place of honor in international affairs.

Hardened war veterans, who had been told that they would be rewarded for their sacrifices at the front but instead confronted unemployment and landlessness, were drawn to fascism's dynamism. So too were veterans eager to escape the boredom and idleness of civilian life, which seemed so squalid in comparison with the high drama of battle. These demobilized soldiers welcomed an opportunity to wear the uniforms of the Fascist militia (Black Shirts), parade in the streets, and fight socialist and labor union opponents. Squads of Fascist Black Shirts (*squadristi*) raided socialist and trade union offices, destroying property and beating the occupants. As socialist Red Shirts responded in kind, it soon appeared that Italy was drifting toward civil war.

Hoping that Mussolini would rescue Italy from Bolshevism, industrialists and landowners contributed large sums to the Fascist party. The lower middle class, fearful that the growing power of labor unions and the Socialist party threatened their property and social prestige, viewed Mussolini as a protector. Middle-class university students, searching for adventure and an ideal, and army officers, dreaming of an Italian empire and hostile to parliamentary government, were also attracted to Mussolini's party. Intellectuals disenchanted with liberal politics and parliamentary democracy were intrigued by his philosophy of action. Mussolini's nationalism, activism, and anticommunism gradually seduced elements of the power structure: capitalists, aristocrats, army officers, the royal family, and the church.

In 1922, Mussolini made his bid for power. Speaking at a giant rally of his followers in late October, he declared: "Either they will give us the government or we shall take it by descending on Rome. It is now a matter of days, perhaps hours." A few days later, thousands of Fascists began the March on Rome. Some members of Parliament demanded that the army defend the government against a Fascist coup. It would have been a relatively simple matter to crush the twenty thousand Fascist marchers, armed with little more than pistols and rifles, but King Victor Emmanuel III (1869–1947) refused to act. The king's advisers, some of them sympathetic to Mussolini, exaggerated the strength of the Fascists. Believing that he was rescuing Italy from terrible violence, the king appointed Mussolini prime minister.

Mussolini had bluffed his way to power. Fascism had triumphed not because of its own strength—the Fascists had only 35 of the 535 seats in Parliament—but because the liberal government, irresolute and indecisive, did not counter force with force. In the past, the liberal state had not challenged Fascist acts of terror; now it feebly surrendered to Fascist blustering and threats. No doubt, liberals hoped that, once in power, the Fascists would forsake terror, pursue moderate aims, and act within the constitution. But the liberals were wrong; they had completely misjudged the antidemocratic character of fascism.

The Fascist State in Italy

Consolidation of Power

In October 1922, when Italy's liberal government capitulated, the Fascists by no means held total power. Anti-Fascists still sat in Parliament, and only four of the fourteen ministers in Mussolini's cabinet were Fascists. Cautious and shrewd, Mussolini resisted the extremists in his party, who demanded a second revolution: the immediate and preferably violent destruction of the Old Order. In this early stage of Fascist rule, when his position was still tenuous, Mussolini sought to maintain an image of respectability and moderation. He tried to convince the power structure that he intended to operate within the constitution, and he did not seek dictatorial power. At the same time, he gradually secured his position and turned Italy into a one-party state. In 1923, the Acerbo electoral law, approved by both chambers of the parliament, decreed that the party with the most votes in a national election (provided that the figure was not less than 25 percent of the total votes cast) would be granted two-thirds of the seats in the Chamber of Deputies. In the elections of 1924, which were marred by Fascist terrorism, Mussolini's supporters received 65 percent of the vote. Even without the implementation of the new electoral law, the opponents of fascism had been enfeebled. Mussolini had consolidated his power.

When socialist leader Giacomo Matteotti protested Fascist terror tactics, Fascist thugs killed him (in 1924). Although Mussolini had not ordered Matteotti's murder, his vicious attacks against his socialist opponent inspired the assassins. Repelled by the murder, some sincere democrats withdrew from the Chamber of Deputies in protest and some influential Italians called for Mussolini's dismissal. But the majority of liberals, including the leadership, continued to support Mussolini. And the king, the papacy, the army, large landowners, and industrialists, still regarding Mussolini as the best defense against internal disorder and Marxism, failed to back an anti-Fascist movement.

Pressed by the radicals within the Fascist party, Mussolini moved to establish a dictatorship. In 1925–26, he eliminated non-Fascists from his cabinet and dissolved opposition parties.

He also smashed the independent trade unions, suppressed opposition newspapers, replaced local mayors with Fascist officials, and organized a secret police to round up troublemakers. Many anti-Fascists fled the country or were deported.

Mussolini then turned on the extremist Fascists, the local chieftains (*ras*) who had led squadristi in the early days of the movement. Lauding violence, daring deeds, and the dangerous life, the ras were indispensable during the party's formative stage. But Mussolini feared that their radical adventurism posed a threat to his personal rule. And their desire to replace the traditional power structure with people drawn from their own ranks could block his efforts to cooperate with the established elite: industrialists, aristocratic landowners, and army leaders. Consequently, Mussolini expelled some squadristi leaders from the party and gave others positions in the bureaucracy to tame them.

Mussolini was less successful than Hitler and Stalin in fashioning a totalitarian state. The industrialists, the large landowners, the church, and to some extent even the army never fell under the complete domination of the party. Nor did the regime possess the mind of its subjects with the same thoroughness as the Nazis did in Germany. Life in Italy was less regimented and the individual less fearful than in Nazi Germany or Communist Russia. The Italian people might cheer Mussolini, but few were willing to die for him.

Control of the Masses

Like Communist Russia and Nazi Germany, Fascist Italy used mass organizations and mass media to control minds and regulate behavior. As in the Soviet Union and the Third Reich,* the Fascist regime created a cult of the leader. "Mussolini goes forward with confidence, in a halo of myth, almost chosen by God, indefatigable and infallible, the instrument employed by Providence for the creation of a new civilization," wrote the philosopher Giovanni Gentile.[18] To convey the image of a virile leader, Mussolini had himself photographed bare-

chested or in a uniform with a steel helmet. Other photographs showed him riding horses, driving fast cars, flying planes, and playing with lion cubs. Mussolini frequently addressed huge throngs of admirers from his balcony. His tenor voice, grandiloquent phrases, and posturing—jaw thrust out, hands on hips, rolling eyes—captivated audiences. Idolatry from the masses, in turn, intensified Mussolini's feelings of grandeur. Elementary school textbooks depicted Mussolini as the savior of the nation, a modern-day Julius Caesar.

Fascist propaganda urged that the grandeur of the Roman Empire be restored through conquest. It also inculcated habits of discipline and obedience: "Mussolini is always right." "Believe! Obey! Fight!" Propaganda also glorified war: "A minute on the battlefield is worth a lifetime of peace." It enticed Italians with a utopian vision—a proud, powerful, and vigorous nation imbued with the martial spirit of their Roman ancestors. The press, radio, and cinema idealized life under fascism, implying that fascism had eradicated crime, poverty, and social tensions. Schoolteachers and university professors were compelled to swear allegiance to the Fascist government and to propagate Fascist ideals, while students were urged to criticize instructors who harbored liberal attitudes. Millions of youths belonged to Fascist organizations, in which they participated in patriotic ceremonies and social functions, sang Fascist hymns, and wore Fascist uniforms. They submerged their own identities in the group.

Economic Policies

Fascists denounced economic liberalism for promoting individual self-interest, and socialism for instigating conflicts between workers and capitalists, which divided and weakened the nation. The Fascist way of resolving tensions between workers and employers was to abolish independent labor unions, prohibit strikes, and establish associations or corporations, which included both workers and employers from a given industry. In theory, representatives of labor and capital would cooperatively solve labor problems in a particular industry. In practice, the representatives of labor turned out to be Fascists who protected the interests of the industrialists. Although the Fascists lauded the corporative system as a creative ap-

*Third Reich was the official Nazi designation for the Hitler regime as the presumed successor of the Holy Roman Empire, 800–1806 (the First Reich), and the German Empire, 1871–1918 (the Second Reich). The Nazis boasted that the Third Reich would last a thousand years.

proach to modern economic problems, in reality it played a minor role in Italian economic life. Big business continued to make its own decisions, paying scant attention to the corporations.

Nor did the Fascist government solve Italy's long-standing economic problems. To curtail the export of capital and reduce the nation's dependence on imports in case of war, Mussolini sought to make Italy self-sufficient. To win the "battle of grain," the Fascist regime brought marginal lands under cultivation and urged farmers to concentrate on wheat rather than other crops. Although wheat production thus increased substantially, total agricultural output declined because wheat was planted on land better suited to animal husbandry and fruit cultivation. To make Italy industrially self-sufficient, the regime limited imports of foreign goods, with the result that Italian consumers paid higher prices for Italian-manufactured goods. Mussolini posed as the protector of the little people, but under his regime the power and profits of big business grew and the standard of living of small farmers and urban workers declined. Government attempts to grapple with the depression were halfhearted. Aside from providing family allowances—an increase in income with the birth of each child—the Fascist regime did little in the way of social welfare.

The Church and the Fascist Regime

Although anticlerical since his youth, Mussolini practiced expediency. He recognized that coming to terms with the church would improve his image with Catholic public opinion. The Vatican regarded Mussolini's regime as a barrier against atheistic communism and as less hostile to church interests and more amenable to church direction than a liberal government. Pope Pius XI (1922–1939) was an ultraconservative whose hatred of liberalism and secularism led him to believe that the Fascists would increase the influence of the church in the nation.

In 1929, the Lateran Accords recognized the independence of Vatican City, repealed many of the anticlerical laws passed under the liberal government, and made religious instruction compulsory in all secondary schools. The papal state, Vatican City, became a small enclave within Rome over which the Italian government had no authority.

Relations between the Vatican and the Fascist government remained fairly good throughout the 1930s. One crisis arose in 1931 when Mussolini, pushed by militant anticlericals within his party, dissolved certain Catholic youth groups as rivals to Fascist youth associations, but a compromise that permitted the Catholic organizations to function within certain limits eased tensions. When Mussolini invaded Ethiopia and intervened in the Spanish Civil War, the church supported him. Although the papacy criticized Mussolini for drawing closer to Hitler and introducing anti-Jewish legislation, it never broke with the Fascist regime.

THE NEW GERMAN REPUBLIC

In the last days of World War I, a revolution brought down the German government, a semi-authoritarian monarchy, and led to the creation of a democratic republic. In October 1918, the German admirals ordered the German navy to engage the British in the English Channel, but the sailors, anticipating peace and resentful of their officers (who commonly resorted to cruel discipline), refused to obey. Joined by sympathetic soldiers, the mutineers raised the red flag of revolution. The revolt soon spread as military men and workers demonstrated for peace and reform and in some regions seized authority. Reluctant to fire on their comrades and also fed up with the war, German troops did not move to crush the revolutionaries.

On November 9, 1918, the leaders of the government announced the end of the monarchy, and Kaiser William II fled to Holland. Two days later, the new German republic, headed by Friedrich Ebert (1871–1925), a Social Democrat, signed an armistice agreement ending the war. Many Germans blamed the new democratic republic for the defeat—a baseless accusation, for the German generals, knowing that the war was lost, had sought an armistice. This legend that traitors, principally Jews and Social Democrats, cheated Germany of victory was created and propagated by the conservative right—generals, high-ranking bureaucrats, university professors, and nationalists, who wanted to preserve the army's reputation and bring down the new and hated democratic Weimar Republic.

ROSA LUXEMBURG SPEAKING IN STUTTGART. A prominent member of the Social Democrats, Luxemburg rejected the argument of revisionists that capitalism could be reformed and revolution avoided. She was sentenced to prison for opposing Germany's entry into the war. Immediately after the war, she emerged as one of the leaders of the newly established German Communist party, or Spartacists. The attempted uprising of the Spartacists in 1919 was crushed, and Luxemburg was murdered by the Free Corps. (© *Topham, The Image Works.*)

In February 1919, the recently elected National Assembly met at Weimar and proceeded to draw up a constitution for the new state. The Weimar Republic—born in revolution, which most Germans detested, and military defeat, which many attributed to the new government—faced an uncertain future.

Threats from Left and Right

Dominated by moderate socialists, the infant republic faced internal threats from both the radical left and the radical right. In January 1919, the newly established German Communist party, or Spartacists, disregarding the advice of their leaders, Rosa Luxemburg and Karl Liebknecht, took to the streets of Berlin and declared Ebert's government deposed. To crush the revolution, Ebert turned to the Free Corps: volunteer brigades of ex-soldiers and adventurers, led by officers loyal to the emperor, who had been fighting to protect the eastern borders from encroachments by the new states of Poland, Estonia, and Latvia. The men of the Free Corps relished action and despised Bolshevism. They suppressed the revolution and murdered Luxemburg and Liebknecht on January 15. In May 1919, the Free Corps also marched into Munich to overthrow the soviet republic set up there by communists a few weeks earlier.

The Spartacist revolt and the short-lived soviet republic in Munich (and others in Baden and Brunswick) had a profound effect on the German psyche. The communists had been easily subdued, but fear of a communist insurrection remained deeply embedded in the middle and upper classes—a fear that drove many into the ranks of the Weimar Republic's right-wing opponents.

In March 1920, the republic was threatened by the radical right. Refusing to disband as the government ordered, detachments of the right-wing Free Corps marched into Berlin and declared a new government, headed by Wolfgang Kapp, a staunch

THE GERMAN INFLATION, 1923. As the value of the mark plummeted, many Germans lost their entire savings, which had taken a lifetime to accumulate. Here children play with now worthless bank notes. (*Hulton-Deutsch Collection/Corbis.*)

German nationalist. President Ebert and most members of the cabinet and National Assembly fled to Stuttgart. Insisting that it could not fire on fellow soldiers, the German army, the Reichswehr, made no move to defend the republic. A general strike called by the labor unions and the socialist parties prevented Kapp from governing, and the coup collapsed. However, the Kapp Putsch demonstrated that the loyalty of the army to the republic was doubtful and that important segments of German society supported the overthrow, by violence, if necessary, of the Weimar Republic and its replacement by an authoritarian government driven by a nationalist credo.

Economic Crisis

In addition to uprisings by the left and right, the republic was burdened by an economic crisis. During the war, Germany had financed its military expenditures not by increasing taxation but through short-term loans, accumulating a huge debt that now had to be paid. A trade deficit and enormous reparation payments worsened the nation's economic plight. Unable to meet the deficit in the national budget, the government simply printed more money, causing the value of the German mark to decline precipitously. In 1914, the mark stood at 4.2 to the dollar; in 1919, at 8.9 to the dollar; and in early 1923, at 18,000 to the dollar. In August 1923, a dollar could be exchanged for 4.6 million marks and in November, for 4 billion marks. Bank savings, war bonds, and pensions, representing years of toil and thrift, became worthless. Blaming the government for this disaster, the ruined middle class became more receptive to ultrarightist movements that aimed to bring down the republic.

With the economy in a shambles, the republic defaulted on reparation payments. Premier Raymond Poincaré (1860–1934) of France took a hard line. In January 1923, he ordered French troops into the Ruhr, the nerve center of German industry. Responding to the republic's call for passive resistance, factory workers, miners, and railroad workers in the Ruhr refused to work for the French. To provide strike benefits for the Ruhr workers, the government printed yet more money, making inflation even worse.

In August 1923, Gustav Stresemann became chancellor. The new government lasted only until November 1923, but during those one hundred days, Stresemann skillfully placed the republic on the path to recovery. Warned by German industrialists that the economy was at the breaking point, Stresemann abandoned the policy of passive resistance in the Ruhr and declared Germany's willingness to make reparation payments. Stresemann issued a new currency backed by a mortgage on German real estate. To reduce public expenditures, which contributed to inflation, the government fired some civil service workers and lowered salaries; to get additional funds, it raised taxes; to protect the value of the new currency, it did not print another issue. Inflation receded, and confidence was restored.

A new arrangement regarding reparations also contributed to the economic recovery. Recognizing that in its present economic straits Germany could not meet its obligations to the Allies or secure the investment of foreign capitalists, Britain and the United States pressured France to allow a reparation commission to make new proposals. In 1924, the parties accepted the Dawes Plan, which reduced reparations and based them on Germany's economic capacity. During the negotiations, France agreed to withdraw its troops from the Ruhr—another step toward easing tensions for the republic.

From 1924 to 1929, economic conditions improved. Foreign capitalists, particularly Americans, were attracted by high interest rates and the low cost of labor. Their investments in German businesses stimulated the economy. By 1929, iron, steel, coal, and chemical production exceeded prewar levels. The value of German exports also surpassed that of 1913. This spectacular boom was partly due to more effective methods of production and management and the concentration of related industries in giant trusts. Real wages were higher than before the war, and improved unemployment benefits made life better for the workers. It appeared that Germany had also achieved political stability, as threats from the extremist parties of the left and the right subsided. Given time and economic stability, democracy might have taken firmer root in Germany. But then came the Great Depression. The global economic crisis that began in October 1929 revealed how weak the Weimar Republic was.

Fundamental Weaknesses of the Weimar Republic

German political experience provided poor soil for transplanting an Anglo-Saxon democratic parliamentary system. Before World War I, Germany had been a semi-autocratic state ruled by an emperor who commanded the armed forces, controlled foreign policy, appointed the chancellor, and called and dismissed Parliament. This authoritarian system blocked the German people from acquiring democratic habits and attitudes. Still accustomed to rule from above, still adoring the power state, many Germans sought the destruction of the Weimar Republic.

Traditional conservatives—the upper echelons of the civil service, judges, industrialists, large landowners, and army leaders—were contemptuous of democracy and were avowed enemies of the republic. They wanted to restore a pre-1914 authoritarian government, which would fight liberal ideals and protect the fatherland from Bolshevism. These traditional conservatives regarded the revolution against the monarchy in the last weeks of the war as a treacherous act and the establishment of a democratic republic as a violation of Germany's revered tradition of hierarchical leadership. Nor did the middle class feel a commitment to the liberal-democratic principles on which the republic rested. The traditionally nationalistic middle class identified the republic with defeat in war and the humiliation of the Versailles treaty. Rabidly antisocialist, this class saw the leaders of the republic as Marxists who would impose a working-class state on Germany.

Right-wing intellectuals often attacked democracy as a barrier to the true unity of the German nation. In the tradition of nineteenth-century Volkish thinkers, they scorned reason and political freedom; glorified instincts, race, and action; and longed for a true German state that would embody order, discipline, and authority. In doing so, they turned many Germans against the republic, eroding the popular support on which democracy depends. As the German historian Kurt Sontheimer puts it,

> The submission of a large part of German intellectual society to the National Socialist *Weltanschauung* [world-view] . . . would have been inconceivable without the anti-democratic intellectual movement that preceded it and that, in its contempt for everything liberal, had blunted people's sensibilities to the inviolable rights of the individual and the preservation of human dignity. . . . Nothing is more dangerous in political life than the abandonment of reason. . . . The intellect must remain

the controlling, regulating force in human affairs. The anti-democratic intellectuals of the Weimar period . . . despised reason and found more truth in myth or in the blood surging in their veins. . . . Had they a little more reason and enlightenment, these intellectuals might have seen better where their zeal was leading them and their country.[19]

The Weimar Republic also showed the weaknesses of the multiparty system. With the vote spread over a number of parties, no one party held a majority of seats in the parliament (Reichstag), and so the republic was governed by a coalition of several parties. But because of ideological differences, the coalition was always unstable and in danger of failing to function. This is precisely what happened during the Great Depression. When effective leadership was imperative, the government could not act. Political deadlock caused Germans to lose what little confidence they had in the democratic system. Support for the parties that wanted to preserve democracy dwindled, and extremist parties that aimed to topple the republic gained strength.

Supporting the republic were Social Democrats, Catholic Centrists, and German Democrats; a coalition of these parties governed the republic during the 1920s.* Seeking to bring down the republic were the Communists, on the left, and two rightist parties, the Nationalists and the National Socialist German Workers' party, led by Adolf Hitler.

---

*The Social Democrats hoped one day to transform Germany into a Marxist society, but they had abandoned revolutionary means and pursued a policy of moderate social reform. The largest party until the closing months of the Weimar Republic, the Social Democrats were committed to democratic principles and parliamentary government. The Catholic Center party opposed socialism and protected Catholic interests but, like the Social Democrats, supported the republic. The German Democratic party consisted of middle-class liberals who also opposed socialism and supported the republic. Although the right-wing German People's party was more monarchist than republican, on occasion it joined the coalition of parties that sought to preserve the republic.

THE RISE OF HITLER

The Early Years

Adolf Hitler (1889–1945) was born in the town of Braunau am Inn, Austria, on April 20, 1889, the fourth child of a minor civil servant. Much of his youth was spent in Linz, a major city in Upper Austria. A poor student at secondary school, although by no means unintelligent, Hitler left high school and lived idly for more than two years. In 1907, the Vienna Academy of Arts rejected his application for admission. After the death of his mother in December 1907 (his father had died in 1903), Hitler drifted around Vienna, viewing himself as an art student. Contrary to his later description of these years, Hitler did not suffer great poverty, for he received an orphan's allowance from the state and an inheritance from his mother and an aunt. When the Vienna Academy again refused to admit him in 1908, he did not seek to learn a trade or to work steadily but earned some money by painting picture postcards.

Hitler was a loner, often given to brooding and self-pity. He found some solace by regularly attending Wagnerian operas (much admired by German nationalists for their glorification of German folk traditions and their stress on a savior, a heroic figure who rescues his people), by fantasizing about great architectural projects that he would someday initiate, and by reading. He read a lot, especially in art, history, and military affairs. He also read the racial, nationalist, anti-Semitic, and Pan-German literature that abounded in multinational Vienna. This literature introduced Hitler to a bizarre racial mythology: a heroic race of blond, blue-eyed Aryans battling for survival against inferior races. The racist treatises preached the danger posed by mixing races, called for the liquidation of racial inferiors, and marked the Jew as the embodiment of evil and the source of all misfortune, all themes that became core Nazi principles.

In Vienna, Hitler came into contact with Georg von Schönerer's Pan-German movement. For Schönerer, the Jews were evil not because of their religion, nor because they rejected Christ, but because they possessed evil racial qualities. Schönerer distributed a postcard carrying his signature, which read: "The Jew is the evil genius of the decline of civilization."[20] Schönerer's followers wore a watch chain with a picture of a hanged Jew attached. Hitler was particularly impressed with Karl Lueger, the mayor of Vienna, a clever demagogue who skillfully manipulated the anti-Semitic feelings of the Viennese for his own political advantage. In Vienna, Hitler also acquired a hatred for Marxism and democracy and the conviction that the struggle for existence and the survival of the fittest are the essential facts of the social world. His years in Vienna emptied Hitler of all compassion and scruples and filled him with a fierce resentment of the social order, which, he felt, had ignored him, cheated him, and condemned him to a wretched existence.

When World War I began, Hitler was in Munich. He welcomed the war as a relief from his daily life, which lacked purpose and excitement. Volunteering for the German army, Hitler found battle exhilarating, and he fought bravely, twice receiving the Iron Cross.

The experience of battle taught Hitler to prize discipline, regimentation, leadership, authority, struggle, and ruthlessness. The shock of Germany's defeat and of revolution intensified his commitment to racial nationalism. To lead Germany to total victory over its racial enemies became his obsession. Like many returning soldiers, he required vindicating explanations for lost victories. His own explanation was simple and demagogic: Germany's shame was due to the creators of the republic, the "November criminals;" and behind them was a Jewish-Bolshevik world conspiracy.

The Nazi Party

In 1919, Hitler joined the German Workers' Party, a small right-wing group and one of the more than seventy extremist military-political-Volkish organizations that sprang up in postwar Germany. Displaying fantastic energy and extraordinary ability as a demagogic orator, propagandist, and organizer, Hitler quickly became the leader of the party, whose name was changed to National Socialist German Workers' party (commonly called Nazi). As leader, Hitler insisted on absolute authority and total allegiance—a demand that coincided with the postwar longing for a strong leader who would set

right a shattered nation. Without Hitler, the National Socialist German Workers' party would have remained an insignificant group of discontents and outcasts. Demonstrating a machiavellian cunning in politics, Hitler tightened the party organization and perfected the techniques of mass propaganda.

Like Mussolini, Hitler incorporated military attitudes and techniques into politics. Uniforms, salutes, emblems, flags, and other symbols imbued party members with a sense of solidarity and camaraderie. At mass meetings, Hitler was a spellbinder who gave stunning performances. His pounding fists, throbbing body, wild gesticulations, hypnotic eyes, rage-swollen face, and repeated, frenzied denunciations of the Versailles treaty, Marxism, the republic, and Jews inflamed and mesmerized the audience. Many listeners—and his speeches generally attracted people already hostile to the Weimar Republic—were swayed by Hitler's earnestness, conviction, and self-confidence. They believed that Hitler and his movement could restore Germany's strength and pride. Hitler instinctively grasped the innermost feelings of his audience: its resentments and its longings. "The intense will of the man, the passion of his sincerity seemed to flow from him into me. I experienced an exaltation that could be likened only to religious conversion," said one early admirer.[21]

In November 1923, Hitler attempted to seize power in Munich, in the state of Bavaria, as a prelude to toppling the republic. The attempt, which came to be known as the Beer Hall Putsch, failed, and the Nazis made a poor showing; they quickly scattered when the Bavarian police opened fire. Ironically, however, Hitler's prestige increased, for when he was put on trial, he used it as an opportunity to denounce the republic and the Versailles treaty and to proclaim his philosophy of racial nationalism. His impassioned speeches, publicized by the press, earned Hitler a nationwide reputation and a light sentence: five years' imprisonment, with the promise of quick parole. While in prison, Hitler dictated *Mein Kampf*, a rambling and turgid work, which contained the essence of his **worldview.**

The unsuccessful Munich putsch taught Hitler a valuable lesson: armed insurrection against superior might fails. He would gain power not by

ADOLF HITLER. In this painting by a German artist, Hitler is idolized as a heroic medieval knight. (*U.S. Army.*)

force but by exploiting the instruments of democracy: elections and party politics. He would use apparently legal means to destroy the Weimar Republic and impose a dictatorship. As Nazi propaganda expert Joseph Goebbels would later express it, "We have openly declared that we use democratic methods only to gain power and that once we had it we would ruthlessly deny our opponents all those chances we had been granted when we were in the opposition."[22]

Hitler's World-View

Some historians see Hitler as an unprincipled opportunist and a brilliant tactician who believed in nothing but cleverly manufactured and manipulated ideas that were politically useful in his drive for power. To be sure, Hitler was concerned not with the objective truth of an idea but with its potential political usefulness. He was not a systematic thinker like Marx. Whereas communism claimed the certainty of science and held that it would reform the world in accordance with rational

principles, Hitler proclaimed the higher validity of blood, instinct, and will and regarded the intellect as an enemy of the soul. Hitler, nevertheless, possessed a remarkably consistent ideology. As Hajo Holborn explains,

> Hitler was a great opportunist and tactician, but it would be quite wrong to think that ideology was for him a mere instrumentality for gaining power. On the contrary, Hitler was a doctrinaire of the first order. Throughout his political career he was guided by an ideology . . . which from 1926 onward [did] not show any change whatsoever.[23]

Hitler's thought comprised a patchwork of nineteenth-century anti-Semitic, Volkish, Social Darwinist, antidemocratic, and anti-Marxist ideas. From these ideas, many of which enjoyed wide popularity, Hitler constructed a world-view rooted in myth and ritual. Given to excessive daydreaming and never managing to "overcome his youth with its dreams, injuries, and resentments,"[24] Hitler sought to make the world accord with his fantasies—struggles to the death between races, a vast empire ruled by a master race, and a thousand-year Reich.

German thought, particularly after Nietzsche, was permeated by the idea of crisis: that Germany and Europe were experiencing a unique historical upheaval. The unexpected loss in World War I intensified the feeling among Germans that the nation required a radical transformation, a new beginning. Hitler conceived himself as a man of destiny leading a movement of world-historical significance; he had been chosen by fate to rescue the nation by imbuing Germans with a rejuvenating ideology, one that was inherent in their primordial past.

Racial Nationalism. **Nazism** rejected both Judeo-Christian and Enlightenment traditions and sought to found a new world order based on racial nationalism. For Hitler, race was the key to understanding world history. He believed that Western civilization was at a critical juncture. Liberalism was dying, and Marxism, that "Jewish invention," as he called it, would inherit the future unless it was opposed by an even more powerful world-view. "With the conception of race

National Socialism will carry its revolution and recast the world," said Hitler.[25] As the German barbarians had overwhelmed a disintegrating Roman Empire, a reawakened, racially united Germany, led by men of iron will, would undo the humiliation of the Versailles treaty, carve out a vast European empire, and deal a decadent liberal civilization its deathblow. It would conquer Russia, eradicate communism, and reduce to serfdom the subhuman Slavs, "a mass of born slaves who feel the need of a master."[26]

In the tradition of crude Volkish nationalists and Social Darwinists, Hitler divided the world into superior and inferior races and pitted them against each other in a struggle for survival. For him, this fight for life, that is, for territory and resources, was a law of nature and of history. The Germans, descendants of ancient Aryans, possessed superior racial characteristics; a nation degenerates and perishes if it allows its blood to be contaminated by intermingling with lower races. Conflict between races was desirable, for it strengthened and hardened racial superiors. It made them ruthless—a necessary quality in this Darwinian world. As a higher race, the Germans were entitled to conquer and subjugate other races. Germany must acquire *Lebensraum* (living space) by expanding eastward at the expense of the racially inferior Slavs.

The Jew as Devil. An obsessive and virulent hatred of Jews dominated Hitler's mental outlook. In waging war against the Jews, Hitler believed that he was defending Germany from its worst enemy, a sinister force that stood in total opposition to the new world he envisioned. In Hitler's mythical interpretation of the world, the Aryan was the originator and carrier of civilization. As descendants of the Aryans, the German race embodied creativity, bravery, and loyalty. As a counterpart, Jews, who belonged to a separate biological race, personified the vilest qualities. "Two worlds face one another," said Hitler in a statement that clearly reveals the mythical character of his thought, "the men of God and the men of Satan! The Jew is the anti-man, the creature of another god. He must have come from another root of the human race. I set the Aryan and the Jew over and against each other."[27] Everything Hitler despised—liberalism, intellectualism, pacifism, parliamentarianism, internationalism, communism, modern art, and individualism—he attributed to Jews.

For Hitler, the Jew was the mortal enemy of racial nationalism. The moral outlook of the ancient Hebrew prophets, which affirmed individual worth and made individuals morally responsible for their actions, was totally at odds with Hitler's morality, which subordinated the individual to the national community. Hitler once called conscience a Jewish invention. The prophetic vision of the unity of humanity under God and the belief in equality, justice, and peace were also contrary to Hitler's creed that all history is a pitiless struggle between races and that only the strongest and most ruthless deserve to survive.

Hitler's anti-Semitism served a functional purpose as well. By concentrating all evil in one enemy, "the conspirator and demonic" Jew, Hitler provided true believers with a simple, all-embracing, and emotionally satisfying explanation for their misery. By defining themselves as the racial and spiritual opposites of Jews, true believers of all classes felt joined together in a Volkish union. By seeing themselves engaged in a heroic battle for self-preservation and racial survival against a demonic enemy that embodied evil, they strengthened their will. Even failures and misfits gained self-respect. Anti-Semitism provided insecure and hostile people with powerless but recognizable targets on whom to focus their antisocial feelings.

The surrender to myth served to disorient the intellect and unify the nation. When the mind accepts an image such as Hitler's image of Jews as vermin, germs, and satanic conspirators, it has lost all sense of balance and objectivity. Such a disoriented mind is ready to believe and to obey, to be manipulated and to be led, to brutalize and to tolerate brutality; it is ready to be absorbed into the collective will of the community. That many people, including intellectuals and members of the elite, accepted these racial ideas shows the enduring power of mythical thinking and the vulnerability of reason. In 1933, the year Hitler took power, Felix Goldmann, a German-Jewish writer, commented astutely on the irrational character of Nazi anti-Semitism: "The present-day politicized racial anti-Semitism is the embodiment of myth, . . . nothing is discussed . . . only felt, . . . nothing is pondered critically, logically or reasonably, . . . only inwardly perceived, surmised. . . . We are apparently the last [heirs] of the Enlightenment."[28]

The Importance of Propaganda.   Hitler understood that in an age of political parties, universal suffrage, and a popular press—the legacies of the French and Industrial Revolutions—the successful leader must win the support of the masses. To do so, Hitler consciously applied and perfected elements of circus showmanship, church pageantry, American advertising, and the techniques of propaganda that the Allies had used to stir their civilian populations during the war. To be effective, said Hitler, propaganda must be aimed principally at the emotions. The masses are not moved by scientific ideas or by objective and abstract knowledge, but by primitive feelings, terror, force, and discipline. Propaganda must reduce everything to simple slogans incessantly repeated and must concentrate on one enemy. The masses are aroused by the spoken, not the written, word—by a storm of hot passion erupting from the speaker, "which like hammer blows can open the gates to the heart of a people."[29]

The most effective means of stirring the masses and strengthening them for the struggle ahead, Hitler had written in *Mein Kampf*, is the mass meeting. Surrounded by tens of thousands of people, individuals lose their sense of individuality and no longer see themselves as isolated. They become members of a community bound together by an **esprit de corps** reminiscent of the trenches during the Great War. Bombarded by the cheers of thousands of voices, by marching units, by banners, by explosive oratory, individuals become convinced of the truth of the party's message and the irresistibility of the movement. Their intellects overwhelmed, their resistance lowered, they lose their previous beliefs and are carried along on a wave of enthusiasm. Their despair over the condition of their nation turns to hope, and they derive a sense of belonging and mission. They feel that they are participants in a mighty movement that is destined to regenerate the German nation and initiate a new historical age. "The man who enters such a meeting doubting and wavering leaves it inwardly reinforced; he has become a link to the community."[30]

Hitler Gains Power

When Hitler left prison in December 1924, after serving nine months, he proceeded to tighten his hold on the Nazi party. He relentlessly used his genius for propaganda and organization to strengthen the loyalty of his cadres and to instill in them a sense of mission. In 1925, the Nazi party counted about 27,000 members; in 1929, it had grown to 178,000, with units throughout Germany. But its prospects seemed dim, for since 1925, economic conditions had greatly improved—Germany's exports had even surpassed those of Britain—and the republic seemed politically stable. In 1928, the National Socialists (NSDAP) received only 2.6 percent of the vote. Nevertheless, Hitler never lost faith in his own capacities or his destiny. He continued to build his party and waited for a crisis that would rock the republic and make his movement a force in national politics.

The Great Depression, which began in the United States at the end of 1929, provided that crisis. Desperate and demoralized people lined up in front of government unemployment offices. Street peddlers, beggars, and youth gangs proliferated; suicides increased, particularly among middle-class people shamed by their descent into poverty, idleness, and uselessness. As Germany's economic plight worsened, the German people became more amenable to Hitler's radicalism. The Nazis tirelessly expanded their efforts. Everywhere, they staged mass rallies, plastered walls with posters, distributed leaflets, and engaged in street battles with their opponents of the left. Hitler promised all things to all groups, avoided debates, provided simple explanations for Germany's misfortunes, and insisted that only the Nazis could establish domestic order, promote economic prosperity, and restore Germany's position as an international power. Nazi propaganda attacked the communists, the "November criminals," the democratic system, the Versailles treaty, reparations, and the Jews. It depicted Hitler as a savior. Hitler would rescue Germany from chaos; he understood the real needs of the Volk; he was sent by destiny to lead Germany in its hour of greatest need. These propaganda techniques worked. The Nazi party went from 810,000 votes in 1928 to 6.4 million in

1930, and its representation in the Reichstag soared from 12 to 107.

The Social Democrats (SPD), the principal defenders of democracy, could draw support only from the working class; to the middle class, they were hated Marxists. Moreover, in the eyes of many Germans, the SPD was identified with the status quo, that is, with economic misery and national humiliation. Swallowing right-wing propaganda, they held the founders and leaders of the Weimar Republic responsible for the defeat in World War I and the diminution of Germany's power in world affairs. The SPD simply had no program that could attract the middle class or give it hope for a better future.

To the lower middle class, the Nazis promised effective leadership and a solution to the economic crisis. For this segment of society, the Great Depression was the last straw, the final evidence that the republic had failed and should be supplanted by a different kind of regime. Germans of the lower middle class craved order, authority, and leadership and abhorred the endless debates and factional quarrels of the political parties. To them parliamentary government was fatally flawed. They wanted Hitler to protect Germany from the communists and from organized labor and to revive the economy. The traumatic experience of the Great Depression caused many bourgeois—until then apathetic about voting—to cast ballots. The depression was also severe in England and the United States, but the liberal foundations of these countries were strong. In Germany they were not, because the middle class had not committed itself to democracy, nor indeed did it have any liking for it. Democracy endured in Britain and the United States; in Germany, it collapsed.

But Nazism was more than a class movement. It appealed to the discontented and disillusioned from all segments of the population: embittered veterans, romantic nationalists, idealistic intellectuals, industrialists and large landowners frightened by communism and social democracy, rootless and resentful people who felt that they had no place in the existing society, the unemployed, lovers of violence, and newly enfranchised youth yearning for a cause. The Social Democrats spoke the rational language of European democracy. The Communists addressed themselves to only a part

of the nation, the proletariat, and were linked to a foreign country, the Soviet Union. The Nazis reached a wider spectrum of the population, and their promise to unite the German people in a racial brotherhood dedicated to restoring German honor and power touched deeper feelings.

And always there was the immense attraction of Hitler, who tirelessly worked his oratorical magic on increasingly enthusiastic crowds, confidently promising leadership and national rebirth. Many Germans were won over by his fanatical sincerity, his iron will, and his conviction that he was chosen by fate to rescue Germany. What a new party member wrote after hearing Hitler speak expressed the mood of many Germans: "There was only one thing for me, either to win with Adolf Hitler or to die for him. The personality of the Fuehrer had me totally in its spell."[31] Many others, no doubt, voted for Hitler not because they approved of him or his ideas, but because he was a strong opponent of the Weimer Republic, which they viewed as weak and contemptible. What these people wanted, above all, was the end of the republic they hated.

Meanwhile, the parliamentary regime failed to function effectively. According to Article 48 of the constitution, during times of emergency the president was empowered to govern by decree, that is, without the Reichstag, the parliament. When President Paul von Hindenburg (1847–1934), the aging field marshal, exercised this emergency power, the responsibility for governing Germany was in effect transferred from the political parties and the Reichstag to the president and chancellor. Rule by the president, instead of by parliament, meant, for one thing, that Germany had already taken a giant step away from parliamentary government in the direction of authoritarianism.

In the election of July 31, 1932, the Nazis received 37.3 percent of the vote and won 230 seats, far more than any other party but still not a majority. Determined to become chancellor, Hitler refused to take a subordinate position in a coalition government. Franz von Papen, who had resigned from the chancellorship, persuaded Hindenburg, whose judgment was distorted by old age, to appoint Hitler chancellor. In this decision, Papen had the support of German industrialists, aristocratic landowners, and the Nationalist party.

As in Italy, the members of the ruling elite were frightened by internal violence, unrest, and the specter of communism. They had abhorred the creation of the Weimar Republic, and the government's ineffectiveness in coping with crises only confirmed their disdain for parliamentary democracy. They thought Hitler a vulgar man, a lowly corporal, and they detested his demagogic incitement of the masses. But they regarded him as a useful instrument to fight communism, block social reform, break the back of organized labor, and rebuild the armament industry. They expected him to break the shackles of the hated Versailles treaty, which the Weimar Republic had passively accepted; restore the strength of the military; and in international affairs pursue a more assertive policy reminiscent of the days of the emperor. They also hoped that the charismatic Hitler would revive the nation's spirit and pride, which had eroded under the republic. And, traditionally anti-Semitic, they welcomed an opportunity to restrict the role of Jews in Germany's political, economic, and cultural life.

Hitler had cleverly reassured these traditional conservatives that the Nazis would protect private property and business and go slow with social reform. They would have preferred a dictatorship under Hindenburg, a respected general who shared their views and upbringing, but a dictatorship under Hitler still seemed to them better than the Weimar Republic, which they had hated since its inception.

Like the Italian upper class, which had assisted Mussolini in his rise to power, the old conservative ruling elite intrigued to put Hitler in power. Ironically, this decision was made when Nazi strength at the polls was beginning to ebb. Expecting to control Hitler, conservatives calculated badly, for Hitler could not be tamed. They had underestimated his political skills, his ruthlessness, and his obsession with racial nationalism. Hitler had sought power not to restore the Old Order but to fashion a new one. The new leadership would be drawn not from the traditional ruling segments but from the most dedicated Nazis, regardless of their social background.

Never intending to rule within the spirit of the constitution, Hitler, who took office on January 30, 1933, quickly moved to assume dictatorial powers. In February 1933, a Dutch drifter with communist leanings set a fire in the Reichstag.

Hitler persuaded Hindenburg to sign an emergency decree suspending civil rights on the pretext that the state was threatened by internal subversion. The chancellor then used these emergency powers to arrest, without due process, Communist and Social Democratic deputies.

In the elections of March 1933, Nazi thugs broke up Communist party meetings, and Hitler called for a Nazi victory at the polls to save Europe from Bolshevism. Intimidated by street violence and captivated by Nazi mass demonstrations and relentless propaganda, the German people elected 288 Nazi deputies in a Reichstag of 647 seats. With the support of 52 deputies of the Nationalist party and in the absence of Communist deputies, who were under arrest, the Nazis now had a secure majority. Hitler then bullied the Reichstag into passing the Enabling Act (in March 1933), which permitted the chancellor to enact legislation independently of the Reichstag. With astonishing passivity, the political parties had allowed the Nazis to dismantle the government and make Hitler a dictator with unlimited power. Hitler had used the instruments of democracy to destroy the Weimar Republic, Germany's first liberal democracy, and create a dictatorship. And he did it far more thoroughly and quickly than Mussolini.

NAZI GERMANY

Mussolini's fascism exhibited much bluster and bragging, but Fascist Italy did not have the industrial and military strength or the total commitment of the people necessary to threaten the peace of Europe. Nazism, in contrast, demonstrated a demonic quality, which nearly destroyed Western civilization.

Hitler's sinister, fanatical, and obsessive personality had a far greater impact on the German movement than Mussolini's character had on Italian fascism. Also contributing to the demonic radicalism of Nazism were certain deeply rooted German traditions, which were absent in Italy: Prussian militarism, adoration of the power state, and belief in the special destiny of the German racial community. These traditions made the German people's attachment to Hitler and Nazi ideology much stronger than the Italian people's devotion to Mussolini and his party.

The Leader-State

The Nazis moved to subjugate all political and economic institutions and all culture to the will of the party. There could be no separation between private life and politics: ideology must pervade every phase of daily life and all organizations must come under party control. There could be no rights of the individual that the state must respect. The party became the state, and its teachings the soul of the German nation. Joseph Goebbels (see below) summed up this totalitarian goal: "It is not enough to reconcile people more or less to our regime, to move them towards a position of neutrality towards us, we want rather to work on people until they are addicted to us."[32] An anonymous Nazi poet expressed the totalitarian credo in these words:

> *We have captured all the positions*
> *And on the heights we have planted*
> *The banners of our revolution.*
> *You had imagined that that was all that we*
> *   wanted*
> *We want more*
> *We want all*
> *Your hearts are our goal,*
> *It is your souls we want.*[33]

The Third Reich was organized as a leader-state, in which Hitler, the *fuehrer* (leader), embodied and expressed the true will of the German people, commanded the supreme loyalty of the nation, and held omnipotent power. As a Nazi political theorist stated, "The authority of the Fuehrer is total and all-embracing . . . it embraces all members of the German community. . . . The Fuehrer's authority is subject to no checks or controls; it is circumscribed by no . . . individual rights; it is . . . overriding and unfettered."[34] Virtually all crucial decisions in foreign affairs were made by Hitler. Yet, at the same time, the Nazi state comprised organizations and individuals competing with one another for influence, power, and plunder.

To strengthen the power of the central government and coordinate the nation under Nazism, the regime abolished legislatures in the various German states and appointed governors who would make certain that Nazi directives were carried out throughout the country. The Nazis took over the civil service and used its machinery to enforce Nazi decrees. In this process of *Gleichschaltung* (coordination), the Nazis encountered little opposition. The political parties and the trade unions collapsed without a struggle.

In June 1933, the Social Democratic party was outlawed, and within a few weeks, the other political parties simply disbanded on their own. In May, the Nazis had seized the property of the trade unions, arrested the leaders, and ended collective bargaining and strikes. The newly established German Labor Front, an instrument of the party, became the official organization of the working class. Although there is evidence that the working class in 1933 would have resisted the Nazis, its leadership never mobilized proletarian organizations. With surprising ease, the Nazis imposed their will on the nation.

Hitler made strategic but temporary concessions to the traditional ruling elite. On June 30, 1934, Nazi executioners swiftly murdered the leaders of the SA (Nazi storm troopers who had battled political opponents) to eliminate any potential opposition to Hitler from within the party. With this move, Hitler also relieved the anxieties of industrialists and landowners, who feared that Ernst Röhm, the head of the SA, would persuade Hitler to remove them from positions of power and to implement a program of radical social reform, threatening their property.

The execution of the SA leaders (including Röhm) was also approved by the generals, for they regarded the SA as a rival to the army. In August, all German soldiers swore an oath of unconditional allegiance to the fuehrer, cementing the alliance between the army and National Socialism. The army tied itself to the Nazi regime because it approved of the resurgence of militaristic values and applauded the death of the Weimar Republic. As the German historian Karl Dietrich Bracher concludes, "Without the assistance of the Army, at first through its toleration and later through its active cooperation, the country's rapid and final restructuring into the total leader state could not have come about."[35]

Economic Life

Hitler had sought power not to improve the living standards of the masses but to convert Germany into a powerful war machine. Economic problems held little interest for this dreamer, in whose mind danced images of a vast German empire. For him, the "socialism" in National Socialism meant not a comprehensive program of social welfare but the elimination of the class antagonisms that divided and weakened the fatherland and blocked the revitalization of German communal and racial ties. Radicals within the party wanted to deprive the industrialists and landowners of power and social prestige and to expropriate their property. The more pragmatic Hitler wanted only to deprive them of freedom of action; they were to serve, not control, the state. Germany remained capitalist, but the state had unlimited power to intervene in the economy. Unlike the Bolsheviks, the Nazis did not destroy the upper classes of the Old Regime. Hitler made no war against the industrialists. He wanted from them loyalty, obedience, and a war machine. German businessmen prospered but exercised no influence on political decisions. The profits of industry rose, and workers lauded the regime for ending the unemployment crisis.

Nazism and the Churches

Nazism conflicted with the core values of Christianity. "The heaviest blow that ever struck humanity was the coming of Christianity," said Hitler to intimates during World War II.[36] Had Germany won the war, the Nazis would no doubt have tried to root Christianity out of German life. In 1937, the bishop of Berlin defined the essential conflict between Christianity and Nazism:

> The question at stake is whether there is an authority that stands above all earthly power, the authority of God, Whose commandments are valid independent of space and time, country and race. The question at stake is whether individual man possesses personal rights that no community and no state may take from him; whether the free exercise of his conscience may be prevented and forbidden by the state.[37]

Nazism could tolerate no other faith alongside itself. Recognizing that Christianity was a rival claimant for the German soul, the Nazis moved to repress the Protestant and Catholic churches. In the public schools, religious instruction was cut back and the syllabus changed to omit the Jewish origins of Christianity. Christ was depicted not as a Jew, heir to the prophetic tradition of Hebrew monotheism, but as an Aryan hero. The Gestapo (secret state police) censored church newspapers, scrutinized sermons and church activities, forbade some clergymen to preach, dismissed the opponents of Nazism from theological schools, and arrested some clerical critics of the regime.

The clergy were well represented among the Germans who resisted Nazism; some were sent to concentration camps or executed. But these courageous clergy were not representatives of the German churches, which, as organized institutions, capitulated to and cooperated with the Nazi regime. Both the German Evangelical (Lutheran) and German Catholic churches demanded that their faithful give Hitler their loyalty; both turned a blind eye to Nazi persecution of Jews. Even before World War II and the implementation of genocide, many Evangelical churches banned baptized Jews from entering their temples and dismissed pastors with Jewish ancestry. During the war both Catholic and Evangelical churches condemned resistance and found much to admire in the Third Reich, and both supported Hitler's war. When Germany attacked Poland, starting World War II, the Catholic bishops declared: "In this decisive hour we encourage and admonish our Catholic soldiers, in obedience to the Fuehrer, to do their duty and to be ready to sacrifice their whole existence."[38] Both churches urged their faithful to fight for fatherland and fuehrer, pressured conscientious objectors to serve, and celebrated Nazi victories.

The German churches, which preached Christ's message of humanity, failed to take a stand against Nazi inhumanity for a variety of reasons. Many German church leaders feared that resistance would lead to even more severe measures against their churches. Traditionally, the German churches had bowed to state authority and detested revolution. Church leaders also found some Nazi ideas appealing. Intensely nationalistic, antiliberal, antirepublican, anticommunist, and anti-Semitic, many members of the clergy were filled with hope when Hitler came to power. They anticipated that Hitler would restore respect for traditional Christian morality, which, they believed, had been undermined by the secularism, materialism, and vice rampant in the republic. And he would declaw the Communists, who had declared war on Christianity. The prominent Lutheran theologian who "welcomed that change that came to Germany in 1933 as a divine gift and miracle"[39] voiced the sentiments of many members of the clergy. Such feelings encouraged prolonged moral nearsightedness, not a revolt of Christian conscience. When the war ended, the German Evangelical church leaders lamented:

> [W]e know ourselves to be one with our people in a great company of suffering and in a great solidarity of guilt. With great pain do we say: "Through us endless suffering has been brought to many people and countries. . . . We accuse ourselves for not witnessing more courageously, for not praying more faithfully, for not loving more ardently."[40]

Shaping the "New Man"

Propaganda had helped the Nazis come to power. Now it would be used to consolidate their hold on the German nation and shape a "new man," committed to Hitler, race, and Volk. Hitler was a radical revolutionary who desired not only the outward form of power but also control over the inner person, over the individual's thoughts and feelings. The purpose of Nazi propaganda was to condition the mind to revere the fuehrer and to obey the new regime. Its intent was to deprive individuals of their capacity for independent thought. By concentrating on myths of the race and the infallibility of the fuehrer, Nazi propaganda sought to disorient the rational mind and give the individual new standards to believe in and obey. Propaganda aimed to mold the entire nation to think and respond as the leader-state directed. Even science had to conform to Nazi racial ideology. Thus, Johannes Stark, a Nobel Prize winner, declared that scientific thought is a function of race:

> [N]atural science is overwhelmingly a creation of the Nordic-Germanic blood component of the Aryan peoples. . . . The Jewish spirit is wholly different in its orientation. . . . True, Heinrich Hertz made the great discovery of electromagnetic waves, but he was not a full-blooded Jew. He had a German mother, from

> whose side his spiritual endowment may well have been conditioned.[41]

The Ministry of Popular Enlightenment, headed by Joseph Goebbels (1897–1945), controlled the press, book publishing, the radio, the theater, and the cinema. A holder of a doctoral degree in the humanities, Goebbels was intelligent and a master in the art of propaganda. Viewing Hitler as a Nietzschean superman, a man of destiny who was inculcating Germans with a saving faith, Goebbels was completely devoted to the fuehrer. He was also vain, cynical, and contemptuous of the very masses he manipulated. But the German people were not merely passive victims of clever and ruthless leaders. "The effective spread of propaganda and the rapid regimentation of cultural life," says Bracher, "would not have been possible without the invaluable help eagerly tendered by writers and artists, professors and churchmen." And the manipulation of the minds of the German people "would not have been effective had it not been for profound historically conditioned relations based . . . on a pseudo-religious exaggerated nationalism and on the idea of the German mission."[42] Although some intellectuals showed their abhorrence of the Nazi regime by emigrating, the great majority gave their support and lent their talents, often with overt enthusiasm, to their leader and to Nazi ideology. Some individuals rejected Nazi propaganda, but the masses of German people came to regard Nazism as the fulfillment of their nationalist longings.

Nazi propaganda saturated the nation. The Nazis tried to keep the emotions in a state of permanent mobilization, for Hitler understood that the emotionally aroused are most amenable to manipulation. Goose-stepping SA and SS (elite military and police) battalions paraded in the streets; martial music quickened the pulse; Nazi flags decorated public buildings; loudspeakers installed in offices and factories blared the Nazi message, and all work stopped for important broadcasts. Citizens were ordered to greet each other with "Heil Hitler," a potent sign of reverence and submission. Nazi propaganda constructed a cult around the person of Hitler, who was portrayed as a charismatic leader chosen by destiny to redeem the fatherland.

The regime made a special effort to reach young people. All youths between the ages of ten and eighteen were urged and then required to join the Hitler Youth, and all other youth organizations were dissolved. At camps and rallies, young people paraded, sang, saluted, and chanted: "We were slaves; we were outsiders in our own country. So were we before Hitler united us. Now we would fight against Hell itself for our leader."[43]

Nazification of Education. The schools, long breeding grounds of nationalism, militarism, antiliberalism, and anti-Semitism, now indoctrinated the young in Nazi ideology. The Nazis instructed teachers in how certain subjects were to be taught; and to ensure obedience, members of the Hitler Youth were asked to report suspicious teachers. Portraits of Hitler, along with Nazi banners, were displayed in classrooms. War stories, adventures of the Hitler Youth, and ancient Nordic legends replaced fairy tales and animal stories in reading material for the young. The curriculum upgraded physical training and sports, curtailed religious instruction, and introduced many courses in "racial science." Decidedly anti-intellectual, the Nazis stressed character building over book learning. They intended to train young people to serve the leader and the racial community—to imbue them with a sense of fellowship for their Volkish kin, that sense of camaraderie found on the battlefield. Expressions of individualism and independence were suppressed.

The universities quickly abandoned freedom of the mind, scientific objectivity, and humanist values. "We repudiate international science, we repudiate the international community of scholars, we repudiate research for the sake of research. Sieg Heil!" declared one historian.[44] Even before the Nazi takeover, many university students and professors had embraced Volkish nationalism and right-wing radicalism. Two years before Hitler came to power, for example, 60 percent of all undergraduates supported the Nazi student organization, and anti-Semitic riots broke out at several universities. Horst von Maltitz observes:

> For seventy years or more, the professors had preached aggressive nationalism, the German destiny of power, hero worship, irrational political Romanticism, and so forth, and had increasingly deemphasized, if not eliminated, the teachings of ethical and humanist princi-

> ples. . . . Essentially neither [professors nor students] wanted to have anything to do with democracy. In the Weimar Republic . . . both groups, on the whole, seemed equally determined to tear down that Republic. The professors did their part by fiery lectures, speeches, and writings; the students did theirs in noisy demonstrations, torch-light parades, vandalism, and physical violence. . . . When Hitler came to power, both professors and students fell all over themselves to demonstrate their allegiance.[45]

"From now on it will not be your job to determine whether something is true but whether it is in the spirit of the National Socialist revolution," the new minister of culture told university professors.[46] Numerous courses on Nazi ideology were introduced into the curriculum. In May 1933, professors and students proudly burned books considered a threat to Nazi ideology, a display of cultural barbarism that gave prophetic meaning to the famous words of Heinrich Heine, the great nineteenth century German-Jewish poet: "wherever they burn books they will also, in the end, burn people." Many academics praised Hitler and the new regime. Some 10 percent of the university faculty, principally Jews, Social Democrats, and liberals, were dismissed, and their colleagues often approved. Many writers, scientists, and artists, the cream of European intellectual life, left Germany. Others served the regime, providing an intellectual justification for Hitler's dictatorship, Nazi racial theories, and the persecution of Jews. Physical anthropologists and biologists were instrumental in erecting a "scientific" foundation for Nazi racism.

Giant Rallies. Symbolic of the Nazi regime were the monster rallies staged at Nuremberg. Scores of thousands roared, marched, and worshiped at their leader's feet. These true believers, the end product of Nazi indoctrination, celebrated Hitler's achievements and demonstrated their loyalty to their savior. Everything was brilliantly orchestrated to impress Germans and the world with the irresistible power, determination, and unity of the Nazi movement and the greatness of the fuehrer. Armies of youths waving flags, storm troopers bearing weapons, and workers shouldering long-

Young Nazis Burning Books in Salzburg, Austria, in 1938. Heinrich Heine, the great nineteenth-century German-Jewish poet, once said that people who burn books end up burning people. (© *Topham/The Image Works.*)

handled spades paraded past Hitler, who stood at attention, his arm extended in the Nazi salute. The endless columns of marchers, the stirring martial music played by huge bands, the forest of flags, the chanting and cheering of spectators, and the burning torches and beaming spotlights united the participants into a racial community. "Wherever Hitler leads, we follow," thundered thousands of Germans in a giant chorus. The Nuremberg rallies were among the greatest theatrical performances of the twentieth century.

Terror. Another means of ensuring compliance and obedience was terror. Its instrument, the SS, had been organized in 1925 to protect Hitler and other party leaders and to stand guard at party meetings. Under the leadership of Heinrich Himmler (1900–1945), a fanatical believer in Hitler's racial theories, the SS was molded into an elite force of disciplined, dedicated, and utterly ruthless men. Myopic, narrow-chested, and sexu-

ally prudish, Himmler contrived a cult of manliness. He envisioned the SS, who were specially selected for their racial purity and physical fitness, as a new breed of knights: Nietzschean supermen who would lead the new Germany.

The SS staffed the concentration camps established to deal with political prisoners. Through systematic terror and torture, the SS sought to deprive the inmates of their human dignity and to harden themselves for the struggles that lay ahead. The knowledge that these camps existed and that some prisoners were never heard from again was a strong inducement for Germans to remain obedient.

Anti-Semitic Legislation

The Nazis deprived Jews of their German citizenship and instituted many anti-Jewish measures designed to make them outcasts. Thousands of Jewish doctors, lawyers, musicians, artists, and

Charles Maurras

Some historians view Action Française, an ultra-nationalist, antidemocratic, and anti-Semitic, organization founded in 1898–99 by Charles Maurras (1868–1952), as a forerunner of the fascist movements that emerged in the aftermath of World War I. In the tradition of early-nineteenth-century French conservatives, Maurras held that the collective takes precedence over the individual: "The primary reality, more real than the individual and more real also than the world," he declared, "is *la patrie,* the Country."* He regarded the religious individualism of the Reformation, the political individualism of the French Revolution, and the cultural individualism of romanticism as forces of national division and discord. The principle of equality, he said, permitted rule by the mediocre and the incompetent.

To save France from class war, political factions, capitalist exploitation, and spiritual disintegration—all consequences of unbridled individualism in his eyes—Maurras championed integral nationalism. It sought the integration of the nation around Catholicism, France's ancestral religion; monarchy, a deeply rooted French tradition; and hierarchy, leadership based on birth and talent. Maurras valued the France of the Old Regime, for it was monarchical, hierarchical, and community minded. Hostile and foreign elements—he meant specifically Masons, Protestants, Jews, alien residents, and recently naturalized citizens—must be deprived of politi-

Roger-Viollet.

professors—many of them prominent figures who had contributed enormously to German intellectual and cultural life—were barred from practicing their professions, and Jewish members of the civil service were dismissed. A series of laws tightened the screws of humiliation and persecution. Marriage or sexual encounters between Germans and Jews were forbidden. Universities, schools, restaurants, pharmacies, hospitals, theaters, museums, and athletic fields were gradually closed to Jews, who were now social pariahs. The Nazi

state also expropriated Jewish property, an act of thievery from which individual Germans and business firms benefited. As a rule, German academic and clerical elites did not protest; many agreed with the National Socialists' edicts. The Jews were simply abandoned.

In November 1938, using as a pretext the assassination of a German official in Paris by a seventeen-year-old Jewish youth, whose family the Nazis had mistreated, the Nazis organized an extensive pogrom not seen in Germany since the

cal rights and influence. Such people, he argued, had no deep roots in the French nation; they could never be truly French. Maurras hoped that army leaders, inspired by the Action Française philosophy, would overthrow the Third Republic and reestablish monarchical rule.

Maurras was strongly anti-Semitic, holding that "Jewish capitalism" and "Jewish democracy" were corrupting the French soul. He attributed a destructive individualism to Judaism, for it had conceived the idea of one God who had endowed everyone with a conscience: "it is in the Law and the Prophets . . . that are to be found the first expressions in antiquity of the individualism, egalitarianism, humanitarianism, and social and political idealism that were to mark 1789."[†] He saw the Jews as agents of revolution and as alien conspirators. Action Française waged a fierce campaign against a pardon for Dreyfus, the Jewish army officer who was falsely convicted of treason. At times, it engaged in organized vandalism and violence against his supporters. For decades Maurras's paper fomented anti-Semitism with vicious editorials such as the following: *"Down with the Jews! Those whom we make the mistake of treating as if they were our equals display a ridiculous ambition to dominate us. They shall be put in their place and it will be our pleasure to do so."*

Student members of the Action Française joined with young royalists to form the Camelots du Roi (hawkers of the king), which sold the Action Française newspaper in the streets, acted as guards at the organization's meetings, and participated in anti-Republic and nationalist demonstrations. The organized violence of Camelots du Roi presaged the fascist terror tactics after World War I. In this sense, the Camelots could be viewed as the first storm troopers.

Support for Action Française came principally from the army, the nobility, the clergy, and middle-class professionals. Between 1910 and 1926, Action membership ranged from thirty thousand to forty thousand. The group posed no threat to the state, but its cult of la patrie, condemnation of democracy, celebration of war, virulent anti-Semitism, employment of organized violence, and call for a leader to resurrect the nation anticipated and coincided with fascism.

After France's defeat in World War II, Maurras supported the authoritarian Vichy regime and denounced the resistance movement. He applauded Vichy's laws that made Jews second-class citizens, and his paper published the hiding places of Jews so that they could be rounded up and sent to German concentration camps. After the liberation of France, Maurras was sentenced to life imprisonment but was released in 1951 for medical reasons.

*Quoted in Michael Sutton, *Nationalism, Positivism and Catholicism: The Politics of Charles Maurras and French Catholics, 1890–1914* (Cambridge: Cambridge University Press, 1982), p. 26.
†Ibid., p. 8.

Middle Ages. Nazi gangs murdered scores of Jews, destroyed 267 synagogues, and burned and vandalized 7,500 Jewish-owned businesses all over Germany—an event that became known as Night of the Broken Glass (*Kristallnacht*). Twenty thousand Jews were thrown into concentration camps. The Reich then imposed on the Jewish community a fine of one billion marks. These measures were a mere prelude, however. During World War II, genocidal murder of European Jewry became a cardinal Nazi objective.

Mass Support

The Nazi regime became a police state, symbolized by mass arrests, the persecution of Jews, and concentration camps that institutionalized terror. Yet fewer heads rolled than people expected, and in many ways life seemed normal. The Nazis established the totalitarian state without upsetting the daily life of the majority of the population. Moreover, Hitler, like Mussolini, was careful to maintain the appearance of legality. By not abolishing the Reichstag or repealing the constitution, he could claim that his was a legitimate government.

To people concerned with little but family, job, and friends—and this includes most people in any country—life in the first few years of the Third Reich seemed quite satisfying. Most Germans believed that the new government was trying to solve Germany's problems in a vigorous and sensible manner, in contrast to the ineffective Weimar leadership. By 1936, the reinvigoration of the economy, stimulated in part by rearmament, had virtually eliminated unemployment, which had stood at 6 million jobless when Hitler took power. An equally astounding achievement in German eyes was Hitler's bold termination of the humiliating Versailles treaty, the rebuilding of the war machine, and the restoration of power in international affairs. It seemed to most Germans that Hitler had awakened a sense of self-sacrifice and national dedication among a people dispirited by military defeat, political weakness, and economic depression. He had united a country torn by class antagonisms and social distinctions and given people a sense of national pride. Workers had jobs, businessmen profits, and generals troops, and the bonds of community had been greatly strengthened—what could be wrong?

Many intellectuals, viewing Hitlerism as the victory of idealism over materialism and of community over selfish individualism, lent their talents to the regime and endorsed the burning of books and the suppression of freedom. To them, Hitler was a visionary, an agent for the rebirth and regeneration of the fatherland, who had shown Germany and the world a new way of life—a new creed.

Thus, having regained confidence in themselves and their nation, many Germans rejoiced in Hitler's leadership, did not regret the loss of political freedom, and remained indifferent to the plight of the persecuted, particularly Jews. Moreover, Hitler's popularity and mass support rested on something far stronger than propaganda and terror, for he had won the hearts of a sizable proportion of the German people. To many Germans, Hitler was exactly as Nazi mythology depicted him, a man of destiny and a savior of the nation who "stands like a statue grown beyond the measure of earthly man."[47]

There was some opposition and resistance to the Hitler regime. Social Democrats and Communists organized small cells. Some conservatives, who considered Hitler to be a threat to traditional German values, and some clergy, who saw Nazism as a pagan religion in conflict with Christian morality, also formed small opposition groups. But only resistance from the army could have toppled Hitler. Some generals, even before World War II, urged such resistance. The overwhelming majority of German officers, however, preferred the new regime, which had restored Germany's military might and pride and had given them the opportunity for professional advancement, or they considered it dishonorable to break their oath of loyalty to Hitler. And most of these officers would remain loyal until the bitter end. Very few Germans realized that they were ruled by evil men driven by an evil ideology, that their country, an advanced industrial society with an impressive tradition of high culture, was passing through a long night of barbarism. Still fewer considered resistance. The great majority of Germans would remain loyal to Hitler and would serve the Nazi regime until its final defeat.

Online Study Center **Improve Your Grade**
Interactive Map: The Growth of Nazi Germany, 1933–1939

LIBERALISM AND AUTHORITARIANISM IN OTHER LANDS

The Spread of Authoritarianism

After World War I, in country after country, parliamentary democracy collapsed and authoritarian leaders came to power. In most of these countries, liberal ideals had not penetrated deeply; liberalism met resistance from conservative elites.

Spain and Portugal. In both Spain and Portugal, parliamentary regimes faced strong opposition from the church, the army, and large landowners. In 1926, army officers overthrew the Portuguese republic that had been created in 1910, and gradually, Antonio de Oliveira Salazar (1889–1970), a professor of economics, emerged as dictator. In Spain, after antimonarchist forces won the election of 1931, King Alfonso XIII (1902–1931) left the country, and Spain was proclaimed a republic. But the new government, led by socialists and liberals, faced the determined opposition of the ruling elite. The reforms introduced by the republic—expropriation of large estates, reduction of the number of army officers, dissolution of the Jesuit order, and closing of church schools—only intensified the Old Order's hatred.

The difficulties of the new Spanish republic mounted: workers, near starvation, rioted and engaged in violent strikes; the military attempted a coup; and Catalonia, with its long tradition of separatism, tried to establish its autonomy. Imitating the example of France (described later in this chapter), the parties of the left, including the Communists, united in the Popular Front, which came to power in February 1936. In July 1936, General Francisco Franco (1892–1975), stationed in Spanish Morocco, led a revolt against the republic. He was supported by army leaders, the church, monarchists, landlords, industrialists, and the Falange, a newly formed fascist party. Spain was torn by a bloody civil war. Aided by Fascist Italy and Nazi Germany, Franco won in 1939 and established a dictatorship.

Eastern and Central Europe. Parliamentary government in eastern Europe rested on weak foundations. Predominantly rural, these countries lacked the sizable professional and commercial classes that had promoted liberalism in western Europe. Only Czechoslovakia had a substantial native middle class with a strong liberal tradition. The rural masses of eastern Europe, traditionally subjected to monarchical and aristocratic authority, were not used to political thinking or civic responsibility. Students and intellectuals, often gripped by a romantic nationalism, were drawn to antidemocratic movements.

Right-wing leaders also played on the fear of communism. When parliamentary government failed to solve internal problems, the opponents of the liberal state seized the helm. Fascist movements, however, had little success in eastern Europe. Rather, authoritarian regimes headed by traditional ruling elites—army leaders or kings—extinguished democracy there.

With the dissolution of the Hapsburg Empire at the end of World War I, Austria became a democratic republic. From the start, it suffered from severe economic problems. The Hapsburg

Empire had been a huge free-trade area. Food and raw materials had been permitted to circulate unimpeded throughout the empire. The new Austria lacked sufficient food to feed the population of Vienna and needed raw materials for its industries. Worsening its plight was the erection of tariff barriers by each of the states formerly part of the Hapsburg Empire. Between 1922 and 1926, the League of Nations had to rescue Austria from bankruptcy. The Great Depression aggravated Austria's economic position. Many Austrians believed that only *Anschluss* (union) with Germany could solve Austria's problems.

Austria was also burdened by a conflict between the industrial region, including Vienna, and the agricultural provinces. Factory workers were generally socialist and anticlerical; the peasants were strongly Catholic and antisocialist. The Social Democrats controlled Vienna, but the rural population gave its support to the Christian Social party. Each party had its own private army: the workers had the *Schutzbund*, and the provincials the *Heimwehr*.

In the early 1920s, under the guidance of its Social Democratic mayor, Vienna introduced a number of social reforms—including free kindergartens, hospitals, and burials, and subsidized housing projects—that significantly improved conditions for the working class. The middle class, which bore the brunt of the tax burden needed to pay for these reforms designed specifically for the working class, saw the Social Democrats, who dominated Vienna, as implacable enemies. During the Great Depression, Chancellor Engelbert Dollfuss (1892–1934) sought to turn the country into a one-party state. In February 1934, police and Heimwehr contingents raided Social Democratic headquarters. When the Social Democrats called a general strike, Dollfuss bombarded worker's strongholds, including huge municipal housing projects, killing 193 civilians. After the workers were subdued, the Dollfuss government tried and imprisoned more than one thousand socialists, outlawed leftist trade unions, and disbanded the Social Democratic party. Austria had joined the ranks of authoritarian states.

When Hitler came to power in Germany, Austrian Nazis pressed for Anschluss. In July 1934, a band of them assassinated Dollfuss, but a Nazi plot to capture the government failed. Four years later, however, Hitler would march into Austria, bringing about the Anschluss desired by many Austrians.

The new Hungary that emerged at the end of World War I faced an uprising by communists inspired by the success of the Bolsheviks in Russia. Béla Kun (1885–1937), supported by Russian money, established a soviet regime in Budapest in March 1919. But Kun could not win the support of the peasants and was opposed by the Allies, who helped crush the revolutionary government. In 1920, power passed to Admiral Miklós Horthy (1868–1957), who instituted a brief white terror, which exceeded the red terror of the Kun regime. During the Great Depression, the Horthy government, which favored the large landholders, was challenged by the radical right, which preached extreme nationalism, anti-Semitism, and anticapitalism and tried to win mass support through land reform. Its leader, Gyula Gömbös (1886–1936), who served as prime minister from 1932 to 1936, sought to align Hungary with Nazi Germany. Wishing to regain territories lost as a result of World War I and aware of Hitler's growing might, Hungary drew closer to Germany in the late 1930s.

Poland, Greece, Bulgaria, and Romania became either royal or military dictatorships. In September 1940, a year after World War II started, the fascist Iron Guard seized power in Romania and engaged in the mass murder of Jews. In January 1941, the Iron Guard was crushed by the military. The new state of Czechoslovakia, guided by President Tomáš Masaryk (1850–1937) and Foreign Minister Eduard Beneš (1884–1948), who were both committed to the liberal-humanist tradition of the West, preserved parliamentary democracy. Its most serious problem came from the 3.25 million Germans living within its borders, primarily in the Sudetenland. The German minority founded the Sudetenland German party, which modeled itself after Hitler's Nazi party. Hitler later exploited the issue of the Sudetenland Germans to dismember Czechoslovakia.

The Western Democracies

While liberal governments were failing in much of Europe, the great Western democracies—the United States, Britain, and France—continued to preserve democratic institutions. In Britain and the United States, fascist movements were merely a nuisance. In France, fascism was more of a threat because it exploited deeply ingrained hostility in some quarters to the liberal ideals of the French Revolution.

The United States. The central problem faced by the Western democracies was the Great Depression, which started in the United States. In the 1920s, hundreds of thousands of Americans had bought stock on credit; this buying spree sent stock prices soaring well beyond what the stocks were actually worth. In late October 1929, the stock market was hit by a wave of panic selling; prices plummeted. Within a few weeks, the value of stocks listed on the New York Stock Exchange fell by some $26 billion. A terrible chain reaction followed over the next few years. Businesses cut production and unemployment soared; farmers unable to meet mortgage payments lost their land; banks that had made poor investments closed down. American investors withdrew the capital they had invested in Europe, causing European banks and businesses to fail. Throughout the world, trade declined and unemployment rose.

When President Franklin Delano Roosevelt (1882–1945) took office in 1933, more than thirteen million Americans—one-quarter of the labor force—were out of work. Hunger and despair showed on the faces of the American people. Moving away from laissez faire, Roosevelt instituted a comprehensive program of national planning, economic experimentation, and reform, known as the New Deal. Although the U.S. political and economic system faced a severe test, few Americans turned to fascism or communism. The government engaged in national planning but did not break with democratic values and procedures.

Britain. Even before the Great Depression, Britain faced severe economic problems. Loss of markets to foreign competitors hurt British manufacturing, mining, and shipbuilding; rapid development of water and oil power reduced the demand for British coal, and outdated mining equipment put Britain in a poor competitive position. To decrease costs, mine owners in 1926 called for salary cuts; the coal miners countered with a strike and were joined by workers in other industries. To many Britons, the workers were leftist radicals trying to overthrow the government. Many wanted the state to break the strike. After nine days, industrial workers called off their strike, but the miners held out for another six months, only to return to work with longer hours and lower pay. Although the general strike failed, it did improve relations between the classes, for the workers had not called for revolution and they had refrained from violence. The fear that British workers would follow the Bolshevik path abated.

The Great Depression cast a pall over Britain. The Conservative party leadership tried to stimulate exports by devaluing the British pound and to encourage industry by providing loans at lower interest rates, but in the main, it left the task of recovery to industry itself. Not until Britain began to rearm did unemployment decline significantly. Despite the economic slump of the 1920s and the Great Depression, Britain remained politically stable, a testament to the strength of its parliamentary tradition. Neither the communists nor the newly formed British Fascist party gained mass support.

France. In the early 1920s, France was concerned with postwar rebuilding. From 1926 to 1929, France was relatively prosperous. Industrial and agricultural production expanded, tourism increased, and the currency was stable. Although France did not feel the Great Depression as painfully as did the United States and Germany, the nation was hurt by the decline in trade and production and the rise in unemployment.

The political instability that had beset the Third Republic almost since its inception continued, and hostility to the Republic mounted. The rift between liberals and conservatives, which had divided the country since the Revolution and grown worse with the Dreyfus affair, continued to plague France during the depression. The French right, particularly the radicals, whose numbers had been increasing since the 1880s, had traditionally rejected the ideals of liberty, equality, individual rights, and parliamentary government associated with the Enlightenment and the French Revolution, and was violently anti-Marxist. Negating liberal ideals and democractic government, the right endorsed an authoritarian and hierarchical system, which would oppose social reform and protect right-wing interests, and extreme nationalism, which would integrate all classes and restore France's greatness. As the leading parties failed to solve the nation's problems, a number of fascistic groups gained strength. On February 6, 1934,

right-wing gangs threatened to invade the Chamber of Deputies. What brought on the crisis was the exposure of the shady dealings of Alexander Stavisky, a financial manipulator with high government connections, including parliamentary deputies and a cabinet minister. Antirepublican forces on the right, with their paramilitary units, saw the scandal as an opportunity to replace the Third Republic with an authoritarian regime. The resulting violence left hundreds wounded and several dead. The whole affair was too poorly organized to constitute a serious threat to the government. But to the parties of the left—socialists, communists, and radicals—the events of February 6–7 constituted a rightist attempt to establish a fascist regime.

Fear of growing fascist strength at home and in Italy and Germany led the parties of the left to form the Popular Front. In 1936, Léon Blum (1872–1950), a socialist, heir of Enlightenment humanism, and a Jew, became premier. Blum's Popular Front government instituted more reforms than any other ministry in the history of the Third Republic. At the time he took office, French workers in many industries were not unionized, worked ten or more hours a day six days a week without vacations, and were poorly compensated. To end a wave of strikes that tied up production, Blum gave workers a forty-hour workweek and holidays with pay and guaranteed them the right to collective bargaining. He took steps to nationalize the armaments and aircraft industries. To reduce the influence of the wealthiest families, he put the Bank of France under government control. By raising prices and buying wheat, he aided farmers. Conservatives and fascists denounced Blum as a Jewish socialist who was converting the fatherland into a communist state. "Better Hitler than Blum," grumbled French rightists.

Despite significant reforms, the Popular Front could not revitalize the economy. In 1937, the Blum ministry was overthrown and the Popular Front, always a tenuous alliance, fell apart. Through democratic means the Blum government had tried to give France its own New Deal, but the social reforms passed by the Popular Front only intensified hatred between the working classes and the rest of the nation. France had preserved democracy against the onslaught of domestic fascists, but it was a demoralized and divided nation that confronted a united and dynamic Nazi Germany.

❖   ❖   ❖

Online Study Center ACE the Test

NOTES

1. Carl J. Friedrich and Zbigniew K. Brzezinski, *Totalitarian Dictatorship and Autocracy* (New York: Praeger, 1961), p. 5.

2. Ibid., p. 7.

3. Hannah Arendt, *The Origins of Totalitarianism* (New York: World, Meridian Books, 1958), p. 469.

4. Karl Dietrich Bracher, *The Age of Ideologies*, trans. Erwald Osers (New York: St. Martin's Press, 1984), p. 83.

5. Friedrich and Brzezinski, *Totalitarian Dictatorship and Autocracy*, p. 13.

6. Zbigniew Brzezinski, *Out of Control* (New York: Charles Scribner's Sons, 1993), p. 19.

7. Quoted in Omer Bartov, *Hitler's Army: Soldiers, Nazis, and War in the Third Reich* (New York: Oxford University Press, 1992), p. 166.

8. Quoted in Arendt, *Origins of Totalitarianism*, p. 330.

9. "All-Russian Communist Party (Bolsheviks), 1919," in *Soviet Communism: Programs and Rules. Official Texts of 1919, 1952, 1956, 1961*, ed. Jan F. Triska (San Francisco: Chandler, 1962), p. 23.

10. V. I. Lenin, "The Immediate Tasks of the Soviet Government," in *The Lenin Anthology*, ed. Robert C. Tucker (New York: Norton, 1975) pp. 448 ff.

11. J. V. Stalin, "Speech to Business Executives" (1931), in *A Documentary History of Communism from Lenin to Mao*, ed. Robert V. Daniels (New York: Random House, 1960), 2:22.

12. Quoted in Isaac Deutscher, *Stalin: A Political Biography* (New York: Oxford University Press, 1966), p. 325.

13. Excerpted in T. H. Rigby, ed., *Stalin* (Englewood Cliffs, N.J.: Prentice-Hall, 1966), p. 111.

14. Quoted in Jonathan Glover, *Humanity: A Moral History of the Twentieth Century* (New Haven, Conn.: Yale University Press, 1999), p. 241.

15. Quoted in Zeev Sternhill, "Fascist Ideology," in *Fascism: A Reader's Guide*, ed. Walter Laqueur (Berkeley: University of California Press, 1976), p. 338.

16. Quoted in John Weiss, *The Fascist Tradition* (New York: Harper & Row, 1967), p. 9.

17. Quoted in F. L. Carsten, *The Rise of Fascism* (Berkeley: University of California Press, 1969), p. 53.

18. Quoted in Max Gallo, *Mussolini's Italy* (New York: Macmillan, 1973), p. 218.

19. Kurt Sontheimer, "Anti-Democratic Thought in the Weimar Republic," in *The Path to Dictatorship, 1918–1933*, trans. John Conway, intro. Fritz Stern (Garden City, N.Y.: Doubleday Anchor Books, 1966), pp. 47–49.

20. Quoted in Joachim Köhler, *Wagner's Hitler: The Prophet and His Disciple*, trans. Ronald Taylor (Cambridge, U.K.: Polity Press, 2000), p. 68.

21. Quoted in Joachim C. Fest, *Hitler*, trans. Richard and Clara Winston (New York: Harcourt Brace Jovanovich, 1974), p. 162.

22. Quoted in Karl J. Newman, *European Democracy between the Wars* (Notre Dame, Ind.: University of Notre Dame Press, 1971), p. 276.

23. Hajo Holborn, *Germany and Europe* (Garden City, N.Y.: Doubleday Anchor Books, 1971), p. 215.

24. Fest, *Hitler*, p. 548.

25. Quoted in Alan Bullock, *Hitler: A Study in Tyranny* (New York: Harper Torchbooks, 1964), p. 400.

26. *Hitler's Secret Conversations, 1941–1944*, with an introductory essay by H. R. Trevor Roper (New York: Farrar, Straus & Young, 1953), p. 28.

27. Quoted in Lucy S. Dawidowicz, *The War Against the Jews, 1933–1945* (New York: Holt, Rinehart & Winston, 1975), p. 21.

28. Quoted in Uri Tal, "Consecration of Politics in the Nazi Era," in *Judaism and Christianity Under the Impact of National Socialism,* ed. Otto Dov Kulka and Paul R. Mendes Flohr (Jerusalem: Historical Society of Israel, 1987), p. 70.

29. Adolf Hitler, *Mein Kampf,* trans. Ralph Mannheim (Boston: Houghton Mifflin, 1962), p. 107.

30. Ibid., p. 479.

31. Cited in Ian Kershaw, "Hitler and the Germans," in *Life in the Third Reich,* ed. Richard Bessel (New York: Oxford University Press, 1987), pp. 43–44.

32. Quoted in David Welch, ed., *Nazi Propaganda* (Totowa, N.J.: Barnes & Noble, 1983), p. 5.

33. Quoted in J. S. Conway, *The Nazi Persecution of the Churches* (New York: Basic Books, 1968), p. 202.

34. Quoted in Helmut Krausnick, Hans Buchheim, Martin Broszart, and Hans-Adolf Jacobsen, *Anatomy of the SS State* (London: Collins, 1968), p. 128.

35. Karl Dietrich Bracher, *The German Dictatorship,* trans. Jean Steinberg (New York: Praeger, 1970), p. 243.

36. *Hitler's Secret Conversations,* p. 6.

37. Quoted in Hans Rothfels, "Resistance Begins," in *Path to Dictatorship,* pp. 160–161.

38. Quoted in Guenter Lewy, *The Catholic Church and Nazi Germany* (New York: McGraw-Hill, 1965), p. 226.

39. Quoted in Hermann Graml et al., *The German Resistance to Hitler* (Berkeley: University of California Press, 1970), p. 206.

40. Quoted in Conway, *Nazi Persecution of the Churches,* p. 332.

41. Excerpted in George L. Mosse, ed., *Nazi Culture* (New York: Grosset & Dunlap, 1966), pp. 206–207.

42. Bracher, *German Dictatorship,* pp. 248, 251.

43. Quoted in T. L. Jarman, *The Rise and Fall of Nazi Germany* (New York: New York University Press, 1956), p. 182.

44. Quoted in Horst von Maltitz, *The Evolution of Hitler's Germany* (New York: McGraw-Hill, 1973), pp. 433–434.

45. Ibid., pp. 438–439.

46. Quoted in Bracher, *German Dictatorship,* p. 268.

47. Quoted in Fest, *Hitler,* p. 532.

Suggested Reading

Applebaum, Anne, *Gulag: A History* (2003). A portrait of Stalin's vast penal network and its inhabitants.

Bracher, Karl Dietrich, *The German Dictatorship* (1970). A highly regarded analysis of all phases of the Nazi state.

Burleigh, Michael, and Wolfgang Wippermann, *The Racial State: Germany 1933–1945* (1991). Persecution of Jews, gypsies, mentally handicapped, and homosexuals; analysis of racially motivated social policies of the Nazi regime.

Fischer, Klaus, *Nazi Germany: A New History* (1995). Probably the best one-volume treatment of Nazi Germany available.

Fritzsche, Peter, *Germans into Nazis* (1998). Tries to explain why Germans were attracted to the Nazi movement.

Jackel, Eberhard, *Hitler's Weltanschauung* (1972). An analysis of Hitler's world-view.

Laqueur, Walter, ed., *Fascism: A Reader's Guide* (1976). A superb collection of essays.

Montefiore, Simon Sebag, *Stalin: The Court of the Red Tsar* (2004). A close-up portrait of Stalin and his circle, drawing on new archival material.

Mosse, George L., *Nazi Culture* (1966). A representative collection of Nazi writings with a fine introduction.

Noakes, J., and G. Pridham, eds., *Nazism 1919–1945* (1983). A useful collection of primary sources in two volumes.

Rees, Laurence, *The Nazis: A Warning from History* (1997). A companion volume to the BBC documentary, its principal virtue lies in the testimonies of former Nazis.

Chapter 31

Thought and Culture in an Era of World Wars and Totalitarianism

Guernica, by Pablo Picasso, a passionate protest against fascism and the horrors of war. (Giraudon/Art Resource, © 2005 Estate of Pablo Picasso/Artists Rights Society (ARS), New York.

- **Intellectuals and Artists in Troubled Times**
- **Existentialism**
- **The Modern Predicament**

Focus Questions

1. Why and how did European intellectual and cultural life convey a mood of pessimism and disillusionment after World War I?

2. How did art and literature express a social conscience during the 1920s and 1930s?

3. What were the different ways that intellectuals struggled with the crisis of European society in an era of world war and totalitarianism?

4. What were some of the conditions that gave rise to existentialism? What are the basic principles of existentialism?

Online Study Center

This icon will direct you to interactive map and primary source activities on the website http://college.hmco.com/pic/perrywc8e.

The presuppositions of the Enlightenment, already eroding in the decades before World War I, seemed near collapse after 1918—another casualty of trench warfare. Economic distress, particularly during the Great Depression, also profoundly disoriented the European mind. Westerners no longer possessed a frame of reference, a common outlook for understanding themselves, their times, or the past. The core values of Western civilization—the self-sufficiency of reason and the inviolability of the individual—no longer seemed inspiring or binding.

The crisis of consciousness evoked a variety of responses. Having lost faith in the purpose of Western civilization, some intellectuals turned their backs on it or found escape in their art. Others sought a new hope in the Soviet experiment or in fascism; still others reaffirmed the rational-humanist tradition of the Enlightenment. Christian thinkers, repelled by the secularism, materialism, and rootlessness of the modern age, urged westerners to find renewed meaning and purpose in their ancestral religion. A philosophical movement called existentialism, which rose to prominence after World War II, aspired to make life authentic in a world stripped of universal values.

INTELLECTUALS AND ARTISTS IN TROUBLED TIMES

Postwar Pessimism

After World War I, Europeans looked at themselves and their civilization differently. It seemed that in science and technology they had unleashed powers that they could not control, and belief in the stability and security of European civilization appeared to be an illusion. Also illusory was the expectation that reason would banish surviving signs of darkness, ignorance, and injustice and usher in an age of continual progress. European intellectuals felt that they were living in a "broken world." In a time of heightened brutality and mobilized irrationality, the values of old Europe seemed beyond recovery. "All the great words," wrote D. H. Lawrence, "were cancelled out for that generation."[1] The fissures discernible in European civilization before 1914 had grown wider and deeper. To be sure, Europe also had its optimists—those who found reason for hope in the League of Nations and in the easing of international tensions and improved economic conditions in the mid 1920s. However, the Great Depression and the triumph of totalitarianism intensified feelings of doubt and disillusionment.

The somber mood that gripped intellectuals in the immediate postwar period had been anticipated by Freud in a series of papers published in 1915 under the title "Thoughts for the Times on War and Death." The war, said Freud, stripped westerners of those cultural restraints that had served to contain a murderous primeval aggressiveness, and it threatened to inflict irreparable damage on European civilization:

> We cannot but feel that no event has ever destroyed so much that is precious in the common possessions of humanity, confused so many of the clearest intelligences or so thoroughly debased what is highest. . . . [T]he war in which we had refused to believe broke out, and it brought—disillusionment. . . . It tramples in blind fury on all that comes in its way, as though there were to be no future and no peace among men after it is over. It cuts all the common bonds between the contending peoples, and threatens to leave a legacy of embitterment that will make any renewal of these bonds impossible for a long time to come.[2]

Other expressions of pessimism abounded. In 1919, Paul Valéry stated: "We modern civilizations have learned to recognize that we are mortal like the others. We feel that a civilization is as fragile as life."[3] "We are living today under the sign of the collapse of civilization,"[4] declared the humanitarian Albert Schweitzer in 1923. In the midst of the depression, Arnold Toynbee wrote: "The year 1931 was distinguished from previous years . . . by one outstanding feature. In 1931 men and women all over the world were seriously contemplating and frankly discussing the possibility that the Western system of Society might break down and cease to work."[5] The German philosopher Karl Jaspers noted in 1932 that "there is a growing awareness of imminent ruin tantamount to a dread of the approaching end of all that makes life worthwhile."[6]

In *All Quiet on the Western Front* (1929), Erich Maria Remarque dealt with the horrors of the war and their impact. A German soldier in the novel ponders the war's effect on youth:

> I am twenty years old; yet I know nothing of life but despair, death, fear, and fatuous superficiality cast over an abyss of sorrow. I see how peoples are set against one another, and in silence, unknowingly, foolishly, obediently, innocently slay one another. I see that the keenest brains of the world invent weapons and words to make it yet more refined and enduring. . . . all my generation is experiencing these things with me. . . . What do they expect of us if a time ever comes when the war is over? Through the years our business has been killing. . . . Our knowledge of life is limited to death. What will happen afterwards?[7]

In the poem "The Second Coming" (1919), William Butler Yeats conveys his sense of the dark times:

> Mere anarchy is loosed upon the world,
> The blood-dimmed tide is loosed, and everywhere
> The ceremony of innocence is drowned;
> The best lack all conviction, while the worst
> Are full of passionate intensity.
> Surely some revelation is at hand
> Surely the Second Coming is at hand.[8]

T. S. Eliot's "The Waste Land" (1922) also expresses a feeling of foreboding. In his image of a collapsing European civilization, Eliot creates a macabre scenario. Hooded hordes, modern-day barbarians, swarm over plains and lay waste cities. Jerusalem, Athens, Alexandria, Vienna, and London—each once a great spiritual or cultural center—are now collapsing.[9]

Other writers and thinkers also focused on the crises facing the Western world. Carl Gustav Jung, a Swiss psychologist, stated in *Modern Man in Search of a Soul* (1933):

> I believe I am not exaggerating when I say that modern man has suffered an almost fatal shock, psychologically speaking, and as a re-

*sult has fallen into profound uncertainty. . . .
The revolution in our conscious outlook,
brought about by the catastrophic results of
the World War, shows itself in our inner life
by the shattering of our faith in ourselves and
our own worth. . . . I realize only too well
that I am losing my faith in the possibility of a
rational organization of the world, the old
dream of the millennium, in which peace and
harmony should rule, has grown pale.[10]*

In 1936, the Dutch historian Johan Huizinga
wrote in a chapter entitled "Apprehension of
Doom":

*We are living in a demented world. And we
know it. . . . Everywhere there are doubts as
to the solidity of our social structure, vague
fears of the imminent future, a feeling that our
civilization is on the way to ruin. . . . almost
all things which once seemed sacred and immutable have now become unsettled, truth
and humanity, justice and reason. . . . The
sense of living in the midst of a violent crisis
of civilization, threatening complete collapse,
has spread far and wide.[11]*

In 1939, as the war clouds darkened, E. M.
Forster, the distinguished British novelist,
lamented:

*During the present decade thousands and
thousands of innocent people have been
killed, robbed, mutilated, insulted, imprisoned. We, the fortunate exceptions, learn of
this from the newspapers and from refugees,
we realize that it may be our turn next, and
we know that all these private miseries may
be the prelude to an incalculable catastrophe,
in which the whole of western civilization . . .
may go down. Perhaps history will point to
these years as the moment when man's inven-
tiveness finally outbalanced his moral growth,
and toppled him downhill.[12]*

The most influential expression of pessimism
was Oswald Spengler's *The Decline of the West*.
The first volume was published in July 1918, as
the war was drawing to a close, and the second
volume in 1922. The work achieved instant noto-

riety, particularly in Spengler's native Germany,
which was shattered by defeat. Spengler viewed
history as an assemblage of many different cultures that, like living organisms, experience birth,
youth, maturity, and death. What contemporaries
pondered most was Spengler's insistence that
Western civilization had entered its final stage
and that its death could not be averted.

According to Spengler, cultures had to pass
through three necessary stages: a heroic youth, a
creative maturity, and a decadent old age. In its
youth, during the Renaissance, said Spengler,
Western culture experienced the triumphs of
Michelangelo, Shakespeare, and Galileo; in its
maturity, during the eighteenth century, Western
culture reached its creative height in the music of
Mozart, the poetry of Goethe, and the philosophy
of Kant. But now, Western culture, entering old
age, was showing signs of decay: a growing materialism and skepticism, a disenchanted proletariat,
rampant warfare and competition for empire, and
decadent art forms. "Of great painting or great
music there can no longer be, for Western people,
any question," Spengler concluded.[13]

To an already troubled Western world, Spengler offered no solace. The West, like other cultures and like any living organism, was destined
to die. Its decline was irreversible and its death
inevitable; the symptoms of its degeneration were
already evident. Spengler's gloomy prognostica-
tion buttressed the fascists, who claimed that they
were creating a new civilization on the ruins of
the dying European civilization.

Online Study Center

Improve Your Grade
Primary Source: A Manifesto for the Twentieth Century?

Literature and Art: Innovation, Disillusionment, and Social Commentary

Postwar pessimism did not prevent writers and
artists from continuing the cultural innovations
begun before the war. In the works of D. H.
Lawrence, Marcel Proust, André Gide, James
Joyce, Franz Kafka, T. S. Eliot, and Thomas

FRANZ KAFKA (1883–1924). The troubled Czech-Jewish writer expressed the feelings of alienation and aloneness that burden people in the modern age. (*Corbis-Bettmann.*)

Mann, the modernist movement achieved a brilliant flowering. Often these writers gave expression to the troubles and uncertainties of the postwar period.

Franz Kafka (1883–1924), whose major novels, *The Trial* and *The Castle*, were published after his death, did not receive recognition until after World War II. Yet perhaps better than any other novelist of his generation, Kafka grasped the dilemma of the modern age. There is no apparent order or stability in Kafka's world. Human beings strive to make sense out of life, but everywhere ordinary occurrences thwart them. They are caught in a bureaucratic web, which they cannot control; they live in a nightmare society dominated by oppressive, cruel, and corrupt officials and amoral torturers. In Kafka's world, cruelty and injustice are accepted facts of existence, power is exercised without limits, and victims cooperate in their own destruction. Traditional values and ordinary logic do not operate.

Our world, thought to be secure, stable, and purposeful, easily falls apart. Like Kierkegaard, Kafka understood the intense anxiety that torments modern people.

In *The Trial*, for example, Josef K., an ordinary man who has no consciousness of wrongdoing, is arrested. "K. lived in a country with a legal constitution, there was universal peace, all the laws were in force; who dared seize him in his own dwelling?"[14] Josef K. is never told the reason for his arrest, and he is eventually executed, a victim of institutional evil that breaks and destroys him "like a dog." In these observations, Kafka anticipated the emerging totalitarian state. (Kafka's three sisters perished in the Holocaust.)

A German-speaking Jew in the alien Slav environment of Czechoslovakia, Kafka died of tuberculosis at an early age. In voicing his own deep anxieties, Kafka expressed the feelings of alienation and isolation that characterize the modern individual. He explored life's dreads and absurdities, offering no solutions or consolation. In Kafka's works, people are defeated and unable to comprehend the irrational forces that contribute to their destruction. Although the mind yearns for coherence, Kafka tells us that uncertainty, if not chaos, governs human relationships. We can be sure neither of our own identities nor of the world we encounter, for human beings are the playthings of unfathomable forces, too irrational to master.

A brooding pessimism about the human condition pervades Kafka's work. One reason for the intensified interest in Kafka after World War II, observes Angel Flores, "is that the European world of the late 30's and 40's with its betrayals and concentration camps, its resulting cruelties and indignities, bore a remarkable resemblance to the world depicted by Kafka in the opening decades of the century. History seems to have imitated the nightmarish background evoked by the dreamer of Prague."[15]

Before World War I, the German writer Thomas Mann (1875–1955) had earned a reputation for his short stories and novels, particularly *Buddenbrooks* (1901), which portrayed the decline of a prosperous bourgeois family. At the outbreak of the war, Mann was a staunch conservative who disliked democracy. After the war, he drew closer to liberalism, supporting the

Weimar Republic and attacking the Nazi cult of irrationalism.

In *Mario and the Magician* (1930), Mann explicitly attacked Italian fascism and implied that it would require armed resistance. In 1931, two years before Hitler took power, Mann, in an article entitled "An Appeal to Reason," described National Socialism and the extreme nationalism it espoused as a rejection of the Western rational tradition and a regression to primitive and barbaric modes of behavior. Nazism, he said, "is distinguished by . . . its absolute unrestraint, its orgiastic, radically anti-humane, frenziedly dynamic character. . . . Everything is possible, everything is permitted as a weapon against human decency. . . . Fanaticism turns into a means of salvation . . . politics becomes an opiate for the masses . . . and reason veils her face."[16]

After Hitler's seizure of power, Mann went to Switzerland and eventually to the United States, where he remained a resolute foe of totalitarianism. In 1938, he described the crisis of reason that afflicted his generation: "The twentieth century has in its first third taken up a position of reaction against classic rationalism and intellectualism. It has surrendered to admiration of the unconscious, to a glorification of instinct. And the bad instincts have accordingly been enjoying a heyday."[17]

In *The Magic Mountain*, begun in 1912 and completed in 1924, Mann had reflected on the decomposition of bourgeois European civilization. The novel is set in a Swiss sanatorium, just prior to World War I. The patients, drawn from several European lands, suffer from tuberculosis and are diseased in spirit, as well as body. The sanatorium symbolizes Europe. It is the European **psyche** that is sick and rushing headlong into a catastrophe.

The Magic Mountain, which ends with the advent of World War I, raised, but did not resolve, crucial questions. Was the epoch of rational-humanist culture drawing to a close? Did bourgeois Europe welcome its spiritual degeneration in the same way that some of the patients in the sanitarium had a will to illness? How could Europe rescue itself from decadence?

D. H. Lawrence (1885–1930), the son of an illiterate British coal miner, was saddened and angered by the consequences of industrial society: the deteri-oration of nature, tedious work divorced from personal satisfaction, and a life-denying quest for wealth and possessions. He looked back longingly on preindustrial England and wanted people to reorient their thinking away from moneymaking and suppression of the instincts. In his works he dealt with the clash between industrial civilization, which regiments human beings in the name of efficiency, and the needs of human nature. Thus in *Women in Love* (1920), the new owner of the family coal mine, determined to utilize modern management techniques in order to extract greater wealth from the business, dismisses the human needs of the workers:

Suddenly he had conceived the pure instrumentality of mankind. There had been so much humanitarianism, so much talk of sufferings and feelings. It was ridiculous. The sufferings and feelings of individuals did not matter in the least. . . . What mattered was the pure instrumentality of the individual. As a man as of a knife: does it cut well? Nothing else mattered.

Everything in the world has its function, and is good or not good in so far as it fulfills this function. . . . Was a miner a good miner? Then he was complete.[18]

In *Lady Chatterly's Lover* (1928), a highly erotic novel, Lawrence affirmed sexual passion as both necessary and beneficial for human well-being and criticized cultural norms that disfigured it with distaste, shame, and guilt.

Like nineteenth-century romantics, Lawrence found a higher truth in deep-seated passion than in reason; this led him to rail against Christianity for stifling human sexuality. Like Nietzsche, he believed that excessive intellectualizing destroyed the life-affirming, instinctual part of human nature. In 1913, he wrote:

My great religion is a belief in the blood, the flesh, as being wiser than the intellect. We can go wrong in our minds. But what our blood feels and believes and says is always true. The intellect is only a bit and a bridle. What do I care about knowledge. All I want is to answer to my blood without fribbling intervention of mind, or moral, or what not. . . . We have got so ridiculously mindful, that we never know that we ourselves are anything.[19]

Shattered by World War I, disgusted by fascism's growing strength, and moved by the suffering of the Depression, many writers became committed to social and political causes. Remarque's *All Quiet on the Western Front* was one of many antiwar novels. In *The Grapes of Wrath* (1939), John Steinbeck captured the suffering of American farmers losing their land when it became the Dust Bowl or driven from it by foreclosure during the Depression. George Orwell's *The Road to Wigan Pier* (1937) recorded the bleak lives of English workers. Few issues stirred the conscience of intellectuals as did the Spanish Civil War, and many of them volunteered to fight with the Spanish republicans against the fascists. Ernest Hemingway's *For Whom the Bell Tolls* (1940) expressed the sentiments of these thinkers.

New art trends emerged, mirroring the trauma of a generation that had experienced the war and lost its faith in Europe's moral and intellectual values. In 1915 in Zurich, artists and writers founded a movement, called *Dada*, to express their revulsion against the war and the civilization that spawned it. From neutral Switzerland, the movement spread to Germany and Paris. Dadaists viewed artistic and literary standards with contempt, rejected God, and glorified unreason. They celebrated nihilism for its own sake. "Through reason man becomes a tragic and ugly figure," said one Dadaist; "beauty is dead," said another. Dada shared in the postwar mood of disorientation and despair. Dadaists regarded life as essentially absurd (*Dada* is a nonsense term) and cultivated indifference. "The acts of life have no beginning or end. Everything happens in a completely idiotic way," declared the poet Tristan Tzara, one of Dada's founders. Tzara elevated spontaneity above reason:

> *What good did the theories of the philosophers do us? Did they help us to take a single step forward or backward? . . . We have had enough of the intelligent movements that have stretched beyond measure our credulity in the benefits of science. What we want now is spontaneity because everything that issues freely from ourselves, without the intervention of speculative ideas . . . represents us.*[20]

For Dadaists, the world was nonsensical, and reality disordered; hence, they offered no solutions to anything. "Like everything in life, Dada is useless," said Tzara.[21]

Dadaists showed their contempt for art (one art historian calls Dada "the first anti-art movement on record"[22]) by producing works that were deliberately senseless, purposeless, and chaotic, and apparently devoid of artistic value. Marcel Duchamp's *Bicycle Wheel* is an example, as is his *Mona Lisa* with a mustache. Despite the Dadaists' nihilistic aims and "calculated irrationality," says the art historian H. W. Janson, "there was also liberation, a voyage into unknown provinces of the creative mind." Thus, Duchamp's painting with the nonsense title *Tu m'* was "dazzlingly inventive [and] far ahead of its time."[23]

Dada ended as a formal movement in 1924 and was succeeded by surrealism. Surrealists inherited from Dada a contempt for reason. They stressed fantasy and made use of Freudian insights and symbols in their art to reproduce the raw state of the unconscious and to arrive at truths beyond reason's grasp. To penetrate the interior of the mind, said André Breton, a French surrealist poet, the writer should "write quickly without any previously chosen subject, quickly enough not to dwell on and not to be tempted to read over what you have written."[24] Writing should not be dictated by the intellect but should flow automatically from the unconscious. Surrealists tried to portray the world of fantasy and hallucination, the marvelous and the spontaneous. Breton urged artists to live their dreams, even if it meant seeing "a horse galloping on a tomato." In the effort to break through the constraints of rationality so that they might reach a higher reality—that is, a "surreality"—leading surrealists such as Max Ernst (1891–1976), Salvador Dali (1904–1989), and Joan Miró (1893–1983) used unconventional techniques and depicted an external world devoid of logic and normal appearances.

Artists, like writers, expressed a social conscience. George Grosz combined a Dadaist sense of life's meaninglessness with a new realism to depict the moral degeneration of middle-class German society. In *After the Questioning* (1935), Grosz, then living in the United States, drama-

HARLEQUIN'S CARNIVAL (1924), BY JOAN MIRÓ (1893–1983). In one of the first surrealist paintings, Miró makes visible an inner world of fantasy and humor populated by an array of imaginary creatures. (*Albright-Knox Art Gallery, Buffalo, New York, Room of Contemporary Art Fund, 1940. Copyright 1991, Artists Rights Society (ARS), N.Y., ADAGP.*)

tized Nazi brutality; in *The End of the World* (1936), he expressed his fear of another impending world war. Käthe Kollwitz, also a German artist, showed a deep compassion for the sufferer: the unemployed, the hungry, the ill, and the politically oppressed.

In a series of paintings, *The Passion of Sacco and Vanzetti* (1931–32), American artist Ben Shahn showed his outrage at the execution of two radicals. William Gropper's *Migration* (1932) dramatized the suffering of the same dispossessed farmers described in Steinbeck's novel *The Grapes of Wrath*. Philip Evergood, in *Don't Cry Mother* (1938–1944), portrayed the apathy of starving children and their mother's terrible helplessness.

In his etchings of maimed, dying, and dead soldiers, German artist Otto Dix produced a powerful visual indictment of the Great War's cruelty and suffering. Service in the German army during World War I made Max Beckmann acutely aware of violence and brutality, which he expressed in *The Night* (1918–19) and other paintings. Designated a "degenerate artist" by the Nazis, Beckmann went into exile. In *Guernica* (1937), Picasso memorialized the Spanish village decimated by Nazi saturation bombing during the Spanish Civil War. *White Crucifixion* (1938) by Marc Chagall, a Russian-born Jew who had settled in Paris, depicted the terror and flight of Jews in Nazi Germany.

Communism: "The God That Failed"

The economic misery of the Depression and the rise of fascist barbarism led many intellectuals to find a new hope, even a secular faith, in communism. They considered the Soviet experiment as a new beginning that promised a better future for all humanity. These intellectuals praised the Soviet Union for supplanting capitalist greed with socialist cooperation, replacing a haphazard economic system marred by repeated depressions with one based on planned production, and providing employment for everyone when joblessness was endemic in capitalist lands. Equating socialism with humanitarianism and capitalism with injustice, they believed that the Soviets were reorganizing society for the benefit of humanity. The American literary critic Edmund Wilson said that in the Soviet Union one felt at the "moral top of the world where the light never really goes out."[25] The British political theorists Sidney and Beatrice Webb declared that there was no other country "in which there is actually so much widespread public criticism and such incessant reevaluation of its shortcomings as in the USSR."[26] To these intellectuals, it seemed that in the Soviet Union a vigorous and healthy civilization was emerging and that only communism could stem the tide of fascism. Many of these deluded people, ignoring or refusing to recognize the reality of Stalin's terror, continued to embrace the Soviet system. For others, however, the attraction was short-lived. Sickened by Stalin's purges and terror, the denial of individual freedom, and the suppression of truth, they came to view the Soviet Union as another totalitarian state and communism as another "god that failed."

One such intellectual was Arthur Koestler. Born in Budapest of Jewish ancestry and educated in Vienna, Koestler worked as a correspondent for a leading Berlin newspaper chain. He joined the Communist party at the very end of 1931 because he "lived in a disintegrating society thirsting for faith," was moved by the suffering caused by the Depression, and saw communism as the "only force capable of resisting the onrush of the primitive [Nazi] horde."[27] Koestler visited the Soviet Union in 1933, experiencing firsthand both the starvation brought on by forced collectivization and the propaganda that grotesquely misrepre-

sented life in Western lands. Although his faith was shaken, he did not break with the party until 1938, in response to Stalin's liquidations.

In *Darkness at Noon* (1941), Koestler explored the attitudes of the Old Bolsheviks who were imprisoned, tortured, and executed by Stalin. These dedicated Communists had served the party faithfully, but Stalin, fearful of opposition, hating intellectuals, and driven by megalomania, denounced them as enemies of the people. The leading character in *Darkness at Noon*, the imprisoned Rubashov, is a composite of the Old Bolsheviks. Although he is innocent, Rubashov, without being physically tortured, publicly confesses to political crimes that he never committed.

Rubashov is aware of the suffering that the party has brought to the Russian people:

> [I]n the interests of a just distribution of land we deliberately let die of starvation about five million farmers and their families in one year. . . . [to liberate] human beings from the shackles of industrial exploitation . . . we sent about ten million people to do forced labour in the Arctic regions and the jungles of the East, under conditions similar to those of antique galley slaves. . . . to settle a difference of opinion, we know only one argument: death. . . . Our poets settle discussions on questions of style by denunciations to the Secret Police. . . . The people's standard of life is lower than it was before the Revolution, the labour conditions are harder, the discipline is more inhuman. . . . Our Press and our schools cultivate Chauvinism, militarism, dogmatism, conformism and ignorance. The arbitrary power of the Government is unlimited, and unexampled in history. Freedom of the Press, of opinion and of movement are as thoroughly exterminated as though the proclamation of the Rights of Man had never been. We have built up the most gigantic police apparatus, with informers made a national institution, and with the most refined scientific system of physical and mental torture. We whip the groaning masses of the country towards a theoretical future happiness, which only we can see.[28]

Pained by his own complicity in the party's crimes, including the betrayal of friends, Ruba-

ANGEL OF HEARTH AND HOME, BY MAX ERNST **(1891–1976).** Ernst formed part of the transition from Dada to surrealism. His paintings expressed a profound anxiety. André Breton called him "the most magnificently haunted mind in Europe." (© 2005 Successio Miro/Artists Rights Society (ARS), New York/ ADAGP, Paris.)

shov questions the party's philosophy that the individual should be subordinated and, if necessary, sacrificed to the regime. Nevertheless, Rubashov remains the party's faithful servant. True believers do not easily break with their faith. By confessing to treason, Rubashov performs his last service for the Revolution. For the true believer, everything—truth, justice, and the sanctity of the individual—is properly sacrificed to the party.

Reaffirming the Christian World-View

By calling into question core liberal beliefs—the essential goodness of human nature, the primacy of reason, the efficacy of science, and the inevitability of progress—World War I led thinkers to find in Christianity an alternative view of the human experience and the crisis of the twentieth century. Christian thinkers, including Karl Barth,

Paul Tillich, Reinhold Niebuhr, Christopher Dawson, Jacques Maritain, and T. S. Eliot, asserted the reality of evil in human nature. They assailed liberals and Marxists for holding too optimistic a view of human nature and human reason, postulating a purely rational and secular philosophy of history, and anticipating an ideal society within the realm of historical time. Reinhold Niebuhr (1892–1971), a leading American Protestant theologian, declared in 1941: "The utopian illusions and sentimental observations of modern liberal culture are really all derived from the basic error of negating the fact of original sin."[29] For these thinkers, the Christian conception of history as a clash between human will and God's commands provided an intelligible explanation of the tragedies of the twentieth century. Karl Barth (1886–1968), the Swiss-German Protestant theologian, called for a reaffirmation of the Christ who inspires faith, the uniqueness of Christianity, and the spiritual power of divine

Profile

Leni Riefenstahl

First achieving fame as a dancer, the strikingly beautiful Leni Riefenstahl (1902–2003) quickly gained further notoriety as an actress and movie director in her native Germany. Riefenstahl first heard Hitler speak in 1932, the year before he gained power; seduced by his passionate oratory, as were many other Germans, she believed he could save Germany. Subsequently, the now-famous cinematic figure requested an audience with Hitler, which was granted. Hitler later commissioned her to produce documentaries about his party, including *Triumph of the Will* (1935), a mesmerizing account of the Nazi party rally at Nuremberg in 1934. Daringly innovative, *Triumph of the Will* enhanced Riefenstahl's reputation as a cinematic genius. Aiming for dynamic, intensely visual effects, she had cameramen moving on roller skates and installed an elevator on a 140-foot flagpole in order to take shots from unusal angles. She also had circular tracks built around the podium from which Hitler spoke. In this way the camera could circle Hitler, generating, she wrote, "new and lively images." Choreographing sweeping panoramic views of parading storm troopers, massed torches, and a forest of Nazi banners with closeups of adoring, near-hysterical spectators and Hitler posing heroically and speaking passionately, Riefenstahl glorified Hitler as a semidivine leader and dramatized the Nazi movement as an irresist-

© CORBIS.

revelation. The true meaning of history, he said, is not to be found in the liberals' view of the progress of reason and freedom or in the Marxist conception of economic determinism. Rather, it derives from the fact that history is the arena in which the individual's faith is tested.

Jacques Maritain (1882–1973), a leading Catholic thinker, denounced core elements of the modern outlook: the autonomy of the individual, the autonomy of the mind, and a nonreligious humanism. He urged that the Christian philosophy of Thomas Aquinas be revived, for he believed that it successfully harmonized faith and reason. Maritain argued that "anthropomorphic humanism," which held that human beings by themselves alone can define life's purpose and create their own values, has utterly failed. Without guidance from a transcendental source, reason is powerless to control irrational drives, which threaten to degrade human existence. Without commitment to God's values, we find substitute faiths in fanatic and belligerent ideologies and unscrupulous leaders.

780

ible and triumphant force. It is likely that this powerful and seductive documentary gained supporters for the Nazis in Germany and throughout the world. *Triumph of the Will* demonstrates convincingly the power and danger of propaganda and the effectiveness of film as a propaganda tool.

Her artistry was further demonstrated in *Olympia* (1937), a documentary of the Olympic games held in Berlin in 1936. Distinguished by dazzling technological innovations, the film is still hailed as one of the finest sports documentaries ever made. Riefenstahl made creative use of cameras on a track to capture racing sprinters and of cameras underwater to show divers slicing into the pool. She deftly slowed and prolonged a shot of a dive, giving the diver the appearance of a swooping bird. She was at her best in personalizing the athlete: the determination and assuredness on the face of Jesse Owens, America's outstanding black track star, and the exhaustion and pain of marathon runners near the end of a grueling race.

After the war, Riefenstahl went through a denazification process and was eventually released from custody. However, her critics, who regarded her contemptuously as "Hitler's propagandist," never forgave her for employing her talents to serve the Nazis. Riefenstahl always protested her innocence, insisting that she had just been doing her art and not glorifying Hitler's ideology. She added that, at the time, she had been politically ignorant and had never joined the Nazi party. Rejecting her claim that *Triumph of the Will* was just art, her critics argued that the film, which radiated such admiration for the Nazi leader and his followers could only have been directed by a person who empathized with the Nazi movement and wanted to convey its message to a wide audience. Critics also noted, among other things, that she had read *Mein Kampf*—so much for her claim of being politically naive—and had sent Hitler a long, flowery congratulatory telegram after Paris fell.

A cultural outcast after World War II, Riefenstahl could not find backers for her film projects. (Ironically, many members of the Nazi party, some of them prominent, returned unhindered to their professions.) She did, however, find an outlet for her creative talents by photographing the Nuba tribe in the Sudan, which earned her praise. And at the age of 72, after starting and completing a course in scuba diving—she had to lie about her age in order to be accepted into the grueling program—Riefenstahl turned to still underwater photography, particularly capturing spectacular reefs in the Pacific, for which she earned additional praise. She died in 2003 at the age of 101. For many people she remains the finest female director of the past century, although a flawed human being who never repented for the evil she had helped promote.

A strong advocate of political freedom, Maritain stressed the link between modern democracy and the Christian Gospels, which proclaimed "the natural equality of all men, children of the same God and redeemed by the same Christ . . . [and] the inalienable dignity of every soul fashioned in the image of God." He insisted that "the democratic state of mind and . . . the democratic philosophy of life requires the energies of the Gospel to penetrate secular existence, taming the irrational to reason."[30] These energies would control the human propensity for self-centeredness, wickedness, and hatred of others. To survive, secular democracy must be infused with Christian love and compassion.

The English Catholic thinker Christopher Dawson (1889–1970) stressed the historic ties between Christianity and Western civilization. He wrote in 1933: "If our civilization is to recover its vitality, or even to survive, it must . . . realize that religion is . . . the very heart of social life and the root of every living culture."[31]

THE NIGHT (1918–19), BY MAX BECKMANN (1884–1950). Max Beckmann's paintings gave expression to the disillusionment and spiritual unease that afflicted postwar Germany. When the Nazis included his works in the Degenerate Art Exhibition (1937), he left the country. In *The Night*, Beckmann, himself a veteran of the front, depicts brutal men engaging in terrible violence. (*Kunstsammlung Nordrhein-Westfalen, Dusseldorf, Estate of Max Beckmann/ © 2005 Artists Rights Society (ARS), New York/VG Bild-Kunst, Bonn.*)

In 1934, the British historian Arnold Toynbee (1889–1975) published the first three volumes of his monumental work, *A Study of History*, in which he tried to account for the rise, growth, breakdown, and disintegration of civilization. Underlying Toynbee's philosophy of history was a religious orientation, for he saw religious prophets as humanity's greatest figures and the world's major religions as humanity's greatest achievement. Toynbee attributed the problems of Western civilization to its breaking away from Christianity and embracing "false idols," particularly the national state, which, he said, had become the object of westerners' highest reverence.

Toynbee regarded nationalism as a primitive religion, inducing people to revere the national community rather than God. This deification of the parochial—tribal or local—community intensified the brutal side of human nature and provoked wars among people sharing a common civilization. To Toynbee, Nazism was the culmination of the worst elements in modern European nationalism, "the consummation . . . of a politico-religious movement, the pagan deification and worship of parochial human communities which had been gradually gaining ground for more than four centuries in the Western world at large."[32] The moral catastrophe of Nazism, he said, demonstrates the inadequacy of liberal humanism, for the Enlightenment tradition proved a feeble barrier to the rise and spread of Nazism. The secular values of the Enlightenment, divorced from Christianity, cannot restrain human nature's basest impulses. For the West to save itself, said Toynbee, it must abide by the spiritual values of its religious prophets.

Reaffirming the Ideals of Reason and Freedom

Several thinkers tried to reaffirm the ideals of rationality and freedom that totalitarian movements had trampled. In *The Treason of the Intellectuals* (1927), Julien Benda (1867–1956), a French cultural critic of Jewish background, castigated intellectuals for intensifying hatred between nations and classes. "Our age is indeed the age of the intellectual organization of political hatreds," he wrote. Intellectuals who stir up hatred between nations, said Benda, do not pursue justice or truth but proclaim that "even if our country is wrong, we must think of it in the right." They scorn outsiders, extol harshness and action, and proclaim the superiority of instinct and will to intelligence; or they "assert that the intelligence to be venerated is that which limits its activities within the bounds of national interest." The logical end of this xenophobia, said Benda, "is the organized slaughter of nations and classes."[33]

José Ortega y Gasset (1883–1955), descendant of a Spanish noble family, gained international recognition with the publication of *The Revolt of the Masses* (1930). According to Ortega, European civilization, the product of a creative elite, was degenerating into barbarism because of the growing power of the masses, for the masses lacked the mental discipline and the commitment to reason needed to preserve Europe's intellectual and cultural traditions. Ortega did not equate the masses with the working class and the elite with the nobility; an attitude of mind, not a class affiliation, distinguished the "mass-man" from the elite.

The mass-man, said Ortega, has a commonplace mind and does not set high standards for himself. He is inert until driven by an external compulsion. He does not enter into rational dialogue with others, defend his opinions logically, or accept objective standards. Faced with a problem, he "is satisfied with thinking the first thing he finds in his head" and "crushes . . . everything that is different, everything that is excellent, individual, qualified, and select. Anybody who is not like everybody, who does not think like everybody, runs the risk of being eliminated."[34] Such intellectually vulgar people, declared Ortega, cannot understand or preserve the processes of civilization. The fascists exemplify this revolt of the masses, for "under fascism there appears for the first time in Europe a type of man who . . . simply shows himself resolved to impose his opinions. This is the new thing: the right not to be reasonable, the 'reason of unreason.'" The danger lay in "the masses . . . having decided to rule society without the capacity for doing so."[35] Rejecting reason, the mass-man glorifies violence: the ultimate expression of barbarism. If European civilization is to be rescued from fascism and communism, said Ortega, the elite must sustain civilized values and provide leadership.

A staunch defender of the Enlightenment tradition, Ernst Cassirer (1874–1945), a German philosopher of Jewish lineage, emigrated after Hitler came to power, eventually settling in the United States. Just prior to Hitler's triumph, Cassirer wrote of the need to uphold and reenergize that tradition: "The age which venerated reason and science as man's highest faculty cannot and must not be lost even for us. We must find a way not only to see that age in its own shape but to release again those original forces which brought forth and molded this shape."[36]

In his posthumous work, *The Myth of the State* (1946), Cassirer described Nazism as the triumph of mythical thinking over reason. The Nazis, said Cassirer, cleverly manufactured myths—of the race, the leader, the party, the state—that disoriented the intellect. Germans who embraced these myths surrendered their capacity for independent judgment, leaving themselves vulnerable to manipulation by the Nazi leadership. Cassirer warned:

In politics we are always living on volcanic soil. We must be prepared for convulsions and eruptions. In all critical moments of man's social life, the rational forces that resist the rise of old mythical conceptions are no longer sure of themselves. In these moments the time of myth has come again. For myth has not been really vanquished and subjugated. It is always there, lurking in the dark and waiting for its hour and opportunity. This hour comes as soon as the other binding forces of man's social life . . . lose their strength and are no longer able to combat the demonic mythical powers.[37]

To contain the destructive powers of political myths, Cassirer urged strengthening the rational-humanist tradition and called for the critical study of political myths, for "in order to fight an enemy you must know him."[38]

Like Cassirer and many other German-Jewish intellectuals, Erich Fromm (1900–1980), a social theorist and psychoanalyst, settled in the United States after the Nazis took power. In *Escape from Freedom* (1941), Fromm explained the triumph of Nazism within the wider context of European history. During the Middle Ages, said Fromm, the individual derived a sense of security from a structured social system, which clearly defined the role of clergy, lords, and serfs, and from a Christian world-view, which made life and death purposeful. Modern westerners have lost this sense of security. Dwelling in impersonal cities, threatened by economic crises, no longer comforted by the medieval conception of life's purpose, they are often tormented by doubts and overwhelmed by feelings of aloneness and insignificance. People try to overcome this "burden of freedom" by surrendering themselves to a person or power that they view "as being overwhelmingly strong;" they trade freedom for security by entering into "a symbiotic relationship that overcomes . . . aloneness."[39] Because modern industrial society has made the individual feel powerless and insignificant, concluded Fromm, fascism is a constant threat. Fromm would meet the challenge of fascism by creating social conditions that lead the individual to be free yet not alone, to be critical yet not filled with doubts, to be independent yet feel an integral part of humankind.

George Orwell (1903–1950), a British novelist and political journalist, wrote two powerful indictments of totalitarianism: *Animal Farm* (1945) and *1984* (1949). In *Animal Farm*, based in part on his experiences with communists during the Spanish Civil War, Orwell satirized the totalitarian regime built by Lenin and Stalin in Russia. In *1984*, Orwell, who was deeply committed to human dignity and freedom, warned that these great principles are now permanently menaced by the concentration and abuse of political power. "If you want a picture of the future, imagine a boot stamping on a human face forever," says a member of the ruling elite as he tortures a victim in the dungeons of the Thought Police.[40]

EXISTENTIALISM

Intellectual Background

The philosophical movement that best exemplified the anxiety and uncertainty of Europe in an era of world wars was **existentialism.** Like writers and artists, existentialist philosophers were responding to a European civilization that seemed to be in the throes of dissolution. Although existentialism was most popular after World War II, expressing the anxiety and despair of many intellectuals who had lost confidence in reason and progress, several of its key works were written prior to or during the war.

What route should people take in a world where old values and certainties had dissolved, where universal truth was rejected and God's existence denied? How could people cope in a society where they were menaced by technology, manipulated by impersonal bureaucracies, and overwhelmed by feelings of anxiety? If the universe is devoid of any overarching meaning, what meaning could one give to one's own life? These questions were at the crux of existentialist philosophy.

Basic Principles

Existentialism does not lend itself to a single definition, for its principal theorists did not adhere to a common body of doctrines. For example, some existentialists were atheists, like Jean Paul Sartre, or omitted God from their thought, like Martin Heidegger; others, like Karl Jaspers, believed in God but not in Christian doctrines; still others, like Gabriel Marcel and Nikolai Berdyaev, were Christians; and Martin Buber was a believing Jew. Perhaps the essence of existentialism appears in the following principles, although not all existentialists would subscribe to each point or agree with the way it is expressed.

1. Reality defies ultimate comprehension; there are no timeless truths that exist independently of and prior to the individual human being. Existence—our presence in the here-and-now—precedes and takes precedence over any presumed absolute values. The moral and spiritual values that society tries to impose cannot define the individual person's existence. Our traditional morality rests on no foundation whose certainty can either be demonstrated by reason or guaranteed by God. There are simply no transcendent absolutes; to think otherwise is to surrender to illusion.

2. Reason alone is an inadequate guide to living, for people are more than thinking subjects who approach the world through critical analysis. They are also feeling and willing beings, who must participate fully in life and experience existence directly, actively, and passionately. Only in this way does one live wholly and authentically.

3. Thought must not merely be abstract speculation but must have a bearing on life; it must be translated into deeds.

4. Human nature is problematic and paradoxical, not fixed or constant; each person is like no other. Self-realization comes when one affirms one's own uniqueness. One becomes less than human when one permits one's life to be determined by a mental outlook—a set of rules and values—imposed by others.

5. We are alone. The universe is indifferent to our expectations and needs, and death is ever stalking us. Awareness of this elementary fact of existence evokes a sense of overwhelming anxiety and depression.

6. Existence is essentially absurd. There is no purpose to our presence in the universe. We simply find ourselves here; we do not know and will never find out why. Compared with the eternity of time that preceded our birth and will follow our death, the short duration of our existence seems trivial and inexplicable. And death, which irrevocably terminates our existence, testifies to the ultimate absurdity of life.

7. We are free. We must face squarely the fact that existence is purposeless and absurd. In doing so, we can give our life meaning. It is in the act of choosing freely from among different possibilities that the individual shapes an authentic existence. There is a dynamic quality to human existence; the individual has the potential to become more than he or she is.

Nineteenth-Century Forerunners

Three nineteenth-century thinkers—Søren Kierkegaard (see Chapter 24), Fyodor Dostoevski (see Chapter 28), and Friedrich Nietzsche (see Chapter 28)—were the principal forerunners of existentialism. Their views of reason, will, truth, and existence greatly influenced twentieth-century existentialists.

Kierkegaard. A Danish religious philosopher and Lutheran pastor, Kierkegaard held that self-realization as a human being comes when the individual takes full responsibility for his or her life. The individual does so by choosing one way of life over another. In making choices, said Kierkegaard, the individual overcomes the agonizing feeling that life in its deepest sense is nothingness.

Twentieth-century existentialists took from Kierkegaard the idea that an all-consuming dread is the price of existence. "I stick my finger into existence," said Kierkegaard, "—it smells of nothing. Where am I? What is this thing called the world? Who is it who has lured me into the thing, and now leaves me here? Who am I? How did I come into the world? Why was I not consulted?"[41] The sense that we live in a meaningless world drives us to the edge of the abyss. This overwhelming dread can cause us to flee from life and to find comfort in delusions. But it can also spark courage since it is an opportunity to make a commitment. For both Kierkegaard and twentieth-century existentialists, the true philosophical quest is a subjective experience: the isolated individual, alone and without help, choosing a way of life to which he or she is deeply committed. Only in this way does the individual become a whole person. Kierkegaard's dictum that "it is impossible to exist without passion"—that our actions matter to us—is at the heart of existentialism.

Dostoevski. Although existentialist themes pervade several of Dostoevski's works, it is in *Notes from Underground* (1864) that he treats explicitly the individual's quest for personal freedom, identity, and meaning and the individual's revolt against established norms—themes that are crucial to the outlook of twentieth-century existentialists.

Nietzsche. Friedrich Nietzsche was an important forerunner of existentialism for several reasons. He stated that philosophical systems are merely expressions of an individual's own being and do not constitute an objective representation of reality; there is no realm of being that is the source of values. Nor does religion provide truth, for God is dead. And, asked Nietzsche, is not this godless world absurd? Nietzsche held that modern westerners had lost all their traditional supports. To overcome nothingness, said Nietzsche, individuals must define life for themselves and celebrate it fully, instinctively, and heroically. Nietzsche's insistence that individuals confront existence squarely, without hypocrisy, and give it meaning—their own meaning—was vital to the shaping of existentialism.

Twentieth-Century Existentialists

Heidegger. The German philosopher Martin Heidegger (1889–1976), generally regarded as the central figure in the development of existentialist thought, presents a problem to students of philosophy. First, Heidegger rejected being classified as an existentialist. Second, he wrote in a nearly incomprehensible style, which obscured his intent. Third, in 1933, Heidegger, recently elected rector of the University of Freiburg, joined the National Socialist party and publicly praised Hitler and the Nazi regime. The following year, he resigned as rector and gave no further support to the Third Reich, although he remained a member of the Nazi party and continued to sympathize with some Nazi ideals. Heidegger's dalliance with Nazism caused some thinkers either to dis-

miss him or to minimize his importance as a valid philosopher.

In his pathbreaking book, *Being and Time* (1927), Heidegger asked: what does it mean *to be*, to say *I am*? Most people shun this question, said Heidegger; consequently, they live inauthentically, merely accepting a way of life set by others. Such people, he said, have "fallen from being;" they do not reflect on their existence or recognize the various possibilities and choices that life offers. Rather, they flee from their own selves and accept society's values without reflection. Neither their actions nor their goals are their own; they have forfeited a human being's most distinctive qualities: freedom and creativity.

To live authentically, declared Heidegger, the individual has to face explicitly the problem of Being; that is, one has to determine one's own existence, create one's own possibilities, and make choices and commitments. Choosing, said Heidegger, is not just a matter of disengaged thought, for the human creature is more than a conscious knower. The authentic life encompasses the feelings, as well as the intellect; it is a genuine expression of a person's whole being.

Coming to grips with death, said Heidegger, provides us with the opportunity for an authentic life. The trauma of our mortality and finiteness, the image of the endless void in which Being passes into non-Being, overwhelms us with dread; we come face to face with the insignificance of human existence, with directionless lives. To escape this dread, said Heidegger, some people immerse themselves in life's petty details or adopt others' prescribed values. But dread of death is also an opportunity. It can put us in touch with our uniqueness, our own Being, letting us take hold of our own existence to make life truly our own.

The authentic life requires, said Heidegger, that we see ourselves within the context of historical time, for we cannot escape the fact that our lives are bound by conditions and outlooks inherited from the past. Human beings are thrown into a world that is not of their own making. They dwell in a particular society, which carries with it the weight of the past and the tensions and conflicts of the present. Without knowledge of these conditions, Heidegger declared, events and things will always impose themselves on us, and we will not have the courage to reject conventions that we had no part in shaping. Although our future is related to the past, it is not determined by it.

Jaspers. Karl Jaspers (1883–1969), a German psychiatrist turned philosopher, was a leading figure in the existentialist movement. Jaspers fell into disfavor with the Nazi regime (he advocated liberal-humanist values, and his wife was Jewish) and lost his position as professor of philosophy at Heidelberg University. Like Kierkegaard, Jaspers held that philosophy and science cannot provide certainty. Also like Kierkegaard, he sought to discover the genuine self through an encounter with life. Like Heidegger, he held that while death makes us aware of our finitude, thereby promoting anxiety, it also goads us to focus on what is truly important and to do so immediately. Jaspers insisted that the individual has the power to choose. To be aware of this freedom and to use it is the essence of being human:

> Man is always something more than what he knows of himself. He is not what he is simply once for all, but is a process; he is . . . endowed with possibilities through the freedom he possesses to make of himself what he will by the activities on which he decides.[42]

Feelings of guilt and anxiety inevitably accompany free will, said Jaspers. Nevertheless, we must have the courage to make a choice, for it is in the act of choosing that the individual shapes his or her true self.

Although Jaspers rejected revealed religion, dogma, and the authority of churches, he did postulate what he called "philosophical faith." He thought of human existence as an encounter with Transcendence: "the eternal, indestructible, the immutable, the source [that] . . . can be neither visualized nor grasped in thought."[43] Jaspers did not equate Transcendence with God in the conventional sense, but the concept is laden with theistic qualities. Although not a traditional Christian, Jaspers was no atheist.

Sartre. The outlook of several French existentialists—Jean Paul Sartre (1905–1980), Maurice Merleau-Ponty (1908–1961), Albert Camus (1913–1960), and Simone de Beauvoir (1908–

1987)—was shaped by their involvement in the resistance to Nazi occupation during World War II. Sartre, the leading French existentialist, said that their confrontation with terror and torture taught them "to take evil seriously." Evil is not the effect of ignorance that might be remedied by knowledge or of passions that might be controlled, said Sartre; rather, it is a central fact of human existence and is unredeemable. Facing capture and death, the members of the French resistance understood what it is to be a solitary individual in a hostile universe. Living on the cutting edge of life, they rediscovered the essence of human freedom: they could make authentic choices. By saying no to the Nazis and resisting them, they confronted existence squarely. They faced the central problem that concerned Sartre: what does it mean to be a human being?

In contrast to Kierkegaard and Jaspers, Sartre defined himself as an atheist and saw existentialism as a means of facing the consequences of a godless universe. Atheistic existentialism, he said, begins with the person and not with God, a preestablished ethic, or a uniform conception of human nature.

For Sartre, existence precedes essence: that is, there are no values that precede the individual metaphysically or chronologically to which he or she must conform. There exists no higher realm of Being and no immutable truths that serve as ultimate standards of virtue. It is unauthentic to submit passively to established values, which one did not participate in making. The individual has nothing to cling to; he or she is thrown into the world "with no support and no aid."[44]

It is the first principle of existentialism, said Sartre, that we must each choose our own ethics, define ourselves, and give our own meaning to our life. Through our actions, we decide how we shall create ourselves. According to Sartre, we are what we do; each individual is "nothing else than the ensemble of his acts, nothing else than his life. . . . man's destiny is within himself." As free conscious beings, we are totally responsible for defining our lives and for giving them meaning and value. "Not only is man what he conceives himself to be, but he is also what he wills himself to be," Sartre said, and "existentialism's first move is to make every man aware of what he is and to make full responsibility of his existence rest on him."[45]

JEAN PAUL SARTRE AND SIMONE DE BEAUVOIR. Sartre and de Beauvoir were two of the principal exponents of existentialism. (*G. Pierre/Corbis-Sygma.*)

In Sartre's view, a true philosophy does not engage in barren discourses on abstract themes; it makes commitments and incurs risks. We are not objectified instruments, determined and shaped by material forces, as Marxism teaches. Nor do unconscious drives determine our actions, as Freud contended. For Sartre, we are not helpless prisoners of our genes, of the environment, of historical forces, or of culture. Rather, we alone are responsible for who we are and for the feelings that torment, trap, and immobilize us. True, the conditions in which we find ourselves impinge on our existence, but it is up to us to decide what to do about them. Thus, said Sartre, a French man or woman had to choose between being a patriot or a traitor during the German occupation. Similarly, an alcoholic made poor choices and continues to make them.

Online Study Center

Improve Your Grade
Primary Source: Existentialism Defined
(Sartre)

We have the capacity to plunge decisively, audaciously into life and constantly to recreate ourselves. We have no control over the fact that we exist; existence is simply given to us. But each individual does decide his or her own peculiar essence. We do so by the particular way we choose to live. The realization that we have the freedom to decide for ourselves what kind of person we are going to be, and what meaning we give to our lives, can be liberating and exhilarating. But it can also fill us with a dread that immobilizes or that leads us to seek refuge in a role selected for us by others. When we abdicate the responsibility of choosing a meaning for our lives, said Sartre, we live in "bad faith."

Camus. Reared and educated in French-ruled Algeria, Albert Camus gained an instant reputation in 1942 with the publication of *The Stranger*, a short novel, and *The Myth of Sisyphus*, a philosophical essay. During World War II, he served in the French resistance. His most important books in the decade after the war were two works of fiction, *The Plague* (1947) and *The Fall* (1956), as well as *The Rebel* (1951), a collection of interpretive essays on historical, philosophical, and esthetic topics.

Camus dealt with the existential theme of the individual struck by the awareness of God's nonexistence and of an impending rendezvous with an eternity of nothingness. Does this mean that my life is without meaning? That my actions do not matter? Camus rejected both suicide and nihilism as responses to this absurdity of existence. Even though existence has no higher meaning and the universe is indifferent to us, we must still accept "the desperate encounter between human inquiry and the silence of the universe."[46] Life may be absurd, but this absurdity is no justification for resignation.

Camus expressed a distaste for abstractions and ideologies because they led their adherents to torture and murder. These beliefs, claiming certainty, cause people to lose sight of their fellows as flesh-and-blood individuals and provide justification for barbarous criminal acts. In 1946, he wrote: "We have seen lying, degradation, killing, deportation, and torture and, each time, it was not possible to persuade those who did it not to do it, because they were sure of themselves and because one does not persuade an abstraction, that is, the representative of an ideology."[47] Ultimately, Camus saw a moralistic humanism that promoted human fraternity and human dignity as a worthwhile response to the absurdity of the human condition. Human beings should aspire to serve "those few values without which a world . . . isn't worth living in, without which a man . . . is not worthy of respect."[48]

For Camus, neither religion nor philosophy provides a basis for human values or can tell us with certainty what is right or wrong. No final authority can be found in a transcendental heaven or in reason's dictates. Thus, when a priest tries to make a condemned man aware of his guilt and his spiritual needs, the prisoner responds: "He seemed so certain about everything, didn't he. And yet none of his certainties was worth one hair of a woman's head."[49] Values may not be absolute or eternal, maintained Camus, but he did urge living by values that advance human dignity and warm human relations; we must find a life-enhancing alternative to the nihilistic conclusion that life is valueless and

meaningless. Reason and experience will never enable us to ascribe a transcendent or ultimate significance to life. Nevertheless, they are effective and helpful guides to escape the nihilistic abyss and to make life worth living.

Religious Existentialism. Several thinkers are classified as religious existentialists, among them Nikolai Berdyaev (1874–1948), an exile from Communist Russia; Martin Buber (1878–1965), a Jew who fled Nazi Germany; and Gabriel Marcel (1889–1973), a French Catholic. During World War I, Marcel served with the French Red Cross, accounting for soldiers missing in battle. This shattering experience brought the sensitive thinker face to face with the tragedy of human existence. A growing concern with the spiritual life led him to convert to Catholicism in 1929.

The modern individual, said Marcel in 1933, "tends to appear to himself and to others as an agglomeration of functions." A person is viewed as an entrepreneur, a laborer, a consumer, a citizen. The hospital serves as a repair shop, and death "becomes, objectively and functionally, the scrapping of what has ceased to be of use and must be written off as a total loss."[50] In such a functional world, maintained Marcel, people are valued for what they produce and possess. If they do not succeed as merchants, bookkeepers, or ticket-takers, people judge them and they judge themselves as personal failures. Such an outlook suffocates spirituality and deprives the individual of the joy of existence. It produces an "intolerable unease" in the individual, "who is reduced to living as though he were in fact submerged by his function. . . . Life in a world centered on function is liable to despair because in reality this world is empty, it rings hollow."[51]

Marcel wanted people to surpass a functional and mechanical view of life and explore the mystery of existence—to penetrate to a higher level of reality. Marcel held that one penetrates ultimate reality when one overcomes egocentricity and exists for others, when one loves and is loved by others. When we exist through and for others, when we treat another person not as an object performing a function but as a "thou" who matters to us, we soar to a higher level of existence. When we are actively engaged with others in concrete human situations, we fulfill ourselves as human beings; when we actively express love and fidelity toward others, life attains a higher meaning. Such involvement with others, said Marcel, provides us with a glimpse of a transcendent reality and is a testimony to God's existence. Marcel maintained that faith in God overcomes the anxiety and despair that characterize the modern predicament. It also improves the quality of human relationships, for if we believe that all people matter to God, they are more likely to matter to us.

THE MODERN PREDICAMENT

The process of fragmentation that had begun in European thought and the arts at the end of the nineteenth century accelerated after World War I. Increasingly, philosophers, writers, and artists expressed disillusionment with the rational-humanist tradition of the Enlightenment. They no longer shared the Enlightenment confidence in reason's capabilities or in human goodness, and they viewed perpetual progress as an illusion.

For some thinkers, the crucial problem was the great change in the European understanding of truth. Since the rise of philosophy in ancient Greece, Western thinkers had believed in the existence of objective, universal truths: truths that were inherent in nature and applied to all peoples at all times. (Christianity, of course, also taught the reality of truth as revealed by God.) It was held that such truths—the natural rights of the individual, for example—could be apprehended by the intellect and could serve as a standard for individual aspirations and social life. The recognition of these universal principles, it was believed, compelled people to measure the world of the here-and-now in the light of rational and universal norms and to institute appropriate reforms. Philosophy had the task of reconciling human existence with the objective order.

During the nineteenth century, the existence of universal truth came into doubt. A growing historical consciousness led some thinkers to maintain that what people considered truth was merely a reflection of their culture at a given stage in history—their perception of things at a specific point in the evolution of human consciousness. These thinkers, called *historicists,*

held that universal truths were not woven into the fabric of nature. There are no natural rights of life, liberty, and property that constitute the individual's birthright; there are no standards of justice or equality that are inherent in nature and ascertainable by reason. It was people, said historicists, who elevated the beliefs and values of an age to the status of objective truth. The normative principles—the self-evident truths proclaimed by Jefferson—that for the philosophes constituted a standard for political and social reform and a guarantee of human rights were no longer linked to the natural order, to an objective reality that could be confirmed by reason. As Hannah Arendt noted, "We certainly no longer believe, as the men of the French Revolution did, in a universal cosmos of which man was a part and whose natural laws he had to imitate and conform to."[52]

This radical break with the traditional attitude toward truth contributed substantially to the crisis of European consciousness that marked the first half of the twentieth century. Traditional values and beliefs, either those inherited from the Enlightenment or those taught by Christianity, no longer gave Europeans a sense of certainty and security. People were left without a normative order to serve as a guide to living—and without such a guide might be open to nihilism. For if nothing is fundamentally true—if there are no principles of morality and justice that emanate from God or can be derived from reason—then it can be concluded, as Nietzsche understood, that everything is permitted. Some scholars interpreted Nazism as the culminating expression of a nihilistic attitude grown ever more brutal.

By the early twentieth century, the attitude of westerners toward reason had also undergone a radical transformation. Some thinkers, who had placed their hopes in the rational tradition of the Enlightenment, were distressed by reason's inability to resolve the tensions and conflicts of modern industrial society. Moreover, the growing recognition of the nonrational—of human actions determined by hidden impulses—led to doubts that reason plays the dominant role in human behavior. The intellect did not seem autonomous and self-regulating but instead seemed subject to the rebellious demands of unconscious drives and impulses. Men's and women's propensity for goodness, their capacity to improve society, and their potential for happiness seemed severely limited by an inherent irrationality. Indeed, civilization itself seemed threatened by people's instinctual needs, as Freud had proclaimed.

Other thinkers viewed the problem of reason differently. They attacked reason for fashioning a technological and bureaucratic society that devalued and crushed human emotions and stifled individuality; these thinkers insisted that human beings cannot fulfill their potential, cannot live wholly, if their feelings are denied. They agreed with D. H. Lawrence's critique of rationalism: "The attribution of rationality to human nature, instead of enriching it, now seems to me to have impoverished it. It ignored certain powerful and valuable springs of feeling. Some of the spontaneous, irrational outbursts of human nature can have a sort of value from which our schematism was cut off."[53]

These thinkers pointed out that reason was a double-edged sword: it could demean, as well as ennoble and liberate, the individual. They attacked all theories that subordinated the individual to a rigid system. They denounced positivism for reducing human personality to psychological laws, and Marxism for making social class a higher reality than the individual. Rebelling against political collectivization, which regulated individual existence according to the needs of the corporate state, they assailed modern bureaucracy and technology. These creations of the rational mind, they claimed, had fashioned a social order that devalued and depersonalized the individual, denying people an opportunity for independent growth and a richer existence. According to these thinkers, modern industrial society, in its drive for efficiency and uniformity, deprived people of their uniqueness and reduced human beings to cogs in a mechanical system.

Responding to the critics of reason, other philosophers maintained that it was necessary to reaffirm respect for the rational tradition, first proclaimed by the ancient Greeks and given its modern expression by the Enlightenment philosophes. Reason, said these thinkers, was indispensable to civilization. What they advocated was broadening the scope of reason to accommodate the insights into human nature offered by the romantics, Nietzsche, Freud, modernist writers and artists, and others who explored the world of feelings, will, and the subconscious. They also stressed the need to humanize reason so that it could never threaten to reduce a human being to a thing.

In the decades shaped by world wars and totalitarianism, intellectuals raised questions that went to the heart of the dilemma of modern life. How can civilized life be safeguarded against human irrationality, particularly when it is channeled into political ideologies that idolize the state, the leader, the party, or the race? How can individual human personality be rescued from a relentless rationalism that reduces human nature and society to mechanical systems and seeks to regulate and organize the individual as it would any material object? Do we, as human beings, have the moral and spiritual resolve to use properly the technological and scientific creations of modern civilization, or will they devour us? Do the values associated with the Enlightenment provide a sound basis on which to integrate society? Can the individual find meaning in what many came to regard as a meaningless universe? World War II gave these questions a special poignancy.

❖ ❖ ❖

Online Study Center ACE the Test

NOTES

1. Quoted in Barbara Tuchman, *The Guns of August* (New York: Macmillan, 1962), p. 440.

2. Sigmund Freud, "Thoughts for the Times on War and Death," in the *Standard Edition of the Complete Psychological Works of Freud*, vol. 14, ed. James Strachey (London: Hogarth Press, 1957), pp. 275, 278.

3. Quoted in Hans Kohn, "The Crisis in European Thought and Culture," in *World War I: A Turning Point in Modern History*, ed. Jack J. Roth (New York: Knopf, 1967), p. 28.

4. Quoted in Franklin L. Baumer, "Twentieth-

Century Version of the Apocalypse," *Cahiers d'Histoire Mondiale* (Journal of World History), 1 (January 1954): 624.

5. Quoted in William McNeill, *Arnold J. Toynbee: A Life* (New York: Oxford University Press, 1989), p. 152.

6. Baumer, "Apocalypse," p. 624.

7. Erich Maria Remarque, *All Quiet on the Western Front*, trans. A. W. Wheen (Boston: Little, Brown, 1929), p. 224.

8. W. B. Yeats, "The Second Coming," in *Collected Poems of W. B. Yeats* (New York: Macmillan, 1956), pp. 184–185.

9. T. S. Eliot, "The Waste Land," in *Collected Poems, 1909–1962* (New York: Harcourt, Brace, 1970), p. 67.

10. Carl Gustav Jung, *Modern Man in Search of a Soul*, trans. W. S. Dell and Cary F. Baynes (New York: Harcourt, Brace, 1933), pp. 231, 234–235.

11. Johan Huizinga, *In the Shadow of Tomorrow* (London: Heinemann, 1936), pp. 1–3.

12. E. M. Forster, "Post-Munich," in *Two Cheers for Democracy* (New York: Harcourt, Brace & World, 1951), p. 21.

13. Oswald Spengler, *The Decline of the West*, trans. Charles F. Atkinson (London: Allen & Unwin, 1926), p. 40.

14. Franz Kafka, *The Trial*, trans. Willa and Edwin Muir (New York: Knopf, 1957), p. 7.

15. Angel Flores, ed., *The Kafka Problem* (New York: Gordian Press, 1975), p. xxi.

16. Thomas Mann, "An Appeal to Reason," excerpted in *Sources of the Western Tradition*, ed. Marvin Perry et al., vol. 2, 5th ed. (Boston: Houghton Mifflin, 1991), p. 366.

17. Thomas Mann, "Schopenhauer," in *Essays of Three Decades*, trans. H. T. Lowe-Porter (New York: Knopf, 1968), p. 409.

18. D. H. Lawrence, *Women in Love* (New York: Penguin Books, 1979), p. 215.

19. Harry T. Moore, ed., *The Collected Letters of D. H. Lawrence* (New York: Viking, 1962), 1:180.

20. Tristan Tzara, "Lecture on Dada (1922)," trans. Ralph Mannheim, in *The Dada Painters and Poets*, ed. Robert Motherwell (New York: Witterborn, Schultz, 1951), pp. 248, 250.

21. Ibid., p. 251.

22. Edward Lucie-Smith, in Donald Carrol and Edward Lucie-Smith, *Movements in Modern Art* (New York: Horizon Press, 1973), p. 49.

23. H. W. Janson, *History of Art*, 2nd ed. (Englewood Cliffs, N.J.: Prentice-Hall, 1977), p. 661.

24. André Breton, *What Is Surrealism?* trans. David Gascoyne (London: Faber & Faber, 1936), p. 62.

25. Quoted in David Caute, *The Fellow Travellers* (New York: Macmillan, 1973), p. 64.

26. Ibid., p. 92.

27. Richard Crossman, ed., *The God That Failed* (New York: Bantam Books, 1951), pp. 15, 21.

28. Arthur Koestler, *Darkness at Noon* (New York: Macmillan, 1941), pp. 158–159.

29. Reinhold Niebuhr, *The Nature and Destiny of Man* (New York: Charles Scribner's Sons, 1941), I:273.

30. Jacques Maritain, *Christianity and Democracy* (New York: Charles Scribner's Sons, 1944), pp. 44, 62.

31. Quoted in C. T. McIntire, ed., *God, History, and Historians* (New York: Oxford University Press, 1977), p. 9.

32. Arnold J. Toynbee, *Survey of International Affairs, 1933* (London: Oxford University Press, 1934), p. 111.

33. Julien Benda, *The Betrayal of the Intellectuals*, trans. Richard Aldington (Boston: Beacon Press, 1955), pp. 21, 38, 122, 162.

34. José Ortega y Gasset, *The Revolt of the Masses* (New York: Norton, 1957), pp. 18, 63.

35. Ibid., p. 73.

36. Ernst Cassirer, *The Philosophy of the Enlightenment*, trans. Fritz C. A. Koelln and James P. Pettegrove (Boston: Beacon Press, 1955), pp. xi–xii.

37. Ernst Cassirer, *The Myth of the State* (New Haven, Conn.: Yale University Press, 1946), p. 280.

38. Ibid., p. 296.

39. Erich Fromm, *Escape from Freedom* (New York: Avon Books, 1965), pp. 173, 246.

40. George Orwell, *1984* (New York: Harcourt, Brace, 1949; paperback, New American Library, 1961), p. 220.

41. Quoted in T. Z. Lavine, *From Socrates to Sartre: The Philosophic Quest* (New York: Bantam Books, 1984), p. 322.

42. Karl Jaspers, *Man in the Modern Age*, trans. Eden and Cedar Paul (Garden City, N.Y.: Doubleday Anchor Books, 1951), p. 159.

43. Quoted in John Macquarrie, *Existentialism* (Baltimore: Penguin Books, 1973), p. 246.

44. Jean Paul Sartre, *Existentialism,* trans. Bernard Frechtman (New York: Philosophical Library, 1947), p. 28.

45. Ibid., pp. 18–19, 38, 42.

46. Albert Camus, *The Rebel*, trans. Anthony Bower (New York: Knopf, 1956), p. 6.

47. Quoted in Roy Pierce, *Contemporary French Political Thought* (New York: Oxford University Press, 1966), p. 125.

48. Quoted in Germaine Brée, *Camus* (New Brunswick, N.J.: Rutgers University Press, 1961), p. 9.

49. Albert Camus, *The Stranger*, trans. Matthew Ward (New York: Vintage Books, 1988), p. 120.

50. Gabriel Marcel, "On the Ontological Mystery," in *The Philosophy of Existentialism*, trans. Manya Harari (Secaucus, N.J.: Citadel Press, 1980), p. 10.

51. Ibid., p. 12.

52. Cited in Harry S. Kariel, *In Search of Authority* (Glencoe, Ill.: Free Press, 1964), p. 246.

53. Cited in Anthony Arblaster, *The Rise and Decline of Western Liberalism* (Oxford: Basil Blackwell, 1984), p. 81.

SUGGESTED READING

See also books suggested for reading at the end of Chapter 28.

Blackham, H. J., *Six Existentialist Thinkers* (1952). Useful analyses of Kierkegaard, Nietzsche, Jaspers, Marcel, Heidegger, and Sartre.

———, ed., *Reality, Man and Existence* (1965). Essential works of existentialism.

Cruickshank, John, ed., *Aspects of the Modern European Mind* (1969). A useful collection of sources in modern intellectual history.

Macquarrie, John, *Existentialism* (1972). A lucid discussion of existentialism.

Wagar, W. Warren, ed., *European Thought Since 1914* (1968). A valuable collection of sources.

Chapter 32

World War II: Western Civilization in the Balance

When the war in Europe ended in May 1945, many areas lay devastated, none more so than the once picturesque German city of Dresden, in which some 50,000 people had perished in a terror bombing by Allied planes in February 1945. Europe was faced with the awesome task of reconstructing a continent in ruins. (The Granger Collection.)

Focus Questions

1. What were Hitler's foreign policy aims?
2. Why did Britain and France pursue a policy of appeasement? With what effect?
3. What was the nature of the New Order that the Nazis established in conquered Europe?
4. What factors led to the defeat of the Nazis?
5. In your opinion, what is the meaning of the Holocaust for Western civilization? For Jews? For Christians? For Germans?
6. What is the legacy of World War II?

Online Study Center

This icon will direct you to interactive map and primary source activities on the website http://college.hmco.com/pic/perrywc8e.

From the early days of his political career, Hitler dreamed of forging in central and eastern Europe a vast German empire that would bring the millions of Germans living there under the rule of the Third Reich. He believed that only by waging a war of conquest against Russia could the German nation gain the living space and security it required and, as a superior race, deserved. War was an essential component of National Socialist ideology; it also accorded with Hitler's temperament. For the former corporal from the trenches, the Great War had never ended. Hitler aspired to political power because he wanted to mobilize the material and human resources of the German nation for war and conquest. Whereas historians may debate the question of responsibility for World War I, few would deny that World War II was Hitler's war.

> It appears to be an almost incontrovertible fact that the Second World War was brought on by the actions of the Hitler government, that these actions were the expression of a policy laid down well in advance in Mein Kampf, and that this war could have been averted up until the last moment if the German government had so wished.[1]

Western statesmen had sufficient warning that Hitler was a threat to peace and the essential values of Western civilization. In the 1920s, Hitler had openly proclaimed his commitment to a war of revenge and expansion, and in the 1930s, he scrapped the Versailles Treaty and openly prepared for such a conflict. But western statesmen failed to rally their people and take a stand until Germany had greatly increased its capacity to wage aggressive war.

THE AFTERMATH OF WORLD WAR I

World War I showed that Germany was the strongest power on the European continent. In the east, the German army triumphed over Russia. In the west, Britain and France could have hoped for no more than a deadlock without the aid of the

Chronology 32.1 ❖ Road to World War II

1931	Japan invades Manchuria
March 1935	Hitler announces German rearmament
October 1935	Italy invades Ethiopia
1936–1939	Spanish Civil War
March 7, 1936	Germany remilitarizes the Rhineland
October 1936	Berlin-Rome Axis is formed
November 1936	German-Japanese anticommunist pact
July 1937	Japan invades China
March 13, 1938	Anschluss with Austria, which becomes a German province
September 1938	Munich Agreement: Britain and France approve Germany's annexation of Sudetenland
1939	Franco establishes a dictatorship in Spain
March 1939	Germany invades Czechoslovakia
April 1939	Italy invades Albania
May 22, 1939	Pact of Steel between Hitler and Mussolini
August 23, 1939	Nonaggression pact between Germany and Russia
September 1, 1939	Germany invades Poland
September 3, 1939	Britain and France declare war on Germany

United States. The Treaty of Versailles weakened Germany but did not permanently cripple it.

In the decade after the war, responsibility for preserving the peace settlement rested essentially with France. The United States had rejected the treaty and withdrawn from European affairs; Soviet Russia was consolidating its Revolution; and Britain, burdened with severe economic problems, disarmed, and traditionally hostile to Continental alliances, did not want to join with France in holding Germany down. France sought to contain Germany by forging alliances with the new states of eastern Europe, which the French hoped would serve as a substitute for alliance with a now untrustworthy Communist Russia. Thus, in the 1920s, France entered into alliances with Poland, Czechoslovakia, Romania, and Yugoslavia. But no combination of small eastern European states could replace Russia as a counterweight to Germany. Against Hitler's Germany, the French alliance system would prove useless.

In the area of international relations, a feeling of hope prevailed during the 1920s. The newly created League of Nations provided a supranational authority to which nations could submit their quarrels. At the Washington Naval Conference (1921–22), the leading naval powers—the United States, Britain, France, Italy, and Japan—agreed not to construct new battleships or heavy cruisers for a ten-year period and established a ratio for these large ships among them. It was hoped that avoiding a naval arms race would promote international peace.

In the Locarno Pact (1925), Germany, France, and Belgium agreed not to change their existing borders, which meant, in effect, that Germany had accepted both the return of Alsace and Lorraine to France and the demilitarization of the Rhineland—two provisions of the Versailles treaty. The Locarno Pact held the promise of a détente between France and Germany. But it was only an illusion of peace, for Germany gave no such assurances for its eastern border with Czechoslovakia and Poland, France's allies.

Other gestures that promoted reconciliation followed. In 1926, Germany was admitted to the League of Nations, and in 1928, the Kellogg-Briand Pact renouncing war was signed by most nations. The signatories condemned war as a solution for international disputes and agreed to settle quarrels through peaceful means. Ordinary people welcomed the Kellogg-Briand Pact as the dawning of a new era of peace, but because the pact contained no clauses for its enforcement, this agreement, too, fostered only the illusion of peace.

Nevertheless, between 1925 and 1930, hopes for reconciliation and peace were high. Recovery from the war and increased prosperity coincided with the easing of international tensions. As evidence of the new spirit of conciliation, France and Britain withdrew their forces from the Rhineland in 1930, four years ahead of the time prescribed by the Versailles treaty.

THE ROAD TO WAR

Hitler's Foreign Policy Aims

After consolidating his power and mobilizing the nation's will, Hitler moved to implement his foreign policy objectives: the destruction of the Versailles treaty, the conquest and colonization of eastern Europe, and the domination and exploitation of racial inferiors. In some respects, Hitler's foreign policy aims accorded with the goals of Germany's traditional rulers. Like them, Hitler sought to make Germany the preeminent power in Europe. During World War I, German statesmen and generals had sought to conquer extensive regions of eastern Europe, and in the Treaty of Brest-Litovsk, Germany took Poland, the Ukraine, and the Baltic states from Russia. But Hitler's racial nationalism—the subjugation and annihilation of inferior races by a master German race—marked a break with the outlook of the old governing class. Germany's traditional conservative leaders had considered but not revoked the civil rights of German Jews and had sought to Germanize, not enslave, the Poles living under the German flag.

In foreign affairs, Hitler demonstrated the same blend of opportunism and singleness of purpose that had brought him to power. He behaved like a man possessed, driven by a fanatical belief that his personal destiny was tied to Germany's future. Here, too, he displayed an uncanny understanding of his opponents' weaknesses; and here, too, his opponents underestimated his skills and intent. As in his climb to power, he made use of propaganda to undermine his opponents' will to resist. The Nazi propaganda machine, which had won the minds of the German people, became an instrument of foreign policy. Nazi propaganda tried to win the support of the twenty-seven million Germans living in Europe and the Americas, outside the borders of the Reich proper. To promote social and political disorientation in other lands, the Nazis propagated anti-Semitism on a worldwide basis and tried to draw international support for Hitler as Europe's best defense against the Soviet Union and Bolshevism. The Nazi anticommunist campaign "convinced many Europeans that Hitler's dictatorship was more acceptable than Stalin's and that Germany—'the bulwark against Bolshevism'—should be allowed to grow from strength to strength."[2]

As Hitler had anticipated, the British and the French backed down when faced with his violations of the Versailles treaty and threats of war. Haunted by the memory of World War I, Britain and France went to great lengths to avoid another catastrophe—a policy that had the overwhelming support of public opinion. Moreover, Britain suffered from a bad conscience regarding the Versailles treaty. Woefully unprepared for war from 1933 to 1938 and believing that Germany had been treated too severely, Britain was amenable to making concessions to Hitler. Although France had the strongest army on the Continent, it was prepared to fight only a defensive war—the reverse of its World War I strategy. France built immense fortifications, called the Maginot Line, to protect its borders from a German invasion, but it lacked a mobile striking force that could punish an aggressive Germany. The United States, concerned with the problems of the Great Depression and standing aloof from Europe's troubles, did nothing to strengthen the resolve of France and Britain. Since both France and Britain feared and mistrusted the Soviet Union, the grand alliance of World War I was not renewed. There was an added factor: suffering from a failure of leadership and political and economic unrest that eroded national unity,

France was experiencing a decline in morale and a loss of nerve. It consistently turned to Britain for direction.

British statesmen championed a policy of appeasement: giving in to Germany in the hope that a satisfied Hitler would not drag Europe through another world war. British policy rested on the disastrous illusion that Hitler, like his Weimar predecessors, sought peaceful revision of the Versailles treaty and that he could be contained through concessions. This perception was as misguided as the expectation of Weimar conservatives that the responsibility of power would compel Hitler to abandon his National Socialist radicalism. Some British appeasers, accepting the view that Nazi propaganda cleverly propagated and exploited, also regarded Hitler as a defender of European civilization and the capitalist economic order against Soviet communism.

In *Mein Kampf*, Hitler had explicitly laid out his philosophy of racial nationalism and *Lebensraum* (living space). As dictator, he had established a one-party state, confined political opponents to concentration camps, and persecuted Jews. But the proponents of appeasement did not properly assess these signs. They still believed that Hitler could be reasoned with. Appeasement, which in the end was capitulation to blackmail, failed. Germany grew stronger and the German people more devoted to the fuehrer. Hitler did not moderate his ambitions, and the appeasers did not avert war.

Breakdown of Peace

To realize his foreign policy aims, Hitler required a formidable military machine. Germany had to rearm. The Treaty of Versailles limited the size of the German army to a hundred thousand volunteers; restricted the navy's size; forbade the production of military aircraft, heavy artillery, and tanks; and disbanded the general staff. Throughout the 1920s, Germany evaded these provisions, even entering into a secret arrangement with the Soviet Union to establish training schools for German pilots and tank corpsmen on Russian soil.

In March 1935, Hitler declared that Germany was no longer bound by the Versailles treaty. Germany would restore conscription, build an air

force (which it had been doing secretly), and strengthen its navy. The German people were ecstatic over Hitler's boldness. France protested but offered no resistance. Britain negotiated a naval agreement with Germany, thus tacitly accepting Hitler's rearmament.

A decisive event in the breakdown of peace was Italy's invasion of Ethiopia in October 1935. Mussolini sought colonial expansion and revenge for the defeat that the African kingdom had inflicted on Italian troops in 1896. The League of Nations called for economic sanctions against Italy, and most League members restricted trade with the aggressor. But Italy continued to receive oil, particularly from American suppliers. Believing that the conquest of Ethiopia did not affect their vital interests and hoping to keep the Italians friendly in the event of a clash with Germany, neither Britain nor France sought to restrain Italy, despite its act of aggression against another member of the League of Nations. The Fascists claimed they were civilizing a backward African nation. In the process, tens of thousands of Ethiopians perished, victims of saturation bombing, poison gas, and mistreatment in concentration camps into which they had been herded.

Mussolini's subjugation of Ethiopia discredited the League of Nations, already weakened by its failure to deal effectively with Japan's invasion of the mineral-rich Chinese province of Manchuria in 1931. At that time, the League formed a commission of inquiry and urged nonrecognition of the puppet state of Manchukuo created by the Japanese, but the member states did not restrain Japan. The invasion of Ethiopia, like the invasion of Manchuria, showed the League's reluctance to use force to resist aggression.

On March 7, 1936, Hitler marched troops into the Rhineland, violating both the Versailles treaty and the Locarno Pact. German generals had cautioned Hitler that such a move would provoke a French invasion of Germany and reoccupation of the Rhineland, which the German army, still in the

MAP 32.1 GERMAN AND ITALIAN AGGRESSIONS, ▶ 1935–1939 German aggression from 1936 to 1939 included the militarization of Rhineland (1936), Anschluss with Austria (1938), and the dismemberment of Czechoslovakia (1938–1939).

ICELAND

Legend:
- Germany and Italy
- Italian possessions in Africa before 1935
- German aggressions, 1935–1939
- Italian aggressions, 1935–1939

0   200   400 Km.
0   200   400 Mi.

NORWAY

SWEDEN

FINLAND

Baltic Sea

ESTONIA

North Sea

DENMARK

LATVIA

Moscow •

Memel •

LITHUANIA

IRELAND

GREAT BRITAIN

London •

NETHERLANDS

Danzig •

EAST PRUSSIA

SOVIET UNION

ATLANTIC OCEAN

Brussels •

BELGIUM

RHINELAND 1936

Berlin •

GERMANY

POLISH CORRIDOR

SUDENTENLAND 1938

Warsaw •

Paris •

LUXEMBOURG

Weimar •

Nuremberg •

Prague •

CZECHOSLOVAKIA 1939

POLAND

Munich •

FRANCE

SWITZERLAND

Vienna •

AUSTRIA 1938

HUNGARY

ROMANIA

PORTUGAL

SPAIN (Civil War, 1936–1939)

• Madrid

Barcelona •

ITALY

YUGOSLAVIA

Black Sea

BULGARIA

• Rome

ALBANIA 1939

GREECE

TURKEY

Mediterranean Sea

A F R I C A

Africa inset:

LIBYA

ERITREA

AFRICA

ETHIOPIA 1935–1936

IT. SOMALILAND

first stages of rearmament, could not repulse. But Hitler gambled that France and Britain, lacking the will to fight, would take no action.

Hitler had assessed the Anglo-French mood correctly. Britain was not greatly alarmed by the remilitarization of the Rhineland. After all, Hitler was not expanding the borders of Germany but only sending soldiers to Germany's frontier. Such a move, reasoned British officials, did not warrant risking a war. France viewed the remilitarization of the Rhineland as a grave threat. It deprived France of the one tangible advantage that it had obtained from the Treaty of Versailles: a buffer area. Now German forces could concentrate in strength on the French frontier, either to invade France or to discourage a French assault if Germany attacked Czechoslovakia or Poland, France's eastern allies. France lost the advantage of being able to retaliate by invading a demilitarized zone.

Three factors explain why France did not try to expel the twenty-two thousand German troops that occupied the zone. First, France would not act alone, and Britain could not be persuaded to use force. Second, the French general staff overestimated German military strength and thought only of defending French soil from a German attack, not of initiating a strike against Germany. Third, French public opinion showed no enthusiasm for a confrontation with Hitler.

The Spanish Civil War of 1936–1939 was another victory for fascism. Nazi Germany and Fascist Italy aided Franco (see page 765); the Soviet Union supplied the Spanish republic. The republic appealed to France for help, but the French government feared that the civil war would expand into a European war. With Britain's approval, France proposed the Nonintervention Agreement. Italy, Germany, and the Soviet Union signed the agreement but continued to supply the warring parties. By October 1937, some sixty thousand Italian "volunteers" were fighting in Spain. Hitler sent between five and six thousand men and hundreds of planes, which proved decisive. By comparison, the Soviet Union's aid was meager. Viewing the conflict as a struggle between democracy and fascism, thousands of Europeans and Americans volunteered to fight for the republic.

Without considerable help from France, the Spanish republic was doomed, but Prime Minister Léon Blum continued to support nonintervention.

He feared that French intervention would cause Germany and Italy to escalate their involvement, bringing Europe to the edge of a general war. Moreover, supplying the republic would have dangerous consequences at home because French rightists were sympathetic to Franco's conservative-clerical authoritarianism. In 1939, the republic fell, and Franco established a dictatorship, imprisoning or banishing to labor camps more than one million Spaniards and executing another two hundred thousand.

The Spanish Civil War provided Germany with an opportunity to test weapons and pilots. It also demonstrated that France and Britain lacked the determination to fight fascism. In addition, the war widened the breach between Italy and Britain and France that had opened when Italy invaded Ethiopia, and it drew Mussolini and Hitler closer together. In October 1936, Mussolini sent his foreign minister to meet with Hitler in Berlin. The discussions bore fruit, and on November 1, Mussolini proclaimed that a Rome-Berlin "Axis" had been created.

One of Hitler's aims was the incorporation of Austria into the Third Reich. The Treaty of Versailles expressly prohibited the union of the two countries, but in *Mein Kampf*, Hitler insisted that an Anschluss was necessary for German Lebensraum. In February 1938, under intense pressure from Hitler, Austrian chancellor Kurt von Schuschnigg promised to accept Austrian Nazis in his cabinet and agreed to closer relations with Germany. Austrian independence was slipping away, and increasingly, Austrian Nazis undermined Schuschnigg's authority. Seeking to gain his people's support, Schuschnigg made plans for a plebiscite on the issue of preserving Austrian independence. An enraged Hitler ordered his generals to draw up plans for an invasion of Austria. Hitler then demanded Schuschnigg's resignation and the formation of a new government headed by Arthur Seyss-Inquart, an Austrian Nazi.

Believing that Austria was not worth a war, Britain and France informed the embattled chancellor that they would not help in the event of a German invasion. Schuschnigg then resigned, and Austrian Nazis began to take control of the government. Under the pretext of preventing violence, Hitler ordered his troops to cross into Austria, and on March 13, 1938, Austrian leaders declared that Austria was a province of the German Reich.

DEATH OF A LOYALIST. In his successful attempt to overthrow the Spanish Republic, General Francisco Franco was aided by Mussolini and Hitler. The Spanish Civil War was another victory for fascism. Photojournalist Robert Capa captured the moment of death of a Loyalist soldier in this famous photograph. (© *Robert Capa/Magnum Photos.*)

Many Austrians welcomed the Anschluss. The idea of a Greater Germany appealed to their Pan-German sentiments, and they hoped that Hitler's magic would produce economic recovery. Moreover, depriving Jews of their rights, property, and occupations had widespread appeal among traditionally anti-Semitic Austrians. The Viennese celebrated by ringing church bells, waving swastika banners, and spontaneously beating, robbing, and humiliating Jews, including tearing Torah scrolls, shearing the beards of rabbis, and forcing whole families to scrub sidewalks. The Austrians' euphoria over the Anschluss and their sadistic treatment of helpless Jews astonished many observers, including the German occupiers.

Czechoslovakia: The Apex of Appeasement

Hitler obtained Austria merely by threatening to use force. Another threat would give him the Sudetenland of Czechoslovakia. Ethnic Germans, numbering some 3.25 million, predominated in the Sudetenland. The region contained key industries and strong fortifications; since it bordered Germany, it was also vital to Czech security. Deprived of the Sudetenland, Czechoslovakia could not defend itself against a German attack. Encouraged and instructed by Germany, the Sudeten Germans, led by Konrad Henlein, shrilly denounced the Czech government for "persecuting" its German minority and depriving Sudeten Germans of their right to self-determination. The Sudeten Germans agitated for local autonomy and the right to profess the National Socialist ideology. Behind this demand was the goal of German annexation of the Sudetenland and the destruction of Czechoslovakia.

While negotiations between the Sudeten Germans and the Czech government proceeded, Hitler's propaganda machine accused the Czechs of hideous crimes against the German minority and warned of retribution. Hitler also ordered his generals to prepare for an invasion of Czechoslovakia and to complete the fortifications along the French border. Fighting between Czechs and Sudeten Germans heightened the tensions. Seeking to preserve peace, Prime Minister Neville Chamberlain (1869–1940) of Britain offered to confer with Hitler, who then extended an invitation.

Britain and France held somewhat different positions toward Czechoslovakia, the only democracy in eastern Europe. In 1924, France and Czechoslovakia had concluded an agreement of mutual assistance in the event that either was attacked by Germany. Czechoslovakia had a similar agreement with Russia, but with the provision that Russian assistance depended on France's first fulfilling the terms of its agreement. Britain had no commitment to Czechoslovakia. Some British officials, swallowing Hitler's propaganda, believed that the Sudeten Germans were indeed a suppressed minority entitled to self-determination. They also thought that the Sudetenland, like Austria, was not worth a war that could destroy Western civilization. Hitler, they said, only wanted to incorporate Germans living outside of Germany; he was only carrying the principle of self-determination to its logical conclusion. Once these Germans lived under the German flag, Hitler would be satisfied. In any case, Britain's failure to rearm adequately between 1933 and 1938 weakened its position. The British chiefs of staff believed that the

nation was not prepared to fight and that it was necessary to sacrifice Czechoslovakia to buy time.

Czechoslovakia's fate was decided at the Munich Conference (September 1938), attended by Chamberlain, Hitler, Mussolini, and Prime Minister Édouard Daladier (1884–1970) of France. The Munich Agreement called for the immediate evacuation of Czech troops from the Sudetenland and its occupation by German forces. Britain and France then promised to guarantee the territorial integrity of the truncated Czechoslovakia. Both Chamberlain and Daladier were praised by adoring crowds in their respective countries for keeping the peace. Hitler considered these Western leaders "little worms."

Critics of Chamberlain have insisted that the Munich Agreement was a tragic blunder. Chamberlain, they say, was a fool to believe that Hitler could be bought off with the Sudetenland. Hitler regarded concessions by Britain and France as signs of weakness; they only increased his appetite for more territory. Second, argue the critics, it would have been better to fight Hitler in 1938 than a year later, when war actually did break out. In the year following the Munich Agreement, Britain increased its military arsenal, but so did Germany, which strengthened western border defenses; built submarines, heavy tanks, and planes; and trained more pilots.

Had Britain and France resisted Hitler at Munich, it is likely that the fuehrer would have attacked Czechoslovakia. But the Czech border defenses, built on the model of the French Maginot Line, were formidable. The Czechs had a sizable number of good tanks, and the Czech people were willing to fight to preserve their nation's territorial integrity. By itself, the Czech army could not have defeated Germany. But while the main elements of the German army were battling the Czechs, the French, who could mobilize a hundred divisions, could have broken through the German West Wall, which was defended by only five regular and four reserve divisions; then they could have invaded the Rhineland and devastated German industrial centers in the Ruhr. (Such a scenario, of course, depended on the French overcoming their psychological reluctance to take the offensive.) And there was the possibility, although probably a slim one, that the Soviet Union would have fulfilled its agreement and come to Czechoslovakia's aid.

After the annexation of the Sudetenland, Hitler plotted to extinguish Czechoslovakia's existence.

Chronology 32.2 ❖ World War II

September 27, 1939	Poland surrenders
November 1939	Russia invades Finland
April 1940	Germany attacks Denmark and Norway
May 10, 1940	Germany invades Belgium, Holland, and Luxembourg
May 27–June 4, 1940	British and French troops are evacuated from Dunkirk
June 22, 1940	France surrenders
August–September 1940	Battle of Britain
September 1940	Japan begins conquest of Southeast Asia
October 1940	Italian troops cross into Greece
April 6, 1941	Germany attacks Greece and Yugoslavia
June 22, 1941	Germany launches offensive against Russia
December 7, 1941	Japan attacks Pearl Harbor: United States enters the war against Japan and Germany
1942	Tide of battle turns in the Allies' favor: Midway (Pacific Ocean), Stalingrad (Soviet Union), and El Alamein (North Africa)
April–May 1943	Uprising of Jews in Warsaw ghetto
September 1943	Italy surrenders to Allies, following invasion
June 6, 1944	D-day—Allies land in Normandy
August 1944	Paris is liberated; Poles rise up against German occupiers
January 1945	Soviet troops invade Germany
March–April 1945	Allies penetrate Germany
May 7, 1945	Germany surrenders unconditionally
August 1945	United States drops atomic bombs on Hiroshima and Nagasaki; Soviet Union invades Manchuria; Japan surrenders

He encouraged the Slovak minority in Czechoslovakia, led by a fascist priest, Josef Tiso, to demand complete separation. On the pretext of protecting the Slovak people's right of self-determination, Hitler ordered his troops to enter Prague. In March 1939, Czech independence came to an end.

The destruction of Czechoslovakia was of a different character from the remilitarization of the Rhineland, the Anschluss with Austria, and the annexation of the Sudetenland. In all these previous cases, Hitler could claim the right of German self-determination, Woodrow Wilson's grand principle. The occupation of Prague and the end of Czech independence, though, showed that Hitler really sought European hegemony. Outraged statesmen demanded that the fuehrer be deterred from further aggression.

Poland: The Final Crisis

After Czechoslovakia, Hitler turned to Poland, demanding that the free city of Danzig be returned to Germany and that railways and roads, over which

Germans would enjoy extraterritorial rights, be built across the Polish Corridor, linking East Prussia with the rest of Germany. Poland refused to restore the port of Danzig, which was vital to its economy. The Poles would allow a German highway through the Polish Corridor but would not permit German extraterritorial rights. France informed the German government that it would fulfill its treaty obligations to aid Poland. Chamberlain also warned that Britain would assist Poland.

On May 22, 1939, Hitler and Mussolini entered into the Pact of Steel, promising mutual aid in the event of war. The following day, Hitler told his officers that Germany's real goal was the destruction of Poland. "Danzig is not the objective. It is a matter of expanding our living space in the east, of making our food supplies secure. . . . There is therefore no question of sparing Poland, and the decision remains to attack Poland at the first suitable opportunity."[3] In the middle of June, the army presented Hitler with battle plans for an invasion of Poland.

Britain, France, and the Soviet Union had been engaged in negotiations since April. The Soviet Union wanted a mutual-assistance pact, including joint military planning, and demanded bases in Poland and Romania in preparation for a German attack. Britain was reluctant to endorse these demands, fearing that a mutual-assistance pact with Russia might cause Hitler to embark on a mad adventure that would drag Britain into war. Moreover, Poland would not allow Russian troops on its soil, fearing Russian expansion.

At the same time, Russia was conducting secret talks with Nazi Germany. Unlike the Allies, Hitler could tempt Stalin with territory that would serve as a buffer between Germany and Russia. Moreover, a treaty with Germany would give Russia time to strengthen its armed forces. On August 23, 1939, the two totalitarian states signed a nonaggression pact, which stunned the world. A secret section of the pact called for the partition of Poland between the two parties and Russian control over Latvia and Estonia (later the agreement was amended to include Lithuania). By signing such an agreement with his enemy, Hitler had pulled off an extraordinary diplomatic coup: he blocked the Soviet Union, Britain, and France from duplicating their World War I alliance against Germany. The Nazi-Soviet Pact was the green light for an invasion of Poland, and at dawn on September 1, 1939, German troops crossed the frontier. Two days later, when Germany did not respond to their demand for a halt to the invasion, Britain and France declared war on Germany.

THE NAZI BLITZKRIEG

Germany struck at Poland with speed and power, implementing tactical concepts of a mobile armored offensive worked out by German military planners between the wars. The German air force, the Luftwaffe, destroyed Polish planes on the ground, struck railways hampering Polish mobilization, attacked tanks, pounded defense networks, and bombed Warsaw, terrorizing the population. Racing across the flat Polish terrain, tanks opened breaches in the Polish defenses, and mechanized columns overran the foot-marching Polish army, trapping large numbers of soldiers. The Polish high command could not cope with the incredible speed and coordination of German air and ground attacks. By September 8, the rapidly moving Germans advanced to the outskirts of Warsaw. On September 17, Soviet troops invaded Poland from the east. On September 27, Poland surrendered. In less than a month, the Nazi **blitzkrieg** (lightning war) had vanquished Poland.

The Fall of France

For Hitler, the conquest of Poland was only the prelude to a German empire stretching from the Atlantic to the Urals. When weather conditions were right, he would unleash a great offensive in the west. Meanwhile, the six-month period following the defeat of Poland was nicknamed the "phony war," for the fighting on land consisted only of a few skirmishes on the French-German border. Then, in early April 1940, the Germans struck at Denmark and Norway. Hitler wanted to establish naval bases on the Norwegian coast from which to wage submarine warfare against Britain and to ensure delivery of Swedish iron ore to Germany through Norwegian territorial waters.

Denmark surrendered within hours. A British-French force tried to assist the Norwegians, but the landings, badly coordinated and lacking in air support, failed. The Germans won the battle of Norway. But the Norwegian campaign produced two positive results for the Allies: Norwegian merchant ships escaped to Britain to be put into service; and Winston Churchill (1874–1965), who had opposed appeasement, replaced Chamberlain as British prime minister. (The German victory in Norway eroded Chamberlain's support in the House of Commons, and he was forced to give up the helm.) Dynamic, courageous, and eloquent, Churchill had the capacity to stir and lead his people in the struggle against Nazism.

On May 10, 1940, Hitler launched his offensive in the west with an invasion of neutral Belgium, Holland, and Luxembourg. While armored forces penetrated Dutch frontier defenses, airborne units seized strategic airfields and bridges. On May 14, after the Luftwaffe had bombed Rotterdam, destroying the center of the city and killing many people, the Dutch surrendered.

A daring attack by glider-borne troops gave Germany possession of two crucial Belgian bridges, opening the plains of Belgium to German panzer (tank) divisions. Believing that this was the main German attack, French troops rushed to Belgium to prevent a German breakthrough, but the greater menace lay to the south, on the French frontier. Meeting almost no resistance, German panzer divisions had moved through the narrow mountain passes of Luxembourg and the dense Forest of Ardennes in southern Belgium. On May 12, German units were on French soil near Sedan. Thinking that the Forest of Ardennes could not be penetrated by a major German force, the French had only lightly fortified the western extension of the Maginot Line. The failure to counterattack swiftly was a second mistake. The best elements of the Anglo-French forces were in Belgium, but the Germans were racing across northern France to the sea, which they reached on May 20, cutting the Anglo-French forces in two.

The Germans now sought to surround and annihilate the Allied forces converging on the French seaport of Dunkirk, the last port of escape. But probably fearing that German tanks would lose mobility in the rivers and canals around Dunkirk, Hitler called them off just as the troops prepared to take the port. Instead, he ordered the Luftwaffe to finish off the Allied troops, but fog and rain prevented German planes from operating at full strength, and British pilots inflicted heavy losses on the attackers. The Allies took advantage of this breathing space to tighten their defenses and prepare for a massive evacuation. While the Luftwaffe bombed the beaches, some 338,000 British and French troops were ferried across the English Channel by destroyers, merchant ships, motorboats, fishing boats, tugboats, and private yachts. Abandoning their equipment on the beaches, the British saved their armies to fight another day. Hitler's decision to hold back his tanks made the miracle of Dunkirk possible.

Meanwhile, the battle for France was turning into an even worse disaster for the French. Whole divisions were cut off or in retreat, and millions of refugees in cars and carts and on motorcycles and bicycles fled south to escape the advancing Germans. On June 10, Mussolini also declared war on France. With authority breaking down and resistance dying, the French cabinet appealed for an armistice, which was signed on June 22 in the same railway car in which Germany had agreed to the armistice ending World War I.

How can the collapse of France be explained? Neither French military leaders, who experienced the debacle, nor historians are in agreement as to the relative strength of the French and German air forces. It is likely that the Germans and the French (including the British planes based in France) had some three thousand planes each. But many French planes—in what still remains a mystery—stayed on the airfields. The planes were available, but the high command either did not use them or did not deploy them properly. Unlike the Germans, the French did not comprehend or appreciate the use of aviation in modern warfare. As for tanks, the French had as many as the Germans, and some were superior. Nor was German manpower overwhelming. France met disaster largely because its military leaders, unlike the Germans, had not mastered the psychology and technology of motorized warfare. French generals had planned for a long war of attrition, a repeat of World War I; they could not cope with the German blitzkrieg. "The French commanders, trained in the slow-motion methods of 1914 to 1918, were mentally unfitted to cope with Panzer pace, and it produced a spreading paralysis among them," says the British military expert Sir Basil Liddell Hart.[4] Put succinctly, the French were badly outgeneraled. One

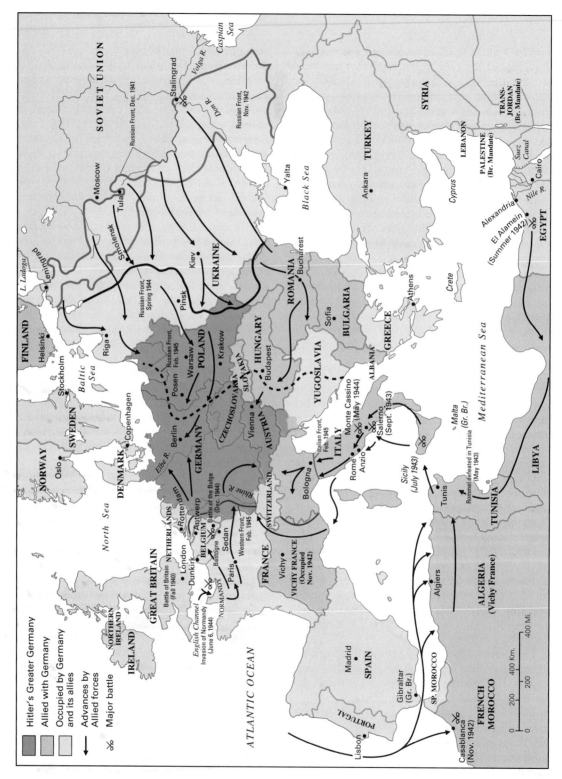

Legend:
- Hitler's Greater Germany
- Allied with Germany
- Occupied by Germany and its allies
- Advances by Allied forces
- Major battle

SOVIET UNION

Russian Front, Dec. 1941

Volga R.

Stalingrad

Russian Front, Nov. 1942

Caspian Sea

Don R.

Moscow

Tula

Smolensk

Yalta

Black Sea

Ankara TURKEY

SYRIA

TRANS-JORDAN (Br. Mandate)

LEBANON

PALESTINE (Br. Mandate)

Suez Canal

Alexandria *Nile R.* Cairo

El Alamein (Summer 1942)

EGYPT

Russian Front, Spring 1944

Kiev

UKRAINE

Pinsk

Bucharest

ROMANIA

Sofia

BULGARIA

Athens

Crete

Cyprus

Mediterranean Sea

L. Ladoga

Leningrad

FINLAND

Helsinki

Riga

Russian Front, Feb. 1945

Posen Warsaw Krakow

POLAND

HUNGARY

Budapest

YUGOSLAVIA

ALBANIA

GREECE

Malta (Gr. Br.)

Stockholm

Baltic Sea

SWEDEN

Copenhagen

DENMARK

Berlin *Elbe R.*

GERMANY

CZECHOSLOVAKIA

SLOVAKIA

Vienna AUSTRIA

Italian Front, Feb. 1945

Monte Cassino (May 1944)

Salerno (Sept. 1943)

NORWAY

Oslo

North Sea

NETHERLANDS

Rotterdam

Antwerp

BELGIUM

Bastogne

Battle of the Bulge (Dec. 1944)

Rhine R.

SWITZERLAND

Bologna

Rome Anzio

ITALY

Sicily (July 1943)

Tunis

Rommel defeated in Tunisia (May 1943)

TUNISIA

LIBYA

GREAT BRITAIN

Battle of Britain (Fall 1940)

London

Dunkirk

Sedan

Western Front, Feb. 1945

Paris

NORMANDY

English Channel

Invasion of Normandy (June 6, 1944)

FRANCE

Vichy

VICHY FRANCE (Occupied Nov. 1942)

Algiers

ALGERIA (Vichy France)

NORTHERN IRELAND

IRELAND

ATLANTIC OCEAN

Madrid

SPAIN

PORTUGAL

Lisbon

Gibraltar (Gr. Br.)

SP. MOROCCO

FRENCH MOROCCO

Casablanca (Nov. 1942)

400 Mi.
400 Km.
200
200
0
0

also senses a loss of will among the French people: a consequence of internal political disputes dividing the nation, poor leadership, the years of appeasement and lost opportunities, and German propaganda, which depicted Nazism as irresistible and the fuehrer as a man of destiny. It was France's darkest hour.

According to the terms of the armistice, Germany occupied northern France and the coast. The French military was demobilized, and the French government, now located at Vichy, in the south, and headed by Marshal Henri Philippe Pétain, the hero of World War I, would collaborate with the German authorities in occupied France, even to the point of passing racial laws and deporting Jews, including two thousand orphans under the age of six, to Nazi murder factories. The leaders of Vichy and their supporters, many of them prominent intellectuals and anti-Dreyfusards in their youth, shared in the antidemocratic, anti-Marxist, and anti-Semitic tradition of the radical right that had arrayed itself against the Third French Republic since the late nineteenth century. Refusing to recognize defeat, General Charles de Gaulle (1890–1970) escaped to London and organized the Free French forces. The Germans gloried in their revenge, and the French wept in their humiliation. The British gathered their courage, for they now stood alone.

Online Study Center

Improve Your Grade
Primary Source: This Was Their Finest Hour (Churchill)

The Battle of Britain

Hitler expected that, after his stunning victories in the west, Britain would make peace. The British, however, continued to reject Hitler's peace overtures, for they envisioned only a bleak

◀ *Map 32.2* WORLD WAR II: THE EUROPEAN THEATER By 1942, Germany ruled virtually all of Europe from the Atlantic to deep into Russia. Germany's defeat at Stalingrad in Russia and El Alamein in North Africa were decisive turning points.

future if Hitler dominated the Continent. "The Battle of Britain is about to begin," Churchill told his people. "Upon this battle depends the survival of Christian civilization. . . . if we fail, then . . . all we have known and cared for will sink into the abyss of a new Dark Age."[5]

With Britain unwilling to come to terms, Hitler proceeded in earnest with invasion plans. A successful crossing of the English Channel and the establishment of beachheads on the English coast depended on control of the skies. Marshal Hermann Goering assured Hitler that his Luftwaffe could destroy the British Royal Air Force (RAF), and in early August 1940, the Luftwaffe began massive attacks on British air and naval installations. Virtually every day during the "Battle of Britain," weather permitting, hundreds of planes fought in the sky above Britain. "Never in the field of human conflict was so much owed by so many to so few," said Churchill of the British pilots, who rose to the challenge. On September 15, hundreds of German planes made an all-out effort to destroy the British air force. The RAF, with virtually every available fighter plane seeing action, shot down sixty aircraft, convincing Hitler that Goering could not fulfill his promise to destroy British air defenses, and on September 17 the fuehrer postponed the invasion of Britain "until further notice." The development of radar by British scientists, the skill and courage of British fighter pilots, the unwillingness of Germany to absorb more losses in planes and trained pilots, and the ability of British industry to replenish losses saved Britain in its struggle for survival. After a succession of spectacular victories, Nazi Germany had suffered its first defeat.

With the invasion of Britain called off, the Luftwaffe concentrated on bombing English cities, industrial centers, and ports in the hopes of eroding Britain's military potential and undermining civilian morale. Every night for months, the inhabitants of London sought shelter in subways and cellars to escape German bombs while British planes rose time after time to make the Luftwaffe pay the price. British morale never broke during the "Blitz."

Britain, by itself, had no hope of defeating the Third Reich. What ultimately changed the course of the war were Germany's invasion of the Soviet Union in June 1941 and Japan's attack on the United States on December 7, 1941. With the

STALINGRAD, FEBRUARY 1943. In the photograph, the Russians are rescuing the bombed-out city of Stalingrad from the Nazi invaders. (*Sovfoto.*)

entry of these two powers, a coalition was created that had the human and material resources to reverse the tide of battle.

Invasion of Russia

The obliteration of Bolshevism and the conquest, exploitation, and colonization of Russia were cardinal elements of Hitler's ideology: in Russia, the Nazi empire would take control of wheat, oil, manganese, and other raw materials, and the fertile Russian plains would be settled by the master race. German expansion in the east could not wait for the final defeat of Britain. In July 1940, Hitler instructed his generals to formulate plans for an invasion of Russia. On December 18, Hitler set May 15, 1941, for the beginning of Operation Barbarossa, the code name assigned for the blitzkrieg against the Soviet Union. Events in the Balkans, however, forced Hitler to postpone the date to the latter part of June.

Seeking to make Italy a Mediterranean power and to win glory for himself, Mussolini had ordered an invasion of Greece. In late October 1940, Italian troops stationed in Albania—which Italy had occupied in 1939—crossed into Greece. The poorly planned operation was an instant failure; within a week, the counterattacking Greeks advanced into Albania. Hitler feared that Britain, which was encouraging and aiding the Greeks, would use Greece to attack the oil fields of Romania, which were vital to the German war effort, and to interfere with the forthcoming invasion of Russia. Another problem emerged when a military coup overthrew the government of Prince Paul in Yugoslavia, which two days earlier had signed a pact with Germany and Italy. Hitler feared that the new Yugoslav government might gravitate toward Britain. To prevent any interference with Operation Barbarossa, the Balkan flank had to be secured. On April 6, 1941, the Germans struck at both Greece and Yugoslavia. Yugoslavia was quickly overrun, and Greece, although aided by fifty thousand British, New Zealand, and Australian troops, fell at the end of April.

For the war against Russia, Hitler assembled a massive force: some four million men, thirty-three hundred tanks, and two thousand planes. Evidence of the German buildup abounded, but a stubborn Stalin ignored these warnings. Desperate to avoid war with Nazi Germany, Stalin would take no action that he feared might provoke Hitler. Consequently, the Red Army was vulnerable to the German blitzkrieg. In the early hours of June 22, 1941, the Germans launched their offensive over a wide front. Raiding Russian airfields, the Luftwaffe destroyed twelve hundred aircraft on the first day, most of them on the ground, a clear example of Stalin's failure to heed warnings provided by an effective Soviet spy network. The Germans drove deeply into Russia, cutting up and surrounding the disorganized and unprepared Russian forces. Contributing to the rout was the poor quality of Russian commanders, a consequence of Stalin's purge of Red Army officers, many of them trained and competent professionals, a few years earlier.

The Russians suffered terrible losses. In a little more than three months, two and a half million Russian soldiers were killed, wounded, or captured, and fourteen thousand tanks destroyed. Describing the war as a crusade to save Europe from "Jewish-Bolshevik subhumans," German propaganda claimed that victory was assured.

But there were also disquieting signs for the Nazi invaders. The Russians, who had a proven capacity to endure hardships, fought doggedly and courageously for the motherland in what Soviet propaganda stressed was a great "patriotic war," and the government would not consider capitulation. At first many Russians, particularly in Ukraine, welcomed the German invaders, who they hoped would liberate them from Stalin's tyranny. But German ruthlessness against the local population, whom Nazi ideology marked for exploitation and servitude, strengthened the resolve of the Russian people. Russian reserve strength was far greater than the Germans had estimated. Increasing the Red Army's strength was the drafting of hundreds of thousands of prisoners from labor camps and the recruitment of hundreds of thousands of women, who saw action as artillery and anti-aircraft gunners, fighter pilots, tank personnel, and snipers. The Wehrmacht (German army), far from its supply lines, ran short of fuel, vehicles, and spare parts and had to contend with primitive roads that turned into seas of mud when the autumn rains came. One German general described the ordeal: "The infantryman slithers in the mud, while many teams of horses are needed to drag each gun forward. All wheeled vehicles sink up to their axles in the

slime. Even tractors can only move with great difficulty. A large portion of our heavy artillery was soon stuck fast. . . . The strain that all this caused our already exhausted troops can perhaps be imagined."[6] Compounding the supply problem were attacks behind German lines by Russian partisans determined to inflict pain on the hated invaders. Conditions no longer favored the blitzkrieg.

Early and bitter subzero weather hampered the German attempt to capture Moscow. Without warm uniforms, tens of thousands of Germans suffered from frostbite; without antifreeze, guns did not fire. The Germans advanced to within twenty miles of Moscow, but on December 6, a Red Army counterattack forced them to postpone the assault on the Russian capital. The Germans were also denied Leningrad, which since September had been almost completely surrounded and under constant bombardment. During this epic siege, which lasted for two and a half years, the citizens of Leningrad displayed extraordinary courage in the face of famine, disease, and shelling that cost nearly one million lives, more than the combined losses of Britain and the United States for the entire war.

By the end of 1941, Germany had conquered vast regions of Russia but had failed to bring the country to its knees. There would be no repetition of the collapse of France. Moreover, by moving machinery and workers east far beyond the German reach, the Soviets were able to replenish their military hardware, which was almost totally destroyed during the first six months of the war. Driven by patriotic fervor—and by fear of the omnipresent NKVD agents searching for malingerers—Russian factory workers, many of them the wives and daughters of soldiers, toiled relentlessly, heroically. Soon they were producing more planes and tanks than Germany. The Russian campaign demonstrated that the Russian people would make incredible sacrifices for their land and that the Nazis were not invincible.

Online Study Center **Improve Your Grade**
Interactive Map: The Nazi Regime, 1942

THE NEW ORDER

By 1942, Germany ruled virtually all of Europe, from the Atlantic to deep into Russia. Some conquered territory was annexed outright; other lands were administered by German officials; in still other countries, the Germans ruled through local officials sympathetic to Nazism or willing to collaborate with the Germans. On this vast empire, Hitler and his henchmen imposed a New Order designed to serve the interests of the "master race."

Exploitation and Terror

"The real profiteers of this war are ourselves, and out of it we shall come bursting with fat," said Hitler. "We will give back nothing and will take everything we can make use of."[7] The Germans systematically looted the countries they conquered, taking gold, art treasures, machinery, and food supplies back to Germany and exploiting the industrial and agricultural potential of non-German lands to aid the German war economy. Some foreign businesses and factories were confiscated by the German Reich; others produced what the Germans demanded. Germany also requisitioned food from the conquered regions, significantly reducing the quantity available for local civilian consumption. German soldiers were fed with food harvested in occupied France and Russia; they fought with weapons produced in Czech factories. German tanks ran on oil delivered by Romania, Germany's satellite. The Nazis also made slave laborers of conquered peoples. Some seven million people from all over Europe were wrested from their homes and transported to Germany. These forced laborers, particularly the Russians and Poles, whom Nazi ideology classified as a lower form of humanity, lived in wretched, unheated barracks and were poorly fed and overworked; many died of disease, hunger, and exhaustion. Many of Germany's most prominent firms collaborated in the enslavement of foreign workers.

The Nazis ruled by force and terror. The prison cell, the torture chamber, the firing squad, and the concentration camp symbolized the New Order. In the Polish province annexed to Germany, the Nazis jailed and executed intellectuals and priests, closed all schools and most churches, and forbade Poles from holding professional positions. In the region of Poland administered by German officials, most schools above the fourth grade were shut down. Himmler insisted that it was sufficient for Polish children to learn "simple arithmetic up to five hundred at the most; writing of one's name; a doctrine that it is a divine law to obey the Germans and to be honest, industrious, and good."[8] The Germans were particularly ruthless toward the Russians. Soviet political officials were immediately executed; many prisoners of war were herded into camps and deliberately starved to death. In all, the Germans took prisoner some 5.5 million Russians, of whom more than 3.5 million perished, primarily from starvation. These prisoners of war were supervised not by the notorious SS, who ran the extermination camps, but by the regular army, the Wehrmacht, whose officers made deliberate decisions to starve Russian prisoners.

German soldiers routinely abused innocents: they stripped Russian peasants of their winter clothing and boots before driving them into the freezing outdoors to die of cold and starvation, slaughtered large numbers of hostages, burned whole villages to the ground in reprisal for partisan attacks, and deported massive numbers of people for slave labor. To the German invaders, drenched in Nazi ideology, the Russians were "Asiatic bestial hordes" led by sinister "subhuman" Jews who aimed to destroy Germany. Recent studies, largely by German historians, demonstrate how committed the Wehrmacht command was to Nazi ideological aims, how willing it was to propagate Nazi ideology among the troops—letters and diaries reveal how ideologically devoted average soldiers were to Nazism—and how implicated both the high command and common soldiers were in war crimes, including the extermination of the Jews.

Extermination

Against the Jews of Europe, the Germans waged a war of extermination. The task of imposing the "Final Solution of the Jewish Problem" was given to Himmler's SS, and they fulfilled these grisly duties with fanaticism and bureaucratic efficiency. In exterminating the Jewish people, the Nazis believed they were righteous and courageous and serving a higher good—the defense of the sacred Volk. In striking at the Jews, they were also destroying essential values of the Western tradition—reason, freedom, equality, toleration, respect for human dignity, and individualism—which they despised and with which the Jews, because of their unique historical experience, were identified.

Regarding themselves as idealists who were writing a glorious chapter in the history of Germany, the SS tortured and murdered with immense dedication. The minds of the SS were dominated by the mythical world-view of Nazism, as the following tract issued by SS headquarters reveals:

> *Just as night rises up against the day, just as light and darkness are eternal enemies, so the greatest enemy of world-dominating man is man himself. The sub-man—that creature which looks as though biologically it were of absolutely the same kind, endowed by Nature with hands, feet and a sort of brain, with eyes and mouth—is nevertheless a totally different, a fearful creature, is only an attempt at a human being, with a quasi-human face, yet in mind and spirit lower than any animal. Inside this being a cruel chaos of wild, unchecked passions: a nameless will to destruction, the most primitive lusts, the most undisguised vileness. A sub-man—nothing else! . . . Never has the sub-man granted peace, never has he permitted rest. . . . To preserve himself he needed mud, he needed hell, but not the sun. And this underworld of sub-men found its leader: the eternal Jew![9]*

Special squads of SS—the *Einsatzgruppen*, trained for mass murder—followed on the heels of the German army into Russia. Entering captured villages and cities, they rounded up Jewish men, women, and children; herded them to execution grounds; and slaughtered them with machine-gun and rifle fire at the edge of open trenches, which sometimes were piled high with thousands of victims, including severely wounded people, who would suffocate to death when the pit was filled with earth. Aided by Ukrainian, Lithuanian, and Latvian auxiliaries, along with contingents from the Romanian army, the Einsatzgruppen massacred some 1.3 million Jews.

Units of the Wehrmacht actively participated in the rounding up of Jews and sometimes in the shootings. Despite the denials of staff officers after the war, evidence from their own files reveals that they knew fully well that the extermination of the Jews was state policy that units of the Wehrmacht were helping to implement.

In Poland, where some 3.3 million Jews lived, the Germans established ghettos in the larger cities. Jews from all over the country were crammed into these ghettos, which were sealed off from the rest of the population. The German administration deliberately curtailed the food supply, and many Jews died of malnutrition, disease, and beatings. In the ghettos, the Polish Jews struggled to maintain community life and to preserve their spirit. They established schools (forbidden by the German authorities), prayed together (also forbidden), organized social services, and kept hidden archives so that future ages would have a historical record of their ordeal.

The mass killings, however, posed problems for the Germans. These murders were too public, whereas the Germans wanted to keep the Final Solution as secret as possible. Furthermore, the face-to-face killing of civilians, including women and children, could be too hard on the psyche of the personnel charged with carrying out such orders. To overcome these problems, the Germans transformed concentration camps, originally established for political prisoners, into killing centers, and they also built new ones for this purpose.* Jews from all over Europe were rounded up—for "resettlement," they were told. The victims dismissed rumors that the Germans were engaged in genocide. They simply could not believe that any nation in the twentieth century was capable of such evil. "Why did we not fight back?"† a survivor asks, and answers: "I know why. Because we had faith in humanity. Because we did not really think that human beings were capable of committing such crimes."[10]

Jammed into sealed cattle cars, eighty or ninety to a car, the victims traveled sometimes for

---

*Some 2.5 million to 3 million Jews were gassed in Nazi death factories built in Poland—Chelmno, Treblinka, Sobibur, Belzec, Lublin, Majdanek, and Auschwitz-Birkenau, the largest.

†Jewish resistance is discussed in the next section of this chapter.

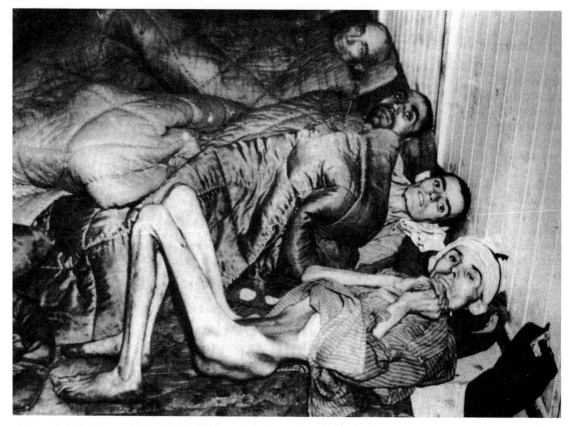

CONCENTRATION CAMP SURVIVORS. Thousands of emaciated and diseased inmates of German concentration camps died in the weeks after liberation by the Allies. These camps will forever remain a monument to the capacity of human beings for inhumanity. (© *Topham/The Image Works.*)

days, without food or water, choking from the stench of vomit and excrement and shattered by the crying of children. Disgorged at the concentration camps, they entered another planet:

> *Corpses were strewn all over the road; bodies were hanging from the barbed-wire fence; the sound of shots rang in the air continuously. Blazing flames shot into the sky; a giant smoke cloud ascended about them. Starving, emaciated human skeletons stumbled forward toward us, uttering incoherent sounds. They fell down right in front of our eyes gasping out their last breath.*
>
> *Here and there a hand tried to reach up, but when this happened an SS man came right*

> *away and stepped on it. Those who were merely exhausted were simply thrown on the dead pile. . . . Every night a truck came by, and all of them, dead or not, were thrown on it and taken to the crematory.*[11]

SS doctors quickly inspected the new arrivals, "the freight," as they referred to them. Rudolf Hoess, the commandant of Auschwitz—the most notorious of the murder factories—described the procedure:

> *The "final solution" of the Jewish question meant the complete extermination of all Jews in Europe. I was ordered to establish extermination facilities at Auschwitz in June,*

1941.... It took from three to fifteen minutes to kill people in the death chamber, depending upon climatic conditions. We knew when the people were dead because their screaming stopped. We usually waited about one-half hour before we opened the doors and removed the bodies. After the bodies were removed our special commandos took off the rings and extracted the gold from the teeth of the corpses....

The way we selected our victims was as follows.... Those who were fit to work were sent into the camp. Others were sent immediately to the extermination plants. Children of tender years were invariably exterminated since by reason of their youth they were unable to work.... We endeavored to fool the victims into thinking that they were to go through a delousing process. Of course, frequently they realized our true intentions, and we sometimes had riots and difficulties due to that fact. Very frequently women would hide their children under clothes, but of course when we found them we would send the children in to be exterminated.[12]

The naked bodies, covered with blood and excrement and intertwined with each other, were piled high to the ceiling. To make way for the next group, a squad of Jewish prisoners emptied the gas chambers of the corpses and removed gold teeth, which, along with the victims' hair, eyeglasses, and clothing, were carefully collected and catalogued for the war effort.* Later, the bodies were burned in crematoriums specially constructed by I. A. Topf and Sons of Erfurt. The chimneys vomited black smoke, and the stench of burning flesh permeated the entire region. Jewish leaders in the United States and Britain, who got word of the killings, pleaded with the Allies to bomb the rail lines to Auschwitz and the gas chambers, but the Allies did nothing. The killing process went on relentlessly. Between 1.1 million

and 1.5 million people died in Auschwitz—90 percent of them Jews. Non-Jewish victims included political prisoners and Soviet prisoners of war.

Auschwitz was more than a murder factory. It also provided the German industrial giant, I. G. Farben, which operated a factory adjoining the extermination facilities, with slave laborers, both Jews and non-Jews. The working pace at the factory and the ill treatment by guards were so brutal, reported a physician and inmate, that "while working many prisoners suddenly stretched out flat, turned blue, gasped for breath, and died like beasts."[13]

Auschwitz also allowed the SS, the elite of the master race, to shape and harden themselves according to the National Socialist creed. The SS relished their absolute power over the inmates. A survivor recalls seeing SS men and women amuse themselves with pregnant inmates. The unfortunate women were "beaten with clubs and whips, torn by dogs, dragged by the hair, and kicked in the stomach with heavy German boots. Then, when they collapsed, they were thrown into the crematory—alive."[14] By systematically overworking, starving, beating, terrorizing, and humiliating the inmates, by making them live in filth and sleep sprawled all over each other in tiny cubicles, the SS deliberately sought to strip prisoners of all human dignity, to make them appear and behave as "subhuman," and even make them believe that they were "subhuman," as the National Socialist ideology asserted. This daily brutalization and humiliation of Jewish inmates produced a psychological distance between the SS and their victims. No sympathy could be felt for people who were frequently depicted as less than human, repulsive lice and vermin. Tormenting and murdering Jews also reinforced the SS's own sense of superiority.

Many concentration camp inmates went mad or committed suicide; some struggled desperately, defiantly, and heroically to maintain their humanity. When prisoners, exhausted, starved, diseased, and beaten, became unfit for work, which generally happened within a few months, they were sent to the gas chambers. Perhaps the vilest assault on human dignity ever conceived, Nazi extermination camps were the true legacy of National Socialism, and the SS, the true end product of National Socialist indoctrination and idealism.

*Between October 1942 and August 1943, reports Simon Wiesenthal, the famed hunter of Nazi war criminals, the Nazis transported from the Treblinka death camp to Berlin 25 freight cars of women's hair, 248 freight cars of clothing, 100 freight cars of shoes, 400,000 gold watches, and 320,000 pounds of gold wedding rings. *The New York Times*, Obituaries, September 21, 2005, p. C18.

Hans and Sophie Scholl

In February 1943, Hans Scholl, age twenty-five, a medical student, and his twenty-two-year-old sister, Sophie Scholl, who was studying biology and philosophy, were executed by the Nazis for high treason. The Scholls belonged to the White Rose, a small group of idealistic students at the University of Munich who urged passive resistance to the National Socialist regime. The White Rose hoped that if more Germans were aware of the Nazi regime's inhumane character, they would withdraw their loyalty.

The Scholls had once been enthusiastic members of the Hitler Youth, but over the years they grew increasingly disillusioned with Nazism. Their outlook was shaped by their anti-Nazi father, by a commitment to the German humanist tradition best represented by Schiller and Goethe, and by Kurt Huber, a professor of philosophy and psychology at their university, who spoke to trusted students of a duty "to enlighten those Germans who are still unaware of

AKG, London.

The SS were often ideologues committed to racist doctrines, which, they believed, were supported by the laws of biology. They were true believers driven by a utopian vision of a new world order founded on a Social Darwinist fantasy of racial hierarchy. To realize this mythic vision of ultimate good, the Jews, whom Nazi ideology designated as less than human but also immensely evil, powerful, and dangerous enemies of humanity, had to be destroyed. The defense of Germany required their extermination. These SS saw themselves as a moral elite dedicated to serving the fatherland. Other SS, and their army of collaborators, were simply ordinary people doing their duty as they had been trained, following orders the best way they knew how. They were morally indifferent bureaucrats, concerned with techniques and effectiveness, and careerists and functionaries seeking to impress superiors with their ability to get the job done. These people quickly adjusted to the routine of mass murder.

Thus, as Konnilyn G. Feig observes, the thousands of German railway workers "treated the Jewish cattle-car transports as a special business problem that they took pride in solving so well."[15] The German physicians who selected Jews for the gas chambers were concerned only with the technical problems and efficiency, and those doctors and scientists who performed unspeakable medical experiments on Jews viewed their subjects as laboratory animals, as the following correspondence between an I. G. Farben plant and the commandant of Auschwitz testifies: "In contemplation of experiments of a new soporific drug we would appreciate your procuring for us a number of women. . . . We propose to pay not more than 170 marks a head. If agreeable, we will take possession of the women. We need approximately 150. . . . Received the order of 150 women. Despite their emaciated condition, they were found satisfactory. . . . The tests were made. All subjects died. We shall contact you on the subject of a new load."[16]

the evil intentions of our government." Hans was also swayed by the persecution of Jews he had witnessed when he was in transport through Poland to the Russian front.

On walls in Munich, the Scholls painted signs: "Down with Hitler," and "Freedom." Stowing their anti-Nazi leaflets in luggage, the students traveled by railroad to several German cities to drop them off. The following excerpts come from three of White Rose's four leaflets:

Who among us has any conception of the dimensions of shame that will befall us and our children when one day the . . . most horrible of crimes—crimes that infinitely outdistance every human measure—reach the light of day? (First leaflet)

Our present "state" is the dictatorship of evil. . . . it is your right—or rather, your moral duty—to eliminate this system. (Third leaflet)

We are trying to achieve a renewal from within of the severely wounded German spirit. This re-birth must be preceded, however, by the clear recognition of all the guilt with which the German people have burdened themselves, and by an uncompromising battle against Hitler. (Fourth leaflet)*

On February 18, 1943, Hans and Sophie were spotted dropping leaflets in the university by the building superintendent, who reported them to the Gestapo. On February 23, Hans, Sophie, and Christoph Probst, also a medical student, were executed. Several days before she died, Sophie stated: "What does my death matter if through us thousands of people will be stirred to action and awakened?" Hans's last words, "Long live freedom," echoed through the prison. Kurt Huber and other members of the group were executed on July 13, 1943.

_____

*Inge Scholl, *Students Against Tyranny,* trans. Arthur R. Schultz (Middletown, Conn.: Wesleyan University Press, 1970), pp. 36, 56, 73, 81–82,.

The German industrialists who worked Jewish slave laborers to death considered only cost-effectiveness in their operations. So, too, did the firms that built the gas chambers and the furnaces, whose durability and performance they guaranteed. An eyewitness reports that engineers from Topf and Sons experimented with different combinations of corpses, deciding that "the most economical and fuel-saving procedure would be to burn the bodies of a well-nourished man and an emaciated woman or vice versa together with that of a child, because, as the experiments had established, in this combination, once they had caught fire, the dead would continue to burn without any further coke being required."[17] Hoess, the commandant of Auschwitz, who exemplified the bureaucratic mentality, noted that his gas chambers were more efficient than those used at Treblinka because they could accommodate far more people. The Germans were so concerned with efficiency and cost that—to conserve ammunition or gas and not slow down the pace from the time victims were ordered to undress until they were hurried into the chambers—toddlers were taken from their mothers and thrown live into burning pits or mass graves.

When the war ended, the SS murderers and those who had assisted them returned to families and jobs, resuming a normal life, free of remorse and untroubled by guilt. "The human ability to normalize the abnormal is frightening indeed," observes the sociologist Rainer C. Baum.[18] Mass murderers need not be psychopaths. It is a "disturbing psychological truth," notes Robert Jay Lifton, that "ordinary people can commit demonic acts."[19]

There have been many massacres during the course of world history. And the Nazis murdered many non-Jews in concentration camps and in reprisal for acts of resistance. What is unique about the **Holocaust**—the extermination of European Jewry—was the Nazis' determination to murder without exception every single Jew who came within their grasp, and the fanaticism, ingenuity, cruelty and systematic way—industrialized mass murder—with which they pursued this goal. Despite the protests of the army, the SS murdered Jews whose labor was needed for the war effort, and when Germany's military position was desperate, the SS still diverted military personnel and railway cars to deport Jews to the death camps.

The Holocaust was the fulfillment of Nazi racial theories. Believing that they were cleansing Europe of worthless life and a dangerous race that threatened Germany, Nazi executioners performed their evil work with dedication, assembly-line precision, and moral indifference—a gruesome testament to human irrationality and wickedness. Using the technology and bureaucracy of a modern state, the Germans killed approximately 6 million Jews: *two-thirds* of the Jewish population of Europe. Some 1.5 million of the murdered were children; almost 90 percent of Jewish children in German-occupied lands perished. Tens of thousands of entire families were wiped out without a trace. Centuries-old Jewish community life vanished, never to be restored. Burned into the soul of the Jewish people was a wound that could never entirely heal. Written into the history of Western civilization was an episode that would forever cast doubt on the Enlightenment conception of human goodness, rationality, and the progress of civilization.

Resistance

Each occupied country had its collaborators, including many right-wing intellectuals, who welcomed the demise of democracy, saw Hitler as Europe's best defense against communism, approved of Nazi measures against Jews, and profited from the confiscation of Jewish property and the sale of war material. In nearly every country occupied by or allied to Nazi Germany, local government officials and the police willingly assisted the Germans in rounding up, hunting down, and deporting Jews to the extermination camps. In Lithuania the local population was responsible for murdering more than half of the country's 140,000 Jewish victims (95 percent of Lithuania's Jewish population perished).

Each occupied country also produced a resistance movement that grew stronger as Nazi bar-

barism became more visible and prospects of a German defeat more likely. The Nazis retaliated by torturing and executing captured resistance fighters and killing hostages—generally, fifty for every German killed.

In western Europe, the resistance rescued downed Allied airmen, radioed military intelligence to Britain, and sabotaged German installations. Norwegians blew up the German stock of heavy water needed for atomic research. The Danish underground sabotaged railways and smuggled into neutral Sweden almost all of Denmark's eight thousand Jews just before they were to be deported to the death camps. The Greek resistance blew up a vital viaduct, interrupting the movement of supplies to German troops in North Africa. After the Allies landed on the coast of France in June 1944, the French resistance delayed the movement of German reinforcements and liberated sections of the country. Belgian resistance fighters captured the vital port of Antwerp.

The Polish resistance, numbering some three hundred thousand at its height, reported on German troop movements and interfered with supplies destined for the eastern front. In August 1944, with Soviet forces approaching Warsaw, the Poles staged a full-scale revolt against the German occupiers. The Poles appealed to the Soviets, camped ten miles away, for help. Thinking about a future Russian-dominated Poland, the Soviets did not move. After sixty-three days of street fighting, remnants of the Polish underground surrendered, and the Germans destroyed what was left of Warsaw.

Russian partisans numbered several hundred thousand men and women. Operating behind the German lines, they sabotaged railways, destroyed trucks, and killed scores of thousands of German soldiers in hit-and-run attacks.

The mountains and forests of Yugoslavia provided excellent terrain for guerrilla warfare. The leading Yugoslav resistance army was headed by Josip Broz (1892–1980), better known as Tito. Moscow-trained, intelligent, and courageous, Tito organized the partisans into a disciplined fighting force, which tied down a huge German army and ultimately liberated the country from German rule.

Jews participated in the resistance movements in all countries and were particularly prominent in the French resistance. Specifically Jewish resistance organizations emerged in eastern Europe, but they suffered from shattering hardships. They had virtually no access to weapons. Poles, Ukrainians, Lithuanians, Romanians and other peoples of eastern Europe with a long history of anti-Semitism gave little or no support to Jewish resisters—at times, even denounced them to the Nazis or killed them on their own. For centuries, European Jews had dealt with persecution by complying with their oppressors, and they had unlearned the habit of armed resistance that their ancestors had demonstrated against the Romans. The Germans responded to acts of resistance with savage reprisals against other Jews, creating a moral dilemma for any Jew who considered taking up arms. Nevertheless, revolts did take place in the ghettos and concentration camps. In the spring of 1943, the surviving Jews of the Warsaw ghetto, armed only with a few guns and home-made bombs, fought the Germans for several weeks.

Italy and Germany also had resistance movements. After the Allies landed in Italy in 1943, bands of Italian partisans helped to liberate Italy from fascism and the German occupation. In Germany, army officers plotted to assassinate the fuehrer. On July 20, 1944, Colonel Claus von Stauffenberg planted a bomb at a staff conference attended by Hitler, but the fuehrer escaped serious injury. In retaliation, some five thousand suspected anti-Nazis were tortured and executed in exceptionally barbarous fashion. Suspended by piano wire from meat hooks, they slowly strangled in front of cameras so that Hitler could observe their excruciating death at his leisure.

TURN OF THE TIDE

The Japanese Offensive

While Germany was subduing Europe, its ally, Japan, was extending its dominion over areas of Asia. Seeking raw materials and secure markets for Japanese goods and driven by a **xenophobic** nationalism, Japan in 1931 had attacked Manchuria in northern China. Quickly overrunning the province, the Japanese established the puppet state of Manchukuo in 1932. After a period of truce, the war against China was renewed in July 1937.

Japan captured leading cities, including China's principal seaports, and inflicted heavy casualties on the poorly organized Chinese forces, obliging the government of Jiang Jieshi (Chiang Kai-shek) to withdraw to Chungking in the interior.

In 1940, after the defeat of France and with Britain standing alone against Nazi Germany, Japan eyed Southeast Asia—French Indochina, British Burma and Malaya, and the Dutch East Indies. From these lands, Japan planned to obtain the oil, rubber, and tin vitally needed by Japanese industry and enough rice to feed the nation. Japan hoped that a quick strike against the American fleet in the Pacific would give it time to enlarge and consolidate its empire. On December 7, 1941, the Japanese struck with carrier-based planes at Pearl Harbor in Hawaii. Taken by surprise—despite warning signs—the Americans suffered a total defeat: the attackers sank 17 ships, including 7 of 8 battleships; destroyed 188 airplanes and damaged 159 others; and killed 2,403 men. The Japanese lost only 29 planes. After the attack on Pearl Harbor, Germany declared war on the United States. Now the immense American industrial capacity could be put to work against the Axis powers—Germany, Italy, and Japan. American factories produced planes, tanks, and ships at a pace and scale that astonished both friend and foe. The American arsenal supplied Britain and the Soviet Union with badly needed equipment.

Defeat of the Axis Powers

By the spring of 1942, the Axis powers held the upper hand. The Japanese Empire included the coast of China, Indochina, Thailand, Burma, Malaya, the Dutch East Indies, the Philippines, and other islands in the Pacific. Germany controlled Europe almost to Moscow. When the year ended, however, the Allies seemed assured of victory. Three decisive battles—Midway, Stalingrad, and El Alamein—reversed the tide of war.

At Pearl Harbor, the Japanese had destroyed much of the American fleet. Assembling a mighty flotilla (eight aircraft carriers, eleven battleships, twenty-two cruisers, and sixty-five destroyers), Japan now sought to annihilate the rest of the United States' Pacific fleet. In June 1942, the main body of the Japanese fleet headed for Midway, eleven hundred miles northwest of Pearl

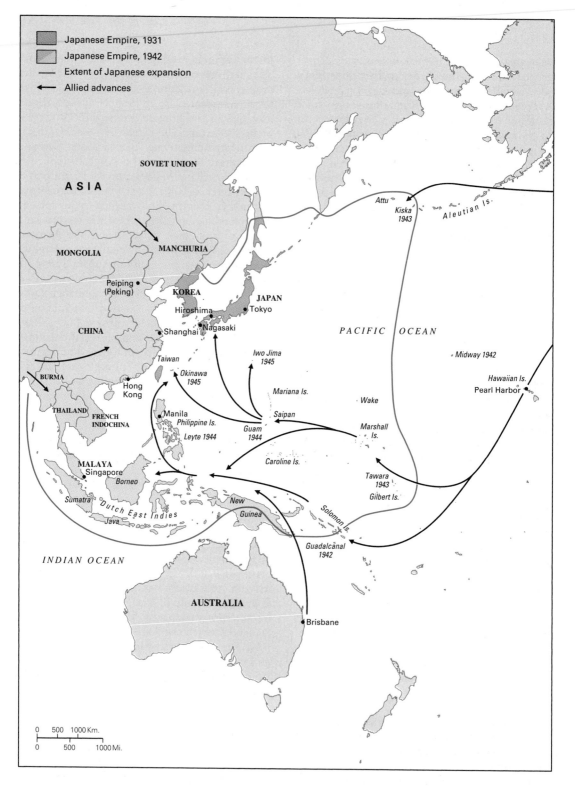

Japanese Empire, 1931
Japanese Empire, 1942
Extent of Japanese expansion
Allied advances

SOVIET UNION

ASIA

MONGOLIA   MANCHURIA

Attu
Kiska
1943   Aleutian Is.

Peiping •
(Peking)
KOREA   JAPAN
Hiroshima   Tokyo •
Shanghai •   Nagasaki

CHINA

PACIFIC OCEAN

Taiwan
Iwo Jima
1945
Okinawa
1945
• Midway 1942

BURMA
Hong
Kong
Mariana Is.
Wake
Hawaiian Is.
Pearl Harbor •

THAILAND
FRENCH
INDOCHINA
• Manila
Philippine Is.
Leyte 1944
Saipan
Guam
1944
Marshall
Is.

MALAYA
Singapore
Borneo
Caroline Is.
Tawara
1943
Gilbert Is.

Sumatra
Dutch East Indies
Java
New
Guinea
Solomon Is.

INDIAN OCEAN
Guadalcanal
1942

AUSTRALIA
• Brisbane

0   500   1000 Km.
0   500   1000 Mi.

Harbor; another section sailed toward the Aleutian Islands, in an attempt to divide the American fleet. But the Americans had broken the Japanese naval code and were aware of the Japanese plan.

On June 4, 1942, the two navies fought a strange naval battle; it was waged entirely by carrier-based planes, for the two fleets were too far from each other to use their big guns or even to see each other. Demonstrating marked superiority over their opponents and extraordinary courage, American pilots destroyed 4 aircraft carriers and downed 322 Japanese planes. The battle of Midway cost Japan the initiative. With American industrial production accelerating, the opportunity for a Japanese victory had passed.

After being stymied at the outskirts of Moscow in December 1941, the Germans renewed their offensive in the spring and summer of 1942. Hitler's goal was Stalingrad, the great industrial center located on the Volga River; control of Stalingrad would give Germany command of vital rail transportation and access to the oil fields of the Caucasus. The battle of Stalingrad was an epic struggle in which Russian soldiers and civilians contested for every building and street of the city. In this urban battlefield, scarred by mile after mile of destroyed buildings and mountains of rubble, the combatants were separated by mere yards, snipers lurked in the maze of ruins, and tough Russian soldiers stealthily and ceaselessly attacked at night with bayonets and daggers; here the blitzkrieg, which had brought the Germans immense success in their earlier offensives, did not apply. Ironically, massive German bombing raids, which had left almost every structure in ruins, provided the Russian fighters with perfect cover from which to harass the enemy. Superior German technical skills and generalship were of no value in close-quarter combat in basements and sewers and amid the rubble and skeletons of buildings. So brutal was the fighting that at night half-crazed dogs sought to escape the city by swimming across the river. One German soldier wrote in his diary at the end of December: "The horses have already been eaten. . . . The soldiers look like corpses or lunatics looking for something to put in their mouths. They no longer take cover from Russian shells; they haven't the strength to walk, run away and hide."[20]

A Russian counterattack in November, planned by General (later Marshal) Georgi Zhukov, who had successfully defended Moscow the previous year, caught the Germans in a trap. Not believing that the Russians had sufficient reserve armies and tanks or the competence to launch a massive counteroffensive, German commanders were taken by surprise. With his soldiers exhausted and desperately short of food, medical supplies, weapons, and ammunition, Friedrich Paulus, commander of the Sixth Army, urged Hitler to order a withdrawal before the Russians closed the ring. The fuehrer refused, persuaded, in part, by the pompous Herman Goering's assurance that his Luftwaffe would be able to supply the beleaguered army by air. It was an empty promise; the lack of available transport planes and terrible winter weather, which limited the number of flights and hampered maintenance crews, who had to work outdoors on primitive Russian airfields, doomed the airlift. After suffering tens of thousands of additional casualties, their position hopeless, the remnants of the Sixth Army surrendered on February 2, 1943. Some 260,000 German soldiers had perished in the battle of Stalingrad, and another 110,000 were taken prisoner. Russian morale soared.

The Soviet high command, which had performed terribly in the early days of the German offensive, distinguished itself at Stalingrad. At the battle of Kursk in July 1943, Russian military leaders again demonstrated an increasing ability to master the technique of modern warfare. Analyzing correctly that the Germans would attack the Kursk salients, Zhukhov turned the area into a fortress. Immense numbers of heavy artillery, mines, antitank ditches, tanks, and planes, including dive-bombers equipped with cannon capable of destroying tanks, were set in place. A huge reserve force was positioned to repair breaches opened by panzer attacks. In an epic encounter, over three hundred German tanks were destroyed in one day. "Soviet success at Kursk . . . was the most important single victory of the war," concludes one military historian. "It was the point at

◀ MAP 32.3 WORLD WAR II: THE PACIFIC THEATER The battle of Midway was a major turning point in the Pacific Theater. The map also shows the island hopping of the Americans that brought them closer to Japan. The battles of Iwo Jima and Okinawa were particularly brutal.

which the initiative passed to the Soviet side. . . . The German front in the east was forced . . . to fall back along its entire length. . . . There was a long way to go to take the fight into Europe and to reach Berlin, but Kursk had unhinged the German front irreversibly."[21]

In January 1941, the British were routing the Italians in northern Africa. Hitler assigned General Erwin Rommel (1891–1944) to halt the British advance. Rommel drove the British out of Libya and, with strong reinforcements, might have taken Egypt and the Suez Canal. But Hitler's concern was with seizing Yugoslavia and Greece and preparing for the invasion of Russia. At the beginning of 1942, Rommel resumed his advance, intending to conquer Egypt. The British Eighth Army, commanded by General Bernard L. Montgomery, stopped him at the battle of El Alamein in October 1942. The victory of El Alamein was followed by an Anglo-American invasion of northwestern Africa in November 1942. By May 1943, the Germans and Italians were defeated in North Africa.

After securing North Africa, the Allies, seeking complete control of the Mediterranean, invaded Sicily in July 1943 and quickly conquered the island. Mussolini's fellow Fascist leaders turned against him, and the king dismissed him as prime minister. In September, the new government surrendered to the Allies, and in the following month, Italy declared war on Germany.

Italian partisans, whose number would grow to three hundred thousand, resisted the Germans, who were determined to hold on to central and northern Italy. At the same time, the Allies fought their way up the peninsula. The fighting in Italy, vicious and costly, would last until the very end of the war. Captured by partisans, Mussolini was executed (April 28, 1945) and his dead body, hanging upside down, was publicly displayed.

On June 6, 1944, D-day, the Allies landed on the beaches of Normandy in France. The invasion force that crossed from England that day consisted of 175,000 soldiers and over 7,000 vessels, including warships, minesweepers, cargo ships, and landing craft—the greatest armada in history. Some 3,700 fighter planes guarded the ships and covered the invasion beaches; another 1,400 transport planes carried parachute battalions or towed gliders filled with infantry equipment. Although they

suspected an imminent landing, the Germans did not think that it would occur in Normandy, and they dismissed June 6 as a possible date because weather conditions were unfavorable. The success of D-day depended on securing the beaches and marching inland. On some beaches the soldiers struggled ashore in the face of intense enemy fire. At Omaha Beach, the Americans almost did not make it. Weighed down by heavy equipment, men drowned as they were tossed by high waves; others were killed or wounded by machine-gun fire before reaching the beach. Much of the heavy armor was lost. Those who stumbled ashore hugged the embankment and sheltered themselves behind whatever barrier they could find to escape the German guns firing from the cliffs. Traumatized by the devastation and death surrounding them, and often leaderless, the soldiers, many of them facing combat for the first time, seemed paralyzed. But amid the chaos, says the official army account,

> At half-a-dozen or more points on the long stretch, they found the necessary drive to leave their cover and move out over the open beach flat toward the bluffs. . . . [T]he decisive factor was leadership. Wherever an advance was made, it depended on the presence of some few individuals, officers and noncommissioned officers, who inspired, encouraged, or bullied their men forward by making the first forward moves. . . . Colonel [George A. Taylor] summed up the situation in a terse phrase: "Two kinds of people are staying on this beach, the dead and those who are going to die—now let's get the hell out of here."[22]

Having established beachheads, the Allies rushed more men and supplies into battle. Still believing that Normandy was only a feint, that the main attack would be directed at Pas de Calais—a deception skillfully promoted by Allied intelligence in the months prior to the invasion— the Germans continued, in what was a fatal blunder, to hold back their crack reserves. Adding to the Germans' woes was the destruction of the French transportation system by Allied planes just prior to the invasion. German troops sent to fortify the defenses at Normandy met delay after delay. Aided by control of the air, the Allies overwhelmed the German defenders. By the end of

HIROSHIMA AFTER THE ATOMIC BOMB. The mass destruction of Hiroshima ushered in a new age. Nuclear weapons gave humanity the capacity to destroy civilization. (*Corbis-Bettmann.*)

July, they had built up their strength in France to a million and a half. In the middle of August, Paris rose up against the German occupiers and was soon liberated.

As winter approached, the situation looked hopeless for Germany. Brussels and Antwerp fell to the Allies; Allied bombers were striking German factories and mass-bombing German cities in terror raids that took a horrendous toll of life. The air war eroded Germany's industrial potential, devastated the transportation system, preventing supplies from reaching the fronts, and caused civilian morale to plummet. Desperate, Hitler made one last gamble. In mid December 1944, he launched an offensive to split the Allied forces and regain the vital port of Antwerp. The Allies were taken by surprise in the battle of the Bulge, but a heroic defense by the Americans at Bastogne, an important road junction, helped stop the German offensive.

While their allies were advancing in the west, the Russians were continuing their drive in the east, advancing into the Baltic states, Poland, and Hungary. Yet German soldiers continued to fight with remarkable skill and determination, inflicting proportionately more casualties than they suffered. They were driven by a fanatic dedication to Hitler and Nazi ideology, loyalty to their comrades and the endangered fatherland, pride in the tradition of German arms, and fear of both vengeful Russians and the SS and other special units that were executing "defeatists."

By February 1945, the Russians stood within one hundred miles of Berlin. Also in February, the Allies in the west were battling the Germans in the Rhineland, and on March 7, 1945, American soldiers, seizing a bridge at Remagen that the Germans had failed to destroy, crossed the Rhine into the interior of Germany. By April 1945, British, American, and Russian troops were penetrating into Germany from east and west. From his underground bunker near the chancellery in Berlin, a physically exhausted and emotionally unhinged Hitler engaged in wild fantasies about new German victories. In mid-April the Red Army's spearhead pushed into Berlin, which Hitler had ordered defended "to the last man and the last shot." The greatly outnumbered defenders—army remnants, elderly recruits, and fanatical Hitler youth—fought tenaciously block by block. As the Russians stormed through the devastated city, SS squads hunted down and lynched deserters and ordinary soldiers for the flimsiest of reasons. The Russians suffered over 300,000 dead and wounded. German casualties were also in the hundreds of thousands, many of them civilians. Hundreds of thousands of Berliners fled west to escape revengeful Russians who murdered, mutilated, raped, and looted in random acts of savagery. On April 30, 1945, with the Russians only blocks away, the fuehrer took his own life. In his last will and testament, Hitler again resorted to the vile lie: "It is not true that I or anybody else in Germany wanted war in 1939. It was wanted and provoked exclusively by those international statesmen who either were of Jewish origin or worked for Jewish interests."[23] On May 7, 1945, a demoralized and devastated Germany surrendered unconditionally.

After the victory at Midway in June 1942, American forces attacked strategic islands held by Japan. American troops had to battle their way up beaches and through jungles tenaciously defended by Japanese soldiers, who believed that death was preferable to the disgrace of surrender. They fought to the last and often killed themselves when confronted with the dishonor of falling into enemy hands. In March 1945, twenty-one thousand Japanese perished on Iwo Jima; another hundred thousand died on Okinawa in April 1945 as they contested for every inch of the island. On August 6, 1945, the United States dropped an atomic bomb on Hiroshima, killing more than seventy-eight thousand people and demolishing 60 percent of the city. President Harry S. Truman said that he ordered the atomic attack to avoid an American invasion of the Japanese homeland, which would have caused hundreds of thousands of casualties.

Truman's decision has aroused considerable debate. Some analysts say that dropping the bomb was unnecessary, that Japan, deprived of oil, rice, and other essentials by an American naval blockade and defenseless against unrelenting aerial bombardments, was close to surrender and had indicated as much. It has been suggested that with the Soviet Union about to enter the conflict against Japan, Truman wanted to end the war immediately, thus depriving the U.S.S.R. of an opportunity to extend its influence in East Asia. On August 8, Russia did enter the war against Japan, invading Manchuria. After a second atomic bomb was dropped on Nagasaki on August 9, the Japanese asked for peace.

The Legacy of World War II

World War II was the most destructive and murderous war in history. The total war waged by the combatants also enveloped civilians, who were victims of reprisals, genocide, slave labor, and aerial bombardment of cities. Estimates of the number of dead range as high as fifty million, including some twenty-five million Russians*—one in three Russians lost a father—who sacrificed more than the other participants in both population and material resources. (In comparison, the United States suffered 400,000 battle deaths.) The war produced a vast migration of peoples unparalleled in modern European history. In accordance with an agreement made with Russia at a conference at Yalta in February 1945, Britain and America compelled some two million Russian prisoners of war, slave laborers, and those who had been recruited into the German army to return to the Soviet Union, many against their will. Ten percent of these deportees were executed and 70 percent sent to Stalin's labor camps. The Soviet Union annexed the Baltic lands of Latvia, Lithuania, and Estonia, forcibly deporting many of the native inhabitants into central Russia. The bulk of East Prussia was taken over by Poland, and Russia annexed the northeastern portion. Millions of Germans fled the invading Russians, who, bent on revenge for the misery the Nazis had inflicted on their kin and

---

*Evidence discovered in recently released Soviet archives has compelled historians to increase substantially this generally accepted estimate.

country, committed numerous atrocities, including indiscriminate killing and mass rape, before Soviet authorities ended the mayhem. Millions more Germans were driven out of Poland, Czechoslovakia, Yugoslavia, Romania, and Hungary, places where their ancestors had lived for centuries, by vengeful eastern Europeans. Moreover, leaders in these countries, driven by nationalist aspirations, welcomed an opportunity to rid their nations of an ethnic minority, particularly since so many of these Germans had aided the Nazi occupiers. In 1945–46, some twelve million to thirteen million Germans were driven westward. Expelled from their homes, often with only a few minutes' warning, they had to leave almost everything behind. Herded into internment camps, they were brutalized by Polish and Czech guards who relished the opportunity to torment Germans. Tens of thousands died from malnutrition, disease, exposure, and mistreatment; thousands more committed suicide.

Material costs were staggering. Everywhere cities were in rubble; bridges, railway systems, waterways, and harbors destroyed; farmland laid waste; livestock killed; coal mines wrecked. Homeless and hungry people wandered the streets and roads. Europe faced the gigantic task of rebuilding. Yet Europe did recover from this material blight, and with astonishing speed.

The war produced a shift in power arrangements. The United States and the Soviet Union emerged as the two most powerful states in the world. The traditional Great Powers—Britain, France, and Germany—were now dwarfed by these superpowers. The United States had the atomic bomb and immense industrial might—its economy, previously suffering from the Great Depression, boomed during the war; the Soviet Union had the largest army in the world and was extending its dominion over eastern Europe. With Germany defeated, the principal incentive for Soviet-American cooperation evaporated.

After World War I, nationalist passions intensified. After World War II, western Europeans progressed toward unity. The Hitler years convinced many Europeans of the dangers inherent in extreme nationalism, and fear of the Soviet Union prodded them toward greater cooperation.

World War II accelerated the disintegration of Europe's overseas empires. The European states could hardly justify ruling over Africans and Asians after they had fought to liberate European lands from German imperialism. Nor could they ask their people, exhausted by the Hitler years and concentrating all their energies on reconstruction, to fight new wars against Africans and Asians pressing for independence. In the years just after the war, Great Britain surrendered India, France lost Lebanon and Syria, and the Dutch departed from Indonesia. In the 1950s and 1960s, virtually every colonial territory gained independence. In those instances where the colonial power resisted independence for the colony, the price was bloodshed.

The consciousness of Europe, already profoundly damaged by World War I, was again grievously wounded. Nazi racial theories showed that even in an age of sophisticated science the mind remains attracted to irrational beliefs and mythical imagery. Nazi atrocities proved that people will torture and kill with religious zeal and machinelike indifference. This regression to mythical thinking and savagery bears out Walter Lippmann's contention that "men have been barbarians much longer than they have been civilized. They are only precariously civilized, and within us there is the propensity, persistent as the force of gravity, to revert under stress and strain, or under temptation, to our first natures."[24] And the behavior of German intellectuals also contained a painful lesson, says German historian Karl Dietrich Bracher: "The intellectuals who supported the Nazis in one way or another all document that the mind can be temporarily seduced, that people can be bribed with careers and fame, that thinking people, especially, are tempted by an irrational cult of action and are peculiarly susceptible to 'one-dimensional' answers and promises of salvation."[25]

The Nazi assault on reason and freedom demonstrated anew the precariousness of Western civilization. This assault would forever cast doubt on the Enlightenment conception of human goodness, secular rationality, and the progress of civilization through advances in science and technology.

The Holocaust was heightened irrationality and organized evil on an unprecedented scale. Auschwitz, Treblinka, Sobibor, and the other death factories represent the triumph of human irrationality over reason—the surrender of the mind to a bizarre racial mythology that provided a metaphysical and pseudoscientific justification for mass murder. They also represent the ultimate perversion of reason. A calculating reason manufactured and organized lies and demented beliefs into a structured system with its own inner logic, and employed sophisticated technology and administrative techniques to destroy human beings spiritually and physically. Science and technology, venerated as the great achievement of the Western mind, had made mass extermination possible. The philosophes had not forseen the destructive power inherent in reason. Historian Omer Bartov poses this disturbing question about the failure of reason and the Western humanist tradition: "What was it that induced Nobel Prize–winning scientists, internationally respected legal scholars, physicians known throughout the world for their research into the human body and their desire to ameliorate the lot of humanity, to become not merely opportunist accomplices, but in many ways the initiators and promoters of this attempt to subject the human race to a vast surgical operation by means of mass extermination of whole categories of human beings? What was there (or is there) in our culture that made the concept of transforming humanity by means of eugenic and racial cleansing seem so practical and rational?"[26]

Both the Christian and the Enlightenment traditions had failed the West. Some intellectuals, shocked by the irrationality and horrors of the Hitler era, drifted into despair. To these thinkers, life was absurd, without meaning; human beings could neither comprehend nor control it. In 1945, only the naive could have faith in continuous progress or believe in the essential goodness of the individual. The future envisioned by the philosophes seemed more distant than ever. Nevertheless, this profound disillusionment was tempered by hope. Democracy had, in fact, prevailed over Nazi totalitarianism and terror. Moreover, fewer intellectuals were now attracted to antidemocratic thought. The Nazi dictatorship convinced many of them, even some who had wavered in previous decades, that freedom and human dignity were precious ideals and that liberal constitutional government, despite its imperfections, was the best means of preserving these ideals. Perhaps, then, democratic institutions and values would spread throughout the globe, and the newly established United Nations would promote world peace.

❖   ❖   ❖

Online Study Center ACE the Test

NOTES

1. Pierre Renouvin, *World War II and Its Origins* (New York: Harper & Row, 1969), p. 167.

2. Z. A. B. Zeman, *Nazi Propaganda* (New York: Oxford University Press, 1973), p. 109.

3. *Documents on German Foreign Policy, 1918–1945*, vol. 6 (London: Her Majesty's Stationery Office, 1956), series D, no. 433.

4. Basil H. Liddell Hart, *History of the Second World War* (New York: Putnam, 1970), pp. 73–74.

5. Winston S. Churchill, *The Second World War: Their Finest Hour* (Boston: Houghton Mifflin, 1949), 2:225–226.

6. Quoted in William L. Shirer, *The Rise and Fall of the Third Reich* (New York: Simon & Schuster, 1960), p. 860.

7. *Hitler's Secret Conversations, 1941–1944*, with an introductory essay by H. R. Trevor Roper (New York: Farrar, Straus & Young, 1953), p. 508.

8. Quoted in Gordon Wright, *The Ordeal of Total War* (New York: Harper Torchbooks, 1968), p. 124.

9. Quoted in Norman Cohn, *Warrant for Genocide* (New York: Harper Torchbooks, 1967), p. 188.

10. Gerda Weissman Klein, *All but My Life* (New York: Hill & Wang, 1957), p. 89.

11. Judith Sternberg Newman, *In the Hell of Auschwitz* (New York: Exposition, 1964), p. 18.

12. *Nazi Conspiracy and Aggression* (Washington,

D.C.: U.S. Government Printing Office, 1946), 6:787–789.

13. Quoted in Joseph Borkin, *The Crime and Punishment of I. G. Farben* (New York: Free Press, 1978), p. 143.

14. Gisella Perl, *I Was a Doctor in Auschwitz* (New York: International Universities Press, 1948), p. 80.

15. Konnilyn G. Feig, *Hitler's Death Camps* (New York: Holmes & Meier, 1979), p. 37.

16. Quoted in Erich Kahler, *The Tower and the Abyss* (New York: George Braziller, 1957), pp. 74–75.

17. Quoted in Steven T. Katz, "Technology and Genocide: Technology as a 'Form of Life,'" in *Echoes from the Holocaust*, ed. Alan Rosenberg and Gerald E. Meyers (Philadelphia: Temple University Press, 1988), p. 281.

18. Rainer C. Baum, "Holocaust: Moral Indifference as the Form of Modern Evil," in *Echoes from the Holocaust*, p. 83.

19. Robert Jay Lifton, *The Nazi Doctors* (New York: Basic Books, 1968), p. 5.

20. Richard Overy, *Why the Allies Won* (New York: Norton, 1995), p. 82.

21. Ibid., p. 96.

22. *Omaha Beachhead*, prepared by the War Department Historical Division (Washington, D.C., 1945), pp. 58, 71.

23. Excerpted in George H. Stein, ed., *Hitler* (Englewood Cliffs, N.J.: Prentice-Hall, 1968), p. 84.

24. Walter Lippmann, *The Public Philosophy* (Boston: Little, Brown, 1955), p. 86.

25. Karl Dietrich Bracher, *Turning Points in Modern Times,* trans. Thomas Dunlap (Cambridge, Mass.: Harvard University Press, 1995), p. 198.

26. Omer Bartov, *Germany's War and the Holocaust: Disputed Histories* (Ithaca, New York: Cornell University Press, 2003), p. 136.

Suggested Reading

Bartov, Omer, *Hitler's Army* (1992). Excellent material on the indoctrination of the German soldier.

Bauer, Yehuda, *A History of the Holocaust* (1982). An authoritative study.

Calvocoressi, Peter, and Guy Wint, *Total War* (1972). A good account of World War II.

Campbell, John, ed., *The Experience of War* (1989). A team of specialists provides a topical approach to the war.

Dear, I. C. B., *The Oxford Companion to World War II* (1995). A superb reference work.

Overy, Richard, *Why the Allies Won* (1995). A brilliant analysis.

Weinberg, Gerhard L., *A World at Arms* (1994). A recent study based on extraordinary knowledge of the sources.

Wiesel, Elie, *Night* (1960). A moving personal record of the Holocaust.

Part Seven

The Contemporary World: The Global Age

Since 1945

1940

1950

1960

1970

1980

1990

2000

Politics and Society

Yalta agreement (1945)
United Nations established (1945)
Marshall Plan for recovery of Europe (1947)
State of Israel established (1948)
North Atlantic Treaty Organization (NATO)
   established (1949)
Division of Germany (1949)
Triumph of communism in China (1949)

Korean War (1950–1953)
European Economic Community (EEC)
   established (1957)
Sputnik launched; space age begins (1957)

Berlin Wall built (1961)
Cuban missile crisis (1962)
Vietnam War (1963–1973)

Détente in East-West relations (1970s)

Gorbachev becomes leader of Soviet Union (1985)
Explosion at Chernobyl nuclear power plant (1986)
Peaceful overthrow of Communist governments
   in Eastern Europe (1989)
Berlin Wall demolished (1989)

Reunification of Germany (1990)
Charter of Paris for a New Europe (1990)
Official end of cold war (1990)
Persian Gulf War (1991)
Yeltsin elected Russian president (1991)
Yugoslav federation breaks up and war begins (1991)
Collapse of the Soviet Union (1991)
Czechoslovakia splits into Czech Republic and
   Slovakia (1993)
European Union ratifies the Maastricht Treaty (1993)
Elections for new Russian constitution and
   parliament (1993)
War breaks out between Russia and Chechnya (1994)
Dayton Agreement ends civil war in former
   Yugoslavia (1995)

Terrorist attacks on World Trade Center and the
   Pentagon (September 11, 2001)

Thought and Culture

Wiener, *Cybernetics* (1948)
Orwell, *1984* (1949)
de Beauvoir, *The Second Sex* (1949)

Camus, *The Rebel* (1951)
Discovery of DNA by Crick and Watson (1951–53)
Djilas, *The New Class* (1957)
Chomsky, *Syntactic Structures* (1957)
Snow, *The Two Cultures and the Scientific
   Revolution* (1959)

Carson, *Silent Spring* (1962)
Pope John XXIII, *Pacem in Terris* (1963)
McLuhan, *Understanding Media* (1964)
Levi-Strauss, *The Savage Mind* (1966)

Solzhenitsyn, *The Gulag Archipelago* (1974–1978)
Wilson, *Sociobiology* (1975)

Creation of the Internet (1983)
Gorbachev, *Perestroika* (1987)

Huntington, *The Clash of Civilization and the
   Remaking of World Order* (1996)
Vatican Commission for Religious Relations with
   the Jews, "We Remember: A Reflection of the
   'Shoah' [the Hebrew name for Holocaust]"
   (1998)

Human genome sequence completed (2001)
Discovery of skull of earliest known hominid
   ancestor that lived in central Africa between six
   and seven million years ago (2002)

Chapter 33

Europe After World War II: Recovery and Realignment, 1945–1989

The Berlin Wall, swiftly erected by the East German Communist regime in 1961, divided the city of Berlin for twenty-eight years. (Corbis-Bettmann.)

- **The Cold War**
- **Building a New Europe**
- **The Soviet Bloc**
- **Decolonization**

Focus Questions

1. What were the origins of and key developments in the cold war?
2. How did Khrushchev and Brezhnev change the Stalinist heritage?
3. What factors fostered growing European unity?
4. Why was World War II followed by decolonization? What were some immediate consequences of decolonization?

Online Study Center

This icon will direct you to interactive map and primary source activities on the website http://college.hmco.com/pic/perrywc8e.

At the end of World War II, Winston Churchill lamented: "What is Europe now? A rubble heap, a charnel house, a breeding ground for pestilence and hate."[1] Everywhere the survivors counted their dead. The material destruction had been unprecedentedly heavy in the battle zones, particularly in the east, where Hitler's and Stalin's armies had fought without mercy to people, animals, or the environment. Industry, transportation, and communication had come to a virtual standstill. Now members of families searched for each other; prisoners of war made their way home.

Europe was politically cut in half; Soviet troops had overrun eastern Europe and penetrated into the heart of Germany. The Yalta agreement of February 1945, signed by Roosevelt, Churchill, and Stalin, turned the prevailing military balance of power into a political settlement. The Soviet Union imposed its grim dictatorship on the Western-oriented countries in eastern and southeastern Europe.

The United States stepped forward as the heir and guardian of the Western tradition. A superpower, it was striving to shape the new world order in the global age that was emerging from the defeat of Germany and Japan. The material wealth of the United States, its industrial efficiency, and the ideals of democratic freedom embedded in its institutions helped rebuild democratic government and generate prosperity in western Europe. The United States also impressed people around the world, inspiring imitation even in hostile countries.

Thus, American influence speeded up the westernization of the world. Japan and Pacific Rim countries were drawn into the mainstream of Western business and culture. Decolonization created a multitude of new states in Asia and Africa, patterned, however painfully, after the Western model of statehood. For better or for worse, all the world's peoples were becoming linked in rapidly increasing political and economic interdependence, a process that was accelerated by immigrants from poor countries streaming toward the rich.

These changes took place over the next decades under the shadow of the cold war, the worldwide ideological conflict between the two victors in World War II, the United States and the Soviet Union. Each offered its form of government and

Chronology 33.1 ❖ Europe, 1945–1989

1945	United Nations founded; eastern Europe occupied by Red Army
1947	Cold war starts; Truman Doctrine; Marshall Plan inaugurated
1948	Stalinization of eastern Europe
1949	NATO formed; first Soviet atomic bomb exploded
1953	Stalin dies
1956	Khrushchev's secret speech on Stalin's crimes; Polish October; Hungarian uprising is crushed
1957	European Economic Community established; sputnik launched—the space age begins
1961	Berlin Wall built, dividing the city of Berlin
1962	Cuban missile crisis
1963–1973	Vietnam War
1964	Khrushchev ousted; a new team of leaders, lead by Brezhnev, succeeds him
1968	Student uprising in France; Czechoslovakia's "socialism with a human face"
1969	American landing on the moon
1979	Soviet Union invades Afghanistan
1982	Brezhnev dies
1985	Gorbachev becomes U.S.S.R. leader
1988	Communist dictatorship in Poland ends; civilian government takes office
1989	Overthrow of Communist regimes in Eastern Europe

guiding ideals as a model for the entire world. While proudly presenting the communist vision as the guide to the future, Stalin remained afraid of Western—especially American—superiority. Trying to help his vast country catch up to Western achievements, he also gave high priority, after his country's losses in two world wars, to external security, expanding his control over the Soviet Union's neighboring states in eastern Europe.

THE COLD WAR

Origins

The cold war (the American financier Bernard Baruch coined the phrase in 1947) stemmed from the divergent historical experiences and the in-

compatible political ambitions of the United States and the Soviet Union. As the European continent lay in a shambles, the proud outsiders to the west and east dominated the global scene. The two superpowers engaged in more than four decades of political and military rivalry that stopped short of outright war. The challenge that started the cold war came before the end of World War II. As the Red Army moved through eastern Europe, the fate of the peoples of that region hung in the balance. Would Stalin treat them as a conquered people, knowing that left to their own devices they would return to their traditional anti-Russian orientation?

As the Red Army occupied Poland, Stalin installed a pro-Soviet regime. Other countries in eastern Europe suffered the same fate. Ever worried about the security of his country's western boundaries, Stalin incorporated most eastern European countries into a buffer zone for protection against Western attack. But alarmed Europeans and Americans interpreted the Soviet occupation as part of a communist expansion that threatened to extend to the rest of the world. Western Europeans, in particular, feared Soviet encroachment, militarily or politically, into their countries. The local populations and their sympathizers in western Europe and the United States viewed the Soviet occupation of eastern Europe as a dire calamity. But short of starting another war, Western countries were powerless to intervene.

For the next forty-five years, the two parts of the Continent would be known as Eastern Europe and Western Europe: two camps of opposing ideologies. To quote Churchill's famous words, "From Stettin in the Baltic to Trieste in the Adriatic, an iron curtain has descended across the Continent."[2] Now the Western democracies had to close ranks against the communist menace. American leaders were profoundly concerned: they had the responsibility of rallying Western Europe, and possibly the world, against universal communism.

Online Study Center

Improve Your Grade
Primary Source: An Iron Curtain Has Descended Across the Continent (Churchill)

Cold War Mobilization

In March 1947, fearing Soviet penetration in the eastern Mediterranean, President Truman proclaimed the Truman Doctrine: "It must be the policy of the United States to support free peoples who are resisting attempted subjugation by armed minorities or by outside pressures."[3] The Truman Doctrine was the centerpiece of the new policy of *containment,* of holding Soviet power within its then-current boundaries. U.S. military and economic support soon went to Greece and Turkey. Thus, a sharp reversal took place in American foreign policy; prewar American isolation gave way to worldwide vigilance against any Soviet effort at expansion.

Later that year, the United States took a major step toward strengthening the West. In June 1947, Secretary of State George C. Marshall announced an impressive program of economic aid, formally called the European Recovery Program but widely known as the Marshall Plan. By 1952, when the plan terminated, it had supplied Europe with a total of $13.15 billion in aid—a modest pump-priming for the subsequent record upswing in U.S., Western European, and even global prosperity. Western Europe recovered, and the United States gained economically strong allies and trading partners.

In 1948, Stalin, seeking greater control in East Germany, cut off access to West Berlin. In response, the United States and Britain organized a massive airlift of supplies to the city, preserving the western outpost in East Germany.

The United States in 1950, with United Nations support, went to war for two years to defend South Korea against an invasion by Communist North Korea and its powerful, ally Communist China. For a time thereafter, hysterical fear of communist infiltration into the U.S. government and among intellectuals gripped the American public. Apprehensions about national security were accompanied by a massive ideological mobilization of American opinion against the communist threat.

The United States strove to contain Soviet power by establishing in 1949 the North Atlantic Treaty Organization. NATO linked the armed forces of the United States, Canada, Portugal, Norway, Iceland, Denmark, Italy, Britain, France, and the Benelux countries (an acronym for Belgium, the Netherlands, and Luxembourg). Greece and Turkey soon joined; West Germany was included in 1956, and Spain in 1982. In response to NATO, the Soviet Union formed the Warsaw Pact, consisting of the armed forces of the Soviet Union and its European satellites.

Arms Race and Space Race

Military alliances and forces were backed up by ever more powerful armaments. Sooner than expected, in 1949, the Soviet Union exploded its own atomic device. Thereafter, the arms race escalated to hydrogen bombs and intercontinental ballistic missiles (ICBMs). Threatened by Soviet

MARSHALL PLAN AID. Since much of Europe lay in rubble at the conclusion of World War II, the U.S. Congress approved the European Recovery Program (the official name of the Marshall Plan) in 1948. The funds were to be used to buy U.S. goods. The earliest aid, however, went toward agricultural assistance and housing construction to alleviate malnutrition and homelessness. (*Bettmann/CORBIS.*)

ICBMs, the United States lost its territorial invulnerability, which its geography had guaranteed until then. The arms race proved a source of profound intellectual and moral alarm. Said Albert Einstein, "The unleashed power of the atom has changed everything save our modes of thinking, and thus we drift toward unparalleled catastrophes."[4] Catastrophe was barely avoided in 1962. When the Soviet Union, under Nikita Khrushchev, prepared to place nuclear missiles in the newly established Communist regime in Cuba, trying to offset U.S. missiles in Turkey, President John F. Kennedy demanded their removal. For a terrifying moment, as the world held its breath, the cold war threatened to turn into a hot nuclear exchange. Fortunately, diplomacy prevailed. A secret deal was struck: Soviet missiles were taken out of Cuba in exchange for the removal of obsolete American missiles from Turkey; in addition, the United States promised not to attack Cuba. The Cuban missile crisis ended peacefully.

The U.S.–Soviet rivalry extended into outer space. In 1957, the Soviet government sent the first *sputnik* (satellite) into orbit around the earth, shocking complacent Americans into a keen awareness of their vulnerability. For some years, the Soviet Union remained ahead in the prestigious field of space exploration, sending the first astronaut, Yuri Gagarin, into orbit in 1961. The United States caught up in 1969 by landing a man on the moon.

All along, science and technology contributed to the escalation of the ominous arms race. Deter-

1972 to a temporary limit on offensive strategic weapons.

The Vietnam War

From the start, the cold war led humanity along the brink of nuclear apocalypse. The conflict remained, however, a *cold* war, because the superpowers abstained from armed confrontation. The United States, however, did get drawn into a protracted hot war with Communist North Vietnam, which, under the leadership of Ho Chi Minh, waged a guerrilla war to take over South Vietnam. If the communists prevailed, apprehensive Americans argued, all the other countries in East and Southeast Asia would fall like dominoes to communist rule. Under President Lyndon B. Johnson, U.S. support of South Vietnam escalated into the undeclared and increasingly unpopular Vietnam War.

The U.S. government shipped to Vietnam nearly half a million soldiers, equipped with chemical weapons and advanced electronic gear. Yet victory eluded the American forces despite the fact that more explosives were dropped on tiny Vietnam than the Allies had dropped during World War II.

Opposition to the war among the American public increased, especially after North Vietnam launched a new wave of attacks early in 1968. Peace talks between the United States and North Vietnam started in April of that year. Despite continuing negotiations, President Richard M. Nixon, elected in late 1968, extended the war by secretly bombing communist bases and supply routes in neighboring Cambodia and Laos. Protests in America mounted until, at last, in 1973, by agreement with North Vietnam, the United States withdrew its forces from the area. In 1975, the North Vietnamese swept aside the inept South Vietnamese army and unified the country under a communist dictatorship. Ho Chi Minh had triumphed against the mightiest nation in the world.

Yet defeat in Vietnam undermined neither America's domestic unity nor its position in the world. American patriotism peaked during the presidency of Ronald Reagan. Despite racial tensions and unresolved problems stemming from generational poverty, the United States continued to stand out as a model of democracy, industrial

THE SPACE PROGRAM. The first American astronauts from Project Mercury in 1961 were ready to venture into space. Front left to right: Walter M. Schirra, Donald K. Slayton, John H. Glenn (later elected a U.S. senator), and Malcolm S. Carpenter. Back left to right: Alan B. Shepard, Virgil T. Grissom, and Leroy G. Cooper. (*Corbis-Bettmann.*)

mined to gain the advantage in order to discourage an enemy attack, each side developed ever more sophisticated weapons and long-range delivery systems that, if used, could have destroyed all civilized life. In addition, other countries were acquiring nuclear arms: England, France, China, Israel, India, and Pakistan. The increasing fear of nuclear war, however, prompted efforts to scale down the arms race.

In 1968, one hundred members of the United Nations signed the Nuclear Non-Proliferation Treaty, promising to abstain from developing nuclear arms; other U.N. members soon joined them. In 1969, the superpowers began the Strategic Arms Limitations Talks (SALT), agreeing in

Legend:
- Territory lost by Germany
- Communist countries
- "Iron Curtain" after 1950
- NATO members
- Nonallied Western countries
- ■ Original Common Market members
- □ Subsequent Common Market members

NORWAY
Oslo
SWEDEN
Stockholm
Baltic Sea
SCOTLAND
N. IRELAND
Belfast
North Sea
DENMARK
Copenhagen
Incorporated into U.S.S.R., 1945
Gdansk (Danzig)
IRELAND
Dublin
GREAT BRITAIN
ENGLAND
WALES
Szczecin (Stettin)
Hamburg
Berlin
Incorporated into Poland, 1945
Warsaw
NETHERLANDS
Amsterdam
The Hague
Allied occupation 1945–1955
E. GERMANY
Established 1949
POLAND
London
Antwerp
Brussels
BELGIUM
Bonn
Frankfurt
Dresden
Prague
0   200   400 Km.
0   200   400 Mi.
Paris
LUX.
W. GERMANY
Established 1949
Nuremberg
CZECHOSLOVAKIA
Strasbourg
Vienna
Munich
AUSTRIA
Allied occupation, 1945–1955
Budapest
FRANCE
SWITZERLAND
Salzburg
HUNGARY
ATLANTIC OCEAN
Geneva
Lyons
Trieste
Zagreb
Bordeaux
Milan
Belgrade
BASQUE
Toulouse
YUGOSLAVIA
Marseilles
ITALY
Elba
VATICAN CITY
Rome
Tirane
Madrid
Corsica
Naples
ALBANIA
Lisbon
PORTUGAL
Barcelona
SPAIN
Defense Treaty with U.S.A., 1953
Sardinia
Gibraltar (Gr. Br.)
Mediterranean Sea
Sicily
GREECE
Adriatic Sea

MAP 33.1 WESTERN EUROPE AFTER 1945 To counter the communist threat from the Soviet Union, Western European countries, formerly enemies, cooperated for their mutual protection. The majority of countries joined NATO for security against communist attack, and six countries within Europe formed the Common Market (the forerunner of the European Union) to facilitate trade and economic integration.

AMERICAN SOLDIERS ON PATROL IN VIETNAM. Americans defended South Vietnam against a threatened takeover by Communist North Vietnam. Between 1964 and 1973, U. S. involvement in the unsuccessful Vietnam War cost over three million Vietnamese lives, killed 58,000 Americans, ruined South Vietnam, and polarized U.S. public opinion over the morality of the war. (*Magnum Photos.*)

productivity, and the good life, much admired around the globe.

BUILDING A NEW EUROPE

U.S. military and economic preeminence after the war prepared the way for the spread of American culture and lifestyle abroad. The languages of Western Europe became permeated with American words and phrases. Young people, especially, favored American popular music, American fashions, and the casual American way of life. Most importantly, however, the United States set a model for economic and political cooperation. As Winston Churchill declared in 1946, "We must build a kind of United States of Europe."[5] After two ruinous world wars, people at last began to feel that the price of violent conflict had become excessive; war no longer served any national in-

terest. Furthermore, the extension of Soviet power made some form of Western European unity desirable, although procommunist sympathy lingered among workers and intellectuals.

Since the countries of Western Europe were not prepared to submerge their separate national traditions under a common government, they started with economic cooperation. Even that began rather modestly, with the creation of the European Coal and Steel Community (ECSC) in 1951. It drew together the chief Continental consumers and producers of coal and steel, the two materials essential for rebuilding Western Europe. The ECSC comprised France, West Germany, the three Benelux countries, and Italy.

Emboldened by the ECSC's success, the six countries in 1957 established the European Economic Community (EEC). Also known as the *Common Market*, it created a free market among the member states and sought to improve living

MAP 33.2 SOUTHEAST ASIA AND THE
VIETNAM WAR In order to prevent the spread of
communism to South Vietnam, the United States
supported the South Vietnamese government in its
war against the communist north. The Ho Chi
Minh Trail was the supply route used by North
Vietnamese Communist guerrilla fighters infiltrating
South Vietnam. When the supply route was bombed,
the war spilled over into Cambodia and Laos.

conditions within them. In 1973, Great Britain,
Ireland, and Denmark joined the original members in what now became the European Community (EC); in 1981, Greece, and in 1986, Spain
and Portugal became members. The EC constituted the largest single trading bloc, conducting
more than one-fifth of the world's commerce.
In this framework of growing cooperation, the
major countries of Western Europe experienced a
political and economic revival, which contributed
to Western superiority in the cold war.

Impoverished by the war and vulnerable in its
dependence on imported food and raw material,
Great Britain lost its leading role in world politics
after 1945; it peacefully dismantled its colonial
possessions. The postwar Labour government, allied with powerful trade unions, provided Britons
with a measure of economic security through social programs and extensive government control
over important branches of the economy. Such
controls, however, placed Britain at a disadvantage vis-à-vis its European competitors, prolong-
ing the wartime austerity.

Under Winston Churchill, the Conservative
prime minister elected in 1951, the British people
started their postwar years of moderate prosperity; in 1959 Churchill's successor, Harold
Macmillan, told his countrymen: "You never had
it so good." Yet the voters were not so sure. For
the next fifteen years they shifted twice from the
Conservatives to the Labour party before electing
Margaret Thatcher in 1978, the first woman
prime minister. She dominated English politics
for the next decade.

The "Iron Lady" fought inflation and rigorously encouraged individual initiative and private
enterprise. During the Thatcher years, the British
economy improved, and London regained its former luster as a financial center. But Britain was
not without severe civic tensions—terrorism by
the Irish Republican Army seeking to drive
Britain from Northern Ireland, and resentment at
the influx of Indians, Pakistanis, West Indians,
and other people from former colonies. In addition, despite their EC membership, the English
clung to their traditional insular detachment from
their neighbors on the Continent.

Across the English Channel, France, liberated
from German occupation, was reorganized democratically under the Fourth Republic and soon
achieved respectable economic growth, despite
frequent changes of government (twenty-six in
twelve years). The short-lived governments assisted in the organization of Western European
defense that laid the groundwork for the European Economic Community, and they promoted
political reconciliation with Germany.

A major problem that France faced in these
years was decolonization. In Indochina, the colonial liberation movement inflicted a resounding
defeat on the French army in 1954. In Algeria,
French settlers and soldiers were determined to
thwart independence. The long and bloody Algerian conflict had serious repercussions.

In 1958, the agitation to keep Algeria under
French control, supported by certain army circles,

reached a dangerous point. To prevent a right-wing coup aided by the army, General Charles de Gaulle stepped forward. He had been the leader of the Free French forces in World War II and president for a brief period after the war. He now restored order and established the Fifth Republic, with a strong executive authority. Aspiring to give France its rightful place in the world, he extended the economic modernization of the early 1950s achieved under the Fourth Republic. He also encouraged the development of science and technology and cemented ties with the new African states that were formerly under French rule. To strengthen patriotic devotion to the nation, he insisted that France have its own nuclear force, and he pulled his country out of NATO. To rescue France from a protracted and divisive conflict, he consented to Algerian independence in 1962 over the protest of the army.

In 1968, domestic opposition erupted dramatically when students and workers, supported by the Communist party, staged demonstrations in Paris, demanding educational reform and social justice. Attempts by the police to break up the demonstrations provoked violent street fights. Alarmed, de Gaulle quickly called a general election, in which a frightened electorate gave him a landslide victory. Unable to revise the constitution in his favor, however, he resigned in 1969.

France produced no leader equal in stature to de Gaulle; his successors could not rally the French people as he had done. The Fifth Republic continued with a government based on a centrist coalition subject to endless friction and attacked by extremists—Communists on the left promoted cooperation with Moscow, while nationalists on the right stirred up hatred toward North African immigrants. In 1981, however, a sudden shift occurred on the left of the political spectrum. The Communists joined forces with the Socialist party and helped to elect its leader, François Mitterrand as president. Now French politics turned socialist; industries and banks were nationalized and government jobs increased. But the socialist remedies applied by Mitterrand failed, forcing the government into a period of austerity by the mid-1980s.

Despite the economic and political uncertainties of the times, Mitterrand maintained the Gaullist tradition. His country was the third largest nuclear power and the fourth largest econ-omy in the world. All along, France was a leading architect of European unity without surrendering its own character.

Italy, half the size of France yet larger in population by a few million, became a democratic republic in 1946. Its government, however, was weak and unstable. The average life span of an Italian cabinet was less than a year. The country offered a sharp contrast between north and south. The north was efficient and prosperous; the south was backward and infiltrated by the Mafia. Centered in Sicily, the Mafia was a source of political corruption and even occasional terror against the government.

The Italian economy proved to be a surprising success despite the fact that the government was perennially in debt and unemployment ran high, especially in the south. Even more than France, Italy was flooded by legal and illegal immigrants from Asia and Africa, straining the country's resources.

In 1945, its cities in ruins, Germany had been defeated, occupied, and branded as a moral outcast. Divided among the four occupying powers—the United States, Britain, France, and the Soviet Union—the German nation was politically extinct. Extensive eastern lands were lost to Poland and the Soviet Union; some territory was returned to France. By 1949, two new and chastened German states had emerged. West Germany (the Federal Republic of Germany), formed from the three western zones of occupation, faced hostile, Soviet-dominated East Germany (the German Democratic Republic). The former capital city of Berlin, inside East Germany, was similarly divided into western and eastern zones of occupation. The partition of Germany signified the destruction of Germany's traditional identity and ambition. The national trauma reached a climax in August 1961, when the East German government suddenly threw up a wall between East and West Berlin and tightly sealed off East from West Germany. West Germany thus became the crucial frontier of the cold war, radiating Western superiority into the Soviet bloc.

The cold war proved a boon to the West Germans; it contributed to their integration into the emerging new Europe and to the reduction of old hatreds. Located next door to the Red Army, the West Germans, along with the Western armed

Margaret Thatcher

Margaret Thatcher (b. 1925), a lower-middle-class grocer's daughter, was an anomaly in the upper-class, male-dominated Conservative party, of which she became the leader in 1975. For four years, while the Conservatives were out of office, she honed the convictions that made her famous. Socialism, she argued, was responsible for Britain's decline; only adhering to free-market principles, dismantling the welfare state, and weakening the trade unions, whose frequent strikes caused widespread misery, would restore prosperity. The Conservative victory in the 1979 election made Thatcher the first woman prime minister in British history. She put her principles into practice.

At first, financial and service industries did well, but unemployment doubled as the government stopped subsidizing inefficient indus-

Jacob Sutton/Getty Images.

forces stationed on their soil, were in a strategic position for defending Western Europe. Moreover, German industrial expertise was indispensable for rebuilding the Western European economy. On this basis, West Germany (far larger than its Communist counterpart to the east and the most populous of all Western European countries) began to build a new political identity.

The architect of the new West Germany was Konrad Adenauer, its chancellor from 1949 to 1963. He sought to restore respect for Germany in cooperation with the leading states of Western Europe and the United States. As a patriot, he reestablished a cautious continuity with the German past; he also shouldered responsibility for the crimes of the Nazi regime and assumed the payment of indemnifications and pensions to the Jewish victims and survivors of the Nazi era, as well as the payment of reparations to the state of Israel, which had been established in 1948. Under Adenauer's guidance, the West Germans also threw themselves into rebuilding their economy;

the whole world soon admired the German "economic miracle." As a result, democracy put down roots among the West German people, strengthening their solidarity with their former European enemies. West Germany was admitted to NATO in 1957 and, together with East Germany, to the United Nations in 1972; it joined France in promoting the European Community.

After the Adenauer era, German voters shifted from center-right to center-left. Chancellor Willy Brandt (1969–1974) took the initiative for an "opening toward the East," contributing to a temporary relaxation of tensions between the superpowers. During these years, West Germany's booming economy and a generous admission policy attracted ambitious "guest workers," many from Turkey. Political extremists did not endanger political stability, except for one party, the Greens, which called attention to the destruction of the environment, industrial pollution, and the dangers of nuclear power. Loosely organized, the Greens expressed a romantic alienation from contries and factories closed. During three years of "Thatcherism," support for her Conservative government eroded. Then came the Argentinian attack on the Falkland Islands, which stirred British patriotism. Military victory under Thatcher's leadership led to her reelection in 1983.

The prime minister aroused strong feelings. She was admired by some and detested by others. Her personal strength was widely recognized; she was known as the "Iron Lady." During her second term in office, she fought successfully for tough laws to limit trade union power; she also dismantled state-owned enterprises and sold off publicly owned housing. Under her leadership, the country's defense was modernized and health care and education were privatized. She also provided vigorous leadership in foreign affairs and forged a partic-

ularly close relationship with President Reagan. Although her inflexibility and self-righteousness made her enemies, the opposition Labour party, lacking strong leadership, could not prevail against her. Her third election victory, in 1987, made her the longest-serving British prime minister in the twentieth century.

Thatcher's opposition to closer integration of Britain in the European Community and a domestic furor over the attempt to replace real estate taxes with an outrageously high local tax led to outright rebellion within her government. In 1990, her leadership was challenged, and she resigned as prime minister in order to preserve party unity.

As Baroness Thatcher in the House of Lords, she remained active in politics throughout the 1990s. However, failing health has restricted her public role in recent years.

temporary society and politics. In 1982, the voters turned conservative, electing the leader of the Christian Democratic Union, Helmut Kohl, chancellor. Kohl continued Adenauer's policy of integrating West Germany, now the most prominent country in Western Europe, into the cold war alliance against Soviet communism.

THE SOVIET BLOC

For Soviet Russia, World War II was another cruel landmark in the succession of wars, revolutions, and crises afflicting the country since 1914. Nothing basically changed after its end. The vast country's weaknesses persisted, even though it had extended its boundaries far to the west. The liberation from terror and dictatorship, which many soldiers had hoped for as a reward for their heroism, never occurred. The epic struggle against the Nazi invaders had further hardened Stalin. Sixty-six years old in 1945, he displayed in

his last years an unrelenting ruthlessness and a suspiciousness that turned into paranoia.

Stalin found no reason to relax control. Wherever he looked, he saw cause for concern. The government, the party, communist ideology, the economy—all were in disarray. Thus, the Soviet Union slid from war into the uneasy peace of the cold war, staggering through the hardships and hunger of the war's aftermath, mourning its dead soldiers, and desperately short of men. A shrill, dogmatic superpatriotism became mandatory for all Soviet citizens. It extolled Russia's achievements, past and present, over those of the West. Even scientists had to submit, sometimes at a fearful cost to research.

Stalin's Last Years

In his last years, Stalin withdrew into virtual isolation, surrounded by a few fawning and fearful subordinates. When on March 5, 1953, the failing dictator died of a stroke, his assistants sighed with relief. Many other people wept. To them, Stalin was the godlike leader and savior of the nation. The human costs of his regime were immense, but of his achievements in raising Soviet power there can be no doubt. By 1949, Soviet Russia possessed the atomic bomb. By 1953, at the same time as the United States, it had the hydrogen bomb as well.

Stalin also bequeathed to his successors a population tamed and even cowed, yet more literate and adapted to urban-industrial life. But one traditional source of insecurity remained: the humiliating comparison with the superior West. Stalin's successors faced a hard task. How could they preserve the Soviet Union's superpower status while reducing the inhumanity of Stalinism?

In addition they had to cope with the consequences of Soviet domination of Eastern Europe. By the end of 1948, virtually all the countries in eastern and southeastern Europe, as well as eastern Germany, had emerged as "people's democracies." The Soviet Union claimed the right to intervene at will in the internal affairs of its satellites. Thus, the pall of Stalinism hung over war-torn and impoverished Eastern Europe. The puppet regimes leveled the formerly privileged classes, curtailing or abolishing private enterprise. The economy was socialized and rigid, and hasty plans were implemented for industrialization and the collectivization of agriculture. Religion and the churches were repressed, and political liberty and free speech stamped out. Even the "proletarian masses" derived few benefits from the artificial revolution engineered from Moscow because Stalin drained the countries under his control of their resources for the sake of rebuilding the Soviet Union. Contact with Western Europe or the United States was banned. Each satellite country existed in isolation, surrounded by borders fortified with barbed wire and watchtowers set along mined corridors. Fear reached deep into every house and into individual souls as little Stalins copied their mentor's style in East Berlin, Warsaw, Prague, Budapest, and Sofia.

The one exception was Yugoslavia, where Marshal Tito set up his anti-Stalinist communist regime with commercial ties to Western Europe. Communist parties elsewhere were guided by Moscow; Soviet troops remained strategically stationed in the area. The Warsaw Treaty Organization (the Warsaw Pact), which was a military instrument for preserving the ideological and political unity of the bloc and for counterbalancing NATO, coordinated the armies of the satellite countries with the Red Army.

After Stalin: Thaw, Détente, Perestroika, and Glasnost

After Stalin's death, a team headed by Nikita Khrushchev (1954–1964) assumed leadership. Khrushchev was the driving force behind the "thaw" that emptied the forced-labor camps and allowed most of the nationalities forcibly resettled during the war to return to their native regions. Privileged Russians were allowed to catch a glimpse of the West. Khrushchev himself visited the United States, observing that "We must study the capitalist economy attentively . . . study the best that the capitalist countries' science and technology have to offer . . . in the interests of socialism."[6] In a secret speech (soon known around the world) at the Twentieth Party Congress in February 1956, Khrushchev even dared to attack Stalin himself. His audience gasped with horror as he recited the facts: "Of the 139 members and candidates of the party's Central Committee who were elected at the 17th Congress (1934), 98 persons, i.e., 70%, were arrested and shot."[7] Without criticizing the Soviet system, Khrushchev acknowledged and rejected the excesses of Stalinism.

Khrushchev's revelations created a profound stir and prompted defection from Communist ranks everywhere. Among the Soviet satellite countries, the first rumbles of protest were heard in June 1956, in Poland. The crisis came to a head in October: would Poland revolt, inviting invasion by the Red Army, or would Khrushchev ease Soviet control? The Soviet boss yielded in return for a Polish pledge of continued loyalty to the Soviet Union. Thereafter, Poland breathed more freely, clinging to its Catholic faith as a cornerstone of its national identity.

Although the "Polish October" ended peacefully, events moved to a brutal showdown in Hungary. On October 20, 1956, an uprising in Budapest led to an anti-Soviet outburst, forcing Soviet troops to withdraw from the country. Next, a moderate Communist government, eager to capture popular sentiment, called for Western-style political democracy and Hungary's withdrawal from the Warsaw Pact. Thoroughly alarmed, and with the backing of Mao and even Tito, the Soviet leaders struck back. On November 4, 1956, Soviet troops reentered Hungary and brutally crushed all opposition.

Reaffirming Soviet superiority in 1959, Khrushchev boasted to alarmed Americans: "We will bury you." In 1962, he claimed that "Soviet society has become the most highly educated society in the world," predicting that by 1970 the Soviet Union would "surpass the strongest and richest capitalist country, the USA, in per capita production."[8] His extravagant promises, however, antagonized wide sections of state and party administration. In October 1964, while he was on vacation, his comrades in the politburo unceremoniously ousted him for "ill health" or, as they later added, his "hare-brained schemes." He was retired and allowed to live out his years in peace.

Khrushchev was succeeded by a group of leaders acting in common. Among these men, Leonid Brezhnev (1964–1982) gradually rose to the fore. Under his leadership, the government of the U.S.S.R. turned from a personal dictatorship into an oligarchy: the collective rule of a privileged minority. Brezhnev's style stressed reasoned agreement rather than command. Soviet officials breathed more easily, and Soviet society in turn grew less authoritarian.

The post-Stalin permissiveness was never without risks, as was shown in Czechoslovakia in 1968. A new group of Communists, led by Alexander Dubček, sought to liberalize their regime. Their goal was a "humanist democratic socialism," or "socialism with a human face"—a Communist party supported by public goodwill rather than by the secret police.

On August 21, East German, Polish, Hungarian, and Soviet troops, under the provisions of the Warsaw Pact, carried out a swift and well-prepared occupation of Czechoslovakia but failed to break the rebellious will of its Communists. While Soviet tanks rumbled through Prague, an extraordinary Czechoslovak party congress secretly met in choked fury. Never had the Soviet leaders encountered such resistance by party members. Nonetheless, the revolt ended in failure. The party was purged, all reforms were can-

celed, and the country was reduced to abject hopelessness. But the Soviet Union paid a high price. A cry of moral outrage resounded around the world; protests were heard even in Moscow.

In the 1970s, international relations entered a limited phase of peaceful cooperation, called *détente*. The Soviet Union had achieved a rough parity in nuclear weapons with the United States; henceforth, it was protected by deterrence just like the United States. For a brief period, the country enjoyed some civic contentment; it inspired Brezhnev's boast that "capitalism is a society without a future."[9] His confidence led in 1979 to the Soviet invasion of Afghanistan, in support of a faltering pro-Soviet regime installed in Kabul, the Afghan capital, following a 1978 coup. Muslim tribal communities, however, opposed Marxist policies, and a countrywide revolt gathered strength. The government's survival became increasingly dependent on Soviet military equipment and advisers.

The massive Soviet invasion failed to establish control outside the major cities. The Soviet army was under constant guerrilla attack by Afghan freedom fighters, the *mujahidin*, drawn from independent tribes normally at war with each other; hatred of the Soviet invaders temporarily united them. The inability of the Soviet forces to build upon popular support, or to train the Afghan army into an effective defense against rebel forces, led to eight years of costly and inconclusive warfare. Afghanistan became a cold war battleground as the mujahidin received arms and assistance from the United States, Saudi Arabia, Pakistan, and other countries, and maintained a strong resistance movement against Soviet forces. Finally a U.N.-brokered agreement resulted in the withdrawal of Soviet forces by 1989.

The domestic backlash in the Soviet Union against the unpopular war, in which fifteen thousand Soviet soldiers died (about one million Afghans perished), was considerable. In addition, the Reagan administration in the United States had used the war as a pretext to begin a massive arms buildup; and especially after the poor showing of Soviet troops in Afghanistan, the Soviets felt obliged to match the huge U.S. defense expenditures. The attempt to do so strained the declining Soviet economy to the breaking point and

A celebration of the Soviet Union's 60th Anniversary. (Bettmann/*CORBIS.*)

was one of the factors leading up to the collapse of the Soviet Union.

The Brezhnev years permitted a relaxation of the authoritarian discipline. The country could be opened, cautiously, to the outside world. Young people, for instance, were allowed access to Western styles of music and dress. More issues of state policy were opened to public debate, and more latitude was granted to artistic expression. Interest in religion revived. Prominent dissidents were still punished, but less brutally than in the past.

The brief era of public satisfaction induced widespread complacency and corruption. Comparisons with the West also caused distaste for the regime. Voices were heard on the street

protesting that Marxism-Leninism "tastes like stale bread." Not surprisingly, economic productivity declined, and opposition stirred among the Soviet satellite states. The Communist claim to superiority faded; the Soviet Union was falling behind in the cold war. One by one, the satellite

MAP 33.3 EASTERN EUROPE AFTER 1945 ▶
During and after World War II, the Soviet Union extended its rule halfway across Europe. Repressive communist governments in Eastern Europe were controlled by Moscow. Yugoslavia, under President Tito, defied Moscow and became a communist state with links to Western Europe and the United States.

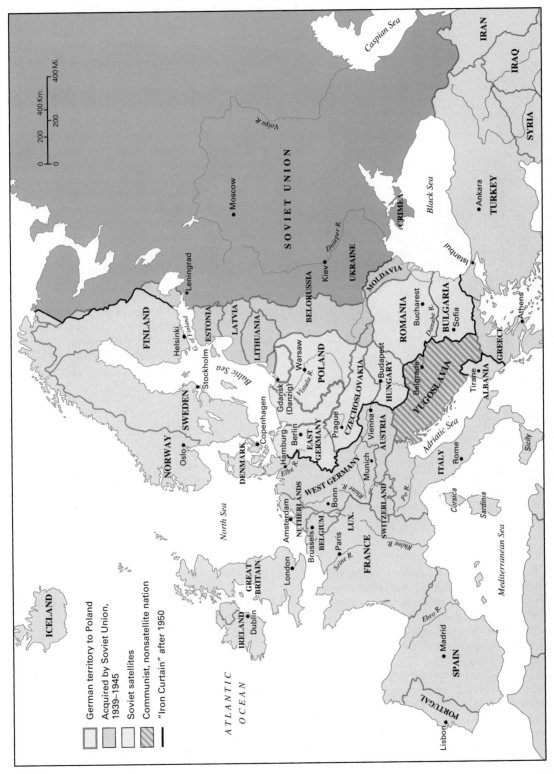

400 Mi.

400 Km.

200

200

ICELAND

IRELAND
Dublin

GREAT BRITAIN
London

ATLANTIC OCEAN

ATLANTIC OCEAN

NORWAY
Oslo

SWEDEN
Stockholm

DENMARK
Copenhagen

FINLAND
Helsinki

G. of Finland

Baltic Sea

North Sea

NETHERLANDS
Amsterdam

BELGIUM
Brussels

LUX.

FRANCE
Paris
Seine R.

Rhône R.

SPAIN
Madrid

PORTUGAL
Lisbon

Ebro R.

SWITZERLAND

WEST GERMANY
Bonn
Munich
Rhine R.
Elbe R.
Hamburg
Berlin

EAST GERMANY
Prague

Gdansk (Danzig)

POLAND
Warsaw
Vistula R.

CZECHOSLOVAKIA

AUSTRIA
Vienna

HUNGARY
Budapest

ITALY
Rome

Corsica

Sardinia

Sicily

Mediterranean Sea

Po R.

Adriatic Sea

YUGOSLAVIA
Belgrade

ALBANIA
Tirane

GREECE
Athens

ROMANIA
Bucharest
Danube R.

BULGARIA
Sofia

MOLDAVIA

LITHUANIA

LATVIA

ESTONIA

BELORUSSIA

UKRAINE
Kiev

Dnieper R.

SOVIET UNION
Moscow
Leningrad

Volga R.

Caspian Sea

CRIMEA

Black Sea

(Istanbul)

TURKEY
Ankara

IRAN

IRAQ

SYRIA

German territory to Poland

Acquired by Soviet Union, 1939–1945

Soviet satellites

Communist, nonsatellite nation

"Iron Curtain" after 1950

843

Jomo Kenyatta (c. 1894–1978) Wearing a leopard skin over his Western-style suit, Kenyatta brandishes a fly whisk, a symbol of authority. Imprisoned by the British for his opposition to colonial rule, he became the leader of independent Kenya in 1963. Under his slogan, *Harambee* (pulling together), he built a strong, stable government and a capitalist-oriented economy. (*Anthony Howard/Camera Press/ Retna.*)

governments in Eastern Europe resumed ties with capitalist states. Brezhnev's successors were old men who survived in office for only a short time. In 1985, at last a younger, energetic Communist, Mikhail Sergeyevich Gorbachev, assumed control, admitting privately that "everything is rotten through and through."

It was the fate of Mikhail Gorbachev to preside over his country's collapse. Self-confident and articulate, he strove to integrate his country into the main currents of modern life through a dramatic retreat from communist theory and practice.

Gorbachev's domestic reforms proceeded under the barrage of two slogans: *perestroika* (restructur-

ing) and *glasnost* (openness). The reforms aimed at "a genuine revolutionary transformation" of Soviet life and institutions.[10] The goals that Lenin and Stalin had tried to reach through totalitarian controls were now to be achieved by voluntary civic cooperation. Perestroika promised to reorganize the state and society and permit Soviet citizens to participate in national affairs. Glasnost, in turn, was to take the Stalinist lid off public opinion and permit at long last an uninhibited discussion of the country's problems. It would rid public thinking of the official propaganda lies and promote open debate. Both perestroika and glasnost sought to transform the Soviet system into a true democracy under the Communist party. Meanwhile, contacts with the outside world increased the yearning for a higher standard of living, and Western ideals, culture, and respect for human rights penetrated Soviet minds as never before. Summed up by Gorbachev as "the most thorough-going upheaval in our country's history,"[11] these changes entailed unforseen perils: the breakup of the Soviet bloc in Eastern Europe and the collapse of the Soviet Union.

DECOLONIZATION

World War II, in which many colonial soldiers loyally fought for their masters, stirred up demands among non-Western peoples for an end to Western colonial rule and for political independence. After all, freedom and self-determination were prominent Allied war slogans. Exhausted by the war, European colonial powers had little strength left for colonial rule. In this setting, a mighty groundswell of decolonization, supported by the ideals of the United Nations, eventually propelled African and Asian lands into independent statehood.

Map 33.4 Former European Colonies ▶
Agitation for independence started after World War I. It gained momentum after World War II and reached a crescendo in the 1960s, resulting in the birth of dozens of new countries. The colonial powers failed to groom their successors for governmental responsibilities, and in some countries independence led to protracted conflicts, extending to the present day.

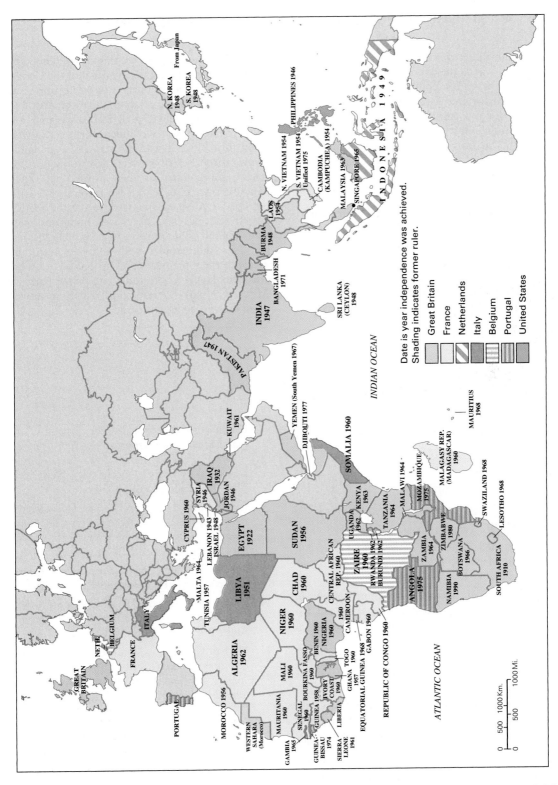

N. KOREA 1948 From Japan
S. KOREA 1948

PHILIPPINES 1946

N. VIETNAM 1954
S. VIETNAM 1954 Unified 1975
CAMBODIA (KAMPUCHEA) 1954
MALAYSIA 1963
SINGAPORE 1965

I N D O N E S I A 1 9 4 9

BURMA 1948
LAOS 1954

BANGLADESH 1971

INDIA 1947

PAKISTAN 1947

SRI LANKA (CEYLON) 1948

YEMEN (South Yemen) 1967

DJIBOUTI 1977

KUWAIT 1961

IRAQ 1932

SYRIA 1946
JORDAN 1946

CYPRUS 1960
LEBANON 1943
ISRAEL 1948

MALTA 1964
TUNISIA 1957

EGYPT 1922

SUDAN 1956

SOMALIA 1960

MALAWI 1964

MOZAMBIQUE 1975

MALAGASY REP. (MADAGASCAR) 1960

MAURITIUS 1968

UGANDA 1962
KENYA 1963
TANZANIA 1964

ZAIRE 1960
RWANDA 1962
BURUNDI 1962

ZIMBABWE 1980
ZAMBIA 1964

SWAZILAND 1968

LESOTHO 1968

ANGOLA 1975

NAMIBIA 1990
BOTSWANA 1966

SOUTH AFRICA 1910

INDIAN OCEAN

Date is year independence was achieved.
Shading indicates former ruler.

Great Britain
France
Netherlands
Italy
Belgium
Portugal
United States

ITALY

LIBYA 1951

CHAD 1960

CENTRAL AFRICAN REP. 1960

CAMEROON 1960

GABON 1960

REPUBLIC OF CONGO 1960

NIGER 1960

EQUATORIAL GUINEA 1968

GREAT BRITAIN
NETH.
BELGIUM
FRANCE

PORTUGAL

MOROCCO 1956

ALGERIA 1962

MALI 1960

MAURITANIA 1960

WESTERN SAHARA (Morocco)

GAMBIA 1965
SENEGAL 1960
GUINEA-BISSAU 1974
GUINEA 1958
SIERRA LEONE 1961
LIBERIA

BOURKINA FASSO 1960
BENIN 1960
NIGERIA 1960
IVORY COAST 1960
GHANA 1957
TOGO 1960

ATLANTIC OCEAN

0   500   1000 Km.
0   500   1000 Mi.

845

Decolonization quickly became a major issue in the cold war as the two superpowers competed with each other for control over the emerging states of Africa and Asia. Both sides, in their ignorance of local cultures, found themselves entangled in the intricacies of local power struggles, especially in tropical Africa, which was frequently involved in protracted civil wars bordering on anarchy.

Online Study Center **Improve Your Grade**
Interactive Map: Decolonization and Independence, 1947–1997

Decolonization often sparked brutal struggles of building modern states among peoples who were utterly unprepared for this effort. For example, in 1960 the Belgians pulled out of the Congo, leaving behind some thirty Congolese university graduates to fill four thousand administrative posts. Moreover, divided by historic, ethnic, and tribal animosities, newly independent states were often torn by civil war. In many African lands, army officers seized power; these ruthless rulers treated the country as their private fief. Thus, Mobutu Sese Seko, who ruled mineral-rich Zaire for thirty-two years, amassed one of the world's largest fortunes and purchased luxurious mansions abroad while poverty raged among his people. Nor did peoples with different traditions adjust to the institutions and procedures of Western democracy. Even today in many parts of Africa, one-party dictatorships remain in power, often dressed up as democracies.

❖   ❖   ❖

Online Study Center **ACE the Test**

NOTES

1. Quoted in Walter Laqueur, *Europe Since Hitler* (Baltimore: Penguin Books, 1970), p. 118.

2. Winston S. Churchill, "Sinews of Peace; Address, March 5, 1946," *Vital Speeches of the Day*, March 15, 1946, p. 3.

3. "The Truman Doctrine," in *Major Problems in American Foreign Policy: Documents and Essays*, ed. Thomas G. Paterson (Lexington, Mass.: Heath, 1978), 2:290.

4. Ralph E. Lapp, "The Einstein Letter That Started It All," *New York Times Magazine*, August 2, 1964, p. 64.

5. Quoted in Roger Morgan, *West European Politics Since 1945* (London: Batsford, 1972), p. 91.

6. *Current Soviet Policies II. The Documentary Record of the 20th Party Congress and Its Aftermath* (New York: Praeger, 1957), p. 141.

7. Nikita S. Khrushchev in *The Crimes of the Stalin Era: Special Report to the 20th Congress of the Communist Party of the Soviet Union*, annotated by Boris I. Nicolaevsky (New York: The New Leader, 1956), p. 20.

8. *Current Soviet Policies IV. The Documentary Record of the 22nd Congress of the Communist Party of the Soviet Union* (New York: Columbia University Press, 1962), pp. 64, 15.

9. Leonid Brezhnev, *Following Lenin's Course* (Moscow: Progress Publishers, 1976), 5:480.

10. Mikhail Gorbachev, "Political Report to the 27th Party Congress," *Current Digest of the Soviet Press*, March 26, 1986, p. 12.

11. Mikhail Gorbachev, "On the Path to a Market Economy; Speech . . . [to] the USSR Supreme Soviet," *Current Digest of the Soviet Press*, October 24, 1990, p. 3.

SUGGESTED READING

Fursenko, Aleksandr, and Timothy Naftali, "*One Hell of a Gamble*": *Khrushchev, Castro, and*

Kennedy, 1958–1964 (1997). An excellent account of the Cuban Missile Crisis.

Mahoney, Daniel J., *De Gaulle: Statesmanship, Grandeur and Modern Democracy* (1996). A perceptive, short biography.

McNamara, Robert S., *In Retrospect: The Tragedy and Lessons of Vietnam* (1995). A candid apology for Vietnam by the secretary of defense who waged the war.

Riddell, Peter, *The Thatcher Decade: Britain in the 1980s* (1989). A *Financial Times* editor analyzes the Iron Lady's policies and leadership style.

Taubman, William, *Khrushchev* (2003) A remarkable portrait of the bumptious leader, his politics, and his country.

Chapter 34

The Troubled Present

The destruction of the World Trade Center's twin towers by members of Al Qaeda, a terrorist organization headed by Osama bin Laden, mobilized the United States to take the offensive against international terrorism. (AP/World Wide Photos.)

- **The Demise of Communism**
- **The Post–Cold War World**
- **Our Global Age: Tensions and Concerns**

Focus Questions

1. What conditions made possible the "revolution" of 1989 in Eastern Europe?
2. What effect did the end of the cold war have on global politics?
3. What are the main problems confronting the European Union?
4. Why has terrorism been described as the "dark side of globalization"?

Online Study Center

This icon will direct you to interactive map and primary source activities on the website http://college.hmco.com/pic/perrywc8e.

Since 1989, momentous events have utterly changed the world. The superpower polarization of world politics ended, and a new, multicentered, unstable world order has emerged. Western civilization and its ideals have been transformed into a transcultural worldwide modernity. At the same time, however, traditional cultural diversity still simmers. The end of the cold war introduced a new uncertainty into human affairs. On the one hand, global interdependence promotes peaceful cooperation; on the other, it causes a clash of cultural traditions, giving rise to contagious violence and extremism.

THE DEMISE OF COMMUNISM

1989: Year of Liberation

The collapse of the Soviet Union, the communist superpower, was one of the most striking events in recent history. The Soviet leaders after Stalin could not reduce the gap in living standards and the quality of life between the Soviet system and Western capitalism. By comparison, the West was making impressive progress. This fact, increasingly recognized throughout the Soviet bloc, undermined its carefully enforced communist conformity. Disloyalty grew throughout the multinational and multiethnic Soviet empire. By the 1980s, it was common knowledge, admitted in the highest ranks of the Communist party, that the Soviet system had stifled rather than advanced creativity and efficiency.

Perestroika and glasnost, promoted by the last Soviet leader Mikhail Gorbachev, spread among the peoples of Eastern Europe, resentful of Soviet domination and worried by widespread economic hardships. During 1989 and 1990, Eastern Europeans showed their distaste for Communist leadership and demanded freedom and self-determination. Poland took the lead.

Traditionally anti-Russian, the Poles had long resented their country's economic decline. The slightest relaxation of Soviet control encouraged Polish nationalism, which always found expression in the Roman Catholic church. When a Polish cardinal became Pope John Paul II in 1978, patriotism surged. In 1980, workers led by an electrician, Lech Walesa, succeeded, with the blessing of the church, in forming an independent labor union,

849

Chronology 34.1 ❖ From Cold War to Globalism

1989	Year of liberation in Eastern Europe; Berlin Wall demolished
1990	Soviet republics call for independence; Soviet economy in crisis; reunification of Germany; Charter of Paris for a New Europe; official end of cold war
1991	Persian Gulf War; Yeltsin elected Russian president; collapse of Soviet Union; Yugoslav federation breaks up and war begins
1993	Czechoslovakia splits into Czech Republic and Slovakia; elections for new Russian constitution and parliament; European Union implements the Maastricht Treaty
1994	South Africa elects multiracial government; war breaks out between Russia and Chechnya
1995	Dayton Agreement ends civil war in Bosnia
1996	Yeltsin reelected president of Russia
1998	Russian currency collapses
1999	Poland, Hungary, and the Czech Republic join NATO; Yeltsin resigns; Chechen war reopens; ethnic cleansing of Kosovo; Serbia bombed
2000	Putin elected president of Russia
2001	Terrorist attack on World Trade Center; war on terrorism in Afghanistan
2003	American-led war on Iraq begins
2004	European Union expands to twenty-five countries

called Solidarity. Pressured by relentless strikes, the Polish government briefly recognized the union, despite threats of Soviet intervention. In December 1981, however, a military dictatorship, under General Wojciech Jaruzelski, imposed martial law.

Solidarity persisted underground until 1988, when public pressure forced Jaruzelski to end his dictatorship and appoint a civilian government. Solidarity was legalized in January 1989; in April the Communist party gave up its monopoly of political power in Poland. In the first free election, Solidarity triumphed, leading to the formation of a noncommunist government. After ten years of struggle, Poland, the largest country in the Soviet bloc, achieved political independence by essentially peaceful means. In December 1990, Lech Walesa was elected president. Encouraged by events in Poland and a resurgence of patriotic feeling, Hungary abolished its Communist bureaucracy in May 1989 and embraced the ideals of democracy and free enterprise.

A more dramatic upheaval occurred in East Germany. On November 6, 1989, when almost a million antigovernment demonstrators crammed the streets of East Berlin, the Communist government resigned. On November 9, in an explosion of patriotic fervor, the Berlin Wall was breached. Young people danced on top of the wall and tens of thousands of East Germans flocked into West Berlin, welcomed with flowers, champagne, and

MAP 34.1 POST–COLD WAR EUROPE AND THE ▶ FORMER SOVIET UNION Instead of the stark postwar division of Europe into three blocs—Western Europe, Eastern Europe, and the Soviet Union—the continent is now a patchwork of independent countries, some with new names. Russia remains the largest country, but the former Soviet Republics have claimed their territory on Russia's eastern and southern borders. Within Europe, East and West Germany have reunited while Yugoslavia has split up.

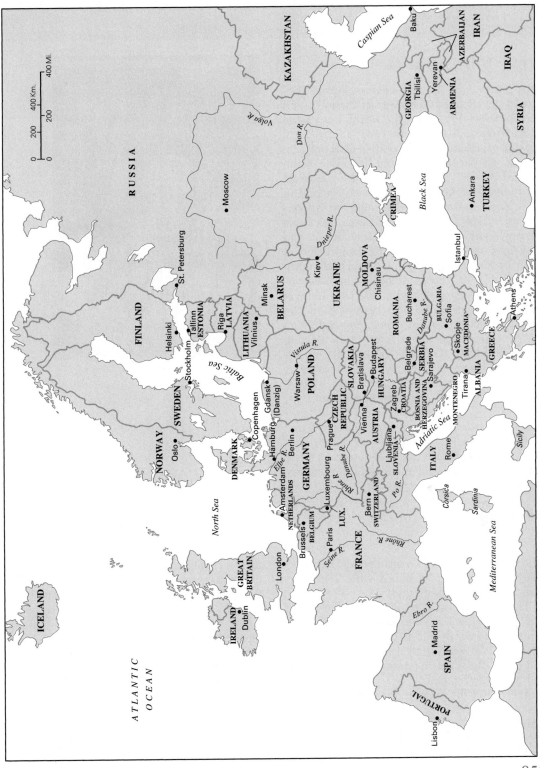

ICELAND

ATLANTIC
OCEAN

IRELAND
Dublin

GREAT
BRITAIN
London

NORWAY
Oslo

SWEDEN
Stockholm

FINLAND
Helsinki

RUSSIA
Moscow
St. Petersburg

KAZAKHSTAN

Caspian Sea
Baku

Volga R.
Don R.

AZERBAIJAN
Yerevan
ARMENIA
GEORGIA
Tbilisi

IRAN
IRAQ
SYRIA
TURKEY
Ankara

Black Sea
Istanbul

CRIMEA

Dnieper R.

UKRAINE
Kiev

MOLDOVA
Chisinau

BELARUS
Minsk

ESTONIA
Tallinn
LATVIA
Riga
LITHUANIA
Vilnius

Baltic Sea

Vistula R.

POLAND
Warsaw

Gdańsk
(Danzig)

DENMARK
Copenhagen

Hamburg
Berlin
GERMANY

Elbe R.

NETHERLANDS
Amsterdam
BELGIUM
Brussels

LUXEMBOURG
LUX.

Rhine R.

FRANCE
Paris
Seine R.

Rhône R.

SWITZERLAND
Bern

CZECH
REPUBLIC
Prague

SLOVAKIA
Bratislava
Vienna
AUSTRIA
HUNGARY
Budapest

Danube R.

SLOVENIA
Ljubljana
CROATIA
Zagreb

Po R.

ITALY
Rome

BOSNIA AND
HERZEGOVINA
Sarajevo

SERBIA
Belgrade

MONTENEGRO
Tirana
ALBANIA

MACEDONIA
Skopje

ROMANIA
Bucharest
Danube R.
BULGARIA
Sofia

GREECE
Athens

Adriatic Sea

Corsica

Sardinia

Sicily

Mediterranean Sea

Ebro R.

SPAIN
Madrid

PORTUGAL
Lisbon

North Sea

400 Mi.
400 Km.
200
200
0
0

851

Pope John Paul II

Pope John Paul II, who died in April 2005, earned the tribute and respect of Catholics and non-Catholics throughout the world. Born Karol Jozef Wojtyla in Poland in 1920, young Karol was an excellent student with a flair for languages. At secondary school he also distinguished himself in athletics and dramatics. At the time of the German invasion of Poland in 1939, Karol was attending Jagiellonian University in Krakow. When the Nazis closed down the university, he worked in a stone quarry and then in a factory. Leaving the factory job in 1942, he studied secretly for the priesthood in the home of Krakow's archbishop and was ordained in 1946, a year and a half after the war had ended. During the next several years, he earned two doctorates in philosophy and theology, one in Rome and the other in Poland, where he taught social ethics. In 1964, he became archbishop of Krakow, was elevated to the College of Cardinals in 1967, and in 1978 became John Paul II, the first non-Italian pope since 1523.

Several distinguishing features characterized Pope John Paul's twenty-six-year pontificate. He journeyed to more than 120 countries to advance spiritual renewal and interfaith relations.

(CORBIS.)

money for buying West German goods. East Germany was ready to be united with West Germany, with Gorbachev's approval.

The exhilaration over breaching the Berlin Wall reverberated in the countries still under Communist rule. By mid-December 1989, a multiparty system was installed in Bulgaria, which had joined the quest for democratic government and private enterprise.

The end of the year produced the final victories in the revolution of 1989. Romania's Nicolae Ceausescu, persisting in his own ruthless dictatorship, had paid no attention to the drift of the times. But on December 21, students disrupted a mass demonstration organized on his behalf in the capital city of Bucharest. The crowd followed the students' lead, and even the army turned against Ceausescu. On December 25, he and his wife were tried and executed. The most repulsive representative of Communist rule, defying to the last the trend toward democratic freedom, had ignominiously fallen.

On the same day, Czechoslovakia joined the triumphant finale of the crusade against communism with the election of Václav Havel as president. The most daring and articulate dissident in his country, Havel had led a swift "velvet revolution" against the Czech Communist government. The election of

As part of his holy mission, he condemned war and violence repeatedly. In Ireland he told the violent Catholic and Protestant factions: "On my knees I beg you to turn away from the path of violence and return to the ways of peace." He protested violations of human rights around the world; denounced oppressive communism; attacked the greed, materialism, and economic injustice fomented by capitalism; and publicly repented for the acts of injustice and intolerance committed by the church in the past two thousand years. He reached out to non-Catholic Christians, Muslims—no other pope had visited a mosque—Buddhists, and Jews. In dramatic fashion, John Paul continued the work of the post-Holocaust church in improving Jewish-Catholic relations. He reaffirmed the Jewish roots of Christianity; condemned anti-Semitism as a sin "against God and man" and lamented past Christian behavior toward Jews; prayed in the synagogue in Rome (the first pope ever to do so); and established full diplomatic relations with Israel and made an official visit to that country, including moving stops at the Western Wall, Judaism's holiest site, and Yad Vashem, Israel's Holocaust memorial, where he paid his respects to the Jewish victims of Nazi persecution. As a young man he had witnessed Nazi brutality against Jews.

Historians credit John Paul for aiding the collapse of communism in Eastern Europe. Soon after his election to the papacy, he visited his native Poland, where huge crowds of admirers turned out to see him. His words—"The exclusion of Christ from the history of man is an act against man"—buoyed the spirits of the intensely Catholic population, giving them hope that the spiritual will prevail over atheistic communism, which, he said, treats people "merely as means of production." His visit helped give rise to Solidarity, a labor movement that challenged Poland's communist rulers.

On certain questions, John Paul was extremely conservative—strongly opposing abortion, contraception, premarital sex, homosexuality, same-sex unions, and ordination of women, and insisting on the inviolability of celibacy for priests. Liberal Catholics faulted the pope's prohibition against condoms, which they felt were necessary for family planning and for protection against AIDS. They also maintained that it was time for the church to admit women to the priesthood and for the church to make celibacy optional. Finally, his papacy came under criticism for its slowness in confronting the problem of sex abuse by priests.

this previously imprisoned dissident playwright, a profound thinker deeply committed to the Western humanist tradition, was a joyous landmark in a momentous year of liberation.

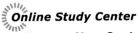

Online Study Center

Improve Your Grade
Primary Source: A Presidential Address to the People of Czechoslovakia on New Year's Day (Havel)

The message spread quickly into Yugoslavia, a fragile federation of six ethnically conscious member republics, among whom Serbia was dominant. Less rigidly controlled than other Eastern European countries, Yugoslavia enjoyed close relations with Western Europe. Yet in 1989, the government could not prevent public protest, encouraged by the news of the Communist downfall in other lands. On December 26, its Communist party caved in and suggested the formation of a multiparty system, which was duly adopted in January 1990. The new freedom soon undermined the unity of the Yugoslav federation—a bitter war would follow.

MIKHAIL GORBACHEV. Soviet leader Gorbachev and his wife visit Vilnius, the capital of Lithuania, following the declaration of independence by the Lithuanian Communist party. Gorbachev warned demonstrators: "If we should separate, it is the end of perestroika." *(Alain Nogues/Sygma.)*

By the end of 1989, except for Albania, where the Communist party held on until free elections in February 1991, all of Eastern Europe had liberated itself from Soviet domination—a breathtaking change, accomplished unexpectedly within a single year and dealing a deadly blow to the Soviet Union itself.

Online Study Center Improve Your Grade
Interactive Map: Democratic Movements in Europe, ca. 1989

The Collapse of the Soviet Union

The repudiation of communism in Eastern Europe intensified the disintegration of Soviet rule at the center. Gorbachev's glasnost released the bitterness accumulated under Stalinist repression, revealed the widespread environmental damage caused by promoting industrial progress at any price, and activated the immense diversity of attitudes and values among the various nationalities that comprised the Soviet Union. As a result, the cohesion of the Soviet Union weakened. Clamoring for independence, the Lithuanians, Latvians, and Estonians set off similar demands among Ukrainians, Byelorussians, Georgians, Armenians, and the peoples of central Asia. Ethnic violence escalated disastrously. The biggest blow to Soviet unity came in 1990, when the Russian republic, the largest member of the Soviet Union, declared its limited independence under the leadership of Boris Yeltsin.

As political fragmentation increased, the Soviet economy, battered by decades of inefficient production and distribution of food and consumer goods, collapsed. The breakdown of effective government led to crime, corruption, and violence—evils always simmering under the surface of Soviet life. In late 1990, a Moscow newspaper described the public mood in grim terms:

> *Our society is in many ways inexorably drifting toward the danger point of ungovernability and decline. Economic collapse, paralysis of political authority, outbreaks of ethnic unrest, the illusory nature of social safeguards, rampant crime, and the visible impoverishment of a starving, tired people, which has spawned a general spiritual emptiness, apathy, bitterness and confusion—these are but a few signs . . . of mounting and potentially explosive public discontent. . . . As the store shelves grow emptier, narrow-minded, rudimentary sentiments have become increasingly prevalent: why the hell do we need this restructuring, all this openness, with pluralism to boot? We'd rather have sausage and order.[1]*

Obviously, the spiritual rebirth and the revolution in people's minds that Gorbachev had hoped for had not occurred. In October 1990, he himself conceded in the face of failure that "unfortunately, our society is not ready for the procedures of a law-based state. We don't have that level of political culture, those traditions. All that will come in the future."[2]

The future, however, deepened the country's disunity. On August 19, 1991, hard-line Communists, hostile to Gorbachev's reforms, staged a coup, imprisoning him in his Crimean vacation home and deposing him as president of the Soviet Union, in preparation for a new Communist dictatorship. Yet the conspirators, all of them high officials appointed by Gorbachev, grossly misjudged popular attitudes. Revulsion against the Communist party was even stronger than the yearning for sausage and order. The KGB's vanguard forces defected to Yeltsin, who led a fervent street protest at risk to his life. The emotional outburst in favor of freedom and democracy quickly spread from Moscow to Leningrad (recently renamed Saint Petersburg, as under the tsars) and other cities. The coup collapsed in less than three days. When Gorbachev returned to Moscow, he faced, as he said, "a different country." The Communist party, now repudiated by Gorbachev himself, was swept aside by public disdain; with virtually no one, including its leaders, believing any more in the Soviet system, it simply dissolved. And so the Soviet Union broke apart.

Within two weeks, twelve of the fifteen union republics—the Baltic republics of Latvia, Lithuania, and Estonia foremost among them—declared their independence. The remaining republics soon followed suit. On December 24, 1991, the Soviet Union was officially dissolved, and Gorbachev was dismissed from office. The only trace left of the former unity was the ill-defined Commonwealth of Independent States (CIS). Holding out the future possibility of becoming a free-trade area for the diverse people of the former Soviet Union, it was eventually joined by all the former Soviet republics, apart from the Baltic States, which preferred to build ties with Western Europe.

The huge empire that for centuries had cast its shadow over Europe and the world perished. Even more significantly, the Soviet system, which had challenged Western ascendancy since the end of World War I, collapsed, together with its ideological presumption of worldwide communist happiness. Freedom, democracy, and private enterprise—the ideals of the American superpower—won the cold war.

The Death of an Ideal

The sudden and unexpected collapse of communism in Eastern Europe in 1989 seemed to discredit Marxism irrevocably. Reformers in Eastern European lands liberated from Communist oppression expressed revulsion for the socialist past and a desire to regenerate their countries with an infusion of Western liberal ideals and institutions and free-market capitalism. Havel, the newly elected president of a free Czechoslovakia, expressed this disillusionment with the past and hope for a new democratic future:

> The worst of it is that we live in a spoiled moral environment. We have become morally ill because we are used to saying one thing and thinking another. We have learned not to believe in anything, not to care about each other, to worry only about ourselves. . . . The previous regime, armed with a proud and intolerant ideology, reduced people into the means of production. . . . Many of our citizens died in prison in the 1950s. Many were executed. Thousands of human lives were destroyed.
>
> Perhaps you are asking what kind of republic I am dreaming about. I will answer you: a republic that is independent, free democratic, a republic with economic prosperity and also social justice.[3]

Marxism is a failed ideology propped up only by force in the few surviving Communist regimes. "Scientific socialism," which claimed to have deciphered the essential meaning and direction of history, is neither scientific nor relevant to current needs. It is merely another idea that was given too much credence and is now ready to be swept into the dustbin of history. Communist ruling elites had believed that Marxism provided a scientific, and therefore accurate, understanding of history and society and that their efforts at social engineering—creating a new and better social order through central planning—accorded with

THE WALL CAME TUMBLING DOWN. The Berlin Wall, symbol of the division of Germany, was breached in November 1989. Young people excitedly clambered onto the partially demolished wall while East and West Berliners thronged the streets. *(Regis Bossu/Sygma.)*

the science of history. They considered force and terror legitimate means of implementing their utopian vision.

Two lessons might be drawn from the failed communist experiment. One is that all theories of history and all visions of the good society are not scientific certainties. Rather, they are human constructs subject to human error. Second, social experiments that are not guided by democratic procedures and humane values, that treat flesh-and-blood human beings as objects to be molded

in accordance with some grand design, produce only suffering and misery.

The political theorist Francis Fukuyama suggests that the decline of communism and the end of the cold war reveal a larger process at work, "the ultimate triumph of Western liberal democracy":

The twentieth century saw the developed world descend into a paroxysm of ideological violence, as liberalism contended first with the remnants of absolutism, then bolshevism and

Fascism, and finally an updated Marxism that threatened to lead to the ultimate apocalypse of nuclear war. But the century that began full of self-confidence in the ultimate triumph of Western liberal democracy seems at its close to be returning full circle to where it started . . . to an unabashed victory of economic and political liberalism. The triumph of the West, of the Western idea, is evident first of all in the total exhaustion of viable systematic alternatives to Western liberalism. . . . What we may be witnessing . . . is the end point of mankind's ideological evolution and the universalization of Western liberal democracy as the final form of government.[4]

THE POST–COLD WAR WORLD

Post-Communist Russia and the Former Soviet Republics

Throughout the 1990s and into the twenty-first century, the Russian Federal Republic has been struggling to bring its political and economic systems into conformity with the Western model while coping with its loss of territory and superpower status. The collapse of the Soviet Union revealed Russia to be a weak, poorly developed society beset by profound problems.

Yeltsin's "Shock Therapy."   Marred by mismanagement, waste, and lack of incentives, the Soviet economic system had failed miserably in comparison with Western capitalism. In order to reform the economy and improve the standard of living of the Russian people, which lagged far behind living standards in Western lands, President Yeltsin, emerging in 1990 as the leader of the new Russia, made a sudden switch in 1992 from a state-run economy to private ownership and a capitalist market system. This precipitous transfer of state firms to private ownership—"shock therapy"—in many ways proved a disaster. The chief beneficiaries of privatization were often the same inefficient managers who had controlled the economy during the Soviet era and amassed wealth by unscrupulous means. Industrial decline, the withdrawal of government subsidies, and ruinous inflation reduced millions of people

dependent on pensions to hand-to-mouth subsistence. Many working Russians also sank into poverty as real wages plummeted some 40 percent from 1992 to 1998. Workers often had to wait two to six months for their paychecks, and unemployment soared. In sum, the achievement of economic security, no less than the attainment of participatory democracy, was likely to be a long and painful process. The Russian economist Georgi Arbatov describes the negative consequences of the attempt to inject capitalism directly into the Russian economy:

The poorly conceived transition program resulted in an unprecedented decline of the national economy. By 1998 Russian GDP was only about one-half its 1990 level, with the crisis spread to virtually all areas of production. Russian industry found itself unable to compete even in its own domestic markets. All of this was accompanied by a sharp reduction in investment and a disintegration of scientific and technological potential. We are now witnessing processes of pauperization and de-intellectualization, accompanied by criminalization, as Russia increasingly takes on the appearance of a Third World republic.[5]

With popular unrest mounting and facing opposition from Communist hardliners, Yeltsin was forced to slow his liberalization of the economy; the social costs—public confusion over bewildering changes, a sharp decline in the standard of living, and the loss of productivity leading to shortages—were too high. "No more experiments," advised slogans spray-painted on walls.

Adding to the intractable problems of the new Russia were soaring crime and corruption. Yeltsin consolidated his power by making alliances with a small group of businessmen, the "oligarchs," who had grown wealthy by acquiring former state-owned enterprises at extremely low prices. They plundered the firms for assets, concentrating Russia's wealth in their own hands, and they gained control of banks "that operate in a pathological fashion." As law enforcement deteriorated, organized crime became a major force in Russian life.

The oligarchs financed Yeltsin's bid for reelection as president, which he won with an astonishing 65 percent of the vote in 1996 despite suffering a heart attack during the election campaign. At age sixty-six and in frail health, Yeltsin could no longer provide effective leadership for his vast fragmented country, and in 1997, he frankly acknowledged the difficulties that he and his country faced: "After creating a new political system, we failed to outfit it with new tools of government, and we ourselves did not learn to govern in a new way."[6]

Nevertheless, by winning reelection with the support of the oligarchs, Yeltsin vanquished the Communists in the Duma, the new legislature. In addition, by permitting the oligarchs to buy up the major state enterprises, he smashed Soviet central planning. It would be impossible in these circumstances to reinstate communism in Russia. But the situation was dangerous because many key enterprises, including banks and the media, were now controlled by unscrupulous oligarchs. In return for their support of Yeltsin, they became an inner political circle in the Kremlin, controlling the country's policies. No wonder Russians began to feel that the government itself had been "privatized."

In August 1998 everything changed. The dysfunctional banking system precipitated a second currency collapse, wiping out Russians' savings and livelihoods. Among the casualties were many of the oligarchs. Some were ruined by the collapse of their banks, others went abroad, and the remainder backed out of public life. Suddenly their political influence, which had been paramount since 1995, diminished dramatically, and a new generation of businessmen began to emerge.

Yeltsin resigned on New Year's Eve 1999. His grasp of events had become increasingly uncertain, and he was obviously incapable of ruling. He thus became the first Russian leader to give up power voluntarily. In his demoralized, bankrupt, and corrupt post-Communist country, Yeltsin contended with problems beyond the capacity of the most astute politician. He made appalling mistakes, but he was determined to go down in history as the man who made the restoration of communism in Russia impossible. It was no mean achievement.

Putin: Clamping Down. Yeltsin's chosen successor, Vladimir Putin, determined to make his mark as a strongman during his short term as Yeltsin's prime minister by reopening the war in Chechnya, a small Islamic enclave in the Caucasus, at war for centuries with the conquering Russians. After two

years of ruthless fighting, at great political damage to Yeltsin, the defeated Russian armies withdrew in 1996, leaving the burden of the final settlement of Chechnya's independence to the future. The war resumed in 1999 when Chechen rebels invaded neighboring Dagestan in an effort to establish a united independent Islamic state in the Caucasus. At the same time, a terrorist attack on apartment blocks in Russian cities killed more than three hundred people and maimed many more. Putin put the blame for the attack on Chechens and stormed into the Caucasus to force the invaders out of Dagestan. The Chechen capital, Grozny, was razed; the main victims were elderly Russian residents, the rebels having already escaped to the mountains. Russian troops took control of the war-devastated Caucasus region, but the Chechen leaders remained at large and continued guerrilla attacks on Russian soldiers.

Vladimir Putin became president of Russia at a time when modest economic stability was beginning to emerge. His objective was to establish a strong centralized state under the rule of law. To this end, he offered a deal to the remaining oligarchs: he would not interfere with their businesses if they would keep out of politics. This agreement was violated by Mikhail Khodorkovsky, the immensely rich owner of the oil group Yukos, who was charged with fraud, embezzlement, and tax evasion and sentenced to nine years in jail. The real reason for his punishment was possibly his financial support of Russian opposition parties and his lobbying and bribery on energy issues in the Duma. His arrest resulted in the dismemberment and auction of the oil group for unpaid taxes. Yukos ended up being absorbed into the state-controlled oil and gas company. This spectacular government takeover sent a chill through the energy sector of the economy and alarmed foreign investors, who worried that property rights might exist only at the whim of the Russian government. But Putin's popularity increased among people resentful of the oligarchs' wealth.

More alarmingly, President Putin steadily increased government control of the media (previously owned by two of the oligarchs) and completely eroded freedom of the press. These actions drew immediate criticism from western countries, which had hoped that Russia would follow a democratic path in allowing a free media and encouraging discussion and criticism of political issues.

The Chechen conflict continued in the background, springing dramatically onto the front pages in October 2002 when pro-Chechen terrorists seized a theater in Moscow in the middle of a performance. In the resulting counterattack, all the hostage takers and 129 hostages were killed by an inept gas attack on the theater by Russian authorities. The worst terrorist attack in Russia took place on the first day of the new school year in 2004. Chechen fighters seized a school in Beslan in the Caucasus and held hundreds of children, parents, and teachers hostage. More than three hundred hostages died, many of them children. The massacre led to worldwide revulsion, and Putin denounced it as part of global Islamic terrorism.

However, the influence of Islamic extremism or of Al Qaeda (see page 868) in Chechnya has been limited; the principal motive of the Chechen fighters is independence from Russia. This is unacceptable to the Russian government; Putin has claimed that there are two thousand potential ethnic conflicts in multiethnic Russia and that granting independence to any region or nationality would weaken the fabric of the fragile country. His tough efficient image shaken by the well-planned Chechen attack, Putin moved to reassert his authority: "[Terrorists] strive for the breakup of the state, for the ruin of Russia[.] I am sure that the unity of the country is the main prerequisite for victory over terror,"[7] he declared, making it clear that unity meant control from the top.

One means of control was to overhaul the country's political system. Kremlin appointees would replace elected governors and other leaders in Russia's eighty-nine regions. This would strengthen the power of the central government in distant regions, where leaders were more accountable to corrupt local interests than to the Kremlin or where leadership was weak and overwhelmed by crime and violence. However, this policy was another example of authoritarianism triumphing over Russia's nascent democracy.

Exhausted by years of turmoil, Russians supported Putin; they appreciated his strong leadership and welcomed his imposed order. In his first

term in office, he won respect for stabilizing the state and economy after the chaos of the Yeltsin decade. He also had the goodwill of the West and the opportunity to turn his country decisively toward a democratic future. After his landslide re-election in March 2004, Putin was beset by problems in his second term—the Yukos takeover, the Chechen attack on the school in Beslan, and popular demonstrations against Russian influence in Georgia and Ukraine. As a result, he shored up his authority and seemed to be taking his country back to one-party rule. His immediate associates in the Kremlin were drawn from the *siloviki*, former security officials who shared his hard-line law-and-order orientation and had no patience for the checks, balances, and uncertainties of democracy.

Russia's international role has shrunk while internal affairs have been the main focus of the government. However, Russia still has a nuclear arsenal, and this gives it a formidable position in the world. Despite misgivings about Western intentions toward Russia and sensitivity about their loss of superpower status, Russians are adopting more positive feelings toward the West.

The gap between Russia and the West remains enormous. Russia is still a huge, poor country riddled with crime and corruption; it is burdened with a crumbling infrastructure, high inflation, and desperate rural poverty. Its health and social services are in crisis due to increasing heart attacks, strokes, and illnesses caused by excessive smoking, drug addiction, alcoholism, drug-resistant tuberculosis, and AIDS. Life expectancy has declined. There are 160 deaths for every 100 births, and the United Nations projects an astounding population decline from about 146 million in the year 2000 to about 104 million by 2050. It is feared that a physically weakened and diminished workforce may undermine Russia's economic recovery.

Unrealistic optimism at the time of the Soviet collapse that Russia would emerge as a free, democratic, and market-oriented state has changed to pessimism. Building a democratic civic society took centuries in the West; Russia in its weakened state cannot achieve that in one generation. But it is in the interests of the West to assist Russia, for if Russia unravels, the whole Eurasian continent will be destabilized.

The Former Soviet Republics. Deep uncertainty prevails in the states that succeeded the former Soviet republics: the European states of Belarus, Ukraine, Moldova, and Georgia; and the Muslim states of central Asia, which include Azerbaijan, Kazakhstan, Turkmenistan, and Uzbekistan. Reorganized through dubious elections, the majority of the states are still dominated by the Communist legacy of overregulated, centrally planned economies. The precipitous breakdown of trading patterns after the Soviet collapse resulted in economic turmoil. The privatization of major industries has proceeded slowly, if at all, and government corruption and regulation have hampered foreign investment, leading to continued impoverishment of the populations of the states. Russia under President Putin still wields considerable influence in the independent countries, supporting rebel movements in Georgia and Moldova and using economic pressure—cheap oil and gas from Russia—to increase dependency and reclaim some of Russia's former superpower status.

Two states that rejected their post-Soviet authoritarian governments were Georgia in 2002 and Ukraine in 2004, through popular protest against fraudulent elections. Georgians staged a bloodless coup against their corrupt and dysfunctional president and installed a western-oriented president, Mikhail Saakashvili, who was better equipped to deal with the problems of a fractured state threatened by ethnic separatist movements. In Ukraine, massive street demonstrations forced a rerun of a presidential election that had been flawed by ballot rigging and open meddling by the Putin administration. The rerun elected a reform candidate, Victor Yuschenko, who pledged to orient his country toward Western Europe and away from Moscow. The protests in both countries were compelling examples for the other post-Soviet states that have made little real progress toward democracy since their independence.

The Muslim countries, however, continue to be governed by repressive one-party governments, and the growth of Islamic extremism has destabilized the region. The Muslim states clustered around the Caspian Sea have extensive oil and gas reserves. Cooperative ventures with western European and American oil companies have given these states access to potential wealth.

Central Asia, located at the intersection of Europe, Asia, and the Middle East, provides porous borders for traffic in weapons, terrorists, and narcotics. After centuries of compulsory unity imposed by tsars and commissars, the diverse and divided inhabitants in the huge area between Europe and East Asia have to learn how to manage by themselves. This is no small task for people untrained in the techniques of civic cooperation required for effective modern states.

Central and Eastern Europe After 1989

After a century of war, occupation, and dictatorship, hopes ran high in the former Soviet satellite countries of central and eastern Europe. Western ideals of freedom and democracy had penetrated deep into the eastern lands and had heightened popular expectations. By 1990, however, the euphoria of the previous year began to vanish. How could democratic government and market economies be adapted to the tension-ridden traditions of that troubled area now suspended between the remnants of Communist rule and the glittering promise of Western life?

The countries that were closest to western Europe geographically—Poland, Hungary, and the Czech Republic—were also closest to Western political and economic systems and eager to move toward full democracy and market economies. Poland achieved a quick but painful transition to a free-market economy; Czechoslovakia followed a similar course. Hungary, the most enterprising of the Communist countries, loosened its economy further. Yet people were unprepared for an open market economy and suspicious of capitalism.

As a result of economic and social insecurities, the pace of privatization of business slowed, most prominently in Poland, where in 1993 a majority voted in favor of leadership under an ex-Communist. A similar trend surfaced in Hungary a year later when the former Communist party, renamed the Hungarian Socialist Workers party, took office after a massive election victory. The Czechs, bound by tradition to western European culture, fared somewhat better; after January 1993, they were relieved of their association with less advanced Slovakia. The Communist party was outlawed, but

FUNERAL IN BOSNIA. A funeral of one of the tens of thousands of Muslim victims of the civil war in the former Yugoslavia, which raged from 1992 to 1995. The principal aggressor was Serbia, intent on seizing territory in Bosnia and Croatia in order to create a "greater Serbia." *(Anthony Suau/Liaison.)*

political disunity among a multiplicity of noncommunist parties prevented effective privatization. Everywhere inflation, unemployment, outdated industrial enterprises, and ignorance of market conditions held down economic development.

Yet after 1995, the economic prospects began to improve with the help of Western aid. Poland, Hungary, and the Czech Republic shifted their economic emphasis from east to west, increasing trade and economic integration with western Europe. The three countries achieved political stability and security through their membership in NATO in 1999 and, together with seven other countries, opened negotiations to join the European Union (see page 864).

In the 1990s, the former Yugoslavia became the most troubled region of Europe. Cobbled together after World War I as an artificial state composed of sharply different ethnic groups dominated by Serbia, Yugoslavia was torn apart by the nationalist ambitions set off by the collapse of the Soviet Union. In July 1991, Slovenia seceded; Croatia and Bosnia attempted to follow in 1992, ending Serbian domination. Because there were large Serbian populations in both Croatia and Bosnia, Yugoslav president Slobodan Milosevic, a Serb nationalist, refused to give up control and unleashed the Serb army, augmented by Bosnian Serbs, on the two countries. Ethnic hatred exploded, centered on Bosnia, a splintered mountainous region. Its major ethnic groups—43 percent Muslim, 17 percent Catholic Croat, and 31 percent Orthodox Serb—were scattered in multiethnic communities; there were few ethnically consolidated areas.

Muslims, Croats, and Serbs ruthlessly fought each other. The Bosnian Serbs, hoping to join with Serbia in a Greater Serbia, conquered 70 percent of Bosnia, conducting a brutal "**ethnic cleansing**" of Muslims while submitting Sarajevo, Bosnia's capital, to bloody bombardment. All sides, but most of all the Serbs, committed heinous atrocities, provoking moral outrage. A U.N. force of sixty thousand peacekeepers vainly tried to halt ethnic cleansing by Serbs.

In August 1995, Croatia went on the offensive to drive Serbs out of its territory, and NATO used its air force for the first time in its fifty-year history, against the Bosnian Serbs. In November 1995, the United States stepped forward, in negotiations held in Dayton, Ohio, to promote peace. The Dayton Agreement proposed a Bosnian government equally shared by Muslims, Croats, and Serbs. As the fighting died down, the U.N. forces were replaced by smaller NATO units, including American troops and even some Russian soldiers. A measure of normality returned to Sarajevo. But the outrageous inhumanities of the Bosnian civil war posed troubling questions. Why were western European countries so reluctant to intervene? Why did the United States enter so late? Can a foreign military presence soften deeply entrenched local hatreds?

Europeans and Americans were forced to reconsider these questions when violence erupted between Serbs and ethnic Albanians in the Yugoslav province of Kosovo. This is a sacred place for Serbs, the site of Orthodox shrines and of the battle of Kosovo in 1389, in which the Ottoman Turks defeated the Serbs, ruling Kosovo until 1912. The Serbs regard the battle as the birth of the Serb nation. Ethnic antagonism has persisted between Serbs and the predominantly Muslim Albanians who form 90 percent of the population of two million. In 1998, President Milosevic, seeking to shore up his power by manipulating Serbian nationalist feelings, sent Serbian forces to crush Albanian separatists fighting for an independent Kosovo.

Repelled by the forced expulsions and massacres of innocent villagers, NATO felt compelled to intervene. Despite a threat of NATO air strikes, Milosevic, a dictator whose hands already were stained with the blood of thousands of victims in Bosnia, refused to allow a NATO peacekeeping force into Kosovo. NATO launched air strikes on Serbia in March 1999. At the same time special Serbian forces, determined to drive Albanians out of Kosovo, stormed into the region. Carrying the practice of ethnic cleansing to a new level of brutality, they terrorized and murdered Albanians, systematically burned villages, confiscated valuables, and compelled their victims to flee the province. Hundreds of thousands of Albanian refugees streamed out of the country into neighboring lands, creating a massive humanitarian crisis.

The unrelenting NATO bombardment of Yugoslavia, expected to be brief and decisive, continued for eleven weeks—so too did the ethnic cleansing of Kosovo—until Milosevic capitulated. Eventually the Kosovo Albanians were allowed to return to their ravaged country. A force of forty thousand NATO and U.N. troops remained in Kosovo to assist with relief efforts, prevent revenge attacks on the remaining Serb population, and enable an administration to be put in place to guarantee Kosovo's autonomy.

The U.N. International Criminal Tribunal for the Former Yugoslavia indicted President Milosevic and Bosnian Serb and Croatian leaders and military commanders on charges of **genocide** and crimes against humanity. President Milosevic ran for reelection in a fraudulent campaign in September 2000. This brazen act sparked massive protests in Belgrade and forced him from office. Facing the threat of a cutoff of Western aid for rebuilding the shattered country, Serbia eventually arrested him and transferred him to the custody of the U.N. Tribunal to face charges. His trial, which began in 2002, is still in progress.

The former Yugoslavia, mired in poverty and dependent on foreign aid, now exists only as a dysfunctional federation consisting of Serbia, Montenegro, and Kosovo. Kosovo, which remains an international protectorate of the United Nations, with NATO and U.N. forces shielding Serbian enclaves from attacks by Muslim Albanians, is bent on eventual independence despite Serbian opposition.

The European Union

Since the end of World War II, the Western European nations have engaged in a slow process of economic, political, and cultural integration. The

GROWING ETHNIC DIVERSITY IN EUROPE. In recent decades, Western Europe has become the home for an increasing number of people from outside the Continent. Turkish guest workers have settled in Germany; millions of people from former colonial possessions in North Africa and sub-Saharan Africa now reside in France; immigrants from India, Pakistan, and the Caribbean, regions once part of the British Empire, now live in Britain. Cultural clashes, competition for employment, criminality, and pressure on welfare services have, at times, led to a xenophobic reaction against immigrants. In the photograph above, President Chirac speaks at a mosque in France. *(AP/World Wide Photos.)*

collapse of Soviet power supplied a sudden jolt for accelerating this trend. In 1991, in the Dutch city of Maastrict, the twelve members of the European Community negotiated the Maastrict Treaty, designed to shape Europe into a unified economic and political force. By 1993, the member states had ratified the treaty and, in recognition of its aims, the European Community became the **European Union (EU)**. The common monetary unit, the euro, competes favorably with the U.S. dollar as a currency for worldwide use. Tied to the global economy with an impact second only to the United States, the new Europe is becoming a powerful presence in world affairs. The majority of EU countries are members of

NATO, which in 2002 admitted its former adversary, Russia, as a junior partner.

Europeans share no common language, identity, or long-term history of cooperation, and each country practices its own form of liberal democracy. Consequently, it has been no easy task to implement the EU's objectives. Many Europeans have unanswered questions about the future of their countries. Are they surrendering their identity, along with their sovereignty, to the EU? Are Europeanization and **globalization** (the latter frequently defined as "American imperialism") going to change irrevocably their national status? The problem is that Europeans do not identify with the EU, personified by remote Eurocrats headquartered in Brussels, Belgium. An unelected European Commission makes the decisions, and the elected European Parliament is a weak institution. The Eurocrats argue that making arcane financial policies more accountable to public opinion would slow the pace of European integration. As the EU moves into new areas—a common economic policy and a projected common foreign policy—decisions will become ever more remote from the ground-floor influence of public opinion in member countries.

The number of Euroskeptics—those who oppose European integration for nationalistic reasons—is increasing. The EU's approval ratings remain under 50 percent, and elections to the European Parliament in 2004 were markedly apathetic. Those who voted used the opportunity to protest against their national governments by increasing the votes cast for Euroskeptic candidates. Even so, there is no lack of European countries eager to join the EU.

On May 1, 2004, the European Union accepted ten new members, eight of which had been former communist countries—the Czech Republic, Estonia, Hungary, Latvia, Lithuania, Poland, Slovakia, and Slovenia—together with Cyprus and Malta. This ambitious enlargement of the EU marked the historic reintegration of a continent that had been divided for forty-five years by the iron curtain and increased the total population of the EU to 450 million people. All the new members had made progress toward a market economy and had demonstrated acceptable standards of democracy and human rights. However, the new countries are much poorer than previous entrants to the EU and naturally hope to increase their prosperity and employment. The experiences of member states with per capita incomes below the EU average that have lifted themselves out of poverty with the help of EU economic assistance, notably Ireland and Spain, have given hope to the new countries that they too can escape economic and industrial backwardness.

Later in the year, the EU began negotiations to admit Turkey to membership. This was a controversial step that the EU had avoided taking for decades. Turkey has a bigger population than any other EU country; it is poorer and less developed than most European lands, and is also

Muslim (although it is a secular state, not a theocracy). If it were to be accepted, it would be the first Muslim country in an organization of nominally Christian members. If it fails to be admitted, despite its heroic measures to conform to the economic and political requirements for membership, the rejection would arouse the anger of the 13 million Muslims in Europe and would increase the appeal of **Islamic radicalism** in Turkey.

One question affecting all Europeans is linked to the worries about identity and change: will immigration transform homogeneous societies into multiethnic, multinational ones? The reluctance of governing political parties to open the immigration question has given far-right-wing parties another reason to attack the EU.

Center-left governments in EU countries are being challenged by the resurgent right wing. In Austria, the ultra-right-wing Freedom party is a member of the governing coalition. In France, with alarming success, Jean Marie Le Pen augmented his anti-immigration platform with an appeal to the "little people ruined by Euro-Globalization." Denmark, Holland, and Portugal all have growing right-wing parties. Many Europeans feel that immigration is a legitimate cause for alarm, for every year thousands of illegal immigrants enter the EU area from all over the world. Some are genuinely fleeing oppression and danger in their own countries; others are in search of jobs; most are unskilled. Unlike the United States, European nations have very limited immigration, so people entering countries illegally have to apply for asylum—that is, they have to prove that they would be in danger if forced to return to their countries of origin. Asylum can be granted on humanitarian grounds, but in most countries it does not extend to would-be immigrants looking for jobs. Although European countries are comparatively prosperous, unemployment is high, and when jobs are few, immigration is seen as a threat.

The treatment of asylum seekers who enter the EU area illegally varies from country to country; the EU is hoping to establish a common immigration policy, a task complicated by growing anti-immigration sentiments. One advantage of having a coherent policy that would give migrants the right to enter the EU legally would be the ability

Contemporary Art

oned individuality and espoused the freedom to express themselves purely through the use of color and abstract, nonrepresentational forms. As the century progressed, each artist felt even more freedom of expression, leading to a proliferation of styles. Artists were also subject to an ever more critical audience. Viewers felt freer in their ability to criticize art and in their efforts to understand the artists and the work they had created.

The most famous abstract expressionist, whose style is known as action painting, was Jackson Pollock (1912–1956). He completed his first action painting in 1950. Pollock poured and splattered his colors on the canvas instead of applying them with a brush or palette knife. He used a liquid paint that he dripped onto huge unstretched canvases spread on the floor. By positioning the canvas on the floor below him, Pollock felt closer to it—he became part of the painting. Able to walk around the canvas, Pollock worked on it from all sides. As he painted, there emerged a harmony, an easy rhythmic give and take between artist and painting, from which the painting acquired a life of its own. His *Convergence* (1952) (Figure 1) may at first seem to be merely an accident, a canvas used as a drop cloth. But each application of color was made in a controlled and studied manner. The artist knew exactly what he was doing every time he dripped, sprayed, or splattered his canvas. One might say that his paintings have a tactile, kinesthetic quality that is evident in the linear, agitated shapes on the canvas, virtually reflecting the motion of Pollock's body as he worked on the canvas below him.

The work of Helen Frankenthaler (1928–) carried further the abstract expressionism initiated by Pollock. It may be characterized as color-field or minimalist painting. In the 1950s, she was impressed with Pollock's work and adapted his technique to her own purposes. She, too, spilled paint on canvas, spreading, rubbing, and brushing colors into expansive shapes. A switch from oil paint to acrylic paints in the sixties enabled her to produce abstract and ethereal effects unlike the energetic

After World War II, myriad styles emerged or continued to develop. The best known of them was abstract expressionism. Art historians cite the realities of the post–World War II era—the aftermath of the atom bomb, the cold war—as the impetus for a number of movements or subgroups of abstract expressionism. The artists shared an outlook that championed

1. Jackson Pollock. *Convergence,* 1952. *(Albright Knox Art Gallery, Buffalo.)*

2. Helen Frankenthaler. *The Bay*, 1963. *(Founders Society Purchase with funds from Dr. and Mrs. Hilbert H. DeLawter. Photograph © 1991 The Detroit Institute of Arts.)*

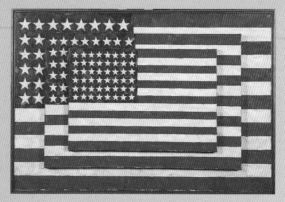

3. Jasper Johns. *Three Flags*, 1958. Encaustic on canvas, 308 7/8 × 45 × 5 in. (784 × 115.6 × 12.7 cm.) *(Fiftieth Anniversary Gift of the Gilman Foundation, Inc., The Lauder Foundation, A. Alfred Taubman, an anonymous donor, and Purchase 80.32 ©Jasper Johns/Licensed by VAGA/New York.)*

linear motion present in Pollock's paintings. In *The Bay* (1963) (Figure 2), Frankenthaler creates a sense of volume, spatial unity, and emotional feeling through the tranquil juxtaposition of translucent colors on a flat, two-dimensional surface.

Abstract expressionism spawned its own antagonists. Pop art was a reaction against nonrepresentational abstract art, which pop artists thought was pretentious and overly serious. Pop artists were influenced by earlier movements that ridiculed the notion of "art for art's sake," scoffed at the idea of the unique art object, and presented ready-made objects such as bicycle wheels and urinals as works of art. The phrase *pop art* was first used in England in the late 1950s to signify paintings that exalted postwar consumerism and celebrated popular culture.

Foremost among the early painters in the pop art movement in the United States was Jasper Johns (1930–). Largely self-taught as an artist, in 1954 he began to paint common objects such as targets, maps, and especially flags.

Four years later he executed one of his most famous paintings: *Three Flags* (Figure 3) is literally three canvases superimposed on each other, creating a reverse perspective, in which the smallest flag moves into the space of the viewer. *Three Flags* is simultaneously a painting and a relief sculpture. The ambiguous meaning of the painting was hotly debated at the time. Was it a realistic representation of the American flag, was it subtle satirical derision of it, or was some esoteric meaning implicit in its seemingly naive obviousness?

The work of sculptors during the second half of the twentieth century reveals both continuity with the sculpture of the pre–World War II period and radical change. Sculptors began to experiment. The major movement from the 1970s was minimalism—simple, symmetrical sculpture made of modern materials that engaged the viewer and, by implication, spurned depicting the human body.

One of the most important minimalist sculptors was David Smith (1906–1965), who flourished during the abstract expressionist era.

4. David Smith. *Cubi XIX. (The Tate Gallery, London/Art Resource, NY.)*

Smith began to sculpt in metal in 1933. During the 1950s and early 1960s, he produced several series of sculptures, including his Cubi series, inspired by cubism. *Cubi XIX* (Figure 4), of 1964, is representative of the series. All the cubis are constructed of monumental cubes, cubic rectangles, and cylinders, which Smith himself constructed out of polished and brushed stainless steel. The carefully balanced cubis are meant to be displayed outdoors,

where they capture and reflect every change in the natural light.

The most famous architect of the early twenty-first century is Frank O. Gehry (1929–). His work is found not only in the United States but also in Japan and several European countries. Gehry's view of architecture has evolved out of his profound interest in painting and sculpture and his friendships with contemporary artists. His theory of architecture embodies the conviction that architecture is an art form among art forms, like painting and sculpture, expressive of human feeling. Known for his innovative use of materials, Gehry is famous for the way he twists, turns, and bends metal into shapes that affect the emotions. One of his most recent ventures, the Guggenheim Museum at Bilbao, Spain (Figure 5), was opened in 1997.

Gehry's Guggenheim Museum is a perfect illustration of his ability to elevate architecture to the rank of an expressive artistic form not bound by the stultifying rules that consigned previous architectural works to the status of mechanically produced, redundant, box-like forms. The Bilbao Guggenheim itself is a work of art, a form of sculptural architecture. The building consists of organically interrelated contrasting shapes composed of a multiplicity of materials, ranging from limestone and glass to titanium. It houses nineteen galleries with thirty-six thousand square feet of exhibition space. It not only attracts numerous visitors—1,300,000 in its inaugural year—but also provides the city of Bilbao with a dramatic architectural centerpiece that has had the intended effect of reinvigorating the Basque region's recession-plagued economy and revitalizing its cultural life.

5. Guggenheim Musuem in Bilbao, Spain *(Superstock.)*

to mitigate the current flood of desperate illegal immigrants. The EU is urging members to view immigrants as an opportunity, not as a threat, because Europe needs to attract legal immigrants to boost economic growth and counter the effects of a low birthrate and, as a consequence, an aging population. By 2030, the EU workforce will have fallen by twenty million, creating a serious labor gap. Meanwhile, workers from the ten new member countries will not be able to work in the original EU countries (except Britain, Ireland, and Sweden) for up to seven years. EU members have taken advantage of existing laws to prevent a possible flood of job-seeking central and east Europeans from moving to more prosperous western states.

At the beginning of 2005, the European Parliament voted to endorse the EU's constitution, which had been agreed upon after months of heated debate, and urged EU governments to follow suit. The constitution was a practical blueprint for streamlining decision making among the twenty-five separate sovereign states and for coordinating economic, employment, diplomatic, and defense policies. At least eleven countries proposed to hold referendums of the constitution, which inevitably faced opposition from Euroskeptics; in addition, each country opposed parts of the document for different nationalistic reasons. But the referendums were scarcely underway in early summer before voters in France and the Netherlands soundly rejected the constitution.

During the first fifty years of the EU's growth and development, national and European concerns were frequently identical, but this was no longer the case. The expansion of the EU to twenty-five members and the possible admission of Muslim Turkey and countries from south-eastern Europe with cultures distant from those of western Europe, all called for a larger surrender of national interest than many countries were prepared to make. Dramatic decisions made by professional politicians without consultation were no longer acceptable.

The defeat of the constitution set off a crisis of confidence within the EU. A summit meeting in June collapsed in a damaging quarrel over the EU's budget. Further expansion of membership is currently on hold while the EU attempts to construct a closer relationship with its citizens and spur economic reform within the EU itself and within its member countries.

The three largest countries in the European Union are France, Germany, and the United Kingdom. France and Germany are the largest countries in terms of area, with populations of 62 million and 83 million respectively; they have traditionally set the agenda for the EU. France and the United Kingdom are nuclear powers. The United Kingdom, with a population of 60 million crammed into its small islands, maintains a special relationship with the United States.

In the United Kingdom, Prime Minister Margaret Thatcher resigned in 1990 in the face of conservative criticism. Her successor, John Major, maintained an uncertain majority in Parliament, increasingly troubled by political scandals and the rising popularity of the Labour party. In the election of 1997, that party, revitalized by Tony Blair, its young and lively leader in close touch with the people, scored an impressive victory. Under his leadership, the Labour party has moved to the political center. It endorsed a pro-business, pro-enterprise policy, limiting benefits for the poor, and jettisoned the old working-class/state-ownership image. This policy has given the country an unusually strong economy, and London is a vibrant worldwide financial center.

Socially, however, the picture is less bright, although the country's infrastructure and public services (particularly health and education) are slowly recovering from years of underfunding and neglect. The industrial north of England has been the recipient of EU funds, which have revitalized this deprived area; from 2004, EU funding will be flowing to the even more neglected new East European states.

In Northern Ireland, where Protestants and Catholics had long been at war with each other, Blair helped to end the conflict and create an elected assembly. After three difficult years, the peace process was finally on track. It was a huge gamble that terrorists and bigots, who have spent decades trying to destroy each other, could act rationally in a democratic assembly. The process came to a halt when the Catholic Irish Republican Army (IRA) was accused of organized crime, including murder. The IRA's political arm, Sinn Fein, the second-largest political party in Northern Ireland, was accused of colluding in the IRA's criminal activities.

After months of pressure from Sinn Fein, the IRA declared that it had "ordered an end to the armed campaign," and that it would pursue its aim of a united Ireland through exclusively political means. The declaration was welcomed in England and the Irish Republic and by the Protestant parties in Northern Ireland. Hope is building that after thirty-six years this conflict, which often targeted civilians in Northern Ireland and England will come to an end.

Britain continues to play an important role in international affairs. It aided the United States, its close ally, in the Gulf War of 1991, when an international coalition led by the United States prevented Saddam Hussein from annexing Kuwait to Iraq. Britain also participated in NATO actions to counter Serbian aggression in the Balkans, and in the war against the Taliban in Afghanistan following the tragic events of September 11, 2001. Prime Minister Blair, despite strong opposition in Britain, supported the United States–led invasion of Iraq in 2003 and committed forces to the coalition. He sees his country as an important bridge between EU and America—a stance that has become increasingly unpopular both in his own country and within the EU. His unwavering support for the war has diminished his popularity, but in the absence of viable opposition, he was reelected in 2005.

France, including the Mediterranean island of Corsica, has the largest territorial state in Europe. Proud of their historical tradition, the French cherish their past and are uneasy about the intrusion of alien ways, especially from the United States.

At home, the socialist François Mitterrand, president until 1995, named Jacques Chirac, a moderate conservative, as his prime minister in 1986. Succeeding Mitterrand as president, Chirac was forced to name a socialist, Lionel Jospin, to head the goverment. The two men were each suited to their jobs, but personal rivalry made for a difficult relationship, especially when Jospin challenged Chirac for the presidency in 2002. A fragmented vote resulted in an upset when Jean Marie Le Pen, the far-right leader of the National Front party, qualified for a runoff election against Chirac. The result sent shock waves through France, where demonstrations against Le Pen gathered force and Chirac campaigned vigorously, claiming that international respect for France would be wrecked if Le Pen—an anti-immigration, anti-EU, antiglobalization, anti-Semitic, racist candidate—won a large proportion of the vote. He received only 18 percent of the vote, but the affair revealed a troubling undercurrent in French society.

Following the policies of de Gaulle, the French government still wants to play its part in world affairs, for instance, opposing American policies in the Middle East. President Chirac's stand against participation in the Iraq war in 2003 bought him renewed popularity in France. At the same time, however, France works closely with NATO to preserve peace in the Balkans. Its chief concern is cooperation with Germany in creating an effective European Union that balances French and German aspirations. Chirac is identified with a vision of a powerful, politically integrated Europe, serving as a French-led counterweight to the United States. The EU, however, is developing into a looser association of countries whose preferred working language is English.

In 2004, President Chirac was at the center of a storm that divided the six million Muslims living in France. A law banned the wearing of symbols of religion in France's traditionally secular schools. Although the symbols included large Christian crosses and Jewish skullcaps, the law was primarily aimed at the headscarves worn by Muslim girls. This reaffirmation of the secular nature of the French state and its insistence on cultural uniformity was at odds with the policies of other EU countries, which accept multiculturalism and tolerate headscarves in schools. The issue was unexpectedly resolved when two French journalists were seized in Iraq by Islamic terrorists. The kidnappers demanded that the law be rescinded, but French Muslims rallied behind the French government and complied with the law in a show of national unity. Headscarves were removed at the beginning of the new school year. (The journalists were later released.)

In the fall of 2005, the suburbs of Paris and scores of other French cities were convulsed by two weeks of rioting by young Muslim males from the bleak housing projects inhabited principally by North African immigrants. That the great majority of rioters were not recent immigrants, but had been born in France, was particularly distressing to officials, for the French government prides itself on creating a uniform French identity that supersedes ethnic and religious orgins. Whatever the aspirations of the government, many French citizens remain resentful of North African immigrant families whom they view as an alien minority that, unlike other immigrants, has failed to integrate into French society. They point to the immigrants' attachment to native cultural traditions, the high costs of welfare payments to Arabs (and blacks from West Africa who also participated in the riots), and the high crime rate among them—Muslims, about 10 percent of the nation, constitute more that 50 percent of France's prison population. The French public was generally outraged by the mayhem and destruction of property—nearly 9,000 cars set afire, and schools, gyms, shops, and churches burned to the ground. Numerous commentators, however, interpreted the riots as a rebellion by a resentful underclass protesting discrimination, segregation, poverty, and a staggering unemployment rate—as much as 40 percent—for young Muslim males.

Germany has the largest population in Europe and is proud of the peaceful reunification of its western and eastern parts in 1990. Helmut Kohl, as chancellor of West Germany, was the architect of the reunited Germany; he poured huge amounts of West German money into what had been the Communist German Democratic Republic, hoping for quick integration. However, attitudes and habits developed under communism have persisted; the seventeen million former East Germans, with no experience of democracy, are somewhat disillusioned more than a decade after unification. Unemployment for them is at 25 percent because communist-era factories have closed and no new industries have been established. The rise in right-wing violence since reunification is particularly severe in the old East Germany, where neo-Nazis and skinheads, usually underemployed and alienated youth, have been responsible for outbreaks of lawlessness and brutality against "outsiders"— immigrants and Jews—whom they regard as parasites draining away the country's resources and diluting its national character.

A hopeful symbol of reunification was the relocation of the German capital from Bonn to Berlin, the traditional German capital city, which for more than forty years had been surrounded by territory under communist control. Greatly expanded, Berlin has become a major European center, with close ties to central and eastern Europe and even Russia.

Kohl's conservative chancellorship ended after sixteen eventful years. In 1998, Germans elected Gerhard Schröder, leader of the Social Democrats, as his successor. Schröder's party formed a coalition with the Greens, who scaled down their environmental and pacifist radicalism. Like England and France, Germany is now ruled by a moderate left-wing government.

The costs of German reunification are still considerable; they have had a dampening effect on German's economy, which has shown little momentum since 1990, and on the EU's overall growth rate. The German government's vision for the future, called Agenda 2010, advocates much needed labor-market reform and tax cuts in order to stimulate demand and cut unemployment, which hit a postwar record in 2005.

Although they lack personal cordiality, President Chirac and Chancellor Schröder followed the same paths in foreign and domestic policy. Both leaders refused to participate in the controversial Iraq war in 2003, a move which soured their relations with the United States but increased their popularity at home. In the EU the former supremacy of France and Germany is waning since new members are unlikely to defer to either Paris or Berlin. In addition, both countries have pressing social-economic problems. High wages and job protection have created high unemployment; excellent health care and social services, plus thirty-five-hour workweeks, have proved unsustainable. The thirty-five-hour workweek had been designed to create more jobs (as well as to give workers more leisure), but it failed to even dent unemployment; output fell, and the work ethic was damaged. Industries and governments recognized that longer work hours and greater flexibility in the labor market were needed in order to make goods more globally competitive. Both the Germans and the French accept the urgent need for reform of social services, but they rebel at the prospect of cuts in benefits and increased costs for services. Schröder was succeeded as chancellor late in 2005 by Angela Merkel, the first woman chancellor, leading a centrist coalition of both major parties in a new attempt to bring about reform.

Our Global Age: Tensions and Concerns

In the twenty-first century, globalization continues relentlessly; the world is being knit ever closer together by the spread of Western ideals, popular culture (particularly American), free-market capitalism, and technology. Government officials and business and professional people all over the world dress in Western clothes. Women follow Western fashions in dress and makeup. People line up to eat at McDonald's, see a Hollywood movie, or attend a rock concert. Everywhere people are eager to adopt the latest technology that originated in the West but is now also manufactured in other, particularly Asian, lands. Advanced technology intensifies the means of communication, not only through television and radio but also with faxes, e-mail, cellular phones, and the Internet.

These developments promote shared interests among individuals and businesses, some of them multinational corporations, throughout the globe, reducing the importance of national frontiers. "Globalization," in the words of one commentator, "is about the disappearance of boundaries—cultural and economic boundaries, physical boundaries, linguistic boundaries—and the challenge of organizing our world in their absence."[8] All of these factors combined are reshaping Western and non-Western societies in a relentless adjustment that causes both deep hardships and possibilities for a better life.

The ideals of freedom and democracy, historical accomplishments of Western civilization, exert a powerful influence worldwide; they are also part of the process of westernization. Unlike technology, they cannot be easily put into practice outside the countries of their origin. However, they inspire human ambitions everywhere. They have even become part of the rhetoric of dictatorships.

At the same time, strong cultural traditions still divide the world. Traditional ways of life, often at odds with the demands of modernization, remain deeply ingrained in many lands. Among people deeply committed to their own cultural traditions or feeling left behind by modernization, the process of globalization has provoked a powerful backlash, nowhere more so than in the Muslim world. The hatred of radical Muslim **fundamentalists** for the West, which they see as a threat to traditional Islam, is a striking example of the clash of cultures in a world being increasingly connected.

On September 11, 2001, nineteen Muslim Arabs, most of them from Saudi Arabia, hijacked four planes: two of them they crashed into the World Trade Center in New York, bringing down both towers; a third plane rammed into the Pentagon in Washington, D.C., causing severe damage; the fourth plane, apparently headed for the White House, crashed in a field in Pennsylvania when passengers heroically attacked the hijackers. In all, almost three thousand people perished in the worst terrorist attack in history. The meticulously planned operation was the work of Al Qaeda, an international terrorist network of militant Muslims, or Islamists, as they call themselves. In 1998, it was responsible for the deadly bombings of the American embassies in Kenya and Tanzania, which killed hundreds, and in 2000, it detonated a bomb next to the U.S. destroyer *Cole* in the harbor of Aden, costing the lives of seventeen American sailors.

The leader of Al Qaeda, Osama bin Laden, scion of an immensely wealthy Saudi family, operated from Afghanistan with the protection of the radical fundamentalist Taliban, who ruled the country, transforming it into a repressive regime based on a rigid interpretation of Islamic law. In particular, the Taliban imposed oppressive rules for women, permitting beatings by male relatives, prohibiting females from working, barring them from schools, and demanding that they wear a garment—the burka—that covered them from head to foot. Violators could be severely beaten, imprisoned, or executed.

When Taliban leaders refused to turn bin Laden over to the United States, President George W. Bush, supported by an international coalition, launched a military campaign whose ultimate goal was the destruction of international **terrorism.** The United States showed a fierce resolve unexpected by bin Laden who thought that the Americans would not risk sending troops to fight in the forbidding Afghan terrain and against people who had defeated the Soviet Union. Local Afghan forces opposed to the Taliban, assisted by American airpower—which proved decisive—defeated the Taliban in a few weeks. The

AFGHANISTAN AFTER THE TALIBAN. After the defeat of the Taliban, which had harbored and encouraged Al Qaeda terrorists, Hamid Karzai became president of an interim government in Afghanistan with the support of the United States. President Karzai struggled to deal with his nation's immense problems: local warlords who resisted the Kabul government, pockets of surviving Taliban fighters, the return of hundreds of thousands of refugees after the ouster of the Taliban, and the destruction, caused by years of warfare and drought, of great stretches of once fertile land. *(Reuters NewMedia Inc./Corbis.)*

new leaders of Afghanistan would no longer permit their country to serve as a haven and training center for radical Islamic terrorists. But the new democratically elected government faces immense problems: local warlords who defy central authority, pockets of surviving Taliban fighters, and a country impoverished by years of warfare, misrule, and drought. Compounding the problems faced by the struggling democracy is the tremendous increase in opium traffic—in 2004, it was estimated that Afghanistan provided 87 percent of the world's illegal opium crop. Drug trafficking has fostered armed militias and corrupt

local officials who impede the progress toward democracy.

On numerous occasions President Bush and his chief advisers declared that the attack on Afghanistan was directed against "evil doers" and not against Muslims in general or their faith. However, bin Laden and his followers view their struggle against the United States as a jihad or holy war against the infidel. Bin Laden and other Arabs from Morocco to Yemen devoted to a militant Islam had fought in Afghanistan to drive out the Soviets. During that conflict, bin Laden and his cohorts drew up plans for the creation of an

Islamic world-state governed by Islamic law, a re-vival of the medieval caliphate. In 1998, bin Laden told his followers that the stationing of American troops in Saudi Arabia, "the land of the two holy Mosques," demonstrated that America "had spearheaded the crusade against the Islamic nation." A religious fanatic and abso-lutist who cannot tolerate pluralism, equal rights for women, and other basic democratic rights, bin Laden wants to drive westerners and Western values out of Islamic lands; he is also a theocrat who would use the state's power to impose a nar-row, intolerant version of Islam on the Muslim world. He and his followers are zealots who are convinced that they are doing God's will. Re-cruits for suicide missions are equally convinced that they are waging holy war against the enemies of God and their centers of evil, for which they will be richly rewarded in Paradise.

To be sure, the actions of bin Laden and his fol-lowers violate core Islamic teachings against killing civilians. At the same time, however, terrorists find religious justification for their actions in Islamic tradition. The early followers of Muhammad, says Bernard Lewis, divided the world

> into two houses: the House of Islam, in which a Muslim government ruled and Muslim law prevailed, and the House of War, the rest of the world . . . ruled by infidels. Between the two, there was to be a perpetual state of war until the entire world either embraced Islam or submitted to the rule of the Muslim state. . . . For Osama bin Laden, 2001 marks the resumption of the war for the religious dominance of the world that began in the sev-enth century. For him and his followers, this is the moment of opportunity. Today America exemplifies the civilization that embodies the leadership of the House of War, and it . . . has become degenerate and demoralized, ready to be overthrown.⁹

The hatred of radical Muslims for the West shows that in an age of globalism the world is still divided by strong cultural traditions. It also reveals how the problems confronting the Middle East—authoritarian governments, the suppres-sion of human rights, rampant corruption, mush-rooming populations, high unemployment, and the ongoing Arab-Israeli conflict—have a global impact. All of these factors have led many disil-lusioned young Muslims to place their hopes for a better life not in democratic reforms but in a radical Islam that promises to restore a glorious past and guarantee entrance to Paradise. Foster-ing religious fanaticism and intolerance are the numerous religious schools financed by Saudi Arabia that have been established in many parts of the Muslim world. In these schools youngsters are given little or no secular education and from an early age are indoctrinated in the tenets of radical Islamism: hatred of the West, holy war against the infidel, the Jew as Devil, and the virtue of martyrdom for the faith.

Before September 11, Al Qaeda operated in Muslim lands from Indonesia to Morocco with little fear of government interference and received huge sums from wealthy Arabs in the Persian Gulf and from worldwide Muslim organizations purporting to be raising funds only for charitable purposes. Al Qaeda members also found a haven in western European lands where they coordi-nated their operations generally unrestrained by the authorities. The destruction of Al Qaeda training camps in Afghanistan; American pres-sure on other lands that had harbored terrorists; the tracking down, capture, and killing of Al Qaeda leaders; and rigorous international efforts to destabilize Al Qaeda's vast financial network have weakened the terrorist organization. But thousands of Al Qaeda fighters crossed from Afghanistan into Pakistan, and the seething dis-content in the Muslim world, particularly among Arabs, provides Al Qaeda with recruits, including zealots willing to inflict maximum casualties on civilians, even if doing so means blowing them-selves up in the process.

After September 11, several Al Qaeda opera-tions were thwarted, including attempts to ex-plode airplanes. But terrorists, either loosely or directly affiliated with Al Qaeda, succeeded in other operations, most of them suicide bombings that killed and wounded thousands of innocents. These terrorist attacks included the bombings of night clubs and restaurants in Bali, Indonesia, frequented largely by Australian tourists; a series of truck-bomb explosions in Istanbul, Turkey that wrecked two Jewish synagogues, the British consulate, and a British bank; the blowing up of four crowded trains in Madrid, Spain; several suicide attacks in Saudi Arabia directed principally at employees of foreign concerns; and suicide bombings of resorts in Egypt and hotels in Amman, Jordan. Abu Musab al Zarqawi, the Jordanian born head of Al Qaeda in Iraq, took responsibility for the attacks in Jordan, which took the lives of at least 57 people, many of whom were attending a wedding. In July 2005, Muslim suicide bombers killed more than 50 people and injured 700 in a terrorist attack on London's transit system. In a second attack two weeks later, the bombs failed to detonate and the suspected suicide bombers were arrested. That the perpetrators of these attacks were British citizens terrorizing their fellow citizens discomforted analysts; they feared that the millions of Muslims dwelling in Europe were potential recruits for extremist Islamic groups, including Al Qaeda, engaged in holy war against the West and that European cities would become targets of fanatical suicide bombers.

With Al Qaeda cells located in some sixty countries with many affiliated groups and freelancers inspired by bin Laden's ideology and eager to attack Western interests, and with bin Laden unaccounted for, international terrorism remains a threat to world stability. Moreover, despite the seizure of Al Qaeda's assets, local cells continue to receive substantial funds from wealthy Arab donors, from money collected from the faithful purportedly for charitable causes, and from criminal activities. Nor do terrorist undertakings require great sums of money. The bombing in Bali cost less than $35,000, the London subway bombings less than $500, and the September 11 attacks under $500,000.

The events of September 11 may have signaled a new type of warfare for a new century. Free and open societies like the United States are vulnerable to attack, less from states that are deterred by America's might—as in the cold war—than by stateless conspiratorial groups employing modern computers, communications and difficult to trace financial operations to organize and finance terrorism. Such groups are not deterred by America's arsenal. And there is the fearful prospect that a rogue state will supply these groups with biological, chemical, and eventually nuclear weapons to wage war by proxy.

DOWNFALL OF A TYRANT. After Baghdad, the capital of Iraq, had been taken by American forces in April 2003, the twenty-foot-high statue of Saddam Hussein was pulled down by Iraqis with the assistance of a U.S. vehicle. *(AP/Wide World Photos.)*

It was just such a fear that led President Bush in March 2003 to order an invasion of Iraq. The war was supported by Great Britain, which provided military assistance, but France, Germany, and Russia strongly opposed the decision. In about three weeks, U.S. and British forces, in an awesome display of operational planning and precision weaponry and suffering minimum casualties, destroyed Iraq's military hardware and decimated its armies. The victorious coalition forces uncovered torture chambers, where "enemies" of Hussein's regime were brutalized, and mass graves, where thousands were slaughtered at the tyrant's command. But vexing problems remained. Could the United States install a democratic regime in a country torn by ethnic, religious, and tribal hatreds; where some Iraqis regarded the Americans as hated occupiers; and where democratic traditions and attitudes were largely lacking? The United States declared that it had invaded Iraq to overthrow a ruthless dictator who had been feverishly amassing an arsenal of biological and chemical weapons and also had been seeking a nuclear capability. America reminded the world that Saddam had used poison gas against Iranian forces and Kurdish rebels in the 1980s, that UN inspection teams had destroyed huge stockpiles of chemical and biological weapons in the 1990s, and that Saddam's regime had not complied with a Security Council resolution ordering Iraq to account fully for its weapons of mass destruction (WMD) program and to cooperate with UN inspectors. Now, warned the United States, there was a danger that Hussein would supply weapons to be used against Americans. However, when no such weapons were found in the months after Iraq's defeat, critics in several lands accused the United States of pursuing a reckless foreign policy. Moreover, coalition forces faced armed opposition from hard-liners loyal to Hussein and his Baath party and from militant Islamists, or Jihadists, many of them Arabs from other lands, particularly Saudi Arabia, who saw themselves engaged in a holy war against hated Americans. American soldiers were confronted with numerous daily guerrilla attacks, but they did succeed in killing and capturing many of the top leadership of the Baath party, including Hussein's two notorious sons, Uday and Qusay, who had routinely imprisoned, tortured, and murdered many Iraqis. And in December 2003, Saddam Hussein was captured.

In 2004–2005, attacks—including suicide bombings—by Hussein loyalists and foreign jihadists increased in scope, frequency, intensity, and sophistication; proving particularly lethal to coalition forces were the larger and better constructed roadside bombs capable of penetrating armored vehicles. The insurgents, who demonstrated effective organization and seemed well financed, targeted both coalition forces and Iraqi officials, soldiers, and police working with the coalition in a deliberate attempt to demoralize and destabilize the new government and its supporters.

They also did not shrink from killing civilians, particularly in Shi'ite neighborhoods. The insur-

gents, predominantly Sunni Muslims who had received favored treatment under Saddam—the ruling elite were virtually all Sunnis—also targeted Shi'ite Muslims, who constitute the majority of the population and had been cruelly oppressed by Saddam. By murdering Shi'ite clerics, pilgrims, and worshippers and bombing their mosques, the insurgents hoped to trigger a sectarian conflict that would make the new Iraq ungovernable. Their frequent suicide car bombings, often in crowded sections, made daily life extremely insecure in parts of the country.

The continued loss of American lives—almost 2,200 by early January 2006—the spiraling cost of pacifying and reconstructing Iraq, and the failure to find weapons of mass destruction led more Americans to question President Bush's policies. But there were also positive signs. Many Iraqis welcomed the end of Hussein's terror and the thousands of reconstruction projects initiated by the United States, including the renovation of hundreds of schools and the greatly improved medical care. And in 2005, millions of Iraqis, defying terrorist threats, participated in three free elections. In the last election in December 2005, religious Shi'ites were the winners, gaining more seats in the assembly than any other party. But most Sunnis had refused to vote, abhorring a Shi'ite and Kurdish-dominated government, and many Sunnis continued to support the insurgency.

The United States had hoped that the toppling of Saddam and the construction of a free, democratic, and viable Iraq would foster the spread of democracy in other parts of the Middle East, defusing radicalism and anti-American sentiments. Although this still remains a possibility, several prospects fraught with danger have emerged. Will Sunnis, hateful of a Shi'ite dominated government, persist with an insurgency which could embroil the country in a prolonged sectarian civil war that delays the departure of American troops? Second, will an Iraq dominated by religious Shi'ites hostile to western democratic ideals, including individual freedom and women's rights, tie itself to the fundamentalist Shi'ite regime in Iran, which regards the United States as the "Great Satan"? Third, Iraq has become a transnational recruiting and training center for Muslim jihadists, many of them tied to Al Qaeda. It is likely that this development will facilitate the growth of an international network of armed, trained, and militant anti-American Islamists.

International terrorism is a major source of concern in today's interconnected world. However, there are others. Western science, medicine, humanitarianism, and economic progress have produced an unprecedented population explosion in Asia, Africa, the Middle East, and Latin America. For countless millennia the world's population remained almost stationary, slowly beginning to grow in the eighteenth century. At the height of Western imperialism, in 1900, the world's population reached 1.6 billion. Fifty years later, it reached 2.5 billion, and by the year 2000, it skyrocketed to 6.1 billion. Despite immense losses of life in two world wars, totalitarian terror, local famines, and other calamities, the world's population nearly quadrupled within a century.

The economic disparity between the rich and the poor, which sharply separates the industrialized from the developing countries, is further cause for concern. According to the World Bank, some 1.1 billion people live in *extreme* poverty—defined as struggling to survive on less than one dollar a day. (Another 1.6 billion people in poverty live on less than two dollars a day.) Each year 8 million poverty-stricken people—some 20,000 a day—perish because they lack safe drinking water, proper nutrition, bednets to protect them from malaria-carrying mosquitoes, adequate hospitals, and life-saving drugs. In many regions of sub-Saharan Africa, the cycle of poverty and death, exacerbated by calamitous civil wars and the ravages of AIDS (some 3 million people worldwide died of AIDS in 2004), has grown more vicious and tragic.

Destructive civil conflicts continue to rage. Strife in the Congo has left some 3.8 million people dead since 1998. More than two decades of warfare in southern Sudan cost 2 million lives before a peace treaty was signed between the government and the rebels. The actions of Arab militias against blacks in Sudan's Darfur region has been called genocidal. Most frightening for the future is the development of weapons of mass destruction by states that do not share Western democratic values. North Korea, a ruthless communist dictatorship, possesses nuclear weapons. Iran, headed by Islamic fundamentalists who support terrorism against the infidel, is moving ahead with plans to build atomic weapons.

But there are also encouraging signs. The cold war has ended, and NATO, the United Nations, and the African Union have provided security forces to quell violent conflicts in several regions. Impressive economic growth in South and East Asia has significantly broadened the middle class and reduced poverty, a testament to the effectiveness of the free market. Democracy has replaced repressive communist regimes in Central and East Europe, and American intervention and pressure has promoted democracy in the Middle East, a region long burdened with authoritarian regimes. Free and fair elections in Afghanistan, Iraq, and the Palestinian territories; the opening of presidential elections in Egypt to more than one candidate; and the granting of a limited vote for municipal councils in autocratic Saudi Arabia may indicate a change—skeptics remain doubtful—in the political landscape in the Middle East, where democracy had been dismissed as an impossible dream. It is hoped that the trend will put pressure to reform on Iran, Syria, and Saudi Arabia, the three most repressive regimes in the region. Democratic institutions and values continue to attract activists thoughout the globe, but promising democratic experiments have also been thwarted by the resurgence of authoritarian forces, notably in the new Russia and several countries in sub-Saharan Africa.

How can peaceful global interdependence be advanced, given the persistent cultural and political differences that divide the world, promoting hatred and inciting violence? How can tiny individuals on our crowded planet gain a sense of control over their personal circumstances as well as over the ever more complex institutions under which they live? How is it possible to gain the world-mindedness that would enable us to be cooperative citizens of our earthly habitat even under grave adversity? Can the present generation of Western peoples, above all, Americans, help shape the development of the global community in accordance with the highest ideals of Western civilization: reason, freedom, and respect for human dignity?

❖   ❖   ❖

Online Study Center ACE the Test

NOTES

1. "Drifting Toward the Danger Point" [from *Izvestia*], *Current Digest of the Soviet Press,* November 21, 1990, p. 26.

2. Quoted in Anthony Lewis, "Et Tu Eduard," *New York Times,* December 21, 1990, sec. A, p. 39.

3. From "Havel's Vision—Excerpts from Speech by the Czech President," *New York Times,* January 2, 1990, p. A13.

4. Francis Fukuyama, "The End of History," *The National Interest,* Summer 1989, pp. 3, 4.

5. Georgi Arbatov, "Origins and Consequences of 'Shock Therapy,'" in *The New Russia: Transition Gone Awry,* ed. Lawrence R. Klein and Marshall Pomer (Palo Alto, Calif.: Stanford University Press, 2001), pp. 173–174.

6. Boris Yeltsin, "Yeltsin Addresses Parliament on the State of the Nation," *Current Digest of the Post-Soviet Press,* April 9, 1997, p. 1.

7. Quoted in Steven Lee Myers, "Opponents Call Putin's Overhaul Plan a Step Back," *New York Times,* September 14, 2004, p. 1A.

8. Tony Judt, "Europe vs. America," *New York Review of Books,* February 10, 2005, p. 41.

9. Bernard Lewis, "Revolt of Islam," *The New Yorker,* November 19, 2001, pp. 52, 62.

SUGGESTED READING

Bhagwati, Jagdish, *In Defense of Globalism* (2004). How globalism works, and how it can work better.

Jack, Andrew, *Inside Putin's Russia* (2004). Increasing stability and increasing authoritarianism under Putin.

Phares, Wallace, *Future Jihad* (2005). Strong on the historical roots of jihad and the strategies of contemporary jihadists.

Reid, T. R., *The United States of Europe* (2004). The development of the European Union, and its potential to challenge the United States.

Epilogue

Reaffirming the Core Values of the Western Tradition

In recent years, modern Western civilization has come under severe attack from several quarters, including religious thinkers, intellectuals loosely called postmodernists, advocates of the poor and oppressed, and militant Muslims. Some religious thinkers deplore the modern age for its espousal of secular rationality, the central legacy of the Enlightenment. These thinkers argue that reason without God degenerates into an overriding concern for technical efficiency—an attitude of mind that produces Auschwitz, Stalin's labor camps, weapons of mass destruction, and the plundering and polluting of the environment. The self without God degenerates into selfish competition, domination, exploitation, and unrestrained hedonism. Human dignity conceived purely in secular terms does not permit us to recognize the *thou* of another human being, to see our neighbor as someone who has been dignified by God; and removing God from life ends in spiritual emptiness and gnawing emotional distress. These critics of the Enlightenment tradition urge the reorientation of thinking around God and transcendent moral absolutes. Without such a reorientation, they argue, liberal democracy cannot resist the totalitarian temptation or overcome human wickedness.

Postmodernism argues that modernity founded on the Enlightenment legacy, which once was viewed as a progressive force emancipating the individual from unreasonable dogmas, traditions, and authority, has itself become a source of repression through its own creations: technology, bureaucracy, consumerism, materialism, the nation-state, ideologies, and a host of other institutions, procedures, and norms. Aversion to a technoscientific culture and to its methodology leads postmodernists to devalue the principle of objectivity in the social sciences and to give greater weight to the subjective, to feelings, intuition, fantasy, to the poetry of life. Postmodernists contend that the evaluation of data and reasoned arguments, no matter how logical they seem, reveal only personal preferences and biases.

In their view, science has no greater claim to truth than does religion, myth, or witchcraft. In a world marked by cultural diversity and individual idiosyncrasies, there are no correct answers, no rules that apply everywhere and to everyone. Moreover, like those who point out the dangers of reason not directed by spiritual values, postmodernists argue that reason fosters oppressive governments, military complexes, and stifling bureaucracies. Nor has it solved our problems.

Expressing disdain for Western humanism, which ascribes an inherent dignity to human beings, urges the full development of the individual's potential, and regards the rational, self-determining human being as the center of existence, postmodernists claim that humanism has failed. The humanist vision of socialist society ended in Stalinism, and liberal humanism proved no more effective a barrier to Nazism than did Christianity. In our own day, they ask, has the rational humanist tradition been able to solve the problems of overpopulation, worldwide pollution, world hunger, poverty and war that ravage our planet? Closer to home, has reason coped successfully with urban blight, homelessness, violence, racial tensions, or drug addiction? Moreover, postmodernists contend that the Western tradition, which has been valued as a great and creative human achievement, is fraught with gender, class, and racial bias. In their view, it is merely a male, white, Eurocentric interpretation of things, and the West's vaunted ideals are really a cloak of hypocrisy intended to conceal, rationalize, and legitimate the power, privileges, and preferences of white, European, male elites.

People who identify with victims of exploitation, discrimination, and persecution throughout the globe also attack the Western tradition. They point to the modern West's historic abuses: slavery, imperialism, racism, ethnocentrism, sexism, class exploitation, and the ravaging of the environment. They accuse westerners of marginalizing the poor, women, and people of color by viewing them as the "other." Furthermore, they condemn the West for arrogantly exalting Western values and achievements and belittling, or even destroying, indigenous peoples and cultures. Finding Western civilization intrinsically flawed, some critics seek a higher wisdom in non-Western traditions—African, Asian, or Native American.

Radical Muslims, who were responsible for or identify with the events of September 11, view Western civilization as a threat to traditional Islam. Their vision of an Islamic society based on a strict interpretation of the Koran clashes head on with core principles of Western democracy—separation of church and state, religious toleration, protection of basic rights, and female equality.

Defenders of the Enlightenment heritage argue that this heritage, despite its flaws, still has a powerful message for us. They caution against devaluing and undermining the modern West's unique achievements: the tradition of *rationality,* which makes possible a scientific understanding of the physical universe and human nature, the utilization of nature for human betterment, and the identification and reformation of irrational and abusive institutions and beliefs; the tradition of *political freedom,* which is the foundation of democratic institutions; the tradition of *inner freedom,* which asserts the individual's capacity for ethical autonomy, the ability and duty to make moral choices; the tradition of *humanism,* which regards individuals as active subjects, with both the right and the capacity to realize their full human potential; the tradition of *equality,* which demands equal treatment under the law; and the tradition of *human dignity,* which affirms the inviolable integrity and worth of the human personality and is the driving force behind what is now a global quest for social justice and human rights.

The modern struggle for human rights—initiated during the Enlightenment, advanced by the French Revolution, and embodied in historic liberalism—continues in the contemporary age. Two crucial developments in this struggle are the civil rights movement in the United States and the feminist movement. Spokespersons for these movements have used ideas formulated by Western thinkers in earlier struggles for liberty and equality. Thus, one reason for the success of Martin Luther King's policy of direct action was that he both inspired and shamed white America to live up to its Judeo-Christian and democratic principles. Although written more than twenty-five years ago, the insights of French social theorist Jacques Ellul still apply:

[T]he essential, central, undeniable fact is that the West was the first civilization in history to focus attention on the individual and on freedom. . . . The West, and the West alone, is responsible for the movement that has led to the desire for freedom. . . . Today men point the finger of outrage at slavery and torture. Where did that kind of indignation originate? What civilization or culture cried out that slavery was unacceptable and torture scandalous? Not Islam, or Buddhism, or Confucius, or Zen, or the religions and moral codes of Africa and India! The West alone has defended the inalienable rights of the human person, the dignity of the individual. . . . The West attempted to apply in a conscious, methodical way the implications of freedom. . . . [T]he West discovered what no one else had discovered: freedom and the individual. . . . I see no other satisfactory model that can replace what the West has produced.*

The roots of these ideals are ultimately found in the West's Greek and Judeo-Christian heritage, but it was the philosophes of the Enlightenment who clearly articulated them for the modern age. To be sure, these ideals are a goal, not a finished achievement, and nothing should make westerners more appreciative of the preciousness of these ideals and more alert to their precariousness than examining the ways they have been violated and distorted over the course of centuries. It is equally true that every age has to rethink and revitalize this tradition in order to adapt it to the needs of its own time.

Therefore, it is crucial in this age of globalism, with its heightened sense of ethnic and cultural diversity, that westerners become sensitized to the histories and traditions of all cultures. But it is equally crucial in an era of global interdependence and tension that westerners continuously affirm and reaffirm the core values of their heritage and not permit this priceless legacy to be dismissed or negated. As the history of our century demonstrates, when we lose confidence in this heritage, we risk losing our humanity, and civilized life is threatened by organized barbarism.

*Jacques Ellul, *The Betrayal of the West,* trans. J. O'Connell (New York: Seabury, 1978), pp. 17–19, 29.

Index

Cyprus, 864
Czechoslovakia: World War I peace settlement and, 713, 714; democracy and, 740, 765, 766; aftermath of World War I and, 796, 797; alliance with France, 796; World War II and, 801–803, 823; 1968 invasion of, 841; end of communism in, 852–853
Czech Republic, 860–861, 864
Czechs: nationalism of, 547, 592, 593; industrialization and, 612; in Austro-Hungarian Empire, 695. *See also* Palacky, Francis

Dadaist, 776
Dagestan, 858
Daimler, Gottlieb, 610
Daladier, Édouard, 802
D'Alembert, Jean, 425, 436
Dali, Salvador, 776
Dalton, John, 562
D'Annunzio, Gabriele, 743
Danton, Jacques, 458
Darby, Abraham, 492
Darby, Abraham, II, 492–493
Darby, Abraham, III, 493
Darby family, 491, 492–493
Dardanelles, 697, 708
Darkness at Noon (Koestler), 778
Darwin, Charles, 563–564
Darwin, Erasmus, 563
Darwinism: natural selection and, 563–564; overview of, 563–564; Christianity and, 564; Social, 565–566, 635–636, 683, 691, 701, 753, 814
Dawes Plan, 749
Dawson, Christopher, 779, 781
Dayton Agreement, 862
de Beauvoir, Simone, 787
de Bonald, Louis, 516
Decembrists, 538
Declaration of Independence, 433, 447, 576
Declaration of Statements and Principles, 577
Declaration of the Rights of Man and of the Citizen, 454, 456–457, 576
Declaration of the Rights of Woman (de Gouges), 576
The Decline of the West (Spengler), 773
Decolonization, 844–846
de Gaulle, Charles, 807, 837, 866
de Gouges, Olympe de, 576
Deists, 413
de Launay, Bernard Jordan, 450
de Maistre, Joseph, 516
Democracy: liberalism and, 521–523; radicalism and, 523; labor and, 613; in post–World War I Europe, 740; United States as model of, 829
Democracy in America (Tocqueville), 522
Denmark: Bismarck and, 589–590; World War II and, 804–805, 816; NATO and, 831; European Community membership, 836; right-wing parties in, 864
Depression of 1873, 607, 615. *See also* Great Depression
Descartes, René, 400–402
Descent of Man (Darwin), 563
Despotism, enlightened, 429–430
Détente, 841

d'Holbach, Paul-Henri Thiry, Baron, 443
Dialectics, and Hegel, 515
Díaz, Porfirio, 656
Dickens, Charles, 496, 559, 560–561
Diderot, Denis, 422, 425, 427, 429
Dimitrijevic, Dragutin, 698
Directory (French Revolution), 469
Disease, 610
Disraeli, Benjamin, 614
Divine right of kings, 368
Dix, Otto, 777
Dollfuss, Engelbert, 765
A Doll's House (Ibsen), 561–562
Domestic system, 497
Dominican Republic, 655
Dostoevski, Fydor, 559, 664–665, 668, 786
Doyle, William, 362, 448
Drama, 560–562. *See also* Literature
Dreyfus, Alfred, 620
Dreyfus affair, 597, 620–621, 652, 767
Droz, Jacques, 541
Drumont, Edouard, 597
Dual Monarchy, 592
Dubček, Alexander, 841
Duchamp, Marcel, 776
du Châtelet, Madame, 415, 419–420
du Cobenzl, Comte, 429
Durkheim, Émile, 670–671
Dutch East Indies, 817
Dutch Republic, 362, 409, 411, 428, 429. *See also* Netherlands
Dynastic state, 360, 462
Dzhugashvili, Iosif. *See* Stalin, Joseph

Eastern Europe: Enlightenment in, 430–432; industrialization in, 486; authoritarian governments in, 765–766; Soviet domination of, 839–844; demise of communism in, 840–844, 849–857, 860; post-communist, 860–867. *See also specific countries*
Eastern Orthodox Church, power of, 625
East Germany (German Democratic Republic): Stalin and, 831; reunification of, 850–851, 866–867
East India Company, 641
Ebert, Friedrich, 746, 748
Economic thought: in Enlightenment, 423–425; liberal, 520–521
Economy: beginning of global, 637–638; in Weimar Republic, 748–749; in Nazi Germany, 757–758; in Russian Federal Republic, 857–859; in central and eastern Europe, 860–867; in European Union, 864. *See also* Commerce and trade
Edict of Nantes, 369, 371
Education: in Enlightenment, 418–420; for females, 419–420; in France, 474; in Soviet Union, 733–734, 737; in Nazi Germany, 760; radical Islam and, 870
Edward VI, king of England, 375
Egypt: Napoleon and, 468; Great Britain and, 638, 651–652, 656; modernization in, 639; elections in, 873
Einsatzgruppen, 811
Einstein, Albert, 679, 681–682
Electricity, 610

Glossary

Absolutism A form of government in which a single ruler and his court possess total and centralized power in the state.

Alliance system The complex web of alliances started in the late nineteenth century by Bismarck's Germany.

Anarchism The radical theory that all forms of government are oppressive and should be abolished. Anarchists denounced capitalist exploitation of workers and envisioned a new social order of individual freedom.

Anathema A person or thing loathed and detested; derived from the religious practice of damning, cursing or excommunicating.

Anomie Purposelessness and social instability as a result of lack of standards or values.

Anticlericalism Opposition to priestly influence in government, education, society, and ownership of land and property. It is most common in countries with a strong Catholic church and exercises an influence on politics in those countries.

Anti-Semitism Extreme fear and hatred of Jews and Judaism based essentially on irrational myths.

A priori A way of thinking that relies entirely on the mind's inherent capacities—as in mathematics—and not on sense experience.

Arête The pursuit of arête, or excellence, was a crucial feature of the ancient Greek outlook.

Authoritarian A government in which authority is centered in a single person or a small group (elite) not constitutionally accountable to the people. Also the political attitude stemming from mistrust of the people or constitutions that favor such a government.

Autocracy The rule of a single head, usually king or emperor.

Bicameral legislature A law-making body that is divided into two parts or two "houses" with different responsibilities.

Blasphemy Scandalous words or actions that are demeaning and hostile to what is considered holy and sacrosanct.

Blitzkrieg Literally "lightning war"; the use of tanks and aircraft to strike swiftly and decisively.

Bolshevik A member of the Marxist revolutionary party that seized power in Russia in 1917.

Bourgeoisie Urban middle class citizens; in Marxist terms, those who own or control the instruments of production.

The Calculus A mathematical system of notation that allows us to depict bodies in motion.

Canon law The officially established rules governing the faith and practice of a Christian church; based on the Roman legal tradition.

Capitalism An economic system in which trade and industry are controlled by private owners or corporations.

Capitalist A person who invests in business enterprise; one who advocates an economy or political system in which investment in and ownership of production, distribution, and exchange of wealth is in the hands of private individuals or corporations.

Cereals production The growing of grain.

Chartist movement Political movement in the 1830s in England that culminated in 1848 with the presentation of a gigantic petition signed by hundreds of thousands of workers and middle class reformers to the Parliament asking for reforms including universal manhood suffrage, the secret ballot, and the abolition of property requirements for members of Parliament.

Chiliasm The religious doctrine that Jesus will reign on earth for 1000 years. Now used to describe a long-term vision of the future.

Citizenship A person, eligible by birth or nationality, for full rights, privileges, responsibilities in a country.

Civil disobedience The political tactic of a group or movement that refuses to obey or comply with laws that are thought to be discriminatory and immoral.

Civilization The intellectual, material, and cultural development of organized human society. The first civilizations are defined by cities, writing, monumental architecture, organized religion, and organized government.

Class The division of society into social strata according to economic or cultural characteristics.

Classical Referring to the culture of ancient Greece and Rome (500 B.C.– 500 A.D.)

Classicism The ancient Greco-Roman intellectual and cultural tradition that valued reason as the avenue to knowledge of nature, ethics, and the human community and aspired to the full development of human talent.

Colonialism The policy of a nation or state that tries to extend its power or authority over other peoples or territories.

Commercial monopoly A situation in which one trader or nation corners the market on a commodity.

Communism 1. An authoritarian system of government with state control of the economy. 2. A doctrine that advocates the overthrow of capitalism by revolution and the establishment of a communist government.

Conscription A general term for involuntary labor but generally in modern times means the requirement by the state that citizens serve in the armed forces.

Conservatism A political and social theory that values traditional institutions and standards.

Constitution The fundamental laws, either written or unwritten, of a political body or state.

Corpuscular The term used often in the seventeenth century to describe what we would call the atom.

Cosmopolitanism Open to influences and interests from all over the world.

Decolonization The process of moving to independence by a colony and the process of granting independence to a colony by the colonial state.

Deist Someone who believes in God but considers him irrelevant to the human situation.

Democracy Government by the population, either directly or through elected representatives.

Demonize The representation of a person, or group of people, as evil or as demons.

Despotism A government with the power to curtail individual liberty and to make and enforce the law without the approval of an elected legislature.

Dialectical conflict A means of arriving at the truth by stating a thesis (or argument), opposing it with a contradictory antithesis, and combining the two arguments into a coherent synthesis.

Dialectics A means of arriving at truth by the exchange of logical arguments.

Diaspora Jews who lived outside Palestine.

Diké Ancient Greek term for the principle of justice that underlies human society, formulated by Solon in 596 B.C.

Diplomatic crisis A conflict over foreign policy between governments.

Dollar Diplomacy The practice of using economic power to "buy" friends and allies in other states.

Dutch Republic What is today the Netherlands.

Dynastic state Traditional leadership of a state by a succession of rulers from the same family.

Ego In psychoanalysis, the conscious part of the psyche that controls thoughts and behavior and is most in touch with the outside world.

Ellipse The oval shape of a planet's orbit.

Empire A large area, usually encompassing different peoples, ruled by a single supreme authority, usually an emperor.

Empiricism The view that knowledge is derived from sense experience.

Ennobled Made noble or aristocratic.

Epic A long poem or other literary narrative celebrating heroic deeds and national glory.

Esprit de Corps Literally "spirit of the group." Comradeship and devotion to a cause that unites members of a group.

Estates The three orders into which French society was divided before the revolution. The First Estate consisted of the clergy, the Second Estate of the nobility, and the Third Estate of the rest of the population.

Ethics 1. Principles of human conduct governed by moral values. 2. Making intelligent moral decisions when confronted with problems.

Ethnic cleansing An attempt to make an area ethnically pure by killing or driving out people of a different nationality or religion.

Eucharist The doctrine essential to Catholicism that the bread and wine are miraculously transformed by the priest into the body and blood of Christ.

European Union (EU) The economic and political integration of 25 European countries for trade and mutual cooperation.

Evolution Darwin's theory, based on empirical evidence, which explained how a wide variety of species emerged over many millennia. The theory holds that human beings have emerged from earlier, lower, nonhuman forms of life. (See natural selection.)

Existentialism A philosophy popular after World War II that emphasized the importance of choosing one's way in a universe devoid of absolutes and indifferent to our existence.

Exodus To leave or immigrate.

Extraterritoriality The right of aliens to be tried according to the laws of their own nation or state rather than by the laws of the state or colony in which they reside or do business.

Fanaticism Extreme, unreasoning belief in something, usually a religion or ideology, that often incites violence against nonbelievers.

Fascism Term used to define antidemocratic, anticommunist, and highly nationalistic and militaristic movements that arose in European countries after World War I.

Feminism A movement against the subordination of women; it aims to achieve the same rights, opportunities, and treatment as men.

Fundamentalism A movement characterized by the strict maintenance of traditional orthodox religious beliefs and principles.

Genocide The planned and systematic extermination of an entire national, racial, or ethnic group.

Gentleman's agreement An informal agreement between individuals or states to do something or recognize something that might not be acceptable in law.

Globalization The spread of western ideals, free-market capitalism, trade, and technology throughout the world.

God-King A king who is believed to be an all-powerful, living god.

The Godly Those who are deemed to be true Christians and therefore destined, or at least the likeliest, to be saved.

Gothic The style of architecture, painting and sculpture in the twelfth through the fifteenth century. Gothic architecture is characterized by lofty vaulted ceilings, large windows and high pointed arches.

Grace The love and protection given to people by God.

Greco-Roman Age The period when the Roman Empire ruled the Mediterranean world and absorbed Greek civilization into its laws, institutions, thought, and art, 30 B.C. to ca. 500 A.D.

Guerrilla A member of a band of soldiers (not in a regular army of a state) who are fighting against a government or a colonial ruler.

Gunboat Diplomacy The name given to the practice of sending ships to intimidate another government.

Hellenic Age Ancient Greek civilization 800 B.C.–323 B.C.

Hellenistic Age The era succeeding Hellenic civilization 323 B.C.–30 B.C., when Greek culture spread through the Near East and was thereby changed.

Hellenization The spread and adoption of Greek language and civilization in the ancient world.

Heresy What is deemed by the authorities to be false religious belief, and therefore those who hold heretical views may be subject to punishment and persecution.

Heterodox Referring to beliefs that are not generally accepted and may be frowned upon or persecuted.

Hierarchy The order of elements (e.g. people) into higher or lower ranks or grades.

Holocaust The systematic extermination of European Jews by Nazi Germany during World War II.

Holy Roman Empire A collection of German speaking states, run by princes, and corresponding roughly with what is today Germany and Austria.

Hubris Excessive pride or arrogance, behavior that for the ancient Greeks produced ruin.

Humanism An approach to life that focuses on the value and worth of human beings and aspires to the maximum cultivation of human talents.

Id The subconscious part of the psyche that is impulsive, instinctual, irrational, and demands satisfaction of primitive needs. Denial of satisfaction results in frustration, anger and unhappiness.

Idealism A school of philosophy that holds that the outer world is not something objective that exists independently of individual consciousness. Rather, the human mind, the knowing subject, determines the form of the outer world.

Idol An image of a god used as an object of worship. A false god.

Incarnation Christian doctrine that Jesus was conceived and born as the Son or God, and is therefore both God and man.

Indigo The plant from which blue dye could be extracted. Indigo was a prized commodity inviting colonial domination in parts of Latin and Central America.

Indirect rule Imperial domination was often exerted indirectly, meaning the local elites and local armies controlled the people in ways that the imperial power wanted.

Individualism Self-reliance and independence in thought and action.

The Inquisition A church-controlled institution that sought to combat heresy and was particularly powerful in Spain and Italy.

Irrational A way of thinking and behaving not derived from reasoning but from impulses, feelings, instincts, and other forces below the level of consciousness.

Islamic radicalism Committed to a fundamentalist vision of Islam, some Muslims seek to create a theocratic state based on a strict interpretation of the Koran. Islamic radicals or jihadists see themselves engaged in a holy war against Western civilization in which terrorism is a legitimate weapon.

Isonomy Ancient Greek term meaning the equality of political rights for citizens of the polis.

Jesuits The "shock troops" of the Catholic Reformation who labored after 1534 to return Europe to the Catholic Church.

Jihad A Muslim holy war against nonbelievers

Judgment Day The day at the end of the world when, according to Christian belief, God will judge all mankind, sending the saved to heaven and the damned to hell.

Kulturkampf The struggle for culture in newly unified Germany (1871) was a campaign by Bismarck for the restriction of the power of the Catholic Church.

Laissez faire An economic theory held by nineteenth century liberals that economic competition should be free from government regulation and allowed to operate according to the laws of supply and demand.

Latifundia Large plantations in the Roman Empire.

Latin Christendom The Christian world in western and central Europe where western civilization developed after the fall of Rome, from 500 A.D. onwards

Lay Piety The religious beliefs and worship of ordinary believers as distinct from the clergy.

Lay preaching The giving of sermons by those who are lay people or laity rather than by ordained members of the clergy.

Lebensraum The German term for "living space." German nationalists deemed the acquisition of certain territories beyond its current borders necessary for the nation's well being.

Lent In the Christian religion, an annual season of fasting that lasts forty days to Easter.

Liberalism A political and social theory founded on individual freedom, equality under the law, and the safeguarding of basic rights from the power of government.

Logic A system of argument based on valid reason and consistent principles.

Logos For Greek philosophers, the fundamental order governing the universe; implanted in every human soul, it enables the individual to live in accordance with natural law. To Christians it means the creative word of God that became a human being in Jesus.

Manumission Granting freedom to a slave.

Maritime Referring to any ventures undertaken at sea; seafaring.

Martyrdom Accepting death or great suffering to demonstrate devotion to one's religion.

Marxism The political and economic theory of Karl Marx based on class conflict between the exploited working class and the capitalist ruling class that owned the means of production and wielded political power. Inevitable revolution would destroy capitalism, and a classless socialist society would emerge.

Mass production Large-scale manufacturing in which labor is specialized.

Mechanical conception of nature All motion occurs in the world because of contact action between bodies, their push and pull.

Mechanism The belief that the universe is analogous to a machine, all of whose parts operate with mathematical precision.

Mechanization Replacement of human labor with machine labor and power technology.

Messiah The anticipated savior and king of the Jewish people, whose coming was prophesied in the Old Testament. Christians believe Jesus Christ to have been the Messiah.

Messianic Age Hopes of ancient Hebrews for an era of peace and justice inaugurated by the Messiah.

Metaphysics The branch of philosophy that attempts to define ultimate reality, or Being.

Militarism The principle or policy of maintaining a strong armed force. Also the glorification of war as heroic and noble.

Millenarian thinking The widespread belief in early modern Europe that the world would end as foretold in the Bible, Christ would return, judge the saved and the wicked, and institute a 1000 year reign of peace.

Modern Referring to historical developments in the West since the fifteenth and sixteenth centuries, the time of the Renaissance.

Modern state The liberal, secular, democratic organization of a state in which citizens have liberty and equality under the law.

Modernism The movement starting in the late nineteenth century that departed from traditional artistic and literary in favor of innovative forms of expression.

Monasticism A secluded religious life of discipline and prayer practiced in a monastery.

Monotheism Belief that there is only one supreme god.

Monroe Doctrine A foreign policy of the United States since 1824 that declares that the United States will not tolerate the establishment or re-establishment of colonies by the European powers in the western hemisphere.

Mosaic law The ancient law of the Hebrews attributed to Moses.

Mystic A person who seeks transcendent union with God through spiritual discipline and surrender of self.

Myth A traditional story that seeks to explain the origins of the world and the actions of supernatural powers.

Mythopoeic thought The creation of imagery and stories that make sense of the world by endowing every object in nature with life or supernatural qualities.

Nationalism A conscious bond shared by a group of people who feel strongly attached to a particular land and who possess a common language, culture, and history, marked by shared glories and sufferings.

Natural law A law derived from nature and implanted in human beings so that they will do what is right and avoid what is wrong, especially in human relations.

Natural philosophy A more accurate term to describe investigation into nature during the Scientific Revolution, gradually replaced by what we call "science."

Natural rights Also called human rights. Basic rights and freedoms to which all people are entitled, including life, liberty, freedom of thought and speech, and legal equality.

Natural selection Darwin's theory which states that organisms more favored by nature than others of its species will have a better chance of survival and passing on their superior traits to their offspring. Over millennia, natural selection causes the death of old species that cannot adjust to the environment and the creation of new species, for genetic changes within a segment of a species can so differentiate its members from the rest of the species that interbreeding is no longer possible. (See evolution.)

Naturalism A literary movement that believed that human character is conditioned by the social environment.

Nazism Ideology of the German Nazi Party under Hitler. Its core principles were racial nationalism, glorification of war, German expansion, anti-Semitism, and idolization of the leader.

Neolithic Age The new Stone Age, beginning around 10,000 years ago with the development of agriculture.

Neo-Platonists The Renaissance followers of Plato who revived his philosophy and whose teachings influenced Kepler and Newton.

New science The term describes the understanding of nature put in place by Copernicus, Galileo, Descartes and Newton, among others.

Nihilism A form of extreme skepticism that rejects all traditional moral and social values and denies the validity of religious beliefs, and traditional truths.

Occupation Military control of territory, nation, or state.

Oikumene The inhabited world, united in a world community.

Old Christians Spaniards who claimed pure Christian ancestry without any intermarriage with Jews or Muslims.

Old Regime The structure of French society before the Revolution, based on clerical and aristocratic privileges under a despotic monarchy.

Oligarchy Rule by the few, a political elite.

Open Door policy The idea that anyone and any state or nation should be allowed to trade without restriction—specifically an American policy toward China at a time that China was being divided by imperialist powers.

Orthodox Referring to beliefs and practices, usually religious, which are generally accepted, taught, and even enforced.

Ostracism Banishment or exclusion from society of a person regarded as dangerous.

Overman For Nietzsche, the exceptional man who aspires to self-mastery; without fear or guilt, he creates his own values and defines his own self, his own life.

Paleolithic Age The Old Stone Age that began with the earliest chipped stone tools made by hunters and gatherers.

Pantheism The belief that nature is the same as God; that the creator and creation are essentially the same and most commonly associated with the seventeenth-century philosopher, Spinoza.

Papacy The office and authority of the pope; the system of church government headed by the pope.

Parlement of Paris Despite the similarity in name with "parliament," the French version was a court that helped to enforce the king's law and registered new ones.

Parochialism A narrow restricted outlook focused on a specific place or on a group of people who share a particular history or culture.

Patricians The noble families of ancient Rome.

Pax Romana The peace, stability and prosperity that characterized the Roman Empire in the first two centuries A.D.

Phenomenal world The physical world experienced by the senses, from which it constructs knowledge and reality.

Philosophy Literally "the love of wisdom." A system of enquiry based on logic and reason;

philosophers searched for basic truths and moral principles for the right conduct of life.

Plebeians The common people of ancient Rome.

Plebiscite A direct vote in which the entire voting public is asked to accept or reject a proposition or a candidate.

Pluralistic Referring to any group or society in which a variety of differing opinions are represented, expressed, tolerated, and perhaps even encouraged.

Polytheism Belief in and worship of more than one god.

Positivism The theory that the scientific method applied to the study of society is the only valid approach to knowledge and precise understanding.

Postmodernism A late twentieth century development that rejects universal principles and seeks the dismantling of all inherited systems and beliefs and that values cultural diversity in the arts and thought. A wide-ranging criticism of the Western tradition as a viable force in the contemporary world.

Productivity A term in economics that refers to how much it costs to produce goods. The less it costs to produce something, the higher the productivity.

Propaganda The deployment of lies, half truths, and myths in all forms of communication in order to win people over to a cause.

Protectorate The practice, common in the era of European imperialism, of a stronger state asserting power over a weaker state or territory. In effect, the protector warns all other powers that the weak state or territory is not available to any other power for colonization.

Providence The power of God acting in the world for, as is usually thought, the good of one and all; often referred to as Divine Providence.

Psyche The mind as the center of thought, emotion, and behavior.

Psychoanalysis The method originated by Freud for treating mental disorders by bringing to light unconscious impulses, desires and memories.

Racist A person who believes that race determines human ability and character, and that one particular race is superior to another.

Radicalism A doctrine advocating extreme change of existing conditions and standards.

Rationalism Reliance on reason as the avenue to knowledge.

Realism The representation in art and literature of social conditions, daily life, and ordinary people as they really are without idealism.

Realpolitik Political practice as a tough-minded, objective means of advancing national interest and power.

Redemption To be saved from the consequences of sin through the sacrifice of Jesus.

Relativism The belief that accepted truths and moral values are not universally valid, but are a matter of individual or group judgment.

Republic The political order in a country where the people or their elected representatives hold supreme power.

Respublica Christiana A universal Christian commonwealth envisioned by the Catholic Church, governed by an emperor under the pope's guidance.

Republicanism Belief in a republican system of government.

Revelation The making known of divine will or truth that was previously hidden.

Ritual A prescribed series of actions or rites used in a religious ceremony.

Romanesque The eleventh- to twelfth-century style of architecture that imitated ancient Roman buildings, with thick walls, rounded arches, and little ornamentation.

Romanticism A literary and artistic movement characterized by the liberation of human emotion with emphasis on the artist's imagination, intuition, and feelings.

Roosevelt Corollary A policy enunciated by Theodore Roosevelt in 1904 stating that European powers should not intervene in any government in the western hemisphere that appeared to be economically or politically unstable.

Royal hegemony The control exercised by a monarch over his or her subjects and territory.

Savior-God Christians view Jesus as both the Savior of mankind and God incarnate, leading humanity from sin to eternal life.

Scholasticism The attempt of medieval theologian-philosophers to explain and clarify Christian teachings by means of concepts and logic derived from Greek philosophy; to prove through reason what was held to be true by faith.

Scholastics Medieval philosopher-theologians who came to dominate the intellectual life of medieval universities.

Scientific Revolution The seventeenth-century movement that overthrew the medieval view of the universe and made physical nature a valid object for experimental inquiry and mathematical calculation.

Secession The act of withdrawing from a state, country, or polity.

Secular Referring to the world we live in as separate from any spiritual world; here and now; this life rather than the afterlife.

Secularization The process by which religious ideas, customs and traditions lose their political and social power in a society.

Self-determination The right of independence or self-government for a nation; also, an individual taking control over his or her life.

Sense perception Knowledge of the material world based on the observation and investigation of nature using the human senses (sight, touch, hearing, taste, and smell).

Skepticism An unwillingness or refusal to believe that something is true or certain unless adequate evidence or proof is provided. It is the opposite of dogmatism.

Social Darwinism The application of Darwin's theory to the study of human society. In the struggle for survival, some maintain, it is natural and beneficial to society for the fittest nations, races, and individuals to survive at the expense of the less fit.

Socialism A social and economic system based on cooperation not competition. The production and distribution of goods would be owned collectively, would benefit the community as a whole, and lift the laboring poor out of poverty and oppression.

Sophrosyne The ancient Greek idea of moderation and self-discipline.

Sovereignty The state's authority, which is absolute in matters of law within its borders.

Spheres of Influence A diplomatic term that describes the area or territory in which a foreign power or powers have great influence.

Stream of consciousness A literary technique that, through a punctuated and spontaneous flow of thought and feelings, attempts to reveal the mystery and complexity of the inner person.

Subsistence Having just enough food, clothing, and shelter to survive. A subsistence economy is one in which people live hand-to-mouth, everything produced is consumed, and there is no surplus.

Suffrage The right to vote.

Sui Generis The only example of its kind, without an equal.

Superman See Overman.

Syndicalism A political/economic philosophy and movement that advocates giving the control of government and industry to workers' federations.

Tabula Rasa A description of the mind as a blank slate before it organizes the impressions gained from experience.

Terror, Reign of The deliberate use of terror by the Jacobin regime to preserve the ideals of the French Revolution by execution of enemies of republican liberty.

Terrorism The use of force or violence against people or property in order to intimidate or coerce societies or governments for political or ideological reasons.

Teutonic cousins Germans and Englishmen (as well as Scandinavians) commonly referred to themselves as descendants of common ancestors—teutonic tribespeople.

Theocracy A country in which the government is dominated by clergy.

Tithe Tenth, referred to by Christians, as the portion of their income or revenues that ought to be given to the support of the Church.

Totalitarianism A form of government that exercises total control over all aspects of life, demanding submission of the individual to the state, and permitting no political opposition.

Tragedy A drama with an unhappy ending caused by human flaws or disastrous circumstances.

Trinity Christian belief in the union of three divinities, Father, Son, and Holy Ghost in one God.

Unconscious, The The inner life of the mind containing memories, repressed desires or passion, not consciously perceived, but affecting conscious thought and behavior.

Universalism 1. The unity and salvation of all people under God 2. Membership of all humanity in a worldwide community.

Utilitarian An ethical theory that all political, economic, and social actions should be directed toward achieving the greatest happiness for the greatest number of people.

Utopian Any visionary system of politics or society, named for Sir Thomas More's *Utopia* (1516).

Vernacular Referring to the language commonly spoken and written in a society.

Volkish thought A late nineteenth century movement glorifying the language, traditions, and history of the Germanic peoples.

World-view The perspective from which an individual or group sees and interprets the world and life. *Weltanschauung* in German.

Xenophobia An unreasoning fear and hatred of foreigners.

Zionism A movement to establish a Jewish state in Palestine, the Jews' ancient homeland.